An Aramaic Wisdom Text from Qumran

A New Interpretation of the Levi Document

by

Henryk Drawnel, S.D.B.

BRILL

LEIDEN • BOSTON

2004

This book is printed on acid-free paper.

Library of Congress Cataloging-in-Publication Data

Drawnel, Henryk.
  An Aramaic wisdom text from Qumran : a new interpretation of the Levi document /
by Henryk Drawnel.
    p. cm. — (Supplements to the Journal for the study of Judaism, ISSN 1384-2161;
v. 86)
    Includes bibliographical references (p.) and index.
    ISBN 90-04-13753-X
    1. Levi document. 2. Manuscripts, Aramaic. 3. Israel. Rashut Ha-Atikot—Library.
4. Bodleian Library. 5. Cambridge University Library. I. Levi document. II. Title.
III. Series

BM488.L48D73 2004
229'.914—dc22   2004045596

ISSN 1384–2161
ISBN 90 04 13753 X

PRINTED IN THE NETHERLANDS

An Aramaic Wisdom Text from Qumran

ᵛSupplements

to the

Journal for the
Study of Judaism

Editor
John J. Collins
The Divinity School, Yale University

Associate Editor
Florentino García Martínez
Qumran Institute, University of Groningen

Advisory Board
J. DUHAIME — A. HILHORST — P.W. VAN DER HORST
A. KLOSTERGAARD PETERSEN — M.A. KNIBB — J.T.A.G.M. VAN RUITEN
J. SIEVERS — G. STEMBERGER — E.J.C. TIGCHELAAR — J. TROMP

ᐯ VOLUME 86

ἀλλὰ πάντα μέτρῳ καὶ ἀριθμῷ καὶ σταθμῷ διέταξας

Wis 11:20

CONTENTS

TABLES

PLATES

PREFACE

The idea to produce a new edition and commentary of the *Aramaic Levi Document* arose during the preparation of the paper due in partial requirement for the doctoral year at the Pontifical Biblical Institute, Rome. The paper dealt with the person of Melchizedek and Levi in the *Letter to the Hebrews* since some relationship between Levi and Melchizedek was observed in the *Document*. While working on the Aramaic composition, I mainly consulted its Cairo Geniza manuscripts with some recourse to the Qumran fragments. Reading the scholarly literature on the *Document*, I noticed that much uncertainty reigned as to its provenance, literary character, and general line of interpretation. Most of the research concentrated on its textual relationship to the Greek *Testament of Levi*, while neglecting the fundamental questions concerning the origins of this Aramaic composition.

The preliminary publication of the Qumran fragments by Kugler (1996a) and the *editio princeps* by Stone and Greenfield (1996a) partially remedied that situation. Kugler published Qumran fragments together with Cairo Geniza manuscripts and Mt. Athos Greek portions of the Aramaic work and undertook a difficult task of restoring its textual form. However, he imposed his own sigla on the Qumran texts and did not publish their photographs, making any comparison with the original texts impossible. He included in his work only those Qumran fragments that supplemented the texts of the composition, especially in its final portion, and omitted the others that overlapped with the Cairo Geniza manuscripts. Although he discussed the authorship and purpose of his reconstructed text, his work intended to reconstruct the "Original Levi" that stood at the source of the whole Levi-Priestly Tradition. He thus treated the *Document* as only one part of his intended proceedings and did not give enough attention to analyze it properly. The publication of the Qumran fragments by Greenfield and Stone concluded a long period of waiting for a comprehensive edition of the composition's oldest manuscripts.

The present monograph continues the scholarly effort of the predecessors who dealt with this difficult and fragmentary composition. It presents the text of the *Document* and tries to find some fundamental answers to its problematics. The result of this inquiry based on a patient study and research lies in front of the reader. Many inconsistencies, misinterpretations, or even mistakes that a critical eye will certainly discover stem not from neglect but from my personal limitations that were not always possible to overcome. However, I console myself that I remained at least partially obedient to the command of Levi, an ideal priest and scribe: "Do not neglect to study wisdom and do not abandon a search for her ways" (*A.L.D.* 90).

Finally, I would like to thank those who helped me in my work by their advice and encouragement. My most heartfelt words of gratitude are directed to Rev. Joseph Sievers, Professor of Jewish History and Literature of the Hellenistic Period at the Pontifical Biblical Institute in Rome, Italy. His patient and kind counsel and direction assisted me in my work and allowed me to bring the whole work to conclusion. The second adviser of the work was Rev. Émile Puech, Director of Research at the Centre National de la Recherche Scientifique in Paris, France. I am greatly indebted to his help and direction in dealing with the Qumran manuscripts, of which he possesses an unsurpassable knowledge and expertise. He showed a vivid interest in the work from its very beginning and his watchful eye and judgment prevented me from committing many mistakes in the painstaking decipherment of the Aramaic texts. To both scholars, however, I am greatly obligated not only for their professional and insightful help, but especially for their friendship and encouragement that changed my work into a profound human experience. I am also very grateful to Mr. Jöran Friberg, a retired professor of mathematics from Chalmers University of Technology, in Gothenburg, Sweden. As an eminent specialist in Babylonian mathematics, he confirmed my conclusions concerning the Babylonian origins of the metrological exercises in the *Document*. Additional expertise was provided by Ms. Eleanor Robson from All Souls College, Oxford. She shared with me a preliminary version of her article about scribal education at Nippur and provided me with several useful observations concerning this theme. I also had the privilege to study the *Testaments of the Twelve Patriarchs* with Mr. John Strugnell, a retired professor of Harvard Divinty School. His vivid intelligence and broad learning inspired my imagination and research to continue the work undertaken. Prof. John Collins from Yale Divinity School read the whole manuskript, made many insightful comments, and accepted the work for publication in this scientific series. Finally, special thanks are due to the professors and staff of the academic institutions where I studied and continued my research, that is: the Pontifical Biblical Institute, Rome; École Biblique et Archéologique Française, Jerusalem; Harvard Divinity School, Cambridge. Last but not least, I would like to express my gratitude to Rev. Paul O'Brien and James Burke and all the parishioners of Infant Jesus-St. Lawrence parish for their hospitality, friendship, and generous support during my stay in Boston.

The photographs of the manuscripts presented in the sixteen plates at the end of this work come from different scientific institutions and have been reproduced here with all necessary permissions. The photographs of the Qumran fragments were made available by Israel Antiquity Authority in Jerusalem; the Cairo Geniza photographs come from the Bodleian Library in Oxford and the University Library in Cambridge, England; the Syriac fragment comes from the British Library in London, England. The microfilm of the Mount Athos manuscript was provided by the Patriarchal Institute for Patristic Studies in Thessaloniki, Greece. I dedicate this book to the memory of my mother Janina.

Kraków, 2004

ABBREVIATIONS

The manuscript sigla introduced and used in the present work indicate different manuscripts preserved in Aramaic, Greek, and Syriac. Verses and line divisions introduced by Charles (1908a: 245–256) have been kept with only minor changes. Some verses have been split up where the literary division of the text imposed it. Line division in Levi's prayer (*A.L.D.* 1a) was first introduced by Milik (1955b: 401) and kept in this study. The Qumran fragments are referred to with the sigla first assigned to them by Milik and then elaborated by M. Stone and J. Greenfield (1996a: 1–72). In two instances, however, it seemed advisable on paleographical grounds to modify them. It is argued that 4Q213a frg. 5 preserves only one column and not two as the editors affirm (Stone and Greenfield 1996a: 35). 4Q214a frg. 2 i is composed of only one fragment, not two, as claimed by Stone and Greenfield who label it 4Q214a frg 2–3 i (1996a: 56).

Since the manuscripts have been republished several times and by different authors, a certain confusion in the assigned sigla remains in the scholarly literature. The present effort to distinguish between different manuscript evidence in a clear and also familiar way tries not to add to the confusion. To the contrary, it is hoped that some clarity may be achieved. A distinction between textual witnesses should facilitate easy reference to different fragments of the same composition. The siglum used for the whole reconstructed work is *A.L.D.*, *Aramaic Levi Document*, denoting language, main personage, and unspecified literary form of the whole composition (cf. § 1.6).

The diacritical signs used in the manuscript section follow those the general Discoveries in the Judaean Desert series use, and the abbreviations of the Qumran manuscripts follow the same DJD series. General abbreviations of biblical books, apocrypha and pseudepigrapha, and transliteration conventions are used in accordance with Patrick H. Alexander, *et al.*, eds. *The SBL Handbook of Style*. Peabody, Mass.: Hendrickson, 1999.

I. *Abbreviations*

A	Aramaic manuscript of the *Document* from the Cairo Geniza: Bodleian and Cambridge fragments
A.L.D.	*Aramaic Levi Document*
B	Syriac manuscript of the *Document*
c.	common; *circa*
CAD	The Assyrian Dictionary of the University of Chicago
conj.	conjunction; conjecture
DJD	Discoveries in the Judaean Desert
E	Greek manuscript of the *Document* from Mt. Athos
emend.	emended
f.	feminine; *folium*
G	Gizeh Greek papyrus of *1 Enoch*
G²	Gizeh Papyrus duplicate of *1 En.* 19:3–21:9
Gᵇ	Chester Beatty Papyrus of *1 En.* 97:6–104; 106–107:3
H	Holiness Code, *Leviticus* 17–26
HALOT	Koehler, L. and Baumgartner, W. *The Hebrew and Aramaic Lexicon of the Old Testament.* 5 vols. Leiden, 1994–2000
l(l).	line(s)
LPT	Levi-Priestly Tradition (*Aramaic Levi Document, Jubilees* 30–32, Greek *Testament of Levi*)
LSJ	Liddell, G. H., Scott, R., Jones, H. S. *A Greek-English Lexicon.* Oxford, 1996
pl.	plural; plate
r.	*recto*
ܣ	Pešiṭta
Sync.	Georgius Syncellus's Greek text of *1 Enoch* (ed. by R. H. Charles. *The Ethiopic Version of the Book of Enoch.* Oxford, 1906).
v(v).	*verso*; verse(s)
>	becomes
*	not attested, but only hypothetical (reconstructed) form

II. *Reconstruction Signs*

אמֹר	letters partially damaged
אמֿר	only a part of the letter is visible
[אמר]	a letter, word, or phrase are missing in the manuscripts

אמר°‎	ink traces of an unidentified letter remain
אמר ‏ᴵ‎	supralinear scribal insertion
†το ηεεσθαι†	text corrupt
{אמר}‎	scribal deletion
<אמר>‎	scribal correction
*אמרᵃ‎	a variant reading in the footnotes
+	word(s) have been added
>	word(s) have been omitted

CHAPTER ONE

ARAMAIC LEVI DOCUMENT: INTRODUCTION

1.1   *A General Presentation of the* Document

Aramaic Levi Document belongs to the Jewish literature of the Second
Temple period. The original composition of this work started from
the reinterpretation of data contained in the Hebrew Bible, although
the document itself eventually did not enter the biblical canon. It
thus belongs to a vast apocryphal literature of the Old Testament
that survived the vicissitudes of independent text transmission. Its
content deals mainly with Levi, his life and activity, and it exegetically develops the biblical account concerning Levi and his brothers.
In *Genesis* 34 Dinah, Jacob's daughter, went to visit the city of
Shechem close to which Jacob's family encamped after the return
from Laban. Once in the city, Dinah met Shechem, the son of
Hamor, who lay with her and defiled her. Hamor then tried to
arrange a marriage between Shechem and Dinah. Jacob's sons cun-
ningly agreed to the proposal under the condition that all the
Shechemites would undergo circumcision. Once the deal was concluded and the Shechemites circumcised, Levi and Simeon killed all
the male inhabitants of Shechem and brought Dinah back to Jacob's
family. Then in *Genesis* 35 the family moved to Bethel and finally
to Hebron where they met Isaac. After a chapter dedicated mainly
to Esau's descendants (*Genesis* 36), in *Genesis* 37 the biblical account
returned to Shechem and its surroundings, where Jacob's sons sold
their brother Joseph into slavery.

The account of the Shechem killing finds its place in the fragmentary *A.L.D.* 1c–2, while Jacob's visit in Bethel is reflected in
A.L.D. 9–10. The final arrival of the family in Hebron and meeting
with Isaac occur twice in the *Document*. In *A.L.D.* 8 the whole family visits Isaac and Levi is blessed by his grandfather; then, in *A.L.D.*
11–13 the family reaches Hebron the second time. Isaac imparts his
blessing to all the members of the family and teaches Levi the priestly
instructions. The selling of Joseph is recounted in *A.L.D.* 3 where
Levi and Simeon are absent while the deal is struck.

The retelling of the biblical data in the *Document* is only the starting point for its composer who intended to depict Levi, the eponymous patriarch of the priestly tribe, as a model priest and scribe.
Most of the material is not inspired by the biblical stories, and many
times it is even at odds with the ritual descriptions of the Pentateuch.
The main difficulty in assessing the full relationship between the
Genesis story and the *Document* stems from the fact that its retelling
of the Genesis account is very fragmentary. Additionally, the preserved textual form of the composition lacks its beginning and its
end. Therefore, the full extent of its biblical inspiration cannot be
exhaustively established.

The preserved text of the *Document*, however, permits one to discern a well-defined structure and literary form of the whole work,
which contains Levi's priestly elevation, his priestly education, and
his address to his children concerning their educational role and eminent social position. The whole composition begins with Levi's prayer
preceded by a short preamble (*A.L.D.* 1a vv. 1–4), in which Levi
prepares himself to enter the presence of God by ablutions and correction of his ways. The prayer (*A.L.D.* 1a vv. 5–19) is composed of
a litany of requests from God concerning Levi's separation from evil,
his personal salvation, and gift of wisdom. Additionally, he prays to
be brought near to God (*A.L.D.* 1a vv. 11, 17) and to execute righteous judgment (*A.L.D.* 1a v. 18). In the context of the whole composition these two demands stand in close connection with Levi's
priestly elevation and execution of his priestly law. Levi then leaves
the place of his prayer, and continues his trip to Jacob (*A.L.D.* 1b).
Meanwhile, he has his first vision, in which he sees a high mountain and the gates of heaven. Unfortunately, the rest of the vision
text is missing. The fragmentary text continues with the story of
Dinah's rape and Levi's preparations to revenge her (*A.L.D.* 1c–2).
Then, the selling of Joseph is recounted (*A.L.D.* 3), and the second
fragmentary vision begins with the condemnation of a woman who
dishonors her family (*A.L.D.* 3a). The vision also contains the description of two opposed kingdoms—the priestly kingdom (*A.L.D.* 3c–4)
and the kingdom of the sword (*A.L.D.* 4–5), while its last part contains Levi's heavenly elevation. Seven angelic beings proclaim his
elevation and assign to him the greatness of eternal peace (*A.L.D.*
6–7). The voyage of the whole family continues to Hebron where
Levi is blessed by Isaac (*A.L.D.* 8). The narration suddenly goes back
to Bethel where Jacob is tithing his properties and Levi's priestly

ordination takes place (*A.L.D.* 9–10). The family returns (*A.L.D.* 11–13) to Hebron and Isaac teaches Levi the order of the holocaust offering in connection with the proper amount of meal offerings (*A.L.D.* 14–61). The amount of meal offerings (*A.L.D.* 31–47) constitutes a metrological exercise on fractions according to the Babylonian sexagesimal system. When Levi finishes his study of priestly and scribal matters, he tells the story of his marriage (*A.L.D.* 62) together with the birth of his sons and grandsons (*A.L.D.* 63–77), and gives a short account concerning the main events in his life up to his death (*A.L.D.* 78–81). Then he addresses his sons in a wisdom poem (*A.L.D.* 82–98), in which he exhorts them to continue to study the scribal and priestly wisdom and to impart the same teaching to future Levitical generations. The last preserved part of the composition contains Levi's speech to his children (*A.L.D.* 99–104), in which he announces to them their future glory and apostasy. The rest of the work is missing.

The beginning of the Levitical tradition according to which Levi as an individual has a priestly status may be deduced from Deut 33:8–11 and Mal 2:4–7. The *Document*, though, is not directly influenced by these passages. The image of Levi as a priest and scribe is never attested in the biblical texts, and is unique to the presentation contained in this Aramaic work. Two compositions found at Qumran, the *Testament of Qahat* and the *Testament of Amram*, are influenced by the *Document*'s literary form and thematics. Their fragmentary state, however, makes more detailed comparison difficult and hypothetical.

Two other literary works preserve the Levitical tradition about Levi as a model priest, and, together with the *Document*, constitute what has been dubbed "Levi-Priestly Tradition" (Kugler 1996a: 2). Their text is related to the *Document*'s account, but their contribution to the interpretation and understanding of the Aramaic work is negligible. The book of *Jubilees* contains a section dedicated to Levi's priesthood (*Jubilees* 30–32) that presents the story of Levi's priestly elevation similar to the *Document*'s narrative. Additionally, in *Jubilees* 21, Abraham transmits to Isaac ritual instructions similar to Isaac's teaching in *A.L.D.* 14–61. The *Jubilees* account, however, lost all the characteristics of a wisdom instruction imparted by a teacher to a student. Additionally, many elements of the *Document*, like Levi's prayer or wisdom poem, are simply absent in *Jubilees*, and any direct textual relationship between the two compositions is unlikely.

The Greek *Testament of Levi*, which is part of the *Testaments of the Twelve Patriarchs*, is a composition close in its text and thematics to the *Document*. It is certain, though, that it underwent several redactional elaborations before it took the final testamentary form in the *Testaments of the Twelve Patriarchs*. The *Testament of Levi* is of little value for the interpretation of the *Document* because of these redactional elaborations that molded its testamentary form and annihilated many literary units of the Aramaic work. The foremost example is the wisdom poem (*A.L.D.* 83b–98), which in *T. Levi* 13 lost all stylistic devices characteristic of Semitic poetry together with its literary structure and order. The following section that discusses previous opinions concerning our composition will also demonstrate how the textual and literary relationship between the *Document*, *Jubilees*, and the *Testament of Levi* dominated the scholarly attention and effort. However, this relationship appears of little importance for the overall understanding of the Aramaic work.

1.2   *Previous Research*

The interpretation and scholarly analysis of the *Document* have been as casual and fragmentary as the manuscript publication itself. First opinions concerning the composition were formulated by the editors of the Cairo Geniza fragments, and scholars took a real interest in it only when its antiquity was further confirmed by the Qumran findings. The delay in the publication of the Qumran manuscripts caused further trouble for even approximate analysis of all manuscript evidence. On the other hand, the discussion concerning the *Document* was overshadowed by the problems in interpreting the *Testaments of the Twelve Patriarchs*. The Aramaic work has been constantly cited as evidence that there existed a Jewish text of the Greek *Testaments* and this evidence spurred further research to reconstruct a Greek text free of Christian interpolations. Some scholars affirmed that the *Testaments* were essentially a Jewish document with Christian interpolations (Charles 1908a, Philonenko 1960—Essene provenance); the others contended that they were essentially Christian in the final redaction but previous stages of literary transmission could be be reconstructed on the basis of literary criticism (Becker 1970 and Ulrichsen 1991). M. de Jonge stated that the final Greek redaction of the *Testaments* was Christian and it was not possible to ascertain previous stages of the literary development (de Jonge 1953b; for the history of research, see Slingerland 1977). The publication and analysis of the fragmentary Qumran manuscripts of the *Document* led him to the same conclusion (de Jonge 1988).

As a text close in its content and general outline to the *Testament of Levi*, the *Aramaic Levi Document* has unceasingly been implicated in this discussion, but rather as a collateral argument that was used to prove or disprove the scholarly opinions on the *Testament*. For some scholars, the Aramaic composition, together with the fragments of the Hebrew *Testament of Naphtali* and *Judah*, is an unquestionable proof that a form of the *Testaments* existed prior to the Christian era and that these texts pointed to the Jewish origins of the *Testaments*. For others, the differences between existing Aramaic and Hebrew texts preclude their direct association with the Greek *Testaments* and a direct literary influence on the latter. Although this discussion helped to sharpen opinions concerning the *Document* and explicate its importance for the knowledge of Second Temple Judaism, it accounted for only one aspect of its possible interpretation, namely, its literary relation to the *Testament of Levi*. A short review of scholarly opinions should demonstrate this tendency.

When the first fragment of the previously unknown composition was published in 1900 by H. L. Pass and J. Arendzen, it became evident that its text was very close to the Greek *Testament of Levi*. The editors placed fragments of *T. Levi* 11–13 alongside the Cambridge fragment of the Aramaic text but, aware of many differences between these two, added the full text of *T. Levi* 11–13 at the end of the article. Bousset (1900) made the very first attempt to compare the Aramaic fragment with the Greek *Testament of Levi*. He analyzed the onomastic midrashim of Merari, Yochebed, and Gershon and pointed to the similarities between the Greek and Aramaic texts. These similarities, together with the convergence of the chronological details in both documents, suggested that the Greek *Testament* and the Aramaic fragment were probably "zwei allerdings stark abweichende Zeugen desselben Textes" (1900: 334).

The discovery of the Koutloumous 39 manuscript of the *Testaments* provided Charles and Cowley (1907) with Greek portions of the Aramaic work and pushed their reflection towards the provisional, but still prevailing, opinion concerning its relationship to *T. Levi*. They postulated that there existed a common source of the *A.L.D.*, *T. 12 Patr.* and the book of *Jubilees*, from which all these three compositions drew some of their material. The assumed date for this source was "not later than 150 B.C." and the opinion that Hebrew was the original language of the composition was argued. The Aramaic and Greek fragments of the *A.L.D.* were thought to be versions of this Hebrew common original (cf. also Charles 1908a: LIV and LVI).

Marinus de Jonge wrote and published his dissertation on the *Testaments* before any of the Qumran *A.L.D.* fragments were made public. In an appendix entitled "The Fragments of a Jewish Testament of Levi," he shortly analyzed the known Aramaic and Greek fragments (1953b: 129–131). He concluded that the Greek translates an Aramaic composition but the Original *Testament of Levi*, which stood behind both the Aramaic fragments and the Greek *Testament of Levi*, was originally written in Hebrew. He also dealt with the Cairo Geniza fragments when analyzing the *Testament of Levi* (pp. 38–52).

When comparing the *Document, Jubilees,* and *Testament of Levi*, he concluded that "there existed a Jewish source and that this source, Original Levi, was used by the author of the Greek Testament of Levi" (p. 52). De Jonge essentially refuted the interpolation theory concerning the origins of the *Testaments* and proposed a "compilation theory," according to which "the present Testament of Levi is a Christian writing for the compilation of which many Jewish elements have been used" (p. 52). He essentially repeated Charles' opinion concerning a written common source for the *A.L.D., Jubilees* and the *Testament of Levi* but his description of the content of the "Original Levi" was very approximate. His conviction that behind *Testament of Levi* there was a written source close in its form to the *A.L.D.* was then shared by Detlev Haupt (1969: 5–6) and Anders Hultgård (1982: 92–122). In his later analysis of the *Document*, de Jonge consistently defended his positions first expounded in his doctoral dissertation (cf. de Jonge 1975: 252–258). He remained convinced that, due to limited knowledge of the text transmission, it was not possible to know much about intermediary redactional stages between the Aramaic Levi and the *Testament of Levi* (de Jonge 1988).

The scholar who pushed the research on the *A.L.D.* in a different direction is Józef T. Milik. By his painstaking work on deciphering and publishing the Qumran scrolls he added greatly to the understanding of the *A.L.D.*, the reconstruction of its form, and a fresh perspective for its interpretation. In a series of articles and publications concerning the Qumran scrolls, he identified and first published manuscripts belonging to the *A.L.D.*, the *Testament of Qahat*, and the *Testament of Amram*. He proved that these three works depended on each other, depicting the life of the first three priestly patriarchs, and in their *Weltanschauung* they were close to the scribal circles responsible for the composition of the Enochic literature.

Milik's first opinions on the *A.L.D.* were expressed in his publication of the Qumran Aramaic portions of the *Levi Document*. He argued that the Aramaic work was of Samaritan origin and the divergences from the *T. 12 Patr.* proved that "les *Test. XII Patr.* sont une composition judéo-chrétienne, utilisant largement les ouvrages juifs proprement dits" (1955b: 406). He made a suggestion that the Geniza manuscripts were copies of a scroll found close to Jericho about 800 A.D. The same opinion was repeated in volume one of the DJD series where he published 1Q21. The fragments of 1Q21 compared with the manuscripts of the Cairo Geniza and *T. Levi* additionally confirmed the opinion that Greek *T. Levi* was a "résumé" of an ancient composition, "certainement antérieure aux Jubilés et au livre d'Hénoch" (1955a: 88).

In 1972 Milik published 4Q'Amram[b c] and entitled it "le livre des Visions de 'Amram," the son of Qahat, son of Levi (1972: 77–97). This text was similar in its visionary form to the Aramaic Levi and, according to the editor, it was known and cited by Origen in his 35th homily on Luke. It was probably written in the second century B.C. At the end of his article, Milik edited another Aramaic fragment from the fourth Qumran cave and identified it as the *Testament of Qahat*, "le fils de Lévi et le père d'Amram" (1972: 97). The existence of these three Aramaic compositions at Qumran attributed to the three priestly patriarchs was also confirmed, according to Milik, by the *Apostolic Constitutions*, vi 16,3, which speak about an apocryphal book, the title of which is τῶν τριῶν πατριαρχῶν. All the fragments of the *Testament of Qahat* were published by É. Puech in *Revue de Qumrân* in 1991 (1991: 23–54) and subsequently in DJD XXXI (2001: 257–282) together with all the manuscripts of the *Visions of Amram* (2001: 283–405).

Only in 1976 did Milik edit another small fragment of the unpublished 4QTestLevi[a] and he contended that the original Testament of Levi "is Samaritan in origin and was composed in the course of the third century, if not towards the end of the fourth" (Milik 1976: 24). Some scholars followed his opinion, usually situating the composition of the composition in the third century B.C. (cf. Stone 1988: 159, n. 2).

In his influential article concerning the pre-Essene literature found
at Qumran, Milik first discussed the Enochic trilogy (Enoch's visions,
chs. 6–19; *Astronomical Book*, chs. 72–82; and Enoch's calendar, similar to 4Q260), then spoke about the two books of Noah (1978:
91–95). The Aramaic *Testament* or *Visions of Levi* with its purported
allusion to the Enochic Visions and an explicit reference to the book
of Noah came next in the chronological order of the composition.
Milik discussed two toponyms of the *A.L.D.* in order to prove its
Samaritan origin and then published some tiny fragments of the
Testament of Judah and *Joseph* together with the *Visions of Jacob* (pp.
96–104). He concluded that all these pseudepigraphic works were
composed in Aramaic; some were of Samaritan origin with a later
developed Judean recension. This abundant Jewish literature, which
used the lingua franca of the successive political powers, developed
in the Persian period, or perhaps even earlier (p. 106). His opinion
concerning the Samaritan origin of the *Levi Document* did not find
many followers in the scholarly world (cf. Kugler 1996b).

Jürgen Becker in his *Habilitationschrift* about the history of the composition of the *Testaments*, dedicated a relatively large section to what
he called *aramäische Levi-Literatur* (1970: 69–105). He underlined that
all the Cairo Geniza fragments, Koutloumous 39 Greek additions
and Qumran findings formed one composition that was different
from the Greek *Testament* and whose traditio-historical relationship
to the latter was yet to be established (pp. 72–76). This was his main
task in the pages that followed but, since not all the Qumran fragments had been published, he decided not to analyze the inner traditio-historical interdependence of different fragments of which the
Levi Literatur was composed (p. 76). He first analysed *T. Levi* 5:3–9:7
and the "Paralleltraditionen," that is Gen 34, *A.L.D.* 1–3c, 4–13 and
Jub. 30–32 (pp. 77–87). He concluded that none of these texts were
directly dependent on *Genesis* or one on the other. Excluding a direct
literary interdependence, he postulated the existence of an oral tradition, the starting point being Gen 34–35. This oral tradition brought
its modification in the process of its retelling, and its transmission
developed into two different but connected lines. One resulted in
two separate Aramaic and *T. Levi* accounts and the other gave rise
to the *Jubilees* version of the story (pp. 84–87).

To further substantiate this thesis he set out to analyze the priestly
instructions of *Jub.* 21, *T. Levi* 9:9–14, *A.L.D.* 14–50, 61, and *A.L.D.*
51–60. He saw a strong connection between *Jub.* 21 and *A.L.D.*

51–60 on one hand, and between *T. Levi* and *A.L.D.* 14–50, 61 on the other (pp. 90–91). By pointing to the existence of two separate sources in the *A.L.D.* priestly instruction and comparing them with *T. Levi*, Becker reaffirmed his thesis that their similarities and differences stemmed not from a common written source but from the oral stage of the transmission of these two compositions, while the elements shared with *Jub.* 21 came from their common oral source (pp. 91–92). Becker's further comparison between *A.L.D.* 62–81 and *T. Levi* 11: 1–12:6 (pp. 93–101) and between *A.L.D.* 78–95 and *T. Levi* 12–14 (pp. 101–13) went along the same line of interpretation. He did not explain the problem of *T. Levi* 4:2 that presupposed knowledge of Levi's prayer.

Becker's analysis introduced some new perspectives for the understanding of the *A.L.D.* in the form available to him. He stated that the *A.L.D.* fragments form a composition that was different from the *Testament of Levi* and not dependent on the latter in its literary form. This observation gave a new thrust to his research, which first started from the literary analysis of the *A.L.D.* in order to compare it with the *Testament of Levi*. Of special interest is also his opinion that, from the literary point of view, the Aramaic composition was "eine in der Ich-Form erzählte pseudoepigraphische Lebensgeschichte Levis, die am Ende eine Abschiedsrede des Jakobsohnes enthält" (1970: 72). The results of the present research confirm Becker's opinion except for his claim that the last part of the *Document* constitutes a testamentary speech. Levi's didactic poem in *A.L.D.* 83b–98 is not a testamentary speech, for the deathbed scenario is completely lacking. After Becker's first steps in the literary analysis of the *A.L.D.*, no further attempts concerning the literary characteristics of the whole composition have been undertaken.

Since he was not interested in the final form of the Aramaic work, Becker did not analyze Levi's prayer (E 2,3; 4Q213a frgs. 1 and 2), which has no counterpart in the *Testament*. But it is this prayer and its literary form that attracted the attention of several scholars. David Flusser analyzed its content and labeled it as an "apotropaic prayer" together with "A Plea for Deliverance" (11QPs[a] col. XIX), Ps 155:1–19 (11QPs[a] col. XXIV), and some rabbinic prayers. The main theme of this type of prayer is "the asking from God to avert personal dangers and that He may grant heavenly bliss" (1966: 201). Seen in the context of the whole *A.L.D.* and the biblical tradition, Flusser's proposal appears not to take into account constitutive elements of Levi's prayer that require another interpretation. He eventually conceded that the prayer of Levi had less in common with rabbinic prayers than the two other Qumran psalms (p. 204).

Jonas Greenfield and Michael E. Stone published the first joint article with their "Remarks on the Aramaic Testament of Levi from the Geniza" (1979). They scrutinized the Geniza manuscripts, corrected many of Charles' readings, and added their comments on some Aramaic terms. They also stated that the language of the Geniza fragments is close to the Aramaic of the Qumran findings. In their opinion, the original language of the composition was Hebrew. In 1985 they published an English translation of all available Geniza and Qumran fragments of the composition (Greenfield and Stone 1985), and their next article used for the first time the expression "Aramaic Levi Document" to indicate all the fragments of this priestly work (Greenfield and Stone 1990). They also added to the understanding of Levi's prayer by commenting on its Greek and Aramaic parts (Stone and Greenfield 1993). They seemed to accept de Jonge's position on the literary dependence between the *A.L.D.* and the *Testament of Levi*, since they tried to situate the prayer within the *A.L.D.* on the basis of *T. Levi* (pp. 249–251, cf. Greenfield and Stone 1990: 154–158). They were also responsible for the publication of the Qumran fragments of the *A.L.D.* from Cave 4 (4Q213, 213a, 213b and 214, 214a, 214b) in the Discoveries in the Judaean Desert series (Stone and Greenfield 1996a: 1–72).

James Kugel (1993: 1–64) proposed to distinguish two different documents in the *A.L.D.* based on two different visions. His analysis of the content of the visions was mainly based on the *Testament of Levi*, in which he underlined the differences between the first vision (chs. 2–5) and the second one (ch. 8). He postulated the existence of these two visions in the *A.L.D.* as well. The first he called "Levi's Apocalypse," the second—"Levi's Priestly Initiation." The first vision described Levi's heavenly ascent, divine instructions and his consecration to be God's servant and minister, and it stemmed from the exegetical interpretation of Mal 2:4–7. The second one contained Levi's consecration to priesthood by seven divine emissaries and did not show any particular interest in the biblical exegesis. Only the latter could pretend to be a part of the priestly trilogy, together with Qahat and Amram compositions found at Qumran. These two visions were woven into one "Aramaic Levi Document," only after the composition of the book of *Jubilees* that was dependent only on the "Levi's

Priestly Initiation" document. Kugel's analysis is too superficial to be accepted. He elaborates the content of the two visions on the basis of the *Testament of Levi*, and transposes the results on the *A.L.D.* On the other hand, the non-visionary content of the *A.L.D.* is hardly noticeable in Kugel's analysis. Kugel's undeniable contribution to the understanding of the *A.L.D.* consists in his emphasis on the exegetical character of the composition.

Kugler's dissertation (1996a) marks an important advance in the knowledge of the *A.L.D.* For the first time, he publishes all Qumran fragments identified by Milik as belonging to the Aramaic *Testament of Levi*. His work represents a very first attempt to reconstruct the textual form of the *A.L.D.* His reconstruction is based not on the text of the Greek *Testament of Levi* but on all available textual witnesses to the Aramaic composition. However, his work is not solely limited to this document. He dealt with the parallel texts that depicted Levi's rise to priesthood and were mainly inspired by the *Genesis* 34 account of the Shechem incident. First, he traced the biblical roots of the tradition (*Genesis* 34; Num 25:6–13; Deut 33:8–11; Mal 2:4–7), and then reconstructed the textual form of the *A.L.D.*, transcribing, translating, and commenting on the Aramaic and Greek texts. He further argued that the *A.L.D.* had only one vision of Levi and not two, as wrongly assumed by previous scholars who based their reconstruction on the text of the *Testament of Levi*. Once the form of the *A.L.D.* was established, he compared it with *Jub.* 30:1–32:9 and the *Testament of Levi*. He concluded that *Jubilees* was not directly dependent on the *A.L.D.*, but on a source similar to it that he called "Levi-Apocryphon." The comparison between the *A.L.D.* and the *Testament of Levi* allowed Kugler to assume the existence and determine the content of a pre-Christian literary work used in the composition of the present *Testament*. He followed the opinion of de Jonge and others that there existed an earlier work before the final redaction of the *Testament of Levi* and called this work "Original *Testament of Levi*". His conclusions concerning especially the assumption of only one vision in the *A.L.D.* and the existence of the Original *Testament of Levi* have been criticized by de Jonge (1997). The criticism of Kugler's one vision theory will be discussed later in this work (cf. § 1.4.3.3).

1.3 *Purpose of the Study*

The review of scholarly opinions presented some general ideas concerning the *A.L.D.* and related literature. The present research does not pretend to solve all the riddles of the *A.L.D.* and Levi-Priestly Tradition (*Aramaic Levi Document; Testament of Levi; Jubilees* 30–32). It also does not intend to reconstruct various literary stages in the transmission of the *Testament of Levi*. Neither does it pretend to reconstruct the common source for all the existing compositions of Levi Priestly Tradition, an attempt undertaken by Kugler in his dissertation. Its main purpose is to gather and analyze all existing manuscripts of the *Document* and write a detailed commentary on the text. The necessity of the undertaking is self-evident—no scholarly work has ever presented all the manuscripts of this ancient work, and no scholarly presentation has extensively dealt with questions concerning its literary form and historical background. One may only wonder that, although Greek parts of the *Levi Document* were first published in 1907, no one has ever discovered the Babylonian scribal background of *A.L.D.* 32a–47. This one fact may suffice as a justification to return to the composition once again and try to interpret it not in the context of the Greek *Testament of Levi*, but as an independent composition with its own ideas to transmit and teaching to impart. Viewing the *Levi Document* as a longer version of the *Testament* appears unjustified in the light of the present research.

Chapter one of this research describes all manuscripts that contain fragments of the *Levi Document* and analyzes their reconstructed order. It should also answer some fundamental questions as to the literary genre of the Aramaic work, its author, date, and purpose of composition. Finally, since Levi's pseudepigraphic work is closely related to wisdom and educational traditions of the ancient Near East, a comparison with Sumerian and Akkadian didactic literature is necessary. The Israelite didactic tradition attested in biblical and extra-biblical sources does not provide any example of Babylonian metrological exercises similar to those found in the *Document* (*A.L.D.* 32a–47).

Chapter two gathers all available manuscript evidence containing different fragments of this Aramaic work. Although separate fragments have been published or republished by different scholars, no publication has fully presented the manuscripts, mainly because many Qumran fragments were not accessible to the scholarly world. There follows a careful scrutiny of all available manuscripts with the intention of deciphering, describing, and bringing together all the fragments available in Aramaic, Greek, and Syriac. Although all the evidence has been published several times by different students of Aramaic literature, the reconstruction of the Qumran witnesses published by Greenfield and Stone has proved to be at times faulty. A comparison between Qumran texts and Cairo Geniza manuscripts appeared to be of particular help in dealing with the reconstruction of the Qumran fragments. A new translation accompanies the text, its fragments being disposed in the order reconstructed in accordance with the available manuscript evidence. It must be stressed that, notwithstanding all the painstakingly undertaken restoration, the *Document* still remains a fragmentary composition. Its beginning and end are lacking, the results of the text reconstruction are, therefore, not a final word concerning the textual form of the whole work. Further research and, hopefully, further manuscript discovery, may shed a new light and change many of the conclusions delineated in this study.

The Commentary presented in the third chapter sets the main ideas of the composition in the context of biblical and extrabiblical ancient literature. Recourse to Sumerian school literature has proven to be of invaluable help for the understanding of the *Document* and its ideas concerning Levitical education. The analysis of literary form and structure of different sections of the composition should help in a better understanding of its literary components and message linked to its literary form. Of particular importance is the observation that Isaac's speech in *A.L.D.* 14–50 is a wisdom instruction intended to teach Levi fundamental priestly duties in connection with metrological knowledge.

Once the text-critical work, literary analysis, and commentary of the whole composition have been completed, overarching conclusions concerning its author, date, place, and purpose of composition may be drawn. Further research is needed, however, to analyze the conclusions reached in this work in the context of other documents dealing with Levi-Priestly Tradition. The person of Levi as an ideal priest was taken over by early Christian generations and his prophetic qualities helped to build an *ex eventu* prophecy in the *Testaments* concerning the coming of a new priest in the person of Jesus Christ. One may also hope that the analysis of the certainly pre-Christian Levi composition will shed some further light on the question and may foster the understanding of Levi's presentation in the Letter to the Hebrews. The *A.L.D.* presents Levi as the priest of God the most high, who receives a tithe as a sign of his priestly election (*A.L.D.* 9). Through the divine election and Isaac's instruction he is the founder of the royal priesthood responsible for upholding the just order (*A.L.D.* 1a v. 18; 3a–7; 14–50). This royal priesthood is then inherited by Qahat (*A.L.D.* 67), and Levi's sons continue their royal rule (*A.L.D.* 99–100). The author of the Letter to the Hebrews demotes Levi from his priestly and royal position by affirming that, in the person of Abraham, Levi has already paid the tithe to Melchizedek, the royal priest without genealogy and a typological forerunner of Christ's priesthood (*Hebrews* 7). By introducing Melchizedek and the tithe motif into the discussion concerning the installation of a non-Levitical priesthood, *Hebrews* 7 appears to react against the vision of Levitical royal priesthood depicted in the *Aramaic Levi Document*.

1.4   *The Text of the* Document

The *Aramaic Levi Document* has been preserved in a very fragmentary state. Beginning in 1896, the manuscripts of this lost composition from the Second Temple period have been found in different places in Greece, Egypt, and Qumran. Some parts of this important work have been preserved only in Greek, and the Aramaic original available to the translators is lost. The most recent findings at Qumran provide the oldest available manuscript evidence, and it often overlaps with other manuscripts of the *Document*. The mutual relationship of the manuscripts and the order of events in the whole composition are not always easy to grasp. The following section intends to help the reader in getting acquainted with all the problems related to the manuscript publication, their paleographical description, and reconstruction of the manuscript order. The paleographic description is based on work with the manuscript photographs provided by the scientific institutions that own them. The description of the Cairo Geniza fragments provided here has benefitted from direct consultation of the originals in Cambridge and Oxford.

1.4.1   *History of Publication*

The publication of different fragments of the *Aramaic Levi Document* has extended over nearly a century. The first identified fragment of this composition was published in 1900, the last in 1996, when both the doctoral thesis of Robert A. Kugler and the official edition of the Qumran fragments in the *Discoveries in the Judaean Desert* series appeared. In 1896 S. Schechter brought to England thousands of different manuscripts from the Geniza of the Qaraite synagogue in Old Cairo. Among them H. L. Pass (1900) identified a fragment of what he considered to be the Aramaic text of the Greek *Testament of Levi*, and published it jointly with J. Arendzen. It was the first fragment of the *A.L.D.* ever made public. It belongs to the Cambridge Taylor-Schechter collection and is composed of two vellum leaves, which, according to the editors, contain passages parallel to *T. Levi* 11–13 that were published alongside its Aramaic counterpart. The editors dated the manuscript to the eleventh century A.D. and also recognized that the first part of the fragmentary leaf (MS A 1c–3) should have occurred earlier in the codex than the second part (MS A 67–96). Additionally, they identified and republished a Syriac fragment of the Aramaic work (MS B) that they found in the *Catalogue of Syriac Manuscripts in the British Museum*, published by W. Wright (1871: 997).

Several years later, R. H. Charles and A. Cowley (1907) republished the Cambridge fragment together with another freshly identified portion of the same composition, one leaf of the Cairo Geniza fragments preserved in the Oxford Bodleian library. The editors also came to know a Greek manuscript of the *Testaments of the Twelve Patriarchs* photographed by Prof. Lake in the Koutloumous monastery at Mount Athos in Greece. One of the additions to the manuscript, not known from previous evidence, corresponded word for word with a part of the Cairo Geniza fragment and had a section that was not covered by the Aramaic fragments. The whole insertion was added by a copyist to the manuscript at *T. Levi* 18:2. The article, however, did not contain its complete text, only the parts that run parallel to the Aramaic fragments.

Charles republished all these Aramaic, Greek, and Syriac fragments of the *A.L.D.* in his edition of the critical text of the *Testaments of the Twelve Patriarchs*. They were brought together in parallel columns in "Appendix III" (1908a: 245–257) that until today constitutes a helpful tool to use and consult. In his introduction to the whole work, Charles describes the Mt. Athos Greek manuscript and gives it siglum *e*. The manuscript was copied probably in the tenth century and contained unique additions to the *Testaments*. These additions were inserted in the text in three different locations: the first in *T. Levi* 2:3, the second in *T. Levi* 18:2, and the third in *T. Ash.* 7:2. The first insertion was published by Charles in his critical apparatus (1908a: 29), the second in his Appendix III where it parallels the Aramaic text, and the third, since its content is undoubtedly Christian, was not published at all. When de Jonge published his final critical edition of the *Testaments* (1978), he also incorporated the manuscript *e* additions except the one at *T. Ash.* 7:2. The latter is not a witness to the *Testaments'* text but an independent exposition of the Trinitarian doctrine and other topics, and was probably inserted in the codex in a wrong place (de Jonge and Hollander 1978: xvii). Additionally, when discussing the composition and redaction of *Testament of Levi* 2–7, de Jonge (1975: 254, n. 24) suggested in a passing remark that in *T. Levi* 5:2 the MS *e* contained a short sentence that most probably comes from the same work preserved in *T. Levi* 2:3 and 18:2 insertions.

In his article in *Revue Biblique* J. T. Milik (1955b: 398–406) published the first fragments of what he called "le Testament de Lévi en araméen" found in the Qumran caves. The first published fragment with the siglum 1Q21 3 overlapped with the Bodleian fragment of the Cairo Geniza manuscript col. a 1, 2 (or 3), 5–6, and 8–9. The second came from the fourth cave. It was composed of two separate leaves and contained the Aramaic counterpart of Levi's prayer in Greek. This prayer constituted the first addition to the *T. Levi* 2:3 in the manuscript Koutloumous 39 published by Charles in 1908. Milik called the former manuscript 4QLévi[b] and adjoined the fuller Greek text of the prayer. He dated this Qumran manuscript at the end of the second or beginning of the first century B.C.

This important article described concisely other unpublished fragments of "le Testament de Lévi en araméen," as Milik labeled them. He mentioned the existence of three manuscripts of this composition at Qumran. The first one consists of only one fragment corresponding to the Bodleian fragment col. a, l. 7–21 (vv. 6–9). The second one (4QLevi[b]) was published in his article. The third was composed of many fragments that corresponded to the Bodleian fragment, col. d, 1–15 (*T. Levi* 18:2 addition, vv. 25–30) and to the Cambridge fragment, col. e, l. 4 to col. f, 19 (vv. 82–95); then, another fragment begins with the last two words of Cambridge f, 23. Finally, he signaled the existence of other fragments of the third manuscript for which he found no parallel in the Cairo Geniza texts.

About eleven years later Milik (1966: 95, n. 2) classified these three manuscripts as belonging to one scroll 4Q213, TestLevi[a]. He also mentioned his identification of further fragments from Qumran Cave 4 (4Q214 or TestLevi[b]) that form a second manuscript of the Levi composition.

Moreover, in 1955, Milik published sixty fragments of the Aramaic *Testament of Levi* in the first volume of the newly inaugurated series *Discoveries in the Judaean Desert* (1955a: 87–91). These were mostly so tiny that their relationship with the known Aramaic and Greek fragments of the Levi composition was hypothetical. 1Q21 3 and 4, however, are matched by Bodleian fragment col. a lines 2–9 and line 15 respectively. Milik also considered possible the connection between the manuscripts of the Cairo Geniza Caraite synagogue and the discovery of the scrolls in the Qumran area around A.D. 800. He suggested that the latter were copies of the former. In another article, however, he did not exclude the possibility of an uninterrupted manuscript tradition that could have lasted even more than ten centuries (Milik 1955b: 405, n. 3).

For a long time, these two publications and the first description of the unpublished manuscripts constituted the sole available information of this Aramaic work found in Qumran. In 1976 Milik published two additional fragments of this composition in his volume dedicated to the Aramaic books of Enoch, labeled them as 4QTestLevi[a] 8 iii 6–7 (4Q213 frgs. 3 and 4 1–4) and situated them in the context of *T. Levi* 14:3–4. He also dated this manuscript to the second century B.C. (1976: 23–24).

Jonas C. Greenfield and Michael E. Stone contributed to a better understanding of the Cairo Geniza manuscript of the *A.L.D.* by publishing an article in which they presented many corrected readings of the Bodleian and Cambridge fragments (1979). They also published a photograph of the Cambridge fragment, commented upon many verses of the text, and stated that "the Aramaic of the Geniza *Testament of Levi* is similar to that of Qumrân Aramaic and is on the whole free of later forms" (1979: 228). In this way, the antiquity of the Geniza fragments was further confirmed.

Subsequently, Joseph Fitzmyer and Daniel Harrington (1978: 80–90) republished the then available Qumran portions of the *A.L.D.* in their *Manual of the Palestinian Aramaic Texts*. Several years later, in his monumental volume *Die aramäischen Texte vom Toten Meer*, Klaus Beyer (1984: 188–209) gathered the then available manuscript evidence and, for the first time, he tried to set the *A.L.D.* fragments in a logical order. He imposed his own sigla (L for Cairo Geniza text, xL for Qumran manuscripts) together with chapter division. His reconstructions of the readings were sometimes dubious and he often created a conflated Aramaic text on the basis of the Greek manuscript *e*. In the *Ergänzungsband* to his first volume (1994: 71–78), Beyer published the remaining parts of the *A.L.D.* from Qumran, without adding any kind of paleographical or textual commentary concerning the manuscripts.

Several years later, É. Puech (1992: 449–501) presented three further Qumranic manuscripts: the first two identified as probably belonging to the Aramaic portions of the *Testament of Levi* (originally named 4QAhA and 4QAhB), the third belonging to the *Testament of Jacob* (4QAJa). Since these two manuscripts were preserved in a very fragmentary state, their exact identification caused many problems, but it was safe to state that their content showed an interest in the Levitical priesthood. One of the fragments described a mysterious person who would make atonement for all the people of his generation (4QTestLévi[d] 9 i 2), a propitiatory action belonging to the priestly prerogatives. Since the connection to the Aramaic fragments of the recognized Levi composition rests solely on the vocabulary level, the general scholarly opinion has been reluctant to accept these fragments as being part of the *Document* (cf. Fitzmyer 1999: 457–458).

Michael Stone and Jonas Greenfield (1993: 247–266) published the Aramaic text of Levi's prayer from Qumran (4QLevi[b]) together with its full Greek version of the Mt. Athos *e* manuscript. They essentially reproduced the text made public by Milik in his 1955 article but added a partial reconstruction of the prayer based on the retranslated Greek text. Their second contribution to the understanding of the prayer was the first attempt of verse by verse philological and literary commentary of the whole text of the prayer. In their article they also announced that it was now their responsibility to prepare the official publication of the remaining fragments of the Levi composition for the DJD series.

As preparation for the DJD series publication, Stone and Greenfield published four articles in *Le Muséon* with the Qumran fragments of the *Document*. They divided the fragments, identified and arranged on the plates by J. T. Milik, into six different manuscripts. Their first article (1994) contained 4Q213; the second (1996b) presented 4Q213a; the third (1996c) had 4Q213b and 4Q214; in the fourth article (1997) they edited the last two manuscripts, 4Q214a and 4Q214b. All these manuscripts were republished with minor changes in the twenty-second volume of the *Discoveries in the Judaean Desert* series (Stone and Greenfield 1996a). The first three articles originated as a result of common work by these two scholars. Since Jonas Greenfield's sudden death on March 20 1995, the task of finishing the publication fell on M. Stone alone, who was helped in the matters of Aramaic grammar and orthography by M. Morgenstern (cf. Stone and Greenfield 1997: 271, introductory note to the article). Morgenstern's notes on grammar and orthography assisted the publication of 4Q214a and 4Q214b in the DJD series and in the fourth *Le Muséon* article (Stone and Greenfield 1997).

Another reference that should be added to the above-mentioned publications is the book by R. A. Kugler (1996a). This is his revised dissertation written under Prof. J. VanderKam and defended at Notre Dame University in May 1994. Kugler collected all the available textual evidence concerning the Levi composition and tried to reconstruct the shape of this fragmentary Aramaic work in order to determine by comparison with *T. Levi* and *Jub.* 30–32 their common source, which he called the "original Aramaic Levi." His dissertation was not conceived as a critical edition of the Qumran fragments, but in order to present his own transcription of the Qumran texts, he had to impose his own sigla of the fragments, which were not yet officially published in the DJD series. Since he did not publish the photographs of the Qumran fragments, any attempt to compare his transcription with the Greenfield and Stone publication of the same manuscripts in DJD will prove how challenging this comparison may be. When presenting the manuscript evidence, he omitted the Greek text of MS E 18,2 wherever it overlapped with the Cairo Geniza fragments. He also did not include the text of the Syriac fragment (MS B). His overall presentation of the manuscripts was therefore not exhaustive.

Three additional fragments have been associated with the text of our composition, they cannot be, however, connected with it in an unequivocal manner. The *Damascus Document* retrieved from the Cairo Geniza contains the words of Levi concerning three nets of Beliar, that is fornication, wealth, and defilement of the temple (CD-A IV 15–19). Although the passage echoes the language of *A.L.D.* 16, it cannot be recognized as a citation of the Aramaic work (Milik 1978: 95), and the correction of its text (Greenfield 1988: 319–322) is not

a sufficient proof that it once belonged to this Levi composition. The
second possible reference to the Aramaic *Document* is found in the
writings of an Egyptian monk, Ammonas, who cited the words of
Levi describing himself as God's servant invested with the gift of the
divine spirit (cf. Tromp 1997: 235–239). It is clear that the citations
attested in the fourth century A.D. Egypt do not come from the available text of the Aramaic work. Their content is, however, close to
the request Levi makes in his prayer for the gift of the holy spirit
(*A.L.D.* 1a v. 8) in his capacity of God's servant (*A.L.D.* 1a vv. 11,
17). The third text associated with the *Document* is a short sentence
attested in *T. Levi* 5:2 (MS E) that presents Levi as a high priest
who makes propitiation for the sins of ignorance of the earth. Although
this short text most probably goes back to an Aramaic original and
shares some characteristics with the MS E 18,2 insertion, it lacks a
clear connection with the Aramaic and Greek portions of the Levi
composition (see the reconstruction of MS E 2,3 in § 1.4.3.3).

From the review of the material concerning the text of the *Document*
some conclusions may be drawn. Although the set of manuscripts
that belong to the Aramaic work has already been published in full,
all the publications present only partial attestations of its available
manuscript evidence and a critical edition of the whole composition
does not exist. On the other hand, the fragmentary state of the work
calls for a comprehensive reconstruction of the respective textual witnesses and assessment of their mutual relationship. The oldest Qumran
witnesses to the *Document*'s text are preserved in a very fragmentary
state and their reconstruction and order must be based on the much
later Cairo Geniza fragments and the Mt. Athos Greek text.

The review of the manuscript publication also indicates that there
are several fragmentary manuscripts representing the *Document*. Two
fragments of the same medieval codex from the Cairo Geniza (MS
A) belong to them; one short Syriac fragment found in a ninth century A.D. Syriac codex (MS B); two Greek insertions into the text of
the MS E that contains the *Testaments of the Twelve Patriarchs* (MS E
2,3 and 18,2); seven fragmentary manuscripts retrieved from the
Qumran caves (1Q21; 4Q213; 4Q213a; 4Q213b; 4Q214; 4Q214a;
4Q214b). In the following sections of chapter one (§§ 1.4.2–1.4.3)
they are paleographically described, then their mutual relationship
and reconstruction help sort out their proper order and textual form.
Chapter two contains their text in the established order and, for the

sake of clarity, overlapping Qumran witnesses are relegated to a separate section.

1.4.2 *Manuscript Description*

1.4.2.1 *The Qumran Fragments*

The fragments are described in the order in which they appear on the plates, not in the order of their disposition in the *Document*'s reconstructed text. The numbers of the photographs and inventory numbers are cited according to Tov, Emanuel *et al.* eds. 2002. *The Texts From the Judaean Desert: Indices and Introduction to the Discoveries in the Judaean Desert Series*. Discoveries in the Judaean Desert 39. Oxford: Clarendon. Pp. 33 (1Q21), 52 (4Q213–214b). Identification and disposition of the fragments on the plates were the work of J. T. Milik. The editors in the DJD series departed from the results of Milik's disposition only in one case. They moved 4Q213a frg. 6 from PAM 43.243 to PAM 43.242 (cf. Stone and Greenfield 1996a: 25). Dimensions are given at maximum for height and width. All of the Qumran *A.L.D.* texts were written on leather.

Table 1. Qumran Manuscripts and their Photographs

Manuscript	PAM Photographs Number	Museum Inventory Number
1Q21 1 and 3–4	40.540	647
1Q21 45	40.490	647
4Q213–4QLevi^a ar	43.241	817
4Q213a–4QLevi^b ar	43.242, 43.243	249
4Q213b–4QLevi^c ar	43.242	816
4Q214–4QLevi^d ar	43.243	370
4Q214a–4QLevi^c ar	43.260	370
4Q214b–4QLevi^f ar	43.260	370

Initially Milik (1955b: 399) indicated the existence of three manuscripts of the *Document* in Qumran Cave 4. In the course of further research he affirmed that they constituted one manuscript 4Q213 and identified a second fragmentary manuscript 4Q214 (1966: 95, n. 2). When transcribing the Qumran fragments, Kugler (1996a: 34–38) divided them into only two manuscripts. The handwriting was for Stone and Greenfield (1996a: 1–72) the main paleographic criterion to divide the Qumran Cave 4 texts into six different manuscripts. Additional restoration of several columns and overlapping

of the Qumran witnesses corroborate this division and confirm Stone
and Greenfield's opinion. The seventh manuscript, 1Q21, comes from
the first Qumran cave and is composed of sixty tiny fragments that
contain very limited textual evidence. Only four of them are of interest for the reconstruction of the *Document*. Several fragments from
Cave 4 preserve their margins and column disposition of the text.
The overall reconstruction based on the Cairo Geniza manuscripts
yields the following results.

Division according to the line length and number of lines in a column:
1. 4Q213 frgs. 1 and 2 (4QLevi[a] ar)—23 lines in a column, 50
   to 60 letter-spaces.
2. 4Q213a frgs. 1 and 2 (4QLevi[b] ar)—18 lines in a column, 50
   to 60 letter-spaces.
3. 4Q213b (4QLevi[c] ar)—the longest line length, more than 70
   letter-spaces, similar to 1Q21 3.
4. 4Q214 frg. 2 (4QLevi[d] ar)—between 30 and 40 letter-spaces.
5. 4Q214a frg 2 (4QLevi[e] ar)—37 lines in a column, 50 to 60
   letter-spaces.
6. 4Q214b frgs. 2–6 (4QLevi[f] ar)—10 lines in a column, 50 to
   60 letter-spaces.
7. 1Q21 3—the longest line length, more than 70 letter-spaces,
   cf. 4Q213b.

1Q21 (Plate I)
Paleography
From the sixty tiny fragments labeled by J. T. Milik 1Q21 (1955a:
87–91, Pl. XVII), only four unequivocally overlap with the *Document*
(frgs. 1, 3, 4, 45). The main criterion to join these mostly tiny fragments was their paleographical homogeneity (cf. Milik 1955a: 87).

Frg. 1
5.8 × 2 cm; one oblong fragment with a clear handwriting. It preserves three lines of the text; in the third line only the tops of some
letters are visible. The leather is torn between lines 1 and 2 in the
right hand side corner of the fragment.

Frg. 3
2.5 × 2.2 cm; the fragment has three lines of the text preserved with
only few letters in the first and third line. In the second line two
words are easily recognizable, the third one is damaged.

Frg. 4

1.8 × 1.2 cm; a tiny fragment with three lines preserved. Few ink dots indicate the existence of line one; line two has two words preserved, while there remains the vertical stroke of a *lāmed* in line three.

Frg. 45

1.7 × 0.7 cm; in the right hand side of this small fragment the leather is warped and partially damaged. Few ink dots indicate line one, while line two has only two damaged words.

4Q213 (Plate II)

The manuscript written in a formal hand is composed of six fragments different in size. Stone and Greenfield (1996a: 3) dated the handwriting at around the middle of the first century B.C.

Frg. 1

10 × 13 cm; two pieces of leather sewn together. The right column preserves twenty one lines of text. The left column is much more fragmentary and preserves nineteen lines. Both columns have the upper margin about 1 cm high. The bottom margin together with the last two lines of the text is torn off (see reconstruction in § 2.2.6). The left column preserves the right margin about 1 cm wide. The scribe does not keep the left margin. The *ʾālep* of וקשטא in 1 i 7 was partially written on the right margin of the second column. Hence it is evident that the text was written after the two pieces of leather had been sewn together. A hook on the margin of the left column between lines 10 and 11 probably indicates the beginning of a new paragraph. A similar hook is observable on the margin of 4Q213a between lines 10 and 11. There is a dot above the final *pê* in line 14 of the right column, and a smaller point above the *tāw* in line 16 of the left column.

Frg. 2

4.5 × 8.6 cm; the fragment preserves the left side of one column. The left margin is sewn to another sheet of which only a fragmentary margin is preserved. Along the left margin, lines 7 through 16, small ink dots appear; they probably served as scribal references for the horizontal ruling. Ink traces on the sheet sewn to the left margin also indicate the presence of the ruling dots. The same procedure is observable on the right margin of 4Q213a frg. 2, lines 5–6

and 11 through 18. Lines 5 and 6 do not have the dots. They probably disappeared in the fold when the sheet was sewn to the second leaf. Hence the supposition that the dots were most probably
added before the two pieces were sewn together.

Frg. 3
2.9 × 3.9 cm; top margin is 1.5 cm high. The fragment is an upper
left side of a column. The left margin preserves seams.

Frg. 4
4.5 × 4.5 cm; the seams on the left side of the fragment indicate
that it preserves the left side part of a column. The leather is warped,
shrunk, and blackened.

Frg. 5
4.2 × 3.5 cm; the bottom margin is 1.6 cm high. The fragment is
a lower left side of a column. In several points the surface of leather
has been erased. It partially preserves 16 lines. The reconstruction
of 4Q213 1 i indicates that this manuscript has 23 lines in each column. That would suggest that 7 lines are now completely lost from
the column represented by the three fragments (4Q213 frgs. 3, 4,
and 5).

Frg. 6
2.3 × 1.8 cm. This tiny fragment is an upper right-hand side part
of a column. The top margin is about 1 cm high. The right edge
has several seams suggesting that the leather preserves the continuation of the preceding column represented by frgs. 3, 4, and 5. The
leather is slightly blackened and it preserves only two words in the
first line. The first word has only tops of the letters visible. Stone
and Greenfield (1996a: 24) claimed that this fragment was not part
of the *Document*. They noted that the handwriting of *ʾālep* and *lāmed*
differed from the rest of the manuscript.

4Q213a (Plate III)
The manuscript is composed of six fragments. It is written in a formal hand, and F. M. Cross ascribed the script to the late Hasmonean
period (Stone and Greenfield 1996a: 27). Milik (1955b: 399) dated
it to the second half of the second century or the beginning of the
first century B.C., and radiocarbon dating of this scroll confirmed his
paleographic judgment (Bonani 1991: 30).

Frg. 1

5 × 10.1 cm; bottom margin 1.7 cm. This is a lower left side of a column, triangular in shape. Holes of the sewing accompany the left edge. It preserves 14 fragmentary lines of the text.

Frg. 2

6.7 × 10.5 cm; right margin 1.4 cm, bottom margin 1.7 cm. This is a lower right side of a column, triangular in shape. Holes of sewing follow the right edge of the leather. It preserves 14 fragmentary lines of the text. Milik (1955b: 400) assumes that both frgs. 1 and 2 had eighteen lines in each column and that the first four lines are missing. The reconstruction of the text fully confirmed his supposition. On the edge of the right margin, lines 5–6 and 11–18, guiding dots indicate the horizontal ruling, a method used also in 4Q213 frg. 2. On the right margin between lines 10 and 11 a horizontally disposed hook indicates the end of a paragraph. A similar paragraph separator exists on the right margin of 4Q213 1 ii between lines 10 and 11.

Frg. 3

4.1 × 2.3 cm. The fragment is joined to the right side part of frg. 4. It preserves five fragmentary lines. The first preserved line, of which only lower parts of letters are visible, continues in the frg. 4, line 4. The first part of lines 4–8 is preserved in frg. 3, the second, in frg. 4.

Frg. 4

6.3 × 4.7 cm; left margin 0.7–1.7 cm, bottom margin 0.3–0.7 cm. The margins indicate that the fragment is a lower left side part of a column.

Frg. 5

4 × 1.6 cm; bottom margin 0.5–0.7 cm. The fragment contains three lines of text, but only three words are legible. It probably comes from the lower part of a column. Stone and Greenfield (1996a: 35) discerned two columns in it. However, line 2, with a large lacuna in the middle, accounts for one continuous text and does not allow us to discern two columns here. No other traces indicate a two columns disposition in the fragment. Milik proposed to join the fragment to the lower right corner of 4Q213a frg. 4, see Kugler 1996a: 80, n. 68. The physical joining, however, is not possible to assess.

Frg. 6
2.3 × 1.3 cm. This tiny fragment preserves three lines of the manuscript, of which only two words are identifiable. The scribal hand
indicates that it belongs to the same manuscript as frgs. 1–5.

4Q213b (Plate IV)
5.8 × 4.1 cm. This single fragment comes from the left side of a
column. The upper and lower parts of the column are missing. The
left margin is only partially preserved. The leather is light. There is
a hole in the leather above the final *pê* in line 3.

Stone and Greenfield (1996a: 38) expressed the opinion that the
color and type of the leather were different from other Qumran
fragments of the *Document*. They also recognized the handwriting as
different from 4Q213a, and belonging to the late Hasmonean type.
One should also note that the line length of the two manuscripts is
different.

4Q214 (Plate IV)
The manuscript is composed of five fragments. Only frgs. 1 and 2
overlap with the Geniza text. The hand of the scribe differs from
other Qumran manuscripts of the *Document*. F. M. Cross, in private
conversation with the editors (Stone and Greenfield 1996a: 44),
described the script as late Hasmonean. Hence the assumption that
the manuscript comes from around the middle of the first century
B.C.

Frg. 1
0.9 × 3.5 cm. A narrow fragment of leather preserving several letters in each line. It comes from the middle of a column. The surface is abraded in the upper left corner. The leather is fair. Line 5
allows the decipherment of the only complete word in the fragment.

Frg. 2
3.6 × 6.9 cm; bottom margin 2 cm. It preserves 10 fragmentary
lines of text. On the right side, lines 3–9, the leather is abraded.
The bottom margin indicates that the fragment contains the lower
part of a column.

Frg. 3
4.8 × 2.2 cm; right margin 1.1 cm. It contains five fragmentary lines
of a column. From the fourth, only the tops of some letters remain.

The fragment comes from the right-hand side of a column. It over-laps with no manuscript of the *Document*.

Frg. 4
1.5 × 2.1 cm. The fragment preserves four lines of writing. It does not overlap with any other witness to the *Document*. The first and last lines preserve respectively bottoms and tops of few letters.

Frg. 5
1.2 × 4.5 cm; an oblong fragment of leather with seven lines pre-served. The second line probably preserves a *vacat*. The identification of the content is impossible. Stone and Greenfield (1996a: 51) excluded it from the Qumran witnesses to the *Document*; the handwriting, in fact, is different from the other fragments. It is not possible to iden-tify any single word.

4Q214a (Plate V)
The manuscript is composed of two fragments. It is written in a for-mal hand and the script belongs to the late Hasmonean period, as pointed out by F. M. Cross (Stone and Greenfield 1996a: 54, n. 3.)

Frg. 1
3.2 × 1.7 cm. The right margin is 0.7 cm wide. The leather is slightly darkened. It contains three fragmentary lines of the text. It comes from the right side of a column, as the presence of the margin indicates.

Frg. 2
4.1 × 4.4 cm; inner margin 0.6–1.1 cm. Leather is blackened and ink partially rubbed out. It contains two fragmentary columns of the text. The scribe did not keep the left margin in the column. The leather is torn between lines 2 and 3 of col. i, and the tear crosses over to the left margin of col. ii. It stops there, however, and does not cut off the upper part of the fragment. Stone and Greenfield (1996a: 56) claimed the contrary and divided the manuscript into two separate fragments.

4Q214b (Plate V)
The manuscript is composed of eight fragments. Although the scribal hand appears to be close to 4Q214a, Stone and Greenfield (1996a: 54) pointed out that the forms of the *mêm*, final *nûn* and *lāmed* are different. Their opinion, however, can be disputed. The script appears to belong to the late Hasmonean period.

Frg. 1
1.6 × 1.7 cm. The leather of this fragment is light in color. It contains three lines of text from the middle of a column. An exact identification of the content is not possible. It does not overlap with any other *Document*'s manuscript.

Frg. 2
1.6 × 1.4 cm. The fragment is tiny and its lower part is joined to the upper side of frg. 3. Together with frgs. 3–6 it is part of one column. Frg. 6 preserves remains of a second column of this manuscript.

Frg. 3
4.7 × 3.8 cm. This fragment, irregular in shape, has its leather slightly blackened in its upper part. Seven fragmentary lines are preserved on the leather. The last three lines continue the text where frg. 6 i breaks off.

Frg. 4
0.6 × 1.5 cm. It has only few letters that indicate the presence of three lines. The reconstruction allows us to confirm the exactness of the disposition on the plate. The first line of this tiny fragment continues line 1 of frg. 1. The final part of the line is found on frg. 5, line 2.

Frg. 5
1.7 × 1.3 cm. It is a left-hand side of a column, preserving three fragmentary lines and tops of the letters from the fourth one. The bottom parts of these letters are preserved on frg. 6. Thus the joining between the two is certain.

Frg. 6
3.6 × 4.0 cm; inner margin 0.3–1.1 cm. It is joined to the bottom part of frg. 5 and preserves a left side of one column and beginnings of four lines of the second column. Leather is white and easy to read.

Frg. 7
1.6 × 0.8 cm. Two lines of text remain on this small fragment. Line one has bottoms of the letters, line 2 only their tops. Location of this fragment within the *Document*'s manuscripts is problematic.

Frg. 8
2.4 × 1.5 cm. It has three lines of text. The tops of the letters in
line 1 are cut off.

1.4.2.2   *The Cairo Geniza Fragments*
A Cambridge, University library, T-S 16.94 (Plates VI and VII).
Parchment. 37 cm × 25.5 cm. The two *folia* of a codex, recto-verso,
come from the end of the ninth or the beginning of the tenth century. There are two columns on each side of the second *folium* and
23 lines in a column. Horizontal and vertical ruling is applied on
both sides of the vellum. The script represents oriental handwriting
leaning towards semi-cursive (see Beit-Arié 1993: 31–34). It is certainly earlier than the square letters of the dated manuscripts of the
10th and 11th centuries, and belongs to the early layer of the Geniza
fragments as typologically described by E. Engel (1990: 311–313, pl.
19). The same hand is recognizable in Oxford MS Heb c 27 f. 56.
According to M. Beit-Arié, "the fragments belong to the earliest layer
of Geniza material" and were written before the turn of the mille-
nium (Greenfield and Stone 1979: 216).

The handwriting of the manuscript indicates that it was written
in the Eastern part of the Mediterranean. The parchment is carefully elaborated. The grains from the hair side were removed; the
parchment was smoothed and glossed, so that there is no difference between the hair side and flesh side of the sheet (cf. Beit-Arié
1981: 26).

The first *folium* (cols. a and b = *A.L.D.* 1c–2; 3) belongs to the
same double leaf as the second, but it is more fragmentary. It preserves in a fragmentary state the last nine lines of the first column
on the *recto* side and the last nine lines of the second column on the
verso side of the leaf. The first fourteen lines are missing on both
sides of the *folium*. It means that two full columns and fourteen lines
are missing between the end of the first preserved column and
the beginning of the second one. To this number should be added
the first fourteen lines from the beginning of the first column on the
recto side. At the bottom of the column there is a partially preserved
ʾālep, which may have a numerical value and indicate the beginning
of the first quire in the codex. The quires in Hebrew medieval codices
were numbered with Hebrew letters (see Beit-Arié 1981: 61). According
to all paleographical data and the content of the fragment, it belongs

to the same codex as MS Heb c 27 f. 56 of the Bodleian library, hence the same siglum has been assigned.

The second *folium* (cols. c–f = *A.L.D.* 66–80; 81–96) lacks the first two lines of the first column on the *recto* side, and the first two lines of the second column on the *verso* side of the leaf. The character of the fold between the first and second leaf suggests that the fragmentary first leaf stood earlier in the codex than the second one. The question arises how many more sheets, composed of two leaves each, stood in between the two.

The bottom margin is about 4.6 cm wide, the top and external margins are about 2.5 cm wide. The two inner margins where the two *folia* are joined amount to a total of 5 cm. The vellum has vertical and horizontal incised lines for the ease of writing. The letters are appended to the horizontal lines. There are only two vertical incisions, at the beginning and end of each column. The external margins of cols. d and e preserve ink dots for horizontal ruling (col d, lines 12–15, 17, 19, 21, 23; col. e, line 1, 3–6, 9, 15–18). Each horizontal incision extends from the external margin of one side of the *folium*, crosses two internal margins, and continues on the following side of the second *folium*. The fragment contains *A.L.D.* 1c–3 and 66–95.

A   Oxford, Bodleian library, Ms Heb c 27 f. 56r.–v. (Plates VIII and IX), catal. no. 2835,27, see Neubauer and Cowley 1906: 274. Parchment. 21.8 cm × 23 cm. This one *folium* of a codex comes from the end of ninth or beginning of the tenth century; there are two columns on each side, with 23 lines in a column. The script represents oriental handwriting leaning towards semi-cursive by the same hand as Cambridge T-S 16.94.

Horizontal and vertical ruling of both sides of the vellum is applied. Each horizontal incision extends from the external margin of the *folium* (cols. b and c) and continues in the inner margin partially preserved in col. d, lines 1–15. On the outer margin of the column b and c there are ink dots for horizontal ruling (col. b, lines 1–11, 17, 20; col. c, lines 1–9; 15–17; 20–23) that crosses over to the external margin. The preserved leaf is the left side of a sheet, the right side being torn off and lost. Hair side and flesh side of the leaf are indistinguishable. There are diagonal ink strokes at the end of several lines (col. a, lines 1, 3, 17; col. b, lines 6, 7, 22; col. c, lines 4, 10, 18, 22; col. d, line 9). The scribe thus filled the remaining space in the line. The fragment contains *A.L.D.* 4–32a.

1.4.2.3 *The Mt. Athos Fragments*

E Athos, Koutloumousiou 39, catal. no. 3108, see Lambros 1966: 1:278. 11th century. Parchment. 19.5 × 29 cm, ff. 275. Each side of the *folium* has two columns of forty lines in each column. It has been assigned siglum *e* in the critical edition of the *Testaments* by Charles 1908a: XI; the *Testaments of the Twelve Patriarchs* are found on ff. 198r.–221r. and ff. 223r.–229r. For the eleventh century minuscule handwriting, see Thompson 1912: 232–245.

The *Testaments* are preceded by a patristic work, Ἀντιόχου μοναχοῦ Ἠθικοὶ λόγοι. They are followed by the *Benedictio Iacobi in XII filios suos* (Gen 48:8–50:26) on ff. 229r.–231r. The *Testament of Levi* is found on ff. 201v.–207v. The insertions described below are found only in this manuscript of the *Testaments*. They are not written on separate *folia* of the manuscript. This fact indicates that the scribe considered them to be integral parts of the *Testament of Levi*. It cannot be proven that the copyist of this manuscript inserted them in the place where they are now found. He may have inherited this form of the *Testament of Levi* from a different manuscript, which is lost today. An erroneous insertion must be excluded for the same copyist left many detailed corrections on the margin of the manuscript up to *T. Jud.* 9:8.

E 2,3 MS Koutloumousiou 39, ff. 201v.–202r. (Plates X and XI). The text of the insertion begins in the line 27 of the first column, continues through the second column on the same verso side of the *folium*. It also occupies the first twelve lines of the first column on f. 202r. Altogether, it is disposed in 66 lines of the manuscript. The insertion directly follows *T. Levi* 2:3 καὶ τείχη οἰκοδόμησεν ἑαυτῆς ἡ κακία; it precedes the final part of *T.Levi* 2:3 καὶ ἐπὶ πύργοις ἡ ἀνομία ἐκάθητο. Although it is so clumsily inserted in the middle of the verse, there is no indication in the manuscript that the Greek scribe was aware of this fact.

E 18,2 MS Koutloumousiou 39, ff. 205v.–207r. (Plates XII through XV). This long insertion starts in line 6 of the first column on 205v. and ends in line 40 of the first column on 207r. It is disposed on three *folia* of the manuscript and its total number of lines amounts to 275. It follows *T. Levi* 18:2 ἐν πλήθει ἡμερῶν; it precedes *T. Levi* 18:3 καί ἀνατελεῖ ἄστρον.

1.4.2.4 *The Syriac Fragment*
B   Add. 17,193 (Plate XVI), British Museum, London, catal. no.
861, see Wright 1871: 997. Parchment, 25.5 cm × 16.5 cm; ff.
1r.–99r. It is dated to 874 A.D. (f. 99r.). It contains 125 short fragments in Syriac that come from different biblical and patristic works.
The title of the whole is, "A Volume of Demonstrations, Collections
and Letters" (*pnqyt' dtḥwyt' wdkwnš' wd'grt'*).

One fragment on f. 71r. contains a citation of the words of Levi
taken from his testament. The citation corresponds to MS A 78–81.
It is preceded by the commentary of Cyril on Isaiah (f. 70r.–v.) and
is followed by some extracts from the writings of Abba Makarios.

1.4.3 *The Order of Manuscripts and their Reconstruction*

Since the *Document* is fragmentary and no single manuscript contains
the whole text, a systematic reflection on the manuscript relations is
necessary. The Qumran texts are fragmentary, but their reconstruction
and order within the *Document*'s structure are facilitated by the comparison with the Cairo Geniza manuscript. The fundamental criterion for the reconstruction is the overlapping between different
manuscripts. However, one should note that the order of the Qumran
texts must sometimes remain arbitrary because there are no overlaps. In that case, the vocabulary analysis of a manuscript or comparison with other compositions of Levi-Priestly Tradition serve as
an indication in discussing its relation to other textual witnesses of
the *Document*.

The comparison with the Greek *Testament of Levi* is considered as
a help, not an obstacle, in the reconstruction of the text and events'
order in the *Document*. Some parts of the *Testament* are a literal translation of what appears in the *A.L.D.*, the others are heavily redacted.
It is undeniable, however, that the *Testament* follows a general outline of the events described in the Aramaic work. Kugler (1996a:
45–51) criticized the comparison with the *Testament of Levi* as a mis-
step in the reconstruction of the text of the *Document*. Although his
reconstruction led to a different order of events in the composition,
his conclusions are not entirely convincing.

1.4.3.1 *A Reconstruction of the Qumran Manuscripts*
Most of the Qumran manuscripts were recovered from the caves in
a fragmentary state, and the *Document*'s fragments are no exception

to the general situation. The fundamental criterion for arranging them in a proper order is their overlapping with the Geniza codex. Wherever the application of this criterion is possible, the given fragment may be securely situated within the order of manuscripts and events based on the aforementioned textual witnesses. Some fragments overlap with other portions of the manuscripts from Qumran, hence their placement within the *Document* creates no difficulty. The remaining portions that do not overlap with any other textual witness appear to be most problematic. Their relation to the whole composition and location within the structure of the text is at best hypothetical.

Since the following fragments overlap with MS A, their connection with the *Document* is easily established. This connection also allows a precise restoration of the Qumran fragmentary evidence on the basis of the MS A text. The overlapping Qumran fragments have been relegated to a separate section (§ 2.2) and presented in the order of their respective location in the fuller text of the MS A.

Table 2. Order of Qumran Manuscripts Based on MS A

MS A	Qumran Manuscripts
A 4–7	= 1Q21 3
A 6–9	= 4Q213b
A 9 ll. 15–16	= 1Q21 4
A 20–23; 25a–b	= 4Q214 1
A 22–24	= 4Q214b 4
A 22–25a	= 4Q214b 5–6 i
A 22–27	= 4Q214b 2–3
A 24–25b	= 4Q214a 1
A 26 l. 4	= 1Q21 45 2
A 25b–30	= 4Q214 2
A 29–31	= 4Q214b 5–6 ii
A 69b–73	= 4Q214a 2 i
A 82–95	= 4Q213 1 i
A 95–96; 98	= 4Q214a 2 ii
A 96 l. 23	= 4Q213 1 ii 1

Since Qumran Cave 4 yielded six manuscripts of the *Document*, it comes as no surprise that some of these fragments overlap as well. The evidence is sometimes reduced to one word or even part of the reconstructed word, it however confirms the textual relation of some

fragments to the *Document*. Thus 4Q213 1 ii overlaps with A 96 and
4Q214b 8 (*A.L.D.* 96–98). It becomes certain then, that the latter
fragment is part of the Aramaic work. 4Q214a 2 ii overlaps with A
95 and 4Q213 2 (*A.L.D.* 97–100), hence the latter text should belong
to the *Document* as well.

Table 3. Overlapping Qumran Manuscripts

4Q213 1 ii 4 and 6	= 4Q214b 8 (*A.L.D.* 96–98)
4Q213 2 5 (*A.L.D.* 97–100)	= 4Q214a 2 ii 5
4Q214 1 5	= 4Q214b 5–6 i 3
4Q214a 1 1	= 4Q214b 2–3 5
4Q214a 1 3	= 4Q214 1 7
4Q214b 2–3 8	= 4Q214 2 3 and 1Q21 45 2
4Q214b 2–3 7	= 4Q214 1 8
4Q214b 5–6 ii 3	= 4Q214 2 8

Several Qumran fragments do not overlap with any other manuscript witness to the composition, and their connection with the
A.L.D. is established mainly on the basis of the paleographic homogeneity with other fragments that overlap with MS A. Vocabulary
contacts with the *Document* together with relation to Levi Priestly
Tradition texts may additionally suggest their location in the Aramaic
text; their overall reconstruction, however, remains hypothetical.

Table 4. Qumran Texts without Parallels

A.L.D. 3a	= 4Q213a 3–4
A.L.D. 3b	= 4Q213a 5
A.L.D. 3c	= 1Q21 1
A.L.D. 101	= 4Q213 3
A.L.D. 102	= 4Q213 4
A.L.D. 103	= 4Q213 5
A.L.D. 104	= 4Q214 3

4Q213a 3–4 (A.L.D. 3a)

Paleographically these two fragments belong together with 4Q213a
frgs. 1–2 (*A.L.D.* 1a–1b). Although they do not overlap with any textual witness of the whole composition, their content indicates some
thematic and vocabulary connection with the *Document*. The first part
of the fragment (4Q213a 3–4 1–6) contains a speech against a woman

who desecrates the name of her father, most probably because of exogamous marriage. A similar reference to a woman who desecrates her father's reputation is found in the halakic regulations against exogamy in *Jub.* 30:5–7 in the aftermath of the Shechem killing. It may only be assumed, that, as in the *Jubilees* text, the angels proclaim the law to Levi when the Shechemites' punishment is over. Hence the fragment should belong to Levi's second vision, which takes place after the Shechem incident.

Another vocabulary connection with the *Document* helps locate this fragment in the context of Levi's second vision. Line 8 speaks about a "tithe of holiness, a sacrifice for God" (מעשר קודש קרבן לאל), and a similar phrase appears in the context of Levi's priestly ordination (*A.L.D.* 9 ll. 18–19). Since the second vision deals with Levi's heavenly elevation (*A.L.D.* 6), it is possible that the tithe motif appears in it as well. In fact, in a later midrashic work (*PRE* 37) the angel Michael introduces Levi before God's presence as a tithe that belongs exclusively to God (see the comment on *A.L.D.* 3a and 9). Note that Levi's priestly ordination in *T. Levi* 8 occurs in his second vision.

Some vocabulary contacts with the *Document* provide another reference as to the fragment's allocation within the manuscript evidence. When line 6 is interpreted in agreement with the preceding negative judgment concerning the shameful conduct of a woman, it claims that the name of her revilement will not be blotted out from her people forever. This negative opinion contrasts with E 18,2 v. 60 (*A.L.D.* 60), where Levi is assured that his name and the name of his descendants will not be blotted out forever. The negative judgment concerning the destiny of those who accept exogamous marriage is opposed by the example of Levi, who follows Isaac's advice to marry within the tribal family (*A.L.D.* 16; 62).

4Q213a 5 (A.L.D. 3b)
Since this tiny fragment is paleographically linked to 4Q213a, and since it contains two words that indicate priestly content, it has been assigned to the text of the *Document*. The two words "eternal priesthood" come from Exod 40:15 and Num 25:13, and agree with the Aramaic composition that assigns to Levi a priesthood that will have no end. The location of the fragment within the second vision is extremely hypothetical.

1Q21 frg. 1 (A.L.D. 3c)

The fragment preserves only three incomplete lines of the text. The second line indicates that somebody is speaking with an unspecified individual promising his sons the priestly kingdom, which will certainly do better than another, not specified kingdom. On the ground of paleographical homogeneity Milik (1955a: 88) assigns this manuscript together with other fragments of the *Document*, some of which overlap with the Cairo Geniza text (1Q21 3 and 4, 45). He observes that the context of the fragment probably corresponds to *T. Levi* 8:11, that is, Levi's heavenly investiture in his second vision. He further notes that line 2 finds an echo in A 19 l. 3 and E 65–67. Grelot (1956: 393–397) accepts Milik's reference to the *Testament*'s text, but he further notes that line two is to be connected with A 4, which describes the kingdom of the sword. 1Q21 1 should, therefore, precede A 4–7, which contains the final part of Levi's second vision. Thus two kingdoms, one of the priesthood and one of the sword, would be conferred to Levi. The interpretation of Grelot drew criticism from Becker (1970: 78–79), whose main objection is the fact that 1Q21 1 is too fragmentary to assume a sure connection with A 4–7.

Although 1Q21 1 is indeed fragmentary, Milik's paleographical judgment connecting 1Q21 1 with 1Q21 frgs. 3, 4, and 45 still stands. Therefore, one should try to find a most probable location for this fragment within the manuscript witnesses of the *Document*. Without accepting Grelot's interpretation concerning a double kingdom theory, the localization of the fragment within the context of the second vision is the most convincing one. Line 2 preserves 2m. sg. suffix that clearly indicates that somebody speaks directly with Levi. In the *Document*, Levi plays the role of the narrator except for Isaac's speech and the angels' speech, probably in the first, and certainly in the second vision. Isaac's speech is preserved in full and does not refer to the priestly kingdom at all. There remain two angelic visions, both preserved in a fragmentary state. The concept of a kingdom (מלכו) appears in A 4 l. 2 and in 4Q213 frg. 2 13 (*A.L.D.* 100 l. 16). In the latter fragment Levi addresses his children, as part of his exhortation. In the former, the seven heavenly messengers speak with Levi in his vision. The context of the angelic address to Levi demanding a direct speech form is the most appropriate one for 1Q21 1. Additionally, 1Q21 1 2 sets a contrast between the priestly kingdom and another kingdom that remains unspecified because the line breaks off. A 4–6 builds a similar contrast between the peaceful characteristics of Levi's priesthood and the kingdom of the sword subject to warlike anxieties. The tenor of both texts remains similar and locating 1Q21 1 within the context of the second vision attested in A 4–7 is still the most reasonable supposition.

4Q213 frgs. 3–5 (A.L.D. 101–103)
4Q213 frgs. 3–5 belong to the same manuscript as 4Q213 frgs. 1 and 2. The handwriting and the analysis of the vocabulary indicate that they are unequivocally parts of the *A.L.D.* Milik (1976: 23, n. 2) compared frgs. 3–4 with *T. Levi* 14:3–4. Although the exact parallelism between the two texts cannot be established, similar wording concerning a sinister future of the Levitical priesthood cannot be overlooked. Frg. 5 is paleographically linked with the preceding two. It most probably contains Levi's warning directed to his sons against some impending evil. The last fragment, 4Q213 6, preserves only two words and from the paleographical point of view one cannot unequivocally state whether it belongs to the same 4Q213 manuscript. Judging from the shape of the *'ālep* and *lāmed*, Stone and Greenfield (1996a: 24) exclude the fragment from the *Document*. Although the decipherment of the fragment in the present work is different, I agree with their conclusion but for a different reason. The fragment cannot be connected with any possible context in the Aramaic work.

4Q214 3 (A.L.D. 104)
Paleographically, the fragment is part of 4Q214 together with 4Q214 1 (*A.L.D.* 22–23, 25) and 2 (*A.L.D.* 25–30). The verbal form in line 3 indicates that somebody is addressing his audience in the second person plural. Since, in the context of the *Document*, that may have happened only in Levi's speech to his children, the fragment has been located at the end of the fragmentary evidence of 4Q213 3–6, which contains Levi's address to his priestly posterity. One might alternatively suppose that Levi talks to his brothers in the missing account of the Shechem incident (*A.L.D.* 1c–2). The text is, however, too fragmentary to allow an unequivocal conclusion.

Table 5. Qumran Fragments without a Clear Connection to the *Document*

4Q213 6
4Q213a 6
4Q214 4
4Q214 5
4Q214b 1
4Q214b 7

Since the fragments are tiny and preserve hardly a single word of their content, the restoration and location in the *Document* have not been possible.

1.4.3.2 *A Reconstruction of MS A*

The two Geniza fragments belong to the same codex as the size of the vellum and the handwriting point out. The Cambridge fragment is composed of one double leaf folded in the middle. The cracks in the fold between the two *folia* allow the supposition that columns a and b precede columns c–f in the codex. Cambridge a (A 1c–2) retells Gen 34, Cambridge b (A 3) deals with the selling of Joseph, and Cambridge c–f (A 66–96) contain Levi's life story and wisdom poem. This order of events is also found in *T. Levi* 6:3–7:4 (Shechem incident) and *T. Levi* 11–13 (life story and wisdom exhortations).

The right margin of the Bodleian *recto* side has been damaged (column a, column d on the *verso* side) so that it immediately starts with the beginning of each line without any right side margin. Lines 14–19 of the column a (*recto*) and d (*verso*) are damaged. The left margin of the *recto* side (column b) and right margin of the *verso* side (column c) are well preserved. They contain several incised horizontal lines that extend to the margin (col. b, lines 1–11, 17, 20; col. c, lines 1–9; 15–17; 20–23) as in the internal margin of the Cambridge fragment. Additionally, it may be noted that ink dots for guiding the ruling of the horizontal lines at the left margin of the *recto* side may be spotted in line 7, 9, 10, 12, 14 to 18, 20, and 21. The *verso* side preserves ink dots in the outer margin of the column c, lines 2 through 22. In the Oriental codices ink dots and pricking for guiding the horizontal ruling were confined only to the outer margin of the sheets (Beit-Arié 1981: 70 and 86). It means that the preserved margins of columns b and c are external margins of a whole sheet with two *folia*. What is preserved is a left part of the *folium*; the right part is torn off and lost. Kugler (1996a: 231) first attracted attention to this detail, but he made a mistake when noting that the cracks occur on the margins of the column a and c of the Bodleian fragment. The right margin of the column a is entirely cut off, while column d preserves only the ends of lines 1–15 without the inner margin.

The quires in Oriental codices were regularly composed of five sheets, each sheet having two *folia* folded in the middle (Beit-Arié 1981: 44). The Cairo Geniza manuscripts indicate that each *folium* contained four columns, two on the *recto* side and two on the *verso* side. These details allow us to reconstruct the quire to which the preserved Aramaic fragments and their Greek translation in E 18,2 belonged, as first attempted by Kugler (1996a: 232–233). The Bodleian fragment (A 4–32a), together with its lost right *folium*, constitutes the innermost sheet 5 in the quire. Since E 18,2 translates A 11–32a and continues where the Aramaic breaks off (vv. 32b–64), it is certain that it constitutes the left side of sheet four lost in Aramaic. The right side of sheet four is also lost, but from the disposition in the quire it is certain that it followed the right side of sheet 3 (Cambridge a–b = A 1c–3). As Kugler rightly noted (1996a: 232, n. 3), it is impossible to assume that the Bodleian fragment (A 4–32a) formed one sheet with E 18,2 v. 32b–64, for, in that case, the end of Levi's vision (Bodleian a = A 4–10) would have to precede directly the account of the selling of Joseph (Cambridge b = A 3). The end of Levi's vision (Bodleian a = A 4–7) indicates that there must have been an additional text in the preceding part of the codex.

The Cambridge fragment constitutes the third sheet of the quire, and, thanks to the Qumran finds, it is certain that the text of the Aramaic work does not end there. The Qumran texts and E 2,3 fill the second sheet, while nothing can be said about the context of the first sheet in the quire.

Table 6. Cairo Geniza Manuscript Reconstruction

Column according to MS A	Content (*A.L.D.* verse numbers)	Preserved Text
Column 1, right side of sheet 1	?	Missing
Column 2, right side of sheet 1	?	Missing
Column 3, right side of sheet 1	?	Missing
Column 4, right side of sheet 1	?	Missing
Column 1, right side of sheet 2	Levi's prayer (1a)	Missing = E 2,3/4Q213a

Table 6. (*cont.*)

Column according to MS A	Content (*A.L.D.* verse numbers)	Preserved Text
Column 2, right side of sheet 2	Levi's prayer (1a)	Missing = E 2,3/4Q213a
Column 3, right side of sheet 2	Levi's first vision (1b)	Missing = 4Q213a 2 11–18
Column 4, right side of sheet 2	Levi's first vision	Missing
Column 1, right side of sheet 3	Shechem account (1c–2)	A (Cambridge a)
Column 2, right side of sheet 3	Shechem account	Missing
Column 3, right side of sheet 3	Shechem account	Missing
Column 4, right side of sheet 3	Selling of Joseph (3)	A (Cambridge b)
Column 1, right side of sheet 4	Selling of Joseph	Missing
Column 2, right side of sheet 4	Selling of Joseph	Missing
Column 3, right side of sheet 4		Missing
Column 4, right side of sheet 4		Missing
Column 1, right side of sheet 5		Missing
Column 2, right side of sheet 5		Missing
Column 3, right side of sheet 5	Levi's second vision	Missing
Column 4, right side of sheet 5	Levi's second vision (3a–3c)	Missing = 4Q213a 3–4, 5; 1Q21 1
Central fold in the quire		
Column 1, left side of sheet 5	End of vision/ ordination (4–10)	A (Bodleian a)
Column 2, left side of sheet 5	Isaac's speech (11–18)	A (Bodleian b)/E 18,2
Column 3, left side of sheet 5	Isaac's speech (19–25b)	A (Bodleian c)/E 18,2
Column 4, left side of sheet 5	Isaac's speech (25b–32a)	A (Bodleian d)/E 18,2
Column 1, left side of sheet 4	Isaac's speech (32a–42)	E 18,2
Column 2, left side of sheet 4	Isaac's speech (43–50)	E 18,2
Column 3, left side of sheet 4	Isaac's speech (51–57)	E 18,2
Column 4, left side of sheet 4	Isaac's speech and marriage (58–64)	E 18,2
Column 1, left side of sheet 3	Levi's children (66–72)	A (Cambridge c)/E 18,2 vv. 65–69
Column 2, left side of sheet 3	Levi's life story (73–80)	A (Cambridge d)
Column 3, left side of sheet 3	Wisdom poem (81–90)	A (Cambridge e)/4Q213 1 i
Column 4, left side of sheet 3	Wisdom poem (90–96)	A (Cambridge f)/4Q213 1 i
Column 1, left side of sheet 2	Wisdom poem	Missing = 4Q213 1 ii

Table 6. (*cont.*)

Column according to MS A	Content (*A.L.D.* verse numbers)	Preserved Text
	(96–98)	1–11/4Q214b frg. 8 2; 4Q213 frg. 2 1–8
Column 2, left side of sheet 2	Future glory (99–100)	Missing = 4Q213 1 ii 12–19; 4Q213 frg. 2 9–16
Column 3, left side of sheet 2	Future apostasy (101–104)	Missing = 4Q213 frgs. 3–5
Column 4, left side of sheet 2	Future apostasy (101–104)	Missing = 4Q213 frgs. 3–5; 4Q214 frg. 3
Column 1, left side of sheet 1	?	Missing
Column 2, left side of sheet 1	?	Missing
Column 3, left side of sheet 1	?	Missing
Column 4, left side of sheet 1	?	Missing

The actual text of the Cairo Geniza manuscripts covers only the sheets three to five, the rest is supplemented by MS E 2,3, MS E 18,2, and Qumran fragments. Levi's prayer and first vision precede the midrashic retelling of the Shechem conquest based on Gen 34. It is followed by the midrashic account of the selling of Joseph based on Gen 37. Both accounts probably amount to an equal number of lines (three columns each?). One can also hypothetically assume that the last two columns of the right side of sheet 5 should contain Levi's second vision whose final part is found in Bodleian a (A 4–7). There follow Levi's ordination and Isaac's speech. There is no doubt that E 18,2 vv. 32a–64 preserves the text of four Aramaic columns of the Cairo Geniza disposition.

Much uncertainty remains as to the content of the right side of the fourth and fifth sheets in the reconstruction. It is certain that the story of the selling of Joseph begins on the right side of sheet three and probably continues on the right side of sheet four, it is impossible to know, however, how long it was and how much space it took in the manuscript. Its length has been hypothetically disposed in three columns of the Geniza text. It is impossible to know whether the story of the selling of Joseph continued up to the beginning of Levi's second vision. It is certain, however, that the vision followed on the right side of sheet five with its ending section on the left side of the same sheet.

Kugler (1996a: 232–233) filled the eight missing columns of the right side of sheets four and five with a different content. He believed that there was only one vision in the *Document*, hence Levi's prayer and vision should be placed in this eight column space. Levi's prayer (E 2,3 and 4Q213a frg. 1 to 2 10) should account for two Geniza columns, and the visionary material (4Q213a 2 11–18 and 4Q213a 3–4) accounts for one and a half. He then assumed that three columns, which probably followed Cambridge c, completed the account of the Shechem incident and introduced Levi's prayer. He allowed for another one and a half columns to terminate the vision account.

This reconstruction can hardly be justified even with a proper credit for its hypothetical nature. According to his reconstruction, the Shechem account should occupy a considerable length of seven consecutive columns, enough space to accommodate easily the biblical Shechem story of *Genesis* 34 retold twice. Never in the midrashic material dedicated to the slaughter of the Shechemites does this incident amount to such a length. To the contrary, it is always greatly shortened. Additionally, he wrongly identified Cambridge b (A 3) as belonging to the Shechem account. According to all probability *A.L.D.* 3 is a midrashic account of the selling of Joseph based on *Genesis* 37. Kugler's opinion about the existence of only one vision cannot be upheld either (see the reconstruction of MS E 2,3 in § 1.4.3.3). The prayer is followed by the first vision that could occupy the other two columns.

The remaining Qumran texts can easily be accommodated in the Cairo Geniza pattern on the left side of sheets three and two. With the help of the reconstructed Qumran fragments 4Q213 1 and 2, it is easy to notice that one column of the Qumran scroll contains two columns of the Cairo Geniza codex. 4Q213 1 i accommodates the text disposed in two columns in Cambridge e and f (A 81–95). Thus, one Qumran column corresponds to one two-column side of the Geniza *folium*. Hence it is possible to tentatively accommodate the additional Qumran evidence in the disposition of the Cairo Geniza manuscript. The end of Levi's wisdom poem occupies one additional column in the Geniza disposition corresponding to the first eleven lines of 4Q213 1 ii. The reconstruction of the latter proves that, similarly to 4Q213 1 i, it also had twenty-three lines. It means that the second part of the Qumran column 4Q213 1 ii together with 4Q213 frg. 2 should also account for another additional column in the Geniza codex.

The Qumran manuscripts also report Levi's prediction of his children's apostasy in 4Q213 frgs. 3–5. These fragments, therefore, must have had their place in the Geniza codex. The seams on the left side of frgs. 3, 4 and 5, together with the upper margin in frg. 3 and a bottom margin of frg. 5, suggest that they are part of one column, which, according to all probability, also had twenty-three lines. It is then probable that this part of Levi's address to his children should account for the other two columns in the Geniza disposition of the codex. There are, however, only sixteen attested lines in these Qumran fragments.

This hypothetical reconstruction of one quire of the Cairo Geniza codex accounts for all the manuscript data available. On the other hand, it points to the probability that the actual size of the whole text of the *Document* could have reached beyond the size of one quire only. And yet, the content of the right *folium* of the first and outermost sheet in the quire remains a mystery. It could have contained the introduction to the whole work, or perhaps another additional story, lost in the text transmission. The left *folium* of the same outermost sheet follows the last fragments of Levi's prediction (left side of sheet 2). It has no preserved text and nothing can be said as to whether the text continues or arrives at its conclusion. Because of the lack of additional manuscript evidence the answer to these uncertainties remains enshrouded in mystery.

1.4.3.3 *A Reconstruction of MS E*

MS E 2,3
Overlap between E 2,3 and 4Q213a frgs. 1–2
E 2,3 vv. 1–11 = 4Q213a 1
E 2,3 vv. 15–19 = 4Q213a 2 5–10

The MS E text of the prayer begins with Levi's ablutions and a short preparation for the prayer. It ends up abruptly in 1a v. 19, when Levi continues to pray in silence. Where the Greek text breaks off, the Aramaic overlapping fragment continues with the description of Levi's departure from the place where he prays, his trip to his father Jacob, and his presence in Abel Main. The last four Aramaic lines tell the reader that Levi lies down, probably falls asleep, and has a vision in which he sees the gates of heaven and an angel.

Here the fragment ends and nothing is known about the content of
the vision.

There are several reasons to consider the prayer and the following vision as preceding the Shechem incident in *A.L.D.* 3. First of
all, the text of the *Testament of Levi* indicates that the prayer and the
first vision (*T. Levi* 2:3–6:2) took place before Levi's vengeance on
the Shechemites (*T. Levi* 6:3–7:4). Additionally, the angelic response
to Levi's prayer in his first vision (*T. Levi* 4:2–3, 5) indicates that
God has heard Levi's requests as formulated in the text of the
Document. God separates Levi from lawlessness (cf. *A.L.D.* 1a v. 13),
accepts him as his son, servant (cf. *A.L.D.* 1a vv. 11, 17, 19), and
minister of his presence (cf. *A.L.D.* 1a vv. 11, 17). The prayer mentioned in *T. Levi* 2:4 says only that Levi prays to be saved, and evidently does not correspond to the angelic answer in *T. Levi* 4:2–3,
5. It is, therefore, plausible to assume that the redactors of the
Testament eliminated Levi's long prayer from their text, but did not
adjust the angelic response to it. The prayer could have once belonged
to the source elaborated by the redactors of the *Testament*, and it
stood there before the beginning of the first vision. The scribe who
reinserted the *Document*'s prayer in *T. Levi* 2:3 before the beginning
of the first vision most probably recognized the connection between
the content of the prayer and *T. Levi* 4:2–3, 5.

There are some further indications that the *Document*'s vision corresponds to the first vision in the literary structure of *T. Levi*. In the
Greek *Testament* the first vision takes place in Abelmaul (*T. Levi* 2:3,
5; cf. 6:1), while *A.L.D.* 1b l. 13 suggests that Levi was in the vicinity of Abel Main when the vision took place. Both accounts mention only one angel appearing to Levi, and in both texts the gates
of heavens are open (*T. Levi* 2:6; *A.L.D.* 1b l. 18). Further comparison is not possible for the Aramaic work breaks off at this point,
while the Greek *Testament* continues with Levi's heavenly journey.

The text of the prayer discloses additional indications that Levi's
prayer and his first vision should precede the Shechem incident. In
A.L.D. 1a v. 18, Levi asks God to make him participate in God's
words in order to carry out a true/righteous judgment. The Shechem
killing becomes in the *Document* a righteous execution of the doers
of violence (*A.L.D.* 78), and may be interpeted as the consequence
of Levi's request to carry out this true judgment. Situating the prayer
after the Shechem incident would make Levi's request for righteous
judgment superfluous and unnecessary. Once the sentence passed on

the Shechemites has been carried out, there is no need to make any request for it. It would also annul the divine authority that justifies the killing as willed by God and obediently executed by Levi and his brothers (cf. *T. Levi* 5:3).

After the Shechem incident when Levi has already been proclaimed a priest, Isaac discloses to Levi the legal content of the "true/righteous law" on which Levi should base his priestly and judicial authority. One of the main criteria to remain ritually pure is to avoid any kind of sexual immorality (זנות). According to the *Document*, Levi's purity essentially consists in maintaining endogamy in family relations (*A.L.D.* 16–17). His request, therefore, to mete out the true judgment in *A.L.D.* 1a v. 18 unequivocally indicates the reason for the killing of the Shechemites: they attempted to establish an exogamous relationship with the tribal family of Jacob. Once the prayer is located before the Shechem story, Levi's request for the true judgment acquires all its importance for his priestly and judicial vocation.

Levi's prayer also contains another request that calls for the location of the prayer before the Shechem incident. In *A.L.D.* 1a v. 13 he asks God to utterly eliminate lawlessness (ἀνομία) from under the heavens. In the autobiographical section of the *Document* Levi affirms that being eighteen years old he killed Shechem and destroyed the doers of violence (*A.L.D.* 78: עבדי המסא). The term המס does not refer to the violent killing of the Shechemites but should be interpreted as referring to Shechem's sexual misdemeanor that disrupts the divinely instituted social order. The Greek counterpart of the term in the LXX is sometimes ἀνομία. Levi's killing of the Shechemites must then be interpreted as a restoration of this order, stemming from his request to eliminate lawlessness on earth. Again, when this request is situated before the Shechem incident, the killing acquires the theological perspective of eliminating lawlessness caused by Shechem's sexual immorality.

Among the scholars who have dealt with the *Document*'s literary relation to the *Testament*, and the order of events in the former composition, only Kugler holds the opinion that the Aramaic composition had one vision, and that the vision followed the Shechem account. He believes that *A.L.D.* 1b is the introduction to the vision whose final section is found in *A.L.D.* 4–7. Kugler points out that while in *T. Levi* 2:3 the first vision takes place in Abelmaul, the *Document* suggests that Levi already left Abel Main (*A.L.D.* 1b l. 13) and he may already have reached Bethel, where his one and only vision probably takes place (1996a: 48). This reconstruction is completely hypothetical, for the text of *A.L.D.* 1b ll. 11–14 is fragmentary and does not warrant what Kugler wants it to say. Although line 13 suggests that Levi is leaving Abel Main, it does not exclude the possibility that he is still close to that location, and there is no indication whatsoever that he already reached Bethel where he has his vision. The most probable location he is heading to is the neighborhood of Shechem, where Jacob dwells before the desecration of Dinah occurs.

Kugler also lightly dismisses the fact that only one angel appears in *A.L.D.* 1b l. 18 and seven in *A.L.D.* 7. He affirms that since little is known of the content of the vision, the narrative could have introduced the other six angels before the final statement that has seven angels leaving Levi in *A.L.D.* 7. Finally, he adds that although *A.L.D.* 1b contains the language characteristic of heavenly journeys, it does not exclude the possibility that Levi received his ordination while earthbound. These two of Kugler's arguments can be easily dismissed for they are based on a weak *argumentum e silentio*, and cannot be proven at all. Additionally, the *Testament of Levi* contradicts Kugler's interpretation, for in Levi's first vision Levi is accompanied by one angel and travels through the celestial realm, while his second vision in ch. 8 has precisely seven angels that complete a solemn rite of Levi's priestly elevation.

When arguing his case Kugler (1996a: 49–50) further concentrates on the translation equivalence of *A.L.D.* 7 ll. 10–13. He accepts Greenfield and Stone's translation of the passage and contends that the expression אף דן (line 13) cannot refer to the first vision, but it should be translated "this very thing" (1996a: 50). It is unfortunate for Kugler that he relied on the translation of Greenfield and Stone and not on his own analysis of the Aramaic passage. Greenfield and Stone's translation was based on their emendation of the text (cf. Greenfield and Stone 1979: 219) and therefore is to be cautiously scrutinized before being accepted as valid. On the other hand, Kugler's rather dogmatic acceptance of the translation does not take into account the context of the passage. The expression אף דן must be rendered as "also this one," if faithfulness to the Aramaic text is to be preserved. Kugler further affirms that the expression "also this one" could refer to Levi's prayer or to another event in the *Document*. This opinion suggests that, in order to prove his point, Kugler dismisses the fundamental criterion for interpretation of any text, that is the immediate context of the phrase. The best reference for the deictic particle דן in *A.L.D.* 7 l. 11 in the context of the whole *A.L.D.* 7 is Levi's visions and their content. Additionally, the mere possibility that Levi had many visions is further confirmed by *A.L.D.* 98, where the expression בחזוין "in the visions" suggests that Levi had more visions (cf. also *A.L.D.* 1b l. 16).

Trying to definitely undermine the reconstruction of the two visions on the basis of the Greek *Testament*, Kugler (1996a: 54–55) compares *A.L.D.* 78 and *T. Levi* 12:5 with *T. Levi* 4:2–6; 5:2–4. The former two texts of the Aramaic work and the *Testament* indicated that Levi was ordained to the priesthood after the killing of the Shechemites. *T. Levi* 12:5 faithfully follows here the text and tradition of the *Document*. *T. Levi* 4:2–6; 5:2–4, however, indicate that Levi was elevated to the priesthood before the killing occurred (*T. Levi* 6:3–5). This discrepancy with *T. Levi* 12:5 and *A.L.D.* 78 is for Kugler proof that the redactors of the *Testament* adjusted the *Document*'s order of events to their own exegetical purposes by recounting the events attested in *A.L.D.* 78 and *T. Levi* 12:5 in a different order.

Kugler's opinion faces some difficulties that must now be considered. First of all, in order to be sure that *T. Levi* 4:2–6; 5:2–4 changes the order of events as attested in the *Document* and *T. Levi* 12:5, one must be convinced that the first vision material (chs. 2–5) in the *Testament* was absent in or totally different from the text of the Aramaic composition. Since the content of the first vision in the Aramaic work is lacking, one cannot know whether the redactor of the *Testament* introduced Levi's angelic elevation in the vision account from another source, or that this angelic elevation was part of the *Testament*'s main source, that is the *Document* itself. In the latter case, the proclamation of Levi's priestly dignity in the *Testament*'s first vision would stem from the *Document*, and could not be ascribed to the activity of the redactor of the *Testament*. In the present fragmentary state of the *Document* this question must remain open. Kugler's opinion is based on the unproven and unprovable assumption that the Aramaic composition did not contain Levi's angelic elevation in the text that followed *A.L.D.* 1b. Additionally, some scholars consider *T. Levi* 4:2–6 and 5:2–4 as belonging to the oldest redactional strata of *T. Levi* 2:3–6:2 (Becker 1970: 261–264; Haupt 1969: 123, only *T. Levi* 4:2–6), hence the possibility that Levi's priestly elevation was mentioned in the *Document*'s first vision cannot be completely excluded.

Another argument for positing Levi's prayer after the Shechem incident is Kugler's understanding of *A.L.D.* 1a vv. 1–2, the lines that stand before the beginning of the prayer. They describe Levi's purification and Kugler understands the garment laundering and a bath in pure water as stemming from the synoptic reading of Lev 15:13 and Num 5:2 (1996a: 57–58). The former is the only one in the biblical text that requires garment laundering and purification bath for a person afflicted with a genital discharge (זב); the latter text classifies the leper, the זב, and the corpse contaminated person together as unfit for cult participation because of their impurity. Reading these two texts synoptically, the author of the *Document* formulated the new rule that required garment laundering and purification bath (Lev 15:13) for Levi who underwent corpse contamination (Num 5:2) when slaughtering the Shechemites. Consequently, the prayer must follow the Shechem incident.

Kugler's argumentation appears to be based on a tautological way of reasoning. Since the prayer stands in the *Document* after the slaughter of the Shechemites, the author reads synoptically the two biblical texts to create a new purification rule concerning corpse contamination. Since he creates a new purification rule concerning corpse contamination, the prayer stands after the slaughter of the Shechemites. This argument goes in a circle for it is based on what it tries to prove: that the prayer and its introductory verses are preceded by the slaughter of the Shechemites partially preserved in *A.L.D.* 1c–2. In order to prove that *A.L.D.* 1a vv. 1–2 denote the purification after corpse contamination, Kugler would have to demonstrate that what preceded was indeed the Shechem story. This he cannot achieve for the simple reason that the preceding text is utterly unknown. Additionally, without this *a priori* assumption, it is not possible to exclude that the synoptic reading of Lev 15:13 and Num 5:2 leads to a creation of the purification rule that concerns the leper or the person with sexual discharge. What should lead the reader in the interpretation of *A.L.D.* 1a vv. 1–2 is the following context of the introduction to the prayer and of the prayer itself. This readily available context suggests that what one deals with is a quest for personal salvation and priestly appointment, and the simplest assumption is that the first preserved verses deal with the purification necessary for a cultic action of standing in prayer before the sanctuary (see comment on *A.L.D.* 1a vv. 1–2). The new rule of garment laundering and body washing was created in accordance with heightened purity exigencies expected from the ideal priest that characterize the whole Aramaic work.

In his reconstruction of the Cairo Geniza fragments (MS A), Kugler found another argument against the theory that the *Document* had two visions. He calculated an eight-column gap between *A.L.D.* 3 (Cambridge b) and *A.L.D.* 4–10 (Bodleian a), and filled it with the continuation of the Shechem killing, Levi's prayer (*A.L.D.* 1a vv. 1–19), and his vision (*A.L.D.* 1b; 3a) that ends in *A.L.D.* 4–7 (Kugler 1996a: 233). He used this reconstruction to prove that there was no room in the eight-column gap for the two vision account (1996a: 58–59). This ingenious attempt is not convincing, for the existing gap might have contained different material and the prayer with the first vision might have been located at the beginning of the reconstructed Geniza manuscript, as it has been presented above in this study. By no means, however, should the Cairo Geniza reconstruction alone arise to the status of an unquestionable proof of the presence or absence of the two visions in the *Document*'s narrative.

Kugler's arguments concerning his one vision theory have proven to be faulty. He tried to discard the generally accepted scholarly opinion, which states that, like the *Testament of Levi*, the text of the *Document* has two visions separated by the account of the Shechem killing. His argumentation is based on a set of assumptions, the foremost of which is the very conviction about a one-vision-theory. His one-vision-theory was already criticized by other scholars (de Jonge 1999: 82–83), and in the present fragmentary state of the *A.L.D.* text, the solution based on the *Testament of Levi* literary outline and the analysis of the prayer's text appears to be the most reasonable one. The prayer (*A.L.D.* 1a) and the following vision (*A.L.D.* 1b) stand before the Shechem incident (*A.L.D.* 1c–2), while *A.L.D.* 4–7 belongs to Levi's second vision.

T. Levi 5:2 (MS E)

De Jonge (1975: 254, n. 24) was the first to suggest that *T. Levi* 5:2 (MS E) belongs to the *A.L.D.* text together with two other insertions into the text of the *Testament* (E 2,3 and 18,2). This is the text of the verse:

καὶ εἶπέν μοι; Λευί σοὶ δοθήσεται ἡ ἱερατεία καὶ τῷ σπέρματί σου τοῦ λειτουργεῖν τῷ ὑψίστῳ ἐν μέσῳ τῆς γῆς καὶ ἐξιλάσκεσθαί σε ἐπὶ ταῖς ἀγνοίαις τῆς γῆς· τότε ἔδωκεν τὰς εὐλογίας τῆς ἱερατείας

... And he said to me: 'To you, Levi, and to your seed will be given the priesthood to minister to the Most High in the middle of the earth,

> and you will make propitiation for the sins of ignorance of the earth';
> then he gave the blessings of the priesthood. . . .

According to Hultgård (1982: 93–94), the verse has been inserted in the wrong place and does not fit the context. He located the original place of the insertion either in *T. Levi* 2:10–12, which ascribes to Levi different priestly functions, or in *T. Levi* 4:4, which begins with the same expression found in *T. Levi* 5:2 (καὶ δοθήσεταί σοι). The probability that *T. Levi* 5:2 (MS E) belongs to the text of the *Document* cannot be lightly dismissed. Since the fragment indicates that only one person speaks to Levi (καὶ εἶπέν μοι), and *A.L.D.* 1b l. 18 mentions only one angel appearing to Levi, this insertion could have been located in the text of Levi's first vision. Moreover, the vocabulary of the fragment indicates many contacts with the text of the *Document* (cf. Λευί/ לוי in E 2,3 v. 17; A 14 l. 8/E 18,2 v. 14; A 83 l. 8; E 18,2 v. 61; δίδωμι in E 2,3 vv. 6, 8, 16; τὸ σπέρμα/ זרע in, e.g. A 17 ll. 17, 19; E 18,2 v. 49; ὕψιστος translates עליון [E 18,2 v. 30], see A 9 l. 20; 13 l. 6).

T. Levi 5:2 (MS E) does not have, however, any overlapping Aramaic material either in Geniza or in Qumran manuscripts. The fact that it appears only in MS E, which has two large portions of the *Document*, does not preclude the possibility that it comes from a different source, or that it was modeled on other parts of the Greek *Testament*. Without an unequivocal proof of its Aramaic provenance and connection to the *Document*, the question whether or not it belongs to the text of the Aramaic work must remain open.

MS E 18,2
Overlap between E 18,2 and A
E 11–32a = A 11–32a
E 66–69a = A 66–69a

MS E 18,2 is a Greek translation of the Aramaic text whose textual form is close to, though not identical with, the Geniza fragments of the *Document*. The Greek text begins in *A.L.D.* 11 with the description of Levi's second visit to Isaac and abruptly ends in *A.L.D.* 69a in the middle of the genealogical account concerning Levi's third son Merari. E 11–32a and 66–69a run parallel to the Aramaic text of the Cairo Geniza fragments, while the intermediate section E 32b–65 is preserved only in the Greek translation. This textual continuity of E 18,2 helps to restore a proper order of the Geniza fragments. When Bodleian d (A 25b–32a) breaks off, the Greek text continues and again runs parallel to Cambridge c (A 66–69a).

Although E 18,2 vv. 32b–65 has no parallel text among the fragments of Qumran manuscripts, the overlapping with the Cairo Geniza fragments makes it clear that the Greek text is a translation from the lost Aramaic portion of the *Document*. Kugler (1996a: 42) tried to prove that this Greek section overlaps with a tiny Qumran fragment, 4Q214 5 (4Q214b 7); his identification, however, remains unsatisfactory (see the reconstruction of 4Q214b 7 in § 2.3).

1.4.3.4 *A Reconstruction of MS B*

This short Syriac fragment overlaps with MS A (B 78–81 = A 78–81). It shares some readings with the Greek *Testament*, and these suggest that it has been influenced by the latter. It is preceded by a short introduction of the Syriac scribe explaining why this particular fragment has been chosen. The scribe was interested in the chronology of Levi's life, hence he chose *A.L.D.* 78–81, that reviews main events of the patriarch's life in a chronological order.

1.4.3.5 *Two Recensions Theory*

When discussing the *Document* and other testamentary literature at Qumran, Milik (1978: 106) suggested that they circulated in two recensions, one Samaritan and one Judean. He did not support his intuition with any convincing proof, but working with all the fragmentary evidence of the Aramaic composition one may point to a few indicators, which can prove that Milik's two recensions theory may lie not too far from reasonable certainty.

When reconstructing the Aramaic text of Levi's prayer, one has to retranslate the extant Greek text into Aramaic and supplement the fragmentary 4Q213a frgs. 1 and 2 by rearranging the recuperated text in the manuscript disposition of the Aramaic fragments. 4Q213 frg. 1 preserves only the left part of a column while the right part, with the beginning of the lines, is lost. While filling in the gaps with the retranslated text of the prayer it becomes evident that much more space is left in lines 8–10, 12–13, 16–17 of the Aramaic fragment. In addition to that, MS E 2,3 v. 9 has a different word order in comparison with the Aramaic fragment that presupposes a more developed text. This procedure of comparing the line length of the Qumran fragment with the retranslated Greek text is not possible for 4Q213a frg. 2 that preserves the beginnings of the broken lines and does not allow for a precise restoration of the line length. The evidence gleaned from the reconstruction of the first column suffices to suppose that the Greek text of the prayer (MS E 2,3) contains a shorter recension in comparison with the longer Aramaic text. This supposition, however, remains hypothetical, for the Aramaic text of the prayer remains fragmentary and the line length of the Qumran manuscript may vary.

When reconstructing 4Q214 1 it also becomes clear that this Qumran fragment contains a shorter text in comparison with MS A 20–25. The reconstruction excludes the existence of the list of the trees fit for the sacrifice attested in MS A and E 18,2. It also supposes that the Qumran fragment omits A 25b ll. 22–23a, lines that do not exist in MS E 18,2, as well. On the other hand, 4Q214b 2–3, 4Q214b 4, and 4Q214b 5–6 i confirm the existence of the tree list at Qumran, while 4Q214a 1 and 4Q214b 2–3 witness to the reading of A 25b ll. 22–23a. Although the omission of A 25b ll. 22–23a may be explained as a case of *homoioteleuton* similar to the one in E 18,2 v. 25a, the omission of the tree list is less likely to be casual or caused by a copyist's error. The probability that 4Q214 frg. 1 belongs to a shorter recension of the *Document* cannot be excluded altogether.

When reconstructing the final part of the wisdom poem and the beginning of Levi's vision of the future (*A.L.D.* 96–100), a discrepancy in the length of textual witnesses is also noticeable. 4Q213 frg. 1 ii and frg. 2 form two complementary elements of one column, while 4Q214a frg. 2 ii and 4Q214b frg. 8 overlap with parts of the former two texts, while 4Q214a 2 ii overlaps with some words in MS A 95. The comparison of 4Q214a 2 with 4Q213 1 ii and 2 makes evident that the former is shorter by omission of *A.L.D.* 97. This difference in the fragmentary manuscript evidence was also noted by Stone and Greenfield (1996a: 72).

The analysis of textual variants in MS A and E 18,2 leads to the conclusion that the Greek text is not based on the text type of the Cairo Geniza fragments. Although the Greek translation is a literal rendering of the Aramaic idiom, many different readings, some omissions or expansions indicate that MS E 18,2 is based on another textual form of the *Document*. Sometimes it preserves ancient readings that underwent some modifications in the MS A text. One can cite several example of that phenomenon, like θεχακ in E 18,2

v. 24, תכבה in 4Q214b 2–3 4, and האנתא in A (cf. also a shorter
form of E 18,2 v. 28 and 4Q214 frg. 2 and the MS A expanded
text). On the other hand, E 18,2 v. 67 transmits a longer text expansion, which, however, goes back to its Aramaic *Vorlage*.

The short Syriac fragment from the ninth century A.D. is of little
value as a source of additional information about the text of the
Document. This citation of *A.L.D.* 78–81 is too short to allow for any
conclusions, and the text is most probably influenced by the Greek
Testament of Levi. From the short introduction of the citation it may
be inferred that the scribe chose this particular fragment because of
his interest in Levi's life span. This short Syriac note is not a decisive proof that there existed a Syriac edition of the whole *Document*.

Since the overall manuscript evidence is fragmentary and previous observations mostly based on text reconstructions, any attempt
to hypothesize the history of the text transmission must remain in
the realm of reasonable probability. The available evidence, however, confirms the antiquity and reliability of the Greek translation
preserved in MS E. The first fragment, E 2,3, preserves a shorter
text in comparison with its Qumran counterpart, and the second
fragment, E 18,2, while closely following the Aramaic text, contains
valuable readings that confirm its antiquity. The differences between
the texts point to the existence of two recensions of the *Document*.
How and when the two recensions arose is uncertain; the presence
of seven different manuscripts in the Qumran library allows for the
supposition, however, that the exegetical activity of the Qumran
scribes left its imprint on the Aramaic work and could have led to
the creation of a second expanded recension.

1.4.3.6 *A Tentative Order of Manuscripts and Events in the* Document
From the preceding discussion of the available evidence, there emerges
an order of the fragments and, consequently, of the events in the
Document. Since the manuscript evidence remains fragmentary, this
order remains hypothetical. It is, however, based on the mutual relationship of the manuscripts that justify and make it plausible.

Table 7. Order of the Manuscripts and Events in *A.L.D.*

Content	*A.L.D.*	Manuscripts	Overlapping Manuscripts
1 Levi's Prayer	1a	E 2,3	4Q213a frgs. 1–2 10
2 First Vision	1b	4Q213a 2 11–18	
3 Shechem Incident	1c–2	A 1c–2	
4 Selling of Joseph	3	A 3	
5 Second Vision	3a	4Q213a 3–4	
	3b	4Q213a 5	
	3c	1Q21 1	
	4	A 4	1Q21 3
	5	A 5	1Q21 3
	6	A 6	1Q21 3; 4Q213b
	7	A 7	1Q21 3; 4Q213b
6 First Visit to Isaac	8	A 8	4Q213b
7 Ordination in Bethel	9	A 9	1Q21 4; 4Q213b
	10	A 10	
8 Second Visit to Isaac	11–19	A 11–19	E 18,2 vv. 11–19
	20	A 20	4Q214 1; E 18,2 v. 20
	21	A 21	4Q214 1; E 18,2 v. 21
	22	A 22	4Q214 1; 4Q214b 2–3; 4Q214b 4; 4Q214b 5–6 i; E 18,2 v. 22
	23	A 23	4Q214 1; 4Q214b 2–3; 4Q214b 4; 4Q214b 5–6 i; E 18,2 v. 23
	24	A 24	4Q214a 1; 4Q214b 2–3; 4Q214b 4; 4Q214b 5–6 i; E 18,2 v. 24
	25a	A 25a	4Q214 1; 4Q214a 1; 4Q214b 2–3; 4Q214b 5–6 i; E 18,2 v. 25a
	25b	A 25b	4Q214 1; 4Q214 2; 4Q214a 1; 4Q214b 2–3; E 18,2 v. 25b
	26	A 26	1Q21 45 2; 4Q214 2; 4Q214b 2–3; E 18,2 v. 26
	27	A 27	4Q214 2; 4Q214b 2–3; E 18,2 v. 27
	28	A 28	4Q214 2; E 18,2 v. 28
	29	A 29	4Q214 2; 4Q214b 5–6 ii; E 18,2 v. 29
	30	A 30	4Q214 2; 4Q214b 5–6 ii; E 18,2 v. 30
	31	A 31	4Q214b 5–6 ii; E 18,2 v. 31
	32a	A 32a	E 18,2 v. 32a
	32b–61	E 18,2 vv. 32b–61	
9 Genealogy and	62–65	E 18,2 vv. 62–65	
Autobiography	66–69a	A 66–69a	E 18,2 vv. 66–69a

Table 7 (*cont.*)

Content	A.L.D.	Manuscripts	Overlapping Manuscripts
	69b	A 69b	4Q214a 2 i
	70	A 70	4Q214a 2 i
	71	A 71	4Q214a 2 i
	72	A 72	4Q214a 2 i
	73	A 73	4Q214a 2 i
	74–77	A 74–77	
	78–81	A 78–81	B 78–81
10 Wisdom Poem	82–94	A 82–94	4Q213 1 i;
	95	A 95	4Q213 1 i; 4Q214a frg. 2 ii 1–2
	96	A 96	4Q213 1 ii 1
	96	4Q213 1 ii 1–4	A 96; 4Q214b 8
	97	4Q213 1 ii 5–8	4Q214b 8
	97	4Q213 2 1–4	
	98	4Q213 1 ii 9–11	4Q214b 8
	98	4Q213 2 5–8	4Q214a 2 ii 5; 4Q214b 8
	98	4Q214a 2 ii 5–6	
11 Perspectives for the Future	99	4Q213 1 ii 12–16; 4Q213 2 9–12	
	100	4Q213 1 ii 17–19; 4Q213 2 13–16	
	101	4Q213 frg. 3	
	102	4Q213 frg. 4	
	103	4Q213 frg. 5	
	104	4Q214 frg. 3	

1.5 *The Language, Author, Date, Place, and Purpose of the Composition*

1.5.1 *The Language*

Since the publication of the first Cairo Geniza fragments of the *Document* (Pass and Arendzen 1900), several scholars have commented on the language represented by the composition. From the presence of Hebraisms in the Aramaic fragments, Charles (1908a: liv–lvii) concluded that they had been translated from Hebrew. He additionally affirmed that the paronomasia in the onomastic midrash on Qahat's name was understandable only when retranslated into Hebrew. De Jonge (1953a: 130–131) essentially repeated Charles' argumentation concerning the Hebrew origin of the Aramaic. He also attempted for the first time to situate the language of the Geniza fragments in relation to Jewish Aramaic dialects. The Aramaic of the fragments would belong to a mixed type with some agreements with the Aramaic of *Targum Onqelos* on the one hand and the Palestinian Targum on the other. Grelot (1955) adopted the opinion that the original language of the *Levi Document* was Hebrew but criticized de Jonge's contention that the Aramaic itself belonged to the mixed type of the language. He argues that de Jonge's classification based on the terminology adopted by Dalman (1905) was no longer adequate for the antiquity of *Targum Onqelos*, and thus the base of Dalman's typology was disproved (1955: 97). These findings call for a new approach to the whole problem of Aramaic dialectology.

When the Qumran *Genesis Apocryphon* was published (Avigad and Yadin 1956), the eminent philologist Eduard Y. Kutscher (1958) wrote a seminal article situating the Aramaic of the Qumran scroll within the history of that language. He concluded that the scroll represented a transitory stage between the Official Aramaic of the biblical books (Ezra, Nehemiah, Daniel) and later phases of Western Aramaic. At the end of the article he mentioned the Aramaic text of the *Levi Document* from the Cairo Geniza and gave the reason why he did not include it in his linguistic analysis: "While there is no doubt that its language is close to that of our scroll, there is also no doubt, for reasons that cannot be explained here, that it was not transmitted in its original form" (Kutscher 1958: 34).

This statement of Kutscher served to substantiate two conflicting opinions concerning the language of the Geniza fragments. Greenfield and Stone (1979: 227–229) contended that the Aramaic of the Levi composition was close to that of some of the Qumran scrolls and blamed medieval copyists for minor mistakes and late forms. Consequently, they classified the language of the composition as belonging to Standard Literary Aramaic. The latter term refers to the diachronic typology of Aramaic elaborated by Greenfield in his earlier articles. He argued that alongside the Imperial Aramaic of the Persian chancellery "there arose an Aramaic which was suited for literary use" (1974: 285). To this category belong the Ahiqar framework story, the Bar Punesh fragment, the Aramaic portions of Ezra and Daniel, the Qumran texts (Tobit, Enoch, Daniel pseudepigrapha), the Geniza version of the *Testament of Levi*, the targums of Onqelos and Jonathan, and *Megillat Ta'anit* (1974: 284–288; cf. Greenfield 1978a).

While agreeing with Kutscher's opinion concerning the language of the Geniza Levi composition, Joseph A. Fitzmyer (1999: 459–464)

criticized its classification with Qumran Aramaic or earlier phases of
the language. He neatly distinguished between the Aramaic of the
Levi Document from Qumran and the one found in the Cairo Geniza
fragments of the same composition. The former belongs to what he
called "Middle Aramaic (200 B.C. to A.D. 200), while the latter should
be classified as 'Late Aramaic' (from A.D. 200 on; for the justification
of the chronological division, cf. Fitzmyer 1971: 22, n. 60; 1979:
57–84). This distinction is based on the presence of late forms in
the Geniza manuscripts that were introduced by later copyists. These
late forms attest that the Cairo Geniza fragments represent a different
historical stage in the development of the language. Fitzmyer also
noted that various manuscripts of the same Levi composition (Qumran,
Cairo Geniza, Greek translation) did not preserve a uniform text but
differed one from the other. This proves that "all these texts are
seen rather to have been at least revisions of, if not completely new
compositions based on, the ancient Jewish Levi text now known to
us from Qumran" (1999: 462).

One cannot but agree with Fitzmyer's opinion that the Cairo
Geniza language shares common features with Late Aramaic and
these features distance the medieval manuscripts from their earlier
Qumran counterparts (see below). These common features, however,
are easily ascribed to medieval copyists and do not necessarily show
that the Cairo Geniza manuscripts contain completely new compositions based on ancient Qumran texts. One can easily notice that
Qumran fragments, Greek translation, and Cairo Geniza manuscripts
have at times different readings (see § 1.4.3.5). It is necessary, however, to underline that they all preserve the same literary composition and are distinct and different from the testamentary form it
took when the process of reinterpretation led to the creation of the
Greek *Testament of Levi*. The continuity of transmission explains the
presence of the early forms in the Geniza manuscripts, like prevalence of *hap'el* over against *'ap'el* as already stressed by Stone and
Greenfield (1979: 229). Late forms in Cairo Geniza manuscripts are
mostly limited to the abundant use of *scriptio plena*, and the presence
of Late Aramaic morphological forms is non systematic and too limited to ascribe the language of the manuscripts to that chronological period. Additionally, the *scriptio plena* is a phenomenon widely
spread already in many Qumran manuscripts and cannot be used
as an unequivocal criterion for late dating of Cairo Geniza language
of the same Levitical composition.

Additionally, the opinion that the *Levi Document* was originally written in Hebrew and then translated into Aramaic must also be rejected. The composition is written in a good literary type of Aramaic and there exists no unequivocal basis for the translation theory. That theory was mainly based on the presence of the Hebrew forms and vocabulary in the Cairo Geniza manuscripts. The Qumran discoveries confirmed the existence of some of the Cairo Geniza Hebraisms in the earlier manuscripts of the *Document*, but this philological phenomenon is shared by all the manuscripts from Qumran and only proves that Hebrew and Aramaic were in constant linguistic contact during the Second Temple period (cf. Fassberg 1992). One also should take into consideration the author's conscious move to reinterpret Hebrew biblical texts in order to create the image of an ideal priest and scribe. Thus the onomastic *midrashim* in *A.L.D.* 62–77 prove that the author was versed both in Hebrew and Aramaic and wrote for the educated class of Levitical priests, presumably well acquainted with both languages.

The Cairo Geniza manuscripts of the *Levi Document* overlap in many places with Qumran fragments of this composition, but the latter are in a much more fragmentary state that impedes an exhaustive analysis of changes that occurred in the process of transmission. However, the list of words that exemplify Late Aramaic morphology of the Cairo Geniza texts may help illustrate their language and, wherever possible, show the difference from Qumran Middle Aramaic forms. As argued earlier, however, Late Aramaic forms are too limited to consider the language of the Cairo Geniza manuscripts as belonging to that historical period.

1. Abundance of *scriptio plena* over *scriptio defectiva*

1c. sing. Perfect: כהנית (A 79 1. 19); קטלית (A 78 1. 17); קרבית (A 9 1. 21); אשלמית (A 10 1. 23);

א = ā (Dalman 1905: 70–71, 151) שארי (A 16 1. 6, in contrast to שרי A 26 1. 3); ראמא (A 76 1. 13, in contrast to רם 4Q213a 2 17 = 1b 1. 17); טאב (A 87 ll. 15, 15; 94 1. 17, in contrast to טב 4Q213a 1 16 = 1a v. 9; 4Q213 1 i 20 = 94 1. 17);

י = e/i (Beyer 1984: 417; Dalman 1905: 71, 75); אליך (A 89 1. 20, in contrast to אלך 4Q213 1 i 10); כהין (A 9 1. 20; 13 1. 5; 17 1. 19, in contrast to כהנין 4Q213 2 12 = *A.L.D.* 99 1. 15); לביש (A 19 1. 2; 20 1. 3); סליק (A 23 1. 15; 31 1. 20; 32a ll. 22, 23); עביד (A

31 l. 17); קאים (A 19 l. 1; 85 l. 12); רחיע (A 20 l. 4, in contrast to
רחע A 21 l. 8; 26 l. 2); שאיט (A 98 l. 21); האיב (A 20 l. 4; 87 l. 16);
אליפו (A 88 l. 18); הקטיר (30 l. 14); מהקריב (A 22 l. 9); היזדהר (A
16 l. 14); מיזדהר (A 22 l. 12);

אינון (A 1c l. 20; A 3 l. 20; A 22 l. 10; A 22 l. 11, in contrast to
אנו]ן in 4Q214b 4 1; A 24 l. 16; A 25a l. 20, in contrast to אנון in
4Q214b 2–3 5); cf הנון (A 82 l. 6) in contrast to אנון in 4Q213 1
i 3 (A.L.D. 82 l. 6); אחזינך (A 15 l. 12); מינך (A 15 l. 13, in contrast
to מן 6 l. 8; 7 l. 9, etc.); מינהון (A 23 l. 14, in contrast to מנהון
4Q214b 5–6 i 3); למיעל (A 19 l. 1); ניעא (28 l. 8); שיתה (32a l. 22,
in contrast to שת A 73 l. 1); בישרא (A 14 l. 11; in contrast to בבשרך
A 18 l. 23; בשר]א 4Q213b 1 = A.L.D. 6); ליה (A 32a l. 21); רתיכין
(A 95 l. 19); שלמיה (A 92 l. 13);

 י = y (Beyer 1984: 417; Dalman 1905: 71); ייקר (A 93 l. 14) and
ויקר (A 89 l. 20), in contrast to יקר in A 71 l. 20; A 88 l. 19, etc.);
יירחה (A 70 l. 17, in contrast to ירחא in A 68 ll. 9, 9); צביין (A 1c
l. 20, in contrast to צבין in A 91 l. 11); תליתוי (A 69a l. 12);

ס for ש (Dalman 1905: 53, 66f, 104; Beyer 1984: 419); סניא (A
69b l. 15; A 92 l. 13; A 95 l. 19); סחי (A 19 l. 2); סימא (A 94 l. 17,
in contrast to שימה in 4Q213 1 ii 3, 3 = A.L.D. 96 ll. 3, 3); עסרין
(A 79 l. 20).

2. Emphatic state instead of the absolute form of the noun, as nor-
mally expected in Official and Middle Aramaic: אנתתא (A 17 l. 16);
חוכמתא (A 88 l. 19; 89 l. 20, in contrast to חכמה in 4Q213 1 i 10;
89 l. 21).

3. Penetration of Hebraic forms
   a. 1c.s. perfect ending in *yôd* in the third-weak verbs: הויתי (A 71
l. 18; 80 ll. 21, 23); הזיתי (A 22 l. 12; 81 l. 2), in contrast to חזית
4Q214b 5–6 i 2 (A.L.D. 22 l. 12); 4Q214a frg. 2 ii 6 (A.L.D. 98
l. 9); שויתי (A 71 l. 19, in contrast to שוית 4Q214a 2 i 4); שריתי (A
82 l. 6); קריתי (A 76 l. 10; 82 l. 5); קראתי (A 69a l. 12).
   b. Final ים- instead of expected ין: מצרים (A 72 l. 1, in contrast
to מצר]ין in 4Q214a 2 i 7; 73 l. 2; 76 l. 12; 80 l. 22). This phenomenon sporadically appears in Biblical and Qumran Aramaic, cf.
Fassberg 1992: 55–56.
   c. Hebraic verbal forms: קראתי (A 69a l. 12, cf. Fassberg 1992: 60).
   d. Hebraic nominal form: אוצר (A 95 l. 22).

e. A Hebrew *qatúl* form for an abstract noun כהונתא (A 9 l. 19, in contrast to כהנותא in A 13 l. 8; A 15 l. 14; A 19 l. 3; A 67 l. 7; 1Q21 1 2 = *A.L.D.* 3c l. 2 = *qātil-ū̃t*)

4. Late pronominal suffix of the first person plural ־ן : ברתן (A 1c l. 20), כואתן (A 2 ll. 22, 23), כולן (A 1c l. 20), אבונן (A 11 l. 3, in contrast to אבונה in A 11 l. 3; אבונא in A 12 l. 4), אחונן (A 3 l. 22), אמרנן (A 1c l. 19); cf. Fitzmyer 1999: 464.

5. Late morphological forms: אינש (A 7 l. 13, in contrast to אנש in 4Q213b 3 and אנ]ש in 4Q213 2 1 = *A.L.D.* 97 l. 4, cf. Fitzmyer 1999: 463–464); שבעתון (A 7 l. 9); אלבשי possessive suffix instead of the object suffix in perfect (A 9 l. 19, cf. Dalman 1905: 47, 359, 362); התחמיון impv. pl. m. in ־ן (Dalman 1905: 348, Beyer 1984: 494); מן with the *nûn* assimilated (A 9 l. 18; 11 l. 2, cf. Dalman 1905: 227); ביש (A 87 l. 16, in contrast to באישא in 4Q213a 1 13 = *A.L.D.* 1a v. 7; *qatíl* Beyer 1984: 528); פקודי (A 83b l. 8); *qittúl* Dalman 1905: 164); רתיכן (A 95 l. 19; *qatíl* Dalman 1905: 149); דמין לקן (A 22 l. 10, in contrast to לקדמין in A 16 l. 14; A 27 l. 4, cf. Schulthess 1924: § 131. 4d); קודם (A 30 l. 16, in contrast to קדמיך in 4Q213a 1 16, 16 = *A.L.D.* 1a vv. 15, 16; *qatl*).

6. Late Aramaic vocabulary: התחמיון (A 2 l. 22) instead of הוא. הכין (A 6 l. 7) in contrast to הי[כה (4Q213b 1).

7. Assimilation of a dental consonant: קמיא (A 68 l. 9, cf. Beyer 1984: 94, n. 1; Dalman 1905: 103, § 15.4.)

The Cairo Geniza fragments also preserved some linguistic traits from the earlier period of the language history.

1. Prevalence of די over ד (only 20 l. 5; 93 l. 15); Qumran text: ד 4x; cf. the Official Aramaic זי (4 Q213 3–4 5 = *A.L.D.* 3a l. 5).

2. Prevalence of *hap̄ʿel* (10 l. 1; 21 ll. 6, 7; 22 ll. 9, 9, 11; 23 l. 14; 25a l. 20; 25b l. 23; 26 l. 3; 27 l. 4; 30 l. 14; 31 l. 20; 72 l. 1; 73 l. 2; 78 l. 15; 80 l. 22; 83b l. 8; 86 l. 13; 87 l. 15) over against *ʾap̄ʿel* (1a v. 7; 9 l. 19; 10 l. 23; 69a l. 11; 71 l. 18; 73 l. 3);

3. 3f.s. suffix—הא־ קניהא (A 94 l. 17, cf. 4Q213a 3–4 6.6; Fassberg 1992: 53);

4. the use of the direct object marker ל, while ית used only twice (13 ll. 7, 7).

The *Document* contains a high number of loan words, a phenomenon not unusual in Aramaic, the *lingua franca* of the ancient Near East in the first millennium B.C. The following discussion presents an exhaustive list of the loan words found in the whole composition.

Hebraisms
Fitzmyer (1999: 464) wrongly considered the Hebraisms in the Cairo Geniza fragments as introduced into the medieval Aramaic text. Some of them were attested in Qumran fragments of the *Document*, while the others turned out in other Qumran Aramaic texts. Hence the presence of the Hebraisms cannot be indiscriminately ascribed to a late medieval copyist.

אוצר (A 95 l. 22); הודשא (A 72 l. 23, attested in Qumran Aramaic, cf. Fassberg 1992: 58); ידיד (A 83b l. 9); כבוד (A 71 l. 21); כילי (A 91 l. 10); לבונה (A 30 l. 14); ניחח (30 l. 16); משפחה (A 17 l. 16; attested in Qumran Aramaic, cf. 4QpapTob[a] ar 2 9); מוסר (A 88 l. 17; A 90 l. 23; 4Q213 1 ii 5 = *A.L.D.* 98 l. 8; attested in Qumran Aramaic, cf. Fassberg 1992: 59); פר (A 32a l. 23); אל עליון (1Q21 1 3 = *A.L.D.* 3c l. 3; 9 l. 20; 13 l. 5; 30 l. 16; cf. Fassberg 1992: 57).

Old Persian Loan Words
נחשירותא (A 4 l. 3; cf. Hinz 1975: 172); סרך (A 30 l. 15; 31 l. 17, cf. Hinz 1975: 221); פתגם (A 15 l. 13; cf. Hinz 1975: 186); רתיכן (A 95 l. 19; cf. Greenfield and Stone 1979: 228).

Akkadian Loan Words
בירה (A 11 l. 2; cf. Kaufman 1974: 44); זמן (A 5 ll. 4, 5, 5, 5, 6, 6; A 73 l. 4; cf. Kaufman 1974: 91); מנה (A 32a l. 23; cf. Kaufman 1974: 69); מח (A 91 l. 6; 95 l. 20; cf. Kaufman 1974: 71); נכסין (A 95 l. 20; cf. Kaufman 1974: 77); שיט (A 89 l. 21; cf. Beyer 1984: 706); שיטו (4Q213 1 i 11 = *A.L.D.* 89 l. 21; cf. Beyer 1984: 706).

Hittite Loan Word
θέρμος, "thermos" (E 18,2 vv. 47, 47; cf. the comment on *A.L.D.* 47).

1.5.2 *The Author*

The Aramaic work was composed by an author whose personal identity remains totally unknown to the modern reader. What follows in this section, therefore, is only a reconstruction based on the analysis of the *Document*'s content together with its cultural and historical background. The work itself was most probably anonymous from the very beginning of its circulation, and the composer(s) remained hidden in the shadow of his (their) own work.

The author of the *Document* belonged to the priestly group of Levitical scribes responsible for the preparation of the Levitical students. He composed a book for this purpose and chose Levi, the eponymous patriarch of the Levitical priestly tribe, as an ideal example of priestly piety, service, and education. When composing his book he heavily relied on the biblical data concerning Levi but adapted them for his own pedagogical needs.

He was well acquainted with dream interpretations and justified Levitical claim to royal and priestly judicial authority with two visionary dreams of the noble patriarch of the priestly tribe (*A.L.D.* 1b; 3a–7). His priestly background is detectable in his perfect knowledge of the Levitical ritual (*A.L.D.* 19–30), which he adapted for his purpose of expressing the ideal of a sapiential order that underlies the description of the holocaust offering (*A.L.D.* 30 and 31). His quality of being a scribe becomes apparent because of his metrological knowledge and the ideal of metro-arithmetical education that he tried to instill into his Levitical students and transmit to his co-teachers (*A.L.D.* 31–47).

He was an expert teacher of metro-arithmetical knowledge and proved it in Isaac's instruction where counting became an important element in Levitical education necessary for upholding the sapiential order (*A.L.D.* 31). Joseph was held in high regard as a pedagogical example of the one who taught scribal skills and wisdom, thus attained glory and greatness, and was associated with kings (*A.L.D.* 90). Hence the future glory of the Levitical priesthood depended on the education they received from their forefathers: Noah (*A.L.D.* 57), Abraham (*A.L.D.* 22; 50; 57), Isaac (*A.L.D.* 12–13, 15), and Levi (*A.L.D.* 83b–84; cf. *A.L.D.* 88). He defined the wisdom teacher as the one who leads the man who studies wisdom (*A.L.D.* 91) and the subsequent praise of the wisdom teacher constituted a central part of the Levitical educational doctrine according to which teaching leads to an extremely high social position not only at home but in any land and country.

The author was also an expert jurist who imparted to Levi a highest judicial authority (*A.L.D.* 14–15; 99). Now Levi and his sons are responsible for upholding the judicial order of the combined priestly and royal authority (*A.L.D.* 3c; 30–31; 67; 100). In two separate visions this authority was grounded in the celestial realm with the heavenly condemnation of exogamy, priestly and royal elevation, and the concept of two kingdoms that stood in sharp opposition with each other. In terms of practical acquisition of this judicial authority, Levi became a student under Isaac to learn his priestly duty of upholding holiness by avoiding exogamy (*A.L.D.* 16), officiating at the altar (*A.L.D.* 19–30), and learning counting necessary for a proper administration of the sacrificial material (*A.L.D.* 31–47). This educational ideal points to the didactic setting of the composition and strengthens the suggestion that the whole *Document* is a text written by a teacher for his pupils who, in turn, are to become teachers and to hold important positions in the society.

The author of Levi's composition was well acquainted with Babylonian school tradition, imitated Babylonian metrological exercises, and adopted the Babylonian practice of metro-arithmetical education in the context of wisdom literature. He must have received his own scribal education in a Babylonian school or was trained in a Levitical didactic system modeled on the Babylonian scribal education. He also belonged to the priestly descendants of the Ezra circle that under the leadership of the Babylonian scribe and priest opted for the separation of Judah from the rest of neighboring nations.

1.5.3   *The Date, Place, and Purpose of the Composition*

1.5.3.1   *The Date*

The earliest Qumran manuscripts of the *Levi Document* are dated to the second half of the second century B.C., while the Cairo Geniza fragments were copied around the beginning of the tenth century A.D. The Syriac fragment was preserved in a manuscript dated to A.D. 874, and the Greek translation was found in the manuscript of the *Testaments of the Twelve Patriarchs* paleographically dated to the eleventh century A.D.

The composition contains no clear allusions to historical events or persons that could help locate the composition in the context of the Second Temple history. Linguistic data allow for classification of the Qumran fragments as belonging to the Middle Aramaic stratum in the linguistic history of the language. Paleographical evidence indicates that the oldest Qumran manuscript (4Q213a) comes from the second half of the second century B.C., thus a *terminus ad quem* is

easily established. Establishing a *teminus a quo* for the composition of
the *Document* is a more complicated task requiring an analysis of comparative data concerning social status of priesthood after the exile
and the Babylonian context of scribal education in the Persian and
Hellenistic periods.

In most cases scholars based their dating of the Aramaic work on
the analysis of its content and comparison with other related texts.
On the grounds of literary criticism Charles and Cowley (1907: 567)
claimed that the *Document* was written not later than 150 B.C., for it
served as a literary source to both the *Testaments of the Twelve Patriarchs*
and the book of *Jubilees*. Ascribing both the priestly kingdom (*A.L.D.*
3c) and the kingdom of the sword in (*A.L.D.* 4b–5) to Levi, Grelot
(1956: 396, 406) affirmed that this image of a sovereign priest and
military commander points to the context of the Maccabean upris-
ing against the Hellenizing religious policy of Antiochus IV Epiphanes.
Beyer (1984: 188–189) followed Grelot's opinion and further suggested that the *Document* was composed not later than the reign of
John Hyrcanus (135–104 B.C.) because, paleographically, Qumran
manuscripts of the *Document* dated from the second half of the second century B.C. Levi's speech in *A.L.D.* 101–102 interpreted as a
warning against the Hellenization of the Jerusalem priesthood suggested the Hasmonean rule as a *terminus ad quem* for the composition of the work (Beyer 1984: 189).

Anders Hultgård (1977: 41–45; 1980: 94–95) modified the opinion of the preceding two scholars by claiming that the Jerusalem
Zadokite clergy composed the *Document* as a reaction against the
Hellenistic tendencies of the pre-Maccabean Jewish priests. By killing
the Shechemites Levi executed God's will with zeal, and thus became
an excellent example of purity and zeal for the Torah. The speech
against his sons in *A.L.D.* 101–102 was for Hultgård an indication
"qu'on se détourne des prêtres qui ont subi l'influence grandissante
de l'hellénisme" (1977: 44). The origins of this particular reinterpretation of Levi's life went back to the third century B.C., but its
literary redaction took place in the first half of the second century
B.C. with some redactional modification during the Maccabean period.
Later on the *Document*'s royal and priestly ideology helped justify the
Hasmonean claim to royal dignity. The Hasmoneans must have
exploited the "Levitical" ideology to further their political agenda
among the circles of Jerusalem Zadokite priesthood, which most probably had recognized the legitimacy of the new dynasty. In Hultgård's

view, the redactional addition to the *Document* in *A.L.D.* 67, which claimed for Qahat both priesthood and kingship, further substantiated the opinion concerning a later exploitation of the *Document* standpoint by the pro-Hasmonean circles.

Hultgård's opinion is nuanced and elaborate, but his reading of the *Document* as an anti-Hellenistic manifesto of the Jerusalem Zadokite priesthood does not find a real confirmation in the text. To the contrary, there are no traces of anti-Hellenistic polemics in the *Document*'s fragmentary text, and Levi's speech to his children in *A.L.D.* 101–102 does not explicitly mention the reasons for the moral corruption of the Levitical priesthood. The *Document* rather suggests that the priestly apostasy occurs when Levi's sons abandon the way of studying wisdom and neglect the pursuit of knowledge.

Basing the *Document*'s dating on Levi's military exploits and royal characteristics of the sons of Levi does not stand a critical scrutiny. Becker (1970: 78–79) convincingly argued against interpreting *A.L.D.* 4b–5 as a text that ascribes to Levi the kingdom of the sword. He observed that the terms used to characterize the kingdom of the sword could hardly describe actual warfare or Levitical priestly duties. He also underlined a great uncertainty surrounding the correct localization of the fragmentary 1Q21 1 (*A.L.D.* 3c) before the description of the kingdom of the sword in *A.L.D.* 4b–5. *A.L.D.* 3c spoke about the priestly kingdom but its connection with the *Document*'s context and with the kingdom of the sword was not assured. Also the reinterpretation of Levi's military expedition against Shechem in Gen 34 could not be unequivocally connected with the context of Maccabean warfare in the second century B.C. The text describing the Shechem killing is very fragmentary (*A.L.D.* 1c–2), and the interpretation of the incident in *A.L.D.* 78 suggests that Shechem had to die because he committed a lawless deed by treating Dinah like a prostitute.

Michael Stone (1987: 578, n. 20) advanced the opinion that the Aramaic work was composed in the course of the third century B.C. "because this document or something very like it must have served as a source for *Jubilees*, which is dated most recently to the first third of the second century B.C.E." An additional indication for an early dating was the *Document*'s non-polemical use of the solar calendar, an attitude totally abandoned in the book of *Jubilees* (Stone 1988: 160, n. 2, 168; cf. Greenfield and Stone 1979: 224–225). Stone underlined the instructional character of the composition, its combination of priestly and royal characteristics in the person of Levi, and the tendency to root the unusual sacrificial practices "in the very oldest and most authoritative priestly sources, Abraham's instructions given to the ancestor of all the true priests on his investiture with the priestly office (para. 50)" (1988: 169). Kugler (1996a: 134–135) followed Stone's argumentation and additionally observes that the incipient dualism found in the composition would suggest its early third century B.C. date.

Józef T. Milik, who published the very first Qumran fragments of the *Document* in 1955, was convinced that "it is Samaritan in origin and was composed in the course of the third century, if not towards the end of the fourth" (1976: 24). He claimed that *A.L.D.* 102 contains the earliest allusion to the *Book of Watchers* (*1 En.* 1–36), and that this attestation of the Enochic composition suggests the early datation of the Aramaic composition. The Samaritan provenance of the *Document* is assured by the toponyms of the ancient kingdom of Israel (1978: 96). Kugler attempted to substantiate Milik's claim of the composition's Samaritan origin by pointing to some possible connections with the Samaritan Pentateuch and later Samaritan writings exalting Levi and Joseph (Kugler 1996b). He was, however, acutely aware that the evidence was indeed slim, and points of comparison not entirely convincing.

All scholars who have debated the *Document*'s date and place of composition have failed to properly analyze its Greek section (*A.L.D.* 32a–47) dealing with different quantities of sacrificed material. Consequently, they have not discovered the Babylonian numerical system on which the section is based. The author of the Aramaic work imitates Babylonian metrological lists used in the elementary stage of scribal education. When asking for the historical period in which the *Document* might have been composed, one has to consider historical data concerning scribal education in Babylon. On the other hand, it is also necessary to situate the composition in the historical period in which the contacts of Jewish priesthood with Babylon were particularly intense. Finally, additional data contained in the work, like the Shechem killing, the combination of priestly and royal power, and educational preparation of the future priests, heads, judges, and kings, also presume a particular social and religious situation in the history of the post-exilic Jewish community in Judea. The combination of these aforementioned elements should lead to certain conclusions concerning the *terminus a quo* for the composition of the *Document*.

Babylonian metrological lists are already attested in the early third millennium B.C. and continued to be used during the Ur III (2112–2004 B.C.) and Old Babylonian (2017–1595 B.C.; cf. Brinkman 1977: 336–337) periods in the scribal school called "tablet house," *é-dub-ba-a* in Sumerian or *bīt tuppi* in Akkadian. They constitute an introductory exercise intended to acquaint the student not only with the names of weights and measures, but with the sexagesimal numerical system on which the Babylonian metrological system is based as well (Waetzoldt 1988: 43). At the same time, by copying the metrological lists the student acquired the fundamental arithmetical knowledge of number fractions which was then used in more complicated mathematical exercises, examples of "applied " mathematics (Nemet-Nejat 1993). After the disintegration of the scribal school system at the end of the Old Babylonian period, much less is known concerning the mathematical training of the scribe. Scribal education most probably continued on the family level (Sjöberg 1975: 160, n. 3) but mathematical training is poorly documented.

Around the middle to the first millennium B.C. there came a revival of Babylonian mathematics most probably caused by a process of cultural cross-fertilization during the period of intense empire building in the eastern Mediterranean (Friberg 1987–90: 582–583). Main elements of scribal metrological and mathematical tradition were preserved from the Old Babylonian period without substantial changes, and school tablets, although in a much restricted number, are well attested (Gesche 2001: 36–42). At the same time, there appeared a mathematical astronomy on a highly sophisticated level. It continued in the Seleucid period with the Babylonian ephemerides for the motion of the sun, moon, and planets (Neugebauer 1983). During the same period there developed a "cosmic" religion, which relied on a zodiacal and horoscopic astrology based on astronomical observations and used to establish the fate of the king or the nation (van der Waerden 1974: 127–204).

The historical context of the missions of Ezra and Nehemiah must be seriously considered as a *terminus a quo* for the formation of the Levitical tradition that eventually led to the composition of the *Document*. This assumption is based on the following arguments.

1. The Babylonian Jew Ezra reached Jerusalem as an official of the Persian king Artaxerxes to complement the Persian policy of supporting and supervising non-Persian cults (Smith 1987: 90). A group of Israelites, priests, Levites, singers, gatekeepers, and temple slaves

accompanied him from Babylon. Scholars debate a precise date of
his mission (458 or 398 B.C.), but for the purpose of this research it
is important to notice that Ezra and his party left Babylon at the
time of renewed interests in Babylonian mathematics in scribal circles of Mesopotamia. It is probable that Levitical priests in exile
were influenced by the revival and brought with them to Judea some
fundamental principles of Babylonian scribal education. On the other
hand, one cannot exclude the possibility that the metrological lists
constituted a scribal heritage transmitted from one generation beginning with the earliest period of Israel's presence in Canaan. Archeological excavations brought to light some examples of Akkadian
thematic noun lists from Old and Middle Babylonian periods in
Israel (cf. Demsky 1990: 162–163).

2. In the Persian royal decree Ezra bears the title of "the priest,
scribe of the law of the God of heaven" כהנא ספר דתא די אלה שמיא
(Ezra 7:12, 21). The conjunction of the two titles, priest and scribe,
in relation with Ezra is also found in Neh 8:9; 12:26, while Neh
8:13 calls Ezra הספר. In Ezra 7:6 he is described as "a scribe (ספר)
skilled in the law of Moses." Similarly, Ezra 7:11 indicates that Ezra
was "the priest (הכהן), the scribe (הספר), learned in matters of the
commandments of the Lord and his statutes for Israel."

The presentation of Ezra as a ספר in the Persian commissioning
letter gave rise to the opinion that Ezra was an official scribe in the
Achaemenid administration, while the specification of his expertise
in the laws of God may be ascribed to the author or redactor of
Ezra-Nehemiah (Schaeder 1930: 39–51). Comparative material from
the Persian period bears witness to the fact that foreigners were
employed as scribes in the administration of the empire, partly on
account of their bi- or multilingual skills (Schams 1998: 54–55).
Administrative skills of a scribe had to include reading and writing
expertise, knowledge of the official administrative language, that is
Aramaic, legal matters and diplomatic letter writing. Whatever Ezra's
position at the Persian court might have been, his designation as a
scribe indicates that he had to receive some formal education to
properly exercise his function. Whether his education included any
metrological training is completely unknown, but, judging from the
Old Babylonian school curriculum in vogue also in the first millennium B.C. (New and Late Babylonian periods), he probably got
acquainted with principles of metric and arithmetical knowledge. It
is worth noting that before leaving the river Ahava in Babylon Ezra

weighed out temple vessels and offerings before the priests' chiefs
and leaders of the people (Ezra 8:24–27). The author of the book
therefore assumed that Ezra possessed knowledge of the metric system and arithmetical calculation. When the returning caravan reached
Jerusalem the gold, silver, and temple vessels were weighed out again
in the temple into the care of the priests and assisting Levites (Ezra
8:33). Then everything was checked by number and weight and the
total weight was recorded in writing (Ezra 8:34). The particular
importance assigned to weights and numbers in the Ezra account is
reflected in the *Document*'s instruction where Isaac admonished Levi
to proceed in order, by weight and measure (*A.L.D.* 30–31) and then
he taught the priestly scribe the knowledge of Babylonian counting
associated with metric system of weights and measures. It is certain
that the author of the composition was a priest who received scribal
education and Ezra's titles of priest and scribe may apply to him
as well.

3. Ezra introduced the marriage reform, the purpose of which was
to eliminate exogamic marriages among the priestly class and lay
people as well (Ezra 9–10). During his mission to Jerusalem, Nehemiah
found out that the practice of exogamous marriages continued and
reintroduced its prohibition (Neh 10:29–31; 13:1–3, 23–30). The
Document fully agrees with these two reformers by reinstating the
endogamous principle for Levi (*A.L.D.* 16), and by interpreting
Shechem's attempt to marry Dinah in Gen 34 as "violence/law-
lessness" (*A.L.D.* 78). Levi then was represented as an ideal priest
who obeyed the endogamous principle by marrying Melcha, a woman
from Abraham's family (*A.L.D.* 62). The motivation for the endogamous family relations is based in the Aramaic composition on the
concept of the "holy seed" זרע קדיש (*A.L.D.* 17) identified with Levi
and his descendants. The same idea was embraced by Ezra who
extends it to the whole nation. The post-exilic community had to
abandon the practice of exogamous marriages (Ezra 9:12) because
the nation as a זרע הקדש could not mix with the neighboring nations
(Ezra 9:2, cf. Weinfeld 1964: 237–239; Williamson 1985: 131–132).

4. Ezra stood at the head of the whole Jewish community in
Jerusalem and Judea and his genealogy is traced back to Aaron to
ensure his connection with the high priestly family (Ezra 7:1–5). The
genealogy, whether historical or not, intends to prove his authority
as the religious reformer and enforcer of the law of Moses (Williamson
1985: 91–92). It also reflects the increasingly prominent role of the

high priests in the political arena in the post-exilic period. The Aramaic papyri from Elephantine attest to the respected position of the Jerusalem high priest Yehohanan who was asked for help in rebuilding the military colonists' temple (Cowley 1967: nos. 30 and 31; cf. Goodblatt 1994: 8–9). Following the same tendency, the *Document* ascribes to the Levitical priesthood a prominent social position by claiming for them judicial, priestly, and royal authority. Levi as a learned priest and scribe (*A.L.D.* 14–61) maintained peace and equity of the priestly rule, which received visionary and heavenly authentication (*A.L.D.* 3a–7), while Levi's sons were called heads, judges, rulers, priests, and kings (*A.L.D.* 99–100). Additionally, the high priesthood over the whole Israel was claimed for Qahat (*A.L.D.* 67).

5. When another Babylonian Jew, Nehemiah, arrived at Jerusalem, the people made a pledge to bring offerings to the priests and a tithe to the Levites who were also entitled to collect the tithe in all the towns (Neh 10:38). In doing this the Levites were to be assisted by an Aaronic priest, and they had to bring one tenth of their tithe to the temple treasury (Neh 10:39). Later on Nehemiah enforced the tithe practice when it was neglected by the inhabitants of Judah (Neh 13:10–13). In the context of the importance of the tithe for the upkeep of the temple personnel and temple cult it comes as no surprise that the tithe motif and metro-arithmetical calculation connected therewith appear as an important motif in Levi's priestly elevation (*A.L.D.* 3a l. 8; 9).

6. In Neh 10:34 (cf. Neh 13:31) the priests, the Levites and the people cast lots in the matter of wood procurement (קרבן עצים) to arrange to bring wood to the temple by families at the appointed times each year to burn it on the altar of the Lord. The wood procurement is not mentioned in the Pentateuch, which merely states that the priest is responsible for arranging wood on the altar (Lev 1:7), the altar fire should burn continually, and the priest should burn wood on the altar every morning (Lev 6:5–6, 12–13). The *Document*'s insistence on the knowledge of the tree species (*A.L.D.* 24) and the wood quantity used for different animals (*A.L.D.* 32a–36) can be seen as a natural development of this post-exilic custom that assigned greater importance to wood in the temple sacrificial system than pentateuchal regulations. Nehemiah's reform also includes priests among those who procure wood for sacrificial use. Consequently, Levi as a scribal priest had to learn the types of sacrificed wood and

how to calculate its weight corresponding to different sacrificed animals.

The process of the religious reforms and political changes in post-exilic Judah led eventually to the reinterpretation of the biblical Levi and his life story in accordance with the new historical circumstances during the Persian dominion in the Trans-Euphrates province. That this process actually started is plainly witnessed by the book of the prophet Malachi that depicted Levi as an ideal priest who possessed the true instruction and walked blameless with the Lord (Mal 2:4–7). The composition of the *Document* stands at the end of this process and can be approximately dated to the end of the fourth or the early years of the third century B.C., in accordance with Milik's suggestion.

Dating the composition of this Aramaic work to that historical period is also related to the observation that the *Document* ascribes a highly elevated political status to the Levitical priesthood. The work was composed to formulate and promote an educational basis of the priestly tradition according to which Levi and his sons become students of the priestly and scribal wisdom in order to occupy the highest social and political positions in post-exilic Israel. They are to be heads, judges, priests, and kings (*A.L.D.* 99–100) and Qahat inherits the high priesthood for the whole of Israel. The description of Qahat's high priestly office in *A.L.D.* 67 draws on Gen 49:10 where Jacob blesses Judah and associates him with the congregation of all nations. In the *Document* Qahat inherits this designation. It is certain, therefore, that the Aramaic work not only promotes the Levitical priesthood to the royal dignity but it also associates the royal blessing of Judah with the office of the high priest. A later redactor added an explanatory gloss preserved only in Greek (MS E 18,2 v. 67) that explicitly states what was already evident in the Aramaic midrashic reinterpretation of Gen 49:10—that Qahat possesses the office of the high priest and king at the same time (MS A 67).

The *Document*'s presentation of the priestly monarchy fits in well with the political situation in Judea around the end of the Persian period and beginning of Greek dominion over the province of Judah in 332 B.C. A Hellenistic ethnographic historian, Hecataeus of Abdera, writing around the end of the fourth century B.C. (Stern 1976: 20), left some remarks concerning the origins of the Judeans. In a passage preserved by the first century B.C. writer Diodorus of Sicily, this Greek historian described the political and religious status of priests and high priests in Judea. His description is commonly held as historically reliable although influenced by Greek ethnographical tradition and political utopianism (cf. Goodblatt 1994: 11, n. 19 and 20; Tcherikover 1959: 58–59).

> The sacrifices that he [Moses] established differ from those of other nations, as does their way of living, for as a result of their own expulsion from Egypt he introduced an unsocial and intolerant way of life. He picked out the men of most refinement and with the greatest ability to head the entire nation, and appointed them priests; and he ordained that they should occupy themselves with the temple and the honours and sacrifices offered to their God. (5) These same men he appointed to be judges (δικαστάς) in all major disputes, and entrusted to them the guardianship of the laws and customs. For this reason (διό) the Jews never have a king, and authority over the people is regularly vested in whichever priest is regarded as superior to his colleagues in wisdom and virtue (φρονήσει καὶ ἀρετῇ). They call this man the high priest, and believe that he acts as a messenger (ἄγγελον) to them of God's commandments. (6) It is he, we are told, who in their assemblies and other gatherings announces what is ordained, and the Jews are so docile in such matters that straightway they fall to the ground and do reverence to the high priest when he expounds the commandments to them. And at the end of their laws there is even appended the statement: "These are the words that Moses heard from God and declares unto the Jews." (Diodorus of Sicily, *Bibliotheca Historica* XL 3; text and transl. Stern 1976: 26–29)

Hecataeus' description of the priests and high priest corresponds to the *Document*'s image of Levitical priesthood. He presented the priests as leaders of the nation and judges in major disputes. Of particular interest is Hecataeus' assertion that *because* (διό) of the priestly leadership in the nation the Jews do not have a king, and his place is taken by the high priest. The Jewish high priest played the function of the messenger of God's commandments and was expected to be superior to his colleagues in understanding and virtue. The correspondence between the *Document* and the Greek historian's account further suggests that Hecataeus had Jewish informants who were his main source of information about Judea and its social structure. This opinion is based on the observation that in his account there are two allusions to biblical verses (Goodblatt 1994: 11).

Another reason to date the *Document* to the early years of the Hellenistic period is the story related by Josephus concerning the marriage between Nikaso, daughter of Sanballat governor of Samaria, and Manasseh, the brother of the Jewish high priest Jaddua (*A.J.*

11.302–347). When the elders of Jerusalem learned what had happened, they gave Manasseh a choice of either divorcing Nikaso or giving up the priestly office "for they considered this marriage to be a stepping-stone for those who might wish to transgress the laws about taking wives and that this would be the beginning of intercourse with foreigners" (*A.J.* 11.307). When Manasseh presented the problem to his father-in-law, the latter promised him that, with the consent of the Persian king Darius III (338–331 B.C.), he would build a temple on Mount Garizim where Manasseh could officiate as a high priest. The unfortunate bride eventually followed this enticing proposal and many priests who lived in exogamous marriages left Jerusalem and joined Manasseh (*A.J.* 11.309–312). Since Darius was defeated by Alexander in the battle at Issos, Sanballat's plan initially did not work out. However, when Alexander laid siege to Tyre and needed military help, Sanballat sent him eight thousand troops and asked permission for his son-in-law to build the temple (*A.J.* 11.313–323). When the permission was granted, Sanballat hastened to build the temple, installed Manasseh as high priest, and nine months later died (*A.J.* 11.324–325).

Josephus' account has often been dismissed as lacking a historical basis (cf. Cowley 1967: 110; Rooke 2000: 222, n. 5). The critics argued that Josephus made up the whole story basing his account on a similar episode mentioned in Neh 13:28. Nehemiah expelled from Jerusalem one of the sons of Jehoiada, the son of Eliashib the high priest because this son, whose name is omitted in the text, married a daughter of Sanballat the Horonite, governor of Samaria. There is a growing consensus among scholars, however, that essential elements of Josephus story are based on historical facts (Mor 1989: 4–5; Hengel 1989: 39–40; Albertz 1994: 527–528). The discovery of the Samaritan bullae and papyri from Wadi ed-Daliyeh have proved that, in addition to Sanballat in the time of Nehemiah, there was another Sanballat, father of the Samaritan governor in the early fourth century B.C. (Cross 1963; 1966; 1974). Since the high offices in the Persian empire tended to be of a hereditary nature, it comes as no surprise that the descendants of Sanballat the Horonite held the governorship of Samaria for several generations. Following Cross's reconstruction it is plausible to accept the governor of Samaria from Josephus' account as a historical person who flourished in the time of Darius III and Alexander the Great. One should also notice that the city of Shechem (Tell Balâṭah), which was abandoned between

480 and 330 B.C., was rebuilt and fortified at the end of the fourth
century, and developed into an important center around 300 B.C.
(Wright 1965: 170–184). The rebuilding of Shechem most probably
resulted from the destruction of rebellious Samaria by Alexander in
331 B.C. and its resettlement with Macedonian mercenaries. The
Samaritans fled Samaria and had to find a new place to live and
worship. It is not improbable that together with the rebuilding of
Shechem they constructed a sanctuary on the top of Mount Garizim,
for archaeological excavations proved that beneath Hadrian's temple structures there exist older layers that perhaps are those of the
Samaritan sanctuary (Hengel 1989: 41–42).

Although the historical image of that period is not perfectly trans-
parent due to the scarcity of available documentation, it constitutes
an important background for the composition of the *Document*. The
author of this priestly composition tried to reinstate the endogamic
principle for the Levitical priesthood in opposition to those priests
who might have defected from the Jerusalem sanctuary on account
of their exogamous marriages, as related by Josephus. Rebuilding of
Shechem and creation of a schismatic sanctuary might have further
infuriated the Jerusalem priestly class and led to the reinterpretation
of the story of *Genesis* 34. Levi's merciless killing of Shechemites guilty
of attempting exogamy was considered an act of priestly heroism
and virtue and unequivocally set the Jerusalem priestly class against
the marriage practices of the schismatic priests in Shechem. The setting of *Genesis* 34 and consequently of the *Document* in and around
Shechem only added to the unequivocal message suggesting that any
compromise in sexual purity and intermarriage had already been
rejected by the founder of the priestly tribe. Since the Aramaic work
is didactic in nature and intends to transmit an idealized image of
a wise priest, the time of a particular crisis among priestly ranks
could have led to its composition and reaffirmation of the endogamic
principle for those who remained faithful to the Jerusalem sanctuary and its standpoint of separation from neighboring nations.

Dating the *Document*'s composition to the early Hellenistic period
stems also from the observation that its Aramaic is free from Greek
influence. Persian loan words prove that the language was under the
influence of the Iranian culture for a considerable period of time.
On the other hand, the presence of a Hittite metrological term
(*A.L.D.* 47) is of great philological interest and witnesses that the

author relied on ancient scribal terminology that either survived in
the local Palestinian culture or resulted from his Babylonian scribal
education.

1.5.3.2   *The Place*

The *Document* does not contain any clear indications as to its place
of composition. The topographical description indicates that the
author was well acquainted with the territory of northern Israel. He
mentioned Shechem (*A.L.D.* 3), Abel Main (*A.L.D.* 1b) and Bethel
as places of Levi's life and activity. Bethel appears as a particularly
suitable place for the composition of this Aramaic text for it plays
an important role in Levi's priestly activity. His second vision probably happened in Bethel, he was ordained and officiated as the
priest of God the most high in Bethel (*A.L.D.* 9), and, finally, Isaac's
instruction suggests that Bethel was the place of Levi's priestly duties
(*A.L.D.* 19).

The composition of the *Document* at Bethel could be consonant
with Milik's opinion concerning the Samaritan origin of the whole
work. There are, however, some weighty arguments that militate
against Milik's suggestion and the Bethel connection. At the time of
Ezra and Nehemiah's restoration Bethel became part of the Yehud
province settled with the lay returnees from Babylon (Ezra 2:28; Neh
7:32), and its connection with the Samaritan tradition is not confirmed
by the historical events of the Persian period. It is also difficult to
imagine that Bethel could have been seriously considered by the
priestly composer of the *Document* to be a place of Levi's priestly
activity (*A.L.D.* 9–10), given the schismatic overtones of Jeroboam's
cult during the monarchic period (cf. 1 Kgs 12:29–33; 2 Kgs 23:15;
Hos 10:15; Amos 3:14). It is evident that Bethel as the place of
Levi's priestly activity is connected with the reinterpretation of Jacob's
story and his unfulfilled vow in Gen 28 to tithe everything that God
would bestow upon him during his stay in Mesopotamia. Since the
Genesis text does not contain any description of Jacob's fulfillment
of this particular vow, Levi's elevation to priesthood and tithe apportioning at Bethel come as a solution of an exegetical problem. On
the one hand Jacob's honor was saved, on the other, Levi found a
place where he could be ordained and exercise the priestly office.
Similarly, mentioning of Shechem in the *Document*'s narrative stems
from the reinterpretation of the biblical story (*Genesis* 34 and 37),

while the toponym Abel Main, if properly localized in the Shechem
vicinity, proves only that the author knew the region well, not that
he was of Samaritan origin.

It then becomes evident that Bethel does not indicate the place
of origin of the *Document* but appears as a literary reference necessary for the proper functioning of the reinterpreted biblical text.
Additionally, the Levitical priest, writing the *Document* from the perspective of the post-exilic period, could not have situated Levi's
priestly ordination and service in Jerusalem for obvious historical reasons. Instead, he used the name of the city of Bethel in his narrative and played consciously on its meaning. While the expression בית
אל in *A.L.D.* 10 denotes a proper noun, the same expression in *A.L.D.*
19 indicates "the house of God," that is, the temple where Levi
fulfilled his sacrificial duties.

Joseph's eminent position in the didactic poem (*A.L.D.* 90) is due
not to the recourse of the Samaritan group to the ancestor of the
Ephraimite tribe (cf. Judg 1:22) but to the reinterpretation of the
Genesis story in accordance with the ideological and didactic perspective of the scribal education adopted by the priestly author of
the *Document*. His quality of a good administrator of Egyptian wealth
is reinterpreted to create an image of the teacher of scribal craft,
instruction, and wisdom who is elevated to royal dignity on account
of his intellectual skills.

A Levitical school in Jerusalem presents an attractive hypothesis
concerning the place where the *Document* might have been composed.
The Jerusalem temple needed a group of educated priests who had
to be versed in sacrificial matters and everyday administration. There
are, however, no historical or archeological records concerning any
kind of Levitical school as an independent institution in the history
of pre- or post-exilic Israel. The text of the *Document* indicates that
education took place in the family milieu, hence a Levitical priestly
family appears as a most probable social context for the composition of the whole work. One could agree that the *Document* witnesses
to the existence of a Levitical school in Judea only under the condition that the term "school" is understood in the context of family
education. Note that 1 Chr 2:55 lists the families of the scribes
(משפחות ספרים) that dwelt at Jabez in the post-exilic Judea. On the
other hand, the content of priestly and scribal education in the
Document suggests that the proper place for its application is indeed
the temple and its administration. Since no evidence concerning a

Levitical school in Jerusalem is available, one should assume that priestly education as presented in the *Document* took place in the family milieu, while thus acquired knowledge could have been used in the administration of both the temple and Judean province. The archeological and literary evidence from Mesopotamia indicates that schooling usually took place in the courtyards of private houses (cf. Charpin 1986: 419–485; Stone 1987: 56–59, 125).

The priestly author responsible for the composition of Levi's pseudepigraphic work created a document that is incomprehensible outside of priestly and scribal education. Levi, the priest and scribe in one and the same person, learned his professional skills from Isaac (*A.L.D.* 12–13; 15) as the prototype of priestly students responsible for the upkeeping of the due sacrificial order. Isaac acquired knowledge that he taught Levi from Abraham (*A.L.D.* 22; 50; 57). Levi in turn addressed his sons in a wisdom poem (*A.L.D.* 83b–98) and stressed the importance of the education of their own descendants (*A.L.D.* 88), their responsibility to teach and study wisdom (*A.L.D.* 90; 98), and the prominent position of the wisdom teacher (*A.L.D.* 91–93). These data indicate that the education was thought of as a process that took part in a family milieu. The metrological section in *A.L.D.* 32a–47 is influenced by Babylonian scribal exercises, this infuence, however, cannot prove the Babylonian composition of the *Document*. It is most probably due to the Babylonian education of the Levitical priests who brought this kind of elementary metro-arithmetical knowledge with them from the exile and adopted it in the administration of the temple and education of their sons. West Semitic metrological terminology used with the Babylonian arithmetical pattern (cf. *A.L.D.* 37–47) also suggests this interpretation.

The presence of a Hittite term in the metrological speculation in *A.L.D.* 47 may result from the influence of the Hittite culture felt long after the fall of the Hittite empire with its capital Ḫattuša in the twelfth century B.C. The Neo-Hittite states continued to coexist with Phoenician and Aramean political entities in Syria in the early first millennium B.C. (cf. Klengel 1992: 187–218); linguistic contacts with Aramaic therefore should not come as a surprise. The presence of the Hittite population in Canaan is well attested on the pages of the Old Testament in the patriarchal and monarchical periods, and even during the exile Ezekiel referred to the parentage of Jerusalem: "your mother was a Hittite and your father an Amorite" (Ezek 16:45; cf. 16:3). The Hittites also appear in the post-exilic accounts of the

Ezra and Nehemiah's stay in Jerusalem (Ezra 9:1; Neh 9:8). When
Ezra learned about the intermarriage practices of the people of Israel
who "have acted according to the abominations of the Canaanites,
Hittites. . . ." It is doubtful whether the list of the nations reflects the
actual historical situation of Judah, for it is partially based on Deut
7:1 (cf. Williamson 1985: 131). The *Document* proves, however, that
an actual linguistic influence has survived to early Hellenistic times,
and the conservative tradition of the priestly family education was
a vehicle of its preservation.

The sociopolitical context of post-exilic Judah also suggests that
the Levitical priesthood with its influence on the creation of the
Judean polity and the importance of the high priest is responsible
for the composition of the *Document*. The Aramaic work presents Levi
as a priest who learns the priestly sacrificial skills and his genealogy
(*A.L.D.* 62–77) concentrates on the establishment of the high priestly
line beginning with Qahat. The role of Levi's other two sons is
greatly reduced. Gershom was excluded from priesthood while Merari
was described as one close to death and no priestly role is assigned
to him. The high priestly line continues with Qahat's son Amram
who espoused Levi's daughter Yochebed. Amram was given a prominent role as the one who would lead Israel out of Egypt (*A.L.D.* 76).
There is no doubt that this midrashic exegesis of his name alludes
to the role of Moses and Aaron in the biblical account of Exodus
(cf. the comment on *A.L.D.* 76). Finally, the priestly and royal rule
assigned to Levitical priesthood and the position of the priests as
judges, heads, and rulers reflects well the historical image of Jerusalem
and Judah in late Persian and early Hellenistic periods.

1.5.3.3 *The Purpose*

There are no historical records as to what was the purpose of composing a document that reinterpreted biblical data and added a considerable section of non-biblical material. The fact that the *Document*
was preserved by Qumran covenanters proves its importance for the
community that was greatly concerned with priestly matters, purity
status of its members, Enochic writings, dualistic world-view, calendar computations, etc. Since the Aramaic work is related to these
particular interests of the Qumran group, its presence there is easily accounted for. The partial overlapping of these themes, however,
does not fully explain the reasons for its composition, which took
place in the years preceding the foundation of the community. The

answer should be sought first of all in its content and in the analysis of some comparative data pertinent to the concepts of education in the ancient Near East. The working hypothesis that may be formulated at the outset of the following discussion is that the *Document*'s composition was caused by educational concerns nurtured by priestly instructors responsible for the preparation of a professional class of priestly administrators and rulers.

The analysis of the content is hindered by the fragmentary state of the manuscript evidence. The beginning and end of the composition are lost, and so some important information concerning its purpose is not available. Additionally, the available manuscripts are fragmentary and their reciprocal order is not always easy to ascertain. The preserved text, however, presents a cogent picture of Levi's life, and its inherent indications suggest the purpose of the composers. The preserved content of the *Document* can be thematically divided into three sections: Levi's pseudepigraphical life story (*A.L.D.* 1a–10; 62–81): his priestly education and that of his descendants (*A.L.D.* 11–61; 82–98); the future destiny of Levitical priesthood (*A.L.D.* 99–104). The largest preserved section deals with priestly education, one should, therefore, begin from its analysis. The section that describes Levi's life is much more fragmentary, especially where it interprets the biblical data (*A.L.D.* 1c–3). Its relation to educational ideals is, however, detectable at several points, and it provides these ideals with an authoritative, moral, and religious framework. The last thematic section forecasts the future of priestly teachers and students in relation to their response to the religious, moral and educational ideals expressed in two preceding thematic sections.

1.5.3.3.1. *Apprenticeship in the Patriarchal Household (*A.L.D. *11–61; 82–98)*

According to the *Document*, Levi's education takes place at Isaac's home in Hebron where the whole family arrives after Jacob fulfills the act of Levi's ordination at Bethel. As soon as Isaac learns that Levi became a priest he begins to teach his grandson priestly matters. The relationship between Isaac and Levi is that of a priestly teacher to a priestly apprentice. When teaching, Isaac indicates how he himself learned priestly matters. His priestly expertise comes from the observation of Abraham's sacrificial ritual (*A.L.D.* 22) and from Abraham's explicit instruction transmitted to him (*A.L.D.* 50). The prescriptions concerning blood stem from the book of Noah that

Abraham read (*A.L.D.* 50). By referring to these patriarchs, the *Document*'s author creates a stream of transmission of the priestly knowledge reaching back to the prediluvian patriarch. By learning Isaac's instruction, Levi becomes the depository of this knowledge and he himself exhorts his descendants to transmit it to future priestly generations (*A.L.D.* 88; 90; 98). The creation of this stream of transmission indicates to the priestly readers of the composition that there exists a set of knowledge that is being handed down from one generation of priestly apprentices to the other. In this way the author of the Aramaic work justifies and motivates the educational experience of priestly students. While studying priestly knowledge, they become part of this stream of transmission that began with the forefathers of the nation. Thus their educational experience is rooted in history, and the knowledge they receive becomes a priestly inheritance (*A.L.D.* 98) that is to be handed down in the same process of transmission (*A.L.D.* 88).

Although the stream of transmission reaches back to Noah, Abraham, and Isaac, priestly education becomes a domain of only the Levitical tribe. While the whole family arrives at Hebron (*A.L.D.* 11), Isaac transmits his teaching to Levi only, after he learns of his priestly consecration. Levi exhorts his sons to teach only their sons (*A.L.D.* 88), and there is no reference to the Levitical function of the teachers of the nation. Levi's son, Qahat, in his *Testament* warns his sons not to abandon priestly inheritance by transmitting it to strangers and half-breeds because this transmission would allow those who do not belong to the priestly tribe to acquire power (cf. *A.L.D.* 13 and 98; 99–100). Additionally, strangers and half-breeds are contrasted in the *Document* with the wisdom teacher whose glorious fate is assured in every land and province (*A.L.D.* 91).

This reluctance to go beyond the limits of the tribal family is motivated first by the rejection of the exogamic principle and endorsement of endogamy for priests. Secondly, the *Testament of Qahat* explicitly affirms that the transmission of priestly inheritance is related to the exercise of power. The same stance may be inferred from the Wisdom poem where Joseph's teaching activity (*A.L.D.* 90) is related to his glorification and elevation to a royal status. Thirdly, professional knowledge shared by all the members of the group creates a sense of identity particular to that group, and sets up boundaries to all those who do not belong to it. In this way, transmission of professional knowledge becomes an important element of creating an identity of a priestly guild that characterizes the professional group and defines its responsibilities in the society to which it belongs but from which it is distinct by virtue of endogamy and education. Another important element adding to this distinction is divine election, which justifies it from the religious point of view (*A.L.D.* 6; 51; 58).

Isaac's instruction contains elements of a priestly curriculum that are deemed important in the education of priestly apprentices. The main themes include avoidance of any kind of impurity, exogamy included (*A.L.D.* 14–18); ritual ablutions accompanying burnt offering ritual (*A.L.D.* 19–30); elementary metrological exercises in the context of the accompanying meal offering (*A.L.D.* 31–47); rules concerning blood (*A.L.D.* 55–57). Elementary metrological exercises (*A.L.D.* 31–47) find their closest parallels in Babylonian school exercises that constitute the very first step in the mathematical education of a scribe. There remains, therefore, little doubt that Babylonian educational practices influenced priestly education in Israel to the extent that it is presented as a part of a curriculum learned by Levi. This presentation may be interpreted as an attempt to appropriate a tradition foreign to post-exilic priestly education. Another possible reason to include the exercise would stem from the author's intention to indicate how metro–arithmetical knowledge may be useful in exercising priestly duties and ministry. The third reason is related to a more general evaluation of scribal knowledge in ancient Mesopotamia. Scribal education and counting are presented as a highly valued knowledge in Mesopotamian learned circles to the extent that even some learned kings boast about their scribal skills acquired in the "tablet house." In consonance with that tradition, the wisdom poem presents scribal craft (metro-arithmetical calculation included) and instruction of wisdom as an ideal to cherish and transmit to future generations as a source of glory and part of priestly inheritance. This particular importance attached in the *Document* to scribal education becomes an important expression of professional pride, glory, and elevated social position stemming from that education. Joseph as a teacher of scribal craft and instruction of wisdom is highly glorified and associated with kings (*A.L.D.* 90). This wisdom education cannot be acquired with military means but must be taught, studied, and sought for. The praise of the wisdom teacher that constitutes the central part of the wisdom poem focuses on the important social function that becomes fundamental for acquiring professional knowledge, priestly identity, elevated social position, and eternal glory.

1.5.3.3.2. *Moral Authority in Education – Levi's life* (A.L.D. *1a–10;* *62–81*)

Since education needs exemplary incarnation of educational ideas, the reinterpretation of Levi's life in the *Document* served this goal. Levi appears as an example of moral, religious, and professional behavior. He corrects his ways (*A.L.D.* 1a v. 2), asks God to purify his heart from every impurity (*A.L.D.* 1a v. 14), be close to Him (*A.L.D.* 1a v. 11), and do God's will by proceeding according to just judgment (*A.L.D.* 1a v. 18). His two visionary dreams (*A.L.D.* 1b; 3a–7) indicate his close relationship with the heavenly realm and divinely justify his priestly vocation. When ordained in Bethel by his father Jacob (*A.L.D.* 9–10), he begins to fulfill his sacrificial duties and bestows priestly blessings upon his father and brothers. The killing of the Shechemites by Levi and Simeon in *Genesis* 34 deserved Jacob's condemnation, while the *Document*'s reinterpretation presented Levi's killing as an act of justice and elimination of the doers of violence (*A.L.D.* 78). While *Genesis* 37 implies that Levi participated in the selling of Joseph, in the *Document*'s account he, Simeon, and Reuben are absent when the selling takes place (*A.L.D.* 3). Thus he is not culpable of this mischief and presents Joseph to his priestly descendants as a teacher whose example should be imitated. His marriage with Melcha (*A.L.D.* 62) proves that Levi followed Isaac's advice and observed the endogamic principle in his life. The midrashim that inerpret the names of Levi's children (*A.L.D.* 63–77) foretell their importance for the priestly service and the destiny of the whole nation. Qahat will hold priestly and royal dignity in Israel, while the marriage of Yochebed and Amram will lead to the liberation of the whole nation from the Egyptian captivity.

1.5.3.3.3. *Purpose of Education* (A.L.D. *99–104*)

The third thematic section of the *Document* presents the goals of Levitical education and election to priesthood. They are to occupy leading political, religious, and judicial positions in the society (*A.L.D.* 99–100). If they abandon the path of rigtheousness and education, they will walk in the darkness of satan and the guilt for the perversion of the moral and cosmic order will be laid on them (*A.L.D.* 101–102). One should also consider here the wisdom poem (*A.L.D.* 83b–98) that presents the acquisition of knowledge and a teaching position in sapiential education as a means of elevation and a way that leads to the observance of justice and truth.

The administration of the province of Yehud with its temple in Jerusalem organized by the Babylonian Jews, Ezra and Nehemiah, called for a class of educated priests able to carry out liturgical and administrative tasks. In this historical milieu the knowledge of priestly ritual and scribal craft, a necessary tool to carry out all kinds of priestly and adminsitrative tasks, became of extreme importance. The composition of the *Document* came as an outgrowth of teaching professional knowledge to priestly apprentices in line with pedagogical methods and educational ideology of the ancient Near East.

The analysis of the content leads to the conclusion that the Aramaic work was composed in order to uphold the scribal hierocracy by the education of the ruling class. The *Document* indicates that the priestly class had an important social and political position stemming from the divine election and professional preparation (contrast the opinion of Rooke [2000]). Its content also suggests that the reforms of Ezra and Nehemiah had a lasting influence in the circles of the Jerusalem priesthood. The priestly class, therefore, cannot be easily ascribed to the assimilationist party opposed to the Judean separatists that rejected intermarriage with non-Judeans (Smith 1987). Additionally, reading the whole Aramaic composition as a manifesto of the Maccabean priests, kings, and warriors (Grelot 1956) only partially explains its data and assumes that both the kingdom of priesthood and the kingdom of the sword belong to Levi. *A.L.D.* 3c–5, however, can be explained differently and more in consonance with the text and other Aramaic literature.

Kugler (1996a: 135–137) affirmed that several themes interwoven in the *Document*'s narrative explain the reason for the composition of the work. He listed Levi's suitability for the priestly office stemming from his passion for his own purity and that of the community; the presentation of priestly practices different from those required from clergy in the Torah; the conjunction of the priestly office with the role of sage and scribe; the dualism of the narrative, especially seen in Levi's prayer (*A.L.D.* 1a). From these themes Kugler draws the conclusion that the author enlarges the notion of priesthood by applying different requirements and adding to the priestly office the exercise of wisdom and scribal skills. By noting the failure of some of Levi's descendants to heed his advice and conform to his model (*A.L.D.* 101–102), the author suggests that some of the priests of his own days have indeed failed. Hence comes Kugler's suggestion that "the author is engaged in a constructive polemic against some form of the priesthood, and in the promotion of his notion of the office's proper character." Behind this polemic there are two distinctive priestly groups, one that does not realize the ideal evinced by Levi and is explicitly accused by Levi's warnings about his apostate descendants; and the other that accepts the norms established in Levi and prizes "purity, wisdom and learning as traits proper to the priesthood. *Aramaic Levi* is a rejection of the former kind of priest, and a plea for acceptance of the latter type."

Although Kugler's opinion concerning the conflict that stands at the origin of the *Document*'s composition has been accepted by some scholars (Boccaccini 1998: 74), his overall explanation of the Aramaic work's purpose is questionnable. Nothing in the text warrants Kugler's assumption that liturgical divergences from the Torah prescriptions connote polemical overtones within the priestly class. Most of these divergences probably stem from heightened purity standards, Babylonian influence, and presentation of metro-arithmetical exercises. Additionally, exegetical tendencies of the author in dealing with the biblical text are palpable in almost every section of the work, and without any polemical intent against a priestly group. The presentation of a dark future for Levi's sons (*A.L.D.* 101–102) is followed by a promise of restoration (*A.L.D.* 102 ll. 8–9), while the dualism found in the Aramaic composition reflects the conception of the whole surrounding reality and does not denote in the *Document* one priestly group with the exclusion of the other. To the contrary, in the admonition of his descendants about their apostasy (*A.L.D.* 101–102) Levi speaks to his sons and grandsons without excluding any particular group (cf. *A.L.D.* 82). Nothing warrants Kugler's opinion that behind this speech there is one group of priests contemporary to the author that failed in carrying out their priestly duties while the other followed Levi's admonitions. The defection of Manasseh, the brother of the Jewish high priest Jaddua, from the Jerusalem priesthood might have indirectly caused the reinterpretation of the Shechem killing in *Genesis* 34 and reaffirmation of the endogamic principle in the *Document*. One cannot claim, however, on the basis of the Aramaic work's content that a priestly group opposes Levi and his conjunction of wisdom and scribal skill with the priestly office. Any kind of education theory and practice presupposes a presentation of instructional standards and goals to be achieved in the formation process. There remains little doubt that the *Document* contains such a presentation exemplified by Levi's life and exhortations. From the educational standards and ideals' mere existence, one cannot easily conclude that they express a conflict within the group targeted in the education.

When speaking about scribal skill, Kugler seems to refer to his translation of ספר with "reading and writing." This rendering first proposed by Greenfield and Stone (1979) needs additional clarification in the context of the *Document*. The Aramaic term denotes all knowledge learned by Levi, metro-arithmetical calculation included. The conjunction of the priestly function with counting and calculation of sacrificial material can hardly appear as a new development in relation to biblical data. What is certainly new in the whole Second Temple history of Levitical priesthood is the *Document*'s attestation of elementary metro-arithmetical exercises common in Mesopotamian education of scribal apprentices. This fact, too, can hardly be explained by a conflict within Levitical priesthood.

1.6   *The Literary Genre*

Since the publication of the first Cairo Geniza fragment of the *Document* the textual closeness to the Greek *Testament of Levi* has been obvious. On the other hand the editors noticed many incongruencies between the two compositions and called the former "an early source of the Testaments of the Patriarchs" (Charles and Cowley 1907: 566) without discussing its literary genre. Reflecting on the composition of the *Testaments*, Marinus de Jonge began his analysis of the Greek *Testament of Levi* "with an examination of the relation between the Aramaic and Greek fragments of *a Jewish Testament of Levi* (italics H.D.) that have been preserved, and the parallel passages in our Greek Testament" (de Jonge 1953b: 38). Although he did not muse on the literary characteristics of the Aramaic work, he suggested its literary form by simply applying the word "Testament" to define it. When J. T. Milik published the first two Aramaic fragments of Levi's prayer and a small fragment from Cave 1 (1Q21 3), he entitled his article as "le Testament de Lévi en araméen" (1955b: 398), but did not discuss the literary characteristics of the *Document*. His subsequent publication of the Aramaic fragments from Cave 1 bore the same title "Testament de Lévi" (1955a: 87). In one of his articles on apocryphal Jewish literature, when referring to the Aramaic composition, he hesitated between the term "Testament" and "Visions" (1978: 95), the overall discussion concerning the literary genre was, however, missing.

In a passing remark Burchard (1965: 283, n. 2) suggested that the siglum "T" meaning "Testament" should not be applied to the *Document*, since it did not contain literary characteristics of a testament. According to him, there existed a connection between the literary style of the priestly composition and the *Genesis Apocryphon* found in the first Qumran cave. Both compositions contain a life story of a patriarch based on the biblical text and told in the first person singular narrative voice. In his analysis of our Aramaic text Becker (1970: 72) followed Burchard's suggestions and affirmed that the composition is a pseudepigraphic life story narrated in the first person singular with Levi's *Abschiedsrede* at its end. The publications and research of Jonas C. Greenfield and Michael E. Stone witnessed to a growing tendency to distance the scholarly research from qualifying the *Document* as a testament. In 1979, these two scholars published an article with their "Remarks on the Aramaic Testament of Levi from the Geniza," but their translation of this fragmentary work six years later bore the title "The Aramaic and Greek Fragments of a Levi Document" (Greenfield and Stone 1985: 457–469).

When Milik published some fragments of a hitherto unknown composition of another priestly patriarch, the "Visions of Amram," he also signaled the existence of the as yet unpublished "Testament of Qahat" (Milik 1972: 77–97). He labeled these two compositions as testaments and grouped them together with the Aramaic *Testament of Levi*. He also argued that these three Aramaic compositions concerning the three priestly patriarchs were mentioned in the *Apostolic Constitutions* vi 16 3.

While discussing the literary characteristics of the testamentary Jewish texts in the Hellenistic and Roman period, Eckhard von Nordheim (1980: 108) commented briefly on the Aramaic work. He affirmed with Burchard that there was not enough evidence to call it a testament. Although verses 81–83 are similar to the formal elements of the introductory section of a testament, it is doubtful whether they are to be considered as a speech of a dying person. On the other hand he noticed against Becker that defining the Aramaic text as a pseudepigraphic life story narrated in the first person singular falls short of precisely identifying and describing the literary form of the composition. Hollander and de Jonge (1985: 21–22) agreed with von Nordheim's opinion that the *Document* could not be called a testament. In relation to the *Testament of Qahat* and *Amram* they pointed out that they are not called "testaments," but together with the Levi composition they "form a series of documents giving priestly final exhortations and visions, preserved in the sectarian priestly circles whose literature was hidden at Qumran (though not necessarily produced by the Qumran sect)."

Kugler's publication of the *Document* termed by him as *Aramaic Levi* did not include any discussion of the literary form of the composition. His only suggestion concerned its supposedly non-apocalyptic character for "the little of the vision report that has survived does not record the revelation of heavenly secrets to Levi" (Kugler 1996a: 46). This comment set in the context of the ongoing discussion of the relation between the *Testament of Levi* and *Aramaic Levi* certainly does not suffice to properly assess the literary genre of the composition. It seems that, being wholly concentrated on the quest to find its final textual form, Kugler decided not to discuss the literary qualities of the *Document* at all.

The review of the preceding opinions concerning the literary "Gattung" of the *Document* shows a growing scholarly consensus that the Aramaic work is not a testament, although it contains testamentary features that later appear in the *Testaments of the Twelve Patriarchs*. Milik's suggestion to read and interpret the composition in connection with the Qahat and Amram documents gained, however, a general acceptance. There is no doubt that the *Levi Document* influenced the vocabulary and content and, most probably, the literary form of the latter two priestly works. On the other hand, a clear answer as to the literary genre of the work cannot be unequivocal due to the fragmentary state of manuscript evidence.

The analysis of the *Document*'s literary form and content allows of the opinion that the composition is a pseudepigraphic text written not only to tell the story of Levi's life, but also to transmit well defined wisdom ideals pertinent to Levitical priestly and scribal instruction. The narration in the whole composition is reported by Levi himself in first person singular and is partially based on the biblical data concerning Levi and his genealogical descendants. Levi tells the history of his life based on the rewritten biblical text of Gen 34 and 37. These portions of the work, however, are very fragmentary, and do not allow any exhaustive analysis concerning their relation to biblical texts. It is certain, however, that the *Document* reinterprets the biblical account to enhance Levi's positive image. The killing of the

Shechemites (Gen 34) is presented as a positive action (*A.L.D.* 1c–3; 78), while Simeon and Levi are absent when Joseph is sold into slavery by his brothers (Gen 37).

The largest preserved sections contain a non-biblical account of Levi's elevation to the status of a learned sage who receives his education from Isaac, his teacher and mentor. In his wisdom instruction (*A.L.D.* 14–61) Isaac appears to be a wisdom teacher who in the form of scribal advice transmits to his pupil Levitical knowledge necessary for upholding the due order of priestly service. The section dedicated to weights and measures (*A.L.D.* 31–47) contains metrological lists of sacrificial material that turn out to be modeled on the Babylonian metro-arithmetical school exercises. Isaac's wisdom instruction contains therefore actual metrological exercises intended to introduce priestly apprentices into the elementary principles of arithmetical thinking.

Levi then tells the story of his marriage and children combining genealogical information with chronological details in a well elaborated literary pattern (*A.L.D.* 62–81). The section contains a series of onomastic midrashim indicating the future fate of his descendants. Its last part (*A.L.D.* 78–81) contains an autobiographical resume of Levi's life. In the year of Joseph's death he solemnly proclaims his didactic poem (*A.L.D.* 82–98), which presents the ideal of scribal metro-arithmetical and wisdom education as a way for his sons to acquire glory, greatness, association with kings, and the glorious status of a wisdom teacher. Joseph is presented as the example of a scribal career of the one who taught scribal craft and wisdom instruction and was elevated to the royal status. Situating the didactic poem in the year of Joseph's death adds greatly to the didactic character of the poem—Levi's sons are to take Joseph's place as teachers of metro-arithmetical wisdom and thus assure the same association with kings for their children. The central stanza of the didactic poem is dedicated to the praise of the wisdom teacher, the one who teaches those who study wisdom. The natural inference from the poem's content is that the only way to the hidden treasures of wisdom leads through studying, teaching, and seeking wisdom.

The last preserved section (*A.L.D.* 99–104) in the form of a prophetic speech with apocalyptic overtones reveals the future of Levi's sons and their destiny already written in the heavenly books. Their future will be glorious; they will inherit the position of judges, rulers, priests and kings, and there will be no end to their kingdom. Such an eminent position in the social structure of the nation should be interpreted as the consequence of their priestly, metro-arithmetical and sapiential preparation—following Levi's example they learn how to preserve the just order of the sacrifices and weights and measures; they also know how to eliminate lawlessness from the society they lead (*A.L.D.* 78).

Levi's prayer (*A.L.D.* 1a) adds to this sapiential ideal a particular trait of personal piety and God's intervention in the life of the priestly sage. Levi requests from God gifts of spirit, wisdom, and understanding (*A.L.D.* 1a v. 8) that refer to practical skills of preparing the sacrifice while exercising metro-arithmetical knowledge of weights and measures. Dualism inherent in the prayer (*A.L.D.* 1a vv. 7–10) is further developed into an image of two contrasting kingdoms standing in opposition one to the other (*A.L.D.* 3c–6). Levi's request from God to eliminate lawlessness from under the heaven (*A.L.D.* 1a v. 13) finds its practical fulfillment in the killing of the Shechemites who are dubbed "doers of violence/lawlessness" (*A.L.D.* 78). The request to be close to God as his servant (*A.L.D.* 1a vv. 11, 17) bears fruit in the heavenly and earthly elevation to priesthood with a special reference to the tithe, which becomes a distinctive symbol of fundamental arithmetic skills (*A.L.D.* 9). The two visionary dreams (*A.L.D.* 1b; 3a–7) serve the same purpose of anchoring the same scribal ideal of royal priesthood in the framework of divine election to the office held by Levi and his sons.

The composition thus contains a series of literary forms that indicate a careful composition by its author: narrative framework formulated in first person singular, prayer, two visionary dreams, rewritten Bible, wisdom instruction, genealogy with onomastic midrashim, autobiographical section, didactic poem, prophetic speech with apocalyptic overtones. The author decided to make a recourse to the patriarch of the priestly tribe in order to give to his own educational perspective an authoritative tone. Thus Levi is the main narrator and this literary fiction indicates that the work can be tentatively classified as a pseudepigraphic autobiography with a didactic poem and prophetic speech at its end. This definition denotes pseudepigraphy as a constitutive element of the literary genre noticeable throughout the whole composition. The autobiography is fictional, draws many details in Levi's life from the biblical account, and develops them into a coherent succession of events.

Moshe J. Bernstein (1999: 3) distinguished the following categories of pseudepigraphy in literary works of the Second Temple period: authoritative, convenient, and decorative pseudepigraphy. Authoritative pseudepigraphy intends to strengthen the authority of the work and its message, and the speaker of the work is a figure of antiquity (e.g. Enoch literature, *Jubilees*; pp. 5–6, 25); convenient pseudepigraphy intends to inculcate morals and values that convey a moral message (testamentary literature; pp. 6, 26); decorative pseudepigraphy is pseudepigraphic by title only and not by content (e.g. Wisdom of Solomon; pp. 7, 25). When applying his classification to the pseudepigraphic texts found at Qumran, Bernstein characterizes Levi's composition as belonging to a group of texts that express authoritative pseudepigraphy together with *Jubilees*, "the Hebrew Testament of Naphtali and the Aramaic fragments of testament-like works assigned to Jacob, Judah and Joseph (very fragmentary) and Qahat and Amram" (1999: 9–10).

Pseudepigraphy as a literary phenomenon distinguishable in the whole work can be classified as "authoritative," in accordance with Bernstein's classification. Levi's life, studies, and exhortations are intended to be a norm in priestly education and world view. Levi is depicted as a candidate for priesthood who expresses his pious attitude in his prayer, eliminates lawlessness, is divinely elected to priesthood, follows the endogamic principle, and studies priestly knowledge under Isaac. His teacher insists that he should keep this teaching of the forefathers and transmit it to his children. Levi then exhorts his children to pursue the same educational ideal to assure a future and glory for the priestly tribe. Study of priestly knowledge thus becomes normative for priestly apprentices, and Levi's life an example to be imitated. In this sense the composition can be classified as didactic. It conjoins wisdom and professional priestly terminology with the idealized autobiography of the priestly patriarch. The pseudepigraphic autobiography ends with a didactic wisdom poem (*A.L.D.* 83b–98) and a speech that prophetically foretells the future of the priestly tribe (*A.L.D.* 99–104).

One should note that the Akkadian literature knows the literary genre of a fictional autobiography that can end with a blessing/curse ending, donation ending, didactic or prophetic endings (Longman 1991). The Akkadian fictional autobiography uses first person singular narrative style and has a three-fold structure: first-person introduction, first-person narrative, and the third item that allows a categorization into subgenres. The narrator is usually a king or god and the autobiography is pseudonymous and fictional. All the texts classified by Longman as belonging to the genre are written in prose and seek to support a particular political or cultic program. The Akkadian autobiography with the didactic third element of its structure ends in a series of first-person admonitions in which the narrator transmits to the next generations what he himself learned from experience. Longman assigned to this category the Adad-guppi autobiography, the Cuthaean Legend of Naram-Sin, and the Sennacherib autobiography. The autobiography with a prophetic ending foretells in its third part the political and social upheavals in a language that comes close to the apocalyptic literature. This subgenre is represented by the Marduk Prophecy, Šulgi prophecy, Uruk prophecy, Dynastic prophecy, and Text A. The *Levi Document* is related to these two literary subgenres of the fictional autobiography. Together with the pseudonymy, the autobiographical developments of the biblical text are a pure literary fiction, and the autobiographical account ends with a didactic (wisdom poem: *A.L.A.* 82–98) and prophetic ending (previsions for the future: *A.L.D.* 99–104). Additionally, the *Document* contains a well defined didactic and cultic program, the execution of which assigns to Levitical priesthood a prestigious political position. It is also worth noting that the *Story of Ahiqar*, wise scribe and counsellor to the kings of Assyria, bears some literary resemblance to the *Levi Document*. In both accounts sapiential instruction is set in the context of a narration that tells the story of a sage in an autobiographical style.

This pseudepigraphic literary work with elements of priestly and scribal metro-arthmetical education is a unique literary composition in the Jewish literature. It undoubtedly influenced the *Testament of Qahat* and *Visions of Amram*, but the fragmentary state of the compositions makes any detailed analysis futile for the purpose of this research. Perhaps these three works that present three succesive priestly patriarchs were composed to influence priestly apprentices who were beginning their studies of priestly matters. Thus they would constitue school literature whose purpose was to present patriarchal priests, students, and rulers as examples to follow and imitate. The Enochic *Astronomical Book* (*1 En.* 72–82) contains Babylonian-style astronomical computations based on arithmetical calculations and knowledge of fractions set in the framework of the wisdom instruction. This particular literary form of the *Astronomical Book* is close to Isaac's wisdom instruction (*A.L.D.* 14–50) that contains metrological data with fraction notations (*A.L.D.* 32a–46a) based on the Babylonian practices in scribal education. Perhaps this wisdom instruction about

astronomy stems from the same Levitical circles interested in impart-
ing to priestly students the rudiments of their professional knowledge
with a recourse to angelic and patriarchal authorities.

The *Levi Document* bears some resemblance to another Aramaic
work that midrashically develops the biblical text. The Aramaic portions of the book of the words of Noah have been fragmentarily preserved in the first seventeen columns of the *Genesis Apocryphon*. It
essentially contains Noah's life story based on the biblical account
but exegetically modified and set in the context of the Watchers' fall
(cols. II–V) and the mystery of evil on the earth (col. I). Noah's
father, Lamech, wonders if his son has been conceived by the Watchers
and, when he consults Enoch, his grandfather, he receives a negative answer to his doubts (cols. II–V). Then in 1QapGen V 29 the
Noahic composition is introduced with the formula "book of the
words of Noah" כתב מלי נוח, and an account in the first person singular follows. As in the *Levi Document*, the narrative standpoint is
pseudepigraphic and autobiographical. Noah recounts the story of
his marriage, birth of his sons, and marriage of his sons (VI 7–10),
and after the flood story he adds the names of his grandsons and
granddaughters (XII 8–12). This genealogical account is close in form
to the description of Levi's children in *A.L.D.* 62–75, although the
literary form of Levi's composition is more elaborate with onomastic midrashim and chronological details. Then, before the flood arrives,
Noah is warned in a vision about its inevitability caused by the sin
of the sons of heaven with women, but his salvation is assured (VI
11–VII 8). In the *Levi Document*, the first fragmentary vision happens
before the Shechem incident and, most probably, it must have contained some instruction as to what to do and how to proceed in the
case of Dinah. Columns XIII–XV of the book contain an elaborate
symbolic vision of an olive and cedar trees. The closing columns
(XVI–XVII) go back to the biblical text and describe the partition
of the earth between Noah's sons. Noah's story in its present Aramaic
form lacks, however, any reference to scribal learning or education.
It cannot be, therefore, classified as a didactic composition written
to transmit a well defined moral and educational ideal.

Autobiography as a literary genre is well attested in the ancient
Egyptian funerary inscriptions commissioned by high ranking royal
officials and composed with the help of learned scribes (Lichtheim
1988). The autobiographical self-presentation of a deceased official
encompasses narrative and declarative records of his life, career, and

personality. They are always presented in positive terms and constitute a way of ensuring access to eternal life. The moral correctness and exemplary behavior are frequently summed up by the concept of "maat" (truth, right, righteousness, justice), a principle of right order by which the gods lived, and which society recognized as a norm of human deeds and actions (Lichtheim 1992: 9–102). Besides the autobiography as a literary genre, there exist in Egyptian literature several royal instructions with autobiographical elements. The two outstanding examples are *Instruction to Merikare* (Brunner 1988: 137–154) and *Instruction of Amenemhet* (Brunner 1988: 169–177) in which royal advice interweaves with examples from the king's life. Of particular interest is the *Instruction of the High Priest of Amun*, Amenemhet (Brunner 1988: 390–391). In the introductory statement the document is presented as an "Instruction," but the content deals with Amenemhet's exemplary life conduct. The autobiographical elements in the composition serve therefore as an instructional example for Amenemhet's priestly sons. Finally, one must mention instructions written by scribal teachers for their pupils. Autobiographical elements, however, do not occur in this type of school compositions (Lichtheim 1976: 168–178; Simpson 1973: 329–347).

The *Levi Document* as a pseudepigraphic composition written from the perspective of a dead person (*A.L.D.* 81) may distantly be related to the Egyptian mortuary autobiography transmitting an ideal of morally correct life. The particular blend of autobiographical data and wisdom instruction concerning professional education is, however, difficult to intercept in the hieroglyphic literature. Rather, the Levitical composition appears to be unambiguously related to ancient Sumerian school literature, which had its formative epoch in the Ur III period and attained its peak in the Old Babylonian times (cf. Kramer 1956; Kraus 1973: 21–27). The existence of the scribal education is also attested in the first millennium B.C., and the Mesopotamian education continued to use the same literary forms and texts (cf. Gesche 2001: 61–198). The tree list in *A.L.D.* 24 reminds the reader of semantically arranged thematic noun lists used in the scribal training of Mesopotamian schoolboys. Metrological lists in *A.L.D.* 32a–46a based on a sexagesimal numeric system imitate metrological lists used in the elementary metro-arithmetical education of the Babylonian scribes. The author of the *Levi Document* includes in Levi's heavenly (*A.L.D.* 3a l. 8) and earthly (*A.L.D.* 9) elevation the tithe motif, which, when compared with numerical pattern of *A.L.D.*

32a–36, may be interpreted as an example of "theological arithmetics" intended to prove an intrinsic connection between priestly
vocation and metro-arithmetical education. A similar "theological"
interpretation of numbers and their fractions is well attested in the
Babylonian literary compositions. The educational ideal intended to
transmit the knowledge of "scribal craft, instruction, and wisdom"
(*A.L.D.* 88; cf. 90 and 98) finds its roots in the Babylonian scribal
training that linked metro-arithmetical education with proverbial wisdom in the earliest stages of education. Joseph's presentation as a
teacher of scribal wisdom who attains glory, greatness, and association with kings (*A.L.D.* 90) finds its echo in Babylonian royal hymns
composed by scribal writers. Whenever a king claims to possess scribal
knowledge and education, his mathematical training is presented as
an important expression of his learning. The literary motif of the
wisdom teacher who sits on the throne of glory is already attested
in the Sumerian school composition that narrates the school vicissitudes of a student. In the same "Schooldays" composition the teacher
predicts a high social status of the student due to his excellent per-
formance at school. Levi's speech directed to his children in *A.L.D.*
99–100 and preceded by the didactic poem concerning scribal education apparently follows the same pattern of reasoning: Levi's sons
will inherit all the important offices in the society, royal dignity and
rule included.

Thus the *Document* probably grew in the Levitical milieu in which
priestly education, metro-arithmetical training, and scribal ideals were
transmitted. The father-son wisdom terminology reflects, in fact, the
teacher-student relationship, similar to *Proverbs* 1–9. The proper context for the education is the Levitical priestly family where, according our Aramaic work, Levi is instructed by Isaac and receives his
formal priestly and scribal training. Levi's pseudepigraphic composition was created to justify the need of this education by its recourse
to the patriarchal traditions of Israelite religion. The instructional
character of the *Document*, however, is not enough to assume that
there existed independent Levitical schools where professional education took place.

The only possible reference to a school in the Old Testament texts
is Sir 51:23 where the writer invites the reader to take up lodging
in his "house of instruction" (MS B בבית מדרשי; cf. Skehan and Di
Lella 1987: 578; Collins 1997: 36–37). Scholars have strived for
decades to prove the existence of schools in the pre-exilic period of

royal administration, but the biblical material remains ambiguous. Klostermann (1908) was the first to propose a school background of Prov chs. 1–9 and his intuition was confirmed by later discoveries of related proverbial material used in the education of Israel's neighboring countries and cultures. The interpretation of biblical evidence ranges from considering most of the biblical texts of the Old Testament as at least indirectly related to the school context (Lemaire 1981: 34–83), to a complete denial of the existence of schools in pre-exilic Israel (Haran 1988). Epigraphical evidence seems to confirm the opinion that schools were indeed functioning as places of literacy and intellectual training (Lemaire 1981: 7–33; Puech 1988).

The Aramaic work indicates, however, that Babylonian influence on Levitical education was at work in the post-exilic Israel, and that scholarly scepticism concerning that influence is not justified anymore. The situation in recent scholarship concerning that subject is well reflected in the book written by James L. Crenshaw: *Education in Israel: Across the Deadening Silence*. It is worthwhile to cite here a passage concerning his opinion about schools in Israel and the relationship with the neighboring cultures.

> None would question the existence of royal scribes in Egypt and Mesopotamia, as well as at Ugarit, but drawing analogies from these empires, more advanced than Israel and Judah, seems inappropriate. Comparative studies invariably confront a fundamental question: Are the two cultures being compared sufficiently alike to justify a transference of ideas and practices from one to the other? The answer to that question in this instance is probably no. The simple fact that both Egyptian and Mesopotamian texts provide ample witness to the existence of schools requires one to ponder the absence of similar attestations in Israel. One hesitates to make much of arguments from silence, but in this case the missing allusions to schools stand out as exceptional and therefore demand an explanation. Why do the lists of royal officials in the biblical record omit any reference to an official in charge of instruction, and why do the sages of Israel never mention schools prior to Ben Sira? (Crenshaw 1998: 108–109)

The *Levi Document* substantially contributes to the ongoing discussion on education in Israel. There remains no doubt that the methods attested in Mesopotamian scribal education influenced the author to the extent that it is presented as an ideal to cherish, study, and transmit to the next generations of priestly apprentices.

The preceding remarks concern the literary form of the priestly work and result from the analysis of its content and literary analysis of singular sections. Dubbing the *Document* as a pseudepigraphic composition with an educational thrust appears as the most reasonable description in accord with the actual data inherent in the text and comparative evidence from Egyptian and Mesopotamian literature. Since the beginning and end of the composition has been lost, the final and ultimate answer to the question of the *Document*'s literary form remains tentative. One may only hope that future discoveries will bring to light the full text of the work and make further analysis and final conclusions possible.

CHAPTER TWO

ARAMAIC LEVI DOCUMENT: THE TEXT

2.1 *Reconstructed Text*

The section 2.1 contains the manuscripts of the *Document* in their order discussed in § 1.4.3. The following table should facilitate the consultation of the Qumran fragments in chapter two, because their presentation here does not follow the order in which they appear on the plates, but rather the order of the reconstructed sequence of events in the composition. The Qumran fragmentary texts that over-lap with other manuscripts of the *Document* have been relegated to a separate section of the chapter (§ 2.2). Those Qumran fragments that do not show a clear link to the reconstructed text of the whole composition are found in § 2.3.

Table 8. Qumran Fragments in Chapter II

Qumran Sigla	A.L.D.	Section
1Q21 frg. 1	3c	2.1.5.3
1Q21 frg. 3	4–7	2.2.2
1Q21 frg. 4	9	2.2.2
1Q21 frg. 45	26–27	2.2.3
4Q213 = 4QLevi^a ar		
frg. 1 i	82–95	2.2.6
frg. 1 ii	96–100	2.1.15 and 2.2.6
frg. 2	97–100	2.1.15 and 2.2.6
frg. 3	101	2.1.17.1
frg. 4	102	2.1.17.2
frg. 5	103	2.1.17.3
frg. 6	non classified	2.3
4Q213a = 4QLevi^b ar		
frg. 1	1a vv. 1–11	2.2.1
frg. 2	1a vv. 14–1b l. 19	2.2.1
frg. 2 11–18	1b	2.1.2 and 2.2.1
frgs. 3–4	3a	2.1.5.1
frg. 5	3b	2.1.5.2
frg. 6	non classified	2.3

Table 8 (*cont.*)

Qumran Sigla	A.L.D.	Section
4Q213b = 4QLevi^c ar	6–9	2.2.2
4Q214 = 4QLevi^d ar		
frg. 1	20–23; 25a–b	2.2.3
frg. 2	25b–30	2.2.3
frg. 3	104	2.1.17.4
frg. 4	non classified	2.3
frg. 5	non classified	2.3
4Q214a = 4QLevi^e		
frg. 1	24–25b	2.2.3
frg. 2 i	69b–73	2.2.5
frg. 2 ii	95–96; 98	2.2.6
4Q214b = 4QLevi^f		
frg. 1	non classified	2.3
frgs. 2–3	22–27	2.2.4
frg. 4	22–24	2.2.4
frgs. 5–6 i	22–25a	2.2.4
frgs. 5–6 ii	29–31	2.2.4
frg. 7	non classified	2.3
frg. 8	96–98	2.2.6

2.1.1 *A.L.D. 1a*[a]

E 2,3 (Pls. X and XI) – Strophic Disposition;
Parallel: 4Q213a frgs. 1 and 2

1 τότε[b] ἐγὼ ἔπλυνα τὰ ἱμάτιά μου,
    καὶ καθαρίσας αὐτὰ ἐν ὕδατι καθαρῷ

2 καὶ ὅλος ἐλουσάμην ἐν ὕδατι ζῶντι·
    καὶ πάσας τὰς ὁδούς μου ἐποίησα εὐθείας.

---

[a] The verses division of the prayer was first introduced by Milik (1955b) and kept in this presentation to avoid unnecessary confusion. Here the number 1a refers to the whole prayer, which is an exception to the verses designation in the *Document* where the first of the two numbers (e.g., 1c l. 15) refers to the verse and the second to the line division. In the prayer text the first number refers to the whole prayer, while the second indicates the verse (e.g., 1a v. 1). This exception seems necessary to avoid renumbering the whole of the *Document* fragmentary text. The numbering system used in the *Document* is explained in *Abbreviations*.

[b] Several lines, or perhaps columns, of lost text precede (cf. 1.4.3.2 and 1.4.3.3). 4Q213a 1 5 has ה[before the beginning of the preserved Greek translation.

3 τότε τοὺς ὀφθαλμούς μου καὶ τὸ πρόσωπόν μου ἦρα πρὸς τὸν οὐρανόν,
  καὶ τὸ στόμα μου ἤνοιξα καὶ ἐλάλησα,

4 καὶ τοὺς δακτύλους τῶν χειρῶν μου καὶ τὰς χεῖράς μου ἀνεπέτασα
  εἰς ἀλήθειαν κατέναντι τῶν ἁγίων καὶ ηὐξάμην καὶ εἶπα

5 ᵉΚύριε, γινώσκεις πάσας τὰς καρδίας,
  καὶ πάντας τοὺς διαλογισμοὺς ἐννοιῶν σὺ μόνος ἐπίστασαι.

6 καὶ νῦν τέκνα μου μετ᾽ ἐμοῦ.
  καὶ δός μοι πάσας ὁδοὺς ἀληθείας·

7 μάκρυνον ἀπ᾽ ἐμοῦ, κύριε, τὸ πνεῦμα τὸ ἄδικον καὶ διαλογισμὸν τὸν
  πονηρὸν καὶ πορνείαν, *καὶ ὕβρινᵈ ἀπόστρεψον ἀπ᾽ ἐμοῦ.

8 δειχθήτω μοι, δέσποτα, τὸ πνεῦμα τὸ ἅγιον,
  καὶ βουλὴν καὶ σοφίαν καὶ γνῶσιν καὶ ἰσχὺν δός μοι

9 ποιῆσαι *τὰ ἀρέσκοντά σοιᵉ καὶ εὑρεῖν *χάρινᶠ ἐνώπιόν σου
  καὶ αἰνεῖν τοὺς λόγους σου μετ᾽ ἐμοῦ, κύριε·

10 καὶ μὴ κατισχυσάτω με πᾶς σατανᾶς
   πλανῆσαί με ἀπὸ τῆς ὁδοῦ σου.

11 καὶ ἐλέησόν μεᵍ καὶ προσάγαγέ με εἶναί σου δοῦλος
   καὶ λατρεῦσαί σοι καλῶς.

12 τεῖχος εἰρήνης σου γενέσθαι κύκλῳ μου,
   καὶ σκέπη σου τῆς δυναστείας σκεπασάτω με ἀπὸ παντὸς κακοῦ.

13 παράδος διὸ δὴ καὶ τὴν ἀνομίαν ἐξάλειψον ὑποκάτωθεν τοῦ οὐρανοῦ,
   καὶ συντελέσαι τὴν ἀνομίαν ἀπὸ προσώπου τῆς γῆς.

14 καθάρισον τὴν καρδίαν μου, δέσποτα, ἀπὸ πάσης ἀκαθαρσίας,
   καὶ προσαροῦμαι *πρὸςʰ σε αὐτὸς·

15a καὶ μὴ ἀποστρέψῃς τὸ πρόσωπόν σου ἀπὸ τοῦ υἱοῦ παιδός σου Ἰακώβ.

15b σύ, κύριε, εὐλόγησας τὸν Ἀβραὰμ πατέρα μου καὶ Σάρραν μητέρα
    μου,

16 καὶ εἶπας δοῦναι αὐτοῖς σπέρμα δίκαιον
   εὐλογημένον εἰς τοὺς αἰῶνας.

ᶜ 4Q213a 1 10 + אנתה.
ᵈ 4Q213a 1 13 >.
ᵉ 4Q213a 1 16 דשפיר ודטב קדמיך.
ᶠ 4Q213a 1 15 רחמיך.
ᵍ 4Q213a 1 18 + מרי.
ʰ 4Q213a 2 5 לע[י]ניך.

17   εἰσάκουσον δὲ καὶ *τῆς φωνῆς[i] τοῦ παιδός σου Λευὶ
γενέσθαι σοι ἐγγύς,

18   καὶ μέτοχον ποίησον τοῖς λόγοις σου
ποιεῖν κρίσιν ἀληθινὴν εἰς πάντα τὸν αἰῶνα,
ἐμὲ καὶ τοὺς υἱούς μου εἰς πάσας τὰς γενεὰς τῶν αἰώνων·

19   καὶ μὴ ἀποστήσῃς τὸν υἱὸν τοῦ παιδός σου ἀπὸ τοῦ προσώπου σου
πάσας τὰς ἡμέρας τοῦ αἰῶνος.
καὶ ἐσιώπησα ἔτι δεόμενος.

TRANSLATION[a]

1 Then **I** washed my garments,
and having purified them in pure water,

2 I also ba**thed** myself completely in running water,
and I made straight **all** my ways.

3 Then **I raised** my eyes and my face **towards heavens**
and I opened my mouth and spoke;

4 and I spread out faithfully **the fingers of my hands and my
hands** in front of the sanctuary and I prayed and **said,**

5 "**O Lord**, you know all the hearts
and all the intentions of the thoughts **you alone know**.

6 And now, my children are with me.
And give me all the **ways of truth**;

7 **remove** from me, o Lord, the unrighteous spirit and **evil** intention,
and turn fornication and pride **away** from me.

8 Let the holy spirit, o Master, be shown to me,
and give me counsel and wi**sdom and knowledge and strength**

9 to do what pleases you and fi**nd grace before you**
and praise your words with me, o Lord.

---

[i] 4Q213a 2 8 צלוה.

[a] The text in bold print in the translation marks the words and phrases preserved in the Aramaic fragmentary manuscript. The *italics* in the translation indicate the portions that have been restored without any manuscript evidence.

10   And **do not allow any satan to rule over me**
     to lead me astray from your way.

11   And have mercy **on me and draw me near to be your**
     servant and to serve you properly.

12   Let there be a wall of your peace around me
     and let your shelter of might protect me from every evil.

13   Therefore, remove and efface lawlessness from under the heavens,
     and eliminate lawlessness from the face of the earth.

14   Purify my heart, o Master, from every impurity,
     and I will raise myself **to** you;

15a and do not turn your face away from the son of your servant
     Jacob.

15b You, **o Lord, bl**essed Abraham my father and Sarah my mother,

16   and you said you would give them **a seed of right**eousness,
     blessed for ever.

17   Listen also to **the voice of your ser**vant Levi
     to be near to you,

18   and make (him) participate in your words
     to do **a true judgment for a**ll eternity,
     (that is) me and my sons for all the generations of the ages.

19   And do not turn aside **the son of your servant from before
     your count**enance for all the days of eternity."
     And I became silent, still praying.

COMMENTS

   L. 1   τότε *then*. This particle may translate both באדין (19 l. 2; 25b
l. 1) or אדין (e.g. LXX Dan 2:15, 19) without difference in meaning. When
this particle stands at the beginning of the sentence it marks the clause as
temporally sequential to what precedes (see *A.L.D.* 1a v. 3; 9 l. 15; 10
l. 22; 22 l. 11; cf. Buth 1990: 34–40). Since the preceding context is lacking, nothing can be said about the relationship of 1a vv. 1–2 introduced
by τότε to the preceding context. Stone and Greenfield (1993: 250) preferred to see the passage as the end of a preceding ceremony, but their
preference cannot be proven for obvious reasons.

   L. 2   ἐν ὕδατι ζῶντι *in running water*. 4Q213a 1 7 reads אתרחע[ת וכל,
hence there is no space for the Greek syntagm. The Aramaic text must
have omitted the syntagm, probably due to the *homoioarcton*, במין חיין—

במין טהרין. Alternatively, the expression במין חיין might stand before the verb in the Aramaic text. For the Hebrew expression מים חיים "running water, see, e.g. Lev 14:6, 51; Num 5:17; 19:17.

L. 4 εἰς ἀλήθειαν *faithfully*. The preposition εἰς after the verb would suggest a local meaning: "towards truth" (so Kugler 1996a: 70). This rendering does not make much sense here for the following noun has an abstract meaning. Here it introduces an accusative of manner, "in truth, truly" (cf. Smyth 1984: § 1686. d.), and most probably translates the Aramaic לקושט, cf. 1QapGen VI 1, 1, 3, 4, 6, 23; cf. also Isa 42:3 where the LXX translates לאמת "faithfully" with εἰς ἀλήθειαν (cf. Beyer 1984: 193, n. 1). Levi's prayerful position is here an expression of his confidence that God hears and accepts his requests.

L. 5 Κύριε *Lord*. 4Q213a 1 10 has אנתה "you" after מרי. This pronoun is attested twice in the sentence (4Q213a 1 10 and 11) and it rhetorically emphasizes God's knowledge of the human heart and mind. MS E omits its first occurrence losing the rhetorical emphasis of the evenly balanced Aramaic counterpart. The omission is probably due to the translator's inadvertence or the pronoun was already absent in the translator's *Vorlage*.

L. 6 τέκνα μου μετ᾽ ἐμοῦ *my children are with me*. Since the context does not indicate the presence of Levi's children during his prayer, MS E's reading does not concord well with the immediate context. Beyer (1984: 190) suggested that the Greek τέκνα μου is a mistranslation of the Aramaic imperative בני, "build," but this opinion produces a strange and unusual phrase and assumes a translator's mistake. It is much easier to assume the correctness of the Greek translation. Although the introduction to Levi's prayer suggests that Levi stands alone before God (*A.L.D.* 1a vv. 1–4), he prays for his children as well (*A.L.D.* 1a vv. 18). Additionally, the syntagm בני "my sons" frequently appears in MS A referring to Levi's children (74 l. 4; 84 l. 9; 88 l. 17; 90 l. 22).

L. 7 καὶ ὕβριν *and pride*. 4Q213a 1 13 does not leave room for the MS E expression because זנותא (πορνεία) is followed by אהד (ἀπόστρεψον). The difference probably points to a different Aramaic *Vorlage* used by the translator.

L. 9 ποιῆσαι τὰ ἀρέσκοντά σοι *to do what pleases you*. According to the reconstruction of 4Q213a 1 16, a similar phrase is repeated at the end of the verse: "what is beautiful and good before you" [.דשפיר ודטב קדמיך]. Stone and Greenfield (1993: 262) assume the omission of the MS E expression by *homoioteleuton* "either at the level of the Aramaic *Vorlage* of the Greek (קדמיך-קדמיך) or in the Greek itself (ἐνώπιόν σου—ἐνώπιόν σου)." The reconstruction of the prayer indicates that 4Q213a 1 15–17 is considerably longer than the Greek text (see Reconstructon of the Aramaic text in § 2.2.1). Hence it should be assumed that the Qumran text expands the Aramaic *Vorlage* of MS E and inserts an expression similar to the one found at the beginning of the line.

L. 9 χάριν *grace*. MS E omits σου, cf. 4Q213a 1 15 רחמיך "your mercy". Stone and Greenfield (1993: 261) emend the Qumran text in accordance with the MS E reading, <רחמי>ן. The emendation is not necessary for the Aramaic is grammatically correct, and the different Greek reading points to a different Aramaic text as in many other cases in the *Document*. On the other hand, in the Qumran texts the final *nûn* sometimes resembles the final *kāp*. The copyist's error is, therefore, likely to occur. Note, that the Greek term usually translates Hebrew חן in the LXX (e.g. Exod 33:17; 34:9; Num 32:5).

L. 9 μετ᾽ ἐμοῦ *with me*. The syntagm does not seem to fit the context of the clause. Perhaps the translator misinterpreted the Aramaic בי "in me."

L. 10 בי תשלט אל *do not allow . . . to rule over me*. Since the noun שטן is masculine, the Aramaic verb should be parsed as 2m. sg. *hapʿel* of שלט; the Greek verb is aorist impv. 3sg. κατισχυσάτω that supposes 3m. sg. *peʿal* ישלט. In the E translation כל שטן is the subject of the sentence, while in Aramaic it serves as object. E probably follows the LXX translation of Ps 119:133b.

L. 11 ἐλέησόν με *have mercy on me*. After this phrase 4Q213a 1 18 inserts מרי "o Lord," which is most probably an expansion.

L. 13 παράδος *remove*. MS E reads παραδως. The *omega* is often misread for *omicron* in the MS and vice versa. De Jonge (1978: 25) unnecessarily corrects to παραδοὺς, blurring thus the meaning. The form is a regular aor. impv. of second person singular from παραδίδωμι. It is parallel to ἐξάλειψον "efface," and shares with it the same direct object, ἀνομίαν "lawlessness." The two verbs form a hendiadys: "utterly destroy."

L. 14 προσαροῦμαι *I will raise myself up*. MS reads separately προς αρουμαι. De Jonge (1978: 25) considered it as corrupt for προσάρωμαι, the aorist subjunctive passive of προσαίρω "to lift, raise up." The emendation is not necessary; the form is a regular future middle of προσαίρω.

L. 14 πρός σε *to you*. 4Q213a 2 5 reads לע]יניך. The *lāmed* and *ʿayin* of 4Q213a 2 constitute the only remnants of the text in the line. MS E would suppose the Aramaic לך, hence the difference between the two readings is patent. The reconstruction "to your eyes" is similar in meaning to MS E, being a metonymic description of God's presence. The difference is best explained by the supposition of a different Aramaic text available to the Greek translator.

2.1.2 *A.L.D. 1b*

For the complete text of 4Q213a 2, notes and reconstruction, see § 2.2.1.

4Q213a frg. 2 11–18 = 4QLevi^b (Pl. III)

11כ (1b)	באדין נגדת ב[ ] [
12	על אבי יעקוב וכד]י [
13	מן אבל מין אדין] [
14	שכבת ויתבת אנה ע]ל [
15	אדין חזיון אחזית] [
16	בחזות חזוא וחזית שמ]יא פתיחין וחזית טור [

17   תחותי רם עד דבק לשמי]א   והוית בה ואתפתחו [

18   לי תרעי שמיא ומלאך חד] אמר לי לוי על [

bottom margin

TRANSLATION

11   (1b)Then I went b[   ]

12   Upon my father Jacob and wh[en   ]

13   From Abel Main, then[   ]

14   I lay down and remained o[n   ]

15   vac   Then I was shown a vision [   ]

16   in the vision of visions. And I saw the heav[ens *split open and I saw a mountain*]

17   Beneath me,   high until it reached the heave[ns *and I was on it and opened*]

18   To me the gates of heavens and an angel[*said to me, "Levi, enter"*]

COMMENTS

     L. 14   ויתבת אנה על] *and I remained o[n.* For the verb יתב with the prep. על, see A 93 l. 14 (*hap'el*); 11QtgJob XXVII 1 (36:7). Here the action is parallel in meaning with שכב "to lie down."

     L. 15   חזיון *vision.* With Milik (1955b: 400) who reads singular; see also 4Q204 frg. 1 vi 5 (*1 En.* 13:8).

     L. 15   אחזית *I was shown.* The verb is an *'op'al* of חזי, cf. 4Q209 frg. 25 3 (*1 En.* 74:1 or 78:10); for the verb חזי in *hap'el*, see A 15 l. 12.

     L. 16   בחזית חזיוא *in the vision of visions.* The first noun is a feminine construct from חזו. The second is a plural form of חזו with a scribal metathesis between the *yôd* and the *wāw*, as Kugler (1996a: 79) points out. For the sg. emph. masc. of חזו, see A 7 ll. 11, 12.

     L. 17   רם *high.* This word might be an adjective or verb. Assuming that what follows has prepositional value, it is probable to consider the form to be an adjective.

     L. 17   דבק ל עד *until it reached.* See 1QapGen XVII 10; cf. 1QapGen XVI 11; XVII 8. 9. 16, etc. The expression may be interpreted as a composite preposition (see Greenfield and Sokoloff 1992: 87), the context, however, is broken and a correct interpretation difficult to assess.

2.1.3   *A.L.D. 1c–2*

MS A (Cambridge a; pl. VI); first 14 lines are missing

15 ‏(1c)דטמאת לב[נ]י יעקב בזנותה על]
16 ‏דברת די כל א[נש יסב לה לאנתה]
17 ‏למעבד כדין בכל[ארעא והתמלכת] [
18 ‏יעקב אבי ורא[ובן אחי על דברהא (דא ?) [
19 ‏ואמרנן להון ב[חוכמה ובי]נה   די ה[וו]
20 ‏צביין אינון בברתן ונהוי כולן א[חין]
21 ‏וחברין (2)נזורו[ן]עורלת בישרכון
22 ‏והתחמיון כו[אתן] ותהון התימין
23 ‏כואתן במילת ק[וש]ט ונהוי לכ[ון]
bottom margin   א

NOTES ON READING

L. 15 ‏דטמאת לב[נ]י. At the beginning of the line the letters are damaged. The reconstructed sequence *dālet–ṭêt* is a reconstruction based on the remaining ink traces. For the particle ‏ד in the *Document*, see 1a vv. 9 (213a 1 16), 9 (213a 1 16), 16 (213a 2 7); 20 l. 5; 87 l. 14 (213 1 i 8); 93 l. 15. The restoration in lines 15–18 follows the text restored by Puech (2002: 514).

L. 16 ‏א[נש. There is space for two letters before the lacuna and no ink traces at all. This space is hypothetically filled with a *nûn* and *šîn*.

L. 17 ‏[והתמלכת]. With Puech 2002: 514. Cf. *T. Levi* 6:3 ἐγὼ συνεβούλευσα τῷ πατρί μου καὶ Ῥουβὴμ τῷ ἀδελφῷ μου. Kugel (1992: 11, n. 16) supposes that Jacob and Reuben report to Levi on their conversation with the Shechemites: "[Then said to me] Jacob my father and Reub[ben my brother: we went to Shechem]. . . ." This restoration is based on the Kugel's supposition that Levi would not want to use the circumcision as a trick and was against the idea. In that restoration only Reuben and Jacob address the Shechemites with a proposal to circumcise and then report the whole affair to Levi. The *Testament*'s text, however, unequivocally indicates that Levi addresses Jacob and Reuben, and not vice versa. Hence it seems better to restore this Aramaic line on the basis of the Greek *Testament*. Kugel's assumption that Jacob and Reuben report to Levi their dialogue with the Shechemites does not have any confirmation either in the biblical text (cf. Gen 34:13–17) or in the *Testament*'s textual tradition.

L. 18 ‏ורא[ובן אחי. Following Greenfield and Stone (1979: 216). The reconstruction is based on *T. Levi* 6:3.

L. 19 ‏די ה[וו]. The *dālet* is certain, the next letter is probably a *yôd* or *wāw*.

L. 23 ‏ק[וש]ט. The tail of the *qôp* remains in the manuscript.

Bottom margin: ‏א. The letter below the last line in the column is an ʾālep without a lower left leg. It is probable that the ʾālep indicates the number of the quire or double leaf of the codex. Single sheets were very rarely numbered in medieval Hebrew manuscripts (see Beit-Arié 1981: 50–68). Beyer (1984: 195) considers the ʾālep here to be the first letter of ‏א[חין "brothers," there are, however, no ink traces of additional letters to confirm his reconstruction.

TRANSLATION

15 (1c)Since she defiled the so[ns *of Jacob with her harlotry,*]

16 therefore every m[an *will take a wife for himself*]

17 in order to act according to the law in the whole[*country. I consulted*]

18 Jacob my father and Re[uben *my brother on (this?) matter*]

19 and we said to them with [*wisdom and* under]standing, because

20 they desired our daughter, so that we all would become b[rothers]

21 or companions: (2)"Circumcise [ ]the foreskin of your flesh

22 and appear like [us] and you will be sealed

23 like us with the circumcision of tr[u]th. And we will be for y[ou]

COMMENTS

L. 15 טמאת *she defiled*. The form is a 3f. sg. *paᶜel* from טמא. For other examples of the verb in *paᶜel*, cf. 1QapGen XX 15, 30; for the woman who ruins the name of her family, cf. *A.L.D.* 3a ll. 3–6; cf. *Jub.* 30:7.

Ll. 15–16 על] דברת די [*therefore*. For this composite conjunction introducing a purpose clause in imperfect, see, e.g. Dan 2:30; 11QtgJob XXXIV 4 (40:8).

L. 17 למעבד כדין *to act according to the law*. This phrase belongs to the legal language and most probably refers to the decision concerning the circumcision of the Shechemites, a necessary legal prerequisite for the arranged marriage (Gen 34:14–15). A similar legal expression occurs in the biblical text: עשה כמשפט ל "to proceed according to the law/manner/legal custom" (Exod 21:9, 31; Lev 5:10; 9:16; Num 15:24; 29:6, etc.; cf. Fishbane 1985: 209–213). Kugler (1996a: 63–64) translates דין as "determination" and affirms that it concerns the agreement between the Shechemites and the sons of Jacob.

L. 19 ב]חוכמה ובי[נה *with [wisdom and under]standing*. The Palestinian targums change the MT במרמה, "with deceit" (Gen 34:13) to בחכמה, cf. also *Gen. Rab.* 80:8. The same change occurs in targums in Gen 29:22 where the syntagm is applied to Laban and his fellow townsmen. Only *Frg. Tg.* C Gen 34:13 follows the Genesis text, בעיצא דרמיו, "with a counsel of deceit." Wisdom is a particular characteristic of Levi's teaching, see, e.g. *A.L.D.* 88 ll. 18, 19; 89 l. 20. Hence it seems appropropriate to restore the lacuna in accordance with the ideological standpoint of the *A.L.D.* and general targumic tradition. Here Levi's wisdom in dealing with the Shechemites consists in acting according to God's will and points to his shrewdness in bringing it about. The context is, however, fragmentary and does not allow an unequivocal interpretation. For the word pair הוכמה ובינה in the MT, see e.g. Deut 4:6; Isa 11:2; 29:14; Job 28:12, etc.

L. 21 והבריו *or companions.* The translation of the *wāw* with "or" is suggested by A 91:7 אה או הבר "brother or companion."

2.1.4 *A.L.D. 3*

MS A (Cambridge b; pl. VII); the first 14 lines are missing

15 (3)[והשיבו למקטל יוס[פ](?) אחי בכל עדן
16 [די השתלח לאח]יא די הוו בשכם
17 [למשאל לשלם] אחי ואחוי דן
18 [שמ]ע[י]ן[די אחוהין בשכם ומה
19 מ]ית יוס[ף ביד עב]די המסא ואחוי
20 אינון יהודה די אנה ושמעון
21 אחי אזלנא לה[ן][ח]דה לראובן
22 אחונן די למדנ[ח א]שר ושור
23 [י]הודה קדמא [ל]משבק עאנא

NOTES ON READING

L. 15 [והשיבו למקטל יוס[פ](?) אחי. (Beyer 1984: 195) fills the lacuna with [שמעון but his reading does not fit the following context where the absence of Simeon is reported (line 20). The visible ink traces of a top part of a letter pointing to the left may suggest a final *pê*. It would fit the proposed reconstruction based on the *Targum Onqelos* Gen 37:18. Lines 15–19 follow the reconstruction of E. Puech (2002: 518).

L. 19 מ]ית יוס[ף בעב]די. The *mêm, wāw/yôd, tāw, yôd* are certain. The next *wāw* is placed on the edge of the lacuna; there also remains the right downstroke of a *sāmek*. The context suggests that it is preferable to read *peʿal perfect* מית and יוס[ף as subject, rather than the noun מות in construct with יוס[ף, with the omission of the predicate היה, cf. Puech 2002: 521.

L. 21 לה[ן][ח]דה. The manuscript preserves the crossbar of a *dālet* and the left leg of a *hê* on the edge of the leather tear. The restored form is a *paʿel* infinitive of אחד "to join" (cf. Jastrow 1950: *s.v.*; Sokoloff 1990: 45).

L. 22 למדנ[ח. The ink traces on the lacuna edge suggest the restoration of a *nûn* and *het*. This restoration would mean that Reuben went from the region of Shechem to northern Galilee.

L. 23 קדמא [ל]משבק. The *ʾālep* at the end of the first word is certain and then the curved downstroke of a *mêm* is visible. The *lāmed* before the infinitive is lost in the lacuna.

TRANSLATION

15 ⁽³⁾[*And they plotted to kill* Jose]ph(?) my brother in every time

16 [*when he was sent to*] the [*broth*]ers who were in Shechem

17 [*to ask about welfare of (?)*]my brothers. And Dan reported

18 [dis]c[uss]i[*ons of his brothers*] in Shechem and how

19 Jose[ph] died [*by the* do]ers of violence. And Judah reported

20 to them that I and Simeon

21 my brother had gone to j[o]in Reuben

22 our brother who (was) on the east of Asher. And [J]udah

23 jumped forward [to] leave the sheep

COMMENTS

L. 17 דן *Dan*. Greenfield and Stone (1985: 461) followed by Kugler (1996a: 65) interpreted דן as a demonstrative pronoun. However, if one accepts Charles' rendering of the word as a proper name (1908b: 228) one is closer to the fragmentary context that abundantly enumerates Jacob's sons: Judah (line 20 and 23), Simeon (line 20), Reuben (line 21).

L. 17 ואחוי *and (Dan) reported*. For the verb see also A 3 l. 19; 84 l. 10.

L. 19 עב[ד]י חמסא *do]ers of violence*. The expression may also mean "deeds of violence." In *A.L.D.* 78 l. 18 it means "doers of violence" referring to the Shechemites. Here, however, it most probably refers to Levi and Simeon.

2.1.5 *A.L.D. 3a–3c*

2.1.5.1 *A.L.D. 3a*

4Q213a frgs. 3–4 = 4QLeviᵇ (Pl. III)

```
⁽³ᵃ⁾] ° [        ] ° [        ] ° [                                    1
א[ וכען י֯[ע]לו מכתשי נברׁיא                                          2
אׁ]נתה ותחׁל֯ל֯ שמה ושם אבוה                                          3
° [ אׁ֯° ׁח ע֯ם ל֯מׁשֿ[ן  ]כה[ ] °֯דה בחׁ]ללה[ אׁבֿהֿתֿא וכל          4
בתוׁ]לה זי חבלת שמה ושֿם אבההתה ואבהֿתֿת לכל אחיה                     5
ולׁ[אׁבוהׁ}אׁ{ ולא מׁהׁמחא שם ׁהׁסדה מן כול עמה}אׁ{ <הׁ> לעלם        6
לׁ]ם לכל דרי עלׁמׁא ומׁ[ ]חֿׁ° קדישׁי֯ן מן עמא°                       7
לׁ° ואׁ]ן[ ]מׁעשר קודש קרבן לאל מן                                   8
                        bottom margin
```

NOTES ON READINGS

L. 1   Kugler (1996a: 77) reads ‏[מן נק[ב]תא‎ [   ]. The ink traces of six letters remain in the manuscript and make any suggestion a mere guess.

L. 2   ‏וכען‎. With Milik (Brown 1988: *s.v.*). Stone and Greenfield (1996a: 33) read ‏אשבען‎ "he besware us". What they read as a *shin* is rather a *wāw* with a right leg of the preceding *ʾālep*. The next letter cannot be a *bêt*, for its horizontal base is too short.

L. 2   ‏י[ע]לו‎. The lower downstroke of a *lāmed* is discernible. The vertical downstroke before the lacuna may be read as a *wāw* or *yôd*.

L. 4   ‏אˢה‎. Kugler (1996a: 77) restores here ‏ב[עליה‎. Between his supposed *ʿain* and the edge of the manuscript enough blank space is preserved to allow the reader to see the horizontal base of the supposed *bêt*. This is not however the case, so his reading is to be abandoned.

L. 4   ‏למשׁ[ ]כה[‎. Kugler (1996a: 77) tentatively reads ‏למש[ר]פה‎. The lower parts of the remaining letters do not permit a full identification of the word.

L. 4   ‏בהן[ללה‎. The *bêt* is to be connected with the traces of the following letter rather than with a *hê* joined to the end of the preceding word. There is no space for an additional word in the lacuna.

L. 4   ‏אבהתא‎. The reconstruction is probable, see Milik 1976: 263.

L. 5   ‏בתו[ן]לה‎. *Lāmed* and *hê* are certain, cf. Beyer 1994: 77.

L. 6   ‏ולˏ[אבוה{א}‎. The second *ʾālep* is crossed out with a vertical line and partially rubbed out. In 1QapGen the 3f. sg. suffix ‏הא‎- coexists with the more frequent ‏ה‎-, cf. Muraoka 1993: 40–41. Since the former occurs rarely, it is probable that the intervention intends to eliminate a form that appeared suspect to the scribe. For the practice of crossing out letters in Qumran MSS, see Tov 1996: 53–56.

L. 6   ‏הסדה‎. Stone and Greenfield (1996a: 33) read ‏הסיה‎. The leather is shrunk but the head of a *dālet* excludes the *yôd/wāw* reading. See Milik's decipherment in Brown 1988: *s.v.*

L. 6   ‏עמה{א}<ה>‎. The scribe attempted to correct an *ʾālep* into a *hê*, for this practice in Qumran scrolls. cf. Tov 1996: 56.

L. 7   ‏ה°[‎. Kugler (1996a: 77) reads here an *ʿain*. A semicircular upper part of a letter is stuck between the *tāw* and the *qôp*.

L. 8   ‏לˢא[ו‎. The long arm of the *lāmed* remains on the leather, then the curved *wāw* precedes the right arm of an *ʾālep* together with a part of its axis. Stone and Greenfield's (1996a: 33) read a *ḥêt* here, but the *ʾālep* is certain.

L. 8   ‏לאל מן‎. Against Stone and Greenfield who read ‏לאלפן‎ (1996a: 33).

TRANSLATION

1   [3a][   ]

2   ]ʾ*a* and now the pla[g]ues of men will [befa]ll

3   ] a woman and she desecrated her name and the name of her father

4]° ᵓ°*h* with *lmš*[   ]*kh* [   ]°*dh* in de[secrating] the fathers. And
every

5 [vir]gin who ruins her name and the name of her fathers, she
also brings shame on all her brothers

6 and on] her father. And the name of her revilement will not be
wiped out from all her people for ever.

7]*lṭ* for all the generations of eternity *wm*[   ]*t°* the holy ones from
the people°

8]*l* and ᵓ[   ] holy tithe, an offering to God from

COMMENTS

L. 5   זי *that*. Note the archaic form of the relative pronoun.

L. 5   חבלת שמה *ruins her name*. This verb in *paᶜel* may mean "to destroy,
ruin" (Dan 4:20; Ezra 6:12), "to kill" (Dan 6:23) "to act corruptly" (about
Watchers 4Q203 8 11; cf. Neh 1:7). It cannot therefore be translated "to
profane" (Stone and Greenfield 1996a: 34). This latter meaning is here
conferred by the verb חלל, see lines 3 and 4. The verb חלל here stands
in paralelism with "to bring shame" בהת in the same line.

L. 5   אבהתת *brings shame*. An ᵓ*apᶜel* perfect of בהת; for the noun from this
root, see 4Q212 1 ii 25 (*1 En.* 91:2) and Milik 1976: 263.

L. 6   חסדה *her shame*. The pronom. suffix ה- may indicate either masc.
or fem. gender. The context suggests the fem. gender for in the same line
there was another 3f. sg. suffix ה⊃- for "her father" אבוה and "her people"
עמהא. For the use of חסד "revilement, shame" in Aramaic, see 4Q196 frg.
6 5 (Tob 3:10 LXX MS S), where Sarah complains about the unjust insults.

L. 8   קרבן לאל מן *an offering to God from*. This expression is best understood as an apposition to the preceding "holy tithe"; for קרבן, see A 9
l. 18, 21; 10 l. 1; 30 l. 15; 4Q547 frg. 1 4; frg. 5 1; 11Q18 frg. 28 4.

2.1.5.2 *A.L.D. 3b*

4Q213a frg. 5 = 4QLevi^b (Pl. III)

(3b)]°°°[   ] 1
]מת[[   ] °[ ]° עם ל[2
vacat   כ]הנות עלמא[3
bottom margin

NOTES ON READINGS

Stone and Greenfield (1996a: 35–36) distinguished two columns in this
fragment. It seems, however, that there is only one column and a *vacat* at

the end of line 3. There are no letters below line three, then the remaining space probably constitute the bottom margin of a column. The leather, however, is torn, and uncertainty as to what follows remains.

L. 3　מה°[. Kugler (1996a: 80, n. 68 and p. 83) does not accept Milik's proposal to join this line to 4Q213a 3–4 7. He rightly argues that the physical joint of the two fragments is not certain. That makes the Milik's opinion dubious.

TRANSLATION

1　(3b)]

°°° [

2　]l with/people [

]°mt[

3　]an eternal priesthood　vacat

COMMENTS

Since it is not possible to make any plausible connection with other fragments in the manuscript, the location of the fragment after 4Q213a 3–4 is extremely hypothetical. The two words that remain suggest the connection with Levi's heavenly elevation in his second vision. In *A.L.D.* 7 the seven angels administer to Levi an "anointing of eternal peace," and line three of the fragment could be seen as the angelic statement about Levi's priestly status.

2.1.5.3　*A.L.D. 3c*

1Q21 1 (Pl. I)

[מֶן דִי לֶהֱוֹין תְּלִיתִין][(3c)　　　　　　　　　　1

לְבֶ]נָיךָ מַלְכוּת כָּהֲנוּתָא רַבָּא מִן מַלְכוּתָ] חֲרַבָּא　　　2

[לְ]אֵ]לֵ[ן עֶ]לָ[י]וֹן[　　　　　　　　　　3

NOTES ON READINGS

The fragment comes from the middle of a column whose beginning and end are lost. It is the biggest piece of sixty minuscule fragments assigned by Milik to the same 1Q21.

L. 2　לְבֶ]נָיךָ. Milik (1955a: 88) reads בִיךְ[. The curved downstroke of the *yôd* is linked to the tail of a *nûn*, cf. Grelot 1956: 396, n. 2.

L. 3　The line is reconstructed in accordance with Milik's (1955a: 88) plausible suggestion.

TRANSLATION

1　(3c)]because they will be three [

2 to] your [s]ons, the kingdom of the priesthood is greater than the
kingdom [of the sword]

3]for [G]od the [most] h[igh

COMMENTS

Milik (1955a: 88) compares this fragment with *T. Levi* 8:11. Line 2 resembles *A.L.D.* 67 l. 7. Compare *Jub.* 16:18; 33:20; *T. Jud.* 21:2–4; Rev 1:6;
5:10; 1Pet 2:5–9; these texts are inspired by Exod 19:6. The fragment,
however, suggests a different perspective by pointing to a contrast between
two kingdoms, with the prevalence on the side of the priestly rule.

2.1.6   *A.L.D. 4–10*

MS A (Bodleian a; pl. VIII)
Parallels: <u>1Q21 3</u> and <u>4Q213b</u>

[ו[שלמא וכל חמדת בכורי ארעא	1
כולה למאכל ולמלכות חרבא פנשא	2
וקרבא ונהשירותא ועמלא	3
ונצפהתא וקטלא וכפנא (5)זמנין תאכול	4
וזמנין תכפן וזמנין aתעמול* וזמנין	5
תנוח וזמנין תדמוך וזמנין תנוד	6
שנת עינא (6)כען הוי לך bהכיןc *רביניך*	7
מן dכולה* והיך יהבנא לך רבות שלם	8
עלמא vac (7)וננדו שבעתון מן לותי	9
<u>ואנה אתעירת מן שנתי אדין</u>	10
אמרת חזוא הוא דן וכדן אנה	11
מתמה די יהוי לה כל חזוה וטמרת	12
אף דן fבלבבe* ולכל fאינש* לא גליתה	13
(8)ועלנא על אבי יצחק ואף הוא כדן	14
[ברכ]ני vac (9)אדין כדי <u>הוה</u> gיעקב*	15
[h[אבי*]מעשר כל מה דיהוה לה כנדרה	16

---

a 1Q21 3 2 העמל.
b 4Q213b 1 הי[כה.
c 4Q213b 1 רביתך.
d 4Q213b 1 כל בש[ר]א.
e 4Q213b 3 בלבבי.
f 4Q213b 3 אנש.
g 4Q213b 4 יעקוב.
h 4Q213b 4; cf. 1Q21 4 אבי יע[קב.

17 [וֹדי כ]ע֯ן֯ אנה הוית קדמי בראש

18 [כהנו]תֹה וֹלֹי ֹיֹמכל* בנוהי יהב קרבן

19 מֹעֹשֹ[ר] לאל ואלבשי לבוש כהונתא

20 וֹמלי ידי והוית כהין לאל עֹל{מין/א} <יון>

21 וֹקרביתֹ* כל קרבנוהי וברכת לאבי

22 בחיווהי וברכת לאחי [10]ֹאדין כולהון

23 ברכוני ואף אבא ברכני ואשלמית

NOTES ON READINGS

L. 1 שלמ]א֯[ו. The margin width of the whole column suggests this restoration.

L. 16 [אבי] מעשר. MS A has here a lacuna and the text in brackets has been restored on the basis of 4Q213b 4. This reading confirms Grelot's reconstruction (1956: 404) against the proposal of Greenfield and Stone (1979: 219) who read [הוה מ]עשר. 1Q21 4 has a variant reading [אבי יע]קב מעשרן.

L. 17 [וֹדי כ]ע֯ן֯. The manuscript preserves the ink traces of the tail of an ʿayin joined to the downstroke of a nûn. Greenfield and Stone (1979: 219) correctly propose [וכ]ע֯ן֯ but the width of the lacuna allows the restoration of an additional word.

L. 18 [כהנו]תֹה. This reading of the lacuna was first proposed by Charles and Cowley (1907: 571) and generally accepted, see also Grelot's reconstruction (1956: 404, n. 4).

L. 19 מֹעֹשֹ[ר]. Greenfield and Stone (1979: 219) read מעש]ר[. Only lower parts of the first three letters exist in the manuscript.

L. 20 לאל עֹל{מין/א} <יון>. The Cairo Geniza manuscript עליון is a scribal correction from עלמין, with an elaboration of the mêm. The correction creates an intermediary form עלמיא by the hesitant scribe, cf. Puech 2002: 525–526, contrast Kugler (1996a: 89 עליון corrected into עלמיא); cf. Lévi (1907: 175), Grelot (1956: 405 עליון), Greenfield and Stone (1979: 220 עלמיא). The mêm is first decomposed into a pê and yôd, yôd and final nûn; these last two letters are changed to ʾālep by the addition of the left leg. The correction to עליון elaborates the pê/mêm with a horizontal bar and and a hook added to the upper arm of the ʾālep in order to create the hook of the final nûn; then the head of pê and wāw become the yôd – wāw sequence. The parallel Qumran reading 4Q213b 6 has also a similar correction לא[ל עֹל{מין<א>}<יון> וא]נה.

TRANSLATION

1 [(4)and] peace, and all desirableness of the first-fruits of the earth,

---

i 4Q213b 5 מן.

j 4Q213b 6 וא]נה מקרב.

2 all of it to eat. But for the kingdom of the sword (there will be) struggle

3 and battle and slaughter and affliction

4 and hissing and killing and hunger. ⁽⁵⁾Sometimes it will eat,

5 and sometimes it will hunger; and sometimes it will toil, and sometimes

6 it will rest; and sometimes it will sleep, and sometimes will depart

7 the sleep of the eye. ⁽⁶⁾Now see how we have made you

8 greater than all, and how we have given you the greatness of eternal

9 peace. vacat   ⁽⁷⁾And those seven departed from me,

10 and I arose from my sleep. Then

11 I said, "This is the vision and I wonder

12 that the whole vision like this one will come true." And I hid

13 also this one in my heart and I did not reveal it to anybody.

14 ⁽⁸⁾And we [we]nt to my father Isaac, and he also thus

15 [blessed] me   vacat ⁽⁹⁾Then, when Jacob

16 [my father] was tithing everything that belonged to him according to his vow,

17 [and because n]ow I was first at the head of the [priesth]ood,

18 then to me from all his sons he gave the offering

19 of tith[e] to God, and he clothed me in the priestly clothing,

20 and he filled my hands. And I became a priest of God the most high,

21 and I offered all his offerings. And I blessed my father

22 in his life, and I blessed my brothers. ⁽¹⁰⁾Then they all

23 blessed me, and also the father blessed me. And I completed

    (Bodleian b, 1) to offer his offerings in Bethel.

COMMENTS

L. 2   כולה   *all of it.* The final *hê* is best taken as a resumptive 3f. sg. suffix and the whole form as standing in apposition to the preceding construct chain; cf. Muraoka and Porten 1998: 247–248.

L. 2   מלכות חרבא   *the kingdom of the sword.* This expression is the subject of the 3f. sg. form of the verbs in v. 5, see Greenfield and Stone 1979: 218. Grelot (1956: 397) interpreted the verbs in v. 5 as 2m. sg. forms, but his interpretation and translation are based on the assumption that the rule of the sword belongs to Levi together with the priestly kingdom. This opinion should be abandoned. The immediate context and vocabulary analysis indicate an intimate connection between vv. 4b and 5. The nouns "toil" עמל and "hunger" כפן from v. 4 are used verbally in v. 5.

L. 2   פנשא   *struggle.* Only the verbal forms *paʿel* and *hitpaʿel* are attested in *Fr. Tg.* MS C Gen 32:25, 26, where it translates Hebrew אבק *nipʿal*, "to fight, struggle."

L. 3   נחשירותא   *slaughter.* This is a Persian loan-word meaning "hunt, fight between wild beasts or heros, carnage," see de Menasce 1956: 213–214. It is attested in western Aramaic also in 4Q246 i 5—a masculine form with a Hebrew nominal suff. ון-, נחשירון. It is also found in Qumran Hebrew in 1QM I 9, 10, 13 נחשיר.

L. 4   נצפתא   *hissing.* Attested in Syriac, *nṣf,* "to hiss," see Brockelmann 1928: *s.v.*, root I. Semantically, it corresponds to the Hebrew noun שרקה "hissing." The Hebrew term denotes derision of the enemies and is always accompanied by שמה "devastation, desolation," see Jer 18:16; 19:8; 25:9, 18, etc. Beyer (1984: 194) translates with "Ächzen," "groaning," but this rendering is inadequate.

Ll. 7–8   הכין רבינך מן כולה   *how . . . everything.* 4Q213b 1 reads [הי]כה רביתך מן כל בשׂר. The Qumran line differs considerably from A. The verb רבי in A 6 l. 7 is 1c. pl. and fits well in the context that suggests the presence of seven angels speaking with Levi (A 7 l. 9). The following verb in A 6 l. 8 is also plural (יהבנא). In 4Q213b 1 the verb is in singular and, consequently, only one person is speaking with Levi. Furthermore, בשׂר is not attested by A, which, however, uses the expression elsewhere (A 14 l. 11, cf. E 18,2 vv. 52, 54; 4Q214b 7 1). Since the MS A plural form fits the context, it is probable that the Qumran text changes the verb to a singular form (contrast Stone and Greenfield 1996a: 39). The preceding lines of the Qumran fragment are lost and nothing can be said about the end of the second vision it contained. The MS A הכין, "so, in this way," comes from the form הא כן attested in *Ahiqar* 145, 164, 184; see Stone and Greenfield 1996a: 39. For the lexeme היכה, see 4Q213b 1; 4Q212 v 23 (*1 En.* 93:14); 1QtgJob XXXI 2.

L. 8   רבות   *greatness.* Usually this Aramaic noun means "greatness," "exaltation"; Greenfield and Stone (1979: 218) pointed out that the Hebrew משח, "to anoint," was translated in the Targums by the Aramaic root רבי, hence their translation *anointing.* The context does not unequivocally confirm this interpretation. In the preceding line the verb from the same root (רבינך

"we have made you great") refers to Levi's glorification, not to his anointing, cf. also *A.L.D.* 90 l. 1.

L. 9 שבעתון *seven.* The numeral with an abbreviated pronominal suffix 3m. pl. הון- with the omission of ה; the phenomenon is attested in the Qumran texts, see בסרכן "in their order" (4Q201 1 ii 1 = *1 En.* 2:1); cf. also Greenfield and Stone 1979: 218–219.

L. 11 חזוא הוא דן *This is the vision.* Following Charles, Grelot (1956: 399) joined the next syntagm וכדן with the sentence and bases his translation on *T. Levi* 8:18 ὅτι τοῦτο ὅμοιον ἐκείνῳ ἐστί: "cette vision est comme l'autre." However, this translation of the Aramaic is grammatically unacceptable, as Greenfield and Stone (1979: 219) observe. Additionally, the Greek sentence in the *Testament of Levi* does not literally correspond to the Aramaic. That suggests some redactional activity and makes any literal comparison suspect.

L. 11 וכדן אנה מתמה *and I wonder... like this one.* In the expression כדן the demonstrative דן refers to the noun חזוה (l. 12) in the emphatic state.

L. 11 די יהוי לה כל חזוה *that the whole vision... will come true.* It is difficult to find the reference to which points לה. Greenfield and Stone (1979: 219) emended לה to לי and connected it with the preceding יהוי saying that "the scribe, scrupulous to avoid a homograph of the *tetragrammaton*, transposed an original *he* at the end of the verb יהוה and the *yôd* of לי." The first objection arises when one understands that Greenfield and Stone based this proposal on their emendation of לה to לי. Secondly, the spelling of הוה with a final *yôd* is normal for Aramaic and is attested in, e.g., A 84 ll. 11, 12; cf. 19 l. 2, 2; 20 l. 3. It seems, therefore exaggerated to assume this kind of scribal transposition that would make the text unintelligible. Grelot (1956: 400) interpreted לה as an "anticipatory suffix" (cf. Bauer and Leander 1962: §74a), and translated: "je m'étonnais (me demandant) ce qu'il adviendrait (cf. *Dan.*, II, 45) de toute cette vision (ל = au sujet de)." Bauer and Leander noted that the anticipatory suffix serves as an indicator of the noun identification, e.g. בָּהּ שַׁעֲתָא "in it, the hour" = "in the same hour," Dan 3:6, 15; 4:30; 5:5. We follow here Beyer (1984: 613) who parses the preposition ל here as *dativus ethicus* and leaves it untranslated (cf. e.g. MS A 14 ll. 8–9; 16 l. 14 אזדהר לך; Beyer 1984: 196). The proposed translation indicates that Levi wonders that the previsions and promises of the vision will come true.

L. 13 אף דן *also this one.* Kugler (1996a: 78) translated "this very thing," and blurred thus the meaning without taking into account the immediate context. His translation reflects the opinion that there is only one vision in the *Document.* Grammatic structure of the sentence and its context do not support his translation. The Aramaic אף דן refers to the vision Levi just finished seeing in his dream. Similarly, the deictic דן in A 7 l. 11 unequivocally refers to the vision.

L. 17 [ו]די כֹ[עֻ]ן *[and because n]ow.* The restoration of די in the lacuna (Puech 2002: 524) suggests that the following clause is coordinated with the preceding וכדי in line 15. The apodosis thus begins with ולי *then to me,* in line 18, with the beginning of the ordination rite.

L. 17 קדמי *first*. Charles (1907: 578) proposed to read קדמי as the ordinal numeral "first." Greenfield and Stone (1979: 219) emended it to קדמה creating thus an idiom הוה קדם corresponding to Hebrew הוה לפני. The emendation itself is then corrected in Stone and Greenfield 1996a: 41, n. 12 to קדמוהי. The hypothetical character of the emendation, which is not based on any other textual evidence and is also grammatically impossible, should be questioned (see Grelot 1983: 106). Charles' proposal seems to explain best the text that purposefully underlines Levi's privileged priestly position.

Ll. 17–18 בראש [כהנו]תה *at the head of the priesthood*. In MS E 18,2 v. 64 ἀπὸ τῆς ἀρχῆς ἱερωσύνης probably translates the same expression with a different preposition. The Greek expression does not necessarily mean "high priesthood" (Greenfield and Stone 1985: 466), for the *Document* knows a technical term for it, כהנותא רבתא A 67 l. 7, rendered by the translator with ἡ ἀρχιερωσύνη ἡ μεγάλη. MS E 18,2 v. 67 preserves a similar expression ἀρχὴ βασιλέων, which implies Aramaic ראש מלכין. In these instances of the lexeme ראש/ἀρχή, the whole expression refers to the priestly and royal status of Levi's family in Israel (see *A.L.D.* 64 and 67; cf. *A.L.D.* 99 l. 13 ראשין "chiefs, rulers"). *T. Levi* 8:11 speaks of three ἀρχαί of Levi's sons meaning three offices or functions reserved for them. The rendering "at the head of the priesthood" (Charles 1908b: 229) is a good literal translation of the Aramaic.

L. 19 אלבשי *he clothed me*. 'Apʿel of לבש with a 1st person. sg. suffix characteristic to Late Aramaic, see 1.5.1 and Greenfield and Stone 1979: 220.

L. 19 לבוש כהנותא *the priestly clothing*. The Aramaic expression here and in v. 19 indicates the set of priestly vestments necessary for the liturgical service, see Exod 28; 39:1–31; Sir 45:8–13. According to 4Q550 2, at the Persian court there were servants responsible of the royal wardrobe עבדי לבוש מלכותא; cf. 4Q550c ii 2.

L. 20 <יון> { א/מין} כהן לאל על{מין} *priest of the God most high*. In Gen 14:18 and in 1QapGen XXI 15 this expression is applied to Melchizedek; in the *Document* it defines Levi's priesthood, see A 13 l. 5. The allusion to Melchizedek is obvious. MS A 17 l. 19 and MS E 18,2 v. 48 further define Levi as a holy priest, כהין קדיש; Levi's descendants as priests, MS E 18,2 v. 49 ἱερεῖς; priests and kings 4Q213 2 12. For the eternal Levitical priest, see 4Q545 frg. 4 19 כהן עלמין; cf. 4Q547 frg. 9 6–7.

L. 20 <יון> { א/מין} אל על{מין} *God the most high*. This Hebrew expression is quite frequent in Aramaic texts, see 1QapGen XII 17; XX 12, 16; XXI 2, 20; XXII 15, 16, 16, 21; 4Q552 frg. 4 2. Here it constitutes an allusion to Gen 14:18–20, cf. *Jub.* 32:1. In MT see Gen 14:22; Num 24:16; Ps 78:35; in *A.L.D.* see also A 13 l. 5; 30 l. 16; MS E 18,2 vv. 51, 58; cf MS E 5:2: ὕψιστος. It is rare in Qumran Hebrew, see 1QHᵃ XII (Sukenik col. IV) 31; 4Q175 1 10; 4Q492 1 13; 11Q14 1 ii 4, 7. It is a common title for God in Hellenistic times, cf. Bertram 1972: 614–619. A related Aramaic phrase אל ועלין "ʾel and ʿelyan" denoting a pair of gods is attested in the eighth century B.C. Sefire inscription (I A 11), see Fitzmyer 1967: 37–39.

118CHAPTER TWO

L. 21 קרבנוהי *his offerings*. The immediate context indicates that the pronom. suffix refers to God. On the other hand, in A 10 l. 1 קרבנוהי may only refer to Jacob. Here Jacob gives to Levi the tithe offering, and Levi, in turn, offers it to God.

L. 23 אבא *the father*. Usually Levi refers to his father with אבי *my father*, only here does he use the noun without the suffix. As Grelot notes (1983: 108), this use concords well with the context of the preceding line in which Levi does not refer to his brothers using 1 person sg. suffix אהי, but אדין כולהון ברכוני. For the NT usage of this familiar expression, cf. Mark 14:36; Rom 8:15; Gal 4:6.

L. 23 The line in a smaller typeface from the next column is brought here to finish the sentence that spans the two columns.

2.1.7 *A.L.D. 11–18*

MS A (Bodleian b; pl. VIII)
Parallel: E 18,2 (Pl. XII)

(11)καὶ ἀνήλθομεν	(11)ואזלנא אל בבית קורבנוהי להקרבה	1
ἀπὸ Βηθὴλ καὶ κατελύσαμεν ἐν τῇ αὐλῇ Ἀβραὰμ	אברהם בבירת ושרינא אל מבית	2
τοῦ πατρὸς ἡμῶν παρὰ Ἰσαὰκ τὸν πατέρα ἡμῶν. (12)καὶ εἶδεν	(12)וחזא אבונה יצחק לות אבונן	3
Ἰσαὰκ ὁ πατὴρ ἡμῶν πάντας ἡμᾶς καὶ ηὐλόγησεν ἡμᾶς,	ובִרכנא לכולנא אבונא יצחק	4
καὶ ηὐφράνθη. (13)καὶ ὅτε ἔγνω ὅτι ἐγὼ ἱεράτευσα τῷ κυρίῳ	לאלa כהן אנה די ידע (13)וכדי וחדי	5
δεσπότῃ τοῦ οὐρανοῦ, ἤρξατο	שארי שמיא למארי* עליון	6
διδάσκειν με τὴν κρίσιν	דין יתי ולאלפאb* יתי לפקדה	7
ἱερωσύνης καὶ εἶπεν· (14)Τέκνον Λευί, πρόσεχε	אזדהר לויc** ל(14)d vac ואמר c כהנותא	8
σεαυτῷ ἀπὸ πάσης ἀκαθαρσίας·	ומןf טומאה כל מן בריe* לך	9

---

a E τῷ κυρίῳ.
b E >.
c E >.
d E + τέκνον.
e E >.
f E >.

Greek	Aramaic	#
ἡ κρίσις σου μεγάλη ἀπὸ πάσης	כל חטא* דינך רב הוא מן כל	10
σαρκός. (15)καὶ νῦν τὴν κρίσιν τῆς	vac (15)וכען [g]ברי* דין	11
ἀληθείας ἀναγγελῶ σοι, καὶ οὐ μὴ κρύψω	קושטא אהוינך ולא אטמר	12
ἀπό σου πᾶν ῥῆμα. διδάξω σε·	מינך כל פתגם לאלפותך[h] דין	13
(16)πρόσεχε σεαυτῷ	כהנותא* [i]לקדמין* היזדהר לך (16)	14
ἀπὸ παντὸς συνουσιασμοῦ καὶ ἀπὸ πάσης ἀκαθαρσίας καὶ ἀπὸ πάσης	[j]ברי* מן כל פחז [k]ומטמאה ומן כל	15
πορνείας. (17)σὺ †πρῶτος† ἀπὸ τοῦ σπέρματος	{זנו}ת[l] ואנת*[m] אנתתא* [n]מן משפחתי* (17)	16
λάβε σεαυτῷ καὶ μὴ βεβηλώσῃς τὸ σπέρμα σου μετὰ †πολλῶν†·	סב לך ולא תחל זרעך עם [o]זניא*	17
ἐκ σπέρματος γὰρ ἁγίου εἶ, καὶ	[p]ארי זרע קדיש אנת [q]וקדיש*	18
τὸ σπέρμα σου ἁγίασον καὶ τὸ σπέρμα τοῦ ἁγιασμοῦ σου ἐστίν· ἱερεὺς	זרעך[r] היך קודשא* [s]ארו* כהן	19
ἅγιος κληθήσεται τῷ σπέρματι	קדיש [t]אנת מתקרי* [u]לכל* זרע	20
Ἀβραάμ. (18)ἐγγὺς εἶ κυρίου καὶ σὺ ἐγγὺς	אברהם (18)קריב אנת לאל [v]וקריב	21

[g] E >.
[h] E >.
[i] E >.
[j] E >.
[k] E + ἀπὸ πάσης.
[l] E σύ.
[m] E πρῶτος.
[n] E ἀπὸ τοῦ σπέρματος.
[o] E πολλῶν.
[p] E + ἐκ.
[q] E καὶ . . . ἁγίασον.
[r] E καὶ τὸ σπέρμα τοῦ ἁγιασμοῦ σου ἐστίν.
[s] E >.
[t] E κληθήσεται.
[u] E >.
[v] E + σύ.

τῶν ἁγίων αὐτοῦ. γίνου　　　　ᵂלכל* קדישוהי ˣכען* {הווי} <אֿᵢהר> דכי　22
καθαρὸς

ἐν τῷ σώματί σου ἀπὸ πάσης　　　　בבשרך מן כל טומאת כל נבר　23
ἀκαθαρσίας παντὸς ἀνθρώπου.

NOTES ON READINGS

L. 3　והוא. The MS has והוא. Charles (1908a: 247, n. a) emends to והוא
in accordance with E 18,2 v. 12.

L. 8　לוי. An accidental ink dot stands slightly above the *yôd*.

L. 11　There is an ink dot at the end of the line.

L. 16　{ת}זנו. The scribe cancelled the *tāw*, correcting thus a Hebraism.

L. 17　זניאן. Against the textual evidence Beyer (1984: 197) restores to
ז[ר]אן, "strangers." His emendation of the gramatically and stylistically correct text is based on a questionable theoretical assumption that "Im Falle
einer Anspielung auf Lev 21, 7. 14 sollten nicht nur die Huren genannt
sein" (p. 197, n. 1).

L. 22　{הווי}<אֿᵢהר> דכי. Greenfield and Stone (1979: 229) have here
אזדכי. Charles (1908a: 247, n. b) restores אזדכי on the basis of E 18,2
v. 18 and *Jub.* 21:16. The manuscript unequivocally shows the right downstroke of a *hê*, the legs of a *wāw* and *yôd*, then one may discern a *dālet*, *kāp*
and *yôd*. The reading was then corrected by a scribe to אזדהר דכי by changing the *hê* into an *ʾālep*, and the two *wāw* into a *hê*; the head of the *yôd*
has been reworked into a *rêš*, while the *zayin* and *dālet* have been added
above the line (Puech 2002: 528).

TRANSLATION

1　to offer his offerings in Bethel. ⁽¹¹⁾And we went

2　from Bethel and we settled in the fortress of Abraham,

3　our father, alongside Isaac our father. ⁽¹²⁾And Isaac our father

4　saw all of us and blessed us

5　and rejoiced. ⁽¹³⁾And when he learned that I was a priest of God

6　the most high, the Lord of heavens, he began

7　to instruct me and to teach me the law

8　of the priesthood. vacat And he said to me, ⁽¹⁴⁾"Levi, beware,

---

ᵂ E >.

ˣ E >.

9 my son, of every impurity and of

10 every sin; your judgment is greater than all

11 flesh. vacat ⁽¹⁵⁾And now, my son, the law

12 of truth I will show you, and I will not conceal

13 from you anything to teach you the law

14 of the priesthood. ⁽¹⁶⁾First of all, beware,

15 my son, of every fornication and impurity and of every

16 harlotry. ⁽¹⁷⁾And you, take for yourself a wife from my family

17 so that you may not defile your seed with harlots,

18 because you are a holy seed. And holy is

19 your seed like the Holy One, for a holy priest

20 you are called for all the seed of

21 Abraham. ⁽¹⁸⁾You are close to God and close

22 to all his holy ones, now be pure

23 in your flesh from every impurity of any man.

COMMENTS

L. 2 בירת אברהם *fortress of Abraham*. This Akkadian loan-word into Hebrew and Aramaic may mean "fortress" (Cowley 6:3; Neh 7:2), "capital city" (Ezra 6:2) or even "temple" (1 Chr 29:1, 19; cf. Neh 2:8); cf. "Abraham's tower" *māḥfadu la-ʾabrahām* in *Jub.* 29:16, 17, 19, and Leslau 1991: 338. In *Jub.* 29:16, 17, 19 Latin has *baris* for Eth. *māḥfad*; the Latin term is a transliterated Aramaic בירה, cf. Rönsch 1874:140–141. The Greek translator chose here an unusual rendering αὐλή, "courtyard". In the LXX it frequently indicates the court of the tabernacle (e.g. Exod 27:9, 9, 12, 13) or of the Jerusalem temple (e.g. 1 Kgs 6:36; 7:46, 49). He might have been influenced by the priestly character of Isaac's speech to Levi, or he understood the place of Isaac's dwelling as a temple.

Ll. 5–6 לאל עליון *God the most high*. E omits עליון. The omission is probably due to the phonetic *homoioarcton* with the preceding noun.

L. 6 מרי שמיא *Lord of heavens*. Similarly to the *Document*, in 1QapGen XII 17 the expression אל עליון stands in parallelism with "Lord of heavens" מרי שמיא. Although שמיא מרי is close in its formulation to מרי שמיא וארעא (1QapGen XII 16, 21), it occurs as an independent title for God, see 1QapGen VII 7; Dan 5:23; *1 En.* 106:11; Cowley 1967: 30:15; cf. Mk 11:30; Luke 15:18, 21; for its occurrence in other Semitic languages, see Fitzmyer 1971: 99. In 1QapGen XXII 16 Melchizedek proclaims Abraham to be blessed by the most high God, Lord of heavens and earth אל עליון מרה שמיא וארעא.

L. 7 לפקדה יתי to *instruct me*. E omits. The omission of this Aramaic expression may be due to a *homoioteleuton* יתי . . . יתי.

L. 7 לאלפא to *teach*. Levi is a disciple here, but in his wisdom poem he recommends to his sons to fulfill a teacher's function where Joseph serves as an example (*A.L.D.* 90 l. 23).

L. 8 לי *to me*. E omits and reads here τέκνον that assumes the Aramaic בר. The phonetic affinity between לי and the following personal name לוי may easily account for the unintentional omission of the copyist. Isaac often addresses Levi with the expression ברי "my son" (A 14 l. 9; 15 l. 11; 16 l. 15; E 18,2 v. 48). E is, however, not consistent in rendering this syntagm, for it omits the two other instances of ברי (A 15 l. 11 and 16 l. 15). On the other hand, E 18,2 v. 48 assumes Aramaic ברי.

L 9 ברי *my son*. E omits. MS A repeats this syntagm. The repetition may be accredited to the maladroitness of the scribe. It might have happened that the ברי omitted in A 13 l. 8 was then put on the margin of the manuscript and then awkwardly inserted in its present position. The E text seems to preserve the original reading.

Ll. 9–10 ומן כל חטא *and of every sin*. E omits. The syntagm מן כל is repeated three times in this verse, the eye of the translator may have easily skipped over one of the three instances. It is not excluded though, that the omission in the Greek translation is due to a *homoioarcton*: ἀπὸ πάσης ἀκαθαρσίας – ἀπὸ πάσης ἁμαρτίας, and/or a *homoioteleuton*: ἀκαθαρσίας—ἁμαρτίας; for a similar expression cf. A 16 l. 15.

L. 11 ברי *my son*, E omits. See A 13 l. 8 and 14 l. 9.

Ll. 13–14 לאלפותך דין כהונתא to *teach you the law of the priesthood*. E διδάξω σε. Here E is faulty. It omits the complement of the verb and what appears to be an infinite final clause in Aramaic is rendered with a finite verb; for a similar problem see A 23 l. 14 להסקה/προσφέρε. Charles (1908a: 247, n. 7) understands the Aramaic as a result clause (ὥστε), but the preposition ל introduces here a final clause that should be rendered in Greek with τοῦ διδάσκειν σε τὴν κρίσιν τῆς ἱερωσύνης.

L. 13 לאלפותך to *teach you*. When a pronom. suffix is attached to a derived infinitive, the latter takes the construct form ות-, a phenomenon known already in Egyptian Aramaic, cf. Muraoka and Porten 1998: 109 and n. 507; cf. also Bauer and Leander 1962: § 35n; 65n; for the form without a suffix, cf. A 13 l. 7 אלפא.

L. 14 לקדמין *first of all*. E omits. This adverbial expression is found in the *Document* preceding an imperative, see A 22 l. 10 and A 27 l. 4 (cf. E 18,2 v. 56), and it is translated by E with the corresponding πρῶτον. E may have had another *Vorlage* here or it has a simple unintentional omission. One may suppose that the Aramaic copyist omitted the adverb and introduced it in a wrong place in A 17 l. 16. Similarly, E 18,2 v. 22 has πρῶτον repeated twice, the first instance not attested in A and inserted awkwardly between a noun and its complement. The latter case suggests a corrupt Aramaic *Vorlage* available to the translator.

L. 15 ברי *my son*. E omits. See A 13 l. 8.

L. 15 וטמאה *and impurity*. MS E reads ἀπὸ πάσης ἀκαθαρσίας *from every impurity*. E supposes מן כל not extant in A. On stylistic grounds, E preserves a better reading, see A 14, where this Aramaic expression is repeated three times; see also A 18 l. 23.

L. 16 אנתתא מן משפחתי *a wife from my family*. E has a reading that does not correspond to A, leaves the verb (λαβὲ/סב) without a direct object, and does not make much sense in the context. E 18,2 v. 62 indicates that Levi fulfills Isaac's counsel, ἔλαβον γυναῖκα ἐμαυτῷ ἐκ τῆς συγγενείας Ἀβραάμ. This sentence closely corresponds to A 17 ll. 16–17. The LXX often translates משפחה with συγγένεια (e.g. Exod 6:14; 12:21; Lev 20:5) and Qumran Aramaic confirms the presence of this term in 4Q196 2 9 (Tob 1:22). It does not preclude the possibility, though, that E closely follows its Aramaic copy of the *Document*, however corrupt it might be. The Greek σπέρμα suggests Aramaic זרע, attested in this verse (lines 17, 18, 20) and presents an alternative to the extant reading.

L. 17 עם זנין *with harlots*. E μετὰ πολλῶν. E has a corrupt reading for πορνῶν, as Charles (1908a: 247, note 12) has already noticed.

L. 18 ארי זרע קדיש אנת *because you are a holy seed*. E introduces the phrase with an ἐκ of origin (ἐκ σπέρματος), whereas A has a nominal sentence without any prepositional relationship. The former points to Levi's holy ancestors, the latter ascribes holiness to Levi only. The Greek preposition might have been suggested by the preceding corrupt πολλῶν. MS A gives a better meaning when compared with the following clause. The text underlines the holiness of Levi and his sons (וקדיש זרעך).

Ll. 18–19 וקדיש זרעך *and holy is your seed*. E has the imperative ἁγίασον (קדש) "sanctify." It is not clear whether the Aramaic prefers here the *scriptio plena* spelling of an imperative, or it should be interpreted as an adjective parallel to קדיש in the preceding nominal sentence. This paralleilism suggests the latter solution as preferable.

L. 19 היך קודשא *like the Holy One*. E has "and it is the seed of your sanctification" καὶ τὸ σπέρμα τοῦ ἁγιασμοῦ σου ἐστίν. Although Charles (1908a: 247, n. 13) considers the Greek clause to be a dittography, E assumes a different Aramaic reading in its translation: והוא זרע קודשך. The Aramaic *Vorlage* of E is probably different. The lexeme קודשא is translated with "the holy place" (Charles 1908b: 229), "holiness" (MS E), or "the Holy One" denoting God (Esh 1957: 71). Since priestly holiness, avoiding of illicit marriage and God's holiness are closely connected in Lev 21:7–8, the latter meaning is preferred. For this meaning in the targums, see Esh 1957: 74–75; Levy 1881: 2:348; cf. also *1 En.* 1:2; 93:11 (4Q212 V 16 קדשא, cf. Milik 1976: 269); 1 Pet 1:15–16.

L. 19 ארו *for*. E omits. The omission of this inferential particle makes the logical connection with the preceding sentence non existent. It is not excluded that ארו might be absent in the *Vorlage* of the translator. MS A connects the clause to Isaac's motivation of Levi's priesthood as the *inclusio* with ארי (A 17 l. 18) would suggest.

L. 20 אנת מתקרי *you are called*. E reads κληθήσεται. It seems that E does not have in its Aramaic text the personal pronoun אנת. The omission could cause the Greek rendering in 3rd person sing. This rendering, however, makes the clause awkward for Isaac's speech directed to Levi continues.

L. 20 כל *all*. Here and in E 18,2 v. 18, the Greek does not translate the Aramaic qualifier כל. E usually translates it accordingly (cf., e.g. A 16 l. 15; 18 l. 23; 30 l. 15); it is probable then, that it was absent from the Aramaic manuscript used by the translator.

L. 21 וקריב *and close*. MS E adds σύ. The Greek personal pronoun suggests a second אנת in the line, which would run וקריב אנת. This is unnecessary for the understanding of the Aramaic nominal clause; the emphatic repetition of the pronoun is nonetheless possible (see A 17 l. 16). The Greek renders the Aramaic clause with a nominal sentence. This rendering suggests that the translator faithfully follows his Aramaic text. MS A construction, however, makes a second אנת unnecessary and stylistically clumsy.

L. 22 כל *all*. E omits. See A 17 l. 20 above.

L. 22 כען *now*. E omits. This particle preceding an imperative is also found in A 6 l. 6 and 88 l. 17. E does not seem to have any reason to omit it, so it may be assumed that the Greek translator did not have it in his Aramaic manuscript.

2.1.8 *A.L.D. 19–25b*

MS A (Bodleian c; pl. IX);
Parallels: MS E 18,2 (Pl. XII), *4Q214 1*, 4Q214a 1, **4Q214b 2–3**, 4Q214b 4, 4Q214b 5–6 i

1	*אל*לבית[a] וכדי תהוי קאים למיעל (19)	(19)καὶ ὅταν εἰσπορεύῃ ἐν τοῖς ἁγίοις,
2	הוי סחי במיא [b]ובאדין תהוי לביש	λούου ὕδατι πρῶτον καὶ τότε ἐνδιδύσκου
3	לבוש כהנותא (20)וכדי תהוי לביש	τὴν στολὴν τῆς ἱερωσύνης· (20)καὶ ὅταν ἐνδιδύσκῃ,
4	הוי תאיב תוב ורחיע ידיך	νίπτου πάλιν τὰς χεῖράς σου
5	ורגליך עד דלא תקרב למדבחא	καὶ τοὺς πόδας σου πρὸ τοῦ ἐγγίσαι τρὸς τὸν βωμὸν
6	*כל דנה[c](21)וכדי תהוי נסב להקרבה	προσενέγκαι ὁλοκάρπωσιν ·(21)καὶ ὅταν μέλλῃς προσφέρειν

---

[a] E ἐν τοῖς ἁγίοις.
[b] E + πρῶτον.
[c] E ὁλοκάρπωσιν.

Greek	Aramaic	#
ὅσα δεῖ ἀνενέγκαι ἐπὶ τὸν βωμόν,	כל די הוה להנסקה למדבחה	7
πάλιν νίπτου τὰς χεῖράς σου καὶ οὺς πόδας σου.	הוי עוד תאב ורחע ידיך ורגליך	8
(22)καὶ ἀνάφερε τὰ ξύλα πρῶτον <ἐ>σχισμένα, ἐπισκοπῶν	(22)ומהקריב אע*יןᵈ *מהצלחיןᶜ ᶠובקר*	9
αὐτὰ πρῶτον ἀπὸ παντὸς μολυσμοῦ·	אינון לקודמין ᵍמן תולעא*	10
	ʰּובאדין הסק ʲאּינוןⁱ* ארי ʲכדנהᵏ*	11
	ᵏחזיתי* לאברהם אבי מיזדהר*	12
(23)ιβʹ ξύλα εἴρηκεν	ˡ(23)מן כל* תרʸעשר ᵐמיני* ⁿאעין* ᵒאמר	13
μοι ἐπὶ τὸν βωμὸν προσφέρε<ιν>,	ᵖלי ᵖדי הוין* ᵠלהסקה* ʳמינהון* ˢלמדבחה*	14
ὧν ἐστιν ὁ καπνὸς αὐτῶν ἡδὺς ἀναβαίνων. (24)καὶ ταῦτα	די ᵗריחא* תנהון בשׁם ᵘסליק* (24)ᵛואלין	15
τὰ ὀνόματα αὐτῶν· κέδρον καὶ ουεδεφωνα	ʷאינון* שמהתהון ארזא ˣודפרנא*	16

ᵈ 4Q214 1 3 עעין.
ᶜ 4Q214b 5–6 i 1 מצלחין.
ᶠ E ἐπισκοπῶν.
ᵍ E ἀπὸ παντὸς μολυσμοῦ.
ʰ E > A 22:11–12.
ⁱ 4Q214b 4 1 [אנו]ן.
ʲ 4Q214b 5–6 i 2 כן.
ᵏ 4Q214b 5–6 i 2 חזית.
ˡ E >.
ᵐ E and 4Q214b 2–3 2 >.
ⁿ 4Q214b 2–3 2 עעין.
ᵒ 4Q214 1 4 + אלין.
ᵖ E >.
ᵠ 4Q214b 5–6 i 3 ל[אסקא.
ʳ E >; 4Q214b 5–6 i 3 מנהון.
ˢ 4Q214b 5–6 i 3 למדבחא.
ᵗ E >.
ᵘ 4Q214b 2–3 3 סלק.
ᵛ 4Q214 1 5–6 > A 24.
ʷ E and 4Q214b 2–3 3 >.
ˣ E ουεδεφωνα.

καὶ σχῖνον καὶ στρόβιλον καὶ πίτυν   17 ^yוסנדא* ^zואטולא* ושוחא* ^{aa}ואודנא*
καὶ ολδινα

καὶ βερωθα †καν† θεχακ καὶ   18 ^{bb}ברותא* ^{cc}ותאאנתא* ואע משחא
κυπάρισσον

καὶ δάφνην καὶ   19 ^{dd}ערא* ^{ee}והדסה* ^{ff}ואעי ^{gg}ודקתא* ^(25a) *אלין^{hh}
μυρσίνην καὶ ἀσφάλαθον.
^(25a)ταῦτα

εἴρηκεν ὅτι ταῦτά ἐστιν ἅ σε   20 ⁱⁱאינון* די אמר ^{jj}עלי די חזין* ^{kk}להסקה*
ἀναφέρειν

ὑποκάτο τῆς ὁλοκαυτώσεως ἐπὶ τοῦ   21 ^{ll}מנהון* לתחות עלתא ^{mm}על מדבחה*
θυσιαστηρίου.

^(25b)καὶ τὸ πῦρ τότε ἄρξῃ ἐκκαίειν   22 ^(25b) ⁿⁿויכדי תנסקת מן אע)א(אלין על

23 מדבחא* ונורא ^{oo}ישרא* לתדלקא

NOTES ON READINGS

L. 19   καὶ μυρσίνην. Charles (1908a: 249) inadvertently omits this expression from his transcription of the Greek manuscript, thus making his notes on the order of the trees somewhat incorrect.

L. 19   ודקתא. Greenfield and Stone (1979: 229) read רדקתא/ד. The *dālet* is rather certain with its equally large vertical leg. The *yôd* in the preceding ואעי has a large horizontal head, and this would suggest to interpret it as a *rêš*. Hence it is plausible to read אע רדקתא, cf. the preceding line אע משחא. of the 4Q214a 1 1 probably reads הדסא as the last item in the list, but the reading is not certain.

^y   4Q214b 5–6 i 4 וסינדא.
^z   E στρόβιλον.
^{aa}   E ολδινα.
^{bb}   E καὶ βερωθα.
^{cc}   E θεχακ; 4Q214b 2–3 4 ותככה.
^{dd}   E καὶ δάφνην.
^{ee}   4Q214b 5–6 i 5 אדסא.
^{ff}   4Q214b 5–6 i 5 ועעי.
^{gg}   4Q214a 1 1 הדסא.
^{hh}   4Q214b 2–3 5 and 4Q214a 1 1 אלן.
ⁱⁱ   E >; 4Q214b 2–3 5 אנון.
^{jj}   E ὅτι ταῦτά ἐστιν ἅ σε.
^{kk}   4Q214 1 6 לאס]קא.
^{ll}   E >.
^{mm}   4Q214a 1 2 מדבחא.
ⁿⁿ   E >.
^{oo}   E + τότε.

L. 22 הֻנֹסֵקֹה. First Charles and Cowley (1907: 573) restored the text [הסקה], but the ink dots make the reading certain, with the right leg of the *hê* on the edge of the lacuna; for a similar wording of lines 22–23a, see A 23 ll. 13–14.

L. 22 (א)יעא. The *ʾālep* was omitted by haplography.

TRANSLATION

1 [19]And whenever you arise to enter the temple of God

2 bathe in water, and then put on

3 the priestly clothing. [20]And when you are clothed,

4 repeat (it) again and wash your hands

5 and your feet before you sacrifice on the altar

6 all this. [21]And whenever you take to sacrifice

7 everything that is fitting to offer on the altar,

8 repeat (it) again and wash your hands and feet.

9 [22]And sacrifice split wood and examine

10 it beforehand for worms

11 and then offer it up, for thus

12 I saw Abraham my father taking precautions.

13 [23]From all twelve types of wood that are fitting

14 he told me to offer on the altar,

15 these whose smell of their smoke goes up pleasantly. [24]And these

16 are their names: cedar and juniper

17 and almond and silver fir and fir and ash,

18 cypress and fig and oleaster,

19 laurel and myrtle and asphaltos.

20 [25a]These are the ones that he told me that are fitting to offer

21 from them un[der] the burnt offering on the altar.

22 [25b]And when you have offered of these trees on

23 the altar and the fire begins to burn them,

(Bodleian d, 1–2) and then you shall begin to sprinkle blood on the walls of the altar.

COMMENTS

L. 1 למעל לבית *to enter the temple.* The expression refers to Levi's liturgical activity in the temple. Note that the Akkadian technical expression for a temple official is *ērib bīti*, lit. "the one who enters the temple," cf. *CAD* E/4:290–292. For the verb עלל followed by the prep., see Dan 6:11: על לביתה "he entered his house."

L. 1 בית אל *the temple of God.* E τοῖς ἁγίοις. The expression בית אל may be understood and translated as the name of a city (E 18,2 v. 11, Βεθήλ; cf. LXX βαιθήλ, e.g. Gen 12:8, 8) or as a "God's house" (LXX οἶκος θεοῦ, e.g. Gen 28:17, 19). E τὰ ἅγια would assume Aramaic קדשא, or בית קדשא, cf. 4QtgLev 2 4 = Lev 16:20 (הקדש). It is not excluded, however, that E translates the Aramaic בת אל since the context clearly suggests this rendering. *T. Levi* 9,11 has τὰ ἅγια. In Aramaic the reference to the place of Levi's ordination is obvious.

L. 2 πρῶτον *first of all.* A omits. See A 16 l. 14 above.

L. 5 תקרב למדבחא כל דנה *you sacrifice on the altar all this.* Instead of כל דנה the Greek translator adds προσενέγκαι ὁλοκάρπωσιν "to sacrifice the burnt offering." This expression is easily interpreted as the direct object of the infinitive ἐγγίσαι, and the whole sentence is grammatically correct. The Aramaic clause is more complicated. Greenfield and Stone (1979: 221) assume that the verb קרב is intransitive and render adverbially the Aramaic כל דנה: "before you draw near at all to the altar." Their adverbial rendering of כל דנה with "at all" does not do justice to the plain meaning of the expression. It is far easier to interpret the verb קרב as a transitive *pa'el* meaning "to sacrifice," see A 9 l. 21, cf. Ezra 7:17. The *lāmed* before "the altar" introduces here an indirect object, indicating place, not direction, see A 21 l. 7; 23 l. 14; 31 l. 20; the expression כל דנה is easily interpreted as a direct object of קרב referring to the detailed description of the sacrificed material beginning with v. 22. Beyer (1984: 198) emends the text: עד דלא תקרב למדבחא [להקרבה] כל עלה "bevor du dich dem Altar näherst, [um darzubringen] jedes beliebige Brandopfer."

L. 7 כל די הזה להנסקה *everything that is fitting to offer.* E ὡς ἀδίαν ἐνέγκε. E has a corrupt text for ὅσα δεῖ ἀνενέγκαι, see Charles 1908a: 248, n. 3.

L. 9 מהצלהין *splitted.* E reads πρoτoυσχισμένα, a Greek neologism or a corrupt form for πρῶτος and σχίζω. Most probably, it is a translator's attempt to render the perfective value of the *hap'el* passive participle, מהצלהין, "that have been split." The Aramaic form is attested by 4Q214b 4–6 i 1 without the *hê*, מצלהין, cf. Bauer and Leander 1962: § 36w and x.

L. 10 מן תולעא *for worms.* E ἀπὸ παντὸς μολυσμοῦ "from any defilement." For this term in the LXX translating חנפה, see Jer 23:15; cf. 2 Macc 5:27; *1 Esdr.* 8:80. MS A concords with *Jub.* 21:13 and *b. Menaḥ.* 85b, where, too, the wood is to be free from worms.

Ll. 11–12 ובאדין ... מיזדהר *And then ... precautions.* E omits two lines, leaving thus the verb εἴρηκεν/אמר in line 13 without its implied subject (Abraham). E 18.2 v. 57 additionally confirms that in his instructions Isaac refers to Abraham as to an authority. MS A is confirmed by 4Q214b 5–6 i 2, which reads כדן חזית לאברהם, and by 4Q214b 4 1, which has [אנו].

L. 13 מן כל תריעשר מיני אעין *From all twelve types of wood.* E omits מן כל and מיני and, even if it causes only a minor shift in meaning, it points here to a difference between its *Vorlage* and A. The preposition מן relating to the offered kinds of wood is also attested in A 23 l. 14 and 25 ll. 21, 22, and similarly not extant in the corresponding E translation. The מין "kind, type," however, is found only here in A and is omitted by 4Q214b 2–3 2, hence its later insertion by a scribe is likely.

L 13 אעין *wood.* 4Q214b 2–3 2 attests another spelling of this word עעין (see also 4Q214b 5–6 i 5 = A 24 l. 19). The Qumran reading represents a stage in the language development before the consonantal dissimilation ‘ ‘ > ‘ ’ occurred, cf. Puech 2000: 609–611.

L. 14 די חזין להסקה מינהון למדבחה *that . . . the altar.* E translates להסקה with an imperative προσφέρε instead of an infinitive. It also omits חזין together with מינהון. MS A is confirmed by 4Q214b 5–6 i 3, which reads ל]אסקא מנהון.

L. 15 ריח תננהון בשים סליק. *smell of their smoke goes up pleasantly.* The Greek renders Aramaic תנן with καπνός, and omits ריח. The Greek lexeme is never used in the LXX in a sacrificial context, see, e.g., Exod 19:18; Josh 8:20, 21; contrast Rev 8:4. The term ריח is also attested in A 30 l. 16 in connection with the sacrifices. For תנן cf. also 11QtgJob XXXVI 5 (41:12), the cultic context is however, absent.

Ll. 15–19 Although 4Q214 frg. 1 preserves only few words, it is possible to notice that it differs from the A text. Lines 4 and 7 cannot be unequivocally identified with any MS A word and the succession of line 5 and 6 suggests that A 24 is not extant in this Qumran witness. Yet, 4Q214a 1, 4Q214b 2–3 3–4 and 4Q214b 5–6 i 4–5 unanimously attest A 24.

L. 16 ארזא *cedar.* *Cedrus libani* (Zohary 1982: 104–104), also identified as *Pinus cedrus* (Löw 1967: 17–26; Löw 1973: 56–60).

L. 16 דפרנא *juniper.* Identified by Löw (1967: 3:33 and 4:550) as *Juniperus drupacea*, in Greek ἄρκευθος. E has ουεδεφωνα, a corrupt transliteration of the Aramaic (confusion between *wāw* and *rêš*), as Charles (1908a: 248, n. 7) noticed; cf. Ethiopic *defrān* in *Jub.* 21:12. MS A is confirmed by 4Q214b 5–6 i 4, which reads ודפ]רנא.

L. 17 סנדא *almond.* Identified by Löw (1973: 374 and cf. Löw 1967: 3:152) as *Amygdalus communis.* E has here a different tree name, σψίνου "mastich" (*Pistacia Lentiscus*, cf. *LSJ s.v.*), see Sus 54. MS A corresponds to Syriac *šgdt'* (cf. Brockelmann 1928: 755a) and Ethiopic *sogād* (*Jub.* 21:12, cf. Dillmann 1955: 398), "almond tree"; cf. Hebrew שקד (Gen 43:11; Num 17:2; Jer 1:1; Qoh 12:5), Greek ἀμύγδαλος (LXX Qoh 12:5) or κάρυον (LXX Gen 43:11; Num 17:2); see also Stone and Greenfield 1996a: 63. 4Q214b 5–6 i 4 reads סינדא confirming thus MS A text.

L. 17 אמולא *silver fir.* MS E has στρόβιλον "stone pine" (*Pinus cembra* in *LSJ s.v.*; cf. *1 En.* 32:4 G). Charles (1908a: 248, n. c), considers Aramaic

to be a corrupt transliteration of the Greek term איסטרוביל×; *Jub.* 21:12
transliterates the Greek term with *saṭarobilon.* The Aramaic name, however,
is most probably a corrupt word for אלטס× with the metathesis of *ḥêt* and
lāmed, a calque from the Greek ἐλάτη, "silver fir" (*Abies cephalonica,* cf. Löw
1973: 83 and *LSJ s.v.*).

L. 17 שוחה fir. Charles (1908a: 248, n. d), conjectures שיש×. The Aramaic
term, however, corresponds to the Arabic *šūḥ, abies cilicica* (Löw 1967: 3:13,
35, 39; Grelot 1955: 98; Zohary 1982: 106–107; cf. Gen 21:15 השיחם/ἐλάτη),
and it belongs to the same family with cypress and cedar. Two additional
forms are also attested אשוחא (*b. Šabb.* 157a) and אשוחא (*Sidra Rabbah* I 265:
12; 380: 11; II 111: 17). Both terms stand in parallelism with cedar (אר×),
cf. Löw 1973: 60.

L. 17 אדונ× *ash.* Charles (1908a: 248, n. 9), considers Greek ολδινα to
be a corrupt transliteration of the Aramaic, while the Aramaic reading is
in turn a corruption for אורנ×. Löw (1967: 2:119–121) argues that the latter term means *laurus nobilis,* laurel, and not ash. In the Mishnah it is
explained with its Aramaic equivalent ער (*m. Parah* 3:8), a term that also
appears in the *Document,* line 19. It is probable that the two terms denote
a similar type of tree. Note that the lexeme אדון means "path, road, way"
(see the emph. אדונ× Aramaic Letter 6:5 in Driver 1957: 27 and 61) and
is a Persian loan word (cf. Hinz 1975: 23). It seems that the scribal corruption in our text led to the introduction of a correct Aramaic form, but
the form is, however, out of context here. Alternatively, the Aramaic reading here is a noun the meaning of which escapes the modern reader.

L. 18 ברותא *cypress.* E transliterates the Aramaic with βερωθα. For other
names of the class *cupressus sempervirens,* see Löw 1967: 26–33; cf. Zohary
1966: 19 and 1982: 106–107.

L. 18 תאנתא *fig.* E has καν θεχακ. While καν appears to be corrupt for
καί, Charles (1908a: 248, n. 10) says that θεχακ is corrupt for the MS A
ותאנתא "fig tree," a corruption similar to Ethiopic *tānāk* in *Jub.* 21:12.
4Q214b 2–3 4 preserves ותככה instead, a reading which confirms the credibility of the E transliteration. It should denote a kind of evergreen tree,
like the other species in the list. Modern Persian has *taqak*—"a tree like a
cypress or pine" (Steingass 1970: 816). In modern Syriac *tkk* means "a
creeping melon plant, or a stem on which melons, marrows and cucum-
bers grow" (Maclean 1901: 320). The fig in the Geniza manuscript is probably a misinterpretation of the word תככה that was not undertood by the
scribe.

L. 18 עץ משחא *oleaster.* Identified by Löw (1967: 1:590; 3:46; cf. Löw
1973: 138) as *Elaeagnus hortensis.* The E κυπάρισσος translates correctly the
Aramaic term (against Charles 1908a: 249). The LXX uses the Greek term
for the Hebrew ארז (Ezek 27:15; 31:3, 8; Job 40:17) or ברש (2 Kgs 19:23;
Isa 55:1; 60:1; Cant 1:17: ברות; cf. Sir 24:14; 50:10); see, however, Isa
41:19, where the LXX seems to translate עץ שמן. The same Hebrew syntagm in 1 Kgs 6:23 and Neh 8:15 is translated by the LXX with ξύλα
κυπαρίσσινα (1 Kgs 6:23 MS A). The Hebr. עץ שמן is rendered as א×
דמשחא by the targums (1 Kgs 6:23, 31, 32, 33; Isa 41:19; Neh 8:15). *Jub.*

21:12 has here *ʿṣa zayt*. The reading thus disagrees with A and is probably a mistranslation of עץ שמן, see Greenfield and Stone 1979: 221, n. 3.

L. 19 ערא *laurel*. It is an Aramaic term for laurel, *laurus nobilis*, see Löw 1967: 122. The asyndeton here surprises, cf. MS E. The scribe must have ommited a *wāw* here, for all the nouns in the verse are coordinated.

L. 19 הדסה *myrtle*. *Myrtus communis*, cf. Löw 1973: 50–51; Löw 1967: 2:257–274; Zohary 1972: 371–372. The transcriptions of MS E 18,2 in Charles and Cowley 1907: 573 and Charles 1908a: 249 inadvertently omitted καὶ μυρσίνην. Although the omission was first signaled by de Jonge (1964: XIII), scholars continue to repeat the erroneous opinion that E preserves the names of only eleven trees, see Grelot 1991: 256, n. 11, Kugler 1996a: 104, n. 151. MS A is confirmed by 4Q214b 5–6 5, which reads אסדא.

L. 19 אעי דקתא *asphaltos*. E ἀσφάλαθον. The Aramaic name is not attested in other literature. Charles (1908a: 248, n. f) conjectured דולבא, a "plane tree," as one of the ten different names applied to the cedar in *b. Roš Haš.* 23a. Lévi (1908: 285) found an equivalent expression קיסין דקיתא in *Tg. Ps.-J.* Gen 21:3, the material reading of the targumic manuscript is not certain, though. The Greek ἀσφάλαθος, meaning "a spinous shrub yielding a fragrant oil" (*LSJ s.v.*), corresponds most probably to קידה לבנה, "a white spinous shrub," cf. Löw 1967: 2:424. Assuming a metathesis between the *dālet* and *qôp* in MS A דקתא, the term could correspond to קידה/ἀσφάλαθος. Puech (2002: 530–531) proposes to read אעי ירדקתא "trees of green," or "evergreen trees"with a haplography of the *yôd*. He further cites *T. Levi* 9:19 where twelve evergreen trees are mentioned (δώδεκα δένδρων ἀεὶ ἐχόντων φύλλα); cf. *Jub.* 21:12–14; *1 En.* 3:1 (14 trees); 4QEnoch[a] 1 ii 5 (Milik 1976: 146–147); *Geoponica* 11:1 (14 trees). Most of the trees in the Aramaic list are evergreen, except for the fig tree (corrupt for תככה?) and the almond tree. Since the tree lists differ in different manuscripts and tradition, it is difficult to unequivocally accept the opinion of Puech. Other proposals remain valid. Note that 4Q214a 1 1 ends the list with הדסא, where the last item from MS A is absent. The preceding context, however, is lacking, and the order of the trees in the Qumran manuscript is different.

L. 20 לי די חזין *me that are fitting*. E ὅτι ταῦτά ἐστιν ἅ σε. Similarly to E 18,2 v. 23, the translator omits חזין and מנהון (line 21, cf. A 23 l. 13). According to Charles (1908a: 249, n. 12) E is probably a corruption for ταῦτά ἐστιν (ἅ εἴρηκέν μοι) ἃ δεῖ. E 18,2 v. 29 translates חזה with καθήκει (cf. E 18,2 vv. 31, 32, 37, 40, 51) but omits it in v. 23; v. 21 is corrupt like v. 31. It is not excluded that E here translates a different form of the Aramaic text.

Ll. 22–23 וכדי . . . על מדבחה *and when . . . on the altar*. E omits by *homoioteleuton* (line 21 על מדבחה and line 23 על מדבחה), cf. Greenfield and Stone 1979: 221. MS A is confirmed by 4Q214a 1 2 (וכ֯) and 4Q214b 2–3 6, which has א[אלן על מדבחא. 4Q214 frg. 1 probably omits the line.

L. 23 τότε. MS E, A omits. E translates באדין as τότε, cf. E 18,2 vv. 19 and 25b, line 1. The term τότε stands here between the subject and the predicate, and that is unusual for the Aramaic word order.

L. 23   The line in a smaller typeface from the next column is brought here to finish the sentence that spans the two columns.

2.1.9   *A.L.D. 25b–32a*

MS A (Bodleian d; pl. IX);
Parallels: E 18,2 (Pls. XII and XIII), *4Q214 1*, **4Q214 2**, <u>4Q214b 2–3</u>, 4Q214b 5–6 ii

ἐν αὐτοῖς, τότε ἄρξῃ κατασπένδειν τὸ αἷμα	בהון וּוהא*[a] באדין תשרא למזרק דמא	1
ἐπὶ τὸν τεῖχον τοῦ θυσιαστηρίου. (26)καὶ πάλιν νίψαι σου τὰς χεῖρας	על כותלי* מדבחהה*[c] *ועוד[d(26)] רחע ידיך	2
καὶ τοὺς πόδας ἀπὸ τοῦ αἵματος, καὶ ἄρξῃ τὰ μέλη ἀναφέρειν	ורגליך מן דמא ושרי להנסקה אבריה	3
ἡλισμένα· (27)τὴν κεφαλὴν ἀνάφερε πρῶτον	מליחין (27)ראשה הוי מהנסק לקדמין	4
καὶ κάλυπτε αυτὴν τῷ στέατι, καὶ μὴ ὀπτανέσθω	ועלוהי חפי תרבא וּלא*[e] יתחזה*[f] לה	5
τὸ αἷμα ἐπὶ τῆς κεφαλῆς αὐτῆς· (28)καὶ μετὰ τοῦτο τὸν τράχηλον,	דם נכסת תורא*[g] (28) ובתרוהי צוארה*[h]	6
καὶ μετὰ τοῦτο τοὺς ὤμους, καὶ μετὰ ταῦτα	ובתר*[i] צוארה* ידוהי*[k] ובתר ידוהי[l]	7
τὸ στῆθος μετὰ τῶν πλευρῶν, καὶ μετὰ ταῦτα	ניא* עם בן דפנא בתר*[m] ידיא*[n]	8

---

[a] E >.
[b] E τὸν τεῖχον.
[c] 4Q214b 2–3 7 מדבחהא.
[d] 4Q214b 2–3 7 ותוב.
[e] 4Q214 2 4 ואל.
[f] 4Q214 2 4 יתחזי.
[g] E ἐπὶ τῆς κεφαλῆς αὐτῆς.
[h] 4Q214 2 5 צו[ר]א.
[i] 4Q214 2 5 בתרהן.
[j] E and 4Q214 2 5 >.
[k] 4Q214 2 5 ידי.
[l] E >.
[m] 4Q214 2 6 ובת[ר]הן.
[n] E and 4Q214 2 5 >.

τὴν ὀσφὺν σὺν τῷ νώτῳ,	[o]ירכאתא* [p]עם שדרת* [q]חרצא*	9
καὶ μετὰ ταῦτα τοὺς πόδας πεπλυμένους σὺν	ובתר [r]ירכאתא* רגלין רחיען עם	10
τοῖς ἐνδοσθίοις, (29)καὶ πάντα ἡλισμένα ἐν ἅλατι ὡς	קרביא [s](29)וכולהון* מליחין במלח כדי	11
καθήκει αὐτοῖς αὐτάρκως. (30)καὶ μετὰ ταῦτα σεμίδαλιν	חזה להון [t]כמסתהון* (30)ובתר דנה נישפא	12
ἀναπεποιημένον ἐν ἐλαίῳ, καὶ μετὰ ταῦτα οἶνον σπεῖσον	בליל במשחא ובתר [u]כולא* חמר נסך	13
καὶ θυμίασον ἐπάνω λίβανον, καὶ ἢ	והקטיר עליהון לבונה [v]ויהוון* כ̊ן̊	14
τὸ ἔργον σου ἐν τάξει καὶ πᾶσα προσφορά σου εἰς εὐδόκησιν	[w]עובדיך* בסרך וכל [x]קורבניך* [לרעו]א	15
καὶ ὀσμὴν εὐωδίας ἔναντι κυρίου ὑψίστου. (31)καὶ ὅσα ἂν	לריח ניחח קודם אל עליו̊ן (31)[וכל די]	16
ποιῇς, ἐν τάξει ποίει ἃ ποιῇς ἐν μέτρῳ	תהוה עביד בסרך הוי עב[ידי [y]במשחה]	17
καὶ στάθμῳ, καὶ μὴ περισσεύσῃς μηθὲν ὅσα οὐ καθήκει.	ובמתקל [z]לא* תותר צבו די ל̇א[חזה]	18
καὶ †τῷ καθηκι τῶν† οὕτως ξύλα	ולא תחסר מן חושבן חזת ד̊[י] א̊ע̊[י]א̊	19
καθήκει ἀναφέρεσθαι ἐπὶ τὸν βωμόν·	חזין להקרבה [aa]לכל די סליק* למדב[חא]	20

---

[o] 4Q214 2 6 ירכתא.
[p] 4Q214 2 6 ושדר]ת.
[q] E >.
[r] E >.
[s] 4Q214 2 7 וכלה[ן.
[t] 4Q214 2 8 כ]מסתן.
[u] 4Q214 2 9 כלא.
[v] 4Q214 2 10 ו]להוא.
[w] E τὸ ἔργον σου; 4Q214 2 10 עבדך.
[x] E προσφορά σου.
[y] E + ἅ ποιῇς.
[z] E καὶ μὴ.

^(32a)τῷ ταύρῳ τῷ τελείῳ   21 ^(32a)לתורא רבא ככר אעין ליה במתקל
τάλαντον ξύλων καθήκει
αὐτῷ ἐν σταθμῷ,

καὶ εἰς τὸ στέαρ μόνον   22 ואם תרבא בלהודוהי סליק שיתה
ἀναφέρεσθαι ἓξ

μνᾶς· καὶ τῷ ταύρῳ τῷ δευτέρῳ   23 מנין ^{bb}ואם פר תוריך* ^{cc}הוא די סליק*

NOTES ON READINGS

L. 4 מליחין. MS A: מליחי. Charles (1908a: 250, n. a) emends to מליחין.
4Q214 2 3 and 214b 2–3 8 here overlap, confirming thus Charles' emendation.

L. 4 ראשה. MS A: ואשה. Following MS E 18,2, Charles (1908a: 250,
n. b) emends to ראשא. His emendation is confirmed by 4Q214 2 3 ראשא;
4Q214b 2–3 8 preserves the two first letters of the word that are also the
last ones of the whole fragment.

L. 6 נכסת תורא. MS A: נסבת תורא. E ἐπὶ τῆς κεφαλῆς αὐτῆς. Lévi (1907:
177, n. 2) emends נסבת to נכסת and translates "le sang de la jugulation du
boeuf." Greenfield and Stone 1979: 222 follow Lévi's emendation תורא
נ<כס>ה, but propose a different translation, "sacrifice of the ox." They
pointed to *Tg. Onq.* Lev 3:9 and 4:10 where the Aramaic נכסה translates
the Hebrew זבח. The corruption is probably due to the metathesis of *sāmek*
and *kāp*, and to the similar and easily confounded form of the *bêt* and *kāp*,
see A 32 l. 21 כבר for ככר/τάλαντον. Note that E must have had a different
Vorlage.

L. 8 ובתר ידיא. MS A: בתר. According to Charles (1907: 580 n. 8), the
text should be emended to ובתרוהי or ובתר דנא. He also proposed another
emendation ניעא (1908a: 250, n. d). 4Q214 2 6 reads here בת[ר]הן; Stone
and Greenfield (1996a: 48) considered it to be a dittography from the preceding line and eliminated it from the reconstruction. One should probably read with the Greek ובתר, cf. also line 6, 7, 7, 10.

L. 9 ירכאתא. There is an ink splash above the 'ālep.

L. 14 כ. Charles (1908a: 250) reconstructs [כל] in the lacuna, but there
should remain some traces of the *lāmed* in the manuscript. The ink traces
on the edge of the leather suggest the *kāp* and *nûn*.

L. 17 [במשחה]. With Beyer 1984: 200; for the Aramaic term, cf. 4Q554
frg. 1 iii 13, etc.

L. 19 אע[י] ד[ן] הזת אע[י]א. There remain the head of a *dālet* with its vertical stroke. The 'ālep proposed by Greenfield and Stone (1979: 230 אע[י]
הזתא) is less probable. The 'ālep and 'ayin in the following word are cer-

---

^{aa} E >.

^{bb} E καὶ τῷ ταύρῳ τῷ δευτέρῳ.

^{cc} E >.

tain. The resulting form חזת is most probably a scribal error for חזה (Puech 2002: 534). Note that the scribe wrote erroneously חזיק instead of חזין in the next line.

L. 20 חזין. MS A: חזיק. Emended with E: καθήκει.

L. 21 ככר. MS A: כבר. Emended with E: τάλαντον.

TRANSLATION

1 and then you shall begin to sprinkle blood

2 on the walls of the altar. (26) And again wash your hands

3 and your feet from the blood and start offering the portions

4 (that have been) salted. (27) First offer up the head

5 and cover it with fat so that the blood

6 of the sacrifice of the bull may not be seen. (28) And after this the neck

7 and after the neck its two forelegs and after its two forelegs

8 the breast with the flanks and after the two forelegs

9 the thigh with the spine of the loin

10 and after the thigh the two hind legs washed with

11 the entrails. (29) And all of them are salted with salt as

12 it is fitting for them, according to what they require. (30) And after this the fine flour

13 mixed with oil; and after everything pour wine

14 and burn upon them frankincense. And thus

15 your deeds will be in order and all your sacrifices [for deligh]t,

16 for a pleasing smell before God the most high. (31) [And whatever]

17 you do, do it in order, [by measure]

18 and by weight. Do not add anything that is not [fitting]

19 and do not fall short of the adequate calculation of the wo[o]d (that is)

20 required to sacrifice everything that is offered on the alt[ar].

21 [32a] For the full-grown bull, a talent of wood by weight.

22 And if its fat alone is offered, six

23 minas; and if a calf of bulls is offered,

(MS E 18,2 v. 32b) fifty minas, and for its fat alone, five minas;

COMMENTS

L. 1 והא בא באדין *and then.* Lit. "and behold, then." For the same expression at the beginning of a sentence, see 1QapGen II 1. Fitzmyer (1971: 79) noted that the particle הא seems redundant before באדין, but points to the "Syriac *hydyn* that developed from *h'* + *'dyn.* The Greek translator renders here the expression as one semantic unit, τότε, omitting והא. The Aramaic expression is preferable for syntactic reasons. The expression here is syntactically related to the preceding circumstantial clauses introduced by כדי (A 25b l. 22), cf. וכדי . . . ובאדין with the *wāw* of the apodosis in *A.L.D.* 19; 1b ll. 12–13 (?).

L. 2 כותלי *walls.* E τὸν τοῖχον. The plural is confirmed by 4Q214b 2–3 7.

L. 4 מליחין *(that have been) salted.* The passive participle absolute in plural absolute form stands in a predicative position in the clause (Puech 2002: 532; cf. 4Q214 2 3 and 214b 2–3 8) and should not be corrected to מליחיה in order to agree with אבריה (Greenfield and Stone 1979: 222).

L. 7 ידוהי *its two forelegs.* The form is most probably a dual here and in line 8 ידיא together with רגלין in line 10, cf. Puech 2002: 533.

Ll. 6–11 MS E differs considerably from A 28. The following syntagms are repeated in Aramaic: צואדה (line 7), ידוהי (line 7), ידיא (line 8), הרצא (line 9), ירכאתא (line 10). Except for הרצא, which seems to be a real omission from the Greek, the other instances are stylistic variants of the two manuscripts. The MS A repetition is spurious and not extant in 4Q214 2, which omits צואדה (line 7) and ידיא (line 8). 4Q214 2 5 and 6 has בתרהן, which seems to stand behind MS A μετὰ ταῦτα (line 9). The overall comparison of A with E and 4Q214 2 gives more credibility to the E translation that appears to reflect the Qumran manuscript more faithfully. The only major problem is caused by the E omission of הרצא (line 9). The bound form of שדרת] in 4Q214 2 6 suggests that הרצא followed it in the intervening lacuna.

L. 8 μετὰ τῶν πλευρῶν *with the flanks.* The Aramaic expression בן דפנא in singular may have resulted from the accidental omission to the *yôd* in בן, cf. Beyer 1984: 199.

L. 8 καὶ μετὰ ταῦτα *and after this.* With MS E. For the Aramaic ידיא בתר, see the note above.

L. 9 עם שדרת הרצא *with the spine of the loin.* E μετὰ τῷ νώτῳ. According to *LSJ,* the Greek lexeme νῶτον means "back, both of men and animals." When speaking of the order of sacrificed pieces, m. *Yoma* 2:3, 7 and m. *Tamid* 4:10 do not mention the *Document* expression but m. *Tamid* 4:6 earlier explains that the spine (שורה) is offered together with the spleen. Most probably, the Greek translation follows a different *Vorlage* here.

L. 11 מליחין *are salted*. Passive participle as predicate, meaning an accomplished action, cf. Segert 1975: § 6.6.3.5.1–2; Palacios 1933: §205a.

L. 12 נישפא *the fine flower*. A nominalized passive participle, cf. 11Q18 frg. 22 4 נ[שיפה. In Syr. *nšyp'* translates Hebr סלת, "fine flour," e.g. 2 Kgs 7:1, cf. Brockelmann 1928: *s.v.* E 18,2 translates with σεμίδαλις, see also E 18,2 vv. 40, 41, 43, 45, 52. The term נשיף is attested in the fourth century B.C. Aramaic ostraca from Idumaea (Eph'al and Naveh 1996, see nos. 3:3; 5:3; 6:2; 7:2; 26:2; 30:1; 48:2; 52:2).

L. 14 ויהוון *and will be*. E τὸ ηεεσθαί. Charles (1908a: 250, n. 1) considers E to be corrupt for τοῦ ἔσεσθαι, and this seems to be a plausible explanation. Yet, when compared with MS A, E should have a καί and a finite verb, not an infinitive. 4Q214 2 10 has the verb in singular, להוא. In accordance with the Qumran text it is perhaps better to emend MS E to καὶ ᾖ. The imperfect יהוון should not be rendered as a jussive "let [all] your actions follow due order (Greenfield and Stone 1985: 464, followed by Kugler 1996a: 97).

Ll. 14–15 כן עובדיך בסרך *thus your deeds will be in order*. E τὸ ἔργον σου ἐν τάξει. E does not translate כן and the subject is singular, agreeing thus with 4Q214 2 10, ולהוא עבדך בס]רך[. The A reading is a legitimate stylistic variant.

L. 17 הוי עב]יד *do it*. After this clause E inserts a relative sentence: ἃ ποιῇς "what you do."

L. 19 א[ע]ין ד]ין הות חושבן *the adequate calculation of the wo[o]d*. Greenfield and Stone (1985: 464, n. d) considered their reading הותא to be a corrupt word, but Beyer (1984: 576) parses it as an emphatic feminine participle הוה with an omission of *yôd*. In this case, however, the following word should be prefixed with a *lāmed*, הו<י>תא לאעין. The form הות results from an accidental corruption of הזה.

L. 19 א[ע]ין חזין להקרבה *the wood (that is) required to sacrifice*. The participle חזין should be interpreted as a predicate of the clause with the omission of the verb היה, similarly to the clause in lines 3–4 אבריה מליחין.

L. 20 לכל די סליק *everything that is offered*. E omits. The repetition of *lāmed* in line 20 (למדב]חא[;לכל; להקרבה) could have caused the translator's omission of the Aramaic syntagm. However, E might have read a different Aramaic text, given the fact that in the next verse it omits a similar Aramaic expression (A 32 l. 23 הוא די סליק).

L. 21 תו]רא רבא *full-grown bull*. The Greek has here the adjective τέλειος "perfect, without spot or blemish" often qualifying sacrificial victims, cf. *LSJ s.v.*; E 18,2 vv. 33, 36; Exod 12:5 LXX (Hebrew תמים). The Aramaic *Vorlage* of MS E may have had here שלימא, which usually translates Hebrew תמים in the targums. The Aramaic reading probably underlies τῷ ταύρῳ τῷ μεγάλῳ in E 18,2 vv. 37, 41.

L. 21 ככר אעין *a talent of wood*. E adds καθήκει "is fitting."

L. 23 ואם פר תורין *and if a calf of bulls*. E καὶ τῷ ταύρῳ τῷ δευτέρῳ "and for the second bull," see E 18,2 vv. 38 and 41. E assumes a different reading: ולתור תרין. The expression פר תורין is a rare syntagm in MT, found only in Judg 6:25. Greenfield and Stone (1985: 464) assume that a copyist of A misread תרין for תורין. This explanation, however, does not account for the presence of a Hebraism פר in the discussed expression. E translates here a slightly different Aramaic text; it assumes a different preposition (*lāmed*) and omits the Aramaic הוא די סליק in the same line. A similar expression in A 31 l. 20 (סליק לכל די) is also absent in E. Therefore, it should not be excluded that A פר תורין is a legitimate variant reading and that the Greek translator had a different text in front of him.

L. 23   The line in a smaller typeface from the next column is brought here to finish the sentence that spans the two manuscripts.

2.1.10 *A.L.D. 32b–64*
MS E 18,2 (Pls. XIII, XIV, and XV)

(32b) πεντήκοντα μνᾶς, καὶ εἰς τὸ στέαρ αὐτοῦ μόνον πέντε μνᾶς·

(33) καὶ εἰς μόσχον τέλειον μ΄ μναῖ·

(34) καὶ εἰ κριὸς ἐκ προβάτων ἢ τράγος ἐξ αἰγῶν τὸ προσφερόμενον ᾖ, καὶ τούτῳ λ΄ μναῖ, καὶ τῷ στέατι τρεῖς μναῖ·

(35) καὶ εἰ ἄρνα ἐκ προβάτων ἢ ἔριφον ἐξ αἰγῶν κ΄ μναῖ, καὶ τῷ στέατι β΄ μναῖ·

(36) καὶ εἰ ἀμνὸς τέλειος ἐνιαύσιος ἢ ἔριφος ἐξ αἰγῶν ιε΄ μναῖ, καὶ τῷ στέατι μίαν ἥμισυ μνᾶν.

(37) καὶ ἅλας ἀποδέδεικται τῷ ταύρῳ τῷ μεγάλῳ, ἅλισε τὸ κρέας αὐτοῦ, καὶ ἀνένεγκε ἐπὶ τὸν βωμόν. σάτον καθήκει τῷ ταύρῳ· καὶ ᾧ ἂν περισσεύσῃ τοῦ ἁλός, ἅλισον ἐν αὐτῷ τὸ δέρμα·

(38) καὶ τῷ ταύρῳ τῷ δευτέρῳ τὰ πέντε μέρη ἀπὸ τῶν ἐξ μερῶν τοῦ σάτου· καὶ τοῦ μόσχου τὸ δίμοιρον τοῦ σάτου·

(39) καὶ τῷ κριῷ τὸ ἥμισυ τοῦ σάτου καὶ τῷ τράγῳ τὸ ἴσον·

(40a) καὶ τὸ ἀρνίῳ καὶ τῷ ἐρίφῳ τὸ τρίτον τοῦ σάτου.

(40b) καὶ σεμίδαλις καθήκουσα αὐτοῖς·

(41) τῷ ταύρῳ τῷ μεγάλῳ καὶ τῷ ταύρῳ τῷ β΄ καὶ τῷ μοσχαρίῳ, σάτον σεμίδαλιν·

(42) καὶ τῷ κριῷ καὶ τῷ τράγῳ τὰ δύο μέρη τοῦ σάτου καὶ τῷ ἀρνίῳ καὶ τῷ ἐρίφῳ ἐξ αἰγῶν τὸ τρίτον τοῦ σάτου. καὶ τὸ ἔλαιον·

(43) καὶ τὸ τέταρτον τοῦ σάτου τῷ ταύρῳ ἀναπεποιημένον ἐν τῇ σεμιδάλει ταύτῃ·

(44) καὶ τῷ κριῷ τὸ ἔκτον τοῦ σάτου καὶ τῷ ἀρνίῳ τὸ ὄγδοον τοῦ σάτου καὶ

ἀμνοῦ καὶ οἶνον κατὰ τὸ μέτρον τοῦ ἐλαίου τῷ ταύρῳ καὶ τῷ κριῷ καὶ τῷ ἐρίφῳ κατασπεῖσαι σπονδήν.

(45) λιβανωτοῦ σίκλοι ἓξ τῷ ταύρῳ καὶ τὸ ἥμισυ αὐτοῦ τῷ κριῷ καὶ τὸ τρίτον αὐτοῦ τῷ ἐρίφῳ. καὶ πᾶσα ἡ σεμίδαλις ἀναπεποιημένη,

(46a) ἢ<ν> ἂν προσαγάγῃς μόνον, οὐκ ἐπὶ στέατος, προσαχθήσεται ἐπ᾽ αὐτὴν λιβάνου ὁλκὴ σίκλων δύο.

(46b) καὶ τὸ τρίτον τοῦ σάτου τὸ τρίτον τοῦ ὑφή ἐστιν·

(47) καὶ τὰ δύο μέρη τοῦ βάτου καὶ ὁλκῆς τῆς μνᾶς ν΄ σίκλων ἐστίν· καὶ τοῦ σικλίου τὸ τέταρτον ὁλκὴ θερμῶν δ΄ ἐστιν· γίνεται ὁ σίκλος ὡσεὶ ις΄ θέρμοι καὶ ὁλκῆς μιᾶς.

(48) καὶ νῦν, τέκνον μου, ἄκουσον τοὺς λόγους μου καὶ ἐνωτίσαι τὰς ἐντολάς μου, καὶ μὴ ἀποστήτωσαν οἱ λόγοι μου οὗτοι ἀπὸ τῆς καρδίας σου ἐν πάσαις ταῖς ἡμέραις σου, ὅτι ἱερεὺς συ ἅγιος κυρίου,

(49) καὶ ἱερεῖς ἔσονται πᾶν τὸ σπέρμα σου· καὶ τοῖς υἱοῖς σου οὕτως ἔντειλον ἵνα ποιήσουσιν κατὰ τὴν κρίσιν ταύτην ὡς σοὶ ὑπέδειξα.

(50) οὕτως γάρ μοι ἐνετείλατο ὁ πατὴρ Ἀβραὰμ ποιεῖν καὶ ἐντέλλεσθαι τοῖς υἱοῖς μου.

(51) καὶ νῦν, τέκνον, χαίρω ὅτι ἐξελέχθης εἰς ἱερωσύνην ἁγίαν καὶ προσ-ενεγκεῖν θυσίαν κυρίῳ ὑψίστῳ, ὡς καθήκει κατὰ τὸ προστεταγμένον τοῦτο ποιεῖν.

(52) ὅταν παραλαμβάνῃς θυσίαν ποιεῖν ἔναντι κυρίου ἀπὸ πάσης σαρκός, κατὰ τὸν λογισμὸν τῶν ξυλῶν ἐπιδέχου οὕτως, ὡς σοὶ ἐντέλλομαι, καὶ τὸ ἅλας καὶ τὴν σεμίδαλιν καὶ τὸν οἶνον καὶ τὸν λίβανον ἐπιδέχου ἐκ τῶν χειρῶν αὐτῶν ἐπὶ πάντα κτήνη.

(53) καὶ ἐπὶ πᾶσαν ὥραν νίπτου τὰς χεῖρας καὶ τοὺς πόδας, ὅταν πορεύῃ πρὸς τὸ θυσιαστήριον· καὶ ὅταν ἐκπορεύῃς ἐκ τῶν ἁγίων, πᾶν αἷμα μὴ ἁπτέσθω τῆς στολῆς σου· οὐκ ἀνήψῃς αὐτῷ αὐθήμερον·

(54) καὶ τὰς χεῖρας καὶ τοὺς πόδας νίπτου διὰ παντὸς ἀπὸ πάσης σαρκός.

(55) καὶ μὴ ὀφθήτω ἐπὶ σοι πᾶν αἷμα καὶ πᾶσα ψυχή· τὸ γὰρ αἷμα ψυχή ἐστιν ἐν τῇ σαρκί.

(56) καὶ ὃ ἐάν ἐν οἴκῳ †ουσης† σεαυτὸν πᾶν κρέας φαγεῖν, κάλυπτε τὸ αἷμα αὐτοῦ τῇ γῇ πρῶτον πρὶν ἢ φαγεῖν σε ἀπὸ τῶν κρεῶν καὶ οὐκέτι ἔσῃ ἐσθίων ἐπὶ τοῦ αἵματος.

(57) οὕτως γάρ μοι ἐνετείλατο ὁ πατήρ μου Ἀβραάμ, ὅτι οὕτως εὗρεν ἐν τῇ γραφῇ τῆς βίβλου τοῦ Νῶε περὶ τοῦ αἵματος.

(58) καὶ νῦν ὡς σοί, τέκνον ἀγαπητόν, ἐγὼ λέγω, ἠγαπημένος σὺ τῷ πατρί σου καὶ ἅγιος κυρίου ὑψίστου· καὶ ἠγαπημένος ἔσῃ ὑπὲρ πάντας τοὺς ἀδελφούς σου.

(59) τῷ σπέρματί σου εὐλογηθήσεται ἐν τῇ γῇ καὶ τὸ σπέρμα σου ἕως πάντων τῶν αἰώνων ἐνεχθήσεται ἐν βιβλίῳ μνημοσύνου ζωῆς·

(60) καὶ οὐκ ἐξαλειφθήσεται τὸ ὄνομά σου καὶ τὸ ὄνομα τοῦ σπέρματός σου ἕως τῶν αἰώνων.

(61) καὶ νῦν, τέκνον Λευί, εὐλογημένον ἔσται τὸ σπέρμα σου ἐπὶ τῆς γῆς εἰς πάσας τὰς γενεὰς τῶν αἰώνων.

(62) καὶ ὅτε ἀνεπληρώθησάν μοι ἑβδομάδες τέσσαρες ἐν τοῖς ἔτεσιν τῆς ζωῆς μου, ἐν ἔτει ὀγδόῳ καὶ εἰκοστῷ ἔλαβον γυναῖκα ἐμαυτῷ ἐκ τῆς συγγενείας Ἀβραὰμ τοῦ πατρός μου, Μελχάν, θυγατέρα Βαθουήλ, υἱοῦ Λάβαν, ἀδελφοῦ μητρός μου.

(63) καὶ ἐν γαστρὶ λαβοῦσα ἐξ ἐμοῦ ἔτεκεν υἱὸν πρῶτον, καὶ ἐκάλεσα τὸ ὄνομα αὐτοῦ Γηρσώμ· εἶπα γὰρ ὅτι πάροικον ἔσται τὸ σπέρμα μου ἐν γῇ, ᾗ ἐγεννήθην· πάροικοί ἐσμεν ὡς τοῦτο ἐν τῇ γῇ ἡμετέρᾳ νομιζομένῃ.

(64) καὶ ἐπὶ τοῦ παιδαρίου εἶδον ἐγὼ ἐν τῷ ὁράματί μου ὅτι ἐκβεβλημένος ἔσται αὐτὸς καὶ τὸ σπέρμα αὐτοῦ ἀπὸ τῆς ἀρχῆς ἱερωσύνης ἔσται τὸ σπέρμα αὐτοῦ.

TRANSLATION

(32b) fifty minas, and for its fat alone, five minas;

(33) and for the bullock without blemish, 40 minas.

(34) And if a ram of the sheep or a he-goat of the goats is offered, and for it 30 minas and for the fat three minas;

(35) and if it is a lamb of the sheep or a kid of the goats, 20 minas and for the fat 2 minas;

(36) and if it is a one-year-old lamb without blemish or a kid of the goats, 15 minas and for the fat one mina and a half.

(37) When salt has been brought forward for the full-grown bull, salt its flesh and offer it on the altar; a seah is fitting for the bull; and if some salt is left over, salt with it the skin.

(38) And for the second bull, five out of six parts of a seah; and for the bullock, two thirds of a seah.

(39) And for the ram, a half of a seah, and the same for the he-goat;

(40a) and for the little lamb and the kid, a third of a seah.

(40b) And the fine flour fitting for them:

(41) for the full-grown bull and for the second bull and for the bullock, a seah of fine flour;

(42) and for the ram and the he-goat, two parts of a seah and for the little lamb and the kid of the goats, a third of the seah; and the oil:

(43) and one fourth of the seah for the bull, mixed with this fine flour;

(44) and for the ram, one sixth of the seah, and for the little lamb the eighth of the seah, and of the lamb, and pour out wine as a drink offering according to the measure of the oil for the bull and ram and kid.

(45) Six shekels of frankincense for the bull and half of it for the ram and one third of it for the kid. And all the mixed up fine flour,

(46a) whenever you offer it up alone (and) not on the fat, the weight of two shekels of incense will be brought on it.

(46b) And one third of the seah is one third of the ephah;

(47) and the two parts of the bath and of the weight of a mina are of fifty shekels; and one fourth of the shekel is the weight of four thermoi; the shekel is of one weight with about sixteen thermoi.

(48) And now, my child, listen to my words and hearken to my commandments, and let these my words not leave your heart all your days, because you are a holy priest of the Lord,

(49) and all your seed will be priests; and command your sons in such a way that they do according to this law as I have shown you.

(50) For thus father Abraham commanded me to do and to command my sons.

(51) And now, my son, I rejoice that you have been chosen for the

holy priesthood and to offer sacrifice to the Lord most high, as it is fitting to do, according to what has been commanded.

(52) When you receive the sacrifice to make before the Lord from every flesh, according to the calculation of the wood accept thus as I order you, and the salt and fine flour and wine and incense accept from their hands for the whole cattle.

(53) And each time wash the hands and the feet, when you approach the altar; and when you exit from the sanctuary, let no blood adhere to your garment; do not cling to it on the same day,

(54) but the hands and feet wash continually from all flesh.

(55) And let not any blood and any soul appear on you, since the blood is the soul in the flesh.

(56) And when you are at home yourself to eat any flesh, hide its blood in the earth first before you eat from the flesh and you will not eat of the blood any longer.

(57) For thus my father Abraham ordered me, because thus he found in the writing of the Book of Noah concerning the blood.

(58) And now, as I tell you, beloved son, you are beloved to your father and a holy one of the Lord Most High and you will be beloved more than all your brothers.

(59) There will be blessing by your seed on the earth and your seed will be brought for all the ages into the book of the memorial of life.

(60) and your name and the name of your seed will not be blotted out for ages.

(61) And now, child Levi, your seed will be blessed on the earth for all the generations of the ages."

(62) And when four weeks were fulfilled for me in the years of my life, in the twenty eighth year, I took a wife for myself from the family of Abraham my father, Melcha, a daughter of Bathuel, son of Laban, brother of my mother.

(63) And she conceived by me, bore the first son, and I called his name Gershom since I said: "my seed will be sojourners in the land where I was born. We are sojourners as it (will be) in the land which is considered ours."

(64) And concerning the child I saw in my vision that he and his seed will be thrown out from the chief priesthood, his seed will be.

COMMENTS

V. 33 The bullock has no amount of wood assigned to its fat, and that is probably due to the unintentional omission of the stereotyped phrase, "and for its fat only—x minas."

V. 37 ἀποδέδεικται *has been brought forward*. MS E: αποδεδεικτω. Charles (1908a: 251, n. 1) considered the Greek to be corrupt for ἀποδείκνυμι, then emended to הורה/βάλλε and translated "sprinkle" (1908b: 231). The corruption affected only the ending of the otherwise regular passive perfect ἀποδέδεικται, and was probably caused by the following article τῷ. If it is true, ἅλας "salt" is the subject of the verb and the καί (*wāw*) before ἅλας introduces a circumstantial clause, cf. Segert 1975: § 7.5.3.3; Muraoka and Porten 1998: 321–322.

V. 37 ἅλισε *salt*. MS E: αλησε, corrupt for aorist impv. ἅλισε from ἀλίζω, "to salt."

V. 37 σάτον *a seah*. A dry measure attested in the LXX in Hag 2:16,16 without a Hebrew correspondence. The Greek term is a borrowing from the Aramaic סאתא, cf. Walters 1973: 327–328; see also Matt 13:33 and Luke 13:21. For the sake of consistency in transliterating the Semitic terms of weights and measures, the term is rendered as "seah" in the translation.

V. 40a τῷ ἀρνίῳ *little lamb*. See E 18,2 v. 40a and also E 18,2 v. 44, where the term is distinct from ἀμνός.

V. 44 καὶ ἀμνοῦ *and of the lamb*. The noun in genitive is out of context here, the preceding nouns (ram, little lamb) being in dative. Grelot (1991: 257, n. 2) considers these two words as an application of the preceding measures concerning the little lamb (ἀρνίον) to the lamb as well. His suggestion is very plausible for, in E 18,2 vv. 40b–44, which deal with the quantity of fine flour applied to the sacrificed animals, ἀμνός is mentioned only in this place.

V. 46a προσαχθήσεται *will be brought*. MS E: προσωχθήσεται. Charles' proposal to read it as a corrupt form of προσενεχθήσεται (1908a: 251, n. 3) is too distant from the attested form. The simplest explanation is to read the form as a passive future of προσάγω, that is προσαχθήσεται, cf. LXX Lev 14:2; the corruption consists in an accidental and frequent shift from *alfa* to *omega*. The verb is very common in LXX Leviticus, has a clear sacrificial meaning and often translates הקריב, e.g. Lev 1:2, 3, 10; 3:1, 1, 3, 7. Additionally, it is also attested at the beginning of the verse and in E 2,3 v. 11.

V. 46b τὸ τρίτον τοῦ σάτου τὸ τρίτον τοῦ ὑφῆ ἐστιν *one third of the seah is one third of the ephah*. Since a seah is a third of an ephah, it is highly probable that the Greek translation is corrupt here.

V. 53 οὐκ ἀνήψῃς αὐτῷ *do not cling to it*. The verb is an aorist active subjunctive from ἀνάπτω *make fast on or to* (*LSJ s.v. I*). Charles (1908b: 232) translated ἀνάπτω *to light up, kindle* (LSL *s.v. II*) and marked the clause as corrupt, *Thou shalt not †kindle it the same day.†* The context, in fact, does not allow his translation, and it is difficult to imagine that Isaac instructs Levi to burn blood. Greenfield and Stone (1985: 465) rendered the verb as a passive form *be not connected with it.* This translation fits the context much better than the preceding one because in v. 53b and 55 Isaac instructs Levi to avoid any contact with blood. The rendering, however, should take into consideration the active form of the Greek verb.

V. 55   καὶ πᾶσα ψυχή *and any soul.* This syntagm is probably an explanatory transposition from the following clause in which blood is identified as the principle of life ψυχή (נפש).

V. 56   καὶ ὃ ἐάν ἐν οἴκῳ †ουσης† *And when you are at home.* The text is corrupt and needs emendation. The expression ὃ ἐάν is a corruption for ὅταν, cf. E 18,2 vv. 19, 20, 21, 52, 53, 53. The latter term translates Aramaic כדי (vv. 19; 20; 21) and is followed by a modal form of the verb. The form ουσης is seemingly the feminine singular present participle from εἰμί in genitive case, but the context would demand a finite modal form ᾖς. The proposed emendation runs as follows: καὶ ὅταν ἐν οἴκῳ ᾖς.

V. 56   σεαυτὸν *yourself.* The reflexive personal pronoun in accusative is awkward here.

V. 59   τῷ σπέρματί σου εὐλογηθήσεται ἐν τῇ γῇ *There will be blessing by your seed on the earth.* Usually the dative as the indirect object of the verb in passive form translates the Aramaic *lāmed.* The verb, however, "to bless" is usually followed by the preposition ב, the Aramaic retroversion should therefore run ובזרעך יתברך בארעא. The preposition ב in בזרעך is best taken in the instrumental sense, while the verb (*'itpa'el*)—impersonally; cf. *Tg. Onq.* Gen 12:3 ויתברכן בדילך כל זרעית ארעא.

V. 63   ὡς τοῦτο *as it (will be).* MS E 18,2 has a corrupt reading τούτῳ. It can be easily explained by a frequent shift in the manuscript between *omikron* and *omega* and vice versa. The pronoun refers to τὸ σπέρμα μου located earlier in the verse.

V. 64   τῆς ἀρχῆς ἱερωσύνης *the chief priesthood.* With Charles (1908b: 233); Beyer translates with "Amt des Priestertums"; Greenfield and Stone "the highpriesthood" (1985: 467). The comparison with A 9 ll. 17–18 suggests the Aramaic ראש כהנותא, cf. E 18,2 v. 67. Charles' translation is a good literal rendering of this expression.

V. 64.   ἔσται τὸ σπέρμα αὐτοῦ *his seed will be.* E attests a dittographic repetition of the syntagm at the end of the verse, see Greenfield and Stone 1985: 466, n. k.

2.1.11   *A.L.D. 65–72*

MS A (Cambridge c; pl. VII);
Parallels: MS E 18,2 (Pl. XV), <u>4Q214a frg. 2 i</u>

---

(65)λ´ ἐτῶν ἤμην ὅτε ἐγεννήθη   [בר שנין תלתין הוית כדי יליד בחיי](65) 1
ἐν τῇ ζωῇ μου,

Greek	#	Hebrew/Aramaic
καὶ ἐν τῷ ι΄ μηνὶ ἐγεννήθη ἐπὶ δυσμὰς ἡλίου.	2	[וביר]חא עשיריא יליד עם מעלי שמש[א
(66)καὶ πάλιν συλλαβοῦσα ἔτεκεν ἐξ ἐμοῦ κατὰ τὸν καιρὸν τὸν καθήκοντα τῶν γυναικῶν,	3	(66)[ ]והו[ן]ה כזמ[נ]א הוה לנשין והוית[ע֗[מ]֗ה
	4	[וה]רֿת עוד [מני וילידת לי ^aבר] אֿחרֿ[*]
καὶ ἐκάλεσα τὸ ὄνομα αὐτοῦ Κααθ. (67)καὶ ὅτε ἐγεννήθη, ἑώρακα ὅτι ἐπ᾽ αὐτῷ	5	[וקרא]֗תי שמה ק֗[הת ^b(67)וחזי]֗ת די לה
ἔσται ἡ συναγωγὴ παντὸς τοῦ λαοῦ καὶ ὅτι αὐτῷ ἔσται	6	[תהו]ה כנשת כל [עמא וד]֗י לה תהוה
ἡ ἀρχιερωσύνη ἡ μεγάλη· αὐτὸς καὶ τὸ σπέρμα αὐτοῦ ἔσονται ἀρχὴ βασιλέων, ἱεράτευμα τῷ Ἰσραήλ.	7	כהנותא רבתא ^cל[כל יש]ראל vacat
(68)ἐν τῷ τετάρτῳ καὶ λ΄ ἔτει	8	vac (68)בשנת ארב[ע ות]לתין לחיי
ἐγεννήθη ἐν τῷ πρώτῳ μηνὶ μιᾷ τοῦ μηνὸς	9	יליד בירחא קמיֿא [בח]֗ד לירח[א]
ἐπ᾽ ἀνατολῆς ἡλίου. (69a)καὶ πάλιν	10	ועוד(69a) vacat [שמש]א עם מדנח
συνεγενόμην αὐτῇ καὶ ἐν γαστρὶ ἔλαβεν, καὶ ἔτεκέν μοι υἱὸν	11	אוספת והוית ע֗[מ]֗ה^d וילידת לי בר
τρίτον, καὶ ἐκάλεσα τὸ ὄνομα αὐτοῦ Μεραρί·	12	תליתי וקראתי שמה מררי ארי
ἐλυπήθην γὰρ περὶ αὐτοῦ.	13	מר לי עלוהי(69b)להדה ארי <u>כדי יליד</u>
	14	הוא מית והווה מריר לי <u>עלוהי</u>

---

^a E >.
^b E + ὅτε ἐγεννήθη.
^c E + αὐτὸς καὶ τὸ σπέρμα αὐτοῦ ἔσονται ἀρχὴ βασιλέων, ἱεράτευμα.
^d E + καὶ ἐν γαστρὶ ἔλαβεν.

15 סניא מן די ימות ובעית והתחננת

16 עלוהי והוה בכל מרר vacat (70)בשנת

17 ארבעין לחיי יילדת ביירהה ᶜתליתיᵃ*

18 (71)ועוד אוספת והויתי עמהא והרת

19 וילדת לי ברתא ᶠושויתי* שמהא

20 יוכבֿד אמרֿת כדי ילדת לי ליקר

21 ילדת לי לכבוד לישראל vacat

22 (72)בשנת שתין וארבע לי לחיי וילדת

23 בחד בחודשא ᵍשביˇעˇיˇאˇ* מן בתר די

NOTES ON READING

Ll. 1–5 Vv. 65 and 66 are reconstructed on the basis of E 18,2 vv. 65–66.

L. 2 [מעלי שמש]א. For the reconstructed syntagm, see Dan 6:15.

L. 3 והו[ה. Beyer (1984: 202) restored עמ[ה but it does not correspond to MS E Greek text. Although A 66 ll. 3–4 is very fragmentary, it seems not to follow the word order of E. The proposal here is no less hypothetical than Beyer's but it attempts to reflect as closely as possible the Aramaic syntax and order of the sentence. Note that the order of the sentence in MS 18,2 does not correspond to the reconstructed Aramaic clause, see Comments on lines 3–4 below. Greenfield and Stone's reading]ה כומ[(1979: 223) cannot be accepted

L. 3 [הוה]. Cf. A 29 l. 12 חזה/καθήκει.

L. 3 וה[מ]ע̇ה̇ [והוית. For the reconstructed expression, cf. lines 11 and 18. One can discern the lower part of an 'ayin and some ink traces of the head of a hê.

L. 4 [וה]ר̇ת. Only tāw and the head of a rêš stand in the manuscript.

L. 4 א̇ה̇ר̇ן̇. One can discern the axis and left leg of an 'ālep and the two legs of the hê. The last two letters are partially abraded.

L. 6 תהוה. Faint traces of the horizontal crossbar of a hê are discernible together with the vertical right leg of this letter.

L. 7 כהנ̇ת̇א̇. Only the lower parts of the first three letters are preserved.

L. 7 ל[כל. The hook of a lāmed is preserved at the border of the intervening lacuna.

ᶜ 4Q214a 2 i 3 ת]ל̇שׁעא.

ᶠ 4Q214a 2 i 4 ושוית.

ᵍ 4Q214a 2 i 6 שב]יˇעא.

L. 9   [א]לירדֹֿ. The horizontal crossbar of the *ḥêt* together with its right downstroke have been preserved in the manuscript. The *yôd* is well visible.

L. 11   עֹ.[מ]הֿ. The left leg of a *hê* together with the beginning of its crossbar are discernible at the end of the lacuna.

L. 12   תליהֹי. No lacuna occurs in this place, the leather, however, is torn and abraded. Only faint ink traces remain from the first *yôd*. One would expect the regular ordinal תליתי, cf. A 3c l. 1; 70 l. 17; 81 l. 2.

L. 13   End of E 18,2.

L. 16   והוה. One should not read a Hebrew form היה (Charles 1908: 253). For a similar *wāw*, cf. A 11 l. 3 אבונן, A 12 l. 4 לכולנא.

L. 19   אמרֹת. Some ink traces remain from the head of a *rêš*.

L. 20   יוכבֹד. Notwithstanding the lacuna in this place, the crossbar of a *dālet* together with its right downstroke are well preserved.

L. 22   וילידת. The *wāw* before the verb causes a syntactic incongruity. It might have been introduced by a scribal mistake similar to A 89 l. 20 ויקר.

TRANSLATION

1 (65) [I was thirty years old when he was born in my life,]

2 [and he was born in the tenth month at sunse]t.

3 (66) [And it happen]ed about the ti[me appropriate for women, and I was] wi[th h]er,

4 [and she concei]ved again [by me and bore me] another [son],

5 [and I call]ed his name [Qahat. (67) And I sa]w that to him

6 [would belo]ng the congregation of all the [people and th]at to him would belong

7 the high priesthood (He and his seed will be a supreme kingship, a priesthood) for [all Is]rael.

8 (68) In the fou[r and th]irtieth year of my life

9 he was born, in the first month on the [fir]st day of the mon[th]

10 at sunris[e]. vacat (69a) And once again

11 I was wi[th] her and she bore me a third son,

12 and I called his name Merari, for

13 I was exceedingly bitter on his account, (69b) for when he was born

14 he was dying, and I was very bitter on his account

15 because he was about to die. And I besought and asked for mercy

16 for him and it was in all bitterness. vacat [(70)] In the fortieth year

17 of my life she gave birth in the third month.

18 [(71)] And again I was with her, and she conceived

19 and bore me a daughter and I gave her the name

20 Yochebed, (for) I sai[d]: "When she was born to me, for the glory

21 she was born to me, for the glory of Israel."

22 [(72)] In the sixty-fourth year of my life she was born to me

23 on the first day of the seventh month after that

(Cambridge d, 1–2) we were brou[ght] to Egypt, in the sixteen[th] year of our entry into the land of Egypt.

COMMENTS

Ll. 3–4

[2](καὶ πάλιν συλλαβοῦσα)   [1]() והו[נ]ה כזמ[נא חזה לנשין [והוית] ע[מ]ה)
[3](ἔτεκεν ἐξ ἐμοῦ)

[1](κατὰ τὸν καιρὸν τὸν   [2]([והע]רת עוד) ([מני [3]וילידת לי בר] אחר[ן)
καθήκοντα τῶν γυναικῶν)

Although A is very fragmentary, it is possible to notice that it does not follow the clause order of the Greek (A: 1–2–3; E: 2–3–1). The translator's eye may have skipped over one part of the sentence because of the *homoioarcton* (והרת–והוה), then, having noticed the omission, he added it at the end of the sentence. E also does not have any direct object of τίκτω (cf. E 18,2 vv. 63 and 69) and the prepositional phrase ἐξ ἐμοῦ should be joined to συλλαβοῦσα (cf. E 18,2 v. 63), τίκτω being usually followed by indirect object in dative (cf. E 18,2 v. 69; *LSJ*, s.v.).

L. 5 והו[נ]ת די לה *[And I sa]w*. MS E adds ὅτε ἐγεννήθη *when he was born*. The width of the intervening lacuna in A does not allow the assumption that this E syntagm was in the A manuscript (כדי יליד). The E *Vorlage* was probably different in this place.

L. 7 αὐτὸς . . . ἱεράτευμα *he . . . priesthood*. A omits. Greenfield and Stone (1985: 466, n. a) affirmed that the MS E reading was lost in A by parablepsis; Grelot (1991: 259, n. 22) assumes that A might have been lacunose and that E clumsily follows LXX Exod 19:6; cf. also Baarda 1988: 219–221. The Greek clause makes clear that it is a translation of a Semitic *Vorlage* different from MS A. Even if someone dispenses the Greek addition as a gloss, it would be an impossible task for him to explain, given our limited knowledge of the manuscript history, on which stage of the textual transmission it entered the manuscript. The sentence fits the overall context that ascribes royal characteristics to the Levitical priesthood (cf. *A.L.D.* 3c l. 2; 67; 99; 100). The clause does not follow Exod 19:6 (LXX) but is inspired by the *Document*'s content and vocabulary. The translator's choice of a rare LXX lemma ἱεράτευμα (Exod 19:6; 23:22; 2 Macc 2:17; cf. 1 Pet 2:5, 9) proves only his acquaintance with the LXX vocabulary in his interpretation of the Aramaic text. It is not enough, however, to posit a *textual* dependence of the Greek version of the *Document* on Exod 19:6. Here is our tentative retranslation of the clause into Aramaic: ראש מלכין כהנותא הוא וזרעה יהוון. It is very probable that the omission was caused by parablepsis and *homoioteleuton*: רבתא כהנותא – כהנותא.

L. 8   ארב]ע *four/r*. E ἐνιαυτῷ. The Greek text has a corrupt reading for τετάρτῳ, cf. Charles 1908a: 253, n. 3.

L. 8   לחיי *of my life*. The Aramaic syntagm is well attested in the biographical section of the composition, see A 70 l. 17; 72 l. 22;75 l. 10; 82 l. 4; see also A 9 l. 22; 81 l. 1. The Greek translator must have omitted it, creating ambiguity.

L. 9   בירחא קמיא *in the first month*. The assimilation of *dālet* in קמאה is common in later targumic literature, cf. Dalman 1905: 103; Beyer 1984: 94, n. 1; contrast A 9 l. 17 (קדמי); 4Q209 7 iii 2 (קדמיא). The introduction of this late form should be ascribed to a medieval copyist.

L. 11   καὶ ἐν γαστρὶ ἔλαβεν *and she conceived*. A omits. The omission is probably due to a *homoioarcton* (והרת) – (והוית).

L. 14   הוא מית *he was dying*. The periphrastic tense with the perfect of הוה indicates here an ongoing process and not a completed action, cf. Grelot 1955: 93; Muraoka and Porten 1998: 205. The imperfect in the next line ימות indicates a similar aspect of the action. *T. Levi* 11:7 MS *b* has ἀπέθανεν "he died," in aorist, while MSS *l, m, e, a, f* read ἀπέθνῃσκεν "he was dying," impf. indicative, thus agreeing with the Aramaic verbs.

Ll. 14–15   והוה מריר ... ימות *And I was ... to die*. Charles and Cowley (1908a: 253, n. a) considered the clause to be a dittograph of the preceding הוא מית ... מר לי (A 69 ll. 13–14). Although the wording of this clause is similar to the preceding sentence, it should be noted that all names of Levi's children have a double explanation, cf. E 18,2 vv. 63–64 (Gershon); E 18,2 v. 67 (Qahat); A 69 ll. 12–15 (Merari); A 71 ll. 20–21 (Yochebed). On the other hand, the reconstruction of 4Q214a 2 i suggests that the syntagm מן די ימות was not extant in this Qumran manuscript. The rest of the clause, however, is part of the Qumran manuscript. The underlined syntagm is present in the Qumran manuscript and the line length supposes the presence of what precedes it in the missing part of the line (see the reconstruction of 4Q214a 2 i in § 2.2.5).

L. 15   ובעית והתחננת *And I besought and asked for mercy*. In 1QapGen XX 12 this syntagm is used in Abraham's sorrowful prayer against the pharaoh Zoan, see also 4Q204 1 vi 18 (*1 En.* 14:7). Grelot (1955: 94) parses the second verb as a *hitpeᶜel* with a passive meaning "recevoir miséricorde, être exaucé," attested in Syriac. His argument is flawed by the assumption that the form translates a Hebrew *nipᶜal*. The verbal form should be parsed as a *hitpaᶜal*, "to entreat, pray for mercy," cf. 1QapGen XX 12; 4Q204 1 vi 18 (14:7); 11QtgJob XXXV 6 (40:27); Charles 1908b: 233.

L. 16. בכל מרד *in all bitterness*. It is an adverbial circumstantial clause similar to במרד (*Tg. Isa* 22:4; 33:7) as pointed out by Grelot (1955: 94). There is no reason, however, to accept his suggestion to displace the expression to its purported original place before ובעית. Its present location at the end of the onomastic midrash sums up Levi's grief and anxiety over the child expressed in the preceding clauses.

L. 17 ביירחה תליתיא *thir[d] month*. 4Q214a 2 i 3 has here a different numeral, probably "ninth," with the omission of *yôd*, תן[שעא. It is probable that the Qumran manuscript preserves different numerals.

L. 19 ברתא *a daughter*. According to Fitzmyer (1999: 462–463), one should expect here an absolute state instead of the emphatic form of the noun. The emphatic state is, however, not impossible, for, among his children, Yochebed is Levi's only daughter.

L. 19 ושויתי שמהא *and I gave her the name*. In A 69a l. 12 and 76 l. 10 the *Document* uses a different verb קרי. Grelot (1955: 95) noted that a similar targumic expression שוי ית שמיה translates the Hebrew וישם את שמו in Judg 8:31. He hesitated between considering the *Document*'s expression as "une variante de traduction" and the possibility that it goes back to the original. The latter solution must be preferred for the alternance between קרי שם and שוי שם is nothing else but a legitimate stylistic variation withing the literary pattern.

L. 20 אמרת *(for) I said*. It is probable that the particle ארי has been omitted before the verb that begins the onomastic midrash, see esp. A 76 l. 11, and also 69a l. 12; 69b l. 13; cf. Grelot 1955: 95.

L. 21 כבוד *glory*. This Hebraism, like the others present in the *Document*, does not prove that the text is a translation from Hebrew (Grelot 1955: 95) nor that the medieval scribe is responsible for them (Fitzmyer 1999: 464). The author of the Aramaic composition is bilingual as all four onomastic midrashim make it clear.

L. 22 לי *to me*. MS A probably makes a mistake by introducing this syntagm before לחיי. Its proper place would be after וילדת at the end of the line, cf. line 21: ילדת לי.

L. 23 The line in a smaller typeface from the next column is brought here to finish the sentence that spans the two columns.

2.1.12 *A.L.D. 72–80*

MS A (Cambridge d; pl. VII);
Parallels: MS B (Pl. XVI); 4Q214a frg. 2 i

1   העלֹנֹ[א] למצרים   vacat   בשנת שת ⁽⁷³⁾

עש[רה למ]עלינה לארע מצרים ולבני 2

נֹשֹ[בת נשין] מֹן בנת אחי לעדן אשריות 3

זמניהון ו[יליד]ו להון בנין vac (74) שם בני 4

נרשון לבֹנֹ̇י ו[שמעי vacat ושם בני 5

קֹהֹת עֹמֹרם ויצהר וחברון ועוזיאל 6

vac ו[שֹׁם בני מררי מחלי ומושי [vac 7

(75)וֹנֹסֹב לה עמרם אנתא ליוכבד ברתי 8

עד די אנה הי בשנת תשעין ואֹ[רֹבע] 9

לחֹוי (76)וקריתי שמה די עמרם כדי 10

יליד עמרם ארי אמרת כדי יליד 11

דנה יֹ{רים} <פק> עמא מן אֹרֹע מֹצרים 12

[כ]דן יתֹקֹרֹא [שמה <עמ]א̇> ראמא vacat 13

(77)ביום חד יליֹדֹ[ו בנ]יֹא הֹוֹא ויוכבד 14

ברתי (78)בר שנין [a]תֹמֹנה עשרה* [b]העלת* (78) 15

לֹאֹרע כנען ובר שנין תֹמֹנה עשרה 16

כדי קטלית [c]אנה* לשכם [d]ונמרת* 17

[e]לעבדי [f]חמסא* vac (79)ובר שנין תשע 18

עשרה כהנית ובר שנין תמנה 19

ועסרין נסבת לי אנתה vac (80)ובר 20

שנין [g]תמנה וארבעין* הויתי כדי 21

[h]העלנא* [i]לאֹרע* מצרים ושנין 22

[j]תמנין ותשע* [k]הויתי חי* במצרים 23

---

a B ܘܗܘܐ ܬ̄

b B ܐܠܝܕ.

c B >.

d B ܘܐܡܪܬ.

e B + ܠܚܠܡܗ.

f B ܕܐܠܒ

g B ܩ̄.

h B ܐܠܝܕ.

i B >.

j B ܛ̄.

k B ܗܘܝܬ.

NOTES ON READING

L. 1   העלנ[א]. For the reconstructed form, see MS A 80 l. 22 העלנא.

L. 2   למעלינה. The reconstructed form (Beyer 1984: 203) is an infinitive with the pronominal suffix. Charles (1908a: 254) reads [ה]עלינה. Puech (2002: 539) proposes an alternative הנ[עלינה]; cf. A 78 l. 15 (העלת) and 80 l. 22 (העלנא).

L. 3   נ[ס]בת נשין מן. A tail of a *nûn* and *sāmek* is preserved at the beginning of the lacuna. The lacuna has been reconstructed on the basis of 1QapGen VI 8.

L. 4   זמניהון. With Kugler 1996a: 112. The head of a *zayin* is well preserved. The downstroke is slightly abraded but easily discernible. The remaining letters in the word are clear.

L. 4   ו[יל]דו. Some traces of the head of a *dālet* remain on the edge of the lacuna. The form is a *peʿîl* perfect of ילד, 3m.pl. with the subject בנין that follows the verb. The suffix -הון refers to לבני in l. 2.

L. 8   ונסב. The tail of a *wāw* and the downstroke of the *nûn* are well preserved, the ink in the following *sāmek* and *bêt* is fair enough to read the letters.

L. 12   י{רים}<פק>. The darkened leather preserves the tops of *yôd* and *rêš* on the edge of the lacuna; then *rêš*, *yôd* and final *mêm* have dots over them, probably signs of the first attempt to change the reading. The scribe transformed the right downstroke of the final *mêm* into the vertical line of a *qôp*, and then he joined the crossbar of the *mêm* with the preceding *yôd* to create the hooked crossbar of the *qôp*. The *rêš* served as material for a *pê* whose base left some ink traces on the edge of the lacuna. The ink at the beginning of the lacuna suggests a *yôd* added by the correcting scribe. The new form introduced by the scribe is a *hapʿel* imperfect 3m. sg. from נפק (cf. Puech 2002: 540).

L. 12   אר̊ע. The *ʾālep* is clear, then only the tops of the letters are distinguishable.

L. 12   מ̊צרים. The ticked head of the *mêm* is left, the rests of the slanted tail of the *ṣādê* appear at the edge of the lacuna, while the rest of the word is well preserved at the end of the line.

L. 13   שמה <עמ[א]>. With Puech (2002: 538). Charles and Cowley (1907: 575) read שמה] עמא[in the lacuna, there is, however enough space for no more than four letters. At the end of the lacuna, there is an ink dot to the right of the following *rêš*, and that suggests a supralinear *ʾālep* rather than a *yôd* read by Greenfield and Stone עמ[י (1979: 226).

L. 14   יליד]ו בנ[יא. The lower hook of a *lāmed* is well preserved, with the downstroke of a *yôd*. There is enough space for four reconstructed letters in the lacuna.

L. 16   תמנה. Pass and Arendzen (1900: 657) read תש[עה. Charles (1908a: 254) argues that the *šin* is written over an erasure. While the *tāw* is damaged, the rest of the letters are clear.

TRANSLATION

1 we were brou[ght] to Egypt, (73) in the sixteen[th] year

2 of our entry into the land of Egypt. And for my sons

3 I to[ok wives] from the daughters of my brothers at the moment corresponding to their

4 ages, and sons w[ere b]orn to them. vac (74) The name of the sons of

5 Gershon, Libn[i and] Shimei; vacat and the name of the sons of

6 Qahat, Amram and Yizhar and Hebron and Uzziel;

7 [vac and] the name of the sons of Merari, Mahli and Mushi. vac

8 (75) And Amram took a wife for himself, Yochebed, my daughter,

9 while I was still living, in the ninety-fou[rth] year

10 of my life. (76) And I called the name of Amram, when

11 Amram was born, for when he was born I said:

12 "This one will {exalt} <lead> the people <out> of the land of E[gy]pt."

13 vacat [Th]us [his name] will be called: "<the> exalted [<peopl]e>."

14 (77) On the same day the [children] we[re bo]rn, he and Yochebed,

15 my daughter. (78) I was eighteen years old (when) I was brought

16 to the land of Canaan and I was eighteen years old

17 when I killed Sheche[m] and destroyed

18 the doers of violence. vac (79) And I was nineteen years old

19 (when) I became a priest and I was twenty-eight

20 years old (when) I took a wife for myself. vac (80) And I was

21 forty-eight years old when

22 we were brought to the land of Egypt, and eighty-

23 nine years I lived in Egy[pt].

COMMENTS

L. 1 הֻעְלֹ[נא] למצרים *we were brou[ght] to Egypt.* The partially reconstructed verb is most probably a first person plural from עלל in *hup'al* perfect. The same root in the same conjugation stands also in A 78 l. 15 (העלת) and 80 l. 22 (העלנא); for the *hup'al* form of the same root see Dan 5:13, 15; cf. Bauer and Leander 1962: § 16h (p. 57) and 48k (p. 167).

Ll. 1–2 בשנת שת עש[רה] . . . מצרים *in the sixteen[th] year . . . Egypt.* There is a *vacat* in the manuscript preceding the clause, and that would suggest joining it to the text that follows (cf. Charles 1908b: 233; Greenfield and Stone 1985: 467; Kugler 1996a: 113). However, the clause has to be read in the context of the preceding sentence dealing with the date of Yochebed's birth. She was born in the sixty fourth year of Levi's life (A 72 l. 22), after the entry into Egypt (A 72 ll. 23–1), in the sixteenth year from that same entry (A73 ll. 1–2). In accordance with the proposed interpretation of the text, the next sentence begins with ולבני "And for my sons." This interpretation perfectly fits the *Document*'s chronology, for Levi is said to enter Egypt being forty eight years old (see A 80). Consequently, the verb in A 73 l. 2 is reconstructed to לֹמֵעלינה in parallelism with the preceding clause די הֻעְלֹ[נא] מן בתר. Only Haupt (1969: 83) and Beyer (1984: 204) follow this interpretation. Joining the clause with the following context and incorrect reconstruction of the lacuna has led to an improbable assumption that Levi's entry into Egypt took place when he was sixteen years old (see Becker 1970: 98; Wise 1997: 29).

Ll. 3–4 לעדן אשויות זמניהון *at the moment corresponding to their ages.* The form אשויות is interpreted as a nominalized infinitive construct *'ap'el* of שוי "to equal, to correspond, to be of the same value," cf. Grelot 1955: 99; Beyer 1984: 704; cf. also the expression שוי זמן ל (*pa'el*) "to set, appoint time for" in 11QtgJob XXXI 2–3 (Job 38:25).

Ll. 10–11 כדי יליד עמרם *when Amram was born.* Charles (1908b: 234) considers the proper name "Amram" (l. 11) as an apposition to the direct object of קריתי (l. 10): "I called the name of Amram, when he was born, Amram. . . ." The proper name, however, is the subject in the circumstantial clause.

L. 15   MS B introductory sentence:

ܬܘܒ ܕܟܡܐ ܚܝܐ ܠܘܝ. ܫܪܒܐ ܕܡܚܘܐ ܡܢ ܕܝܬܩܐ ܕܝܠܗ.

ܐܡܪ ܠܘܝ ܒܕܝܬܩܐ ܕܝܠܗ ܗܟܢ.

twb d-km' ḥy' lwy. šrb' d-mḥw' mn dytq' dylh. 'mr lwy b-dytq' dylh hkn. "Concerning how (long) lived Levi; a story which is reported in his testament. Thus said Levi in his testament."

The small Syriac fragment of *A.L.D.* is composed of three short introductory sentences and the actual citation of the *Document* that runs parallel to A 78–81. These introductory remarks demonstrate the interest of the Syriac scribe in Levi's life span. They also give the modern reader an insight into the literary genre of the whole work, at least, as it was understood in the ninth century A.D. at which the manuscript is dated. The scribe uses twice the lexeme *dytq'* which is a Syriac borrowing of the Greek διαθήκη, cf. Brockelmann 1928: 152a. This use would suggest that the Aramaic work was considered to be a "testament," most probably under the influence of the Greek *Testament of Levi*. The Syriac text follows closely A 78–81 but it shares some readings with the Greek *Testament*.

Table 9. Chronology in *A.L.D.* 78–81

	A 78–81	B 78–81	T. Levi 12:5
Entry into Canaan	18	8	8
Killing of Shechem	18	18	18 (cf. 2:2 "about twenty")
Priesthood	19	19	19
Marriage	28	28	28 (= T. Levi 11:1)
Entry into Egypt	48	40	40
Years in Egypt	89	90	——
Total life span	137	137	137 (= 19:4)

Essentially, B closely follows the A text. There are, however, some variants that should be commented upon. A 78 l. 15 says that Levi was eighteen years old when he left for Canaan. *T. Levi* 12:5 affirms that he was only eight and thus agrees with B which gives exactly the same age. On the other hand, B states that Levi was forty years old when he entered Egypt and this date is confirmed by *T. Levi* 12:5. However, A with its 48 years and 89 years spent by Levi in Egypt makes a perfect calculation of one hundred thirty seven years of Levi's life span. B does not give a correct number of years Levi spent in Egypt and *T. Levi* 12:5 omits it completely.

Ll. 17–18 וגמרת לעבדי המסא *and destroyed the doers of violence.* B *w-'wbdt l-klḥwn 'bdy 'wl'*. The meaning of A and B is similar with variation in the word choice. The B variant *'wl'* "lawlessness" instead of המסא suggests that both terms are synonyms referring to the lawlessness commited by the Shechemites. MS B has *klḥwn*, which corresponds closely to the Genesis text where Levi and Simon kill all men, cf. Gen 34:25 "and they killed all the males" ויהרגו כל זכר.

2.1.13 *A.L.D. 81–90*
MS A (Cambridge e; pl. VI);
Parallels: MS B (Pl. XVI); 4Q213 1 i

ܚܢܝ ܟܠܗ ܓܠܝ ܚܠܡܝ   (81)   והוו* כל ⁿיומי חיי** שבע ותלתין ומאה (81)a   1

2   שנין וחזיתי לי בנין תל[י]תיין] עד

ᵃ B >.

ᵇ B ܚܝ.

3 די לא מיתת vacat ⁽⁸²⁾ובש[נ]ת מאה[ו][ת]מני

4 עשרה לחי היא שנ[תא]די מית בה

5 יוסף אחי קריתי לבנ[י ו][לבניהון

6 ושריתי לפקדה ^cהנון* כל די הווה

7 עם לבבי ^(83a)עניח ואמרת לבנ[י] [שמ]ע[ו][ן]^(83b)

8 למאמר לוי אבוכון והציתו לפקודי

9 ידיד אל ⁽⁸⁴⁾אנה ^dלכון* מפקד בני ואנה

10 קושטא לכון מהחוי חביבי ⁽⁸⁵⁾ראש

11 ^eעובדיכון* יהוי קושטא ועד

12 עלמא יהוי קאים ^fעמכון* ^gצדקה*

13 ^hוקושטנ[א* הן] ת[ז][ר]ע[ו][ן תנהעלון

14 עללה בריכה ו[ן][מא][בא]* ⁽⁸⁷⁾^jדי זרע*

15 ^kמאב טאב* ^lמ[ה]נעל* ודי זרע

16 ביש עלוהי האיב זר[ע]ה vacat

17 vacat ⁽⁸⁸⁾וכען ^mבני* ספר ⁿמוסר*

18 ^oחוכמה* אליפו לבניכון ותהוי

19 חוכמתא עמכון ליקר עלם

20 ⁽⁸⁹⁾די ^pאליף* ^qחוכמתא* ^rויקר* היא

21 בה ודי שאיט חוכמתא ^sלבשרון*

22 מתיהב vacat ⁽⁹⁰⁾חזו ^tבני ליוסף אחי

23 [ד]מאלפא ספר ומוסר חכמה

---

c 4Q213 1 i 3 אנון.

d 4Q213 1 i 5 לכן.

e 4Q213 1 i 6 כל עבדכן.

f 4Q213 1 i 7 עמ[כן.

g 4Q213 1 i 7 צדקתא.

h 4Q213 1 i 7 וקשטא.

i 4Q213 1 i 8 וט[נ]בה.

j 4Q213 1 i 8 דזרע.

k 4Q213 1 i 8 טב טב.

l 4Q213 1 i 8 מעל.

m 4Q213 1 i 9 >.

n 4Q213 1 i 9 ומוסר.

o 4Q213 1 i 9 וחכמה.

p 4Q213 1 i 10 אלף.

q 4Q213 1 i 10 הכמה.

r 4Q213 1 i 10 יקר.

s 4Q213 1 i 11 לב[סרון ולשיטו.

t 4Q213 1 i 11 + לכן.

NOTES ON READING

L. 1   ותלתין ומ̇אה. The tops of the letters are preserved on the edge of the parchment.

L. 2   תל[ל]יתין. The upper arm of a *lāmed* is recognizable at the beginning of the lacuna.

L. 13   ת̇ו̇[ר̇]ע̇ן. The top of a *tāw* and *zayin*, two parallel legs of an *'ayin* and the head of a *wāw* and *nûn* appear in the manuscript.

L. 13   תנהעלון. The manuscript preserves some faint traces of the letters in this lacuna. The existing space between the *nûn* and the *'ayin*, and a vertical downstroke preserved there suggest a *hê*. The resulting verbal form is a regular *hap'el* תהנעלון with a metathesis between the *nûn* and the *hê*; for the *hap'el* of עלל without metathesis, see line 15: מהנעל.

L. 14   ו[ט̇א]בא. The basis of the *bêt* is visible but the *ṭêt* and *'ālep* are lost in the lacuna. For the spelling of the lexeme see line 15. 4Q213 1 i 8 has וט[בה.

L. 15   מ̇ה̇נעל. *Mêm* and *hê* are damaged by the lacuna but easily discernible.

L. 17   ו̇כען. The lower downstroke of the *wāw* remains in the manuscript.

L. 18   אליפו. MS: אפילו. Also here a metathesis occurs. Pass and Arendzen (1900: 659, n. 1) emend to אליפו.

L. 20   ו̇יקר. The *wāw* is absent in 4Q213 1 i 10. This scribal addition also appears in A 72 l. 22 (וילידת) causing syntactic incongruity; cf. also A 93 l. 14 ייקר.

TRANSLATION

1   (81) And all the days of my life were one hundred thir[t]y-seven

2   years, and I saw my sons of the thi[rd generation] before

3   I died vacat (82) In the [hundred and eigh]teenth

4   y[ear] of my life, this is the y[ear] in which

5   my brother Joseph died, I called [my] sons [and] their sons

6   and I began to command them everything that I had

7   intended. (83a) I spoke and said to my sons: [(83b) Hear]

8   the word of Levi, your father, and obey the commands

9   of God's beloved. (84) I myself command you, my sons, and I myself

10   show you the truth, my beloved. (85) Let the principle

11   of all your actions be truth and for

12 ever let justice be established with you.

13 (86) And [if you s]ow tru[th], you will reap

14 a blessed and [go]od harvest. (87) Whoever sows

15 good, reaps good, and whoever sows

16 evil, his seed returns upon him.

17 vacat (88) And now, my sons, teach scribal craft, instruction,

18 wisdom to your children, and let

19 wisdom be with you for eternal glory.

20 (89) Whoever studies wisdom, will (attain) glory

21 through her, but the one who despises wisdom, becomes an object of

22 disdain. vacat (90) Consider, my sons, Joseph my brother

23 [who] taught scribal craft and the instruction of wisdom,

(4Q213 1 i 12) to glory, and to greatness, and to kings [on their thrones he was joined.]

COMMENTS

L. 2 [וחזיתי לי בנין תל]יתיין and I saw sons of the thi[rd generation]. The sentence is related to Gen 50:23 that recounts last moments before Joseph's death: "And Joseph saw Ephraim's children of the third generation" (בני שלשים).

L. 17. ספר מוסר חוכמה scribal craft, instruction, wisdom. 4Q213 1 i 9 adds a *wāw* before מוסר and חוכמה, while the Geniza text prefers an asyndeton; see A 90 l. 23 where the same two terms appear in the construct state, cf. *A.L.D.* 98 l. 8; Prov 15:33.

Ll. 20–21 ויקר היא בה will (attain) glory through her. Greenfield and Stone interpret the syntagm בה as referring to wisdom and give the preposition an instrumental value: "through it" (1985: 468). Charles and Cowley (1907: 583) followed by Kugler (1996a: 120) translate the clause: "she is an honour in him"; cf. Beyer 1984: 207 "dem ist sie eine Ehre."

L. 21 די שאיט the one who despises. 4Q213 1 i 11 reads לב]סרון ולשיטו מתיהב, "becomes an object of [con]tempt and disdain." It is probable that A not preserve ולשיטו, due to an accidental omision in the text transmission. While the verbal form of the root שוט is frequent in the targumic literature (Levy 1881: *s.v.*), the noun is attested in Syriac (*šyṭwtʾ* and *šywṭwtʾ* "contemptio," cf. Brockelmann 1928: *s.v.*) and Mandaic (*šuta, šituata, etc.* "contempt, shame," cf. Drower and Macuch 1963: 454). The roots שוט and

בשר form a poetic word pair, see Form and Structure of *A.L.D.* 82–98 in § 3.10.

L. 21. לבשרון *disdain*. 4Q213 1 i 11 reads a *sāmek* instead of a *šîn*: לב[ן]סרון. Greenfield and Stone (1979: 227) consider the Geniza spelling to be "a hypercorrection, the root being בסר." The nominal form with the suffix ־ון is frequent in Middle Aramaic, while the usual Aramaic form בוסרן is found in Late Aramaic and Syriac, cf. Sokoloff 1990: *s.v.*; Brockelmann 1928: *s.v.* The verb from the same root is attested in 4Q542 1 i 6: יבסרון עלכין *and they will despise you*; cf. Puech 2001: 274.

L. 23 The line in a smaller typeface from the next column is brought here to finish the sentence that spans the two manuscripts.

2.1.14   *A.L.D. 90–96*
MS A (Cambridge f; pl. VI);
Parallels: <u>4Q213 1 i</u>, <u>4Q213</u> 1 ii and <u>4Q214a 2 ii 1–2</u>

1	[ליקר ולרבו ולמלכין על כורסיהון]
2	[מתחד הוא אל תמחלו חכמתא]
3	[למאלף ולאורדתה ל]א תשב[ן]קן
4	לב[עא] (91)די ^aמאלף* חוכמ]ה נבר דן[י]
5	אלף [חכמה כל י]ומוהי א[ריכין]
6	וסנה ל[ה שמ]עה לכל ^bמא[חי*]
7	ומדינה[ן די]ן ^cעללי* לה אח או חבר
8	הוי בה [ולא מ]תנכר ^dהוא* בה
9	ולא דמ[ה בה]לנכרי ולא דמה
10	בה לכילא[י]מן די כולהון יהבין
11	לה בה יקר [ב]די ^eכולה* צבין
12	למאלף מן חוכמתה (92)רחמוד[י]ן vacat
13	^fסניאין* ושאלי ^gשלמיה* רברבין
14	(93)ועל כורסי ייקר מהותבין לה
15	בדיל למשמע ^hמילי* חוכמתה*

---

^a 4Q213 1 i 14 <מהלך>.
^b 4Q213 1 i 15 מח.
^c 4Q213 1 i 15 יחך.
^d 4Q213 1 i 16 >.
^e 4Q213 1 i 17 כלא.
^f 4Q213 1 i 18 סניאין.
^g 4Q213 1 i 18 שלמה.
^h 4Q213 1 i 19 מלי.

16 עׄוׄתׄר רב די יקׄר היא חוׄכמתה (94)

17 וׄסׄיׄמׄאׄ* ᵏטׄאׄבׄאׄ* לכל קׄנׄׄיׄהׄאׄ (95) הׄן

18 יאׄתׄוׄן מׄלׄכׄיׄן תׄקׄׄיׄפׄׄיׄן ועׄם רב

19 וׄחׄיׄל וׄפׄרשיׄן ורתיכין סׄנׄׄיׄאׄן

20 עמׄהׄוׄן וׄיׄנׄסׄבׄׄוׄן נכׄסׄׄי מאׄׄת

21 וׄמׄׄדׄׄיׄׄנׄׄה דׄׄיׄׄבׄׄוׄׄזׄׄוׄׄן כׄל די בׄהׄׄון

22 אׄׄוׄצׄרׄׄי חׄׄוׄכׄׄמׄתׄׄא לׄׄא יׄׄבׄׄוׄׄזׄׄון

23 ולׄׄא יׄׄשׄׄכׄׄחׄׄון (96) מׄׄטׄׄׄמׄׄׄוׄׄׄׄרׄׄׄׄיׄׄׄׄה וׄׄׄׄלׄׄׄׄא

NOTES ON READING

L. 1–2 [על כורסיהון מתחד הוא] The line 1 is partially supplemented with
the text from 4Q213 1 i 12. The Qumran text does not fill fully the MS
A lacuna but leaves enough space to account for about three or four additional words. The proposed restoration (Puech 2002: 545) is more consonant with *T. Levi* 13:9 σύνθρονος ἔσται βασιλέων. Note the connection
with A 93 l. 14 where the wisdom teacher is seated on the throne of glory
(ייקר כורסי).

L. 3 [קן] ל[א תשבן]. According to 4Q213 1 i 13, Levi is speaking to his
children, so the verb should be put in jussive plural parallel to תמחלו from
the preceding line. The ink traces at the edge of the lacuna do not suggest, however, the presence of a *lāmed* from the particle אל, typical to a
jussive. On paleographical grounds, the ink traces on the edge of the leather
suggest an *ʾālep*, hence the restored form ל[א. It is not excluded that the
latter form was introduced by a copyist, cf. MS A 27 l. 5 לא and the corresponding Qumran fragment with אל (4Q214 2 4). For שבק followed by
an infinitive with its complement, see, e.g., 1QapGen XIX 15, 16, 19. In
the reconstruction here the width of the lacunas in lines 2 and 3 dictates
placing the proposed syntagm ולאארהתה, a direct object of בקרה (l. 4), in
the emphatic position at the beginning of the clause.

L. 4 לבן]עא. On the basis of 4Q213 1 i 13, Kugler (1996a: 119 and
123) reads למאלף. The space of about one line between למאלף and נבר in
4Q213 1 i 13–14 excludes this restoration. The vertical downstroke of a
bêt with its oblique base are the last ink traces before the lacuna. The reconstructed form is an infinitive *peʿal* לבן]עא "to seek," without the preformative
mêm. The infinitive without a prefixed *mêm* is most probably a genuine Aramaic form attested elsewhere (cf. Ezra 5:3, 13 לבנא and comments in Muraoka and Porten 1998: 108, n. 498; cf. also Muraoka 1983–84: 98–99). For בעי
in the *Document*, cf. *A.L.D.* 69b l. 15; [90 l. 4]; 97 ll. 5, [7]; 4Q214b 1 3.

ⁱ 4Q213 1 i 19 חכמתה̇.
ʲ 4Q213 1 i 20 וׄשׄׄיׄמׄׄה; 4Q213 1 i 20 + לכל] יׄדׄעׄׄה.
ᵏ 4Q213 1 i 20 טׄׄבׄׄה.

L. 4 ‫ה]כמן מאלף‬. For the proposed restoration, cf. Puech 2002: 547. 4Q213 1 i 14 reads <‫מהללך‬>, which appears to be a scribal correction of the underlying *pa'el* participle ‫ מאלף‬from ‫ אלף‬"to teach," hence the reading here. For the explanation of the Qumran correction, see § 2.2.6 and bibliographical references there. In the Geniza manuscript Greenfield and Stone (1979: 230) read a *nûn* at the end of the lacuna - ‫[ן‬. The ink traces may suggest a left downstroke of a *hê*. The proposed reading ‫ ה]כמן‬is a conjecture, which, however, explains the ink traces on the leather and is consonant with the overall syntax of the sentence. The *pa'el* of ‫ אלף‬can be construed with double accusative, as is the case here. Note that when the Qumran scribe introduced his correction of the text, he probably omitted ‫ ה]כמן‬to adjust the meaning of the clause.

L. 5 ‫א]ריכין‬. Ink traces of the right legs of an *'ālep* appear in the text.

L. 7 ‫עלל‬. There are two ink dots on the edge of the leather, one beneath the other. The lower belongs most probably to an *'ayin* with its long tail slanted from upper right to lower left, cf. the *'ayin* in line 6; the upper might belong to the curved leg of a *lāmed*. The reconstructed form is an active participle masculine of *pe'al* from the root ‫ עלל‬"to enter," frequent in the *Document* (see, e.g., A 3a l. 2; 8 l. 14; 19 l. 1; 73 l. 2). Beyer (1984: 206) proposes to read ‫א]ל‬, but the reading does not correspond to the remaining ink traces.

L. 7 ‫אח או חבר‬. Although only lower parts of the following letters remain, the reading ‫ חבר‬is certain, the *rēš* being well preserved.

L. 10 ‫לכילא]י‬. For the suggested reading, see Puech 1991: 39 and 2001: 273.

L. 11 ‫ד]רי‬. With 4Q213 1 i 17. Charles (1908a: 256) has ‫א]רי‬. What Charles reads as a *rēš* may also be a *dālet*, the horizontal part of its head being torn by the lacuna.

TRANSLATION

1 [to glory, and to greatness, and to kings *on their thrones*]

2 [*he was joined.* Do no]t [neglect to study]

3 [wisdom *and* do not] aban[don]

4 a se[arch *for her ways.*] [91] [Whoever teaches wisdo]m (to) a man wh[o]

5 studies [wisdom, all] his days are l[ong]

6 and hi[s fa]me spreads. Whichever la[nd]

7 or province he enters, he is a brother or companion

8 in it, [and he is not] considered a stranger in it,

9 and he is not simil[ar to] a stranger [in it], and he is not similar

10 in it to a half-bree[d], for they all give

11 him glory in it; (this is) [be]cause they all desire

12 to learn from his wisdom. vacat [92] Hi[s] friends

13 are many, and his well-wishers are great ones.

14 [93] And they seat him on the throne of glory

15 in order to hear the words of his wisdom.

16 [94] Great wealth of glory is wisdom,

17 and a good treasure for all who acquire her. [95] If

18 mighty kings come and a great army,

19 and soldiers and horsemen and numerous chariots

20 with them, then they will carry away the possessions of the land

21 and province, and they will plunder everything that is in them,

22 the treasuries of wisdom they will not plunder

23 and they will not find [96] her hidden places and (they will) not

(4Q213 1 ii 1–3) enter her gates, and [they will] not[and] they will [not] be able to conquer her walls, [   ]and not[and] they will [not] see her treasure.

COMMENTS

L. 1 ליקר ולרבו ולמלכין *to glory, and to greatness, and to kings.* The Qumran text does not fill fully the MS A lacuna but leaves enough space to account for about three additional words. Stone and Greenfield (1996a: 8) propose to begin the new sentence with ולמלכין and restore ולמלכין [יעט הוה "and he did advise kings." The repetition of the *lāmed,* however, suggests a stylistic unity of the whole expression. The restoration here is more consonant with *T. Levi* 13:9 σύνθρονος ἔσται βασιλέων.

L. 2 אל תמחלו *Do no]t [neglect.* The MS A text is supplemented by 4Q213 1 i 13; for the verb מחל, see also *A.L.D.* 102 l. 6, and the comment on *A.L.D.* 90 in § 3.10.2.

L. 4 לב[עא *a se[arch].* Literally: "to seek."

L. 4 מאלף חוכמ[ה [די] *[Whoever teaches wisdo]m.* This line is partially supplemented by 4Q213 1 i 14, see Notes on Readings above. Note that the following section of the poem (vv. 91–93) describes the glorious fate of the wisdom teacher. The literary analysis of the poem indicates that the praise of the wisdom teacher stands in the center of the poetical construction (stanza IV).

L. 6 וסנה ל[ה שמ[ע]ה *and hi[s fa]me spreads.* The verb סנה is an active participle from סני "to come, to go" with an indirect object לה (cf. Beyer

1984: 644; for a *lāmed* after verbs of physical movement, cf. Muraoka and Porten 1998: 270). Here it metaphorically refers to the growing extension of the wisdom teacher's fame.

L. 16 חוכמתה *wisdom*. The Qumran fragment 4Q213 1 i 20 inserts here an additional clause לכל[ידעיה] "for all [who know it]." It thus preserves the poetical parallelism with the following line לכל קניהא *for all who acquire it*. The copyist of MS A must have accidentally omitted the line.

L. 18 ועם רב *and a great army*. The Hebrew equivalent of the expression usually refers to a multitude of people (cf. Gen 50:20; Num 21:6; Deut 2:21; Josh 17:14, 15, 17, etc.), but it may also denote military units (cf. Deut 20:1; Josh 11:4). The latter meaning corresponds well to the *Document*'s context.

L. 20 וינסבון *then they will carry away*. Here begins the apodosis of the conditional sentence that begins in lines 17–18: הן יאתון מלכין תקיפין *If mighty kings come*.

L. 22 אוצרי הוכמתא *the treasuries of wisdom*. The Hebrew term אוצר in plural may mean "supplies" (Neh 12:44; 2 Chr 8:15), or "storehouses" (Neh 13:12, 13). It may also refer to "treasuries" of the palace (cf. e.g. 1 Kgs 14:26; 15:18; 2 Kgs 12:19; 16:8; 18:15; 24:13) or the temple (cf. e.g. 1 Kgs 7:51; 14:26; 15:18; 2 Kgs 12:19; 24:13; cf. Ezra 2:69; Neh 7:70). Additionally, it denotes one's personal wealth (cf. Jer 15:13; 17:3). In the cosmic perspective the heavens are God's storehouse (cf. Deut 28:12; 32:34; Jer 10:13, etc.). Here the term metaphorically denotes the place where hidden wisdom is stored.

L. 23 The line in a smaller typeface from the next column is brought here to finish the sentence that spans the two manuscripts.

2.1.15 *A.L.D. 96–100*
4Q213 1 ii and frg. 2 (Pl. II);
Parallels: <u>4Q214a frg. 2 ii</u> and <u>4Q214b frg. 8</u>; MS A 96 l. 23

top margin

ולא[	(96)מ̲ט̲מ̲ו̲ר̲י̲ה̲ ולא יעלון תרעיה ולא[	1
ולא[	] ולא [ ] ישכחון למכבש שוריה	2
[	יהזון שימׄחׄה שימתה נ̇[נ]דׄהׄ[	3
[כל]אנ[ש די](97)	ולא איתי כ̲ל̲ מחיר נדדה ו̇ל̲[א	4
[ ]ת̇ה̇[	בעא חכמׄה̇[חכ]מתא י̇[שכח	5
[ ]ל̇° א[	מטמרה מנ̇ה̇[פ̲ל	6
[ ]ן כל בעי[ן	] ולא הס[י]ר̇[	7
(98)וכען בני [ספר ומוסר	בקשט]	8
חזית בחזוין די]תרתון אנון	חכׄמה ד̇ אלפׄ[ו	9
[רבה תתנון	וׄת̇ה̇[ן	10
וׄי̇[קׄר̇ vacat	]קׄ 11

אנ]ן (99)   12   [אף בספריא
קר]ית   13   תה]ווֿן ראשין ושפטין
ודא]נין   14   ב[ועבדין
]   15   [אף כהנין ומלכין
תה]ווֿן   16   שׁ[(100)[ ]ן מלכותכן
תהוא]   17   יק]ֿל ולא איתי סוף
ליק]רכן   18   ולא [תהעבר מנכן עד כל
ד]ריא   19   ]ן ביקר רב

TRANSLATION

1 (96) her hidden places, and they will not enter her gates, and [they will] not[and]

2 they will [not] be able to conquer her walls, [   ]and not[and]

3 they will [not] see her treasure. Her treasure c[orresp]onding to it (?)[   ]

4 and [n]o price is adequate for it and [not   (97)every] ma[n who]

5 looks for wisdom, [wis]dom he will [find   ] th[ ]

6 her hidden place from it/him pl[   ]ʾ l[   ]

7 and not la[c]k[   ]n all who see[k]

8 truly [(98)And now, my sons,] scribal craft and instruction

9 of wi[s]dom that you (?) tea[ch/learn   I saw in visions that] you will inherit them

10 and t[   ]great you will give

11 [and g]lory   vacat

12 (99)ʾn[   ]also in the books

13 I re[ad   [you will b]e heads and magistrates

14 and ju[dges   ]b and servants/doing

15 [   ]also priests and kings

16 you will be[come   (100)]n your kingdom

17 will be   glo]ry and there will be no end

18 to [your] gl[ory   and it will [not] pass from you until all

19 ge[nerations   ]n with great glory

COMMENTS

Here begins the section of the *Document* preserved only in Qumran manuscripts (*A.L.D.* 96–104). For the separate text of these two Qumran fragments, notes and their reconstruction, see § 2.2.6. For reasons to locate them in the *Document*'s structure, see § 1.4.3.1; for a detailed commentary, see § 3.10.2 and § 3.11.1. There follows the strophic disposition of the whole wisdom poem *A.L.D.* 83b–98.

2.1.16 *A.L.D. 83b–98—Wisdom Poem: Strophic Disposition*

The following reconstruction is based on all available manuscript evidence. For the literary analysis of the poem, see Form and Structure in § 3.10.

[A 83–96]; 4Q213 1 i – 4Q213 1 ii 1–9; *4Q213 2 1–8*; 4Q214a 2 ii 1–5; 4Q214b 8)

1	[83b]שמעו למאמר לוי אבוכן	והציתי לפקודי ידיד אל]
2	[84]אנה לכן [מפקד בני	ואנה קשטא לכן מהחוי חביבי]
3	[ראש] כל עבדכן [לדוה קשטא[85]	ועד עלמא להוה קאם עמ]כן צדקתא
4	[86]וקשטא [הן תזרעון	תנהעלון עללה בריכה וט]בה
5	[87]דזרע טב	טב מעל
6	ודי זרע באיש	עלוהי חב זר]עה vacat
7	[88]וכען ספר ומוסר וחכמה [אלפו לבניכן	ותהוה חכמתא עמכן ליקר עלם
8	[89]די אלף חכמה	יקר [היא בה
9	[ודי שאט חכמא	לב]סרחון ולשיטו מתיהב
10	[90]חזו לכן בני [ליוסף אחי	די מאלף הוא ספר ומוס]ר חכמה
11	ליקר ולרבן ולמלכין	[על כורסיהון מתחד הוא vacat]
12	אל תמזגלו חכמתא למאלף	[ולאחרתה אל תשבקו לבעא]
13	[91][די] <מהלך> גבר די אלף חכמה	כל [יומוהי אריכין]
14	וסנה לה שמע]א	לכל מת ומדינה די יהך לה
15	[אה או חבר הוא בה	ולא הוא מתני]כר בה
16	ולא דמא בה לנכרי	ולא [דמא בה לכילאי]
17	[מן די כלהן י]הבין לה בה יקר	בדי כלא צבין [למאלף מן חכמתא]
18	[רחמו]הי שגיאין[92]	ושאלי שלמה רברבין]
19	[93]ועל כרסי יקר מהחבין לה	בדיל צבי]ן למשמע מלי חכמתה
20	[94]עתר רב די יקר היא חכמתא לכל]ידעיה	ושימה טבה [לכל קניה]
21	[95]הן יאתון מלכין תקיפין	ועם [רב ו]חיל [ופרשין]
22	[ורתיכין סגיאין עמהן	וינסבון נכסי מת ומדינה]

אוצרי חכמתא לא יבוזון]	[ויבוזון כל די בהן 23
ולא יעלון תרעיה	[ולא ישכחון] מטמורייה<sup/> (96) 24
[ולא] ישכחון למכבש שוריה	[ולא] 25
[ולא] יחזון שימתה	[ולא] 26
ולא איתי כל מחיר גנזה	[שימתה נ[נ]ד̇ה̇] 27
(97) כל /אנ̇/ש די [בעא חכמה]	[ו[לא 28
] [תה]	[הכ]מתא י[שכח 29
] א[ל̇° [	[מטמרה מנה [פל 30
] [ז̇ כל בעי[ן	[ולא הס[ן]רן[31
(98) וכען בני ספר ומוסר חכמה די אלפ[ו	[ ] בקשט 32
ות̇] [	חזית בחזוין די][תרתון אנון] 33
[ ]	[רבה תתנון] 34
	vacat קך [י] 35

TRANSLATION

1 (83b)Hear the word of Levi, your father — and obey the commands of God's beloved.

2 (84)I myself command you, my sons, — and I myself show you the truth, my beloved.

3 (85)Let the principle of all your action be truth — and for ever let justice be established with you.

4 (86) And if you sow truth, — you will reap a blessed and good harvest.

5 (87)Whoever sows good, — reaps good,

6 and whoever sows evil, — his seed returns upon him.

7 (88)And now, my sons, scribal craft and instruction and wisdom teach your children, — and let wisdom be with you for eternal glory.

8 (89)Whoever studies wisdom — will (attain) glory through her,

9 but the one who despises wisdom, — becomes an object of contempt and disdain.

10 (90)Consider, my sons, Joseph my brother — who taught scribal craft and the instruction of wisdom,

11 to glory, and to greatness and to kings | on their thrones he was joined.

12 Do not neglect to study wisdom | and do not abandon a search for her ways.

13 (91) Whoever guides a man who studies wisdom, | all his days are long

14 and fame comes to him. | To whichever land or province he goes,

15 he is a brother and companion in it, | and he is not considered a stranger in it,

16 and he is not similar to a stranger in it | and he is not similar in it to a half-breed,

17 for they all give him glory in it; | (this is) because they all desire to learn from his wisdom.

18 (92)His friends are many | and his well-wishers are numerous.

19 (93)And they seat him on the throne of glory | because they want to hear the words of his wisdom.

20 (94)Great wealth of glory is wisdom for all who know it, | a good treasure for all who acquire it.

21 (95)If mighty kings come, horsemen | and a great army and soldiers and

22 and numerous chariots with them, | then they will carry away the possessions of the land and province,

23 and they will plunder everything that is in them. | The treasures of wisdom they will not plunder

24 and they will not find (96)her hidden places | and they will not enter her gates

25 and [they will] not[conquer her walls | and] they will [not] be able to

26 and not[| and] they will [not] see her treasure.

27 Her treasure c[oresp]onding   and no price is adequate for it
    to it (?) [   ]

28 and [not   (97)every] ma[n who] looks for
                                      wisdom,

29 [wis]dom he will [find   ]*th*[   ]

30 her hidden place from   ] ᵓ *l* [   ]
    it/him *pl*[

31 and [he] does not la[c]k[   ]*n* all who see[k]

32 truly [   ]   (98)And now, my sons, scribal
                                      craft and instruction of wi[s]dom
                                      that you (?) tea[ch/learn]

33 [I saw in visions that] you   and y[ou will
    will inherit them

34 [   ]great you will give   [   ]

35 [and g]lory   vacat

2.1.17 *A.L.D. 101–104*

2.1.17.1 *A.L.D. 101*

4Q213 frg. 3   =   4QLeviᵃ (Pl. II)

top margin

[⁽¹⁰¹⁾ ל[כ]ן̇ כל עממיא	1
שמשא ש̇[ה]רא ו̇כוכביא	2
]מן̇	3
[ל̇ש̇הרה	4
[ ]	5

NOTES ON READINGS

L. 1 Milik (1976:23) does not transcribe this line in his reconstruction, but see his reading in Brown 1988: *s.v.*

L. 1 ל̇[כ]ן̇. Stone and Greenfield (1996a: 21) read an ᵓ*ālep* at the end of the lacuna. A bend to the left rather points to a *nûn*, cf. Milik's reconstruction in Brown 1988: *s.v.*

L. 2 The reconstruction is based on 1QapGen VII 2; cf. also Milik 1976: 23.

L. 4 [ל̇ש̇הרה. Milik (1976: 23) restores שהרה וכ[. The upper arm of a *lāmed* is, however, visible before the *šîn*, see also Milik's reading in Brown 1988: *s.v.*

TRANSLATION

1   [(101)] for [you] all the nations
2   sun, m]oon and stars
3   ]from (?)
4   ]for its moon
5   ]   [

COMMENTS

For reasons to locate this fragment in the *Document*'s structure, see
§ 1.4.3.1; for a detailed commentary, see § 3.11.2.

2.1.17.2 *A.L.D. 102*

4Q213 frg. 4   =   4QLevi^a (Pl. II)

כן תחשב̇ו̇ן][(102)	] 1
א] הלא קבל [ל]מ̇ה̇ך̇ ל]̇	] 2
נא] ועל מן תהוא ח̇ובתא	] 3
הלא] עלי ועליכן בנ̇י ארו ידעונ̇ה̇	] 4
א]ר̇דחת קש̇°א תשבקון וכל שבילי	] 5
ת̇מהלון ותהכון בחשוך̇ שטן][	] 6
מ]ן ח̇ן̇ש̇]וכה תהא עליכן] ̇ו̇ת̇הכון	] 7
שנ̇]יא [ט̇ע̇ן ומ̇]ל̇ל̇ [ו̇]תהוון לשכלין	] 8
תהו̇ו̇]ו̇ן כ̇]ל ק̇]שיט̇ן]י̇ן ו̇]ת̇כהל̇]ון	] 9

NOTES ON READINGS

L. 2   ]ל ל̇מ̇ה̇ך̇ [. Milik (1976: 23) reads ה̇נ̇ו̇ך̇ but only the final *kāp* may
easily be discerned. An ink dot may be spotted at the beginning of the
lacuna. Since the leather is shrunk, the intervening lacuna could have contained two or even three letters. On the edge of the leather there comes
a horizontal base of probably a *mêm*. Next, two small dots before the final
kāp are probably remnants of two downstrokes of a *hê*. Since the beginning
of the word is lost in the lacuna, the reconstruction remains hypothetical.

L. 4   ידעונה. Kugler (1996a: 120) reads ידעתה. The manuscript, however, clearly indicates the horizontal base of a *nûn* joined to the following
hê. The downstroke of a *wāw* is stuck between the *ʿayin* and *nûn*.

L. 6   בחשוך̇. Milik in Brown 1988: *s.v.* reads בחשו]כא. The vertical downstroke of the final *kāp* is also extant in the manuscript and runs parallel to
the preceding *wāw*.

L. 6   שטן. Kugler (1996a: 120) reads here שטן. The *śîn* is easily recognizable, then only the tops of the letters are preserved.

L. 7   ח̇ן̇ש̇]וכה. With Stone and Greenfield 1996a: 22. Milik in Brown
1988: *s.v.*, followed by Beyer (1994: 77) and Kugler (1996a: 120), reads עקה
רבה "great oppression." This reading is quite dubious for the manuscript

does not seem to have a *qôp* but a *mêm* and final *nûn* distinctly separated from the next word. There follows a *ḥêt* with the right upstroke overlapping the crossbar; one letter is lost in the lacuna and there come *wāw*, *kāp* and *hê*.

L. 8 שֹׁגֹֹ[יא]שֹׁעֹן. For *śîn* and *gîmel* in the same word, see 4Q213 1 i 18. The ink traces on the edge of the lacuna suggest the left downstroke of a *ṭêt*. The verb טען should mean "to claim against, to plead" (Sokoloff 1990: 229). Another reading, for example a *ḥêt*, is also possible.

L. 8 וֹמֹ[לל]ל. A *wāw* precedes the *mêm*; some traces of the upper arm of the second *lāmed* remain under the *'ālep* in the preceding line.

L. 8 לשכלין. Stone and Greenfield (1996a: 22) have לשפלין. However, a *kāp*, not a *pê* is discernible, see Milik in Brown 1988: *s.v.*

L. 9 קֹ[שׁישֹֹׁ]ין. Stone and Greenfield (1996a: 22) here read only a *śîn*, and do not indicate the discernible upper parts of a *yôd* and *ṭêt*.

L. 9 וֹ[תֹכֹהֹלֹ]ון. Two horizontal and semicircular strokes of two letters suggest a *tāw* and *kāp*. Then, on the edge of the torn leather, ink traces may be read as a *hê*. The downstroke of the final *nûn* from the preceding line preserves some traces of the upper arm of a *lāmed*.

TRANSLATION

1 [(102)]thus you will darken[

2]' did not he accept[to] go to?[

3]*n*' and on whom will the guilt be

4] is that not on me and on you my sons, behold they will know it

5 the p]aths of righteousness you will abandon, and all the ways of

6] you will neglect and you will walk in the darkness of satan

7]*mn* da[r]kness will come upon you [   ] and you will walk

8]great[ly]he pleaded and he s[ai]d: "You will become intelligent

9 you will be]come a[ll t]ruthfu[l and]you will be ab[le

COMMENTS

For reasons to locate this fragment in the *Document*'s structure, see § 1.4.3.1; for a detailed commentary, see § 3.11.2.

2.1.17.3 *A.L.D. 103*

4Q213 frg. 5 = 4QLevi^a (Pl. II)

עֹמֹהֹון בֹ[ר]שֹׁעֹא[(103)]   ] 1

ש[נ]איכן אדין ידי[ם]בכן   ] 2

°°[ ]ל̊שנין בכן מן כל מ[   ] 3

bottom margin

NOTES ON READING

L. 1 [עמ̊ה̊ון. Only lower parts of five letters remain in the manuscript. First, the base of an *'ayin/śîn* and *mêm/bêt* are discernible. Then, two parallel downstrokes suggest a *hê*. Finally, there comes the downstroke of a *wāw* before the tail of a final *nûn*. Since the context is broken, one may translate as either "with them," or "their people."

L. 1 ש̊א[ר]ב. Stone and Greenfield (1996a: 23) have [°ע̇א   פ̊. The bottom horizontal stroke of a *pê* or *bêt* is noticeable. Then, the leather is erased and only a tail of probably a *śîn* still remains. The last two letters are certain.

L. 3 [לשׁנין. A tiny dot before the *śîn* could be interpreted as the tail of a *lāmed*. The overall reconstruction is hypothetical.

TRANSLATION

1   [(103)]with them/their people (?) by the [e]vil one

2   those who h]ate you. Then he will aris[e] against you

3   ]languages against you from every m[

COMMENTS

For reasons to locate this fragment in the *Document*'s structure, see § 1.4.3.1; for a detailed commentary, see § 3.11.2.

2.1.17.4   *A.L.D. 104*

4Q214 frg. 3   =   4QLevi^d (Pl. IV)

[   ]°[ ]°[   ] 1

[ארו מן יקר בא̊ר̊[עא(104) 2

[אנה די תמרון לי ̇ ̇ ד[ינה 3

[יקירין מן נשׁיא̊] 4

[ה̊ל̊[א]ל̊[ ]ל̊] 5

NOTES ON READING

L. 2 בא̊ר̊[עא. The downstroke of probably a *rêš* suggests this reconstruction.

L. 3 ̇ ד[ינה. One may hypothetically assume that initially the scribe omitted the particle ד֗י because of the *homoioteleuton* with the following noun, ד[ינה "Dinah," or perhaps ד[ינא "judgment."

L. 3 ד[ינה. Stone and Grenfield (1996a: 49) read a *hê*. The horizontal part of the head is attached to the right downstroke, and that points to a *dālet*.

L. 5 הל[א. The crossbar of a *hê* and the *lāmed* are well preserved on the edge of the leather.

TRANSLATION

1]°[ ]°[   ]

2 (104)Behold, more than glory in [the] coun[try   ]

3 I, when you tell me that D[inah   ]

4 more glorious than the women   ]

5 [   ]*hl*[   ]*l*[   ]

COMMENTS

For reasons to locate this fragment in the *Document*'s structure, see § 1.4.3.1; for a detailed commentary, see § 3.11.2.

2.2   *Overlapping Qumran Texts*

The Qumran texts that overlap with other manuscript evidence have been located here with their respective notes and reconstructions. For the convenience of the comparison with non-Qumranic manuscript evidence, the order of their presentation follows the reconstructed literary form of the *Document* and its verse numbering.

2.2.1   *A.L.D. 1a–1b*

4Q213a frg. 1   = 4QLevi^b (Pl. III)

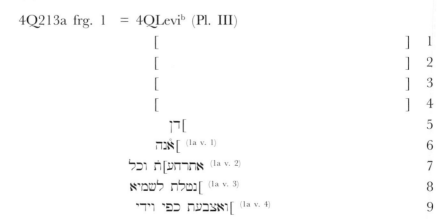

[	] 1
[	] 2
[	] 3
[	] 4
]דן	5
]א̊נה (1a v. 1)	6
אתרחע[ת וכל (1a v. 2)	7
]נטלת לשמיא (1a v. 3)	8
]ואצבעת כפי וידי (1a v. 4)	9

[אמרת ^(1a v. 5) מרי אנתה 10

א]נתה בלחודיך ידע 11

[^(1a v. 6) אָרחת קשט ^(1a v. 7)]ארחק 12

[באיש° וזנותא דחא 13

ה]כמה ומנדע ונבורה ^(1a v. 8) 14

לא]שכחה רחמיך קדמיך ^(1a v. 9) 15

[דשפיר ודטב קדמיך 16

ו]אל תשלט בי כל שטן ^(1a v. 10) 17

ע]לי מָרי וקרבני למהוא לכה ^(1a v. 11) 18

bottom margin

NOTES ON READING

L. 6 אנה[. The left leg of an ʾālep is joined to the following nûn, the rest of the letter is torn.

L. 12 אָרחת[. A tear comes across the word; only an ink dot close to the downstroke of the rêš indicates the preceding ʾālep.

L. 13 באיש°[. The yôd is disproportionately large and high, rising slightly above the line. The base of the bêt is attached to the following ʾālep.

L. 15 ונבורה. A tear comes across the gîmel and continues obliquely leftwards to the next line separating the head of the final kāp in קדמיך from its tail.

L. 16 דשפיר[. Only the left part of dālet's head is preserved.

L. 18 ע]לי מרי. The lāmed and yôd are well preserved. The lower parts of the following letters are torn off, except for the second yôd that is fully preserved.

L. 18 למהוא. The mêm is a correction on the previous kāp - למה < לכה.

4Q213a frg. 2 = 4QLevi^b (Pl. III)

[   ] 1

[   ] 2

[   ] 3

[   ] 4

[לען ^(1a v. 15) 5

[מרי ב]רכה ^(1a v. 16) 6

[זרע דק]שט ^(1a v. 17) 7

[צלות עב]דך ^(1a v. 18) 8

[דין קשט לכ]ל° ^(1a v. 19) 9

[לבר עבדך מן ק]דמיך 10

[באדין נדת ב]^(1b) vac   ° 11

12 על אבי יעקוב וכד]י   [

13 מן אבל מין vac אדין]   [

14 שכבת ויתבת אנה ע]ל   [

15 vac אדין חזיון אחזית]   [

16 בחזות חזיוא וחזית שמ]יא   [

17 תחותי רם עד דבק לשמי]א   [

18 לי תרעי שמיא ומלאך חד]   [

bottom margin

NOTES ON READING

L. 11 Here starts a new section indicated by a *vacat* of about only two letters and by a hook written on the margin between lines 10 and 11. A similar sign may be found on the margin of 4Q213 1 ii 11.

L. 12 וכד]י. The vertical downstroke of a *dālet* is joined to the preceding *kāp*. Milik (1955b: 400) reads a *yôd*.

L. 15 חזיון. Fitzmyer and Harrington (1978: 90) read חזוין. The sequence *yôd-wāw* is, however, certain in the manuscript.

L. 16 חזיוא. With Milik 1955b: 400. Fitzmyer and Harrington (1978: 90) followed by Stone and Grenfield (1996a: 30) change the sequence to *wāw-yôd*, חזויא, but the text rather clearly indicates a *yôd-wāw* sequence.

Reconstruction of 4Q213a frg. 1 = 4QLevi^b

1   [   ]

2   [   ]

3   [   ]

4   [   ]

5   [דן   ]

6   באדין [אנה^(1a v. 1)   ]

7 [רחעת   לבושי וטהרת להון במין טהרין^(1a v. 2) ובמין חיין אתרחע]ת וכל

8 [ארחתי ישרין עבדת(   ) (?) vac ^(1a v. 3) אדין עיני ואנפי]נטלת לשמיא

9   [(   ) ^(1a v. 4) ואצבעת כפי וידי ופומי פתחת ומללת]

10 [אושטת לקשט קדם בית אל(   ) וצלית ו]אמרת^(1a v. 5) מרי אנתה

11 [ידע כל לבביא(   ) וכל עשתנת רעיוניא א]נתה   בלהודיך ידע

12 [וכען בני עמי(   ) ^(1a v. 6) והב לי כל]ארחת קשט^(1a v. 7) ארחק

13 [מני מרי רוחא די עולא(   ) ועשתן ב]איש וזנותא דחא

14 [מני^(1a v. 8) יתחזיני מרי רוח קודשא ועטה וה]כמה ומנדע וגבורה

15 [הב לי ^(1a v. 9) למעבד דשפיר לך ולא]שכחה רחמיך קדמיך

16 [ולשבחה מליך עמי מרי)(   )(למעבד]דשפיר ודטב קדמיך

17]](la v. 10)(   )ו[אל תשלט בי כל שטן

18 [לאטעיה לי מן ארחך)(   )(ורחם ע]לי מ^ארי וקרבני(la v. 11)
למהוא לכה

bottom margin

NOTES ON THE RECONSTRUCTION

Placing the retranslated Greek text of Levi's prayer (MS E 2,3) in the disposition of the Aramaic manuscript demonstrates that the line length of the latter exhibits a longer text in comparison with the Greek version. Round brackets indicate where the Qumran text has purported expansions of the Greek. This observation demonstrates that the Greek text was translated from an Aramaic manuscript shorter than the Qumran text.

The difference between the two textual witnesses comes as no surprise for MS E 18,2 differs in a number of points from the Cairo Geniza manuscript. It cannot be unequivocally proven that the Greek version of the prayer preserves an older text, but the expansion of the Aramaic manuscript may be easily explained by the exegetical tendency of the Qumran scribes. The seven Qumran manuscripts of the *Document* differ in a number of points and do not attest a wholly uniform text (see § 1.4.3.1 and § 1.4.3.5).

Ll. 1–6   The first four missing lines suggest that the extant text was preceded by some kind of introductory account that served as a narrative setting to the prayer. A short notice about Levi's prayer in *T. Levi* 2:4 is also preceded by a general introduction to the testament in *T. Levi* 1:1–2:3. Levi's preparation to the prayer known from MS E 2,3 begins at the end of line 6.

L. 8   The remaining space in the line allows the supposition that the Qumran text is probably ten to fifteen letter-spaces longer.

L.12   The remaining space allows us to assume the presence of at least three additional words absent in Greek.

L. 13   According to the Qumran line length, there should be two additional words in the lacuna. It is possible that the list of Levi's requests in E 2,3 v. 7 was longer or disposed in different order. That the Greek list differs from the Aramaic is additionally confirmed by the omission of the expression καὶ ὕβριν in Aramaic.

L. 15   The line length allows the supposition that the list of requested faculties is one word longer.

Ll. 15–16   The Greek ποιῆσαι τὰ ἀρέσκοντα σοί (למעבד דשפיר לך) is situated at the beginning of line 9 in the Greek translation, hence its proper localisation in the Qumran disposition is line 15. What one then reads at the end of line 16 ([למעבד]דשפיר ודטב קדמיך) is an alternative expression not extant in Greek.

Ll. 17   E 2,3 v. 9 ends with μετ' ἐμοῦ, κύριε and the following line 10 starts with καὶ μὴ κατισχυσάτω με πᾶς σατανᾶς that corresponds to the end of line 17 in the Aramaic manuscript: ו[אל תשלט בי כל שטן. Consequently, not only the end of Qumran line 16 is not extant in Greek but the first part of the line 17 as well. The Aramaic text is much longer than the *Vorlage* of E 2,3 v. 9.

L. 18 The length of reconstructed line 18 suggests that the Aramaic text was about two words longer in comparison with E 2,3 v. 10.

Reconstruction of 4Q213a frg. 2 = 4QLevi[b]

1   [עבד ולמפלחך בטב ^(1a v. 12)לההוא שור שלמך סחור לי]

2   [וטלל נבורתך יטללני מן כל באישא ^(1a v. 13)על כן]

3   [קח חמסא ומחי לה מן תחות שמיא ונמר חמסא]

4   [מן אנפי ארע ^(1a v. 14)טהר לבבי מרי מן כל טמאה ואנה אנטיל]

5   לע[נ]יניך ^(1a v. 15)ואל תפנה אנפיך מן בר עבדך יעקב אנתה]

6   מרי ב[ברכת לאברהם אבי ולשרה אמי ^(1a v. 16)ואמרת למנתן להן]

7   זרע דק[שט בריך לעלמין ^(1a v. 17) (?) vacat ואף שמע לקל]

8   צלות עב[דך לוי למהוא קריב לך ^(1a v. 18)ותחברני למליך למעבד]

9   דין קשט לכ[ל עלם יתי ובני לכל דרי עלמין ^(1a v. 19)ואל תהעדי]

10   לבר עבדך מן ק[דמיך כל יומי עלמא ושקטת ועוד צלית]

11   ^(1b)באדין נגדת ב]   vac כ   [

12   על אבי יעקוב וכד]י   [

13   מן אבל מין vac אדין]   [

14   שכבת ויתבת אנה ע]ל   [

15   אדין חזיון אחזית]   vac [

16   בחזות חזיוא וחזית שמ]יא   פתיחין וחזית טור   [

17   תחותי רם עד דבק לשמי]א   והוית בה ואתפתחו   [

18   לי תרעי שמיא ומלאך חד]   אמר לי לוי על   [

bottom margin

NOTES ON RECONSTRUCTION

Ll. 1–4 The first four lines are missing, and their restoration depends on the retranslated text of E 2,3. The reconstruction of the retranslated text confirms Milik's suggestion that the manuscript had eighteen lines in a column. The first three lines, however, seem to be too short when filled with the retranslated text and compared with lines 5–6 and 8–10. It would confirm the same tendency of the Qumran text to expand the shorter text of the prayer attested in E 2,3.

L. 7 This line is too short for the manuscript standard line length. At least two additional words should be assumed as present in the Qumran text but absent in the Greek version. However, one cannot exclude the possibility of a *vacat* before ואף.

L. 10 קן]דמיך. Stone and Greenfield (1996a: 30) reconstructed קן]דם.
E 2,3 v. 19 suggests 2m.sg. pronominal suffix.

L. 10   This is the last line of Levi's prayer. The rest of the preserved
eight lines deals with Levi's trip to his father Jacob (lines 11–14) and the
beginning of his vision (lines 15–18).

L. 11 נגדת. The verb נגד here means "to go, to set out to," and it may
be followed by a preposition, see 1QapGen XIX 8; 1QapGen XXII 4
למדיתון נגדו מלכיא ארהא; 11QtgJob XXXVI 3–4.

L. 14   Comparing this line with *1 En.* 13:7, Milik (1955b: 405) reconstructs דן ע]ל מי. It seems, however, more probable that Levi has his vision
close to Abel Main, see line 13.

Ll. 16–18   The proposed readings in the lacunae follows Milik (1955b: 404)
who restores the text on the basis of *T. Levi* 2:4–5 (β recension). Placing
this reconstructed text in the Qumran MS disposition proves that some
words are missing and the Qumran text was longer than Milik supposed.

4Q213a frg. 1 5–18 and frg. 2 5–10 (reconstruction)
Parallel: MS E 2,3

דן[⁵

⁽¹ᵃ ᵛ· ¹⁾τότε ἐγὼ ἔπλυνα τὰ ἱμάτιά μου, καὶ καθαρίσας αὐτὰ ἐν ὕδατι καθαρῷ
[באדין] ⁶אנה] רחעת לבושי וטהרת להון במין טהרין[

⁽¹ᵃ ᵛ· ²⁾καὶ ὅλος ἐλουσάμην ἐν ὕδατι ζῶντι καὶ πάσας τὰς ὁδούς μου ἐποίησα
εὐθείας.
ובמין חיין אתרחע]ת וכל ⁷[ארחתי ישרין עבדת]

⁽¹ᵃ ᵛ· ³⁾τότε τοὺς ὀφθαλμούς μου καὶ τὸ πρόσωπόν μου ἦρα πρὸς τὸν οὐρανόν,
καὶ τὸ στόμα μου ἤνοιξα καὶ ἐλάλησα,
[אדין עיני ואנפי] נטלת לשמיא ⁸[ופומי פתחת ומללת]

⁽¹ᵃ ᵛ· ⁴⁾καὶ τοὺς δακτύλους τῶν χειρῶν μου καὶ τὰς χεῖράς μου ἀνεπέτασα
εἰς ἀλήθειαν κατέναντι τῶν ἁγίων. καὶ ηὐξάμην καὶ εἶπα·
ואצבעת כפי וידי] אושטת לקשט קדם בית אל וצלית ¹⁰[אמרת⁹

⁽¹ᵃ ᵛ· ⁵⁾Κύριε, γινώσκεις πάσας τὰς καρδίας, καὶ πάντας τοὺς διαλογισμοὺς
ἐννοιῶν σὺ μόνος ἐπίστασαι.
מרי אנתה] ידע כל לבביא וכל עשתוני רעיוניא ¹¹[נתה בלחודיך ידע]א

⁽¹ᵃ ᵛ· ⁶⁾καὶ νῦν τέκνα μου μετ᾽ ἐμοῦ. καὶ δός μοι πάσας ὁδοὺς ἀληθείας·
[וכען בני עמי והב לי כל ¹²ארחת קשט]

⁽¹ᵃ ᵛ· ⁷⁾μάκρυνον ἀπ᾽ ἐμοῦ, κύριε, τὸ πνεῦμα τὸ ἄδικον καὶ διαλογισμὸν τὸν
πονηρὸν καὶ πορνείαν, καὶ ὕβριν ἀπόστρεψον ἀπ᾽ ἐμοῦ.

אַרחק] מני מרי רוחא די עולא ועשחונא ⁱ³[באישⁱ וזנותא דחא [מני

(1a v. 8)δειχθήτω μοι, δέσποτα, τὸ πνεῦμα τὸ ἅγιον, καὶ βουλὴν καὶ σοφίαν καὶ γνῶσιν καὶ ἰσχὺν δός μοι

[יתחזיני מרי רוח קודשא ועטה ¹⁴וח]כמה ומנדע ונבורה [הב לי

(1a v. 9)ποιῆσαι τὰ ἀρέσκοντά σοι καὶ εὑρεῖν χάριν ἐνώπιόν σου καὶ αἰνεῖν τοὺς λόγους σου μετ᾽ ἐμοῦ, κύριε·

[למעבד דשפיר לך ¹⁵ולא]שכחה רחמיך קדמיך [ולשבחה מליך עמי מרי ¹⁶למעבד] דשפיר ודטב קדמיך

(1a v. 10)καὶ μὴ κατισχυσάτω με πᾶς σατανᾶς πλανῆσαί με ἀπὸ τῆς ὁδοῦ σου.

ו]¹⁷אל תשלט בי כל שטן [לאטעיה לי מן ארחך]

(1a v. 11)καὶ ἐλέησόν με καὶ προσάγαγέ με εἶναί σου δοῦλος καὶ λατρεῦσαί σοι καλῶς.

[ורחם ¹⁸ע]לי מרי וקרבני למהוא לכה [עבד ולמפלחך בטב]

(1a v. 12)τεῖχος εἰρήνης σου γενέσθαι κύκλῳ μου, καὶ σκέπη σου τῆς δυναστείας σκεπασάτω με ἀπὸ παντὸς κακοῦ.

[להוא שור שלמך סחור לי וטלל נבורתך יטללני מן כל באישא]

(1a v. 13)παραδοὺς διὸ δὴ καὶ τὴν ἀνομίαν ἐξάλειψον ὑποκάτωθεν τοῦ οὐρανοῦ, καὶ συντελέσαι τὴν ἀνομίαν ἀπὸ προσώπου τῆς γῆς.

[על כן קח חמסא ומחי לה מן תחות שמיא ונמר חמסא מן אנפי ארעא]

(1a v. 14)καθάρισον τὴν καρδίαν μου, δέσποτα, ἀπὸ πάσης ἀκαθαρσίας, καὶ προσάρωμαι πρὸς σε αὐτός·

[טהר לבבי מרי מן כל טמאה ואנה אנטיל ⁵ לע]יניך

(1a v. 15a)καὶ μὴ ἀποστρέψῃς τὸ πρόσωπόν σου ἀπὸ τοῦ υἱοῦ παιδός σου Ἰακώβ.

[ואל תפנה אנפיך מן בר עבדך יעקב]

(1a v. 15b)σύ, κύριε, εὐλόγησας τὸν Ἀβραὰμ πατέρα μου καὶ Σάρραν μητέρα μου,

[אנתה] ⁶מרי ב]רכת לאברהם אבי ולשרה אמי]

(1a v. 16)καὶ εἶπας δοῦναι αὐτοῖς σπέρμα δίκαιον εὐλογημένον εἰς τοὺς αἰῶνας.

[ואמרת למנתן להן ⁷זרע דק]שט בריך לעלמין]

(1a v. 17)εἰσάκουσον δὲ καὶ τῆς φωνῆς τοῦ παιδός σου Λευὶ γενέσθαι σοι ἐγγύς,

[ואף שמע לקל ⁸צלות עב]דך לוי למהוא קריב לך]

^(1a v. 18)καὶ μέτοχον ποίησον τοῖς λόγοις σου ποιεῖν <u>κρίσιν ἀληθινὴν εἰς</u>
<u>πάντα</u> τὸν αἰῶνα, ἐμὲ καὶ τοὺς υἱούς μου εἰς πάσας τὰς γενεὰς τῶν αἰώνων·

[וחברני למליך למעבד] ⁹דין קשט ל֯כ֯]ל עלם יתי ובני לכל דרי עלמין]

^(1a v. 19)καὶ μὴ ἀποστήσῃς <u>τὸν υἱὸν τοῦ παιδός σου ἀπὸ τοῦ προσώπου σου</u>
πάσας τὰς ἡμέρας τοῦ αἰῶνος. καὶ ἐσιώπησα ἔτι δεόμενος.

[ואל תהעדין] ¹⁰לבר עבדך מן ק֯]דמיך כל יומי עלם ושקטת ועוד צלית]

NOTES ON RECONSTRUCTION

L. 4   τῶν ἁγίων. Stone and Greenfield (1993: 257) reconstruct קדישא.
The expression בת אל that denotes a sanctuary in A 19 l. 1 seems preferable.

L. 5   διαλογισμοὺς ἐννοιῶν. LXX Ps 145:4 has διαλογισμός for the Aramaic
*עשתנה "thought, plan," see Wagner 1966: 93. For רעין see, e.g., Dan 2:29,
30; 4:16. The term διαλογισμός also appears in E 2,3 v. 7.

L. 11   Here ends 4Q213a 1.

L. 12   סחור לי. For this expression, see 5Q15 1 i 1.

L. 12   ומלל. See 4Q201 1 ii 7 (*1 En.* 4); 11QtgJob XXXVI 29.

L. 12   ישללני. See Dan 4:9.

L. 13   חמסא. The Greek ἀνομία often translates the lexeme חמס, see
LXX Isa 53:9; 59:6; Ezek 7:23; 8:17, etc; *1 En.* 9:1 (Sync.) = 4Q201 iv 8.
The Aramaic term is also attested in A 3 l. 19 and 78 l. 18.

L. 13   מן תחות שמיא. For the reconstructed syntagm, see Jer 10:11.

L. 13   נמר חמסא. See A 78 l. 17–18.

L. 14   אנטיל. See Dan 7:4.

L. 14   לע]יניך. This is the beginning of 4Q213a 2. For the reconstructed
syntagm, cf. Dan 4:34; 7:4.

2.2.2   *A.L.D.* 4–9

1Q213 (Pl. I)

⁽⁴⁾פנשא וק]רבא [ונחשירותא	1
⁽⁵⁾]ת֯עמל וזמנין תנ֯]וח	2
רבות שלם [ע֯למא ⁽⁷⁾]ן	3

NOTES ON READING

L. 3   ]ן [ע֯למא. Milik (1955a: 88) reads ש]לם ע֯ל]מא and places a question mark above the *mêm*. The remaining part of the letter resembles rather
a medial, not a final *mêm*, hence the present reconstruction.

1Q213—reconstruction

Parallel: MS A 4–7

⁽⁴⁾]למאכל ולמלכות הרבא פנשא וק]רבא [ונחשירותא ועמלא ונצפהא	1
וקטלא וכפנא ⁽⁵⁾זמנין]	

2 [תאכול וזמנין תכפן וזמנין] תֹעמל וזמנין תנֹ[וח וזמנין תדמוך וזמנין
תנוד שנת עינא ⁽⁶⁾כן רבינך מן]

3 [כולה והיך יהבנא] לֹךְ שֹׁ[לם עלמא vacat ⁽⁷⁾ונגדו שבעתון מן לותי
ואנה אתעירדת מן שנתי [

NOTES ON THE RECONSTRUCTION

L. 1 וק[רבא. Milik (1955a: 89) hesitates whether to reconstruct ח[רבא
(A 4 l. 2) or וק[רבא (A 4 l. 3). He opts for the first proposal, but the line length
of his reconstruction becomes too long. Starting the reconstruction with
וק[רבא seems preferable. The line length approximately corresponds to 4Q213a.

L. 2 This line overlaps with A 5 ll. 5–6.

L. 3 לֹךְ שֹׁלם. Milik (1955a: 89) reconstructs עֹלֹמא] שלם רבות לך [יהבנא,
being, however, convinced, that "les traces des lettres ne correspondent pas
bien à la lecture imposée par le contexte." Puech (2003) proposes to read
a šin after the final kāp. This reading most probably omits רבות found in
MS A 6 l. 8: יהבנא לך רבות שלם עלמא.

1Q214 (Pl. I)

] [		1
⁽⁹⁾אבי יע[קב מעשר]		2
]לֹ[		3

NOTES ON READINGS

L. 1 The lower part of the preceding line is still preserved; there are
no ink traces, though.

1Q21 4—Reconstruction

Parallel: MS A 9:15–16

1 [ ] [ ]

2 ⁽⁹⁾אבי יע[קב מעשר] הוה כל מה דיהוה לה כנדרה אף כען הוית
קדמי בראש]

3 כהנותא ו]לֹ[י מכל בנוהי יהב קרבן מעשר לאל ואלבשי לבוש כהונתא
ומלי ידי]

The fragment is a part of A 9 ll. 15–16 but it preserves a different
word order. MS A and 4Q213b 4 read אבי יעקב. Compare T. Levi
9:3 where the Greek is close to 1Q21 4 2.

4Q213b = 4QLevi^c (Pl. IV)

⁽⁶⁾ הי]ךֹהֹ רביתך מן כל בשֹׁר]	1
⁽⁷⁾ [אֹנה אתעירדת מן שנתי אדין	2

‫ה̇ אף דן בלבבי ולכל אנש לא]‬ 3

‫⁽⁹⁾ כ]ד̇י הוה יעקוב אבי מעשר‬ 4

‫ה̇ ולי מן בנוהי יהב]‬ 5

‫לא]ל̇ ע̇ל}מין<א{ >יון< וא]נה‬ 6

NOTES ON READING

L. 1 ‫הי]כ̇ה רביתך‬. The tops of several letters are torn making the decipherment difficult. Additionally, the leather is shrunk and difficult to read. Only the base of a *kāp* remains, then the following two downstrokes suggest a *hê*. The next downstroke is slightly curved to the right and might be interpreted as a *rêš* with traces of its head, but it cannot be an *ʿayin*. Then there comes the partially erased base of a *bêt* with some remains of its head. This reconstruction would yield the phrase, ‫רביתך‬ "I have exalted you," cf. ‫רבינך‬ in A 6,7. Kugler (1996a: 80) reads the whole line as follows: ‫כהונותך מן כל בשר‬ and translates: "Your priesthood is over all flesh". His reading ‫כהונותך‬ raises some objections. This word is never spelled with two *wāw* neither in Qumran nor in MS A. It is attested either as ‫כהנותא‬ (e.g. 1Q21 1 2; A 13 l. 8) or ‫כהנותא‬ (4Q542 1 i 13; A 9 l. 19, etc.). From a purely grammatical point of view, Stone and Greenfield (1996a: 38) offer a better reading, ‫רעיתך‬, "I have preferred you". Paleographically, however, the general shape of what they read as an *ʿayin* is different from that letter in this manuscript, see lines 2 and 4.

L. 2 ‫אנה‬[. There remains the left leg of an *ʾālep* together with its left arm.

L. 6 ‫לא]ל̇ ע̇ל}מין<א{ >יון< וא]נה‬. Only the tops of the letters remain, the rest is torn. There is the arm of a *lāmed* at the beginning, then follow *ʿayin* and *lāmed*. The scribe first wrote ‫עלמין‬ then corrected his first reading to ‫עלמיא‬ then to ‫עליון‬. The head of the *mêm* is discernible with the *ʾālep* corrected to a *nûn*. Some erasures occur in the *ʾālep* and *nûn*. Note that a similar correction occurs in A 9 l. 20, ‫לאל על}מין/א{ >יון<‬, where the copyist made several adjustments.

L. 6 ‫וא]נה‬. The tops of *wāw* and *ʾālep* are well preserved.

4Q213b – reconstruction
Parallel: MS A 5–9 and 1Q21 3

‫⁽⁵⁾וזמנין תנוח וזמנין תדמוך וזמנין תנוד שנת עינא ⁽⁶⁾כען חזי לך הי]כ̇ה‬ 1
‫רביתך מן כל בשר̇[א]‬

‫והיכה יהבנא לך רבות שלם עלמא ⁽⁷⁾וננדו שבעתון מן לותי ו]א̇נה‬ 2
‫אתעירת מן שנתי אדין‬

‫אמרת חזוא הוא דן וכדן אנה מתמה די יהוה לה כל חזוא וטמר]ת̇‬ 3
‫אף דן בלבבי ולכל אנש לא‬

‫נליתה ⁽⁸⁾ועלנא על אבי יצחק ואף הוא כדן ברכני ⁽⁹⁾אדין כ]ד̇י‬ 4
‫הוה יעקוב אבי מעשר vac‬

[כל מה דיהוה לה כנדרא וכען אנה הוית קדמי בראש 5
כהונת]ה ולי מן בנוהי יהב

ל[קרבן מעשר לאל ואלבשי לבוש כהונתא ומלי ידי והוית כהן לא] 6
עליון וא[נה הוית]

(7) [מקרב]

NOTES ON THE RECONSTRUCTION

The column width spans about 70 letter-spaces that is close to the line length of the reconstructed 1Q21 3.

L. 1　The preserved Qumran text is different from the Geniza manuscript, cf. A 6 ll. 7–8 in § 2.1.6.

L. 5　A 9 l. 18 adds כל before בנוהי.

L. 6　וא[נה הוית מקרב]. MS A has וקרבית; one is, therefore, tempted to read וא[קרבת], an 'ap'el of קרב attested in A both in its 'ap'el (e.g. A 10 l. 1) and pa'el (A 20 l. 5) forms. In this case, however, one should expect some ink traces of the lāmed in כל, which follows the verb in A 9 l. 21, except if one reads here the construction וא[נה הוית מקרב or וא[נה קרבת.

2.2.3　A.L.D. 20–32

1Q21 45 (Pl. I)
Parallels: MS A 26–27; 4Q214 2–3; 4Q214b 2–3 8

```
]°[      ]°°[                                          1
מל[]דׄ֯ין (27) ראשא]  (26 l. 4)                        2
```

NOTES ON READINGS

Line 2　preserves only one full word, but the preserved text allows a connection with MS A 26–27. Additionally, this tiny fragment overlaps with 4Q214 2 3 and 4Q214b 2–3 8.

4Q214 frg. 1 = 4QLeviᵈ (Pl. IV)

```
] דׄ[(20 l. 5)                                          1
] חׄ[(21 l. 7)                                          2
]עא[(22 l. 9)                                           3
]ןׄילׄאׄ[                                               4
]ןׄבדׄמׄ[(23 l. 14)                                     5
]קׄסאלׄ[(25a l. 20)                                     6
]דׄהדל[(25b l. 23)                                      7
]כׄ[(25b l. 2)                                          8
```

NOTES ON READING

L. 1   ]ךֿ[. There remains only a downstroke of a letter, the upper part is torn. Following the reconstruction of the fragment, one should read here a final *kāp*.

L. 2   ]חֿ[. Only the head and the right leg of a *ḥêt* remain, the left part of the letter is abraded.

L. 3   ]עֿא[. The two arms of an *ʿayin* are well preserved, only its tail is lost.

L. 4   ]אליןֿ[. The ink traces indicate a left part of an *ʾālep* with its two legs and a part of its axis. The downstroke of the final *nûn* is thick and its top touches the preceding *yôd*. The usual orthography of אלין in Qumran is without the *yôd*. exceptions, however, do occur, see, e.g., 4Q531 frg. 7 4, 5; 4Q543 16 3.

L. 7   ]להדֿ[. The manuscript preserves *lāmed* and *hê*, the vertical stroke of the third letter may come from a *dālet* or *hê*. The restoration is tentative and follows the context of the passage in MS A. Stone and Greenfield (1996a: 45) have לס, but the comparison with the preceding line does not allow us to read a *sāmek* here.

L. 8   ]כֿ[. The head of a *kāp*, either medial or final, remains on the edge of the leather.

4Q214 frg. 1—reconstruction
Parallel: MS A 20–25

1   ‏וכדי‎ ‏(21)‎ ‏האב‎ ‏(20)‎‏תוב ורחע ידיך ורגלין]ך [עד די לא תקרב למדבחא כל דנה‎

2   ‏תהוא נסב להקרבה כל די]הֿ[זה להנסקה למדבחא הוי עוד תאב‎

3   ‏ורחע ידיך ורגליך (22)‏ומהקרב]אֿעֿ[ין מהצלחין ובקר אנון‎

4   ‏לקדמין מן תולעא (23)‏תרי עשר אעין]אלינֿ[אמר לי‎

5   ‏די חזין להסקה מנהון ל]מֿדבחֿ[א די ריח תנגהון בשים סלק‎

6   ‏אלין אנון די אמר לי די חזין]לֿאסקֿ[ה מנהון לתחות (25a)‎

7   ‏עלחא על מדבחא (25b)‏ונורא ישרא]להדֿ[לקא בהון והא‎

8   ‏באדין תשרא למזרק דמא על]כֿ[ותלי מדבחא‎

NOTES ON THE RECONSTRUCTION

The reconstruction of this tiny piece of the manuscript indicates that it preserves a text shorter than MS A and closer to MS E 18,2 textual form.

L. 1   MS A text seems to be too long for the Qumran line disposition.

L. 4   A 22 ll. 11–12 is not extant in E 18,2 v. 22. Assuming the same absence in the Qumran fagment, the line length and overall reconstruction become perfectly balanced.

L. 4   Although absent in MS A and the Greek translation, the pronoun אלך fits the context by referring the reader to the previous A 22 ll. 9–10, which first mentions wood for the sacrifice. Additionally, one should follow the Greek text and omit מן כל [ ] מיני (A 23 l. 13) to preserve the correct line length.

L. 5   The line of the reconstructed text does not leave any space for A 24. It should be assumed that the verse is absent from the Qumran fragment and A 25 directly follows A 23.

L. 5 ל[מֹדבֹחֹ]א. This word also overlaps with 4Q214b 5–6 i 3 למדבחא.

L. 7 E 18,2 omits the Aramaic clause A 25b ll. 22–23a. When the same omission is applied in this reconstruction, the line length fits perfectly.

L. 7 Hand transcription of the text suggests to reconstruct א[להֹדֹ]לקֹא rather than]להד[לקֹהֹ. The infinitive overlaps with 4Q214a 1 3 לֹ[הֹ]דֹלֹ[קֹא.

L. 8 The reconstruction allows the observation that the noun כ[ותלֹי overlaps with 4Q214b 2–3 7 כותלי.

4Q214 frg. 2 = 4QLevi^d (Pl. IV)

(26)] קֹ [(25b)	1
ר]נֹליך מֹן[	2
מליחֹ[ן יֹ]ן [(27)]ראשא הֹ[וי	3
א] ואל יתחזי לֹ[(28)	4
א] ובתרהן ידיא[	5
בת]הֹן ירכתא ושדר[ת	6
רחי[ן]ען עם קרביא [(29)]וכלהֹ[ן	7
לה[ן]ן כ]מסתן vac [(30)]ובֹ[תר	8
ו]בֹתֹרֹ כלא חמר נ[	9
ו]להוא עבדך בס[ן]רֹך	10

bottom margin

NOTES ON READING

L. 1 קֹ[. The head of a *qôp* is partially excised, but its tail is well preserved. No letter follows on the leather of the preserved line, the *qôp* then is the last letter of the preceding word.

L. 3 הֹ[וי. Stone and Greenfield (1996a: 46) read לֹ[קֹ]דֹמין. The remaining downstroke of a letter does not descend below the line, hence it cannot be read as the tail of a *qôp*. It is most probably the downstroke of a *hê* as the MS A text suggests.

L. 4 א[. The surface of the leather is abraded at the beginning of lines 3–7.

L. 7 וכלהֹ[ן. The upper arm of the *lāmed* is partly rubbed off but its hook is well preserved. The left downstroke of the *hê* and its crossbar are torn off.

L. 8 כ]מסתן. The left leg of the *tāw* is unusually thick because of a scribal correction. There follows a large vacat.

4Q214 frg. 2—reconstruction
Parallel: MS A 25–30; 1Q21 45; 4Q214b 2–3 8

[(25b)]באדין תשרא למזר]קֹ [דמא על כתלי מדבחה]	1
[(26)]ועוד רהע ידיך ור]נֹליך מֹן[דמא ושרי]	2

3 [להנסקה אבריא מליחן]ן (27)[ראשא ה]ני מהנסק]

4 [לקמדין ועלוהי חפי תרב]א ואל יתחזי ל]ה דם]

5 [נכסת תורא (28)ובתרוהי צור]א ובתרהן ידיא] ובתרהן

6 [ניעא עם בן דפנא ובת] רהן ירכתא ושדר]ת תרצא]

7 [ובתרהן רגלין ר]חין ען עם קרביא (29)וכלהן] מליחין]

8 [במלח כדי חזה לה]ן] כ]מסחן vac]וב]תר דנא נשיפא [

9 [בליל במשחא ו]בֿתֿר כלא חמר נֿ]סך והקטיר]

10 [עליהן לבונה ו]להוא עבדך בס]רך וכל קרבניך]

bottom margin

NOTES ON THE RECONSTRUCTION

The column width and the line length of about 30–40 letter-spaces are shorter than in other Qumran manuscripts of this Aramaic work (50–60 letter-spaces). This manuscript preserves a text closer in its textual form to MS E 18,2, for a detailed comparison, cf. MS A 28 in § 2.1.8.

L. 3 [ראשא]. מליחן[]ן]. The expression partially overlaps with 4Q214b 2–3 8 and 1Q21 45 2 מל]יחין ראשא.

L. 4 ואל יתחזי. MS A 27 l. 5 reads ולא יתחזה.

L. 5 ובתרהן. The Qumran line omits צוארה repeated by A 28 l. 7.

L. 6 ושדר]ת. MS A 28 l. 9 reads עם שדרת.

L. 10 ו]להוא עבדך. MS A 30 ll. 14–15 uses plural forms and adds "thus": ויהוון כן עובדיך.

4Q214a frg. 1 = 4QLevi^c (Pl. V)

1 הֿדֿסֿא (24) (25a)אלן א] [

2 על מדבחא vacat ו]כֿ(25b) [

3 ל]ה]דֿל]קה [

NOTES ON READINGS

L. 1 הדסא. The remaining lower parts of the two first letters differ from the *dālet*, *qôp* and *tāw* of דקתא in MS A. The downstroke of a letter at the edge of the leather is that of a *sāmek*. Since the remaining ink traces are minimal, the proposed reading is only a conjecture, which, however, corresponds to the actual remains.

L. 2 על מדבחא. A large empty space at the beginning of the line is puzzling because, following MS A 25a l. 21, the Qumran text should read עלהא. On the other hand, the *vacat* that follows in the Qumran manuscript is justified for MS A 25b l. 22 begins a new sentence here.

L. 3 ל]ה]דל]קה. The upper arms of the *lāmed* are well preserved; the whole reading is reconstructed on the basis of the MS A text.

4Q214a frg. 1—reconstruction

Parallel: MS A 24–25; <u>4Q214 1 7</u>; <u>4Q214b frgs. 2–3 5</u>

1   ⁽²⁴⁾הֹדֹסֹא ^(25a)אֱלֵן אַ]ינון די אמר לי די חזין להסקה מנהון לתחות עלתא[

2   על מדבחא vacat ^(25b)וֹכ]די הנסקת מן אעי אלין על מדבחא ונורא ישרא[

3   לֹ]הֹ]דֹלֹ]קֹא בהון והא באדין תשרא למזרק דמא על כותלי מדבחא[

NOTES ON THE RECONSTRUCTION

The Qumran fragment corresponds to A 24 l. 19–25b l. 2. The line length covers about 50 to 55 letter-spaces, a usual size in the Qumran manuscripts of the *Document*.

L. 1 A 24 l. 19 reads דקתא. The term הֹדֹסֹא at the end of v. 24 means that either the list ended with this tree, or the syntagm was repeated, אדסא ועי הֹדֹסֹא. It is also possible that the position of the names of the trees in the list were interchanged.

L. 3 לֹ]הֹ]דֹלֹ]קֹה overlaps with 4Q214 1 7, לֹהֹדֹ]לקא[.

2.2.4 *A.L.D. 22–31*

4Q214b frg. 2–3 = 4QLevi^f (Pl. V)

1   ] וֹבֹ]אֹדֹ]יֹ]ן [

2   ⁽²³⁾תרי ע]שר עעין א[

3   סֹלֹק ⁽²⁴⁾ואֹלֹין שמֹה]

4   [בֹרֹותא ותככהֹ]

5   ^(25a)אֱלֵן אֱנון די אֱ[

6 ^(25b)אֱסקֹ]ת מֹ]ן עעי]א אֱלֵן עֱלֹ מֹדֹבֹחֹא וֹ]נֹ]וֹרֹ]א

7   עֱלֹ כותלי מדבחא ⁽²⁶⁾ותוֹבֹ]

8   אֱבֹרֹ]יֹה] מֹ]לֹי]חֹין ⁽²⁷⁾רֹאֹ]שֹא

NOTES ON READINGS

L. 1 וֹבֹ]אֹדֹ]יֹ]ן. Most of the line is torn off, only the lower parts of three letters are visible. Stone and Greenfield (1996a: 64) read a *sāmek* and a final *nûn*. However, the two parallel strokes can hardly belong to a *sāmek*. Following MS A text one should read a left leg of an *'ālep* and the down-stroke of a *dālet*.

L. 3 סֹלֹק ואֹלֹין. The upper parts of the letters are torn off, but the exact identification does not cause any problem.

L. 5 אֱ. The left leg of an *'ālep* together with the beginning of its axis remain on the edge of the leather.

L. 5 אֱנון. The scribal dot above the *'ālep* is probably an ink splash; the leather is partially abraded.

L. 5]א̊. The right upper arm of an *’ālep* is preserved, the rest, how-ever, is torn off.

L. 6]ן מ̊[ת̊ק̊ס̊א. The tops of *tāw*, *mêm*, and *nûn* remain on the edge of the leather. Stone and Greenfield (1996a: 64) do not transcribe them.

L. 6 ע̊ל̊ מדבח̊א̊. The tail of an *‘ayin* and *lāmed* remain on the edge of the tear; Stone and Greenfield (1996a: 64) omit the *‘ayin* in their tran-scription. The *mêm* and *dālet* are well preserved, the tops of the other let-ters are damaged.

L. 6 ו̊[נ̊]ר̊[א. The bottom of the *wāw* is visible, then, after the lacuna, only a small ink dot suggests the end of the downstroke of a *rêš*.

L. 7 מדבחא. The *ḥêt* is damaged, but the whole reading is certain.

L. 8]א̊ב̊ר̊[יה]. The leather preserves ink traces of an *’ālep*, a clear *bêt*, and the head of a *rêš*, cf. A 26 l. 2.

L. 8 מ[לי]ח̊ין. The right part of a *mêm* is well preserved, then the cross-bar of the *ḥêt*, the *yôd*, and the final *nûn* remain on the leather.

4Q214b frg. 4 = 4QLevi^f (Pl. V)

]א̊נ̊ו̊[^(22 l. 11)	1
]ı̊ ר̊ לי[^(23 l. 13–14)	2
]א̊ ı̊[^(24 l. 16)	3

NOTES ON READINGS

Milik located this small fragment on the plate between frgs. 2–3 and 5–6 and this location and restoration are based on A 22–24.

L. 2 ר̊[. The downstroke of the *rêš* is partially damaged.

L. 3]א̊ ı̊[. The manuscript preserves only two separate ink dots from the tops of two letters. The second one may be identified as the right arm of an *’ālep*. All is restored on the basis of MS A.

4Q214b frg. 5–6 i = 4QLevi^f (Pl. V)

]ן̊ מצלח̊ין ^(22)	1
כדן חזית לאברהם[	2
ל̊[אסקא מנהון למדבחא ^(23)	3
ודפ[רנא וסינדא̊ ^(24)	4
ע[ר̊א אדסא ועעי	5
לתחות עלחא[^(25a)	6

NOTES ON READINGS

This is the first of the two columns that have survived in the fragment. 4Q214b frg. 2–3 and 4 preserve other parts of the right column. In the left column, only few letters of the text survive.

L. 1 מִצְלֹחִין. Only the upper parts of *ṣādê* and *lāmed* remain in the manuscript on the edge of a lacuna.

L. 2 לאברהם. The upper arm of a *lāmed* is partly rubbed; its hook touches the following *ʾālep*. The right downstroke of the final *mêm* remains on the edge of the leather.

L. 3 ל]אסקא. The left leg of an *ʾālep* together with the upper part of its axis stand on the edge of the leather.

L. 4 וסינדא. A tear runs across this word; the upper part of a *dālet* is certain, and an *ʾālep* more probable than a *hê* without its horizontal head.

L. 6 לתחות עלהא. The tops of the letters allow full identification of these two words.

4Q214b frg. 2–3, frg. 4 and frg. 5–6 i – reconstruction
Parallels: <u>MS A 21–27</u>; 1Q21 45; <u>4Q214 1 5 and 8</u>; <u>4Q214 2 3</u>; <u>4Q214a 1 1</u>

1 [⁽²¹⁾למדבחא הוי עוד תאב ורחע ידיך ורנליך ⁽²²⁾ומהקרב עעי]ן מִצְלֹחִין

2 [ובקר אנון לקדמין מן תולעא וב]אֹד[י]ן [אסק] אֹנֹו[ן ארו]כדן הוית לאברהם

3 [אבי מזדהר ⁽²³⁾מן כל תרי ע]שר עעין א[מ]רֹ לֹי[ן די חזין ל]אסקא מנהון למדבחא

4 [די ריח תננהון בשים] סלק ⁽²⁴⁾ואל]ן שמה[תהו]ן א[רזא ודפ]רנא וסינדא

5 [ואטולא ושוחא וארזנא] בֹרֹותֹהֹ ותככֹהֹ [ועעא משחא ע]לֹרֹא אדסא ועי

6]   vacat?   [⁽²⁵ᵃ⁾אֵלֹן אֵנֹוֹן די א[מר לי די חזין לאסקא מנהון]לתחות עלהא

7 [על מדבחא ⁽²⁵ᵇ⁾וכדי אסק]ת מֹן [עע]ין]א אֹלֹן עֹל מֹדבֹחֹא וֹ[נ]וֹרֹ [א ישרא לֹאדלקֹא]

8 [בהון והא באדין תשרא למזרק דמא]עֹל כֹותֹלֹי מדבֹחֹא ⁽²⁶⁾ותוֹב [רחע ידיך]

9 [ורנליך מן דמא ושרי לאסקא] אברֹ[יֹה] מֹ[לי]חֹיֹן ⁽²⁷⁾רֹאֹ[שא הוי מסק לקדמין]

10 [ועלוהי חפי תרבא ולא יתחזי לה דם נכסת תורא ⁽²⁸⁾ובתרוהי צורא

NOTES ON THE RECONSTRUCTION

The line length oscillates between 62 and 55 letter-spaces. 4Q214b 5–6 i preserves the end of the lines in the manuscript, whereas frg. 2–3 ll. 1–5 and frg. 4 belong to the right side of the column. 4Q214b 2–3 ll. 6–8 (7–9 in the reconstruction) constitute the next three lines of the text.

L. 2   Albeit A 22 ll. 11–12 is omitted in E 18,2 v. 22, line 2 in the reconstruction confirms the presence of these two MS A lines in 4Q214b 4 1 and 5–6 i 2.

L. 3   MS A 23 l. 12 has מן כל תריעשר מיני אעין. The Qumran text omits מיני, "kinds of". This omission concords with E 18,2 v. 23 which has a shorter text ιβ' ξύλα and omits כל מן found in MS A. This last syntagm, however, is to be kept in the reconstruction, if the line length should correspond to the Qumran verse disposition.

L. 3   The expression למדבחא in 4Q214b 5–6 i 3 overlaps with 4Q214 1 5 (ל]מדבח[א).

L. 4   ‏ואל[ן שמֹה[תהון. MS A adds ‏אינון after ‏ואלין, E 18,2 v. 24 follows the Qumran reading.

L. 5   ‏ותככה. A 24 l. 18 reads ‏ותאנהא.

L. 6   This line is too short at its beginning. One should assume another noun suggested by the construct ‏עי, and a *vacat* in the Qumran manuscript.

L. 6   ‏אלן אנון. This expression partially overlaps with 4Q214a 1 1 (‏אלן ‏א]).

L. 8   ‏כותלי. 4Q214b 2–3 7 partially overlaps with 4Q214 1 8 ([‏כֹ]ותלי).

L. 8   ‏ותוב. A 26 l. 2 reads ‏ועוד instead.

L. 9   ‏מ]לי[חין רא]שא. 4Q214b 2–3 8 overlaps with 4Q214 2 3 (‏מליחֹ[ן]) ‏רא]שא, and with 1Q21 45 2 (‏מל[יחין ראשא).

L. 10   This reconstructed line is probably the last one in this column, then the text continues in the second column preserved in 4Q214 5–6 ii, see below. The reconstruction of these two columns allow the supposition that this manuscript has ten lines in each column. Note, however, that line 10 could have been located at the top of the next column.

4Q214b frg. 5–6 ii = 4QLevi^f (Pl. V)

‏[^(28)	1
‏[^(29)	2
‏כמ]סתהון ^(30)	3
‏לבו]נה	4
‏א[ל ^(31)	5
‏הֹ]ותר	6

NOTES ON READINGS

This is a second column of the fragmentary 4Q214b 5–6. The leather preserves only few letters at the beginning of four lines.

Ll. 1–2   The existence of the first two lines in the column is postulated on the basis of the comparison with the first column in 4Q214b 5–6 i.

L. 3   ‏כמ]סתהון. The downstroke and base of a *kāp* followed by remains of a letter remain at the edge of the leather; the rest of the line is torn.

L. 6   ‏הֹ]ותר. There remains only an ink dot on the edge of the lacuna. The restoration is based on MS A 31.

4Q214b frg. 5–6 ii—reconstruction
Parallels: MS A 28–34; 4Q214 2

1   ‏[^(28)ובתרהון ידיא ובתרהון ניעא עם בן דפנא ובתרהון ירכתא עם שדרת הרצֹא]

2   ‏[ובתרהון רגלין רחיען עם קרביא ^(29)וכלהון מליחין במלה כדי הוה להון]

3   ‏כמ]סתהון ^(30)ובתר דנה נישפֹא בליל במשחא ובתר כלא המר נסך והקטר עליהון]

4   לבו[נ]ה ולהוא כן עבדך בסרך וכל קרבנך לרעוא לריח ניחח קדם]

5   א]ל עליון (31)וכל די תהוה עבד בסרך הוי עבד במשחא ובמתקל ולא]

6   ת]ותר צבו די לא חזה ולא תחסר מן חשבן הזהא די עעין חזין להקרבה]

7   [לכל די סליק למדבחא (32a)לתורא רבא ככר עעין לה במתקל ואם תרבא]

8   [בלחודוהי סליק שתה מנין ועם פר תורין הוא די סליק (32b)חמשי ך מנין]

9   [ואם תרבא בלחודוהי חמשא מנין (33)ואם תורא רבא ארבעין מנין (34)ואם]

(10) [דכרא מן ענא או צפירדא מן עזיא הוא די סליק ולה תלתין מנין ולתרבא]

NOTES ON THE RECONSTRUCTION

The remaining letters allow the hypothetical reconstruction of the whole column. This manuscript corresponds to A 28–32a and the last two lines of the reconstruction contain the text known today only from E 18,2 vv. 32b–34. The first two lines in the column cover A 28 ll. 7–29 l. 12. However, a shorter form of verse 28 attested by E 18,2 v. 28 and 4Q214 2 was used in the reconstruction. Although the upper and lower margins are lost, the reconstruction of the second column points out that the manuscript probably had ten lines in each column. Once the missing text between the end of the first column (4Q214b 2–3 8 = line 9 in the reconstruction) and the beginning of line 3 in 4Q214b 5–6 ii is filled with MS A 27–29, it becomes evident that it accounts for only three lines of the Qumran manuscript—one tentatively located at the bottom of 4Q214b 2–3 and two at the top of 4Q214b 5–6 ii. It is highly improbable that the Qumran text is substantially longer than the MS A manuscript.

2.2.5   A.L.D. *69–73*

4Q214a frg. 2 i = 4QLevi^c (Pl. V)

אר]ו[(69b) כדי	1
ע]לוהי	2
ש]עא(70)	3
א]א̊ ושוית(71)	4
ב̊]שנת(72)	5
יעא [	6
מ̊צ̊]ר[י̊]ן[(73)	7

NOTES ON READINGS

L. 1   אר]ו̊[כדי̊. There are some ink traces on the edge of the fragment. The *wāw* is identified mainly on the basis of the comparison with MS A text. The *yôd* is rubbed but the reading is certain.

Ll. 2–3   The leather is partially torn between line 2 and 3.

L. 3   שׁעא[. The ink traces on the edge of the leather cannot belong to a *yôd* (Stone and Greenfield 1996a: 56), for the stroke does not have the hooked top characteristic to this letter. It might constitute the left part of a *šîn* with part of a slanting stroke on the right. Since the surface of the leather above the letters is partially damaged, one may assume that the scribe tried to correct ת]שׁעא to ת]שׁיעיא with the two *yôd* written above the line. The reconstruction remains hypothetical.

L. 4   א[. The ink dot on the edge of the leather can be recognized as the left upper part of the axis of an *’ālep*.

L. 5   בשׁנת[. Only an ink dot of the *bêt* has survived on the right of the *šîn*.

L. 7   [מצ̇]ר]י̇[ן]. Faint ink traces on the edge of the leather indicate the presence of some letters.

4Q214a frg. 2 i—reconstruction
Parallel: MS A 69a–73

1 כדי ואר]ן (69b) לחדה עלוהי לי מר ארו מרדי שמה וקראת תליתי [בר

2 עלוהי] והתחננת ובעית סניא עלוהי לי מריר והוה מת הוא [יליד

3 ת]שׁעא בירחה ילידת לחיי ארבעין בשנת (70) vacat מרד בכל [והוה

4 ושׁיית בֿרת]א לי וילידת והרת עמהא והוית אוספת ועוד (71) vacat (?)]

5 בשנת (72)] לישראל לכבוד לי ילידת ליקר כדי אמרת יוכבד [שמהא

6 שב]יֿעא בחודשא בחד ולידת   לחיי וארבע [שתין

7 [מצ̇]ר]י̇[ן] לארע למעלינא עשרה שת בשנת (73) למצרין העלנא די בתר [מן

NOTES ON THE RECONSTRUCTION

Stone and Greenfield (1996a: 57) wrongly assume that the column width is limited to 39–40 letter-spaces. The line length oscillates between 50 and 55 letter-spaces. They also left out lines 1 and 2 from their reconstruction.

L. 2   To keep the line length the clause מן די ימות (A 69b l. 15) has to be omitted. Note that in A 69b the information about Merari's death appears twice, cf. A 69b l. 14 (מת הוא).

L. 3   ת]שׁעא. Note the unusual ending of the ordinal. A 70 l. 17 reads תליתן[י], but the surviving ending is different. The *‘ain* suggests "nine" for "ninth" (תשׁיעיא).

L. 4   There is either an additional word or a *vacat* at the beginning of the line.

L. 6   The spurious לי after וארבע has been omitted in the reconstruction. The Qumran text must have had two or three additional words in this line, or a *vacat* compensated for an omission. Note the unusual ending of the numeral שב]יֿעא. One would expect שׁביעיא.

2.2.6 *A.L.D. 82–100*

4Q213 frg. 1 i = 4QLevi^a (Pl. II)

vacat[	1
מ]ֹית בה[(82)	2
א]ֹנון[	3
לבני[(83)	4
א]ֹנה לֹכן[(84)	5
שֹ כל עבדכן[(85)	6
וקשטֹא (86)צדקתֹא [ ] כֹן[	7
ומ]ֹבה (87)דזרע טב טב מֹעֹל	8
וכען ספר ומוסר וחכמה (88)vacat זר]ֹעֹה	9
ליקר עלם (89)די אלף חכמה יקר[	10
לב]ֹסרון ולשיטו מתיהב (90)הזו לכן בני	11
ומוס]ֹר חכמה ליקר ולרבו ולמלכין	12
אֹל תמחלו חכמתא למאלף[	13
מֹאֹלֹפֹ}<מֹהֹלֹךֹ> נבר די אלף חכמה כל (91)[	14
שמע]ֹא לכל מת ומדינה די יהך לה	15
מתנ]כֹֹֹֹֹר בה ולא דמא בה לנכרי ולא	16
יֹ]הֹבין לה בה יקר בדי כלא צבין	17
רחמן]הֹי שניאין ושאלי שלמה רברבֹין (92)	18
וֹ]ֹן (93)למשמע מלי חכמתֹה	19
לכל [(94)ידעיה ושימה טֹבה	20
תֹקֹיפֹין ועם [רב]חֹיֹל (95)[	21

NOTES ON READINGS

L. 2 מֹית[. The ticked head of a *mêm* with its left oblique stroke is well preserved.

L. 3 אֹנון[. The ink traces of the *'ālep* are partly erased; the final *nûn* is damaged.

L. 4 לבני[. The arm of a *lāmed* and the ticked head of a *bêt* are discernible; see *bêt* in line 8.

L. 5 לֹכן. The hole in the leather damages the letters; there remain the damaged arm and foot of the *lāmed* together with the base of the *kāp*.

L. 6 שֹ[. There are light remains of the bottom of a downstroke. According to the Geniza text, it is a *šîn*.

L. 7 There is a lacuna between עמ]כֹן and צדקתא. A *vacat* is plausible here, for the leather is torn in such a way that the remaining space accomodates only two large letters, or even less; thus Greenfield and Stone's (1996a: 9) reading [קאם] must be abandoned

L. 7 וקשטא. The ʾālep crosses over the stitching and is written partly on the margin of the next column. It proves that the text was copied only after the sewing of singular leaves took place.

L. 8 וט[בה. The shape of the head and base is that of a bêt and not a kāp, as Stone and Greenfield (1996a: 5) incorrectly transcribe and reconstruct.

L. 10 אלפ. The pê has an unusually large base – it is a final pê converted by the scribe into the shape of a median letter, see also למאלפ (line 13 – corrected from the final pê); אלפ (line 14); 4Q213 2 9, 12, 14.

L. 13 אל[. A left leg and a part of the axis of an ʾālep is preserved, the rest is lost in the tear.

L. 14 <מהלך>{מאלפ}[. Only tops of the letters have survived, the surface of the leather being abraded. A ticked head of a mêm may be discerned, then the ink traces suggest a hê as a correction of an ʾālep or ʿayin; a yôd hangs above the hê, and there follows the thick arm of a lāmed. The last letter is a final pê (cf. אלפ in line 10) corrected into a final kāp. Its huge head distinct from that of a regular pê fills the space between the two words. The scribe most probably changed a more familiar paʿel participle מאלף "the one who teaches" to מה<י>לך, a participle hapʿel of הלך "the one who guides/directs/leads," cf. 4Q542 1 i 12 and comment in Puech 1991: 42. This initial mistake that led to the correction was caused by the homoioteleuton with the next אלף.

L. 14 אלף חכמה. There is an ink dot on the leather above the line between pê and ḥêt.

L. 15 שמע[א. The left curved leg of an ʾālep departs from the diagonal axis almost entirely lost in the lacuna.

L. 16 מתנ[נ]בר. A dot from the base of a kāp and a tick of the horizontal crossbar of a rêš are preserved on the edge of the tear.

L. 18 שניאין ושאלי. Yôd is partially effaced, the lower part of the wāw damaged, while the left leg of the second ʾālep is abraded.

L. 18 רברבין. The last three letters are damaged, but the overall reading is certain.

L. 19 הכמתה. The surface of the leather is warped and partially abraded. The first three letters are damaged but the reading is certain. The tāw is well preserved, then the right leg of a hê (see line 8) touches the tāw, the rest of the letter, however, is lost.

L. 20 טבה. The left and right strokes of the ṭêt are partially preserved on both edges of the lacuna, the last two letters are certain.

L. 21 חיל[. Although the leather is torn, there remain the heads of ḥêt, yôd, and a part of a lāmed.

4Q213 1 i—reconstruction
Parallel: [MS A 81–95]

1	[(81)וחזית לי בנין תליהאין עד די לא מיתת	vacat [
2	[(82)ובשׁנת מאה ותמנֹי אשׁרה לחיי היא שׁתא דין] מית בה

3 [יוסף אחי קרית לבני ולבניהן ושרית לפקדה [אנון

4 [כל די הוא עם לבבי (?) vacat ⁽⁸³⁾עניִת ואמרת [לבנִי

5 [שמעו למאמר לוי אבוכן והציתו לפקודי ידיד אל ⁽⁸⁴⁾[אנה לכן

6 [מפקד בני ואנה קשטא לכן מהחוה חביבי ⁽⁸⁵⁾רא]שׁ כל עבדכן

7 [להוה קשטא ועד עלמא להוה קאם עמ]כֹן [צדקתא ⁽⁸⁶⁾וקשטֹא

8 [הן תזרעון תנהעלון עללה בריכה וט]בֹה ⁽⁸⁷⁾דזרע טב טב מעל

9 [ודי זרע ביש עלוהי חאב זר]עֹה ⁽⁸⁸⁾vacat וכען ספר ומוסר וחכמה

10 [אלפו לבניכן ותהוה חכמתא עמכן ⁽⁸⁹⁾ליקר עלם די אלף חכמה יקר

11 [היא בה ודי שאט חכמתא לב]סרון ולשיטו מתיהב ⁽⁹⁰⁾חזו לכן בני

12 [ליוסף אחי די מאלף הוא ספר ומוס]רׁ חכמה ליקר ולרבו ולמלכין

13 [על כרסיהון מתחד הוא vacat]אֹל תמחלו חכמתא למאלף

14 [ולארחתה אל תשבקו לבעא ⁽⁹¹⁾די]מٔאٔלٔף <מٔהٔלٔךׁ> נבר די אלף חכמה כל

15 [יומוהי אריכין וסנה לה שמע]א לכל מת ומדינה די יהך לה

16 [אח או חבר הוא בה ולא הוא מתנ]כֹּרׂ בה ולא דמא בה לנכרי ולא

17 [דמא בה לכילאי מٔן די כלהן י]חٔבין לה בה יקר בדי כלא צבין

18 [למאלף מן חכמתה ⁽⁹²⁾רחמו]הי שניאׁין ושׁאٔלׁי שלמה רברבٔין

19 [ועל כרסי יקר מהתבין לה בדיל צבי]ן למשמע מלי חכמתה ⁽⁹³⁾

20] vacat ⁽⁹⁴⁾עותר רב די יקר היא חכמתה לכל] ידעיה ושימה טֹבה

21 [לכל קניה ⁽⁹⁵⁾הן יאתון מלכין]תٔקٔיפٔיٔן ועם [רב ו]חٔיٔל

22 [ופרשין ורתיכין שניאין עמהן וינסבון נכסי מת ומדינה]

23 [ויבוזון כל די בהן אוצרי חכמתא לא יבוזון ולא ישכחון]

1 [⁽⁹⁶⁾מטמוריה ולא. . .

NOTES ON THE RECONSTRUCTION

The reconstruction indicates that this Qumran manuscript had two additional lines (22–23) preserved in A 95. The last two words of A 95 l. 23 are extant at the beginning of the new column in 4Q213 1 ii 1, which contains the continuation of 4Q213 1 i. It also becomes evident that the line length in 4Q213 1 i roughly corresponds to two lines of the Cairo Geniza text. For the purpose of a correct reconstruction, the orthography of the Geniza manuscripts has been changed in conformity with Qumran spelling. The examples of *plene* spellings in Cairo Geniza manuscripts have been listed in § 1.5.1.

L. 1 The *vacat* at the end of the line indicates the beginning of a new section, cf. A 81 l. 3.

L. 4   Since the line is too short in the reconstruction, a possible *vacat* might have occurred before עניח.

L. 6   כל עבדכן. A 85 l. 10 omits כל.

L. 7   The A text is also too short to fill the Qumran line. A 85 l. 12 reads an absolute form צדקה, whereas the Qumran text has this word in the emphatic state.

L. 9   The Qumran text and A 87 l. 17 have a *vacat* before the beginning of the new section.

L. 9   וכען. A 88 l. 17 adds בני after וכען.

L. 9   ומוסר וחכמה. A 88 ll. 17–18 omits the *wāw* before מוסר and חכמה.

L. 10   חכמה. A 89 l. 20 reads an emphatic state חוכמתה.

L. 10   יקר. A 89 l. 20 has a *wāw* before יקר, and that causes a syntactical incongruity and should be deleted.

L. 11   לכן. A 90 l. 22 omits.

L. 12   [מאלף הוא]. The line length makes it necessary to add הוא after מאלף, cf. Stone and Greenfield 1996a: 9.

L. 13   The reconstructed MS A text is shorter than the Qumran line. Since the narrative switches to an exhortation in A 90 ll. 2–4, a *vacat* may be assumed before the switch occurs.

L. 14   <מהלך>. In A 90 l. 2 there is a left downstroke of a *hê* at the end of the lacuna, and that suggests a different reading, probably [הכמ]ה. Since the Qumran scribe corrected the reading (see Notes on Readings above), he probably adjusted his text and omitted the word that became semantically spurious in the corrected sentence.

L. 15   Instead of עלל "to enter" (A 91 l. 7), the Qumran MS has יהך "to go."

L. 19   צבי[ן]. This word must have been accidentally omitted in A 93 l. 15; cf. A 91 l. 11. With this reconstruction, all the words fit within the line perfectly and the syntax runs much more smoothly. The preposition בדיל requires a finite verb but is followed in A 93 l. 15 by an infinitive למשמע. According to Stone and Greenfield (1996a: 11), the word בדיל is to be omitted and thus למשמע is preceded by לה מהתבי[ן]. This proposal should be abandoned.

L. 20   לכל] ידעיה. MS A omits the syntagm which stands in poetical parallelism with לכל קניהא (A 94 l. 17). A *vacat* or an additional word probably occurs at the beginning of the line.

L. 21   Although the leather is shrunk, the length of this line can be precisely established on the basis of A 95.

4Q213 frg. 1 ii = 4QLevi^a (Pl. II)

top margin		
ולא]	מטמומריה ולא יעלון תרעיה ולא](96)	1
ולא]	ישכחון למכבש שוריה [ ] ולא	2
[	יחזון שימחה שימחה נ[נ]דה]	3
[	ולא איתי כל מחיר ננדה ו[לא](97)	4

[בעא חכמ֯ה֯] הכ[מחא י֯[שכה   5

[מטמרה מנד]   6

[ולא חס[ין֯[ד֯]   7

[בקשט [(98)   8

[חכ֯מה ד֯'אלפ[ו   9

[י֯ת֯ת֯]   10

[   ] כ֯11

[אנ[(99)   12

[קד֯]ית   13

[ודא֯]נין   14

[   ]   15

[ת֯ה֯]וו[(100)ן֯   16

[תהוא֯]   17

[לי֯ק֯]רכן   18

[ד֯]ר֯יא   19

NOTES ON READINGS

L. 1   תרעי֯ה. There is a small dot above the *hê*.

L. 3   שימ֯תה. With Stone and Greenfield 1996a: 14. Only the top of the third letter with its right downstroke is preserved. Milik (Brown 1988: *s.v.*) reads שיחתה "its fodder". Kugler (1996a: 119) reads a *dālet*, שידחה and translates "its box," see his note on p. 125. The beginning of a base and the slanting stroke on the left make the *mêm* certain.

L. 3   ] נ֯ד[נ]֯ה. Before the lacuna there remains an angular bend of a letter, probably a *nûn*. The head of the *dālet* is easily discernible together with the crossbar and right leg of a *hê*.

L. 4   כ֯ל מחיר. The upper part of the *lāmed* is preserved on the edge of the leather together with the bottom of the right downstroke of a *kāp*.

L. 4   ו֯[לא. Only the downstroke of a letter has survived. Given the frequency of *wāw* in this section, it seems to be the most plausible reading.

L. 5   י֯[שכה. The head of a *yôd* remains in the manuscript. For the *ʾapʿel* impf. of the same root, cf. A 95 l. 23; 4Q213 1 ii 2 (*A.L.D.* 96 l. 2).

L. 8   בקשט. A part of the head of a *bêt* together with a *qôp* are preserved on the leather.

L. 9   חכ֯מה. Remains of the base of a *kāp* are visible, while the *ḥêt* is almost complete. There is a small ink dot above the *hê*.

L. 9   אלפ[ו. The remaining angular base of a letter may be a median *pê*. The supralinear ד֯' seems to be written by the first scribe.

L. 11   On the margin of the manuscript between lines 11 and 12 there is a hook with its horizontal crossbar truncated by the lacuna; a similar sign appears on the margin of 4Q213a 2 10 (*A.L.D.* 98). Scribal signs placed on the manuscript margins have been detected elsewhere in the Qumran manuscripts, and they indicate the end or beginning of a paragraph, cf. Tov 1996: 47 and 71, fig. 1.3.

L. 12　אנ]. The right downstroke turning to the left remains at the edge of the leather. It may be a *nûn* or *bêt*.

L. 14　ודא]נין. The *'ālep* is certain. The overall reading follows the reconstruction by Milik (cf. Brown 1988: *s.v.*)

L. 16　תה]וון. There is a small accidental dot in the manuscript above the *tāw*. The next letter attached to the *tāw* could be a *hê*.

L. 17　תהוא. The reading is certain, but only the right leg and a part of the axis of an *'ālep* are visible.

L. 18　ליק]רכן. The *lāmed* and *yôd* are easily discernible, then comes the rounded tip of a *qôp*.

L. 19　ד]ריא. The manuscript indicates some faint traces of a vertical downstroke of what might be a *dālet/wāw/...*. The proposed reconstruction is hypothetical.

4Q213 frg. 2 = 4QLevi^a (Pl. II)

כל [אנ]ש די] [(97)	1
[　　　　] תה][	2
[　　　]א לי°[	3
[　　ן כל בעי]ן[	4
]ספר ומוסר[(98)	5
]תרתון אנון[	6
]רבה תתנון[	7
וי]קר　　　　vacat	8
]אף בספריא[(99)	9
תה]וון ראשין ושפטין	10
]ב ועבדין[	11
]אף כהנין ומלכין[	12
ש][ ]ן[מלכותכן[(100)	13
יק]ר ולא איתי סוף	14
ולא]תעבר מנכן עד כל	15
]ן ביקר רב[	16

NOTES ON READINGS

L. 1　כל [אנ]ש. The right arm of the *'ālep* is cut off but the reading is certain. The curved base of a letter may belong to a *nûn* or *pê*.

L. 3]° ל א[. The *'ālep* and *lāmed* seem not to belong to the same word, there is a dot in between.

L. 5 ס̇פר[. The *sāmek* is lost except for a part of its hook.

L. 9 א̇פ[. The scribe uses the usual *pê*, instead of the final *pê*, cf. also line 12 and 14; 4Q213 1 i 10, 13, 14.

L. 10 מלא[כ]י̇ן. The *yôd* and final *nûn* are well preserved, while there are some traces of the head of a letter before the *yôd*. The *kāp* is probable and suggested by the context.

L. 12 א̊פ[. There remain some traces characteristic to an *'ālep*, its left leg, a part of its axis, and the top of the right arm.

L. 13 ש̇[ ]ן̇[. The ink traces suggest the slanting stroke of a *śin* rather than an *ᶜayin*.

L. 16 בי̇קר]ן[. The ink traces suggest a final *nûn*, the right downstroke of the *bêt* and its base are damaged by the lacuna.

4Q213 1 ii and frg. 2—reconstruction
Parallels: MS A 96, 4Q214a frg. 2 ii and 4Q214b frg. 8

			top margin	
ולא[			(96) מ̇ט̇מ̇וריה ולא̊ יעלון תרעיה ולא̇]	1
ולא[			ישכחון למכבש שוריה [ולא̇]	2
[			יחזון שימ̇תה שימחה נ̇[נ̇]ד̇ח̊]	3
1		(97) [כל̇ [אנ̇]ש̇ די̇]	ולא איתי כל̊ מחיר ננדה ו̇]לא	4
2		[תה] [	בעא חכמה̇] חכ]מחא י̇]שכח	5
3		[א לי̇°] [	מטמרה מנד̇ה] פל	6
4		[ן כל בעי̇ן] [	ולא הסן̇]ר̊]	7
5		(98) וכען בני [ספר ומוסר	ב̇קשט]	8
6		חזית בחזוין די]ת̇רתון אנון	חכ̇מה ד̇ אלפ̊]ו	9
7		[רבה תתנון	י̇ת̇]	10
8		ו̇י̇ק̇ר vacat	]כ	11
9		א̊פ בספריא]	(99) אנ̇]	12
10		תה]ו̇ו̇ן ראשין ושפ̇טין	קר̇]ית	13
11		ב ועבדין]	ודא̇]נין	14
12		א̊פ כהנין ומלכין]	]	15
13		(100) ש̊] [ן̇] מלכותכן	תה]ו̇ו̇ן	16
14		יק̇]ר̊ ולא איתי סוף	תהוא̊]	17
15		ולא [תעבר מנכן עד כל	לי̊ק̇]רכן	18
16		ן בי̊קר רב]	ד̇]רי̊א	19

NOTES ON THE RECONSTRUCTION

The fragmentary text in these two fragments indicates that it contains the end of Levi's wisdom poem and the beginning of his speech directed to his children. Since both 4Q213 1 ii and 4Q213 1 i belong to the same manuscript, it is fair to assume that the number of lines in the column in 4Q213 1 ii is the same as in reconstructed 4Q213 1 i. This means that 4Q213 1 ii had twenty three lines. 4Q213 1 i is sewn to 4Q213 1 ii and the left margin of 4Q213 2 has also seams with a blank margin of the following column. Since 4Q213 1 ii and 4Q213 2 form together one column, the preserved stitchings on its both sides indicate that it was added between two separate leaves of the manuscript. It sometimes happened at Qumran that one leaf of the leather was inserted to serve as only one column. The sheets were ruled before sewing.

On the right margin of 4Q213 1 ii between lines 11 and 12 a scribal hook indicates the beginning of a new paragraph. Hence, the *vacat* of 4Q213 2 8 probably corresponds to the line 11 in 4Q213 1 ii, the last line of the paragraph. It would mean that the wisdom poem ends with an exhortation similar to A 88 ll. 17–18. Levi exhorts his sons to teach scribal craft, instruction, and wisdom (4Q213 2 5 together with 4Q214a 2 ii 5 and 4Q213 1 ii 9). The following paragraph deals with the future of Levi's children. The reconstruction of 4Q214a 2 ii indicates that 4Q213 2 5 should immediately follow 4Q213 1 ii 3. Yet, the wisdom poem in 4Q213 1 ii 4 continues and makes this restoration impossible. 4Q214a 2 ii probably witnesses a shorter ending of the wisdom poem, cf. the reconstruction of 4Q214a 2 ii below.

4Q214a frg. 2 ii = 4QLevi^c (Pl. V)

1	[וֹמדִינה](95)
2	לא ישכחון]
3	טבה ו[ל]ל]א
4	מנה ול]א
5	(98)ולכען בני ספר ו]
6	חזית בחזוין ד]י
7	[000000

NOTES ON READINGS

L. 1 וֹמדִינה. The reading is certain, Stone and Greenfield's decipherment (1996a: 58 וֹמדִיהא) does not find confirmation in the manuscript.

L. 3 א[ל]ל]ו. It seems that the ink remains could fit the proposed reading.

L. 4 ו]ל. The *wāw* is certain, then the arm of the *lāmed* and its hook are partially preserved at the edge of the leather.

L. 5 ספר. The ink traces are characteristic to the *sāmek* in this manuscript.

L. 6 בחזוין. Although the leather is partially folded, all the letters are discernible and the reading is certain. There follows the head of a *dālet*.

4Q214a frg. 2 ii—reconstruction
Parallels: A 95:21–23, <u>4Q213 1 ii 1–3, 9</u>

⁽⁹⁵⁾וּמְדִי֗נָֿה [וישׂתון כל די בהן אוצרי חכמתא לא יבוזון ⁽⁹⁶⁾<u>ומטמוריה</u> [		1
[לֹא ישׂכֿחוֹן] ולא יעלון תרעיה ולא		2
[ולא ישכחון למכבש שוריה ולא טבה וֹ[ל]אֿ		3
[מנה ולֹ[אֿ ולא יחזון שׂימתה שׂימתה		4
[⁽⁹⁸⁾וֹכֿען בני֗ ספֿר וֹ[מוסר חכמה די אלפו		5
[חזית בחזוין ד]י֗		6
[ ]°°°°°°		7

NOTES ON THE RECONSTRUCTION

This is the second column of 4Q214a 2. The first column breaks up at the beginning of Cambridge d (A 73 l. 2). The second column begins with the last words attested in A 95 l. 23 at the end of Cambridge f fragment. It means that three columns of Geniza text, d, e and f, (A 73 l. 2–95 l. 21) should fit in the space between the end of the first and beginning of the second column of 4Q214a 2. Assuming an average 60 letter-space line length of this Qumran manuscript, it would mean that the line number of the first Qumran column would amount to about 30 missing lines and 7 extant, the longest column length attested among Qumran manuscripts of the *Document*. 4Q213 frgs. 1 and 2 each have twenty three lines in a column, 4Q213a frgs. 1 and 2 preserve each eighteen lines in a column. 4Q214b frg. 2–3, frg. 4 and frg. 5–6 i and ii reconstructed together have ten lines in a column. Compare the 34 lines of 1Q*Genesis Apocryphon*.

L. 1   The lines of this fragment correspond to the final part of the wisdom poem. The reconstruction begins with וּמְדִי֗נָֿה found in A 95 l. 21.

L. 2   The expression לֹא ישׂכֿחוֹן] precedes ומטמוריה, hence the word order diverges from both A 95 l. 23 and 4Q213 1 ii 1. The reconstructed line length (about 55 letter-spaces) is also found in other Qumran manuscripts of the *Document*, see, e.g., 4Q213 1 i.

Ll. 3–4   The fragmentary words in these two lines do not overlap with any other manuscript witness.

L. 5   This line partially overlaps with 4Q213 2 5. In the reconstruction of the latter in combination with 4Q213 1 ii, 4Q213 2 5 constitutes the second half of 4Q213 1 ii 8. It means that the text of 4Q214a 2 ii 5 immediately preceded by that of 4Q213 1 ii 3 is shorter by about four and a half lines (4–8a = *A.L.D.* 97) in comparison with the reconstruction of 4Q213 1 ii and 4Q213 2.

4Q214b frg. 8 = 4QLevi^f (Pl. V)
Parallels: <u>4Q213 1 ii 4, 6</u>

[‏ולא[ן אֹיתֹי כוֹל מֹ]חֹיר ננדה ו‎ (96 l. 4)   1

[‏מ[ן]טמרא מנה פֹ]‎ (97 l. 6)   2

[‏מ[ן]וֹסֹר ח[כֹ]מה‎ (98 l. 9)   3

NOTES ON READINGS

L. 1   This line corresponds to 4Q213 1 ii 4 and line 2 to 4Q213 1 ii 6 (מטמרה מנה). Following the reconstruction of 4Q213 1 ii and 4Q213 2, it is certain that there is not enough space to accommodate 4Q213 1 ii 5 and 4Q213 2 1–2 in the space of the first two verses in 4Q214b 8. The latter is apparently one line shorter than the former ones.

L. 2   מ[ן]טמרא. Stone and Greenfield (1996a: 70) read מ[ן]טמריא. The *yôd* is, however, absent in the manuscript, cf. 4Q213 1 ii 6 מטמרה.

L. 2   פ[. The ink traces suggest a *pê*, the rest of the word is torn. 4Q214a 2 ii 4 has a different reading ולא[.

L. 3   מ[ן]וסר ח[כ]מה. The ink traces and the space allow the reconstruction of the last three letters of מוסר. Then the crossbar of the *ḥêt* is certain, and the partially rubbed downstroke probably belongs to a *kāp*.

2.3   *Non Classified Fragments*

The Qumran fragments presented here were assigned by Milik to the plates containing the *Document*'s manuscripts but they do not overlap with any other textual witness and their fragmentary state does not allow us to ascertain their unquestioned relation to the Levi's composition. It is, however, possible that they belong to the portions of the *Document* that are lost.

4Q213 frg. 6 = 4QLevi[a] (Pl. II)

‏כאֹבֹ רֹם אל]‎   1

NOTES ON READINGS

Stone and Greenfield (1996a: 24) have כמֹבֹרך and do not propose any translation. Kugler (1996a: 120) reads כהכים. The *kāp* is certain; then comes the right leg and part of the axis of an *ʾālep* followed by the head of a letter, probably a *bêt*. Then come *rêš* and final *mêm*. Remains of a light downstroke are possible after the *bêt*.

TRANSLATION

1   like an exalted father, do not/God[

COMMENTS

It is impossible to connect this fragment with any part of the available text and content of the *Document*.

4Q213a frg. 6 = 4QLevi^b (Pl. III)

‏אמרת מא[	‏]‏	1
vacat [	‏]‏	2
[ ]ל̊[	‏]‏	3

NOTES ON READINGS

The fragment probably preserves the left part of the lines in a column.

L. 2. The blank space between lines is probably a *vacat*.

L. 3]ל̊[. The arm of a *lāmed* has survived on the edge of the leather. The rest of the line is torn and missing.

TRANSLATION

1	[	]I said/she said what (?)	
2	[	] vacat	
3	[	] *l*[	]

COMMENTS

L. 1 The line is fragmentary, the parsing of the verb remains uncertain.

4Q214 frg. 4 = 4QLevi^d (Pl. IV)

‏]דֹנֹהֹ[	1
‏א/ה]בריןֹ ‏°[	2
‏]וֹ רבה ‏כהנ]ה	3
‏כ ‏צֹרֹיֹהֹ[ןֹא	4

NOTES ON READINGS

L. 1]דֹנֹהֹ[. The ink traces suggest the presence of three letters, the base of a medial *nûn* is the only probable decipherment. The reconstruction is hypothetical.

L. 4 א[ןֹצֹרֹיֹהֹ. Only tops of the letters have survived. Stone and Greenfield (1996a: 50) read]מריה[, the *mêm*, however, is impossible. The downstroke to the right with slanting one on the right top favor the reading *ṣādê*. For the reconstruced term אוצר, see A 95 l. 22.

TRANSLATION

1	]this[
2	] me[n
3	]high p[riest
4	]its [tre]asures *k*°[

4Q214 frg. 5 = 4QLevi^d (Pl. IV)

] יׄי [	1
] vacat [	2
[כיה]	3
[א טבח]	4
[רׄם ליש]ראל	5
[אׄטׄיׄין]	6
]° שם[	7

NOTES ON READING

It has been impossible to connect this fragment with any other witness of the *A.L.D.* Stone and Greenfield (1996a: 51) affirm that its handwriting is too different to be ascribed to 4Q214.

L. 1   ] יׄי [. Either *yôd* or *wāw* are possible.

L. 6   ]אׄטׄיׄין[. There remains the left downstroke of an *’ālep* or *lāmed*, then *yôd* and *wāw* follow the *ṭêt*. Read perhaps an *’ap‘el* of נטי "they will bend," (cf. Jastrow 1950: *s.v.*).

TRANSLATION

]*yn* [	1
] vacat [	2
]*kyh*[	3
]’ good[	4
]exalted for *Is*[rael	5
]*they will bend*[	6
]*name* °[	7

4Q214b frg. 1 = 4QLevi^f (Pl. V)

[מין מן כו]ל	1
מן]כׄול לביך [	2
[בׄעׄוׄ מׄצׄליׄן]	3

NOTES ON READINGS

L. 2   כֹּל[. Two ink dots from the upper and lower crossbar of the *kāp* remain at the edge of the leather.

L. 3   ]בֹ֒ע֒וֹ מֹצֹלִי֒ן[. Only the tops of the letters are preserved in the line. The *bêt* and *ʿayin* are the most probable readings followed by a *wāw*. Then there come the slanting head of *mêm* and remains of the head of a *ṣādê*. The *lāmed* is certain; then there probably comes the *yôd*; the *ʾālep*, however, is also possible.

TRANSLATION

1   ]*myn* from a[ll

2   from]all your hearts[
                               ]they sought, praying[

This fragment has no evident parallel with any known text of the *Document*.

4Q214b frg. 7 = 4QLevi^f (Pl. V)

1   [מ֒ן כול בשר]א

2   [מֹשחא ו֒]

NOTES ON READINGS

L. 1   ]מֹן כול[. Except for an ink dot of the base the *mêm* is lost, but the whole reading is certain. Kugler (1996a: 42) reads תכל and connects the expression with E 18,2 vv. 51–56; his reading, however, is incorrect—there is no *tāw* and כול is certain.

L. 2   ]מֹשחא ו֒[. The preserved tops of the letters permit to read the sequence *m-š-ḥ-ʾ*.

TRANSLATION
4Q214b frg. 7 = 4QLevi^f

1   ]more than all flesh[
2   ]measure/oil and[

COMMENTS

L. 1   The expression "from every flesh" is extant in A 14 ll. 10–11, 4Q213b 1 and E 18,2 v. 52. The word of the second line is also attested in A 24 l. 18; 30 l. 13 and 1Q21 37 2. The combination of the two lines is, however, difficult to locate in the *Document*. It might be connected with the description of Levi's priestly elevation, cf. A 6 and *T. Levi* 8:4.

L. 2   Because of the lack of context it is impossible to distinguish between two meanings of the lexeme משח.

CHAPTER THREE

ARAMAIC LEVI DOCUMENT: COMMENTARY

3.1 *Levi's Prayer—A.L.D. 1a*

Form and Structure

The composition (1a vv. 5–19) is written in a balanced prose and does not exhibit the characteristics of regular line parallelism found in Hebrew poetry. It is presented as a prayer in 1a v. 4 (ηὐξάμην "I prayed") and 1a v. 17 (צלות "prayer") and the whole text is divided into two parts, 1a vv. 5–15a and 1a vv. 15b–19. The beginning of the two sections is marked off by similar expressions, "you, Lord" (1a v. 5: κύριε/מרי אנתה; 1a v. 15b: σύ, κύριε/מרי [אנתה); 1a v. 15a and 1a v. 19a end the two parts with a similar clause ("do not turn—do not turn"). Both sections are formally similar—they are made up of a series of requests with verbs in imperative, except for 1a vv. 15b–16 that evokes God's blessing of Abraham and Sarah.

Formal elements of the prayer suggest that its literary form shares some features with the individual lament category of the Hebrew Psalter (e.g. *Psalms* 3–7; 13; 17; 22; 25; 38; 31, etc.). According to Gunkel's description of this literary genre (1998: 152–186), there are several constitutive elements of this type of psalmic song. The invocation of God's name stands at the very beginning of the composition and places the *orans* in the immediate presence of God (e.g. Ps 3:2; 5:2; 6:2). The lament may take a form of complaint against God or enemies, or it simply describes the distressful situation of the *orans* (e.g. Ps 3:2–5; 5:10; 6:3–4, 7–8; 10:1–18). The most important part of the genre is the supplication or request for help (e.g. Ps 3:8; 5:2, 9, 11; 13:3–4; 22:11, 19–21), and is joined to affirmation of trust in God as a basis for deliverance from oppression (e.g. Ps 13:5; 16:8; 22:3–5; 25:15). The psalm usually ends with the vow to praise and serve God when the crisis is past (e.g. Ps 13:6; 22:22–31; 26:12; 27:6).

From the review of the literary elements of the genre it becomes clear that the *Document*'s prayer presents a modified version of this literary type. Like the psalmic songs, the composition begins with the invocation of God's name (1a v. 5, "Lord"), and its major part

contains supplications (verbs in imperative), the goal of which is to
receive God's salvation and to be accepted into an intimate relationship with the Lord (1a vv. 6b–15a, 17–18). The basis for the
hope of being heard by God is rooted in the evocation of Abraham
and Sarah's covenantal blessing and promises (1a vv. 15b–16). The
lament, however, does not appear in the composition, but a "negative petition" is introduced instead (Westermann 1981: 185). It uses
the verbs that appear elsewhere in the individual lament songs in
the complaint: "do not turn away" (1a v. 15a); "do not cast off"
(1a v. 19; cf. Ps 27:9; 55:1, 11; 69:17; 102). In his analysis of the
historical development of the lament genre, Westermann (1981: 201)
classified this type of evolved literary composition as "petitionary
prayer without a lament," and cited as examples *3 Macc.* 6:1–15; *4
Ezra* 8:20–36; *Ps. Sol.* 12; Tob 3:1–5 (1981: 204, n. 94). There
remains little doubt that Westermann's definition corresponds to the
literary character of Levi's prayer.

David Flusser classified Levi's prayer as belonging to the "apotropaic"
type of literary composition alongside 11Q Psᵃ Plea for Deliverance
(11Q5 xix) and other rabbinic prayers. He stated that "the theme
of these prayers is the asking from God to avert personal dangers
and that He may grant heavenly bliss" (1966: 201). He then pro-
ceeded to draw a comparative table of topics that are common in
this type of prayer (1966: 203). The article makes it clear that Flusser's
approach consists in the analysis of the common thematic motifs and
not in the description of common literary characteristics of these
compositions. Hence his conclusions are not valid for establishing
the literary genre of Levi's prayer, although they help understand
the continuity of traditional prayer motifs inherent in works coming
from different historical epochs.

A narrative introduction in first person singular precedes the prayer
and is syntactically divided into 1a vv. 1–2 and 3–4. The repetition
of τότε in 1a vv. 1 and 3 might indicate either a discontinuity between
1a vv. 1–2 and 3–4 or mere progress of the narrative. In the former case Levi's purification and washing should be connected with
the preceding section that is totally missing. The latter interpretation seems preferable for neither the topic nor syntactic structure
impedes to read 1a vv. 1–2 as an introduction to the prayer. To
the contrary, this introductory liturgy that conjoins bodily ablutions
and moral conversion harmonizes well with the content of the prayer.
It expresses the *Document*'s tendency to interpret priestly purity as

dependent on one's moral action and God's intervention (1a v. 14; cf. also the comment on *A.L.D.* 1a vv. 1–2 below).

Stone and Greenfield (1993: 249) suggested that 1a vv. 1–2 describe the end of a ceremony rather than introduction to the prayer because Levitical ablutions usually follow cultic activities. The *Document*, however, does not confirm their opinion for in *A.L.D.* 19–21 several ablutions are requested exactly before the beginning of sacrificial activities. Also Num 8:7 and 21 indicate that clothes laundering and body washing of the Levites are necessary prerequisites of their consecration for the liturgical office in the tent of meeting. Additionally Exod 29:4 points out that Moses has to wash Aaron and his sons before putting on them priestly garments.

The section that follows the prayer (*A.L.D.* 1b) indicates that Levi, while going to his father Jacob, has a visionary experience. Since *A.L.D.* 1b ll. 11–14 is only a connective narrative between the prayer and the vision, it is certain that *A.L.D.* 1a vv. 1–19 constitutes a direct preparation to the visionary and revelatory experience that follows in 1b ll. 15–18. However, the prayer is not only an introduction to the vision, but it sketches out a specific description of Levi as God's holy servant who aspires to priestly (*A.L.D.* 1a vv. 11, 17) and judicial authority (*A.L.D.* 1a v. 18), rooted in God's revealed wisdom and spirit (1a v. 8) and dependent on God's purification of his servant (*A.L.D.* 1a v. 14). In this quest for God's intervention Levi is confronted by the threat of fornication, pride, and by the rule of the satanic spiritual power (*A.L.D.* 1a vv. 7, 10). His request to eliminate lawlessness from the earth (*A.L.D.* 1a v. 13) summarily expresses all forces opposed to God and to his lawful order. This soteriological conflict delineated in the prayer finds its solution and continuation in the following narrative about Levi's life and his priestly and royal elevation. By executing the doers of lawlessness (*A.L.D.* 78; cf. *A.L.D.* 1c–2) Levi becomes a guardian of divinely established legal principle of endogamy. By following Isaac's instructions he upholds the liturgical and metro-arithmetical order that reflects his royal and priestly authority (cf. *A.L.D.* 14; 30; 31; 46b–47; 99; 100). His royal priesthood of eternal peace (*A.L.D.* 3c–4; 6) is opposed to the sinful kingdom of the sword (*A.L.D.* 4–5). The judicial authority conferred to him by the heavenly elevation (*A.L.D.* 6) and earthly ordination (*A.L.D.* 9) is higher than any other human power (*A.L.D.* 14) and passes to his priestly descendants (*A.L.D.* 99; 100).

3.1.1 *Introductory Narrative—A.L.D. 1a vv. 1–4*

A.L.D. 1a v. 1 *Then I washed my garments. A.L.D.* 1a vv. 1–2 describe the purification rite that considerably differs from Levi's ablutions in *A.L.D.* 19–21 set in the context of Levi's sacrificial activity. Here the description recalls Lev 15:13 which rules that a man with sexual discharge (זב) should wash his clothes and bathe his body in running water to be clean again. Although the preceding context in the *Document* is missing, one could hardly connect Levi's purification with the circumstances set out by the biblical text. Kugler (1996a: 57–58) argued that the ablution refers to Levi's purification after corpse contamination in the killing of the Shechemites. The purification rite would result from the author's reading of Lev 15:13 in the light of Num 5:2 that "classifies the leper, the זב, and the corpse-contaminated together as persons too impure for cultic participation." However, Kugler's interpretation is based on the assumption that Levi's prayer stands in the structure of the whole composition after the Shechem incident (*A.L.D.* 1c–2). Being concentrated on proving the location of the prayer after the Shechem killing, Kugler ignores the immediate context of Levi's ablution (1a v. 2b "I made straight all my ways") and evident vocabulary relation between 1a vv. 1–2 and the prayer (see Form and Structure above). Additionally, since the LXX text omits ζῶντι in its rendering of the masoretic מים חיים in Lev 15:13, the connection of the latter with the *Document*'s ablution remains only a probability.

A.L.D. 1a v. 2 *I also bathed myself completely in running water.* The expression ἐν ὕδατι ζῶντι, lit. "in living water," is a Septuagint version of מים חיים that indicates water gushing from a spring (Gen 26:19; Jer 2:13; 17:13; Cant 4:15; cf. Zech 14:8). The "living water" is, therefore, best rendered as "flowing water" in contrast to standing water or water coming from a cistern. The "living" water in the Pentateuch is used only in the purification rites of a leper (Lev 14:5–6, 50; Num 19:17) or a man with a sexual discharge (זב Lev 15:13; LXX omits ζῶντι). Again, there is no evidence in the *Document* that these circumstances apply to Levi. Following the accepted interpretation, one should assume that bathing in running water is a sign of Levi's moral purification (1a v. 2b "I made straight all my ways") and preparation to enter the presence of God in his prayer. It is not clear whether Levi enters an actual torrent with running water, or, perhaps, the expression ἐν ὕδατι ζῶντι, which stands in parallel with ἐν ὕδατι καθαρῷ "in pure water," denotes only the quality of the purification water used for the ablution. In the latter case the preposition ἐν (ב) should have an instrumental value "with living water." Note that in *m. Miqw.* I 1–8 the "living water" has the highest purification quality and is used to prepare the holy water for the remission of sin (לקדש מהן הטאה). The local meaning of ἐν (ב) seems more appropriate, for the verse assumes that Levi washes his whole body in the water.

It seems that later baptismal traditions preferred to administer ritual washing in actual running water or rivers, like the baptism of repentance administered by John in the Jordan river (Matt 3:1–6; Mark 1:4–8; Luke 3:3–6). Washing of the body in running water is a fundamental element in the Mandaean baptismal rite (Segelberg 1958: 38–39). One of the Greek Sybilline texts reports a baptismal rite very similar to the *Document*'s text.

> Ah, wretched mortals, change these things, and do not lead the great God to all sorts of anger, but abandon daggers and groanings, murders and outrages, and wash your whole bodies in perennial rivers (ἐν ποταμοῖς λούσασθε ὅλον δέμας ἀενάοισιν). Stretch out your hands to heaven (χεῖράς τ'ἐκτανύσαντες εἰς αἰθέρα) and ask (αἰτεῖσθε) forgiveness for your previous deeds and make propitiation for bitter impiety with words of praise; God will grant repentance (μετάνοιαν) and will not destroy. He will stop his wrath again if you all practice honorable piety in your hearts. (*Sib. Or.* IV 162–170; text Geffcken 1902: 100; trans. Collins 1983: 388)

In an eschatological and apocalyptic context the author of the fourth Sibylline Oracle exhorts his audience to repentance and baptism. The latter should consist in washing the entire body in perennial (lit. ever-flowing) rivers and in stretching out the hands to heavens (lit. "in the air"). The baptized should also ask forgiveness from God who will grant them repentance and spare their lives. God's forgiveness is warranted only if the moral conversion is joined to the body washing and prayerful request of the petitioners. The baptism pericope is set in the context of human impiety (*Sib. Or.* IV 153–161) and God's imminent judgment (*Sib. Or.* IV 171–192). The performed rite is strikingly similar in its structure and meaning to the *Document*'s narrative. Levi washes his body in running water (1a v. 2a), and the washing stands in the context of his moral conversion (1a v. 2b). He positions himself in front of the sanctuary with his eyes and face raised to heavens (1a v. 3) and his hands outstretched in front of the sanctuary (1a v. 4). There follows a petitionary prayer that does not specifically deal with forgiveness of sins but amply discusses Levi's personal salvation from evil and purification requested from God. Although the eschatological elements are not so evident in the context of Levi's ablution and prayer, Levi's judicial function in exercising God's judgment is evident (cf. *A.L.D.* 1a v. 18; 14; 99).

The Jewish background of the Sibylline baptismal rite has long been assumed (Brandt 1910: 87–90; Thomas 1935: 46–60), and the parallelism with the *Document* confirms this opinion. On the other hand, the conviction that Levi's ablution should be interpreted as a purification rite from human sinfulness finds an additional confirmation. It is noteworthy that Levi's prayer for personal salvation in *T. Levi* 2:4 stems from the observation that he sees "all men corrupting their ways" (*T. Levi* 2:3). If one assumes a similar text in the *Document* preceding the ablution, then Levi's moral conversion in *A.L.D.* 1a vv. 1–2 appears as a reaction to the corruption of the human race. Since the prayer and its introduction precede Levi's ordination (*A.L.D.* 9–10), the purification rite before the Levitical ascendancy to royal priesthood may serve as an adequate preparation for the future

priest proclaimed holy by Isaac (*A.L.D.* 17) and close to God's holy ones
(*A.L.D.* 18). Note that in *T. Levi* 8:5 during the liturgy of the heavenly ordination one of the angels washes Levi with pure water. Also Levi's ablution
and prayer in *A.L.D.* 1a vv. 1–19 is ultimately directed towards his priestly
elevation for they prove his fitness for office. Much, however, remains
unknown because of the fragmentary nature of the *Document*'s first and second vision.

and I made straight all my ways. The clause is an adaptation of Isa 40:3,
an exhortation to prepare the way of the Lord and make straight his path.
Here it refers to Levi and metaphorically indicates his intent to correct his
behavior in order to follow the way of God. It is also similar to another
biblical expression "straight path" (דרך ישרה) that usually expresses walking according to God's will and his law (cf. 1 Sam 12:23; Jer 31:9; Hos
14:10; Ps 107:7; Prov 12:15; 14:12; 16:25; Ezra 8:21, etc.; for the metaphorical meaning of the Hebrew lexeme דרך in the Old Testament as a way
of life with ethical connotation, cf. Zehnder 1999: 326–336; 484–503). The
comparison with the text of the prayer and the rest of the *Document* confirms
the ethical interpretation of the sentence. Levi asks God to reveal to him
all the ways of truth (1a v. 6) and not to be led astray from God's path.
In *A.L.D.* 102 l. 5 his sons abandon the path of truth and walk in the
darkness of satan.

The connection between washing of the entire body and correcting Levi's
ways implies a moral, not cultic, interpretation of the cleansing. This particular perspective that conjoins ablutions with moral purification is well
attested in the prophetic writings. Isa 1:15–17 establishes a link between
washing and conversion from doing evil in order to make the prayer acceptable: "When you spread forth your hands, I will hide my eyes from you;
even though you make many prayers, I will not listen; your hands are full
of blood. Wash yourselves (רחצו/λούσασθε); make yourselves clean (הזכו/
καθαροὶ γένεσθε); remove the evil of your doings from before my eyes; cease
to do evil, learn to do good" (cf. Ps 18:21; 24:3–5). The whole section of
1a vv. 1–19 finds its explanation and justification in this Isaian text: in
order to make the prayer (1a vv. 5–19) acceptable and make the spreading forth of hands (1a vv. 3–4) meaningful, they must be preceded by conversion and ablution (1a vv. 1–2). Levi's life becomes a concrete expression
of Isaiah's exhortatory exclamation, and the prophetic piety of the future
ideal priest is thus firmly established.

Washing of garments in 1a v. 1 presented as a purification rite (καθαρίζω)
should also be interpreted in the same perspective of a moral purification.
In the text of the prayer Levi implores God to purify (καθαρίζω) his heart
from every impurity (1a v. 14). In the biblical prophetic tradition pollution
of one's garment becomes a symbol of moral incongruity. Isa 64:5 speaks
of becoming "like one who is unclean (כטמא), and all our righteous deeds
are like a polluted garment" (כבגד עדים). In Zech 3:4–5 the high priest
Joshua has to take off unclean clothes, the indication of his iniquity, and
his vesting with a clean turban and garments becomes a symbol of divine
acceptance.

A.L.D. 1a v. 3 *Then I raised my eyes and my face towards heavens. A.L.D.* 1a vv. 3–4 constitutes the immediate introduction to the prayer when Levi takes up a position of an *orans*. First he raises up to the heavens his eyes and countenance (1a v. 3); then he stretches his fingers and his hands towards the sanctuary (1a v. 4). The former action is a classical *topos* for the beginning of a prayer. In Dan 4:31 Nebuchadnezzar begins his prayer in this way, the young man of *1 Esdr* 4:58 does exactly the same, turning his face towards Jerusalem, and in *4 Bar* 6:2 (4) Baruch repeats the same gesture (cf. John 11:41). The latter, instead, seems to be rare and unusual.

A.L.D. 1a v. 4 *and I spread out faithfully the fingers of my hands and my hands.* The closest parallel text appears in *Jub.* 25:11, Rebecca's blessing of the Lord and of her son Jacob. "Then she (Rebecca) lifted her face to heaven, extended the fingers of her hands (*ʾaṣābəʿa ʾədawihā*) and opened her mouth." The similarity with *A.L.D.* 1a vv. 3–4 is striking. Levi lifts up his face and eyes to heavens (1a v. 3), extends his fingers and his hands (1a v. 4) and opens his mouth to speak (1a vv. 3, 4). Extending the fingers towards God might have been an intermediary stage in the development towards the priestly tradition recorded in the Babylonian Talmud, according to which the priest is bound to extend the joints of his fingers when turning in prayer to God (*b. Soṭah* 39b, cf. Jacobson 1977: 259).

Spreading out the hands towards the heavens or the sanctuary is also a common sign for the beginning of a prayer in the Hebrew Bible. Although the Greek ἀναπετάννυμι (1a v. 4a) occurs neither in LXX nor in NT, MT often uses the expression פרש כפים "to stretch out the hands" to indicate the prayerful attitude (see 1 Kgs 8:22,38,54; Ezra 9:5; Isa 1:15; Ps 41:21; Job 11:13; cf. 11QPsᵃ XXIV 3). The closest example is the prayer of Solomon before the consecration of the temple in 1 Kings 8. Solomon spreads out his hands towards the heavens at the beginning of the prayer (v. 22), recommends to the pious Israelites to spread out their hands in prayer towards the Temple (v. 38), and even when he ends his prayer, he rises from his knees with his hands still spread up to the heavens (v. 54). Levi's pious position, therefore, recalls either the king himself or the king's clear recommendation of this prayerful position.

in front of the sanctuary. In E 18,2 the Greek syntagm τῶν ἁγίων (v. 4) translates either קדישין, "holy ones" (A 18 l. 22; cf. *A.L.D.* 17), or בית אל, "sanctuary" (A 19 l. 1; cf. *A.L.D.* 53). It seems more probable that Levi stands in prayer in front of the sanctuary like Solomon in 1 Kgs 8:22, and Levi's position with his hands stretched out strengthens this interpretation. It is unlikely that Levi stands before the holy ones (Greenfield and Stone 1985: 459) and, instead of speaking with them, directs his prayer to God. An unquestioned mention of an angel occurs later in *A.L.D.* 1b l. 18 (4Q213a 2 18). Consequently, it is improbable that there is any connection with the high priest Joshua, who stands before an angel (Zech 3:1–10), as Kugler (1996a: 73) suggested.

and I prayed and said. The introductory formula ηὐξάμην καὶ εἶπα is a modified biblical introduction to a prayer, εὔχομαι εὐχὴν λέγων (see LXX:

Gen 28:20; 1 Sam 1:11; 2 Sam 15:8; 2 Kgs 20:2; cf. 2 Macc 9:13; *T. Levi*
2:4). The Aramaic ואמרת that underlies the Greek καὶ εἶπα here, usually
introduces direct speech (see *A.L.D.* 7 l. 11; 13 l. 8; 71 l. 20; 76 l. 11; 83a
l. 7). The addition of the verbs of speaking at the end of 1a v. 3 and 1a
v. 4 is probably due to the poetic parallelism between the two verses.

3.1.2   *The Prayer—A.L.D. 1a vv. 5–19*

A.L.D. 1a v. 5 *O Lord*. Our composition does not employ the Tetragrammaton
at all. God's titles in the *Document* belong to the common stock of Second
Temple theological terminology: κύριε = מרי 1a v. 5 (4Q213a i 10); 1a v.
11 (4Q213a 1 18); 1a v. 15 (4Q213a 2 6) (for κύριος without an Aramaic
equivalent, cf. 48; 52; for אל, cf. A 3a l. 8; 9 l. 19; 83b l. 9; for אל עליון,
cf. A 9 l. 20; 13 l. 5; 30 l. 16 [κύριος ὕψιστος, E 18,2 vv. 30, 51, 58]; for
קודשא as God's title, cf. A 17 l. 19). The Aramaic מארי is rendered with
δεσπότης in 13 l. 6 (for the Greek δεσπότης only, cf. also 1a vv. 8, 14). This
Greek lexeme appears frequently in Jewish Hellenistic prayers (e.g. Jdt 9:12;
2 Macc 15:22; 3 Macc 6:9, 10; cf. Tob 8:17). Several of God's titles are
enumerated in the related Aramaic *Testament of Qahat* (4Q542 1 ii 1–3).

you know all the hearts. The remaining fragment of the Aramaic text allows
the reader to find an exact parallel in 1 Kgs 8:39b (2 Chr 6:30), where
Solomon expresses the same conviction that only the Lord knows the human
heart. Therefore he is able to repay humankind according to its conduct.
However, *A.L.D.* 1a v. 5 introduces the theme of God's knowledge of the
human heart not to seek reward from God but to present him with a whole
list of demands, which especially deal with spiritual gifts and endowments.
The difference in comparison with Solomon's prayer is striking. Solomon
first praises God's faithfulness (vv. 23–26), then he asks God that his prayer
(vv. 27–30) and the prayers of the people in different situations may be
heeded and accepted (vv. 31–53). Levi's prayer is rather self-centered and
concerns his separation from evil (1a vv. 7, 10, 12–13), spiritual gifts (1a
vv. 6, 8–9, 14–15a) and introduction into priestly office (1a vv. 11, 17–18).
Only once in *A.L.D.* 1a v. 18b does he include his sons into the litany of
different requests, while *A.L.D.* 1a v. 6 merely states that his children assist
him while he prays. It seems that Levi's prayer is modeled on Solomon's
prayer in terms of vocabulary in order to suggest a certain parallelism
between the two persons: Solomon, the wisest king of Israel on the one
hand and Levi, the wisest priest in Israel on the other. Solomon prepares
the temple for consecration; Levi prepares himself for priestly ordination.

all the intentions of the thoughts you alone know. This is the last clause in 1a
v. 5. One may correctly ask if there is any connection between 1a v. 5
(God's knowledge of the human heart) and the rest of the prayer (a set of
requests). At first sight there appears to be none, but upon closer scrutiny
one may understand this statement about God's knowledge of the human
heart and mind as Levi's invitation addressed to God to intervene in his
life and, one may say, in his inner self. God's knowledge of the human
heart is directed towards a goal, that is, a just retribution (cf. 1 Kgs 8:39).

Since God knows human intentions, he may repay Levi according to all human ways. One is, therefore, not surprised that Levi's first request concerns the "ways of truth" as a condition to assure God's favor for himself (see 1a v. 9). Levi also asks God to purify his heart (1a v. 14), a request that may be fulfilled only by the one who knows the human heart.

A.L.D. 1a v. 6 *And give me all the ways of truth.* After the introductory statement in 1a v. 5 Levi begins his litany of various requests (1a vv. 6–14, 17–19). The expression "ways of truth" (4Q213a 1 12 ארחת קשט) also appears in Levi's instructions of his children in *A.L.D.* 102 l. 5 (4Q213 frg. 4 5), when he predicts their future apostasy from the "ways of truth". It essentially expresses Levi's commitment to God and rejection of the forces that oppose him (*A.L.D.* 1a v. 10). In the Enochic literature it indicates the way of final salvation preserved for the righteous ones (see *1 En.* 104:13 fənāwāta rət' = ὁδοὺς τῆς ἀληθείας; cf. *1 En.* 91:18, 19; 92:3; 94:1; 99:10; 104:13; 105:2; ארח קשטא 1QapGen VI 2; 4Q212 frg. 1 ii 18 [*1 En.* 91:18]; 4Q212 frg. 1 iv 22 [*1 En.* 91:14]; 4Q212 frg. 1 v 25 [*1 En.* 94:1]).

The Aramaic קשט is also synonymous to the Hebrew צדקה, with which it stands in poetical parallelism in *A.L.D.* 85 l. 12 (see Tob 1:3). This concept of קשט/ἀλήθεια becomes characteristic of Levi's person and his priesthood (see 1a v. 16 [4Q213a 2 7]; 1a v. 18 [4Q213a 2 9]; *A.L.D.* 15 l. 12; 84 l. 10; 85 l. 11; 86 l. 13; 97 l. 8; 102 l. 2). Levi may thus be compared to Enoch who is named "the scribe of righteousness" (*1 En.* 15:1: bə'si ṣādq wa-ṣaḥāfē ṣədq/ἄνθρωπος ἀληθινὸς καὶ γραμματεὺς τῆς ἀληθείας [G]). Additionally, both Levi and Enoch study scribal craft (cf. the comment on *A.L.D.* 88). Levi in *A.L.D.* 31–47 is versed in the knowledge of the weights and measures and their fractions, while Enoch uses his arithmetical skills in the astronomical calculations (*1 En.* 72–82).

A.L.D. 1a v. 7 *the unrighteous spirit and evil intention . . . fornication and pride.* The following three verses 7–9 should be treated as a unit. They set forth a contrast between the unrighteous spirit and the spirit of holiness, between the evil thought, adultery, pride and the gift of counsel, wisdom, knowledge, and might. This moral and spiritual dualism is probably one of the earliest sketches of this sort in the literature of the Second Temple period. It is further developed in *A.L.D.* 3c–5, where the priestly kingdom is contrasted with the kingdom of the sword.

The concept of an unrighteous spirit is absent from the LXX but it appears in 1QS IV 23, which states that the spirit of truth and unrighteousness (רוחי אמת ועול) fight in the human heart. 1QS IV 9 indicates the spirit of unrighteousness (רוח עולה) as the source of many vices, pride (גוה) included (see 1QS IV 20; cf. *T. Reu.* 3:6: πνεῦμα ἀδικίας). Our verse mentions pride (ὕβρις) as well, a term frequently occurring in the Wisdom literature (Prov 11:2; 13:10; 14:3, 10, etc.; in the context of a prayer: Esth 13:12; 3 Macc 2:3; 6:12).

The concept of the evil thought/intention (διαλογισμὸν τὸν πονηρὸν = באישא[; cf. 1a v. 5) is absent from the LXX but it appears twice in the

NT in Matt 15:19 and Jas 2:4. In Matt 15:19 it is accompanied just as in *A.L.D.* 1a v. 7 by πορνεῖαι in the list of the things that come out of the human heart and defile human beings, as opposed to eating with unwashed hands that does not defile humankind. The list in *A.L.D.* 1a v. 7 stands in clear contrast with the following verse describing the true image of an ideal high priest. The list in 1a v. 7, therefore, should rather be considered as a list of qualities and spiritual values that are not compatible with his priestly vocation. In fact, Isaac instructs Levi not to have anything to do with harlots (*A.L.D.* 17 l. 17) and with sexual immorality or fornication (*A.L.D.* 16 ll. 15–16).

CD-A IV 17 identifies זנות as one of Belial's nets about which Levi spoke (CD IV 15). It is difficult to be sure that CD referred to our composition. However, it is also undeniable that Levi speaks about fornication in *A.L.D.* 1a v. 7 (זנותא 4Q213a 1 13) as of a thing to avoid. It is not possible to exclude, that the author of CD was influenced by the *A.L.D.* but a clear reference to the *Document* is difficult to prove.

The first verb in the line is "to remove," (ארחק *'ap'el* 4Q213a 1 12 = μάκρυνον MS E 2,3). Its Hebrew counterpart frequently appears in the book of Psalms (e.g. Ps 55:8; 88:9), Job (e.g. Job 11:14; 13:21), and Proverbs (e.g. Prov 4:24; 30:8). The Hebrew counterpart of the second verb "turn away, repel" הדחא (4Q213a 1 13) usually refers to the actions of the wicked, never with God as subject (see Ps 35:5; 36:13; 62:4; 118:13; 140:5; Prov 14:32).

A.L.D. 1a v. 8 *Let the holy spirit, o Master, be shown to me.* The whole verse is related to Isa 11:2 (see below). In the LXX "to show" δείκνυμι usually translates הראה, e.g. Gen 12:1; 41:25. The prayer of Eleazar in 3 Macc 6:15 uses exactly the same form of the verb δειχθήτψ (aorist impv. passive, 3s.): "Let it be shown to all the Gentiles that you are with us, O Lord. . . ."
and give me counsel and wisdom and knowledge and strength. This line is related to Isa 11:2 that describes the gifts imparted to the shoot from the stump of Jesse. It is the only place in the Hebrew Bible where all the elements of *A.L.D.* 1a v. 8 are reflected (spirit, counsel, wisdom, knowledge, might). Two additional traits of the spirit in Isa 11:2, that is understanding (בינה) and fear of the Lord (יראת יהוה), are omitted by *A.L.D.* 1a v. 8. The Aramaic text also develops the Isaian verse and adapts it to the character of Levi's prayer. In the Isaian verse the concepts of counsel, wisdom, knowledge, and might qualify the spirit that is to repose on the stump of Jesse. Levi in his prayer separates these qualities and lists them independently from the mention of the spirit. They do not qualify the spirit but acquire a stronger dimension of the gifts equal to the gift of the spirit. When considered in the context of the prayer, the whole list of *A.L.D.* 1a v. 8 is set in clear contrast to the things to avoid expounded in the preceding verse. The Isaian text is certainly elaborated upon in the prayer and it helps to sketch a moral and spiritual dualism characteristic in the whole of Levi's prayer. Hence, only secondarily one may think about the messianic interpretation of the passage. If it is messianic, it should be qualified as describing the qualities of a priestly messiah, in the sense that all these gifts

requested by Levi are necessary for his priestly appointment. On the other hand, by adapting to his purposes the Isaian text, the author of the *Document* undoubtedly connected to Levi, to a priestly person, traits ascribed to a Davidic salvific individual. It seems to be a conscious exegetical move, for it has already been pointed out that Levi's prayer exhibits several vocabulary borrowings from Solomon's prayer of the temple consecration (cf. the comment on *A.L.D.* 1a vv. 4, 5).

The parallel between Solomon and Levi comes to the fore when one reads Solomon's request in his prayer to God in 1 Chr 1:9: "Give me now wisdom (הכמה) and knowledge (מדע) to go out and come in. . . ." This verse is an interpretation of 1 Kgs 3:9a where Solomon asks God for an understanding heart to judge the people. The wording of *A.L.D.* 1a v. 8b is close to the Chronicler's interpretation of Solomon's prayer and this parallelism indicates pointedly that the *A.L.D.* follows exegetical tendencies already inherent in the Hebrew Bible.

Kugler (1996a: 73, n. 48) proposed Prov 8:10–14 as a more reliable possibility for the biblical paradigm of the *A.L.D.* verse. Although the four terms of *A.L.D.* 1a v. 8 appear in the proposed passage, there is no mention of the fifth one, that is of the spirit. Certainly, Levi asks for the same items that are praised by Lady Wisdom and his priesthood is in clear connection with the wisdom teaching. Stylistically, however, there cannot be established any clear connection with Prov 8 and the wisdom motifs present in Levi's speech to his children have no literary links whatsoever to this Wisdom speech.

It seems, therefore, that Levi takes upon himself the characteristics of the future salvific figure that is to come from the tribe of Judah. These characteristics when ascribed to Levi make him an example of a salvific figure coming, however, from a different tribe (cf. Collins 1995: 83–95). Is this verse to be considered as an indication of a developing Levitical messianism? All these characteristics are later ascribed to the Davidic Messiah in 1QSb V 25, 4QpIsaᵃ frgs. 8–10 11–12, 18 and *Ps. Sol.* 17:37 (for the relation between the messiah and the spirit in apocryphal Jewish literature, cf. Chevalier 1958: 10–52).

A.L.D. 1a v. 9 *to do what pleases you*. The whole of *A.L.D.* 1a v. 9 is a purpose clause composed of three infinitives that qualify the two preceding main clauses (1a v. 8). The reader learns that Levi asks for all these spiritual gifts in order to please God in his acts, to find grace before him, and praise his words. The first two clauses in the verse are common expressions of God's favour in the OT; the third one "to praise (αἰνεῖν) your words" seems to have a liturgical connotation in the context of Levi's prayer. When compared with 1a v. 11 (λατρεῦσαι) and 1a v. 17 (γενέσθαι σοι ἐγγύς), this verb points to Levi's future function as a priest of God the most high (*A.L.D.* 9 l. 20). For the syntagm "to praise (God's) words" αἰνέω λόγον, see LXX: Ps 55:11; Sir 21:15; cf. Dan 2:23; 4:37; 5:23 (שבח).

The Aramaic *Vorlage* of the verse (4Q213a 1 16 "to do what is. . . . good before you") allows the comparison with Levi's wisdom poem, where he declares as good the harvest of truth (*A.L.D.* 86 l. 13–14) and treasure of wisdom (*A.L.D.* 94 l. 17). Truth and wisdom also define Levi's priestly vocation (cf. *A.L.D.* 1a vv. 8 and 18).

A.L.D. 1a v. 10 *And do not allow any satan to rule over me.* The verse is an exegetical adaptation of Ps 119:133b (cf. Sir 33:21 Hebrew MS E). The psalm states: "and do not allow any iniquity (און) to get dominion (תשלם) over me." 4Q213a 2 17 changes "iniquity" to "satan" (שטן). Change of prospective is rather clear. Iniquity of the Hebrew text gives places to an adversary that leads astray from the way of the Lord. Some texts of the Hebrew Bible indicate that in the celestial sphere there are spiritual beings whose job is to accuse people before God (*Job* 1–2; Zech 3:1–7), or who may become adversaries of humanity (Num 22:22–35; 1 Chr 21:1; cf. Day 1988). The heavenly adversary of humanity, however, is still a member of the heavenly court and cannot be classified as belonging to the category of a spiritual world opposed to God. The noun שטן may also refer to a merely human being, like in 1 Kgs 11:14, where by God's decree Rezin the Edomite, becomes Solomon's foe (cf. 1 Sam 29:4; 2 Sam 19:17–24; 1 Kgs 5:16–20).

The expression "any satan" (lit. "every satan") in the *Document* should be understood as referring to a category of evil spirits. *A.L.D.* 1a vv. 7–8 implies a dualistic notion of the spiritual world, so the noun "satan" certainly belongs to the category of unrighteous spirits (1a v. 7; see also 1QH^a XXII [Sukenik frg. 4] 6 כל שטן משחית; XXIV [Sukenik frg. 45] 2 כל שטן ומשחית. Additionally, in *A.L.D.* 102 l. 6 the noun "satan" is qualified by "darkness," which recalls the angel of darkness, Melchireša', from the *Testament of Amram* (cf. below and the comment on *A.L.D.* 102).

to lead me astray from your way. A close example of the satan's misleading power is 1 Chr 21:1 that replaces Yahweh's wrath (אף) of 2 Sam 24:1 with Satan (שטן) as the driving power in David's census of the people. Behind this substitution lies the Chronicler's theological principle that it is not God but an evil spirit that misleads David. The other example is even more appropriate. The high priest Joshua stands before an angel and Satan stands at the angel's right side to slander Joshua. This kind of misleading and slander Levi prays to avoid when he asks God that no satan has power over him to " lead me astray (πλανῆσαι) from your way." Additionally, the book of Revelation presents a striking parallelism with the *Document*. Rev 12:9 describes Satan, an appellative already become a proper name, as the one who "leads astray the whole world (ὁ πλανῶν τὴν οἰκουμένην ὅλην). The development from the strictly personal level in the prayer to the cosmic and universal character of Satan's dominion took place within Second Temple Judaism (cf. the Enochic *Book of the Parables*, especially *1 En.* 54:6). In *1 En.* 37–71 Satan has already been mentioned as a class of evil spirits (40:7; 53:3; 56:1, etc.); its role, however, is different from the present verse (see Charles 1912: 78, note on 40:7). The Qumran Plea for Deliverance (11QPs^a Plea) exegetes Ps 119:133b in a similar way and parallels "satan" with the "unclean spirit" (v. 15: רוח טמאה).

It is noteworthy that the *Testament of Amram* has already a full-blown division of the spiritual world between the two classes of angelic beings represented by Melchizedek and Melchireša'. These two exercise their power (שלט cf. 4Q543 frgs. 5–9 3; frg. 10 1; 4Q544 frg. 1 12, 12; frg. 2 16; 4Q546 frg. 4 2) over the whole of humanity. The first is ruler over Amram and the sons of light (4Q544 frg. 2 16), the second rules over all darkness (4Q544 frg. 2 14–15; frg. 1 13 = 4Q543 frgs. 5–9 5). This composition evidently develops the ideas on the nature of the spiritual world already present in Levi's prayer (*A.L.D.* 1a vv. 7–10). Additionally, satan is also connected with darkness in Levi's vision of his children's future (cf. *A.L.D.* 102 l. 6). The presentation of the spiritual world in the *Document* is close to the *Testament of Amram*'s dualistic perspective.

A.L.D. 1a v. 11 *and draw me near.* Levi's request refers to his future role as priest of God the most high (*A.L.D.* 9; 13). The expression "to draw near" (cf. *A.L.D.* 1a v. 17) refers to his future priestly elevation, and some biblical texts confirm this interpetation. *Ezekiel* 43 and 44 describe the restoration of the cult in the new Temple. Ezek 43:19 defines the role of the Levitical priests in the future temple: "You shall give to the Levitical priests of the family of Zadok, who draw near to me to minister to me, says the Lord GOD, a bull for a sin offering." Ezek 44:10–14 deals with the Levites who have strayed from the Lord together with the rest of Israel and sinned with idolatry. Hence, they cannot draw near to God to serve as priests (v. 13) and their role is reduced to be gatekeepers and temple servants (v. 11). On the other hand, Ezek 44:15 states that the Levitical priests, the Zadokites, who have remained faithful to God when Israel strayed away (בתעות/ἐν τῷ πλανᾶσθαι; cf. Ezek 48:11), are to draw near to God (יקרבו/προσάξουσιν) to minister to him (לשרת/λειτουργεῖν). In the context of these statements in Ezekiel, it comes as no surprise that Levi asks not to be led astray (πλανῆσαι) by satan for that would disqualify him from the priestly vocation. He then asks God to draw him near (1a v. 11: προσά-γαγέ μέ/קרבני; cf. 1a v. 17) to be God's servant and to serve (λατρεῦσαι; cf. E 5:2 in § 1.4.3.3) him in a proper way.

In Exod 29:4 Moses makes Aaron and his sons approach (הקרב) the tent of meeting to initiate them in the priestly office (cf. Exod 40:12, 14; Lev 8:6, 13, 24). In Num 16:9–10 Moses addresses the rebellious Levites: "Is it too small a thing for you that the God of Israel has separated you from the congregation of Israel, to bring you near (להקריב) to himself, to do service in the tabernacle of the Lord, and to stand before the congregation to minister to them; and that he has brought (ויקרב) you near him, and all your brethren the sons of Levi with you?" This passage appears in a controversial context of the Korah rebellion, when the Levites unsuccessfully aspire to priesthood. When defining the conditions of Levi's priesthood in the *Document*, Isaac states that Levi is close (קריב) to God and to His holy ones (*A.L.D.* 18 l. 21). That statement implies that Levi's prayer has been heard and that he has been granted a particular priestly status of closeness to God. This expression and idea could also have developed from texts like Num 1:51; 3:10, 38; 17:28; 18:7. Num 1:51 states that only the Levites take down or pitch the tent of meeting and anyone else that comes near (הקרב) will die. The Aaronic priesthood is reserved to his family and whoever else comes near (הקרב) will die as well (Num 3:10, 38; 17:28; 18:7). All these observations strengthen the initial intuition that Levi in his prayer asks for the priestly appointment.

to be your servant. A certain innovation to the list of Levi's requests is his demand to become God's servant (δοῦλος), certainly pointing to his future priestly and liturgical duties. The Greek translation of עבד with δοῦλος (1a v. 17 [4Q213a 2 8]; 1a v. 19 [4Q213a 2 10]) does not follow the general Septuagint tendency to use παῖς for this word (see, e.g., Gen 9:25, 26, 27; 12:16). The idea of closeness to God is strictly bound in the *Document* to the concept of being God's servant, as 1a v. 11 and 1a v. 17 point it out. 4Q213a 2 8 preserves the Aramaic צלות עב]דך לוי, "prayer of your ser[vant Levi]," an expression that might well serve to define Levi's whole address to God and his particular relationship with the creator. It is plausible to affirm that this type of "Yahweh's servant" terminology was applied for the first time to a priestly character. Levi is conscious of being God's παῖς (1a v. 17) and son of God's παῖς Jacob (1a vv. 15 and 19). In the Hebrew Bible virtually every prominent figure of the national history was called God's servant. However, application of Isa 11:2 to Levi suggests that his being God's servant is additionally interpreted in light of the Isaian text about the ideal king who rules wisely (cf. *A.L.D.* 1a v. 8).

and to serve you properly. The Greek text reads here λατρεύω. In the LXX the terms λατρεύω and λειτουργέω usually translate the Hebrew עבד, but the translators usually distinguish between non-priestly and priestly activities. The term λατρεύω is used in a general context concerning relationship with God (see, e.g. Ex 3:12; 4:23; 7:16,26; 8:16; cf. Daniel 1966: 66–76); the technical term for Levitical service in the LXX is λειτουργέω (see, e.g. Exod 28:35, 43; 29:30, etc.). Num 16:9 applies both terms to Levitical service.

A.L.D. 1a v. 12 *a wall of your peace around me.* This line formulates a peculiar image of Levi being surrounded by a wall of peace and protected by the shelter of God's might in order to be free from every evil. It suggests Levi's total separation from evil as God's work accompanied by the protection of God's peace. There is no direct OT parallel to this verse; compare, however, Job 1:10 where Satan reproaches God for putting a hedge around Job (שׂוך/περιφράσσω). The image of a protecting wall may be contrasted with *T. Levi* 2:3, which states that "unrighteousness had built for itself walls and lawlessness sat upon towers." Living in the shelter of God's might recalls Sir 34:16, where this privilege is reserved for those who love him.

A.L.D. 1a v. 13 *remove and efface lawlessness from under the heavens.* Levi turns now his attention to the existence of lawlessness in the world (cf. *A.L.D.* 1a v. 7). He calls for God's final intervention in dealing with the problem of evil in the world. The *orans* in Ps 51:11 asks God to blot out his sins

(עונתי/ἀνομίας) and Isa 43:25 expressly states that it is God who blots out the sins of the people (פשעיך/ἀνομίας σου). Levi, however, enlarges the perspective and does not limit the annihilation of evil only to his personal life or to the life of the people. The purpose of this request is to eradicate evil from the whole earth. The eschatological prospective is clearly on the horizon of his prayer. Killing of the Shechemites explains what Levi intends by his request. In *A.L.D.* 78 ll. 17–18 Levi states that he has destroyed the doers of violence (חמסא). The latter term is sometimes translated into Greek with ἀνομία, "lawlessness" (Isa 53:9; 59:6; Ezek 7:23; 8:17, etc.; *1 En.* 9:1 Sync = 4Q201 1 iv 8), found also in this verse. Consequently, the Shechem incident in the *Document* should be interpreted in the light of *A.L.D.* 78 l. 17–18 and *A.L.D.* 1a v. 13. By killing the doers of lawlessness Levi becomes an instrument of God's intervention on behalf of the oppressed (Dinah) and against the perpetrators of lawlessness (Shechemites).

A.L.D. 1a v. 14 *Purify my heart, o Master, from every impurity*. The wording recalls the introduction to the prayer when Levi washes and purifies his garments in pure water. Now the perspective is enlarged for he asks God to purify his heart from every impurity. Levi's request echoes God's promise to purify the Israelites from their impurities in Ezek 36:25 as a precondition of giving them a new spirit and a new heart of flesh. What is to be understood by the "impurity" ἀκαθαρσία is best explained by Isaac's speech in which he explains to the newly ordained priest the conditions of his priesthood. In *A.L.D.* 14 ll. 9–10 uncleanness is paralleled with sin (חטא), then in *A.L.D.* 16 ll. 15–16 with fornication (פחז) and with harlotry (זנות). Levi's request is supplemented here by his wish to be lifted up to God. This clause is similar to another request by Levi to be close to God in *A.L.D.* 1a v. 17 and to be led into God's presence to become his servant in *A.L.D.* 1a v. 11.

The wording of *A.L.D.* 1a vv. 13–14 is very close to the Enochic *Book of Watchers*. *1 En.* 10:20 stands in the section of the book in which God's command is delivered to the angel Raphael to execute the divine sentence on Azazel, the children of the Watchers, and the Watchers themselves (*1 En.* 10: 4–22). Raphael should then cleanse the earth after the flood: "And you, cleanse the earth from all uncleanness, and from all unrighteousness, and from all sin and godlessness: and efface all the unclean things that have been done upon the earth (Eth: from off the earth)" καὶ σὺ <u>καθάρισον</u> τὴν γῆν <u>ἀπὸ πάσης ἀκαθαρίας</u> καὶ ἀπὸ πάσης ἀδικίας καὶ ἀπὸ πάσης ἁμαρτίας καὶἀσεβείας, καὶ <u>πάσας τὰς ἀκαθαρσίας</u> τὰς γινομένας ἐπὶ τῆς γῆς <u>ἐξάλειψον</u> (G; Eth. adds: <u>ἀπὸ τῆς γῆς</u>). The underlined words are found in 1a vv. 13–14 of the *Document*. Curiously, Levi asks God for himself and for the whole earth exactly the same as God ordered Raphael to do in relation to the whole earth, that is, to exterminate evil in all its forms. Levi's request however, goes one step further. He asks God to cleanse his heart from all uncleanness. The reason for the existence of evil is sought not in the angelic world but in the human heart (cf. *A.L.D.* 1a v. 7 "the evil thought"). This ethical concept of purity of heart is parallel to the teaching of Jesus (Matt

5:8 οἱ καθαροὶ τῇ καρδίᾳ) and becomes normative for early Christianity (1 Tim 1:5; 2 Tim 2:22; Titus 1:15; Jas 4:8).

A.L.D. 1a v. 15a *and do not turn your face away from the son of your servant Jacob.* This sentence is a classical clause of a Hebrew prayer (Ps 27:9; 69:18;102:3; 132:10; 143:7; Tob 3:6, etc.). The definition of the *orans* as a servant (עֶבֶד/παῖς) is found in Ps 69:18 and our verse is probably an elaboration of this psalm verse. Levi's prayer specifies the *orans* as the *son* of your servant *Jacob*. The expression "servant Jacob" (עֶבֶד יַעֲקֹב) is common in the Deutero-Isaian texts (Isa 41:8; 44:1, 2, 21; 45:4; 48:20) but is also found in other biblical books (Jer 30:10; 46:27, 28; Ezek 28:25; 37:25). In the Deutero-Isaian texts Jacob is portrayed not only as a father of the nation but as an idealized servant of Yahweh who represents either a nation or an individual. It seems certain that the Servant theology of Deutero-Isaiah tended to underline a particular relationship between Yahweh and his elect—would it be an individual or the whole nation as such. In the case of Levi's prayer, the author of the *A.L.D.* undoubtedly follows this tendency of the Deutero-Isaian theology. First, he states that Levi is the "son of your servant Jacob" (1a v. 15), then he applies the title of the "servant" to Levi (1a v. 17), and finally he again underlines that Levi is the son of God's servant without mentioning Jacob by name (1a v. 19). One should note that these are the only explicit definitions in the entire prayer of who Levi is.

A.L.D. 1a v. 15b *You, o Lord, blessed Abraham my father. A.L.D.* 1a vv. 15a and 19 form an *inclusio* by repeating the expression "and do not turn away your face from the son of your servant (+ 'Jacob' in 1a v. 15a)." In the center of the inclusion stands *A.L.D.* 1a v. 17 that defines the nature of Levi's prayer. Being God's servant, he asks God to be close to him, that is, to be God's priest. Levi offers his prayer as a servant but asks for the privilege of becoming a priest. This seems to be the message of *A.L.D.* 1a v. 17, crucial for the understanding of the passage. The idea of his priesthood is further delineated in *A.L.D.* 1a v. 18: Levi shares the knowledge of God's words and purposes and this sharing enables him to do a true judgment. These two characteristics are to last forever and are to be shared by Levi's children. In this way, the eternal and genealogical priesthood is delineated and requested from God.

God's blessing of Abraham is always connected with the promise of a numerous progeny (Gen 12:2; 22:17) similarly to *A.L.D.* 1a v. 16 (זֶרַע— 4Q213a 2 7). God's promise to give Abraham countless descendants (Gen 15:4–5) is the starting point of the covenant stipulation in Gen 15. God blesses Sarah in Gen 17:16 and announces that she will bear a son. This verse belongs to the covenant stipulation account and it also stresses the blessing God will impart to Sarah's son (בֵּן). Although it does not expressly use the term of "progeny" (זֶרַע), it is the only place in the OT where Sarah is blessed by God and where the promise of an offspring is made both to Sarah and to Abraham who is God's interlocutor. Hence, it is appropriate to state that *A.L.D.* 1a vv. 15b–16 is inspired by Gen 17:16.

A.L.D. 1a v. 16 *a seed of righteousness, blessed for ever.* It is not certain that the author of the *Document* was thinking of Isaac when talking about a "seed of righteousness (= 4Q213a 2 7—זרע דק]שט) blessed for ever." Considered in the context of the prayer and of the whole of *A.L.D.*, this designation properly fits Levi himself. The concept of "truth/justice" קשט characterizes his judgment (4Q213a 2 9 = *A.L.D.* 1a v. 18) and is paralleled with his priesthood (*A.L.D.* 15 l. 14). Isaac also calls Levi's descendants "blessed (εὐλεγόμενος) for all the generations of the ages" (*A.L.D.* 61; cf. *A.L.D.* 59). By pointing to God's promise to Abraham and Sarah of a righteous offspring, the author reinterprets the biblical tradition that has concentrated on Isaac and his descendants and lets the reader understand that God promised to Abraham a priestly progeny that is Levi and his sons. Additionally, by invoking Abraham, Levi's famous ancestor, he firmly establishes Levi's priestly legacy in the patriarchal covenantal account. Note that in Gal 3:16 Paul reinterprets God's promises to Abraham and applies the expression καὶ τῷ σπέρματί σου (Gen 12:7; 13:15; 17:7; 24:7) to Christ.

A.L.D. 1a v. 17 *Listen also to the voice of your servant Levi.* The following *A.L.D.* 1a vv. 17–18 constitute Levi's most important requests concerning the nature of his future priestly service and define his status as God's servant in the context of judicial authority. The copulative particle δέ "then" suggests continuation of the preceding thought. The Greek opening expression in 1a v. 17 ("listen also to the voice") is a typical psalmic formulation of the *orans* (e.g. Ps 27:7; 28:2; 64:2; 130:2, etc.). However, the Qumran manuscript speaks here about "the prayer of your servant Levi" (4Q213a 2 8—עב]דך לוי צלות). The Aramaic word for "prayer" is absent from the MT. The overall formulation of the line strongly recalls 1 Kgs 8:30, where Solomon asks God to make his prayer acceptable (ושמעת אל תחנת עבדך/εἰσακούσῃ τῆς δεήσεως τοῦ δούλου σου; cf. 2 Chr 6:21). Some influence of Solomon's prayer on the *Document* has already been noticed (cf. the comment on *A.L.D.* 1a vv. 4, 5, and 8), and this present comparison strengthens the previous intuitions. Levi's name is inserted to further define his dignity as God's servant.

to be near to you. The formal request to be close to God does not find any direct parallel in the MT. The sacerdotal character of the request seems evident in the context of the prayer and the rest of the *Document*. Being close to God (ἐγγύς = קרי־ב, see *A.L.D.* 18 l. 21, 21 and the Greek counterpart) implies God's action to bring Levi close to Him, a request formulated in *A.L.D.* 1a v. 11 (4Q213a 1 18—קרבני). The request to be close to God and be brought to this closeness by God himself implies that Levi asks God for an adequate appointment to the priesthood and that appointment is granted to him as Isaac's instructions suggest (cf. also *A.L.D.* 1a v. 11).

A.L.D. 1a v. 18 *and make (him) participate in your words.* The first expression in the sentence is quite puzzling. It has no counterpart either in the MT or the LXX. Levi prays to participate in God's words as a prerequisite to do a true judgment. It probably implies that his future actions are to be based on God's judicial decrees and decisions. In Dan 2:5, 8; 3:22, 28; 6:13 מלה indicates the royal judicial "decree." Similarly, God's λοωγος (מלה) in the *Document*'s verse should rather be interpreted as denoting God's "decree" or "command." *A.L.D.* 48 ends the set of Isaac's instructions with an exhortation to listen to his words (λόγους) and consider his commandments (ἐντολάς μου) with reference to moral and cultic regulations transmitted to Levi (*A.L.D.* 14–47). Levi's request may also be compared with Enoch's activity who proclaims "words of justice" מלי קושטא 4Q204 frg. 1 vi 8 (*1 En.* 13:10 G λόγους τῆς δικαιοσύνης) based on the visionary revelation concerning the fate of the Watchers, cf. 4Q204 frg. 1 vi 9 (*1 En.* 14:1 G Βίβλος λόγων δικαιοσύνης).

This interpretation is further confirmed by *T. Levi* 18:2 that is related to this verse of the *Document*. To the new priest raised up by God "all the words of the Lord will be revealed; and he will execute a judgment of truth upon the earth . . ." πάντες οἱ λόγοι κυρίου ἀποκαλυφθήσονται· καὶ αὐτὸς ποιήσει κρίσιν ἀληθείας ἐπὶ τῆς γῆς. Revelation of God's words precedes the execution of the righteous judgment (cf. *A.L.D.* 15).

to do a true judgment. This final clause expresses the goal of the preceding request to participate in God's judicial authority. The expression "true judgment" (דין קשט κρίσιν ἀληθινήν) plays an important role in the *Document* and defines Levi's judicial authority. Isaac begins to teach Levi the priestly law (דין כהנותא *A.L.D.* 13 l. 7) that is paralleled with the true law in *A.L.D.* 15 (דין קושטא/κρίσιν τῆς ἀληθείας). When Isaac ends his teaching, he further admonishes Levi to instruct his children according to this law (κρίσιν ταύτην) Levi has just heard (*A.L.D.* 49). The content of Isaac's teaching deals with priestly purity (*A.L.D.* 14–18), holocaust sacrifice (19–30), accompanying meal sacrifice (31–46a), and metrological relations between weights and measures (46b–47), also with redactional addition of Noachic commandments concerning blood (51–57). The underlying concept of the "true law" instruction is, however, "order" סרך (30–31), and the whole section *A.L.D.* 14–47 appears as a conscious attempt to define Levitical priestly דין as rooted in the observance of that sapiential order.

Levi's request here to do the just/true judgment reflects, therefore, the *Document*'s concept of Levitical justice according to which a due order must be followed. The sinful behavior that destroys the just order in the *Document* is lawlessness ἀνομία (*A.L.D.* 1a v. 13) and its synonym—violence חמס committed by the oppressors of Dinah (*A.L.D.* 78; cf. *A.L.D.* 3). Killing the Shechemites, therefore, appears as an element of Levitical priestly and royal duty to do a true judgment by eliminating the doers of violence (*A.L.D.* 78). Thus, the kingdom of the sword (*A.L.D.* 4b–5), which symbolizes the havoc and disorder produced by violent oppression, is opposed by the kingdom of priesthood (*A.L.D.* 3c l. 2; cf. 67; 90; 99) based on eternal peace (*A.L.D.* 6) and the exercise of the orderly true judgment.

The *Document*'s expression "righteous judgment" finds some echo in the use of this expression in the *Apocalypse of Weeks*. In the eighth week of the world history, a sword is given to the righteous to carry out just judgment

(דין קשוט) against the wicked (4Q212 1 iv 16 = *1 En.* 91:12). The expression here denotes a punishment of the wicked in the eschatological times, while its second application in the Apocalypse refers to the law in a general sense. In the ninth week, "righteousness and the righteous judgment ([דין קשוט) will be revealed (יתגלא) to all the sons of the whole earth" (4Q212 1 iv 19–20 = *1 En.* 91:14). It is clear that the *Apocalypse* expression corresponds semantically to the *Document*'s use. It does not denote one particular decree or statute but is a general term for the law, on the one hand, while it also refers to the punitive activity of the just on the other. The knowledge of the "true judgment" is also necessary for the elimination of the "doers of evil" who will disappear only afterwards (4Q212 1 iv 20–21 = *1 En.* 91:14). Levi kills the "doers of violence," and his action can be interpreted as exercising the "righteous judgment" (cf. *A.L.D.* 1a v. 18), a function of the just in the eighth week of the world history. Isaac also hands him down the true judgment that becomes Levi's law or a criterion of his priestly and scribal activity.

The Aramaic קשט may mean either "truth" or "justice" and the Greek translator renders it as the adj. δίκαιος "just" in *A.L.D.* 1a v. 16 (4Q213a 2 7) or as the adj. ἀληθινός "true" in *A.L.D.* 1a v. 18 (4Q213a 2 9), or as the noun ἀλήθεια "truth" in *A.L.D.* 1a v. 6 (4Q213a 1 12) and 15 l. 12 (cf. *A.L.D.* 1a v. 4). In *1 Enoch* the term is usually translated as δικαιοσύνη/δίκαιος (4Q201 v 3 =*1 En.* 10:3 Sync.; 4Q206 3 21 = *1 En.* 32:3 G; 4Q204 5 ii 22 = *1 En.* 106:18 Gᵇ; see also 4Q196 17 ii 3 and 5 = Tob 13:6 S). In one place, however, 4Q204 1 v 4 = *1 En.* 10:16 (G), it is rendered by two lexemes, δικαιοσύνη and ἀλήθεια. Since in the *Document* the Aramaic term in the expression "true/just judgment" conveys the idea of a legal order that must be obeyed (סרך *A.L.D.* 30; 31), its semantic range overlaps with the Hebrew צדק "a just order" reflected by the created universe and by the legal teaching of the Old Testament (Schmid 1968). Dexinger (1977: 150–152) goes a step further and claims that the Aramaic expression קשט דין in the Aramaic *Apocalypse of Weeks* translates the biblical משפט אמת (Zech 7:9), משפט צדק (Deut 16:18), or משפט וצדקה (2 Chr 9:8).

In the Old Testament the judicial authority is often expressed by the formula "to do judgment and justice" עשה משפט וצדקה, where the subject is usually a royal figure (2 Sam 8:15; 1 Kgs 10:9; Jer 22:3; 23:5; cf. Isa 9:6; Jer 33:15; Isa 42:4 "till he [God's servant] has established justice in the land" עד ישים בארץ משפט). In the vision of an ideal Israel in Ezek 40–48, the prophet addresses the princes of Israel with an admonition concerning their execution of social justice. They are to observe the year of release (45:8; 46:16–18), remove heavy impositions (45:9), regulate taxes (45:13–17), and establish the value of weights and measures (45:9-12). These actions that follow the Mesopotamian pattern of the royal social responsibility are summarized in a prophetic saying in Ezek 45:9 "Thus says the Lord God: Enough, O princes of Israel! Put away violence and oppression, and execute justice and righteousness (המס ושד הסירו ומשפט וצדקה עשו) . . ." Note that this plan for an ideal future is partially reflected in the *Document*.

In *A.L.D.* 46b–47 the value of weights and measures is established and *A.L.D.* 78 indicates that killing of the Shechemites is considered as a removal of the doers of violence.

One should also note that the Aramaic קשט in the *Document* corresponds semantically to the Akkadian *kittu* (A 1b 2' and 3' in *CAD* K vol. 8) "truth, correct procedures," a term synonymous with *mišaru* "justice, just order." The same Akkadian term *kittu* refers to the Babylonian just weights and measures (*kittu* A 1d in *CAD* K vol. 8), and is thus related to קשט in the קשט דין (*A.L.D.* 15), a term that denotes priestly injunctions and a long section on weights and measures (*A.L.D.* 31–47) in Isaac's instruction.

The semantic correspondence with the Akkadian expression suggests that Levi's request to do the true judgment is most probably rooted in the common ancient presentation of the ruler as an upholder of the just order in the society. The just king (*šar mīšarim*) upholds the social order by his legislative reforms, and by exercising justice, he becomes a guarantor of the order in the cultic, legal, and military domains with consequences in the nature of the whole universe (Schmid 1968: 24–46). The royal judicial authority is often expressed by the formula "establish justice and truth in the country" *mišaram (kittam) ina matim šakānum* (Weinfeld 1985: 34–44; for *dīn kittim* expressing the same royal responsibility of Nebuchadnezzar II, cf. Lambert 1965: 5, 8). Both terms *mišarum* and *kittum* are associated with the sun-god Shamash (Dossin 1955: 4) and *kittum* could be given as a gift to the earthly king: "I am Ḫammu-rabi, the just king (*šar mīšarim*), to whom Shamash has granted the truth" (*kīnātim*, lit. "true things," meaning "laws"; CH 25b:95–98, text and transl. Driver and Miles 1955: 98–99, 289).

The *Document*'s expression "to do a true judgment" finds its Egyptian counterpart in the ethical and religious ideal of those who do "maat" (*m3ˁt*) in their life. The term may mean "right/rightness, truth, justice," or "order," and the pharaoh is the one who is responsible for upholding *maat* on behalf of the gods whom he represents (Schmid 1968: 46–49). It is frequently found in the autobiographical tomb inscriptions where it expresses a sapiential, ethical and religious ideal that the dead boast to have accomplished in their lifetime (Lichtheim 1992: 9–102). Note that Levi as the main narrator in the *Document* speaks from beyond the grave, for his death is reported in *A.L.D.* 81.

A.L.D. 1a v. 19 *And I became silent, still praying*. The final sentence formally states the end of Levi's vocal prayer. In 1Qap Gen XX 16 Abraham ends his prayer in a similar way: "and I wept and became silent," ובכית והשית.

3.2   First Vision—A.L.D. 1b

Form and Structure

4Q213a frg. 2 10 (*A.L.D.* 1a v. 19) is the last line of the prayer. A scribal hook on the margin between lines 10 and 11 indicates the beginning of a new section. The following three lines (*A.L.D.* 1b ll. 11–14) connect the prayer to the vision, which begins in *A.L.D.* 1b l. 15. Stylistically, באדין in *A.L.D.* 1b l. 11 and אדין in *A.L.D.* 1b l. 15 mark off the section that shortly describes Levi's departure from the place of his prayer and a trip to his father Jacob. The scribe indicated the beginning of the vision with a *vacat* in *A.L.D.* 1b l. 15.

The section is fragmentary and only the right part of the column survives. *A.L.D.* 1b l. 12 suggests that after leaving the place of his prayer Levi has gone to his father Jacob, to Abel Main (?). The next two lines indicate that Levi leaves Abel Main and then something happens that induces him to lie down. *A.L.D.* 1b l. 15 is already a beginning of the visionary dream. These four lines form a literary passage between the prayer and the vision.

V. 1b *Then I left [.* Kugler (1996a: 82) assumes that Levi is at Abel Main at the time of his prayer and supports this opinion by making a reference to *T. Levi* 2:3–4. He then situates the following vision at Bethel, citing *T. Levi* 8:1–2 and *Jub.* 32:1. However, the place of the prayer is not explicitly mentioned in the *Document.* The vision probably took place in a locality close to Abel Main, as suggested by *A.L.D.* 1b l. 13, perhaps on Mount Garizim. The Greek *Testament of Levi* contains some topographical information that might confirm this opinion. *T. Levi* 2:3 affirms that Levi finds himself in Abelmaul, while *T. Levi* 2:5 identifies the place of his first vision as the mountain of the Shield in Abelmaul. *T. Levi* 6:1 adds some precise details affirming that the mountain of the Shield (Garizim, according to Milik 1978: 97) is near Gebal (Ebal), to the right of Abila. Since the *Testament*'s names Abelmaul and Abila are most probably variants of the Aramaic Abel Main in the *Document* (Milik 1978: 96–97), one may assume with *T. Levi* 6:1 that Levi has his first vision on the mountain of the Shield close to Abel Main or Abelmaul from the Greek *Testament* (*T. Levi* 2:5). The exact localization of the place in the *Document* is hindered by the fragmentary state of the Qumran manuscript. It is highly probable that Levi's *second* vision only took place in Bethel (cf. Form and Structure of *A.L.D.* 3a–7 in § 3.5).

Assuming, therefore, that Levi's first vision close to Abel Main and his second vision at Bethel, the following sequence of his travels up to the point of Isaac's instructions (*A.L.D.* 11–61) may be reconstructed. One can easily notice that Levi travels on the north-south horizontal axis.

1. Prayer	(*A.L.D.* 1a)
2. Trip to his father Jacob	to Abel Main? (*A.L.D.* 1b)
3. Vision close to Abel Main	Mt. Garizim? (*A.L.D.* 1b)
4. Shechem incident	Shechem (*A.L.D.* 1c–2)
5. Selling of Joseph close to Shechem	Levi-east of Asher (*A.L.D.* 3)
6. Second vision	Bethel (*A.L.D.* 3a–7)

7. Visit to Isaac in Hebron	heading south (*A.L.D.* 8)
8. Ordination in Bethel	heading north (*A.L.D.* 9–10)
9. Second visit to Isaac in Hebron	heading south (*A.L.D.* 11–61)

The autobiographical section (*A.L.D.* 78–80) additionally mentions his arrival to Canaan (*A.L.D.* 78) and descent to Egypt (*A.L.D.* 80). Levi's visionary dreams (*A.L.D.* 1b and 3a–7) constitute the vertical axis of his experience, but, due to their fragmentary state, it is impossible to know whether he travels through the heavens like in the first vision in *T. Levi* 2:5–5:3.

Upon my father Jacob. The syntagm "my father," אבי, is well documented in the book of Genesis (cf. Gen 19:34; 20:12; 22:7; 24:7. 38, etc.). However, none of Jacob's sons addresses him directly with this form. A frequent designation of Jacob is "Jacob, their father," יעקב אביהם (see Gen 42:29, 36; 45:25, 27; 46:5; cf. Gen 47:7; Isa 58:14). Levi usually speaks about Jacob in the *Document* with the fixed expression "my father Jacob," (here and 1Q21 4) or "Jacob my father" (*A.L.D.* 1a v. 18; 9 l. 15 = 4Q213b 4; 1Q21 29 1). Its roots undoubtedly reach back to the book of Genesis, as cited biblical evidence suggests. Only once the syntagm אבי without a personal name is used (*A.L.D.* 9 l. 21; cf. *A.L.D.* 58). Additionally, *A.L.D.* 10 l. 23 has אבא, 'the father' (cf. *A.L.D.* 50 "father Abraham"). It most probably constitutes the earliest attestation of this Aramaic word that appears transliterated in the Greek of the NT (Mark 14:36; Rom 8:15; Gal 4:6). There is no reason to suppose that in *A.L.D.* 10 l. 23 a later scribe changed אבי to אבא (see Grelot 1983: 107–108).

The expression אבי also designates Levi's grandfather Isaac (*A.L.D.* 8 l. 14; 11 l. 3; 12 l. 4), or his great-grandfather Abraham (*A.L.D.* 11 l. 3; *A.L.D.* 1a v. 15; cf. *A.L.D.* 62). Similarly, Gen 28:13 uses the syntagm אב to designate Jacob's grandfather Abraham. For other occurrences of the word, see *A.L.D.* 22 l. 12; E 18:2:50, 57—Isaac about his father; *A.L.D.* 83 l. 8—Levi about himself, addressing his children; "fathers": *A.L.D.* 3a ll. 4 and 5; "her father": *A.L.D.* 3a ll. 3 and 6.

From Abel Main. Because *A.L.D.* 1b ll. 11–14 are fragmentary, it is not clear where Levi's vision occurs. However, it is possible to suggest that it takes place close to Abel Main. The crucial question is how to localize this toponym. Milik (1978: 96) identifies the place as the water source called in Arabic 'Ein Beit el-Mâ situated 1 km west from the modern city of Nablus. It is located in the valley between mount Ebal and Garizim and other toponyms confirm its connection with Levitical traditions. The nearby hill is called Tell Kumra, "Priestly Hill" and Râs el-Sifâr, "Scribes' Promontory." If Milik's identification is correct, then the sequence of events in these fragmentary verses correctly corresponds to the topographic description. Levi leaves the place of his prayer, heads up to meet his father in the neighborhood of Shechem, probably in Abel Main located close to mount Garizim. After having left Abel Main, he has a vision on Mount Garizim.

I lay down and remained. The expression "to lie down and remain" (שכב ויתב 1b l. 14) as well as its Hebrew equivalent is absent in MT. The opening of the vision is very solemn. The same root (יתב) appears five times in

A.L.D. 1b ll. 15–16. Levi probably sees a mountain the summit of which reaches heavens. The visionary character of his experience points to prophetic and apocalyptic elements in the *Document* (cf. *A.L.D.* 7; Isa 1:1; Ezek 12:27; 13:16). The passive voice in *A.L.D.* 1b l. 15 ("I was given a vision") suggests God's activity and Levi's openness to God's message.

Then I was shown a vision. A.L.D. 1b ll. 15–18 find their closest parallel in *T. Levi* 2:5–6. This parallelism with the *Testament* text suggests again that one deals here with the beginning of the first vision. However, the Aramaic fragment points to another source of possible inspiration, at least for the opening part of the vision. The present research has already proven that the *Document* exhibits some textual closeness to the *Book of the Watchers* (*1 En.* 6–36; cf. *A.L.D.* 1a v. 14). The comparison between *A.L.D.* 1b ll. 13–18 (4Q213a 13–18) and *1 En.* 13:7–9 certainly indicates not a literary dependence of the former on the latter, but the vocabulary contacts are undeniable.

Table 10. Levi and Enoch as Visionaries

4Q213a 2 13–18 (*A.L.D.* 1b)	*1 Enoch*
line 13—Abel Main	= 13:9: Abel Mayyâ (Milik 1976: 196)
line 14—sitting down	= 13:7
line 15—a vision	= 13:8 (4Q204 1 vi 5)
line 16—visions	= 13:8
line 17—a high (mountain?)	absent
line 18 gates of heavens	= 4Q204 1 vi 4: gates of the pa[lace]; cf. 9:2 (4Q201 iv 10)
line 18—an angel	13:8: a voice

This parallelism indicates that the author of the *Document* was wittingly building on the Enochic visionary tradition in order to adapt it to his own purposes: creation of a priest and visionary in one person. One important difference between the two visions is obvious, that is, the place where it happens. Enoch has his vision at the foot of Mount Hermon, close to the "waters of Dan" (*1 En.* 13:7). When he awakes, he goes to the Watchers gathered in Ἐβελσατά (אבל מיא Abel Mayyâ according to Milik 1976: 196) and tells them the vision, which essentially concerns the rejection of the Watchers' petition and proclamation of the imminent judgment (14:4–8). Nickelsburg (1981: 588–590; 2001: 248–250) has noted the parallelism between the visionary experience of Levi in the *Testament of Levi* 2–7 and the *Ethiopic Enoch* 12–16. He, however, locates Abel Main of the *Testament* in the same geographic aera of Mt. Hermon where Enoch's vision took place.

Levi probably receives his first vision close to Abel Main on his way to his father Jacob in Shechem (cf. *A.L.D.* 1b l. 13). Although the name of the place does not literally and geographically correspond to the Enochic account, a reader acquainted with the Watchers' myth cannot miss the connotation with the proclamation of the impending judgment to the Watchers.

This suggestion indicates a line of interpretation of the fragmentary text of Levi's first vision. Enoch has a vision concerning the fate of the Watchers, fallen angels who commit fornication with women (*Jub.* 7:21; cf. *1 En.* 6:2 etc.) They also perpetrate "violence" on the earth (חמסה—4Q201 iv 8 = *1 En.* 9:1; cf. 9:9; 13:2). Levi has a vision that most probably deals with a similar problem. In his vision he must have received God's instruction concerning the fate of the Shechemites who became "doers of violence" (*A.L.D.* 78 l. 18 עבדי חמסא; cf. *A.L.D.* 3 l. 19) through the sin of Shechem, son of Hamor, who treated Dinah, Levi's sister, like a harlot (Gen 34:31 כזונה; cf *A.L.D.* 16 l. 16; *A.L.D.* 1a v. 7 [4Q213a frg. 1 13]). Levi, who already knows God's sentence from his first vision, advises his father and brother how to execute it (*A.L.D.* 1c–2).

This hypothetical reconstruction of the content of Levi's first vision is suggested by *T. Levi* 5:3. An angel leads Levi to the earth, gives him a shield and a sword and tells him to execute vengeance on Shechem because of Dinah. In the *Testament of Levi*, however, any parallelism between Enoch and Levi's visions completely disappears.

3.3   *Shechem Incident—A.L.D. 1c–2*

Form and Structure

The fragment is a midrashic interpretation of the Shechem incident described in Gen 34. In this Genesis chapter, Shechem, Hamor's son, sexually abuses Jacob's daughter Dinah. He falls in love with her and wants to marry her. However, Jacob's sons lay a trap for him and for the city's inhabitants by asking them to be circumcised. Once they agree and become circumcised, Simeon and Levi kill all the male Shechemites and bring back Dinah to their father's house. Jacob is angry with his two sons, whom he later curses in Gen 49:5–7. However, they object that it is not allowed to treat Dinah like a prostitute.

A.L.D. 1c–2 is very fragmentary and covers only Gen 34:13–17. The Cairo Geniza manuscript evidence suggests that the story was well elaborated and probably occupied about four columns of the manuscript (cf. § 1.4.3.2). It is impossible to know what it contained but, judging from the fragment itself, it midrashically developed the Genesis text. Comparing *A.L.D.* 78 ll. 16–18 and the parallel texts (*Jub.* 30; *T. Levi* 6–7), it is likely that it also contained the description of the killing of the Shechemites.

When one compares the Genesis account and the Apocrypon text, reasons for the killing become patent. Gen 34:5 and 13 states that

Shechem polluted (טמא) Dinah by lying with her (v. 2). Then, the responsibility is extended to all the inhabitants of the city (v. 27 טמאו) and cited as the main reason for the killing. Finally, Simeon and Levi respond to Jacob's objections, "Should he treat our sister as a harlot (כזונה)?" When defining Levi's priesthood, Isaac enumerates three traits that the ideal priest should shun: fornication (פחז), impurity (טמאה) and harlotry (זנות) (*A.L.D.* 16 ll. 15–16). The last two concepts correspond to the motivation the Genesis text provided to justify the killing.

V. 1c *Since she defiled*. The broken sentence refers most probably to Dinah and her sexual intercourse with Shechem (Gen 34:1–3). The woman who ruins the name of her family is mentioned in *A.L.D.* 3a ll. 3–6; cf. *Jub.* 30:7. The prohibition of defilement (טומאה) by an improper family relationship is discussed in the *Document* in relation to Levi in *A.L.D.* 141.9; 16 l. 15; 18 l. 23. The *Document* reinterprets here the *Genesis* account where the Shechemites are those who defile Dinah (cf. Gen 34:5, 13, 27).

they desired. In Gen 34, only Shechem desires (v. 8 חשק) and loves (vv. 3, 19 אהב) Dinah; the *Document*'s change to a verb in plural was probably suggested by the verb in plural in Gen 34:27 "they defiled" טמאו that implies a collective responsibility of the inhabitants of Shechem.

so that we all would become b[rothers] or companions. The clause is a reinterpretation of Gen 34:16 "and we will become one nation" והיינו לעם אחד. The Hebrew counterpart of the Aramaic word pair א[חין] וחברין is not attested in MT. In Ezek 37:16, 19 חבר denotes members of one nation, and the *Document* suggests the same interpretation—after the circumcision the Shechemites will become one nation with the sons of Jacob, members of the same covenant (cf. *A.L.D.* 2). This meaning is additionally suggested by *A.L.D.* 91 where the wisdom teacher is treated by other nations not as a stranger but as a brother or companion. The Aramaic form in plural "companions" חברין is attested in Dan 2:13, 17, 18, 21; it may also refer to members of the same political alliance (see 1QapGen XXI 26, 28; XXII 17).

V. 2 *the foreskin of your flesh*. This sentence is related to Gen 17:11 (ונמלתם את בשר ערלתכם), cf. Gen 17:14, 23, 24, 25; Lev 12:3; *Jub.* 15:14, 24, 26, 33). Its biblical context suggests that the circumcision is understood here as a sign of the covenant God made with Abraham. The word order in the syntagm עורלת בשרכון, however, is changed and, consequently, its semantic value is enlarged. Circumcision would relate here to the whole human body (see Ezek 44:7 ערלי לב וערלי בשר "uncircumcised in heart and body"; cf. Deut 10:16 and Jer 4:4 ערלות לבבכם, "foreskins of your heart"; cf. also 1QS V 5, 26; 1QpHab XI 13; 4Q177 II 16; 4Q434 1 i 4; 4Q435 1 1; 4Q504 4 11). Alternatively, it is also possible to suggest that the lexeme בשר is to be understood as an euphemism for the male *pudenda*. This meaning is attested in Syriac and semantically corresponds well to the context that requires actual, not metaphorical meaning (ܣ: Lev 15:2, 3, 19;

cf. Gen 17:14; Ezek 16:26; cf. Brockelmann 1928: *s.v.*; Payne Smith 1879: 553 "per euphemismus ܐܬܡ de pudendis viri et feminae").

and appear like [us]. The lexeme חמי belongs to the stock of Late Aramaic vocabulary. Here it seems to convey the idea of belonging to one nation (see ולא יתחמי בכנישתהון דישראל *Tg. Neof.* Exod 20:13, 14, 15, 16, 17; *Tg. Neof.* Deut 5:17). It is found together with *hitpaʿal* חבר in *Tg. Neof.* Deut 5:20mg. אנשא ... ולא יתחבר. The *Document*'s expression "appear like us" התחמיון כו[אתן] probably corresponds to "you will be like us" תהיו כמנו in the biblical account (Gen 34:15).

you will be sealed. Also Rom 4:11 understands circumcision as a seal. Later rabbinic literature attests the same concept (*b. Šabb.* 137b "he sealed (חתם) his offspring with the sign of the holy covenant; cf. *Tg. Cant.* 3:8; *Pirqe R. El.* 31; *Exod. Rab.* 19:5).

circumcision of tr[u]th. This expression may have a certain bearing on the interpretation of Rom 4:11 where Paul discusses the relationship between circumcision and righteousness. Note that the semantic field of the Aramaic קשט incorporates the meaning of both "truth" and "justice" in its range (cf. the comment on *A.L.D.* 1a v. 18). The term "circumcision" מילה is also a first attestation of later rabbinic usage of this word for circumcision (cf. Exod 4:26 מולה).

Circumcision of the Shechemites is not mentioned in *Jub.* 30; Josephus *A.J.* 1.337–340; *L.A.B.* 8:7. Some commentators suggest that the Jewish authors were probably perplexed by the fact that the sons of Jacob used this religious sign of the Abrahamic covenant as a trap for the Shechemites (cf. Holladay 1989: 189). The context of the story in the *Document* is fragmentary, but the circumcision of the Shechemites undoubtedly appears in the text. It is impossible to know if, similarly to *T. Levi* 6:7, the Aramaic text considered the killing of the Shechemites a sin. Judging from Levi's comment on the killing in *A.L.D.* 78 l. 16–18, it is hardly the case here. For a similar positive evaluation one can also compare *T. Levi* 5:3–4 where the killing is considered as the execution of a divine order (cf. *T. Levi* 6:8–11). In *Jub.* 30:5 the judgment against the Shechemites was decreed in heaven in response to the shameful thing they committed in Israel. Then *Jub.* 30:17 considered the killing as righteousness for Levi and Simeon, while in *Jub.* 30:23 their action of righteousness, justice, and vengeance was recorded in heaven as a blessing. Levi's elevation to the priesthood in *Jub.* 30:18 comes as a response to the fact that Levi was zealous to execute righteousness, judgment, and vengeance on those who rose against Israel.

3.4 *Selling of Joseph—A.L.D. 3*

Form and Structure

This fragment does not constitute a thematic continuation of *A.L.D.* 1c–2 that midrashically interprets the Shechem story based on Gen 34. In *A.L.D.* 3 ll. 19–21 Judah states that Levi and Simeon are absent because they have gone to meet Reuben. Since in Gen 34 these two brothers are the main agents in the killing of the Shechemites, it is unimaginable that the midrashic text simply eliminates them from the account together with the third brother, Reuben. The text of the Cairo Geniza manuscript also indicates that between *A.L.D.* 1c–2 and *A.L.D.* 3 two and a half columns are missing. It is improbable that the account based on Gen 34 continues for so many verses in the *Document*.

The expression "in Shechem" בשכם (*A.L.D.* 3 l. 16) denotes the proper name of a place, not a personal name of the son of Hamor from Gen 34. The line is broken, but the preceding verb "they were" הוו does not leave any doubt as to the interpretation of the following syntagm. *A.L.D.* 3 l. 18 repeats the expression with probably the same reference to a place; the context, however, is fragmentary. In the Pentateuch one finds the expression "in Shechem" בשכם referring to the name of the city only twice in Gen 37:12, 13. This is the chapter that tells the story of Joseph's betrayal and selling by his brothers. Jacob sends his beloved son Joseph to his brothers who are tending the sheep in Shechem. Joseph first reaches Shechem, does not find his brothers there, and, informed by a man, continues to Dothan (Gen 37:14–17). When his brothers see him arrive, they plot to kill him, throw him into a pit, and finally, sell him to the passing caravan of Midianite traders (Gen 37:18–28). Reuben returns to the pit and does not find Joseph, while the brothers report to their father Jacob that a wild beast devoured Joseph (Gen 37:29–36).

The names of Jacob's sons in the *Document*'s fragment also suggest a narrative based on Gen 37. Reuben actively takes part in the incident, defending the life of Joseph (Gen 37:21–22, 29–30). Judah is the one who counsels the brothers to sell Joseph and not to kill him (Gen 37:26–27). Levi and Simeon, however, are not expressly named in the Genesis story, although their presence is certainly assumed by the narrator. An additional connection with Gen 37 is suggested by the fact that Judah in *A.L.D.* 3 l. 22 tends the sheep (ענאא) before he leaves them to proceed to another type of activity. Similarly, Gen 37:12 and 13 indicate that the brothers are tending sheep (צאן) in Shechem. Finally, Dan reports about Joseph being in peril of death by the doers of violence (*A.L.D.* 3 ll. 17–19), thus corroborating the narrative connection with Gen 37. The circumstances in which Joseph finds himself unequivocally suggest the context of his selling by his brothers.

Once the connection with Gen 37 has been indicated, a tentative interpretation of the fragment may be undertaken. Since the manuscript lacks the beginning and continuation of the story, and since *A.L.D.* 3 ll. 15–19 are only partially preserved, the tentativeness of the interpretation must be stressed. The few words that remain in *A.L.D.* 3 ll. 15–17 suggest that they deal with Levi's brothers (lines 15 and 17) and that the action is somewhat connected to the city of Shechem. Then probably Dan (lines 17–19) and Judah (lines 19–22) make a report to their brothers. Finally Judah jumps up and leaves the sheep. The rest of the story is lacking.

V. 3 *And Dan reported.* The verse is fragmentary and subject to two interpetations. Dan here probably accuses Simeon and Levi for the killing of Joseph. It is suggested by the expression "in Shechem" בשכם and "do]ers of violence" עב]די המסא (cf. *A.L.D.* 78 l. 18). The expression "doers of violece" could well apply to the two brothers accused by the biblical text of committing violence against the Shechemites. Gen 49:7 condemns Levi and Simeon and their "weapons of violence" (cf. *A.L.D.* 78). Dan's report that Joseph actually died might concern his being thrown into the pit by the two brothers, which was tantamount to his death. Some targumic and rabbinic texts expressly accuse Simeon and Levi of plotting to kill Joseph (see *Tg. Ps.-J.* Gen 37:19 and 49:7; *Tg. Neof.* Gen 49:6 mg.; *Gen. Rab.* 98:5). *Midr. Prov.* ch. 1 (Buber 1893: 44) states that it was Simeon and Levi who threw Joseph into the pit (see Ginzberg 1998: 5:328–329). It is, however, difficult to assume Levi's hostility towards Joseph in the *Document*, for he presents Joseph as an example to imitate in *A.L.D.* 90. Alternatively, the expression "doers of violence" refers to all the brothers who plot to kill Joseph and throw him into the pit.

And Judah reported to them. Judah's report adduces an important piece of information that helps understand the whole passage. He reports to the other brothers (*A.L.D.* 3 l. 20 אינון) that Levi and Simeon have gone to Reuben who was on the east of Asher, that is in western Galilee. Judah's words are easily explained in the context of Gen 37. The brothers plot to kill Joseph (Gen 37:18–20) but Reuben wants to save him and advises the brothers not to kill him but to throw him into a pit (vv. 21–22). The brothers follow his advice; however, they finally sell Joseph to the passing caravan of the Ishmaelites (vv. 23–28). It is Judah who suggests this move to his brothers (vv. 26–27). Then Reuben returns to the pit where Joseph has been thrown, does not find the boy, and despairs (v. 29). The biblical text clearly indicates that Reuben is not present at the selling of Joseph.

I and Simeon my brother had gone to j[o]in Reuben. Reuben is absent during Judah's speech and it is exactly the moment when Judah takes the initiative by jumping up and leaving the sheep (*A.L.D.* 3 ll. 22–23). The absence of Reuben during the selling of Joseph is also attested by Josephus (*A.J.* 2.31) who states that Reuben "departed in search of grounds suitable for pasturage." Other texts confirm the absence of Reuben during the selling of Joseph (*T. Sim.* 2:9; *T. Zeb.* 4:5; *Gen. Rab.* 84:15, 19; *Pirqe R. El.* 38).

The absence of Simeon and Levi solves an important exegetical problem concerning the role of the two brothers in the selling of Joseph. Gen 37:29–30 suggests that only Reuben is absent when the rest of the brothers sold Joseph into slavery. That means that Levi and Simeon also participate in the deal. This fact would denigrate the picture of an ideal priest who is called "a holy priest for all the seed of Abraham" (*A.L.D.* 17 ll. 19–21). Additionally, in his didactic poem Levi holds Joseph in high esteem. In *A.L.D.* 90 Joseph is an example of a wise man who, because of his teaching activities, is greatly honored and exalted. Levi also proclaims the poem itself in the year in which Joseph died (*A.L.D.* 82 ll. 4–5). Levi's participation in an action against Joseph is hardly justifiable by the *Document*. The easiest solution to this problem was to affirm that Levi was absent when the selling of Joseph took place. In fact, the *Testaments* are quite coherent in this respect. While many brothers accuse themselves for their participation in the selling (*T. Sim.* 2:6–14; 4:2; *T. Zeb.* 1:5; 2:1; 2:1–3:3; ch. 4; *T. Dan* 1:4–9; *T. Gad* 1:9; 3:3), Levi is never mentioned as being present or taking part in the action. Similarly to the *Document*, the *Testaments* hold Joseph in high esteem (see *T. Sim.* 4:4; 5:1; 8:3–4; *T. Levi* 13:9; *T. Benj.* 3:1, 3–8; 5:5). *T. Sim.* 2:9 states that Simeon was absent when Joseph was sold, confirming thus Judah's statement in *A.L.D.* 3 ll. 19–22. However, he is not exonerated from the guilt of plotting to kill Joseph (see *T. Sim.* 2:7). His absence allows Judah to sell Joseph.

And [J]udah jumped forward [to] leave the sheep. The broken text of the manuscript does not allow the reader to be sure that Judah's involvement here concerns the selling of Joseph. However, the comparison with Gen 37:26–27 where Judah gives his brothers this advice suggests this development (cf. *T. Sim.* 2:9). The initiative belongs to him, for he is also the eldest among his brothers when the first three, Reuben, Simeon, and Levi, are absent (cf. Philo *Ios.* § 15–16).

3.5 *Heavenly Elevation—A.L.D. 3a–7*

Form and Structure

The second vision is preserved in a fragmentary state. *A.L.D.* 3a contrasts the virgin who defiles the name of her family (lines 1–6) with "the holy ones from the people" (lines 7–8). *A.L.D.* 3b preserves in full only two words concerning eternal priesthood, a clear reference to Levi and his descendants. *A.L.D.* 3c compares the kingdom of the high priesthood given to Levi's sons with another, non specified kingdom. The fourth part of the vision is attested in *A.L.D.* 4–7, and describes the kingdom of the sword and Levi's heavenly elevation by seven angelic beings who appear to be the main speakers in the vision. *A.L.D.* 7 ends the vision with the report of Levi's awakening from a visionary dream and his amazement concerning its content. This last verse is the only clear indication that the literary form of this fragmentary text may be classified as a visionary dream. Levi's first vision (*A.L.D.* 1b) is most probably also received in a dream as *A.L.D.* 1a v. 14 would suggest. Any extensive discussion of the literary form of the visions is impossible, since they are both preserved in a very fragmentary state.

Levi's first vision takes place in a location close to Abel Main (cf. *A.L.D.* 1b l. 13), probably on Mount Garizim. Then Levi is in Shechem where the killing takes place and he leaves with his brother Simeon for the region of Asher to meet his brother Reuben. Further information is lacking because the text is fragmentary. One may only assume that before traveling to Isaac (*A.L.D.* 8), he stops at Bethel and has his second vision. There are several arguments for that location as the place of the second vision. *Jub.* 32:1 indicates that Levi has a vision in Bethel. He falls asleep and dreams that "he—he and his sons—had been appointed and made into the priesthood of the most high God for ever." The content clearly suggests Levi receives the heavenly ordination, and a similar event happens in the second vision in the *Document*. Additionally, the sentence of *Jub.* 32:1 is almost literally cited in *T. Levi* 8:3b as an angelic speech inaugurating his heavenly ordination. This sentence in the *Testament* belongs to Levi's second vision. MS *k* of the *Testament* also indicates Bethel as the place of the vision (ὄντος μου ἐν Βεθὴλ *T. Levi* 8:1). This manuscript together with MS *b* belongs to the oldest stage of the text transmission of the *Testaments* (see de Jonge and Hollander 1978: xxxiv). They form the same family I, but MS *k* constitutes an independent witness to the text. Lastly, the closing section of the vision, *A.L.D.* 7, corresponds closely to the closing section of the second vision in *T. Levi* 8:18–18. Although the content of the second vision in the *Document* and the *Testament* differ considerably, both texts recount Levi's heavenly elevation. Additionally, the Greek *Testament* and the book of *Jubilees* preserve the same order of events based on Gen 35 (cf. Hultgård 1977: 24, Endres 1987: 158–159):

1. Jacob's family goes to Bethel	*Jub.* 31:1–4; *T. Levi* 7:4; (*A.L.D.* 1a?)
2. Vision in Bethel	*Jub.* 32:1; *T. Levi* 8:1 (MS *k*); *A.L.D.* a–7 (?)

3. Visit to Isaac in Hebron	*Jub.* 31:5–32; *T. Levi* 9:1–2; *A.L.D.* 8
4. Second stay in Bethel	*Jub.* 32; *T. Levi* 9:3–4; *A.L.D.* 9–10
5. Second visit to Isaac in Hebron	*Jub.* 33:1, 21; *T. Levi* 9:5–14; *A.L.D.* 11–61

Although *Jub.* 30–32 speak of only one vision of Levi, one must notice that these chapters eliminate many other elements that appear in the *Document*. Levi's consecratory prayer (E 2,3) and his earthly election and consecration by Jacob (*A.L.D.* 9–10) take place in Bethel. The assumption therefore, that the second vision also takes place in Bethel perfectly harmonizes with the ideological stance of the *Document*. Bethel is considered to be a privileged place of contact between heaven and earth and a sanctuary in which Levi discharges his priestly duties (cf. *A.L.D.* 19).

V. 3a *she desecrated her name.* The whole fragment thematically falls into two parts. The first six lines probably halakically comment on the Dinah story (Gen 34), for they condemn the conduct of a woman who profanes the good reputation of her family as shameful. The wording of *A.L.D.* 3a ll. 3–4 recalls *Jub.* 30:7. This chapter of *Jubilees* retells and halakically comments on the Dinah story in Gen 34. In an angelic speech the Israelite virgin's profanation is retold and condemned (*Jub.* 30:1–6, 24–26) and exogamic marriage is chastised (*Jub.* 30:7–17, 21–22). The killing also becomes a reason why the sons of Levi are elevated to the priesthood (*Jub.* 30:18–20). Although very fragmentary, lines 1–6 are close in their contents to the chastisement of exogamic marriages in the book of *Jubilees*. Lines 7–8 shift to a positive exposition concerning the "holy ones from the people."

A.L.D. 3a ll. 1–2 are too fragmentary to yield any positive meaning. *A.L.D.* 3a ll. 3–4 deal with a woman who defiles (חלל) her name and the name of her father. The proper biblical background to this statement is Lev 21:9. The biblical verse decrees that a daughter of a priest who profanes (Hebrew חלל) herself by playing harlot (לזנות), profanes the name of her father and is to be burned. Although the Qumran fragment does not mention the reason of the desecration, the sexual misconduct, that is intermarriage, seems to lie in the background. In *A.L.D.* 17 l. 17 Levi is warned not to profane (חלל) his seed with harlots (זניאן). *A.L.D.* 3a l. 3 is similar to the comment on the story of Dinah in *Jub.* 30:7 in which a woman who married a foreigner is to be burned because "she has defiled the name of the house of her father" '*ark*ʷ*asat sǝma beta 'abuhā*. Similarly to the *Jubilees'* account, this Qumran fragment does not limit the precept to the daughter of a priest, but applies it to "every virgin" (*A.L.D.* 3a ll. 4–5).

[vir]gin who ruins her name. A.L.D. 3a ll. 5–6 continue the same theme of dishonoring the name of one's family but the subject seems to be any virgin. The expression "to ruin the name" חבל שם is parallel to the following *'apʿel*

of בהת ("to bring shame"), and refers to the virgin's shameful conduct. *Jub.*
30:5 and 7 also use the concept of shame (*ḥafrat*) in the Dinah story, but
applie it to the Shechemites and the Israelite man respectively. Finally, the
record of a virgin's revilement will last for ever (line 6). This sentence sets
the virgin's future in sharp contrast with the future of Levi and his sons
in the *Document*.

And the name of her revilement will not be wiped out. This line is a continuation of the preceding discussion on the virgin who brings shame on her
family. The feminine suffixes in אבוהא and עמהא refer to the virgin from
the preceding line, hence the *hê* in חסדה is also to be interpreted as 3f.sg.
pronominal suffix. The Aramaic חסד "shame, revilement" fits the context
of the preceding lines that speak about shame and ruin the virgin brings
on her family. The whole sentence is an adaptation of the biblical phrase
"to blot out the name" שם מחה, found in Deut 9:14; 29:19; 2 Kgs 14:27;
Ps 9:6; 109:13. It conveys the idea of extermination as a divine punishment for sin. Here, however, the name of the virgin's revilement is to be
preserved forever. That suggests that her sin is not pardonable and she will
not receive mercy from God (see Jer 18:23; Ps 109:14; Neh 3:37).

Thus her example is set as contrasting with the glorious and pious future
of the Levitical priestly lineage. *A.L.D.* 60 repeats the line almost literally
but in relation to Levi and his offspring: "Your name and the name of
your seed will not be blotted out (ἐξαληφθήσεται) for ever." In the LXX,
the Greek ἐξαλείφω "blot out" translates Hebrew מחה, e.g. Gen 7:4, 23,
23; 9:15. The Aramaic verb in *A.L.D.* 3a l. 6 מחי *hitpeʿel* has the same meaning in the targumic literature, "to be blotted out" (see Jastrow 1950: *s.v.*).
The revilement of a virgin who brings shame on her family should be set
in contrast with the example of Yochebed, Levi's daughter, discussed in
the *Document*. She does not bring shame on her father Levi, but glory (*A.L.D.*
71) by marrying Levi's grandson Amram (*A.L.D.* 75). In the context of the
Document, marriage within one tribal family stands in sharp contrast with
Isaac's prohibition to desecrate Levi's seed with harlots (see *A.L.D.* 17).
Levi's progeny is supposed to glorify its fathers' name. Thus Qahat in his
Testament admonishes his sons that by being holy and pure from all min-
gling and by preserving the inheritance, they will give him a good name
and joy to Levi, Isaac, and Abraham (4Q542 1 i 8–13). In another Qumran
text of Levitical inspiration a mysterious priestly person establishes a joy-
ous name to his father (4Q541 24 ii 5).

Particular importance is assigned to profaning the name of the family
(*A.L.D.* 3a ll. 3–6). Contrast 4Q542 1 i 10, where the descendants of Qahat
are supposed to assure him a "good name" through their proper behavior
(cf. 4Q541 24 ii 5; 4Q196 17 ii 15 [Tob 13:11]).

for all the generations of eternity. *A.L.D.* 3a ll. 7–8 shift to another subject, a
positive prophecy concerning "the holy ones from the people" (line 7). The
vocabulary indicates some contacts with MS A and its possible meaning
should be first confronted with the parallel texts within MS A itself. The
first part of *A.L.D.* 3a l. 7 is missing. Although in a fragmentary context,
the expression "all generations of eternity" defines the everlasting charac-

ter of the Levitical priesthood. The same expression is reflected in *A.L.D.*
1a v. 18 and *A.L.D.* 61: εἰς πάσας τὰς γενεὰς τῶν αἰώνων, although the last
Greek word is in plural. These two cases refer to the future of Levi and
of his descendants and imply that they will enjoy the privilege of righteous
judgment and blessing without limits in time (see 4Q542 1 ii 4; 4Q543 2
3; 4Q545 4 19). The expression appears elsewhere in an eschatological context (see 4Q212 ii 17 [*1 En.* 91:18]; iv 18 [*1 En.* 91:13]; LXX Tob 13:2;
14:5; cf. 4Q202 ii 15 [*1 En.* 9:4 G]; Tob 1:5; Eph 3:21). Qumran Hebrew
texts often use the expression דורות עלם (see 1QHᵃ VI 6 [Sukenik XIV];
IX 18 [Sukenik col. I]; XIV 11 [Sukenik VI]; 4Q252 v 4 [about the dura-
tion of messianic royal covenant]; 4Q504 1–2 ii 11 [Puech XIII]; 7 3
[Puech XIII]).

Thus, the lexeme עלם/αἰών most probably implies a timeless perspective
for Levitical priesthood (see *A.L.D.* 1a v. 16 "a seed of righteousness blessed
for ever" [εἰς τοὺς αιῶνας = לעלמין, cf. Dan 2:4, 44; 3:9, etc.]; *A.L.A* 1a v.
18 "righteous judgment for ever" [εἰς πάντα τὸν αἰῶνα]; *A.L.D.* 1a communion with God "all the days of the world" [πάσας τὰς ἡμέρας τοῦ αἰῶνου =
כל יומי עלמא; see Isa 63:9; 1QHᵃ IX 15]; *A.L.D.* "eternal priesthood" [עלמא
כהנות; cf. Exod 40:15; Num 25:13; 1QSb III 26]; *A.L.D.* 59 Levi's descendants remembered in the book of memorial of life "for all ages" [ἕως πάντων
τῶν αἰώνων = עד כול עלמיא; cf. 1QapGen XXI 14]; *A.L.D.* 85 l. 12 the
justice received "for ever" [עד עלמא cf. Dan 7:18 and *A.L.D.* 60, in pl.];
A.L.D. 88 l. 19 wisdom as "eternal glory" of Levi's children [ליקר עלם; cf.
1QSb III 4]). When speaking about the future of his children in *A.L.D.*
100 l. 17 (4Q213 2 15) and *A.L.D.* 100 l. 18 (4Q213 1 ii 18), Levi states
that there will be no end to their glory, ולא איתי סוף ליק[רכן. The *Document*
knows other words designating time that do not have any eschatological
connotation in the composition: עדן *A.L.D.* 3 l. 15; 73 l. 3 (see Dan 6:11,
14; 7,22; Ezra 5:3; זמן *A.L.D.* 5 ll. 4, 5, 5, 5, 6, 6; 73 l. 4; cf. Dan 6:11,
14; 7:25, etc).

the holy ones from the people. The mention of the holy ones is most probably a reference to Simeon and Levi, whose vengeance upon the Shechemites
is praised in *Jub.* 30:6, 17 and rooted in God's will. The slaughter of the
Shechemites is also a decisive argument in the choice of Levi's descendants
to priesthood in *Jub.* 30:18. Additionally, the adjective "holy" קדיש characterizes Levi in a particular way (see *A.L.D.* 17 ll. 18, 20).

holy tithe. Since *A.L.D.* 3a l. 8 is fragmentary, it is difficult to interpret
this expression, the context of the whole *Document* should be, therefore, considered. The tithe motif reappears a second time in *A.L.D.* 9 that reports
Levi's priestly investiture and ordination. A comparison with *A.L.D.* 9 should
be helpful for the understanding of the whole line 8 here.

A.L.D. 9 ll. 18–19
ולי מכל בנוהי יהב קרבן מֹעשֹ]ר[לאל

A.L.D. 3a l. 8
[מעשר קודש קרבן לאל מֹן   ]ל וחן[

238 CHAPTER THREE

These vocabulary contacts indicate that the tithe of holiness is an allusion to Jacob's tithing at Bethel (*A.L.D.* 9) and to Levi's metro-arithmetical skills he learns from Isaac (cf. *A.L.D.* 9 and 32a–36). In the Bodleian fragment the gift of the tithe to God is assigned to Levi and thus, Jacob's action becomes a clear sign of Levi's election to the priestly office. Assigning the tithe to Levi is the first element of Levi's priestly ordination in *A.L.D.* 9. There follow the investiture with the priestly garb and filling of hands, an idiomatic expression for the priestly ordination. It seems, therefore, that the tithing was not only the occasion for Levi's priestly elevation but that, in fact, it was an integral part of the ritual.

Kugler (1996a: 84, n. 87) similarly suggests that "the phrase מעשר קודש קרבן לאל reflects angelic ordination of Levi to the priesthood as a 'holy tithe, an offering to God'. . . . " He makes a recourse to the book of *Jubilees* 32, where in fact the motif of Levi as a human tithe is fundamental to his elevation to the priesthood (cf. the comment on *A.L.D.* 9). The author of *Jubilees* introduces the idea of Levi as a human tithe, a literary motif related to the *Document* description, and reads it in the light of Num 3:44–45 that sets the Levitical tribe apart as a ransom for all Israelite males. This obser- vation by Kugler needs a correction, though. The expression "tithe of holi- ness" in the *Document* is related to Lev 27:30. The verse states that "all the tithe of the land . . . is holy to God" . . . . קדש ליהוה כל מעשר הארץ (see also Lev 27:32; 2 Chr 31:6, 12).

Lev 27:32 unites in one verse the concept of the tithe, the ordinal num- ber "tenth," a synonym of the tithe, and the concept of holiness. In *Pirqe R. El.* 37, when the choice of Levi as the holy tithe is reported, the pas- sage of Leviticus is cited twice. The choice of Levi for the priesthood is justified in the following way:

> Jacob wished to cross the ford of the Jabbok, and he was detained there. The angel said to him: Did you not speak thus—"I will surely give a tenth to you" (Gen 28, 22)? What did Jacob do? He took all the cattle in his possession which he had brought from Paddan Aram, and there were five thousand and five hundred sheep. And the angel spoke again to Jacob: Do you not also have sons and you did not tithe them (to me)? What did Jacob do? He separated the four firstborns (בכורות) of the four mothers and eight were left. He started from Simeon and ended with Benjamin who was still in his mother's womb. And again he began with Simeon and ended with Levi and Levi happened to be the holy tithe to the Lord (מעשר קדש לה) as it is said "the tenth will be holy to the Lord (העשירי יהיה קדש לה)" (Lev 27, 32).
> Rabbi Ishmael says: All the firstborns (בכורות) when they are per- ceptible to the eye must be tithed. But Jacob tithed in the reverse: he started with Benjamin who was still in the mother's womb and Levi happened to be holy to the Lord (ועלה לוי קדש לה). And about him the Scripture says: the tenth will be holy to the Lord (Lev 27,32). (transl. Friedlander 1981: 283–284)

The tithe mentioned in the context of the positive prophecy concerning the "righteous" and "saints" in *A.L.D.* 3a l. 8 appears to make an allusion to Levi's elevation to the priesthood. It may also be supposed that this fragment of the *Document* is actually set within Levi's vision, since his elevation to the priesthood by the angels in connection with the tithe motif is attested in later Rabbinic tradition and targumic interpretation. In *Pirqe R. El.* 37 Levi is presented as מעשר קדש לה׳ and Michael, the angel, introduces him before God as a special God's portion of the tithe: חלק מעשרך.

> Michael, the angel, went down and took Levi and brought him up before the Holy-Blessed-He (cf. *T. Levi* 2:6; 5:1) and he spoke before Him: "O, Sovereign of the world, this is your lot (גורלך) and portion of your tithe (חלק מעשרך)". And He stretched out His right hand and blessed him, so that the sons of Levi might serve before Him in the land like the ministering angels in heaven. Michael spoke before the Holy-Blessed-He: "O, Sovereign of all the worlds, does the king not provide the food for his servants?" Therefore, He gave to them, to the sons of Levi every holy thing which is offered to His Name, according to what is said: They will eat from God's sacrifices and from his portion (Deut 18, 1). (transl. Friedlander 1981: 283–284)

an offering to God from. The tithe of holiness is presented as an offering to God, an expression that might also be an allusion to Jacob's tithing at Bethel. The tithe assigned to Levi in *A.L.D.* 9 is precisely indicated with the same formula. In addition to that, the very first priestly action of Levi is that of a sacrifice he presents to God (וקרבית כל קרבנוהי *A.L.D.* 9). Therefore, the probability is even higher that the tithe mentioned in *A.L.D.* 3a l. 8 was meant to define the priestly character of the "holy ones" and, according to all indications, should be read in the context of Levi's priestly ordination (cf. *A.L.D.* 9–10).

V. 3b *an eternal priesthood.* The expression כהנות עלמא is related to Exod 40:15 and Num 25:13. In the former text, Moses is to anoint Aaron and his sons so that they may have an eternal priesthood. The latter reference concerns Aaron's grandson, Phinehas (cf. Exod 6:25), and his role in Num 25. Israel plays the harlot (זנה) with the Moabite women in Sittim, and as a consequence, begins worshipping Baal of Peor (Num 25:1–2). God tells Moses to kill all the men who worshipped Baal and a plague strikes twenty four thousand people in Israel (vv. 3–5, 9). When another man brings a Midianite woman to the camp, Phinehas kills both of them and as a consequence, the plague stops (vv. 6–8). Mindful of Phinehas' zeal, God stipulates with him a covenant of peace (vv. 10–12) and then the text adds: "And it shall be to him, and to his descendants after him, the covenant of a perpetual priesthood, because he was jealous (קנא) for his God, and made atonement (ויכפר) for the people of Israel" (Num 25:13).

Although there are some similarities between Levi's and Phinehas' story, the expression "eternal priesthood" included, one should be cautious to draw too close a parallelism. Phinehas kills the Israelite man and a Midianite woman out of his zeal for God (קנא Num 25:13). In the *Document* the word קנא does not appear even once, which, however, may be due to the fragmentary state of the manuscript. Phinehas' zealous act brings about propitiation for the sons of Israel and he thus eliminates idolatry and exogamy from Israel, whereas the *Document* interprets the Shechemites' sin as "violence" (*A.L.D.* 78 l. 17), caused by an exogamous relationship with Dinah. Israel's sexual and ritual prostitution in Num 25:1–2 may be interpreted as an idolatrous impurity liable to extermination (Exod 22:19). It is, however, not codified in the P document as טמא. Only Josh 22:17 does suggest that Israel has not yet been purified (הטהר) from the Peor idolatry. However, neither טמא nor חמס appears in the account or in later retellings of the Phinehas' story (see Ps 106:28–31; Sir 45:23–24; 1 Macc 2:26, 54; *4 Macc* 18:12; *Hel. Syn. Pr.* 8:4–5 = *Constitutiones Apostolorum* 7.39:3). Prophetic literature sees a connection between impurity and idolatry (see, e.g., Jer 2:23; Ezek 20:7, 18, 26, 31; 22:3–4; 23:7, 13–14, 17, 30; 36:25, 29, 33; 37:23; Ps 106:36–40; cf. Gen 35:2; Hos 5:3–4; 6:10), this prophetic interpretive strategy, however, is absent in the *Document*.

The term עלם is well attested in the *Document* (see the comment on *A.L.D.* 3a). The other term, כהנותא is also frequent (*A.L.D.* 3c l. 2; 9 ll. 18, 19; 13 l. 8; 15 l. 14; 19 l. 3; 59; 64; 67 l. 7). According to the *Document*, Levi's election to royal priesthood is eternal and should have no end (cf. *A.L.D.* 1a v. 18; 3a; 61; 100). In 1QSb III 26 the expression ברית כהנת [עלם] (Num 25:13) is applied to the eschatological priests, sons of Zadok. 1QM XVII 3 applies it to Eleazar and Itamar as a confirmation of their priestly election instead of Nadab and Abihu (cf. Lev 10:1; Num 3:4; 17:1–5; 26:61).

V. 3c *they will be three*. The numeral "three" in this fragmentary line induced Grelot (1956: 395) to interpret it in the light of *T. Levi* 8:11–14, 17 that discusses three different offices ascribed to Levi's sons. This interpretation is probable, for later in the *Document* Levi ascribes different function to his sons (*A.L.D.* 99–100). There is also a common point between *A.L.D.* 3c l. 2 and the later description of the future of Levi's sons in *A.L.D.* 100 l. 16. Both verses speak about priestly kingdoms, and, additionally, *A.L.D.* 99 l. 15 parallels Levitical priestly and royal offices.

the kingdom of the priesthood. The expression is inspired by Exod 19:6 where the expression "kingdom of priests" ממלכת כהנים is followed by "holy nation" גוי קדוש and refers to all Israel. The whole nation, therefore, becomes a priestly kingdom during the stipulation of the covenant at Mount Sinai. This understanding, however, belies later separation of the priestly and royal offices during the period of the monarchy. Hence, all the targums translate the expression with two distinctive nouns "kings and priests" מלכין וכהנין (see Camponovo 1984: 411). *Jub.*16:18 reflects the same understanding of the biblical text (cf. *Jub.* 33:20; Rev 5:10). The LXX translates the phrase with the no less difficult βασίλειον ἱεράτευμα (see Exod 23:22), which may be rendered with "royal priesthood" (βασίλειον as an adjective—only 2x in the LXX) or by asyndetic two nouns "kingdom, priesthood" (βασίλειον as a noun—22x in the LXX, with different meanings, however; cf. *A.L.D.* 67). In the first case the Hebrew meaning is inverted, in the second, the lack of coordination in Greek is hardly acceptable. 2 Macc 2:17 suggests the second interpretation.

However difficult the understanding of the Greek text may be, only the LXX (MSS) renders the second member of the expression with an abstract noun ἱεράτευμα. This word is unknown in extra-biblical Greek, and in the LXX it always reflects Exod 19:6 (Exod 23:22; 2 Macc 2:17). It is, there-fore, difficult to be sure of its Hebrew *Vorlage*, if any existed at all. The word is additionally found in *A.L.D.* 67 and, like in the LXX, it is asyn-detically paralleled with the kingship, although the Greek expression is different (ἀρχὴ βασιλέων) and its Aramaic counterpart does not exist. 2 Macc 2:17 alludes to Exod 19:6 but inserts the article before each notion and uses a conjunction between them: τὸ βασίλειον καὶτὸ ἱεράτευμα (see, how-ever, 1 Pet 2:9). This reading supports the conviction that Exod 19:6 should be read as two nouns. In this case, one may assume that the LXX trans-lated two abstract nouns, ממלכת כהנה, "the kingdom of priesthood," but did not render the *nomen rectum* כהנה by an appropriate genetive form. The use of a neologism ἱεράτευμα, instead of ἱερατεία, a frequent term used for the Aaronide priesthood (Exod 29:9; 35:19; 39:19 (41), etc.), might suggest that another kind of priesthood is understood here (see Camponovo 1984: 385).

The *Document* goes in a completely opposite direction in its interpreta-tion of Exod 19:6 than the book of *Jubilees* and targumic tradition. It does not differentiate between priestly and royal functions, but ascribes them both to Levi and his sons. Levi's prayer (*A.L.D.* 1a) indicates how royal and priestly characteristics converge in one person. The fragmentary *A.L.D.* 3c l. 2 ascribes to the sons of Levi only the kingdom of priesthood greater than another non specified kingdom while *A.L.D.* 67 ascribes to Qahat the royal and high priestly office. After the Wisdom poem, Levi ascribes to his sons the future role of priests and kings as well (*A.L.D.* 99) and establish-ment of their kingdom (*A.L.D.* 100). The conjunction of Levi's two judicial characteristics, the "righteous law" and the "law of priesthood" in *A.L.D.* 13–15, suggests the conjunction of priestly and royal offices as well. The role of a priest and king is, therefore, strictly connected in the *Document* and ascribed exclusively to the Levitical tribe. Additionally, it is expressly cast into an unspecified future, adding an eschatological character to this conjunction of two offices.

The term "kingdom" מלכות most probably refers to exercising the royal function (cf. Dan 8:23) and does not denote a territory (Dan 1:20; 9:1; 10:13, etc.) or length of one's rule (Dan 1:1; 2:1; 8:1, etc.). It is qualified by the noun in emphatic state, "the priesthood" כהנותא. The latter concept refers in the *Document* either to Levi (*A.L.D.* 9 l. 18; *A.L.D.* 51; cf. *A.L.D.* 64) or to his son Qahat (*A.L.D.* 67 l. 7; cf. E 18,2 v. 67). Levi's son, Gershom, does not inherit it (*A.L.D.* 64). It further qualifies the word "law" דין (*A.L.D.* 13 l. 8; 15 l. 14) or "garment" לבוש (*A.L.D.* 9 l. 19; 19 l. 3). The priesthood and royal power are both ascribed to Qahat in *A.L.D.* 67.

Additionally, some characteristics of the founder of the royal tribe, that is Judah, are ascribed to Levi's son, Qahat, in *A.L.D.* 67.

The verse states that the priestly kingdom is being offered to Levi's children and that their kingdom will do better than another kingdom. The *Document* speaks of the kingdom of Levi's children in *A.L.D.* 100 l. 16. Additionally, *A.L.D.* 99 l. 15 affirms that they will be kings and priests. Thus, Levi's speech to his sons after the Wisdom poem further defines the character of this priesthood. Levi's royal function consists most probably in exercising the "righteous law" taught to him by Isaac (cf. *A.L.D.* 15). To the eschatological high priest in 1QSb III 6 God should assign kingdom and probably the eternal priesthood. The eschatological priest in 1QSb IV 25–26 officiates in the temple of the kingdom בהיכל מלכות. The expression most probably refers to the heavenly temple as the place of God's residence and of his kingdom. The priest by his service is, therefore, similar to the "angels of the face" (v. 26) and is in direct contact with God's kingship. The third time the lexeme מלכות is applied in the eschatological rule of the Qumran community to the "prince of the Congregation," that is a Davidic messiah. 1QSb V 21 states that God "will renew the covenant of the Community with him to establish the kingdom of his people (מלכות עמו) for ever." 1QSb V 25 describes the Prince of the Congregation with the language of Isa 11:2. In the *Document* this Isaian verse is applied to Levi (see *A.L.D.* 1a v. 8), and that clearly suggests that the image of a wise ruler is transferred to Levi and his descendants (cf. *A.L.D.* 67 and E 18,2 v. 67).

Because *A.L.D.* 3c l. 2 is broken, it is not possible to be sure what the other kingdom compared with the priestly one consists in. The only other possible reference within the *Document* is the "kingdom of the sword" in *A.L.D.* 4 l. 2. *A.L.D.* 3c l. 2, however, implies that the kingdom of the priesthood will be greater than the other dominion. The greatness of the Levitical line is assured by angelic elevation (*A.L.D.* 6), Levi's "judgment" (*A.L.D.* 14 l. 10), and teaching of scribal craft and wisdom (*A.L.D.* 90; cf. *A.L.D.* 88 and 98).

[G]od the [most] h[igh]. The restored expression qualifies the priesthood of Levi in the *Document* (see *A.L.D.* 9 l. 20; 13 l. 5). This is the last line of the Qumran fragment 1Q21 1.

V. 4 *and] peace. A.L.D.* 4–7 fall thematically into four parts. *A.L.D.* 4 ll. 1–2a finishes the sentence the beginning of which is lost. The tone is positive and most probably concerns the Levitical sacrifices. *A.L.D.* 4 ll. 2b–6 describes the kingdom of the sword and its activity. *A.L.D.* 6 contains a final remark concerning Levi's priestly elevation. *A.L.D.* 7 is the closing part of the whole second vision.

The reference to peace (שלמא) in this fragmentary sentence suggests that the discourse concerns Levi and his priesthood. "Eternal peace" characterizes his priestly elevation (*A.L.D.* 6 l. 8), and God's "wall of peace" is to protect him from every evil (*A.L.D.* 1a v. 12).

and all desirableness of the first-fruits of the earth. The expression is related to 1 Sam 9:20 ("all desirableness of Israel") and Num 18:13 ("first fruits of everything in their land . . . everyone clean of your house . . . may eat it"). The first biblical text is Samuel's prophetic statement concerning Saul's royal elevation. The second text deals with priestly portions (תרומה) assigned to Aaron and his sons (Num 18:8–19; cf. Lev 7:14, 32; Num 5:9; 18:28; Ezek 44:30; 48:10, 12; Neh 10:38; 13:5). This divine commandment is cast back to the times of Levi. The whole preserved sentence is similar to 4Q504 1–2 IV (Puech XV) 9–14. When the nations bring all desirableness of their countries to Jerusalem (ארצם כול חמדת) a period of peace (שלם) and blessing will follow, without opponent (שטן) or evil attack; all will eat and be replete. In the text of the *Document* peace and prosperity described in *A.L.D.* 4 ll. 1–2 characterize the priestly kingdom (*A.L.D.* 3c l. 2) contrasting the kingdom of the sword in *A.L.D.* 4b–5.

all of it to eat. All the desirableness of the first-fruits in the priestly kingdom is given for consumption (למאכל). Though the root אכל also exists in the description of the kingdom of the sword (*A.L.D.* 5 l. 4), it is there contrasted by the concept of "hunger" כפן repeated twice (*A.L.D.* 4 l. 4; 4 l. 5). The latter is a permanent characteristic of the rule of the sword, as the list in *A.L.D.* 4b suggests.

But for the kingdom of the sword. *A.L.D.* 4b is to be read in connection with the following v. 5. These two verses describe troubling activity of the kingdom of the sword. Since *A.L.D.* 3c l. 2 compares the priestly kingdom with another, not specified royal rule, the present passage has been compared with Levi's priestly dominion. Grelot (1956: 396) ascribes the kingdom of the sword to Levi, and Becker (1970: 79) understands it as reflecting Judah's bellicose activities. Neither opinion seems to reflect properly the description of the kingdom of the sword in *A.L.D.* 4b–5.

Levi's kingdom and rule are characterized by the concept of peace (*A.L.D.* 4 and 6). The priestly dominion fights against the rule of the sword that symbolizes the reign of lawlessness and sin on the earth. Levi's violent actions at Shechem are seen as restoring peace by the elimination of lawlessness. *A.L.D.* 78 states that Levi killed (קטלית) the Shechemites and interprets it as eliminating those who perpetrate violence. This killing is made in accordance with Levi's plea to eliminate lawlessness from the earth (*A.L.D.* 1a v. 13) and is positively valued in the *Document*.

Additionally, the overall description of the rule of the sword does not concord with other details concerning the description of Levitical priesthood. Levi is given all the first fruits to eat (*A.L.D.* 4 ll. 1–2), but the kingdom of the sword is characterized by rotating periods of hunger (*A.L.D.* 4 l. 4; 5 l. 5). Levi's priestly dominion is characterized by peace (*A.L.D.* 4 l. 1; 6 l. 8), whereas the kingdom of the sword is described in terms suggesting extreme violence. Finally, alternating periods in the rule of the sword stand in contrast with evidently unchanging and eternal characteristics of Levitical priesthood, e.g., greatness of eternal peace (*A.L.D.* 6 l. 8), eternal priesthood (*A.L.D.* 3b l. 3; cf. 3a l. 7). Curiously, 4Q562 1 1–2 excludes from the priestly ordination the wicked who act "by the sword or war" (בחרב ובקרב). Since Levi kills the Shechemites with a sword (cf. Gen 34:26), he could hardly qualify for priesthood. The Qumran text is, however,

fragmentary and the connection between the wicked and priestly elevation
is not sure.

The eschatological interpretation of the conflict between the priestly kingdom and the rule of the sword is suggested by some terms in *A.L.D.* 4–5
used to describe an eschatological upheaval elsewhere. In the *Apocalypse of
Weeks*, the period of the sword begins in the eighth week, which is the first
in the eschatological period of human history (*1 En.* 91:12; cf. 90:19). The
sons of the Watchers are exterminated by the sword (*1 En.* 14:6; cf. 4Q531
7 5) and perish in a war of annihilation (קרב אבדן 4Q202 iv 6 = *1 En.* 10:9).

battle and slaughter. The Hebrew equivalents of the two terms "battle" קרבא
and "slaughter" נחשירותא are found together in the *War Scroll* in the description of the eschatological battle between the sons of light and Kittim (1QM
I 9; נחשיר alone in 1QM I 11, 13). Similarly, in 4Q246 i 5 a great slaughter (נחשירון) in the provinces (cf. ii 3) accompanies the intervention of the
king of Assyria and Egypt, before the establishment of an eternal kingdom
of God's people when the rule of the sword will cease (ii 4–6).

affliction. The Hebrew equivalent of עמל in MT usually refers to human
work, toil, but it may also describe violent activity of the enemy (see, e.g.,
Isa 59:4; Ps 7:17; 10:7; 55:11; Job 15:35). The context in the *Document*
indicates the latter meaning of the term. 4Q318 2 ii [viii] 7 similarly lists
oppression (עמל), sword (חרב) for the king, and famine (כפן line 8) for the
Arabs in an astrological prediction of the future.

hissing. The rare term נצפתא is best compared with the Hebrew feminine
noun שרקה (see Comments in § 2.1.6). Like in MT, "hissing" is accompanied by nouns indicating destruction and killing and is best understood as
being a term announcing impending doom. In *Jub.* 20:6 fornication, uncleanness, and pollution of sin will make the life of Abraham's descendants a
hissing (Lat. *sibilationem*, cf. VanderKam 1989b: 117, note) and the sword
will destroy their children.

hunger. The Aramaic כפן "hunger" indicates here a period of punishment.
Its biblical Hebrew counterpart, רעב, is often attested with "sword" חרב to
indicate God's coming punishment of the sinners (see Isa 51:19; Jer 5:12;
11:22; 14:12, 13, 15, 16, 18, etc). The eschatological punishment of the
end of days will also be characterized by famine (see 4QpIsa^b II 1 and
4QpPs^a III 2–5; cf. λίμος in Matt 24:7; Mark 13:8; Luke 21:11; Rev 6:8;
18:8).

V. 5 *Sometimes it will eat, and sometimes it will hunger.* The verse describes
changing periods in the rule of the sword. A contrast is set between eating and hunger, toil and repose, sleep and sleeplessness. This set of usual
human activities in the rule of the sword describes the changing fate of
those who are subject to it, most probably sinners. Periods of prosperity
follow periods of anxiety. Parallelism to the situation of the Giants is noticeable. They devour human property, humans, and each other (*1 En.* 7:3–5)
There is not enough food for them to eat (4Q531 1 6; 4Q532 2 10). After
the deluge, when they become evil spirits, they neither eat food nor become

thirsty (*1 En.* 15:11b). The expression "sleep of the eye will flee" finds its biblical counterpart in Gen 31:40 (cf. Esth 6:1; Dan 6:19). It is, however, well attested in the *Book of the Giants*. In 4Q530 2 ii+6–12(?) 4 the Giants are terrified because of their visions and sleep flees their eyes (ונדת שנת עיניהון). On the other hand, in 4Q530 frg. 1 i 6, one of the Giants falls asleep (דמך) most probably because, as the next line states, the vision has made his eyelids heavy. Thus the *Book of the Giants* connects their sleep and sleeplessness with visions that announce their future doom and destruction. These antithetical statements seem to express the Giants' anxiety and restlessness caused by insecurity concerning their future. The motif of eating bread as expression of the same anxiety is also present in the Qumran text of the book and in the Manichean Fragment "L". In the fragmentary 4Q530 1 i 6 one reads the following statement about bread: "]great [an]ger. And I shall sleep, and bread[" ואהוה דמך לחם] ק[צף שניא. The Manichean fragment "L" of the same composition runs: "Darauf sprach *Sām* zu den Giganten: 'Kommt herbei, daß wir essen und froh sind.' Von Kummer aßen sie kein Brot. Sie schliefen ein" (Sundermann 1984: 497).

and sometimes it will toil and sometimes it will rest. The contrast between toiling and rest in the rule of the sword may be understood as changing periods of punishment and relative repose. 4Q246 ii 4 and 6 envision a repose (l. 4 ינוח/יניח?; l. 6 יסף) from the rule of the sword as a sign of eschatological peace and rule of the people of God (cf. 4Q212 ii 16).

A.L.D. 5 indicates, therefore, unquestionable vocabulary contacts with the *Book of the Giants*. It is, however, unlikely that the rule of the sword is uniquely limited to the uncertain future of the Giants doomed to destruction. It rather expresses the same anxiety and restlessness caused by those who perpetrate the sin of uncleanness and sexual immorality. Watchers, Giants, and Shechemites certainly belong to this category. According to *Jubilees*, the rule of the sword on earth begins only with God's decision to exterminate the Giants with the sword (5:7). They slay each other and are destroyed in a fratricidal war (*Jub.* 9:7). God is instrumental in establishing this punishment, for he not only decrees it but also sends *his* sword among them. In the same sense, Levi executes punishment on the Shechemites with the sword (Gen 34:25–26), but is not subject to the sword and punishment because of his holiness (*A.L.D.* 17; 18–21) and faithful observance of the marriage law (*A.L.D.* 16–17; *A.L.D.* 62).

The dualism inherent in the vision of the priestly kingdom opposed to the kingdom of the sword is later reflected in the *Visions of Amram* (4Q543–4Q549), a third part of the Levitical patriarchal trilogy. Amram can see in his vision two angelic beings, Melchizedek and Melchireša', the former rules over the dominion of light, the latter's dominion is darkness. Melchizedek, king of justice, appears to be Amram's protector, and is depicted in 11QMelch as an eschatological high priest. Although the name of Melchizedek is restored and does not actually figure in the *Visions*, the idea of two contrasting dominions from *A.L.D.* 3c–5 is repeated and transposed to the realm of heavenly beings. Note that the *Document* uses the metaphor of darkness to indicate Levitical future apostasy and sinfulness (*A.L.D.* 102), while Levi is called the "priest of the God most high" a title that unequivocally alludes to the Melchizedek's designation in Gen 14:18 (cf. *A.L.D.* 9).

A similar idea of two opposed royal dominions has survived in the Mandaean creation account. According to the *Book of John* XIII 50 (Lidzbarski 1915), two kings are created, the king of this world, and the king from outside the world. The king of this world wears a crown of darkness, holds a sword in his hand, and kills his sons with it, while his sons kill each other. The king from outside the world places a crown of light on his head and takes Kuštā (truth) in his hand; then, he teaches his sons and his sons teach each other.

This unusual theological perspective in the Mandaean religious thought (Rudolph 1965:91–93) appears to be closely related to the *Document*'s dualism. The mutual killing of the earthly king's sons reflects the kingdom of the sword in the *Document*, its killing, battle, and slaughter (*A.L.D.* 4b). The particular connection between the Kuštā and mutual teaching of the second king's sons finds its echo in Isaac's instruction of Levi in the law of truth (קושטא דין *A.L.D.* 15) and in the studying and teaching ideal of the Wisdom didactic poem (*A.L.D.* 83b–98).

V. 6 *how we have made you greater than all.* The final statement in the vision concerns Levi and his priestly elevation. In 4Q213b 1 (*A.L.D.* 6) Levi is proclaimed greater than all flesh. This elevation consists in his greatness of eternal peace (*A.L.D.* 6 l. 8) and in the administering of his priestly and righteous judgment, which is also the greatest among humans (see *A.L.D.* 14 l. 10). Since the root רבי may mean in the targumic literature either "to make great, magnify" or "to anoint," it is probable that a play on words occurs in this verse. The angels magnify Levi (רבינך) and give him anointing/greatness (רבות) of eternal peace. For the whole expression "anointing of eternal peace," cf. *T. Ps.-J.* Exod 40:15 רבותהון לכהונת עלם. However, the meaning "to anoint" occurs only in the targumic literature; it is not at all certain that it should apply to the *Document* as well. The immediate context does not warrant this supposition. The *Document* also ascribes "greatness" (רבו) to Joseph (see 4Q213 1 i 12 = *A.L.D.* 90 l. 1). The term is associated there with "honor, glory" (יקר) and "kings" (מלכין); note that while Isaac blesses Levi's descendants in *Jub.* 31:14, he uses similar terminology: "The descendants of your sons will be like them (= angels of the presence and the holy ones) in honor, greatness, and holiness. May he make them great throughout all ages."

the greatness of eternal peace. The expression "eternal peace" does not appear in MT. According to Lévi (1907: 175 n. 4), it is an allusion to Num 25:12–13 and came as a fusion of בריתי שלם and ברית כהנת עלם. In *A.L.D.* 1a v. 12 the wall of God's peace becomes a symbol for Levi's separation from evil and communion with God (see also *A.L.D.* 6 l. 8; cf. *A.L.D.* 92 l. 13). Here the "eternal peace" characterizes Levi's priestly elevation administered by angels. For this expression in Qumran, see 1QHᵃ XIX (Sukenik

XI) 27; for a similar expression שלם עלמים in the context of eschatological blessings, see 1QS II 4; 4Q403 1 i 26; 4Q404 2+3AB 8. Eternal peace becomes a particular characteristic of Levi's priesthood; it is worth noting that with the appearance of the new priest in *T. Levi* 18:4 peace will reign on the earth. In *T. Dan* 5:11, a savior coming from the tribe of Levi and Judah will bestow on those who call on him eternal peace (εἰρήνην αἰώνιον). In 1QSb III 21 God establishes the peace of the eschatological high priest for all everlasting ages: יסד שלמכה לעולמי עד. As peace becomes a symbol of Levi's separation from evil in *A.L.D.* 1a v. 12, so the lack of peace is a sign of separation from God and sinfulness (cf. Isa 48:22; 57:21). The fallen Watchers will experience no peace (see *1 En.* 12:5 [cf. 1Q24 8 2]; 13:1, 16:4); the same is valid for sinners (see *1 En.* 5:4 [4Q201 ii 14]; 94:6; 98:16; 99:13; 102:3; 103:8).

The term "greatness" appears in a priestly context in the *Apocalypse of Weeks*. In the eighth eschatological week of the world history, the just will carry out the just judgment against the wicked, and at its close they will gain riches in justice (4Q212 1 iv 15–18 = *1 En.* 91:12–13). Then there will be built the temple of the kingship of the Great One in his glorious greatness (ברבות זוה 4Q212 1 iv 18 = *1 En.* 91:13). The priestly application of the term is also found in the targumic literature. Jacob in *Tg. Ps.-J.* Gen 49:3 tells Reuben that originally the rights of the first-born and the greatness of priesthood and royal rule (בכורותא ורבות כהונתא ומלכותא) belonged to him. Since he has sinned with Bilhah, the rights of the first-born have been given to Joseph, kingship to Judah, and priesthood to Levi. In the *Document*, Levi receives both priestly and royal rule and in 4Q379 1 2 his name is placed at the beginning of the list of Jacob's sons before the name of Reuben and Judah. It seems therefore, that the rights of the first-born have also been transferred to him in this composition of the Second Temple period. Additionally, 4Q225 2 ii 11–12 and 4Q226 7 4–5 list the generations coming from Abraham, and Levi is described as the son of Jacob, the third generation. No names of other sons of Jacob appear in this list.

V. 7 *And those seven departed from me.* The seven persons who leave Levi after having delivered their message are most probably angels. They may be the same angels who appear to Levi and in an elaborate manner ordain him to the priesthood in *T. Levi* 8:2. The seven angelic beings appear for the first time in the apocalyptic literature in *1 En.* 20:1–8. They are described as "the holy angels who keep watch" (v. 1), a definition that recalls Dan 4:10, 20 "watcher and holy one" עיר וקדיש. Note that in *A.L.D.* 18 l. 22 Levi is declared close to the God's holy ones קדישוהי. Thus Levi is praised by angels who in *1 Enoch* are faithful to God and who execute judgment on the fallen Watchers and their progeny (see *1 En.* 10).

I arose from my sleep. 1QapGen XIX 17 ends a vision in a similar way (see 4Q547 frg. 9 8; cf. *T. Levi* 5:7a; 8:18a; *1 En.* 13:9). Then Levi states in a kind of soliloquy that this dream he has just had is a vision and that he is amazed (מתמה *hitpeʿel* part. from תמה) by what he saw (cf. *1 En.* 25:1;

26:6 [4Q205 1 ii 8 אֵת[מהת = ἐθαύμασα G]; 1QapGen XX 9; in MT cf. Hab 1:5; Ps 48:6; Qoh 5:7; also Rev 17:6, 7).

And I hid also this one in my heart and I did not reveal it to anybody. *T. Levi* 8:19 translates the sentence literally (cf. also *T. Levi* 6:2). The sentence finds its Aramaic parallel in 1QapGen VI 12 וטמרת רזא דן בלבבי ולכול אנוש לא אחויתה, "Then I hid this mystery in my heart and did not recount it to anyone." It is the end of the vision Noah has about the activity of the sons of heaven (line 11).

Although in the *Document* the word רז, "mystery," does not appear, the parallelism with the *Genesis Apocryphon* indicates that Levi's vision is a revelation concerning things known to God alone, and revealed to his servant. In apocalyptic thinking God knows mysteries that are revealed only to his chosen ones. Levi is the recipient of this hidden heavenly revelation mediated by the angels. The revelation concerns the interdiction of exogamous marriage and Levi's eternal priesthood that is contrasted with the terrible fate of sinners under the rule of the sword. The conflict between the latter and Levi's priesthood most probably sets the stage for the future developments concerning the role of an eschatological high priest in dealing with the problem of evil. Levi's second vision is not only revelatory in character but it probably accomplishes his priestly elevation. Therefore, when he is ordained by Jacob, he already stands at the head of the priesthood even before the beginning of the consecratory rite (see *A.L.D.* 9). The *Testament of Amram* uses the expression "the mystery of his work" רז עובדה that refers to the description of an ideal Levitical priest, most probably Aaron (cf. 4Q545 frg. 4 15), and resumes the essence of his apocalyptic priesthood.

The second channel of revelation destined to reach Levi is Isaac's teaching. Levi's grandfather is a depository of priestly wisdom that he reveals to his grandson only when he learns about Levi's priestly elevation (*A.L.D.* 13) and does not hesitate to unveil it completely (*A.L.D.* 15 l. 12: "I will not conceal" לא אטמר). Those who want to acquire it with military power will not find its hiding places (*A.L.D.* 96 l. 25 מטמריה). The priestly instructions are grounded in Abraham's authority (*A.L.D.* 22; 50; 57) and come from the time of the prediluvian patriarch Noah through the knowledge of his books (*A.L.D.* 57). This twofold revelation transmits priestly wisdom to Levi, who in the didactic poem (*A.L.D.* 83b–98) exhorts his children to study and teach it to the next priestly generations.

3.6   *First Visit to Isaac—A.L.D. 8*

V. 8 *and he also thus [blessed] me.* Although the text suggests that all the brothers went to meet Isaac, only Levi is blessed by him. This is the first step in fulfilling the angelic promises concerning Levi's elevation that, unfortunately, are preserved in a fragmentary state. The sentence "he also according to this one blessed me" relates to the preceding vision and assumes that Levi has already been blessed by the seven angelic beings.

The double visit to Isaac in the *Document* gives Isaac the same opportunity to impart his blessing twice. Isaac first blesses Levi and only Levi in *A.L.D.* 8, and his choice to bless Levi points to Levi's privileged status among the other sons of Jacob. During the second visit in *A.L.D.* 11–61 he imparts his blessing to all the Jacob's sons (*A.L.D.* 12 l. 4) but he passes his teaching to Levi when he learns about his priesthood (*A.L.D.* 13).

The rite of blessing is an integral part of Levi's ordination (cf. *A.L.D.* 9 ll. 21, 22; 10 l. 23, 23). God's blessing is intrinsically connected with Abraham's election and his descendants (cf. *A.L.D.* 1a vv. 15, 16). By concentrating Isaac's blessing on Levi, the *Document* also suggests that promises given to Abraham are fulfilled in Levi, a holy seed and blessed for ever (see *A.L.D.* 1a vv. 15b–16; *A.L.D.* 59, 61; cf. *A.L.D.* 86 l. 14, "blessed harvest for those who sow justice"). *T. Juda* 25:1–2 states that at the resurrection of the patriarchs Levi will be the first among his brothers and God will bless only Levi. The other brothers will be blessed by the angel of the presence (Judah), the powers of the glory (Simeon), the heaven (Reuben), etc.

Thus in *A.L.D.* 8 Isaac's blessing is imparted to Levi even before his earthly ordination. This move underlines Levi's privileged position among his brothers and the reader is not surprised that in the next verse Jacob chooses Levi for priesthood rather than Reuben or somebody else. On the other hand, after his priestly ordination Levi imparts his priestly blessing to his father during his lifetime (*A.L.D.* 9 l. 21). This priestly blessing is additionally motivated by the blessing of the patriarch who in the *Document* is a depository of patriarchal priestly knowledge (see *A.L.D.* 11).

The first visit to Isaac is also present in *T. Levi* 9:1–2, but the narrative there seems to be influenced by *Jub.* 31. It states that only Levi, Judah, and Jacob have gone to Isaac and that Isaac does not want to go to Bethel with them. These two points are not extant in *A.L.D.* 8 but are part of the *Jubilees'* account. The content of Isaac's blessing bestowed on Levi and his descendants in *Jub.* 31:13–17 is not extant in *A.L.D.* 8, but is reflected in several places of the *Document*: an everlasting blessing upon Levi and his sons (*Jub.* 31:13—*A.L.D.* 61); great honor and glory (*Jub.* 31:14—*A.L.D.* 4; 90; 100); approaching God to serve him (*Jub.* 31:14—*A.L.D.* 1a vv. 11, 17; 18); like the angels of the presence and like the holy ones (*Jub.* 31:14—*A.L.D.* 18); honor, greatness, and holiness (*Jub.* 31:14—*A.L.D.* 6; 17; 48; 51; 90); princes, judges, and leaders (*Jub.* 31:15—*A.L.D.* 99); declaring God's words and judging his verdicts (*Jub.* 31:15—*A.L.D.* 1a v. 18; 99); blessing all the descendants of the beloved (*Jub.* 31:15—*A.L.D.* 9; 59); eating at God's table for ever (*Jub.* 31:16—*A.L.D.* 4).

3.7   *Ordination in Bethel—A.L.D. 9–10*

Form and Structure

The flow of the narrative in the first person singular continues, but the change of topic and some formal elements indicate a shift to another theme in the account. The whole section *A.L.D.* 9–10 is in fact dedicated to Levi's earthly ordination at Bethel, a final stop for Jacob's family before they reach Isaac in Hebron.

The structure of *A.L.D.* 9–10 may be outlined as follows:

1. lines 15–16:   Jacob's tithing according to his vow
2. lines 17–18a   Levi's autopresentation as the first in the priestly office
3. lines 18b–19a   Levi's election as receiver of the tithe
4. lines 19b–20   Priestly investiture and "filling of the hands"
5. lines 21–22   Levi's priestly action
6. lines 22–1   Exchange of blessing, end of the ritual in Bethel

The syntactical structure of this composite sentence is rather simple. *A.L.D.* 9 starts with an adverb אדין, which marks stylistically and syntactically a new section of text. At the beginning of *A.L.D.* 10 the same adverb opens the second section of the ordination at Bethel thus indicating a stylistic caesura from the preceding line. The subordinating conjunction כדי (*A.L.D.* 9 l. 15) introduces a circumstantial clause upon which depends the following relative clause דיהוה (*A.L.D.* 9 l. 16b). The main sentence follows, introduced by אף כען (*A.L.D.* 9 l. 17) and composed of eight clauses coordinated by a series of *wāw*. The subordinated circumstantial clause "when Jacob was tithing . . . according to his vow" (*A.L.D.* 9 ll. 15–16) sets the stage for the whole scene of Levi's ordination. In other words, Jacob's tithing at Bethel represents an event that is constantly at the background of the ceremony.

From the literary point of view, Levi's ordination is modeled on Gen 14:18–20 in which Abraham meets Melchizedek, a king of Salem and a priest of God the most high. Within this short story one may find some elements corresponding to *A.L.D.* 9:

1. a patriarch meets a king and priest in one and the same person;
2. the tithe is apportioned by a patriarch to the royal priest;
3. the tithe applies to all the belongings of the patriarch;
4. the priest serves the God most high;
5. the priest gives a blessing to the patriarch.

Additional elements absent in Gen 14:18–20 are the investiture, filling of the hands and mentioning of the sacrifice. *A.L.D.* 9–10 appears to be an example of the adaptation of the Melchizedek tradition to

an ideal priest, incorporated within the genealogical tradition of
Jewish priestly descendants.

V. 9 *when Jacob [my father] was tithing everything that belonged to him*. The
Document's claim that Jacob tithes everything what was his is based on Gen
28:22 where Jacob states: "and of all that thou givest me I will give the
tenth to thee (עשר **אעשרנו לך**)." *Jub.* 32:2 pushes further the consequences
of this statement, and also includes the people who accompany Jacob from
Harran into the tithing procedure. Consequently, his sons are tithed as well,
and Levi becomes a human tithe to God (*Jub.* 32:3).

One whole section of the *Document* (*A.L.D.* 32a–47) is a metro-arithmetical exercise on weights and their fractions, and the knowledge of ספר
"scribal craft" that includes calculation skills is praised in Levi's didactical
poem (see the comment on *A.L.D.* 88). In the context of the *Document*, therefore, Jacob's action of tithing (עשר) underscores his skills of calculation exercised in the context of Levi's ordination. They reappear in the parallel
description of Levi's ordination in *Jub.* 32:3 where Jacob counts (*ḥollaqᵘa*)
his sons starting from already conceived but not yet born Benjamin.

according to his vow. This statement alludes to Jacob's stay in Bethel (Gen
28) where he takes a vow according to which he would tithe all his property if God would bring him back safely to the land of his father. Gen
28:20 explicitly states that Jacob's pledge was a vow offered to God, "Then
Jacob made a vow (ידר נדר), saying, 'If God will be with me. . . .'" When
coming back from Harran Jacob has not fulfilled his vow, or at least the
Genesis account does not mention it at all. The *Document* supplies then the
biblical story with a detail that proves Jacob's faithfulness to his pledge,
and Bethel is mentioned at the end of the ordination scene (*A.L.D.* 10 l. 1).

I was first at the head of the [priesth]ood. Levi's statement establishes a genealogical priesthood in which Levi is the first person who holds this office. In
his second vision Levi is elevated to the royal priesthood by angels (*A.L.D.*
6; cf. *A.L.D.* 3c); he, therefore, appears in the description of his earthly
ordination as a priest already. The genealogical priestly line then continues in the *Document* with nomination of Qahat as the royal high priest
(*A.L.D.* 67) and exclusion of Gershon from the priestly office (*A.L.D.* 64).
The clause also explains why with his earthly ordination Levi acquires
Melchizedek's title of "priest of God the most high" (see below). Melchizedek
was the first priest (כהן) ever mentioned in the Genesis account; in order
then to enhance Levi's position as the first person to hold the priestly office,
Melchizedek's title is ascribed to Levi.

then to me from all his sons he gave the offering of tith[e] to God. Assigning the
tithe to Levi becomes a sign of his election to the priesthood from among
his brothers and the first step in his priestly ordination; there follow his
investiture and "filling of hand," an idiomatic expression for priestly consecration (see below). In *A.L.D.* 3a l. 6 the tithe is somehow connected with
Levi's heavenly elevation, but, since the text is fragmentary, its precise function is difficult to assess.

The biblical evidence supports choosing Levi as the tithe recipient. In Num 18:21–24 the Levites receive the tithe as their inheritance (נחלה) in return for their service in the tent of meeting (cf. Deut 26:12); they have to pay a tenth of their tithe (מעשר מן המעשר) to the priests (Num 18:26), and in post-exilic Judea they are responsible for the tithe collection from the people in the rural towns (Neh 10:38; cf. 2 Chr 31:12). Additionally, since in *A.L.D.* 9 Levi bears the title of the priest of the God most high (cf. *A.L.D.* 13 l. 6), Gen 14:17–20 must have influenced the description of Levi's ordination. This biblical story conjoins Abraham's meeting of the royal priest Melchizedek with the apportioning of the tithe.

In the context of the *Document*, however, assigning the tenth part of Jacob's possessions to Levi acquires a more particular meaning, connected with the economic and liturgical aspect of tithe administration in Israel. In any arithmetical calculation the term מעשר expresses a tenth part of a given unit, or in other words, it denotes 1/10 fraction of a given totality (cf. Ezek 45:11, 14). When Jacob "tithes" (הוה מעשר) his property, he makes an operation to the completion of which the knowledge of simple arithmetical calculation is necessary. By assigning the 1/10 fraction of his property to Levi, Jacob not only fulfills his vow made to God, but also connects Levi, and consequently Levitical priesthood, with the knowledge of arithmetical calculation. The inclusion of the מעשר in the ordination account makes this knowledge essential to, and intrinsically bound with, exercising Levitical priestly office.

The following section of the *Document* fully confirms this interpretation. In *A.L.D.* 32a–47 Levi studies fractions by learning a Babylonian type of metro-arithmetical school exercise. In order to make the connection between the metro-arithmetical knowledge and Levitical priesthood more evident, the author of the *Document* introduces the מעשר within the ordination account, and then in *A.L.D.* 32a–36 creates a numeric pattern in which talent fractions and mina multiples form a regular arithmetical ratio 1:10. One possible reason for having this particular pattern in the exercise on fractions is to reflect the numeric structure of the מעשר, one-tenth of a given unit. A similar method of associations between mathematical and theological concepts was used by the Babylonian and Akkadian scribes who assigned different numbers to different divine names (cf. Livingstone 1986: 17–70; for the numerical plays on fractions and their symbolic meaning in the Babylonian literature cf. Glassner 1992: 115–127).

The parallel description of Levi's ordination to the priesthood in *Jub.* 32:3 makes the connection between Levi and the tithe even more explicit. Jacob counts his sons backward starting from already conceived but not yet born Benjamin and comes up to Levi, who turns out to be the tenth according to his father computation (cf. the comment on *A.L.D.* 3a). The result of Jacob's computation appears to be the only reason for Levi's priestly ordination, which follows on the heels of the counting. The full metro-arithmetical context of Levi's priestly election and ordination is, however, absent from the book of *Jubilees*, for in its reinterpretation of Levi apocryphal tradition it omits the whole metro-arithmetical exercise.

and he clothed me in the priestly clothing, and he filled my hands. These two actions constitute two further elements of priestly ordination, echoing the biblical description of Aaron's ordination where Moses leads the whole ceremony. In Exod 29 Aaron's ordination is made up of several actions including washing, changing the clothes, offering the sacrifices and filling the hands. The ordination lasts seven days (Exod 29:35) and it takes place in front of the tent of meeting (Exod 29:4). Except for the idiomatic use of the expression "to fill one's hand," (Exod 29:9, 29, 33, 35) there is barely any similarity with *A.L.D.* 9. In Exod 29, there are also many sacrifices offered but the only sacrificer is Moses. Aaron and the Levites are passive observers of the rite itself. Exod 28:41 is far closer to *A.L.D.* 9 for it connects the filling of Aaron's hands with the investiture and the context itself underlines the importance of the priestly vestments which are described in detail. Lev 21:10 is the closest definition of the high priest to *A.L.D.* 6 and 9. He is defined as being chosen from among his brothers, his hands are filled and he wears the priestly garment. For other occurrences of the idiomatic expression for priestly ordination "to fill one's hands," see Exod 32:29; Lev 8:33; 16:32; Num 3:3.

And I became a priest of God the most high. In 1QapGen XXII 15 the expression כהן לאל עליון is applied to Melchizedek (cf. Gen 14:18 כהן לאל עליון); in *A.L.D.* 13 l. 5 it defines Levi's priesthood. The allusion to Melchizedek is obvious. *A.L.D.* 17 l. 19 further define Levi as a holy priest כהן קדיש (*A.L.D.* 48 ἱερεὺς ἅγιος), and Levi's descendants are to be priests (*A.L.D.* 49 ἱερεῖς), or priests and kings (*A.L.D.* 99 l. 15 כהנין ומלכין; for the eternal Levitical priest, see 4Q545 4 19 כהן עלמין; cf. 4Q547 9 6).

I offered all his offerings. Immediately upon his ordination Levi proceeds to fulfill his duties as the priest who acts on behalf of God the most high. In the biblical sacrificial tradition, the חטאת sacrifice accompanies the consecration of the altar and of the priests (Exod 29:10–14, 36; Lev 8:14–17), the beginning of Aaron's sacrificial activities (Lev 9:8–11, 15), or the consecration of the Levites (Num 8:12). The author of the *Document*, however, does not seem to follow this biblical detail for he does not specify what kind of sacrifice Levi offers in Bethel. Note that the *Testament of Amram* also reports about Levi's sacrificial activity with an implicit reference to Jacob: "e[v]erything that Levi, his son, offered o[n the altar]" [ברה ע]ל מדבחא כ[ו]ל די קרב לוי (4Q547 8 2).

Indicating that upon his ordination Levi takes up his priestly responsibility seems to be rather an alternative way of stating his priestly elevation. From the very nature of the priesthood there flows the duty of offering sacrifice to God. In *A.L.D.* 10 l. 1 the narration of Levi's ordination ends with a similar formula קרבית קרבנוהי "to offer his sacrifices"; one has, therefore, the impression that this expression simply summarizes the whole ordination account in Bethel. The use of the expression in the targumic literature confirms this interpretation. The Aramaic קרב קרבן (*hapʻel, itpaʻal,* or *paʻel*) in *Tg. Onq.* and *Tg. Ps.-J.* always translates the biblical idiom for priestly ordination מלא יד "to fill one's hand" (Exod 28:41; 29:9, 29, 33, 35; 32:29; Lev 8:33; 11:32; 21:10; Num 3:3). *Tg. Neof.* renders it with שלם ית קרבן יד.

Since the *Document* has already introduced the expression מלא יד in *A.L.D.* 9 l. 20, the following קרב קרבן in *A.L.D.* 9 l. 21 and 10 l. 1 should be regarded as an additional component of Levi's priestly ordination.

And I blessed my father in his life. By blessing his father and brothers Levi fulfills his fundamental priestly duty and privilege (cf. the Aaronic blessing in Num 6:23–27, and also Lev 9:22, 23; Deut 21:5; 1 Chr 23:13; 2 Chr 30:27; Sir 50:20). Pronouncing blessings on the people was also a primary Levitical function (Deut 10:8; 2 Chr 30:27). Reuben in his testament exhorts his sons to approach Levi to receive a blessing from him: "And approach Levi in humbleness of heart, that you may receive a blessing from his mouth. For he will bless Israel and Judah" (*T. Reu.* 6:10–11). When Isaac blesses Levi's descendants in *Jub.* 31:15, he also elaborates on their future functions: "The blessing of the Lord will be placed in their mouths, so that they may bless all the descendants of the beloved."

V. 10 *in Bethel.* The name of the place itself is surely of Canaanite origin and probably was one of the cult places in Canaan raised to the status of a king's sanctuary by Jeroboam I (cf. 1 Kgs 13:26–33; Amos 7:13). Later Jewish tradition identified Bethel with the Jerusalem Temple (see *GenR* 68:12; 69:7). Amos 4:4 indicates a connection between Bethel and the tithes being brought there. As was earlier demonstrated, the concept of the tithe is somehow present in Levi's second vision (*A.L.D.* 3a) and defines his heavenly received priesthood. Now, in the earthly liturgy, Jacob's tithing in Bethel is the starting point of the whole ceremony (*A.L.D.* 9).

It is probable that Bethel remained a cultic place during the Second Temple period, and that the Jacob tradition at Bethel served to revive the hope for the future national restoration (cf. Hos 12:3–5; Zech 7:2 and the comment in Pfeiffer 1999: 80–82). It should be stressed, however, that the proper noun "Bethel" in the *Document* denotes the temple, lit. "house of God," as the place of Levi's sacrificial practices and learning (cf. *A.L.D.* 19). This pun suggests that the priestly connotations of this proper name were decisive for the author of the *Document* who chooses it as the place of Levi's second vision (*A.L.D.* 3a–7), and priestly ordination (*A.L.D.* 9). Consequently, any reference to a historical reality behind the name of the place should be considered with caution, and the toponym is not an indication of the Samaritan origin of the *Document* (cf. § 1.5.3.2).

3.8 *Wisdom Instruction—A.L.D. 11–61*

Form and Structure

A.L.D. 11–61 is the longest and best preserved part of the *Document*. *A.L.D.* 11–32a is preserved both in Aramaic and Greek, while the Aramaic text of *A.L.D.* 32b–61 is lost. It mainly deals with the legal injunctions concerning holocaust offering and accompanying meal

offering. The narrative introduction (11–13) connects Levi's ordination at Bethel and the arrival of the whole family at Hebron where
Isaac begins to teach Levi the priestly wisdom.

In the Old Testament the Hebrew root חכם often denotes the
skills of religious craftsmanship (Isa 3:3; 40:20; 1 Kgs 7:13; *Exodus*
28–36 [P]; cf. Müller and Krause 1980: 378–379). Although the root
is absent in Isaac's instruction (cf., however, *A.L.D.* 1a v. 8; 88 l.
18, 19; 89 l. 20, 21, etc.), the vocabulary and thematics of the whole
section 14–61 suggest that it should be classified as a wisdom instruction concerning priestly knowledge and craftsmanship. The sapiential relation "teacher—disciple" is established between Isaac and Levi,
the former addressing the latter with the typical wisdom address "my
son" (ברי 14 ll. 9, 9; 15 l. 11; 16 l. 15; τέκνον μου 48; cf. 51; 58;
61). Isaac is the one who teaches (אלף 13 l. 7; 15 l. 13) and com-
mands/instructs (פקד 13 l. 7; ἐντέλλομαι 48) Levi concerning the
priestly order of the sacrifices; he also "shows" (*'ap'el* הוי 15 l. 12; cf.
ὑποδείκνυμι 49) this whole teaching (כל פתגם 15 l. 13) to the priest
of the most high God. The Aramaic term which often refers to a
revelatory activity of an angelic figure here applies to Isaac's teaching. Isaac's knowledge is based on the instruction received from
Abraham (ἐντέλλομαι 50; 57; cf. 22), and Levi, in turn, is supposed
to instruct his children (ἐντέλλομαι 49; פקד 82 l. 6; 84 l. 9).

The wisdom instruction is defined with legal terminology as "the
law of truth" (15 l. 12), or "the law of the priesthood" (15 l. 13),
and the connecting idea underlying the priestly instruction is the prescription to do everything "in order, measure and weight" (30; 31).
This particular phrase, stemming from the biblical sapiential world-
view and widely used in the apocalyptic literature, is the organizing
principle of *A.L.D.* 19–47. Sacrificial instructions in *A.L.D.* 19–30
concerning the burnt offering present a carefully elaborate plan of
gradual proceedings and culminate in Isaac's exhortation to do everything in order, by measure and weight (*A.L.D.* 30). The section dedicated to weights and measures of the sacrificed material (31–47)
organizes their due order (סדך *A.L.D.* 31) in the form of metro-arithmetical lists embedded in the text of the exposition (32a–46a). These
constitute an exercise in a proper metro-arithmetical calculation (חשבן
31 l. 19; λογισμός 52) and establish relations between the integers of
the used measures and their fractions applied to the sacrificed material. In short, *A.L.D.* 31–47 appears to be a metrological scholarly
instruction intended to teach not only the quantity of the sacrificed

material but also the knowledge of fractions and arithmetical ratios between metrological units. Instructions concerning professional education replete with technical terminology were already known in ancient Sumer. The composition "Farmer's Almanac" depicts a farmer who adresses his son teaching him in a series of instructions how to cultivate the field in the course of yearly agricultural activities: "In days of yore a farmer instructed his son (as follows)" (Kramer 1963: 340; cf. Kramer 1981: 65–69).

This kind of "scientific" wisdom instruction intended for priestly apprentices shares vocabulary contacts and formal literary parallels with the *Astronomical Book* of the Enochic corpus (*1 En.* 72–82). The angel Uriel passes down the astronomical knowledge to Enoch, but the vision context is totally absent in the book. The basic form indicating Uriel's transmission of knowledge is the expression "Uriel showed to me (*'ar'ayani*)" (*1 En.* 72:1; 74:2; 75:3, 4; 78:10; 79:2, 6; 80:1; 82:7; cf. Rau 1974: 157). Some of these examples stress that Uriel shows Enoch the totality (*kʷəllu*) of the astronomical knowledge (*1 En.* 72:1; 74:2; 79:2, 6; 80:1; cf. *A.L.D.* 15). The calculation חשבן (4Q209 25 3 = *1 En.* 74:1 or 78:10; cf. *A.L.D.* 31 l. 19) concerning the movements of the celestial bodies belongs to the astronomical order (סרך *1 En.* 2:1 = 4Q201 ii 1; cf. *A.L.D.* 30–31), sign of the obedience of all of creation to God.

The transmission of the astronomical teaching is rooted in the sapiential "father–son" relationship (*1 En.* 76:14; 79:1; 82:1; cf. *A.L.D.* 14 ll. 9, 9; 15 l. 11; 16 l. 15; 49) expressing the fundamental connection between the teacher and the student (Rau 1974: 431–432); cf. 4Q209 26 6: "And now I show to you, my son" וכען מחוה אנה לך ברי (*1 En.* 79:1; cf. *A.L.D.* 84). The astronomical knowledge is equated with wisdom and a commandment to hand it down to future generations is issued (*1 En.* 82–83; cf. *A.L.D.* 49; 83b–84; Rau 1974: 431). The main part of *1 En.* 72 describes the variation of the length of daylight and night during the year (vv. 8–32), with an introduction concerning the twelve "gates" on the horizon through which the sun rises and sets (72:2–7); the chapter ends with the description of the sun's role in the universe (vv. 33–37). Neugebauer (1985: 392–396) demonstrated that the core of the chapter (vv. 8–32) is composed of twelve strictly parallel sentences that verbally present the arithmetical pattern concerning the movement of the sun on the firmament during the year. The Aramaic fragments of the *Astronomical Book* (4Q209) contain this material in the same form of a verbally presented astronomical table (cf. also *1 En.* 74 and Neugebauer's exposition in 1985: 399–401). A similar stylistic device is used in *A.L.D.* 32a–46a, which contains numerical patterns embedded in the text of the narrative. One should note, however, that the *Document's* lists are metrological in nature. On the other hand, a recourse to Babylonian tradition palpable in both texts cannot be overlooked. While the arithmetical schemes of *1 En.* 72–82 could have been inspired by Babylonian astronomical tradition (Albani 1994), the *Document's* metrological sequences follow the pattern of Babylonian scribal exercises (cf. the comment on *A.L.D.* 32a–36).

The formal similarity between the *Astronomical Book* and Levi's wisdom instruction is further noticeable in the use of fraction numbers in both texts. From the purely pedagogical point of view Levi's learning precedes the astronomical teaching in *1 En.* 72–82. The student has to learn the principles of sexagesimal counting by studying metrological lists before passing to more complicated astronomical computation (cf. the comment on *A.L.D.* 31). Given literary similarity with *A.L.D.*, it is probable that the *Astronomical Book* originated in an educational context where a recourse was made to a prediluvian patriarch and his son to underscore the importance of astronomical knowledge and father-son (teacher-pupil) relationship. The angel Uriel's role of the one who "shows" to Enoch astronomical knowledge may be paralleled with Isaac's educational function of "showing" sacrificial and metrological order to Levi (cf. the comment on *I will show you* in *A.L.D.* 15).

The structure of *A.L.D.* 11–61 may be presented in the following way:

    I. Introductory narrative—Second trip to Isaac (11–13)

   II. Wisdom instruction
   1. Priestly purity and holiness (14–18)
   2. Due order of sacrificial activity (19–30)
      2.1 Ablutions (19–21)
      2.2 Wood for the burnt offering (22–25a)
      2.3 Burnt offering of the bull (25b–30)
   3. Proper order of weights and measures (31–47)
      3.1 Wood (31–36)
      3.2 Salt (37–40a)
      3.3 Flour, oil, frankincense (40b–46a)
      3.4 Metrological table (46b–47)
   4. Isaac's final exhortation (48–50)

III. Redactional additions (51–61)
  1. Wood, frankincense, purity, blood (51–57)
  2. Levi's glorious future (58–61)

The introductory narrative brings all the family back to Isaac in Hebron (*A.L.D.* 11–13). Isaac's instructions begin with the statement concerning Levi's judicial authority and purity requirements necessary for the ideal priest (*A.L.D.* 14–18). The attention is focused on the matters of avoiding sexual impurity and sin, marrying a woman from one's tribal family, and declaring Levi's holiness. Ritual injunctions begin with the ablution rite (*A.L.D.* 19–21), deal with the holocaust sacrifice (*A.L.D.* 22–30), and describe corresponding quantities of wood (*A.L.D.* 31–36) and of accompanying meal offering (*A.L.D.* 37–46a). *A.L.D.* 31–47 is also a metro-arithmetical exercise in establishing proper ratios of weights and measures according to the Babylonian numeric system applied to West Semitic metric terminology. The section ends with a metrological table (*A.L.D.* 46b–47) and Isaac's sapiential formula to keep and transmit his teaching to the future priestly generations (*A.L.D.* 48–50); the latter text constitutes the closing element of the whole wisdom instruction (*A.L.D.* 14–50). The unifying concept of the exposition termed as the law of truth/priesthood (*A.L.D.* 15) is סרך "order" (*A.L.D.* 30; 31), a term that applies to Levi's observance of endogamy and avoidance of sexual immorality (*A.L.D.* 14–18), to his offerings (*A.L.D.* 19–30) and metro-arithmetical knowledge of weights and measures (*A.L.D.* 31–47). Isaac's instructions essentially deal only with the holocaust offering and cereal/meal offering but omit others like communion sacrifices (זבח/שלמים), the sacrifice for sin (חטאת), or the reparation sacrifice (אשם). The selective approach to the sacrificial system expounded in the Pentateuch and the reinterpretation of many of its rules stems from the author's intent to create the idealized image of the Levitical "supreme priesthood" (9; 64) based on the observance of the legal due order. One should also take into account the pedagogical thrust of the instruction which sets high professional standards for Levi and all priestly apprentices who should act in order, by measure and weight (*A.L.D.* 30; 31).

Repetition of several themes in the closing part of Isaac's speech (51–61) induced Becker (1970: 87–91) to consider it as a second speech (51–59), different from the first one (14–50, 61) but parallel to *Jub.* 21. However, *A.L.D.* 51–61 stems from the redactional activity aiming at rooting Isaac's teaching in the authority of Noah. *A.L.D.*

51–54 is based on *A.L.D.* 14–50; *A.L.D.* 55–57 does not represent literary contacts with *Jub.* 21 but with *Jub.* 7:30–33, the Noahic injunctions concerning blood (cf. *A.L.D.* 51–61).

3.8.1 *Introductory Narrative—A.L.D. 11–13*

V. 11 *We settled in the fortress of Abraham.* From Bethel the whole family moves to Abraham's fortress, and settles there (שׁרי/καταλύω = *T. Levi* 9:5), where Isaac lives. The arrival of Jacob's family to Mamre is based on Gen 35:27. The book of *Jubilees* expands one trip from Bethel to Mamre in Gen 35 into three distinct occasions on which Jacob visits his father. The first one concerns mainly Levi and Jacob and the blessing they receive from their grandfather (*Jub.* 31; cf. *A.L.D.* 8). The second one has Jacob and Leah leave the Tower of Eder Ephrathah only to explain how Reuben's sin with Bilhah remained unnoticed by Jacob (*Jub.* 33:1; cf. *T. Reu.* 3:13). Only the final arrival of the whole family in Mamre in *Jub.* 33:21–33 corresponds to the biblical account (Gen 35:23–27). *Jub.* 33:21 stands in close parallelism with *A.L.D.* 11, whereas *Jub.* 33:23b essentially repeats *A.L.D.* 12. Although in the Genesis account Isaac dies after the arrival of the whole family (Gen 35:28–29), the *Document* does not indicate a testamentary setting of Isaac's speech. The contrary is true for Abraham's instructions in *Jub.* 21:1.

The biblical text does not explain why and when Isaac moves to Mamre. *Jub.* 29:17, 19 notices this omission and makes Isaac move to the "tower of his father Abraham" even before Jacob comes back from Mesopotamia. The presence of Isaac in the place where Abraham lived, died, and was buried has a particular importance in the *Document*. Isaac is the heir of Abraham's priestly knowledge and he bases his priestly instructions on the authority of his father (*A.L.D.* 22 l. 12; *A.L.D.* 50, 57). It is, therefore, important that Levi receives this patriarchal priestly teaching in the place that recalls Abraham, who inherits Noachic priestly knowledge (*A.L.D.* 57).

V. 12 *and blessed us and rejoiced.* *A.L.D.* 8 concentrates Isaac's blessing on Levi only. Here the whole family (כולנא) enjoys this patriarchal sign. Thus Levi is blessed again, this time with the rest of his brothers. The priestly teaching in the following verses, however, is passed on to Levi only. Isaac's rejoicing expresses simple contentment because of his family's arrival (see *Jub.* 33:23, cf. *Jub.* 26:23). In *T. Levi* 18:14 Isaac rejoices together with Abraham and Jacob, in the context of eschatological salvation brought about by the new priest. In 4Q545 frg. 1a i 7 Amram rejoices during the feast before giving a speech to Aaron; 4Q541 frg. 2 ii 5, "and you will much rejoice" ותחדה; in 4Q542 1 i 10 Qahat's sons will give to him a good name, and joy to Levi, Isaac and Jacob, if they follow the teaching of their forefathers (cf. 4Q548 frg. 1 7, 13).

V. 13 *And when he learned that I was the priest of God the most high.* What provokes Isaac to pass on to Levi his priestly teaching is the information that

Levi has become priest of the most high God, Lord of heavens (מרי שמיא).
No visionary revelation is supposed (see *T. Levi* 9:3). Levi is a priest of the
most high God, an expression which recalls Gen 14:19 and the priesthood
of Melchizedek (see *A.L.D.* 9 l. 20). Another title of God qualifying Levi's
priesthood is "Lord of heavens." It suggests a particular relationship with
the heavenly realm, as is clear from Levi's visions (see *A.L.D.* 1b ll. 16–18;
cf. *A.L.D.* 1a v. 3; *A.L.D.* 1a v. 13). *A.L.D.* 18 underlines Levi's closeness
to God and God's holy ones.

Isaac's instructions, therefore, are transmitted to a visionary priest who
remains in close contact with the heavenly sphere. They do not constitute
a heavenly "revelation" but are firmly rooted in the patriarchal tradition,
which reaches back to the times of Noah (cf. *A.L.D.* 57). Hence, the *Document*
affirms that priestly knowledge of prediluvian patriarchs is handed down to
Levi. In Gen 8:20 Noah comes out of the ark and offers a burnt offering
only from ritually clean animals (טהר). He thus becomes a bridge between
prediluvian priesthood and postdiluvian continuation of sacrificial activity.

It is not clear how Noah's instructions which, according to the *Document*,
were written down in his book (see *A.L.D.* 57) have been revealed to him.
His visionary experience in the *Genesis Apocryphon* informs him of the source
of human corruption (1QapGen VI 11–20) and he knows the eternal law
concerning marriage (1QapGen VI 8). His priestly knowledge is taken for
granted (1QapGen X 13–17). Isaac's priestly instructions deal with the laws
concerning marriage, holocaust and cereal offerings, and laws concerning
blood consumption. They may be easily tracked back to the biblical lore
and tradition, but the *Document* roots them in the Noahic tradition or "book."

he began to instruct me and to teach me the law of the priesthood. In the context
of the *Document* Levi is supposed to command (ἐντέλλομαι) this law (lit.
"judgment" κρίσις, see E 18,2 vv. 13, 14, 15) to his priestly descendants
(*A.L.D.* 48). His didactic poem is not a literal but metaphorical fulfillment
of Isaac's command. Levi teaches (פקד *A.L.D.* 82 l. 6; 84 l. 9) his children
his commandments (83b l. 8 פקודין; cf. 4Q196 14 i 8 = Tob 6:16), which
he himself learnt from Isaac, but they are summarized in the poem by the
obligation to teach and study scribal craft that includes calculation skills,
then instruction, and wisdom. In this context Isaac's sacrificial teaching and
metro-arithmetical wisdom may be understood as Levitical "wisdom" and
Levitical "Torah."

The verb "to instruct" recalls the testamentary setting in the book of
Tobit (see פקד in 4Q198 frg. 1 2 [Tob 14:3]; cf. 4Q196 frg. 11 2 [Tob
5:1]; 4Q197 4 ii 12 [Tob 6:16]—an angel recalls Tobit's commandment
about marrying a woman from the family, cf. Tob 4:13). The *Testament of
Qahat* has the *Document*'s word pair פקד and אלף in Qahat's instructions
(see 4Q542 frg. 1 i 13 and frg. 1 ii 1; cf. 4Q542 frg. 1 ii 10), while Amram
on his deathbed begins to instruct his children (4Q543 frg. 1a, b, c, 2).

the law of the priesthood. *T. Levi* 9:7 understands the Aramaic expression
(*A.L.D.* 13 l. 7; 15 l. 13) as "priestly Law" νόμος ἱερςούνης; similarly, the
term חכמה in *A.L.D.* 93 l. 15 is translated in *T. Levi* 13:4c with νόμος, compare *T. Levi* 13:2b (corresponding probably to *A.L.D.* 88 ll. 18–19) and 13

l. 3a (corresponding probably to *A.L.D.* 89 l. 20). The priestly law is further defined in the following *A.L.D.* 14–15, but it encompasses all of Isaac's instructions (*A.L.D.* 14–61). The expression is unique in all the literature of the period. Note that in the priestly writings of the Pentateuch, the Hebrew תורה may also mean "ritual" describing different sacrificial rites (Lev 6:2, 7, 18; 7:1, 11), or "instruction" when dealing with impurity prescriptions (Lev 11:46; 12:7; 13:59; 14:2, 32, 54, 57; 15:32; cf. Begrich 1936). The term דין as relating to a legal set of instructions is attested in the Elephantine documents. The expression "law of divorce" דין שנאה (Kraeling 1953: 7:39) refers to the legal stipulations previously set forth that should be enforced when the divorce takes place (cf. Kraeling 1953: 220; Rabinowitz 1956: 55).

According to the *Document*, the patriarchs teach the priestly law from one generation to the other. This teaching activity, therefore, is different from the biblical account where Levi and his tribe teach Israel God's ordinances (see Deut 33:10). Isaac teaches (אלף; cf. *A.L.D.* 15 l. 13) Levi the priestly law and his teaching assures freedom from moral and ritual impurity (*A.L.D.* 14–18) and transmits a proper order of liturgical activity (*A.L.D.* 19–30) together with metro-arithmetical knowledge (*A.L.D.* 31–47), an element of priestly and royal glory (*A.L.D.* 88; 90; 98). A later redactor rooted this Levi's knowledge in the teaching of Noah by adding a section concerning blood (*A.L.D.* 55–57). This priestly knowledge intended to uphold a proper order of priestly activity is fundamental to assure the priestly righteousness and wisdom (*A.L.D.* 84–86; 90 ll. 2-4; 102). Levi warns his sons against corruption of their priestly vocation by abandoning the way of studying wisdom (cf. *A.L.D.* 90 and 102). Isaac's teaching of the sapiential order can be seen as a counterpart to the Watchers' fall and corruption. When the Watchers descended to earth, they committed fornication and started revealing and teaching their wives illicit knowledge (*1 En* 7:1; 8). Their knowledge causes "violence" חמסה (4QEnᵃ 1 iv 8 = *1 En.* 9:1) on the earth (for the verb אלף *paʿel*, referring to the Giants' teaching in the *Book of Watchers*, see 4Q201 iii 15 [*1 En.* 7:1]; iv 1, 4 [*1 En.* 8:3]; 4Q202 iii 1, 2, 2, 3, 4 [*1 En.* 8:3]).

And he said to me. Levi is the only recipient of priestly teaching. He passes on this teaching only to his sons (*A.L.D.* 83a). The priestly class, is, therefore, the only recipient of the sacrificial and metro-arithmetical knowledge (*A.L.D.* 19–47). This tendency is in contrast to the biblical tradition. Although only the priests are allowed to discharge sacrificial duties, the entire sacrificial system is revealed to all Israelites (see Lev 1:2; 7:37–38; 21:24; cf. Weinfeld 1963: 61–63). The revelation of heavenly visions in the *Document* is restricted exclusively to Levi (cf. *A.L.D.* 7). The related *Testament of Qahat* similarly limits the transmission of Levitical inheritance to priestly descendants only. Qahat warns his sons not to transmit their inheritance (ירותתכון, cf. *A.L.D.* 98) received from the fathers to strangers (נכראין, cf. *A.L.D.* 91 l. 9), and their property to half-breeds (כילאין, cf. *A.L.D.* 91 l. 10), for that would cause their humiliation and derision (4Q542 1 i 4–7). Thus those who live among them would become their "heads" ראשין (4Q542 1 i 7), and that means they would take their position as rulers (cf. *A.L.D.* 99–100).

A similar idea that only the priestly class possesses priestly knowledge is attested in some Akkadian ritual texts from the Seleucid era. The colophon to the third tablet describing a rite performed by a *kalû*-priest states, "This ritual, which you perform, (only) the properly *qualified* person (30) shall view. An outsider who has nothing to do with the ritual shall not view (it); if he does, may his remaining days be few! The informed person (*mūdū*) may show (this tablet) to the informed person (*mūdū*). The uninformed (*lā mūdū*) shall not see (it)—it is among the forbidden things of Anu, Enlil, and Ea, the great gods" (Pritchard 1969: 336; Thureau-Dangin 1921: 16–17). Neugebauer (1983: 1:18) published two astronomical cuneiform tablets whose colophons contain an analogous formula. Priestly scribes also wrote the tablets in the Seleucid era, and the closing formula expresses the same tendency to keep also this type of priestly knowledge within the priestly circles (Neugebauer 1983: 1:12).

The common person is barred not only from seeing the ritual but from viewing the text of the ritual as well. The "informed person" or *mudû* is "the expert in a specific craft" (*CAD* M 2:165), and it can refer to a priest. The Akkadian word is a passive participle of *wdʿ*, a root whose West Semitic counterpart ידע is well attested in the *Document*. Note, in *A.L.D.* 1a v. 8 Levi asks God for knowledge (מנדע); here Isaac begins to teach Levi his priestly knowledge only when he learns that Levi has become a priest.

3.8.2   *Priestly Purity and Holiness—A.L.D. 14–18*

The passage is marked off with an *inclusio* of מן כל טומאה, *A.L.D.* 14 l. 9 and 18 l. 23. The inner *inclusio* of the verb זהר *hitpeʿel* impv., and מן כל טומאה in *A.L.D.* 14 ll. 8–9 and 16 ll. 14–15 (cf. Comments on טומאה, line 15, in § 2.1.7) splits the section into two. Additionally, the last phrase of the preceding narrative "to teach the law of the priesthood" (*A.L.D.* 13 ll. 7–8) is repeated in *A.L.D.* 15 ll. 13–14 at the end of the first part of the section. With the repetition of the term "impurity" טומאה at the beginning, middle, and end, the dominant topic of the section is indicated. Impurity (טומאה) is a negative value contrasted by Levi's "law" (first section *A.L.D.* 14–15) and his sexual behavior and holiness (second section *A.L.D.* 16–18).

V. 14 *beware, my son, of every impurity and of every sin.* This statement corresponds to Levi's request in his prayer to purify his heart from every impurity (*A.L.D.* 1a v. 14). The parallel with Levi's prayer indicates that especially moral impurity is envisioned. Here the parallel expression "every sin" suggests the same interpretation. The example of the Shechemites is for the author of *Jubilees* a reminder to the Israelites not to commit sin or transgress the commandments or covenant (*Jub.* 30:21). They are also warned to abandon every way of impurity (*Jub.* 30:22 *kʷəllu fənnāwihā larəkʷs*). Here Isaac's first warning should then be read with the same generalizing tendency (cf. Rev 19:2). Only later in *A.L.D.* 16–18 the definition of moral purity is restricted to sexual misconduct. The Noahic tradition ascribes the beginning of impurity on earth to the activity of the Watchers (see *Jub.* 7:21). Isaac's exhortation also recalls the example of Job, who affirms that he is pure (cf. *A.L.D.* 18 l. 22) and without sin: [זכ]י אנה ולא חטא לי 11QtgJob XXII 3 (Job 33:9).

Thus the verse sets contrast between the realm of impurity and sin on one side and Levi's law and judgment on the other. Impurity and sin certainly belong to the rule of the sword as described in *A.L.D.* 4b–5. Levi's judgment should be interpreted in relation to his plea for the true/righteous judgment (*A.L.D.* 1a v. 18), Shechem incident (*A.L.D.* 1c–2; 78), description of the priestly rule (*A.L.D.* 3c–4a), and his priestly elevation (*A.L.D.* 6).

my son. The term ברי (14:9, 9; 15:11; 16:15; τέκνον μου 48; cf. 51; 58; 61) stems from the wisdom language where the image of a father who instructs his son becomes a metaphor for the teacher–disciple relationship (see, e.g., Prov 1:8, 10, 15; 2:1; 3:1; *Ahiqar* 18; 30; 30; 82; 127; 149, etc.). It is obvious that Isaac is Levi's grandfather, but he appears here also as a wisdom teacher who transmits a kind of knowledge particular to the priestly profession (cf. *A.L.D.* 13). Levi in his wisdom poem (*A.L.D.* 83b–98) takes on himself the same role of a teacher who exhorts his sons/disciples to learn and teach scribal craft, instruction, and wisdom transmitted to him by Isaac. Note that the central part of the poem (*A.L.D.* 91–93) is dedicated to the praise of the wisdom teacher.

your judgment is greater than all flesh. The term דין attested in other Semitic languages mainly belongs to legal terminology (see Hamp and Botterweck 1997: 187–189). In the MT it often stands in synonymous relationship with משפט (1 Sam 24:16; Isa 3:13; 10:2; Jer 5:28; 21:12; 22:16; Ps 7:9; 9:5, 9; 72:2; 76:9; 140:13; Prov 31:9), and preserves its basic forensic meaning (see Boecker 1964: 85, n. 7). The subject of דין is the king (Jer 21:12; 22:16; Ps 72:2; Prov 20:8; 31:5, 8) or high priest in a royal function (Zech 3:7; cf. Gen 15:4; Qoh 6:10). The meaning of the term in the *Document* corresponds to the OT use. Levi in his prayer is depicted with royal terminology, and the priestly dominion (*A.L.D.* 3c l. 2 מלכות כהנותא) assures royal, priestly, and judicial authority for his children (see *A.L.D.* 99–100; cf. *A.L.D.* 67). One cannot, therefore, translate the term here as "your liability" (Greenfield and Stone 1979: 220), for Levi is the subject and not the object of legal proceedings in the *Document*. His priestly rule encompasses also the judicial role (cf. Ezra 7:25–26).

The test case of this role is the Shechem story when Levi kills the Shechemites and thus eliminates violence/lawlessness (*A.L.D.* 78). His judgment is "greater than all flesh" also because he receives heavenly appointment to his priestly office and is elevated by the angels more than all flesh (*A.L.D.* 6; cf. 4Q213b 1). His particular elevation is due to the fact that he participates in God's judicial function of eliminating lawlessness from the earth (cf. *A.L.D.* 1a v. 13), as indicated by the Shechem incident (*A.L.D.* 78). Levi's request to participate in God's words in order to execute just judgment (*A.L.D.* 1a v. 18) has been accepted. No other patriarch has ever received the same privilege. Enoch announces to the Watchers God's sentence (*1 En.* 12:4–13:3; 14:4–7), Noah is saved from the coming flood (*1 En.* 10:1–3 *Jub.* 5:19), but they do not receive judicial powers like Levi. Levi's judicial authority finds its development in the *Testament of Qahat*, where in an eschatological context his sons will rise to judge the judgment למדן דין (4Q542 1 ii 5; see *Jub.* 31:15).

Levi is not the supreme judge, who establishes rules or laws for his judgment. He acts in accordance with God's sentence and thus carries out God's punishment on the sinners, administering a righteous judgment (*A.L.D.* 1a v. 18; 1c–2; 78). A similar role is ascribed to the righteous in the *Apocalypse of Weeks*. In the eighth week a sword is given to the righteous to execute just judgment (למעבד דין קשוט) on the wicked (*1 En.* 91:12 = 4Q212 iv 15–17). It is the last punitive act in the rule of the sword (cf. *A.L.D.* 4b–5). A similar function is ascribed to the Son of Man in *1 En.* 69:27. The sum of judgment is given to him and he causes the destruction of the sinners. In Dan 7:22 the Ancient of Days comes and the דין is delegated to the holy ones; then the gift of the kingdom follows (cf. 2 Thess 1:5; see also John 5:22 where Jesus receives the judicial authority (κρίσιν) from the Father, cf. 5:27, 30; 8:16). In *1 En.* 92:1, which serves as the introduction to Enoch's epistle, this patriarch is called the "judge of the whole earth" *makʷannəna kʷəllu mədr*. The verse is partially preserved in 4Q212 1 ii 22–24, but it does not confirm Enoch's juridic role.

Note that Levi's judicial authority is set in the context of exhortations concerning purity. Exercising his priestly authority is based on the ritual and moral correctness before God. Judging between pure and impure is the essence of priestly tasks. Lev 10:10 admonishes Aaron, "You are to distinguish between the holy and the common, and between the unclean and the clean" (cf. Ezek 22:26; 44:23). To exercise this task Levi must be on the side of holiness and purity (cf. the comment on *A.L.D.* 17 and 18). Additionally, the strict observance of the liturgical order (19–30) and the knowledge of weights and measures (*A.L.D.* 31–47) necessary to administer the sacrifice in a proper way constitute another dimension of Levi's judicial authority.

Priestly judicial authority is attested already in the pre-exilic period. In Deut 17:9 the Levitical priests are responsible for legal decisions together with a judge at the central cultic place (cf. Deut 19:17; 21:5). In Ezek 44:24 priests participate fully in legal jurisdiction, "In a controversy they shall act as judges (יעמדו לשפט), and they shall judge it (ושפטהו) according to my judgments." In the post-exilic period this development has increased (cf. Bentzen 1930/31: 280–286). Note that in *A.L.D.* 99, Levi's sons receive the functions of magistrates and judges (שפטין ודא[ני]ן).

V. 15 *the law of truth.* The expression is related to the concept of "true judgment" first met in Levi's prayer (*A.L.D.* 1a v. 18). While in the prayer it certainly denotes execution of the judgment based on the participation in God's words, here it means a set of instructions that, once revealed by Isaac, become a criterion of proper liturgical action and scribal metro-arithmetical wisdom. They constitute a normative code of laws that are to be held if the priestly law (דין כהנותא) is to remain a "law of truth" (דין קשטא). The term דין denotes here law in the general sense on which Levi's judicial activity (*A.L.D.* 14 l. 10 דינך) as a priest and scribe is based; he carries it out whenever necessary (*A.L.D.* 1a v. 18 למעבד] דין קשט). This interpretation also explains the conjunction of the royal and priestly office in one person. Levi not only is a depository of the priestly law, he also interprets and executes it.

This "law of truth" is synonymous with the "law of priesthood" (cf. *A.L.D.* 13 ll. 7–8). Isaac's speech provides some synonyms to these two terms: *A.L.D.* 48 "my words" λόγους μου paralled by "my commandments" τὰς ἐντολάς μου; *A.L.D.* 49 "this law" τὴν κρίσιν ταύτην; *A.L.D.* 51 "what has been commanded" τὸ προστεταγμένον. This legal teaching is related to Abraham's commandments (ἐντέλλομαι *A.L.D.* 50; 57) found by him in the book of Noah (*A.L.D.* 57).

I will show you, and I will not conceal from you anything. The root חזי "to see" refers in the *Document* to Levi's visionary experience (cf. *A.L.D.* 1b ll. 14–15); the term "to conceal" כמר also appears in the context of Levi's second vision (cf. *A.L.D.* 7 l. 13). In the Aramaic New Jerusalem fragments an angelic being (?) "shows" (ʾapʿel חזי) to the seer measurements (משחה) of the temple (4Q554 1 ii 21= 2Q24 1 3–4; 4Q554 1 iii 20–21). Here, however, the ʾapʿel of חזי appears in the context of Isaac's sapiential teaching (ברי "my son," cf. *A.L.D.* 14; 16) and apparently does not refer to any visionary experience. Isaac's "showing" of the law of truth/justice intends to teach (אלף, cf. 13 l. 7) a proper order (סרך) of the burnt offering together with right weights (מתקל) and measures (משחה). The fragmentary Aramaic *Astronomical Book* contains a similar semantic function of the ʾapʿel of חזי. When Enoch transmits to his son Methuselah all the astronomical knowledge, he concludes in the following way, "Their complete explanation I have sh[own to you, my son, Methuselah.]" שלמהון ופרשהון אח]זית לך ברי מתושלח] (4Q209 23 2 = *1 En.* 76:14). Similarly, the archangel Uriel's transmission of astronomical knowledge to Enoch is expressed by the formula "Uriel showed to me" (ʾarʾayani *1 En.* 72:1; 74:2; 75:3, 4; 78:10; 79:2, 6; 80:1; 82:7), or "he showed to me all . . . (ʾarʾayani kʷəllu *1 En.* 72:1; 74:2; 79:2, 6; 80:1). Note that the Ethiopic ʾarʾaya "to show" is a causative (CG) of rəʾya "to see."

In the light of this evidence the clause *I will show you and I will not conceal from you anything* should be dubbed a "teacher's opening formula" standing at the beginning of the wisdom instruction concerning a cultic ritual. The wisdom instruction ends with a corresponding "teacher's closing formula" in *A.L.D.* 48–49 where Isaac commissions Levi to observe the transmitted judicial order (κρίσις) and to teach it to his descendants. Note that in *A.L.D.* 49 the Greek ὑπέδειξα "I showed" supposes the Aramaic ʾapʿel of חזי; the correspondence with *A.L.D.* 15 is, therefore, unmistakable.

Rau (1974: 431) detected the presence of the opening and closing sapiential formulas in the last section of the Enochic *Astronomical Book*. "Bei 82,1a–b haben wir eine Lehreröffnungsformel vor uns, während 81,1 und 81,2 Lehrabschlußformeln sind. Da zum Lehrabschluß der Auftrag zur Weitertradierung gehört, sind 81,5d–f und 81,6c–f (7–9) wahrscheinlich

keine Lehrbeauftragungsformeln, sondern müssen dem Lehrabschluß zuge-
ordnet werden. Entsprechend ist in 76,14 und 79,1 der andere Teil der
Abschlußformel von 82,1–2 erhalten. Beide Teile von 82,1 und 82,2 kon-
nten somit auch isoliert voneinander verwendet werden." His observation
further confirms the formal parallelism between Isaac's teaching in *A.L.D.*
14–50 and the *Astronomical Book*.

V. 16 *of every fornication and impurity and of every harlotry*. This verse indicates
that Levi should avoid sexual impurity and the next one explains what sexual impurity means. The rare term פחז denotes wanton and reckless behavior in Judg 9:4 and Zeph 3:4 (cf. פחזות in Jer 23:32; Greenfield 1978b:
35–40). Its meaning in Gen 49:4 is difficult to grasp, but it probably refers
to Reuben's sexual sin with his father's concubine, Bilhah. Here it stands
parallel to זנות/πορνέια, (cf. Sir 41:16 MS B mg.) and indicates sexual misconduct (cf. the MS E συνουσιασμός and 4 Macc 2:3; Sir 23:6 LXX). In
4Q202 iii 1 = *1 En.* 8:2, because of the fallen Watchers' teaching, the
people are led astray and commit fornication ([זי]פח = ἐπόρνευσαν G).
Isaac's teaching has to prevent the spreading of this sin among Levitical
priesthood.

The two terms "impurity" and "harlotry" are never attested together in
MT but appear frequently in the book of *Jubilees*. In *Jub.* 7:20 Noah instructs
his children to avoid fornication, uncleanness, and iniquity and holds responsible the Watchers who through the illicit intermarriage caused the flood
and made the beginning of uncleanness. They sinned because they trans-
gressed the law of their ordinances (see *1 En.* 15:3–4). This Noahic interpretation of the Watchers' sin implies that there is a particular law established
for the angels, and that the angels first broke it even before humanity did.
Jub. 20:3b states that the angels should keep themselves from all fornication and uncleanness. The Watchers' example, therefore, teaches the consequences of not obeying the law assigned by God both to humanity and
to the angels. By not obeying these laws the whole of humanity risks to
undergo again God's judgment. Abraham in his instructions (*Jub.* 20:5)
essentially repeats the Noahic opinion adding the example of the Sodomites:
"And he told them of the judgment of the giants (cf. דין 4Q530 2 ii+6–12(?)
2, 18), and the judgment of the Sodomites, how they had been judged on
account of their wickedness, and had died on account of their fornication,
and uncleanness, and mutual corruption through fornication." Eventually,
uncleanness and fornication come to signify human sinfulness (see *Jub.* 23:14,
17; 30:21; cf. *A.L.D.* 14). The Genesis account of the Shechem incident
suggests, that the Shechemites defiled Dinah (טמא v. 5, 13, 27) by treating
her as a harlot (כזונה v. 31). In the light of Noahic tradition and the *Document*
itself, these biblical statements fully justify the killing of those who commit
uncleanness and fornication, and their punishment constitutes God's judgment (cf. *A.L.D.* 1a v. 18) for their sin.

V. 17 *a wife from my family*. Marrying a woman from the patriarch's family (משפחה) is a rule that Abraham observes for his son Isaac (Gen 24:38,

40). Levi is obedient to this command and marries Melcha, a woman from Abraham's family (*A.L.D.* 62 συγγενεία), daughter of Bathuel, son of his mother's brother, Laban (cf. *A.L.D.* 62). Also Tobit (Tob 4:12) orders his son Tobiah to marry a woman from his father's tribe (φυλή) and not a stranger. He further notes that Noah, Abraham, Isaac, and Jacob, married women from among their brothers (ἐκ τῶν ἀδελφῶν αὐτῶν) and thus they were blessed in their children and their posterity will inherit the land. Tobit's teaching traces the origin of this custom to Noah, but the book of Genesis does not tell us anything about the genealogy of Noah's wife (Gen 7:13; 8:18). However, *Jub.* 4:33 explains that he married Emzara, the daughter of his father's brother Rakiel (cf. 1QapGen VI 7). According to *Jub.* 4:15, marrying a daughter of the father's brother (πατράδελφος, cf. VanderKam 1989b: 25, n.) starts with Malalael in the second week of the tenth jubilee, when the Watchers descended to earth. In 1QapGen VI 8–9 Noah applies this custom to his three sons and proclaims to act "according to the law of eternal ordinance (דת חוק עלמא), which the Highest [commanded] to humankind." When Levi takes wives for his sons from the daughters of his brothers, he scrupulously follows the same commandment (cf. *A.L.D.* 73). However, his grandson, Amram, marries Yochebed, Levi's daughter and sister of Amram's father, Qahat. Also Levi does not follow literally the Noahic law for he marries a daughter of Bathuel, son of Laban, Levi's maternal, not paternal uncle (cf. the comment on *A.L.D.* 62). The *Damascus Document* presents a connection between Levi and the prohibition of brother–sister marital relationship. CD IV 15 ascribes to Levi the words about Belial's three nets, one of which is harlotry (זנות). It further defines harlotry as bigamy (IV 20–V 6), illicit sexual relations with a menstruating woman (V 7), and marrying the daughter of one's brother or sister (V 7–11). Thus Levi is depicted as the one who defends lawful family relationships.

so that you may not defile your seed with harlots. The sentence is related to Lev 21:15a that refers to the high priest, the meaning, however, seems different. In Lev 21:13–15, the high priest can marry a virgin from his people but not a widow, divorced, or polluted harlot (חללה זנה), so as not to profane his seed. Here, the statement not to defile Levi's seed with harlots is a statement in favor of endogamy. Any woman who does not belong to the tribal family (cf. *A.L.D.* 17; 62 משפחה/συγγένεια) is a female outsider (זונה; cf. *A.L.D.* 1a v. 7 [4Q213a frg. 1 13]). This meaning corresponds to Lev 21:13–15 only under the condition that the term זונה in Leviticus also refers to a woman who does not belong to the tribal family. The biblical text is, however, not clear in this respect (cf. Zipor 1987: 259–267). This marital rule is a basis for Levi's priestly holiness and for the sanctification of his descendants, as the rest of the *Document's* verse indicates. Levi's holiness and that of his offspring is also discussed elsewhere in the *Document* (see *A.L.D.* 48, 58; cf. *A.L.D.* 51; 4Q542 frg. 1 i 8).

because you are a holy seed. The motivation that introduces the prohibition of improper marital relationships leading to defilement is the fact that Levi and his sons are a holy seed. The book of Ezra extends this motivation against exogamy to the whole nation: "The people of Israel and the priests

and the Levites have not separated themselves (נבדלו) from the peoples of
the lands with their abominations, from the Canaanites, the Hittites, the
Perizzites, the Jebusites, the Ammonites, the Moabites, the Egyptians, and
the Amorites. For they have taken some of their daughters to be wives
for themselves and for their sons; so that the holy race has mixed itself
(והתערבו זרע הקדש; cf. 4QMMTᶜ IV 9–11) with the peoples of the land.
And in this faithlessness (מעל) the hand of the officials and chief men has
been foremost" (Ezra 9:1–2). In *A.L.D.* 17 the expression זרע קדיש denotes
only Levi and his descendants, but the motivation to observe endogamy is
the same both in Ezra and in the *Levi Document*—the fear to profane the
holy seed (cf. Hayes 1999; see also Neh 13:28–29 about defiling the priesthood through exogamy).

And holy is your seed like the Holy One. Not only is Levi a holy priest of
God but his descendants as well. The idea of Levitical holiness is rooted
in God's holiness and depends on proper marital relationships (see Lev
21:7–8). The whole of Israel is also called to be free from impurity and
holy as God is holy (cf. Lev 11:44–45; 20:26). The holiness of Israel depends
on observing proper marital relationships (Lev 20:7–21) and dietary laws
(Lev 11; 20:24–26).

for a holy priest you are called. Although the OT often speaks about
sanctification of the priests (e.g. Exod 19:22; 28:3, 41), the *Document*'s expression "a holy priest" has never been used there. Levi's holiness is greatly
stressed in the *Document*. He has been elected for a holy priesthood (*A.L.D.*
51), and he is a holy one of the most high God (*A.L.D.* 58). He requests
the gift of the holy spirit (*A.L.D.* 1a v. 8) and is an ardent foe of uncleanness (*A.L.D.* 1a v. 14). In *A.L.D.* 48 Isaac confirms Levi's holiness once
again. When 4Q545 frg. 4 16–19 describes a future ideal priest, most probably Aaron himself (cf. 4Q545 4 15), its description is similar to that of
Levi in the *Document*: "He is a holy priest (כהן קדיש הוא) [for God the most
high, thus (?)] holy will be for him all his descendants for all et[ernal] generations [and God's beloved/messenger] the seventh among the men of
[His] pleasure [he will be na]med, and he will be called [God's chosen
one for] he will be chosen as eternal priest" (cf. 4Q 546 18 2; 4Q547 frg.
6 1; Puech 2001: 342–344).

V. 18 *You are close to God and close to all his holy ones.* Being close to God
and to his holy ones is a response to Levi's request to be close to God in
A.L.D. 1a v. 17 (cf. *T. Levi* 2:10). That would assume that Levi's life and
liturgical service is parallel to the heavenly liturgy of the angels (see Zech
3:7; *Jub.* 30:18; 31:14; cf. 1QSb IV 24). A similar idea of closeness in connection with liturgical service is expressed by the expression כוהני קורב
"priests of the inner sanctuary" (4Q400 1 i 8, 17, 19, etc.) denoting angels.
Additionally, the term "his holy ones" indicates most probably angels (cf.
qəddusān 1 En. 1:9; 12:2; 14:23; "Watchers and holy ones" 4Q206 frg. 2 ii
5 [*1 En.* 22:6]; Dan 4:10, 20). Grelot (1991:255, n. 11) suggests that the
expression "his holy ones" may also be parsed as a neuter; it would thus
refer to the holy things of the cult and the sanctuary. Given the parallelism
with God, this interpetation is less probable.

be pure in your flesh. Isaac's exhortation to be pure (דכי) from any impurity of every man is a closing statement of the section. Here purity means not only marrying within the boundary of one's tribal family, but the accent is laid on every kind of impurity (see *A.L.D.* 1a v. 14). In the *Testament of Qahat* this virtue has also a prominent role and is a dominant characteristic of Levitical priesthood. In 4Q542 frg. 1 i 8–9 Qahat addresses his sons with the following words, [ער]ברוב כול מן ודכין קד[י]שין והוא "and be ho[l]y and pure from all [min]gling" (cf. 4Q542 frg. 1 i 10 בלבב דכא, "with a pure heart"; 4Q542 frg. 1 i 13 ודכ[ו]והא, "and purity," listed together with righteousness, holiness and priesthood).

The lexeme [ער]ברוב] (4Q542 frg. 1 i 9) proceeds from the verb ערב "to mingle" with a reduplication of the last two consonants, a phenomenon common in Semitic languages (see *Tg. Onq.* Num 11:4 MS y[b] עירברבין; *Tg. Cant* 1:12 עירברובין "mixed multitudes"; cf. Puech 2001: 275). The reading in the *Testament of Qahat* refers to the prohibition of exogamy as unlawful mixing of two different species. Note that in the Samaritan Targum Lev 19:19 and Deut 22:9 the *Testament* term translates the Hebrew כלאים (cf. כילאי in *A.L.D.* 91 l. 10). In *1 En.* 10:9 the Giants are called in Ethiopic *manzərān* (G μαζηρέους), which is a transliterated Hebrew ממזינין with the Greek equivalent κίβδηλοι (G, Sync.). The meaning of the Hebrew term is "bastard" (Deut 23:3); "mongrel people" (Zech 9:6). The Giants are called so because they are an offspring of heavenly and earthly creatures.

The expression "every impurity of any man" כל טומאת כל נבר is similar to the one found in Sarah's prayer in 4Q196 frg. 6 9 (Tob 3:14) דכיה אנה בנרמי מן כ[ל] טמאה [נבר]. Here it might be a hidden allusion to the defilement of the Giants, נברין (see 4Q530 1 i 8; frg. 2 ii+6–12(?) 3, 13, 15, 20, 21; frg. 7 ii 3; frg. 14 2; 4Q531 frg. 1 2, 3; frg. 7 4; the giants/watchers (?) defile themselves, 4Q531 frg. 1 1, אטמיו, cf. frg. 6 4; for the sexual defilement of the Watchers, cf. *1 En.* 7:1; 9:8; 10:11; 15:3–4; *Jub.* 4:22; 7:21).

The Qumran eschatological rule for the end of days accepted the necessity of being free of any impurity as a criterion of acceptance into its ranks. 1QSa II 3–4 affirms that "no man who is afflicted by any one of the human defilements (טומאות האדם) shall enter the congregation of these." The reason for this rule is the presence of angels of holiness in their midst (see 1QSa II 8–9, cf. 1QM VII 4; Licht 1965: 264). The presence of the angels is also a cause of heightened rules of purity in the War Scroll (see 1QM VII 6; cf. 1QM XII 7–9; Schiffman 1984: 383–384). In a similar way, being close to God's holy ones in the *Document* requires from Levi to be pure form every human impurity.

3.8.3 *Due Order of Sacrificial Activity—A.L.D. 19–30*

3.8.3.1 *Ablutions—A.L.D. 19–21*

Levi's first three ablutions stand at the beginning of the section exclusively dedicated to the sacrificial duties (19–47). Ablutions are mentioned in *Jub.* 21:16 but in the structure of the chapter they are positioned in a less logical manner after the description of the wood for the sacrifice (21:12–15). The *Jubilees* text describes three ablutions, two before approaching the altar (cf. *A.L.D.* 19 and 20), but the third one after the sacrifice is offered. The description of three ablutions is also mentioned in *T. Levi* 9:11. The first one concerns bathing (λούομαι) before entering the sanctuary and is based on *A.L.D.* 19, the second assumes washing (νίπτω) during the sacrifice and distantly reminds the reader of *A.L.D.* 26; the third one speaks of washing when Levi finishes or accomplishes (ἀπαρτίζω) the sacrifice, and is most probably influenced by *Jub.* 21:16, which speaks about an ablution after the sacrifice. The *Document* mentions the fourth ablution in *A.L.D.* 26.

V. 19 *to enter the temple of God.* Levi probably has his second vision in Bethel (cf. Form and Structure in § 3.5), and he is ordained to the priesthood in the same place (*A.L.D.* 10), and now Isaac orders him to enter בית אל, the house of God. The play on the meaning of this proper name is evident. In the biblical account the site is a place of Jacob's visionary dream (Gen 28:10–22); he calls it "house of God" בית אלהים and "gate of heaven" שער השמים (v. 17) and changes its name from Luz to Bethel (v. 19). Levi's ordination takes place in Bethel on the occasion of Jacob's payment of his vow to God to tithe all his possessions in exchange for God's protection (cf. *A.L.D.* 9). The play on the meaning of this place conjoins Levi's priestly function with the place of his heavenly and earthly ordination. Thus he remains "close to God and to his holy ones" (*A.L.D.* 18) in exercising his priestly functions.

bathe in water. Levi washes his entire body in a ritual purification before undertaking priestly functions in the temple. Bathing in water (סחי במיא) before putting on priestly vestments reminds the reader of Aaron's consecration (Exod 29:4; 40:12; Lev 8:6; cf. *A.L.D.* 1a v. 2) or Yom Kippur liturgy (Lev 16:4, 24). In parallelism with these texts, the preposition ב is best understood as having a local ("in"), not instrumental ("with") meaning (see also *A.L.D.* 1a v. 2; for the verb סחי "to bathe" in later Aramaic dialects, cf. Greenfield 1991: 590–591).

Cultic norms in Israel prescribed only washing of hands and feet before discharging sacrificial duties (Exod 30:19–21). Curiously, both the *Document* and *Leviticus* 16 set higher standards for the ritual ablutions. *Leviticus* 16 requires two bathings in conjunction with vesting, one before (v. 4), another after sacrificial activities (v. 24), the *Document*, only one, but on every occasion, when entering the sanctuary. Both texts apparently develop the biblical norm that orders washing of hands and feet before entering the sanctuary (see Exod 31:19–20).

V. 20 *repeat (it) again and wash your hands and your feet.* The second ablution takes place after the vesting but before the beginning of the sacrificial duty.

Kugler (1996a: 104) wrongly affirms that it has no biblical basis whatsoever. It partially concords with the biblical norm in Exod 30:19–20 that requires washing of hands and feet before approaching the altar. The third ablution has no biblical basis.

V. 21 *And whenever you take to sacrifice . . . wash your hands and feet.* The third ablution requires washing of hands and feet after being in physical contact ("to take" נסב; cf. *A.L.D.* 52 "to receive" παραλαμβάνω) with the sacrificed offerings. The expression "everything that is fitting to offer on the altar" refers not only to the wood (23:14; 25a:20; 31:19–20) but most probably to all the sacrificed material, compare *A.L.D.* 52 and the use of the impersonal verb חזה/καθήκει for salt (*A.L.D.* 29 l. 12; 37), flour (40b), and for all the sacrificial activity (*A.L.D.* 51). A fourth ablution of hands and feet is necessary after sprinkling the blood on the walls of the altar (*A.L.D.* 26). *Jub.* 21:16 requires washing of hands and feet after the completion of the sacrifice. This affirmation most probably comes as a consequence of the *Document*'s third and fourth ablutions, which take place after being in physical contact with the sacrifice (cf. also Lev 16:24). The two additional ablutions in *A.L.D.* 53a and 54 belong to the redactional additions to Isaac's speech and are of secondary nature. The obligation of washing hands and feet before approaching the altar in *A.L.D.* 53a may be tracked back to *A.L.D.* 20; it clarifies the latter in line with its biblical foundation in Exod 30:19–21. *A.L.D.* 54 places the same action in the context of blood contamination (cf. *A.L.D.* 53b; 55), which recalls *A.L.D.* 26.

3.8.3.2 *Wood for the Burnt Offering—A.L.D. 22–25a*

This section is dedicated to the preparation of the wood on the altar. After the first introductory verse, the paragraph is marked off with an *inclusio* occurring between *A.L.D.* 23 ll. 13–14 and *A.L.D.* 25a, which roots the list of twelve types of wood in Abraham's authority. This section has its parallel text in *Jub.* 21:12–15, where it is found in a reverse order after the description of the sacrifice (21:7–11) and before the necessary ablutions (21:16). The *Document*'s text proceeds in a more logical way: ablutions (*A.L.D.* 19–21), wood (*A.L.D.* 22–25a), sacrifice (*A.L.D.* 25b–47). *T. Levi* 9:12 abbreviates the section of the *Document* by indicating only the number of the trees (12) and by rooting the instruction in Abraham's authority.

The analysis of the relationship between the list of trees in the *Document* and in *Jubilees* is hampered by the corruption of the Aramaic and Ethiopic text. *Jub.* 21:12 names fourteen trees (thirteen according to VanderKam 1989b: 124, n.; cf. *1 En.* 3:1; *Geoponica* 11:1), whereas the *Document* has only twelve. The *Jubilees* text contradicts the *Document* when stating that no split wood is to be placed on the

altar (21:13). Isaac instructs Levi that split wood is to be sacrificed
(*A.L.D.* 22 l. 9). *Jub.* 21:13–14 adds that wood must be tested for its
appearance, it should be dark, strong, without any defect. The *Document*
only states that it should have no worm in it. The trees are fragrant
to produce a pleasant smell (*A.L.D.* 23 l. 15; cf. *Jub.* 21:13b–14), and
whether they are evergreen (*1 En.* 3:1; *Geoponica* 11:1) plays no role
in the *Document*.

V. 22 *And sacrifice split wood.* Isaac orders Levi to offer (*hap'el* of קרב 22
l. 9; 31 l. 20 and סלק *A.L.D.* 22 l. 11; 23 l. 14; 25a l. 20; 25b l. 22; cf.
T. Levi 9:12) wood, which indicates the importance of wood in the *Document*'s
sacrificial ritual. Additionally, a biblical expression "pleasant smell" applied
for the sacrifice (see *A.L.D.* 30 l. 16) is modified in *A.L.D.* 23 l. 15 to "smell
of their smoke goes up pleasantly." It refers to the smoke of different types
of wood burnt on the altar. The Essene text CD-A XI 19 lists wood offering
(עץ) together with burnt offering (עולה), cereal offering (מנחה), and incense
offering (לבונה). Lev 1:7 and 6:5 order the priest to place wood on the altar
to offer the holocaust in the first case, and to upkeep the fire on the altar
in the second. For the wood sacrifice at Qumran, see the comment on
A.L.D. 24.

split wood. É. Puech (1971: 5–19) proposed to translate the root *ṣ-l-ḥ* in
Hebrew and Aramaic with "to penetrate" (Gen 41:38; 2 Sam 19:18) hence
"to penetrate with fire, to burn" (Amos 5:6; Sir 8:10, MS A). This would
be its earlier meaning in comparison with later Syro-Palestinian dialects
that often translate the Hebrew בקע "to split." He further claims that the
Document אעין מהצלחין is best translated with "inflammable wood" in the
sense: "qu'on peut enflammer et faire brûler, prévus pour cet office, non
'qui s'enflamment facilement' . . ." (p. 16). He also discards as late the Greek
translator's rendering of the root by the verb σχίζω "to split." This interpretation is interesting but may only be accepted with some difficulty. Isaac
claims in the *Document* that he saw his father Abraham prepare wood for
the sacrifice in the same manner (see below), and the biblical text, in fact,
provides a justification of this claim. In Gen 22:3 Abraham splits (בקע) the
wood for the offering, hence the meaning of the root *ṣ-l-ḥ* in the *Document*
should rather refer to this action of Abraham.

and examine it beforehand for worms. The verb בקר "to examine carefully"
is used here in a technical sense of testing the wood for imperfections, in
this case worms, that would eliminate it from sacrificial usage. In Lev 27:33
this term is used for examination of the animals presented as a tithe, while
in Mishnaic Hebrew it denotes examining an animal for imperfections (Levy
1876-89: 1:255). It has been contended that the verb בקר in the *pi'el* in 2
Kgs 16:15 and Ps 27:4 denotes the action of examining the intestines of
sacrificial animals, a divination practice frequent in the ancient Near East
(Loretz 1993: 515–521). It may be suggested that the *Document*'s usage of
the term is an extension of this sacrificial practice to wood as cultic material. Note that wood, like the animal, must first be split in order to be

examined. The similarity is, however, limited to the formal element only, for the divination was practiced in order to forecast future events, while wood examination serves the purpose of eliminating material not fit for the sacrifice because of worms.

for like this I saw Abraham my father. Isaac recalls Abraham's authority for the instructions concerning wood fitting for the holocaust (see also *A.L.D.* 23 and 25a). The only biblical fundament for this assertion may be found in Gen 22. Before Abraham leaves for mount Moriah, he splits the wood for the holocaust (Gen 22:3 עלה עצי ויבקע). *Tg. Onq.* translates the Hebrew בקע with צלח, the Aramaic term used here for split wood (*A.L.D.* 22 1. 9). *Tg. Ps.-J.* Gen 22:3 develops the Genesis text stating that Abraham split the wood of olive tree (זיתא), fig tree (תאנתא) and palm-tree (דיקלא) and that this type of wood is fitting (חזיין) for the holocaust. Although only the fig tree is expressly mentioned in the *Document*'s list (24 l. 18), the *Targum Pseudo-Jonatan* links to Abraham's holocaust a list of trees fitting for the sacrifice. In the light of this evidence, it is certain that the list of the trees fitting for the sacrifice in the *Document* originated in the reflection on Gen 22, Abraham's only holocaust sacrifice, which Isaac could actually see (*A.L.D.* 22 l. 12 חזית). Kugler's opinion, that the whole section 22–25a originated in the midrashic reflection on Lev 1:7 which "instructs the priest to arrange the wood on the altar in an orderly fashion" (1996a: 104), does not find any confirmation in the text of the *Document*.

V. 23 *smell of their smoke goes up pleasantly.* The idea that the sacrificed wood produces a sweet smell is absent in the biblical tradition but is attested in the Mesopotamian *Gilgamesh Epic.* After the raven does not return to the ship, Utnapishtim says: "Then I let out (all) to the four winds and offered a sacrifice. I poured out a libation on the top of the mountain. Seven and seven cult-vessels I set up. Upon their pot-stands I heaped cane, cedarwood, and myrtle. The gods smelled the savor, the gods smelled the sweet savor, the gods crowded like flies about the sacrificer" (Gilgamesh XI 155–161; Pritchard 1969: 95). Note that the sweet odor does not come from the sacrificed meat but from the wood burnt on the altar (cf. de Vaux 1964: 40–41). Additionally, the account has a list of sacrificed wood. These two points strongly suggest a relationship between the *Document* and the tradition expressed by the Babylonian text.

V. 24 *And these are their names.* The list of twelve tree names belongs to the educational priestly lore transmitted to Levi by Isaac. By teaching Levi a tree list, Isaac follows a well-known practice in the ancient Mesopotamian scribal education, according to which apprentice scribes had to learn thematic noun lists grouped according to their semantic range. Tree lists used in scribal education are already attested in archaic Uruk (Englund and Nissen 1993: 103–112; Nissen 1981: 103–104; cf. Nissen and Damerow 1993: 105–106) and continued to constitute a constant element in Babylonian school training. They were part of a larger category called UR₅.RA (= *ḫubul-lum*, "interest-bearing loan"), a Sumerian term appearing in the first line of a list of objects written originally in Sumerian but later accompanied by Akkadian equivalents (Cavigneaux 1980–83: 626–628; for the *ḫubullum* lists in the scribal education at Ugarit, cf. Krecher 1969: 137–139). The lists essentially served to master Sumerian, a language of scribal education, but they also contained metrological sections of the type found in *A.L.D.* 32a–46a (see the comment on *A.L.D.* 32a–36). Some Sumerian literary texts used in the Nippur *edubba* contain passages that seem to be exercises in the vocabulary of one specific semantic field (plants, parts of a chariots, cultic boat, different kinds of fish, stones) related to the thematic noun lists (cf. Veldhuis 1997: 126–129).

Although in the *Document* the tree list is transmitted to Levi to teach him an adequate sacrifice preparation, the educational character of Levi's priestly training should not be overlooked. Mesopotamian thematic noun lists and *A.L.D.* 24 serve the same educational goal—an adequate professional preparation. They are also an expression of scribal educational activity that begins with naming and categorizing empirical phenomena. The same educational spirit is also represented in the *Document*'s metrological section (*A.L.D.* 32a–46a), which teaches Levi metrological notations and arithmetical calculation. In ancient Canaan, fragments of thematic noun lists (*ḫubullum*) dated to Old and Middle Babylonian periods were found in archeological excavations at Hazor, Gezer, Taʿanak, and Shechem (cf. Demsky 1990: 162–163).

Lists of different kind exist also on biblical pages, but a tree list in an unequivocal teaching context has never been attested in the Old Testament books (Scolnic 1995). However, the knowledge of tree lists is ascribed to Solomon in 1 Kgs 4:32–33 as a sign of his wisdom and encyclopedic learning: "He also uttered three thousand proverbs; and his songs were a thousand and five. He spoke of trees, from the cedar that is in Lebanon to the hyssop that grows out of the wall; he spoke also of beasts, and of birds, and of reptiles, and of fish."

The verse names twelve different trees, and that number may be haphazard or purposive. It is curious to notice that the twelve tribes of Israel offer (הקריב, see *A.L.D.* 22) wood on the altar of the ideal temple on the festival of the wood (11QT^b VI 11–18; 11QT^a XXIII 1–3). During six days of the celebration, two tribes each day offer their portions, starting with the tribes of Levi and Judah. Then the burnt offering executed by the high priest follows on behalf of the twelve tribes (11QT^a XXIII 3–XXIV 16). The sacrifice for the Levites precedes the one on behalf of the tribe of Judah. The idea of the festival of the wood stems most probably from Neh 10:35 (cf. Neh 13:31) where the priests, Levites and the people determine by lot the procurement of wood for the temple (cf. Josephus, *B.J.* 2.425). It seems very probable that it influenced the description of the festival of the wood in the *Temple Scroll*. 4Q365 frg. 23 5–6 adds the prescription of wood offering at the end of the festival list in Lev 23.

A.L.D. 52 coins a separate name for the wood offering, "reckoning of wood" λογισμὸς τῶν ξυλῶν; see 31 l. 19 חושבן. This term sets wood apart, differ-

entiating it from the rest of the sacrifice, and underlines the importance of
the fitting kind and weight (32a–36) of sacrificed wood.

The Mishnah declares all wood acceptable for the sacrifice, except the
olive and the vine (*m. Tamid* 2:3). The same verse lists as preferable the
fig, the walnut and oleaster. *Sipra* Nedaba 6:4 speaks of the carob, palm
and sycamore (cf. also *t. Menaḥ.* 22a; *b. Tamid* 29b). The *Document*'s tradition of restricting the number of acceptable wood to twelve is not attested
in rabbinic literature.

V. 25a *un[der] the burnt offering on the altar*. *A.L.D.* 25a l. 21 expressly names
the kind of sacrifice that is being prepared, that is the burnt offering עלהא.
It is further accompanied by cereal, libation, and frankincense offerings (see
A.L.D. 30). No other kinds of sacrifice are mentioned. Also in the decree
of king Cyrus (Ezra 6:2–12), only burnt offerings are mentioned, "And
whatever is needed—young bulls, rams, or sheep for burnt offerings to the
God of heaven, wheat, salt, wine, or oil, as the priests at Jerusalem require—
let that be given to them day by day without fail . . ." (Ezra 6:9). In the
Aramaic writings of the Jewish Elephantine colony in the fifth century B.C.
only cereal, frankincense, and burnt offerings are attested (see Cowley 1967:
30:21, 25, 28). Another text, however, states that animal offerings are not
administered (see Cowley 1967: 33: 10–11; cf. Porten 1968: 289–293). Note
that in the description of the *Heavenly Jerusalem*, the bull sacrifice and the
corresponding cereal sacrifice are also included (11Q18 frg. 13; frg. 28).

The *Document*'s choice of the burnt offering is probably motivated by pedagogical interests of the author who intends to teach priestly students not
only the proper order of the sacrificial proceedings (*A.L.D.* 30), but metro-
arithmetical calculations as well. Additional offerings usually accompanying
the holocaust sacrifice constitute an excellent occasion for expounding metro-
arithmetical exercises on capacity unit fractions in *A.L.D.* 37–44. Wood and
frankincense quantities in *A.L.D.* 32a–36 and 45–46a belong to the same
category of metro-arithmetical exercises dealing, this time, with weight units.

3.8.3.3 *Burnt Offering of the Bull—A.L.D. 25b–30*

The section describes the burnt offering of a bull with accompanying meal (*A.L.D.* 30 l. 12), libation (30 l. 13), and incense (30 l. 14)
offerings. It is well embedded in the texture of the preceding and
following passages. *A.L.D.* 25b ll. 22–23a repeats the last clause of
the preceding section concerning wood. The closing sentence (*A.L.D.*
30 ll. 14b–16) underlines the necessity of keeping due order (בסרך
עובדיך) so that all of Levi's sacrifices may be accepted by God. It
thus introduces the next section on weights and measures which picks
up the expression "in order" בסרך and the root "to do" עבד in the
opening sentence (*A.L.D.* 31 l. 17). Proceeding in due order becomes
an important point linking the first part of sacrificial injunctions
(*A.L.D.* 19–30) with the second (*A.L.D.* 31–47).

In *Jub.* 21:7–11 Abraham's sacrificial instruction reverses the order of the *Document* by locating the section before the description of wood qualified for sacrifice (vv. 12–14). The sacrifice is qualified as peace offering, and the accent is laid on sacrificing the fat (vv. 7–8). Then some rules concerning eating meat follow (v. 10) with the injunction to add salt of the covenant to every oblation (v. 11). The section only remotely recalls the *Document*'s description of the burnt offering, and constitutes a secondary development of the well-structured *Document*'s passage. *T. Levi* 9:13–14 concentrates on offering every clean beast and bird together with first fruits and wine; every sacrifice should be salted. While the latter injunction reminds the reader of *Jub.* 21:11, sacrificing every clean animal points to Noah's sacrifice after the deluge (see Gen 8:20). Thus where *Jub.* 21:10 and *A.L.D.* 57 refer to Noah explicitly, the *Testament* connects Levi's sacrifice with the Noahic sacrificial tradition in an implicit manner.

V. 25b *you shall begin to sprinkle blood.* The blood dispensation begins after the fire begins to kindle the wood on the altar. Lev 1:5b orders the blood dispensation before the fire is kindled (Lev 1:7; cf. 1:11b). The *Document* does not imply that the fire is to be kindled. It only says that the blood sprinkling should begin when fire begins to kindle the wood. Lev 6:6 states that the fire should always (תמיד) burn on the altar. Blood in *A.L.D.* 25b is sprinkled on the sides of the altar, an action similar to Lev 1:5b which speaks of throwing the blood round about (סביב) and against it (על), cf. Exod 29:16; Lev 8:19; 9:12.

Biblical laying of hands on the head of the animal (Lev 1:4) and its slaughtering (Lev 1:5a) by the offerer are omitted in the *Document*. Additionally, the offerer's action of flaying and cutting the animal into pieces (Lev 1:6) is also omitted. The reason might be that these actions belong to the offerer and not to the priest.

V. 26 *wash your hands and your feet from the blood.* An ablution after the blood dispensation is another innovation in regard to the biblical text. It is most probably justified by being in physical contact with the animal's blood dashed against the altar, an action that can be handled only by a priest. The contact with blood, the most sacred element of the sacrifice, calls for another ablution (cf. Lev 16:24; *Jub.* 21:16). Note that blood dashed on the sides of the altar in the burnt sacrifice (עלה) may have an expiatory function (Lev 1:4), the context in the *Document*, however, does not allow us to interpet the rite in this sense. In *A.L.D.* 54 washing of hands and feet is set as a rule because of contact with the sacrificed animals (cf. *A.L.D.* 52) and in the context of immunity from the blood contamination (*A.L.D.* 53b and 55). 11QT[a] XXVI 10 affirms that after the sin offering of the Yom Kippur liturgy the high priest "shall wash his hands and his feet from the blood of the sin-offering."

start offering the portions (that have been) salted. Several biblical texts state that the sacrifice should be offered in pieces (נתחים, cf. Exod 29:17; Lev 1:6, 8, 12; 8:20; 9:13; 1 Kgs 18:23, 33), the *Document* adds, however, some modifications. *A.L.D.* 29 explains that all the pieces must be salted with a corresponding quantity of salt. Quantity of salt appropriate for different animals is laid out in *A.L.D.* 37–40a (cf. *A.L.D.* 52). The bull sacrifice in the heavenly Jerusalem also requires salt for all its parts (see 11Q18 13 2). Noah adds salt to his sacrifice after the flood (1QapGen X 17). Similarly to the *Document*, 11QT^a XXXIV 10–11 commands salting of different pieces of the animal before burning them on the altar.

In Ezekiel's visionary "law of the temple" (Ezek 43:12) the need to salt the burnt offering is spelled out (Ezek 43:24; cf. Josephus, *A.J.* 3.227). The Mishnah also states that the pieces of the *Tamid* burnt offering should be salted (see *m. Tamid* 4:3). Lev 2:13 orders only cereal offerings to be salted but together with all other offerings (קרבן, cf. *Jub.* 21:11; *T. Levi* 9:14b; 11QT^a XX 13). By applying salt to the burnt offering, the *Document*'s ruling corresponds closely to Ezekiel's text.

V. 27 *First offer up the head and cover it with fat.* The injunction is similar to Lev 1:8 where the head is first in order, but then it is implied that fat (פדר) is offered afterwards, without covering the head. For the understanding of fat (תרבא/στέαρ) as a separate part of the sacrifice, cf. *A.L.D.* 32a–36.

the blood of the sacrifice of the bull may not be seen. This ritual prescription is not attested in the biblical pages. *A.L.D.* 55 and 56 have a similar injunction concerning blood. It should not appear on Levi's garment, and the blood of the animals has to be covered with earth. This particular preoccupation stems from the conviction that blood constitutes the life of the animal (cf. *A.L.D.* 55).

the sacrifice of the bull. Only the burnt offering of the bull is presented in the *Document* (see תורא *A.L.D.* 32a ll. 21, 23; ταῦρος *A.L.D.* 37, 37, 38, 41, 41, 43, 44, 45). It is also attested in the temple of the *Heavenly Jerusalem* (see 11Q18 frg. 13 1; frg. 28 5).

V. 28 *And after this the neck.* A detailed order of the sacrificed pieces is exposed in *A.L.D.* 28–29. Only the last command to sacrifice the feet washed together with the entrails recalls Lev 1:9a which orders a similar obligatory washing (cf. Lev 1:13; 8:21; 9:14; Exod 29:17). It is, therefore, most probable that the whole order of the sacrificed pieces in *A.L.D.* 27–28 is a midrashic development of Lev 1:8–9a. The additional statement on the salt necessary for the sacrifice of the bull in *A.L.D.* 29 finds its development in *A.L.D.* 37–40a. The list of the sacrificed pieces of the burnt offering may also be found in *m. Yoma* 2:3, 7 and *m. Tamid* 4:2–4 (cf. 11QT^a XXIV 1–4). In the Yom Kippur liturgy the pieces of the bull offering were brought to the altar by 24 priests who were chosen by lot (*m. Yoma* 2:7). The accent, however, is laid not on the order of the sacrificed pieces but that every piece is assigned to a different priest. The resulting order is as follows: head, [right] hind leg, rump, [left] hind leg, breast, neck, two forelegs, two flanks, and entrails. The *Document* adds thigh and spine of the loin. The hind legs are to be washed with the entrails. The same injunction is found in the description of the bull sacrifice in the *Heavenly Jerusalem* (see 11Q18 frg. 13 2).

For the Aramaic יד "foreleg," cf. *b. Ḥul.* 58b; *m. Yoma* 2:3; *m. Tamid* 4:3, etc. The Aramaic ניעא "breast" is an equivalent of Hebrew חזה (cf. Cairo Geniza targum, MS Vatican Ebr. 440 Lev 7:30, 30 in Klein 1980: 1:184; Syriac *n ' '* in Brockelmann 1928: *s.v.*). The Aramaic בן דפנא should be translated as "ribs" (see *b. B. Meṣiʿa* 23b; cf. Syr. *dfnʾ* in Brockelmann 1928: 162). For the lexeme שדרה "spine," see, e.g., *m. Ḥul.* 3:2; for הרצא "loin," cf. *Tg. Onq.* Deut 33:11; pl. in Exod 12:11; 28:42.

V. 29 *salted with salt . . . according to what they require.* The command to offer up the salted portions is mentioned in *A.L.D.* 26 and formulated here explicitly. Salt quantities corresponding to different animals are discussed later in the *Document* (cf. the comment on *A.L.D.* 37–40a).

V. 30 *And after this the fine flour mixed with oil.* The verse is divided into two parts; the first one (*A.L.D.* 30 ll. 12–14a) deals with fine flour, wine, and frankincense offering; the second one (*A.L.D.* 30 ll. 14b–15) constitutes a final statement on Levi's liturgical activities in *A.L.D.* 19–30. The phrase "fine flour mixed with oil" denotes the cereal offering מנחה (Exod 29:40; Lev 2:5; 23:13; Num 7:13, 19, 25, 31, 37, etc.; see also 1QapGen X 16). The cereal offering accompanying the burnt offering is described in Lev 2:1–16. Then, the libation offering of wine follows (see *A.L.D.* 44; 52; cf. Exod 29:40; Lev 23:13; Num 15:5, 7, 10, etc.). The frankincense offering is the last one which accompanies the burnt offering (see also *A.L.D.* 45; 46a; 52). All these three accompanying elements are enumerated in Lev 2:1, the beginning of the description of the cereal offering (Lev 2:1–16). Burnt offerings are accompanied by cereal and communion offerings in Lev 7:37; Num 29:39; Josh 22:23; 1 Kgs 8:64; 2 Kgs 16:13; Ezek 45:15, 17; 2 Chr 7:7. The cereal offering accompanies also Noah's sacrifice after the flood (see 1QapGen X 16). Proper quantities of fine flour, frankincense, and wine corresponding to different sacrificed animals are indicated later in the *Document* (see *A.L.D.* 40b–47). It is interesting to notice that according to 1 Chr 9:29 Levites are in charge of the fine flour, wine, oil, incense, and spices.

and thus your deeds will be in order. The last sentence of the section positively evaluates Levi's liturgical activity with the common biblical phraseology. The sacrifices are to be acceptable to God as a pleasant smell (cf. Gen 8:21; Exod 29:18, 25, 41; Lev 1:9, 13, 17, etc.). A true innovation is the statement that Levi's liturgical actions must be done in due order בסרך. This statement explains why the whole section is so well structured (ablutions, wood, blood, pieces of the bull) and why the preposition בתר "after" is so often used in *A.L.D.* 29–30 (7 x). A similar injunction to follow a due order in every liturgical action in *A.L.D.* 31 opens a second part of Isaac's speech concerning weight and measure of the sacrificed material. The first part then (*A.L.D.* 19–30) ends in the same way in which the second (*A.L.D.* 31–47) begins. The adverbial expression "in order" בסרך is semantically related to the biblical term ערך "to set in order, to arrange," in reference to priestly liturgical action (Gen 22:9; Exod 27:21; 40:4, 23; Lev 1:7, 8, 12, etc.). There remains little doubt, therefore, that the purpose of Isaac's instruction is to give Levi a proper liturgical order necessary for a priest whose judicial authority is greater than that of all flesh (*A.L.D.* 14 l. 10). The description of Noah's sacrifice in the *Genesis Apocryphon* implies that this prediluvian patriarch sacrificed also according to a proper sacrificial order (1QapGen X 13–17). The existence of this order is inferred from the subsequent expressions: "first" לקדמין (1QapGen X 14); "after that" בתרה (line 14); "secondly" תניאנא (line 14); "thirdly" תליתי (line 15). The first expression is also found in a sacrificial context in *A.L.D.* 16 l. 14; 22 l. 10; 27 l. 4; the second in *A.L.D.* 28 ll. 6, 7, 7, 8, 10; 30 ll. 12, 13.

Ezra 8:34 underlines the importance of a proper order as to the number and weight of the temple utensils. The injunction, however, that Levi's work be in order, in measure, and by weight (*A.L.D.* 31) to be acceptable to God stems from the Wisdom tradition according to which God created all things in order. Wis 11:20 affirms about God's activity in the world, "But thou hast arranged all things by measure and number and weight" ἀλλὰ πάντα μέτρῳ καὶ ἀριθμῷ καὶ σταθμῷ διέταξας (cf. Job 28:25; 38:5; Isa 40:12; *1 En.* 43:2, etc.).

The concept of God's order (סרך/τάξις) inherent in the creation is a cornerstone of Enochic theology. The specific term expressing this order is סרך as attested in 4Q201 1 ii 1 (*1 En.* 2:1 τάξις G). When discussing a relationship between body and spirit, *T. Naph.* 2:3 adds the principle that "by weight and measure and rule all the creation of the Most High (is made)." All things are good because they were created in order (ἐν τάξει), and harmony together with purposefulness of different parts of the human body that serve as an example of this order (*T. Naph.* 2:8). The *Testament* description deals with the human body, but the exhortation to act in order is identical with the *Document* statement (*T. Naph.* 2:9; *A.L.D.* 30 l. 15). Nothing is to be done disorderly (*T. Naph.* 2:9b ἄτακτον) because it causes a change of the law of God (*T. Naph.* 3:2b). Subsequently, there come examples of those who changed their order (τάξις): the Gentiles through their idolatry (3:3), the Sodomites and Watchers who changed the order of their nature (3:4–5). To be wise and intelligent, one must know the order of God's commandments and the laws of every activity (*T. Naph.* 8:10).

The lexeme סרך has several specialized meanings in the Qumran scrolls. 1QM uses it to indicate a battle formation of the whole congregation (III 3; XIII 1) or of a particular unit (VII 1; see Yadin 1962: 148–150). In 1QS it may refer to the whole sect (I 16), to the set of rules in vigor in the group (V 1; VI 8; cf. I 1), or to a hierarchical disposition within the group (II 20; V 23; see Licht 1965: 66). However, the Qumran scrolls do not use the adverbial expression בסרך in connection with liturgical priestly action. In CD A VII 8 the expression סרך התורה "rule of the Torah," refers to the Torah and its interpretation. (For a comprehensive discussion of the term in Qumran literature, see Schiffman 1975: 60–68.)

3.8.4   *Metrological Order of Weights and Measures—A.L.D. 31–47*

The lexeme עבד "to do" and adverbial syntagm בסרך "in order" in *A.L.D.* 31 are picked up from the preceding verse and serve as hook-words with the preceding section *A.L.D.* 19–30. They also introduce the same dominant thought from the preceding description of the sacrifice, that is, an injunction to keep a due order. This order now concerns proper measures (משחה) and weights (מתקל) of the offered material. First, the weight of wood necessary for different animals is discussed (*A.L.D.* 32a–36), and then appropriate measures of salt (*A.L.D.* 37–40a), fine flour (40b–45), and weights of frankincense (*A.L.D.* 45–46a). The section is marked off with a rationale of dry measures and weights (*A.L.D.* 46b–47). Neither the book of *Jubilees* nor the *Testament of Levi* contain anything that corresponds to the detailed rationale of the *Document*. Given the precise nature of measurements and their ratios in the section, one has the impression that it is written not only to establish the proper amount of sacrificed material, but also to teach a just system of weights and measures necessary for a correct priestly sacrificial activity (see *A.L.D.* 31 and 46b–47; cf. Ezek 45:10 "You shall have just balances, a just ephah, and a just bath.").

3.8.4.1   *Wood Quantity—A.L.D. 31–36*

V. 31 *do it in order, [by measure] and by weight.* Preoccupation with the appropriate quantity of sacrificed material underlines Levi's quality as a righteous priest who follows a due order. Some biblical texts stress the necessity not to falsify weights and measures (see Deut 25:14; Prov 20:10; Amos 8:5). Lev 19:35–36 prohibits any wrongdoing in judgment, in measures of length or weight or quantity במשפט במדה במשקל ובמשורה. The measures used by the people must be just. This aspect of social justice and moral responsibility is transposed in the *Document* into the realm of liturgical and metro-arithmetical priestly activity. According to 1 Chr 23:29, one of the Levitical duties in the temple is to assist the priests in dealing with the cereal offering and with all measures of quantity and size כל משורה ומדה. The *Document* assigns to Levi, the priest, this responsibility and prohibits adding or diminishing anything from the required amount to keep his work within the norms of priestly justice (דין כהנותא *A.L.D.* 15). Although the weights and measures in *A.L.D.* 31–47 do not concern the cultic measurements of the ideal temple (Ezek 40–48; 4Q554 frg. 1 iii 13, 17, 20, 21, 22; frg. 2 i 16; frg. 2 ii 16; 5Q15 frg. 1 ii 2, 3, 4; cf. Chyutin 1997: 71–112), their purpose is similar. They constitute a legal norm of acceptable worship of the Lord of heavens (*A.L.D.* 13) based on a metrologically established order.

Do not fall short of the adequate calculation of the wo[o]d. The second part of the verse (*A.L.D.* 31 ll. 19–20) is a direct introduction to the description of different quantities of wood adequate for different animal sacrifices in 32a–36. The term חושבן "calculation" (cf. *A.L.D.* 52) indicates the metro-arithmetical computation Levi is supposed to carry out when bringing wood to the altar. The same term appears in the Aramaic text of the *Astronomical Book* of Enoch (*1 En.* 72–82), and it refers there to the calculation of the movements of heavenly bodies (cf. Kvanvig 1988: 61–62). In 4Q209 frg. 25 3–4 (*1 En.* 74:1 or 78:10?) Archangel Uriel shows to Enoch "another calculation" (ח[ש]בון אחרן) concerning the new moons; in frg. 26 6–7 (*1 En.* 79:2?) the term appears in the recapitulation of the calendrical and astronomical laws. The resulting astronomical order of these calculations will last for ever (*1 En.* 72:1) but danger of deviation always exists and leads to disastrous consequences (*1 En.* 80:2–8). Both in the *Document* and in the *Astronomical Book* the term has a technical meaning implying an arithmetical calculation and in both compositions the resulting order cannot be changed without the risk of deviating from the proper norm (cf. סרך "order" in *A.L.D.* 30).

It is certain that the metro-arithmetical calculations of the whole section *A.L.D.* 31–47 constitute a scholarly exercise designed for the priestly students in order to initiate them in simple computational practices. On a more advanced level, these practices based on calculations in the Babylonian style were a necessary tool for establishing the movement of celestial bodies according to the norms of Babylonian mathematical astronomy (cf. Neugebauer 1969: 97–137; 1975: 373–379; Hunger 2001: 311–316). It comes, therefore, as no surprise that "scribal craft" ספר, a term that resumes all metro-arithmetical exercises described in *A.L.D.* 31–47, is studied both by Levi and by his sons on the one hand, and by Enoch, recipient of the "divinely" revealed astronomical knowledge, on the other (cf. the comment on ספר in *A.L.D.* 88). Basic metro-arithmetical knowledge gained by Levi in the instruction of his grandfather Isaac is then used in more sophisticated astronomical calculations ascribed eventually to Enoch (on the literary parallelism between the Enochic *Astronomical Book* and *A.L.D.* 14–50, cf. Form and Structure of *A.L.D.* 11–61 in § 3.8; for the relationship between the *Astronomical Book* and Babylonian astronomy, cf. Albani 1994: 173–269; for the opinion that the Enochic writings originated in Levitical priestly circles influenced by Mesopotamian culture, cf. Kvanvig 1988: 135–143 and 330–342).

Vv. 32a–36

Table 11. Talent Fractions and Mina Multiples

Animal	Wood for the Flesh (Talent Fractions)	Wood for the Fat (Mina Multiples)
תּורא רבא/ ὁ ταῦρος ὁ τελείος	כּכר/τάλαντον	שׁיתה/ἓξ
פּר תּורין ;ὁ ταῦρος ὁ δεύτερος μόσχον τέλειον	πεντήκοντα μ′	πέντε ―――
κριός ἐκ προβάτων ἢ τράγος ἐξ αἰγῶν	λ′	τρεῖς
ἄρνα ἐκ προβάτων ἢ ἔριφον ἐξ αἰγῶν	κ′	β′
ἀμνὸς τέλειος ἢ ἔριφος ἐξ αἰγῶν	ιε′	μίαν ἥμισυ

Animal	Wood for the Flesh (Talent Fractions)		Wood for the Fat (Mina Multiples)
full-grown bull	a talent	= 1 (= 60)	six (minas)
calf of bulls	fifty (minas)	= 5/6	five (minas)
bullock	40 (minas)	= 2/3	four (minas)
ram or he-goat	30 (minas)	= 1/2	three (minas)
lamb or kid	20 (minas)	= 1/3	two (minas)
lamb or kid	15 (minas)	= 1/4	one and a half (mina)

The table indicates that the wood quantity is measured according to the Babylonian sexagesimal metric system, where one talent (ca. 30 kg) is made up of sixty minas, ca. 0.5 kg each (see Powell 1992: 906). The ratio between wood for the fat and wood for the flesh is a regular 1:10. The talent is frequently attested on the biblical pages, but never in connection with the amount of sacrificed material. The mina is attested in Ezek 45:12 (LXX) where its value is indicated as of 50 shekels (see *A.L.D.* 47). The purpose of this schematic representation of wood weights exceeds a simple intention of giving a priestly instruction that deals with the ritual description. It makes rather clear that behind particular amounts of wood there stands a metro-arithmetical order to follow, and this order must be meticulously observed (see *A.L.D.* 31). When compared with the mathematical tradition of the Old Babylonian period, the numerical system of the first column, the amount of wood assigned for the sacrificed animal, appears to be modeled on a Babylonian type of metro-arithmetical school exercise.

Babylonian school mathematics grew out of the economical and administrative needs of the third and second millennium b.c. society which, with the development of city-states and economic prosperity, needed a group of specialized scribes capable of carrying out administrative tasks based on their literacy and knowledge of computation. The mathematical training reached its apogee in the Old Babylonian period with the flourishing of the scribal school (*edubba*) and its doctrine. The method of teaching may be described as "applied" mathematics consisting of the metro-arithmetical computation of given entities, and taking the concrete form of table texts, tables of constants (also known as coefficient lists), and problem texts (cf. Nemet-Nejat 1993: 18–25). At the elementary level, the scribal education was based on the use of multiplication tables, division tables, and tables of measures.

The first necessary step in mathematical education was the knowledge of weights and measures and their sexagesimal structure. The student first met them when studying and copying thematic noun lists (*ḫubullu*, cf. the comment on *A.L.D.* 24) usually divided in six divisions at Nippur (Robson 2002: 330–332). The first division, list of trees and wooden objects, contained the main capacity measures in descending order. When presented units were larger (c. 1.500–18.000 litres) they were contextualized in relation to boat capacity.

279	giš-ma₂-60-gur	Boat of 60 gur capacity (1 gur = c. 300 litres)
280	giš-ma₂-50-gur	Boat of 50 gur capacity
281	giš-ma₂-40-gur	Boat of 40 gur capacity
282	giš-ma₂-30-gur	Boat of 30 gur capacity
283	giš-ma₂-20-gur	Boat of 20 gur capacity
284	giš-ma₂-15-gur	Boat of 15 gur capacity
285	giš-ma₂-10-gur	Boat of 10 gur capacity
286	giš-ma₂-5-gur	Boat of 5 gur capacity
287	giš-ma₂-tur	Small boat

(Veldhuis 1997: 157)

Weights were briefly treated in the list of trees and wooden objects, but were more exhaustively presented as stone weights in the section dedicated to stones.

178	na₄-1-gú	Weight of one talent
179	na₄-50-ma-na	Weight of 50 minas
180	na₄-40-ma-na	Weight of 40 minas
181	na₄-30-ma-na	Weight of 30 minas
182	na₄-20-ma-na	Weight of 20 minas
183	na₄-15-ma-na	Weight of 15 minas
184	na₄-10-ma-na	Weight of 10 minas
185	na₄-5-ma-na	Weight of 5 minas
186	na₄-3-ma-na	Weight of 3 minas
187	na₄-2-ma-na	Weight of 2 minas
188	na₄-1-ma-na	Weight of 1 mina
189	na₄-2/3-ma-na	Weight of 2/3 mina
190	na₄-1/2-ma-na	Weight of 1/2 mina
191	na₄-1/3-ma-na	Weight of 1/3 mina
192	na₄-10-gín	Weight of 10 shekels
193	na₄-5-gín	Weight of 5 shekels
194	na₄-3-gín	Weight of 3 shekels

195	na$_4$-2-gín	Weight of 2 shekels
196	na$_4$-1-gín	Weight of 1 shekel
197	na$_4$-2/3-gín	Weight of 2/3 shekel
198	na$_4$-1/2-gín	Weight of 1/2 shekel
199	na$_4$-1/3-gín	Weight of 1/3 shekel
200	na$_4$-igi-4-gál	Weight of a quarter (shekel)
201	na$_4$-igi-5-gál	Weight of a fifth (shekel)
202	na$_4$-22 1/2-še	Weight of 22 1/2 grains
203	na$_4$-20-še	Weight of 20 grains
204	na$_4$-15-še	Weight of 15 grains
205	na$_4$-10-še	Weight of 10 grains
206	na$_4$-5-še	Weight of 5 grains
206a	na$_4$-3-še	Weight of 3 grains
206b	na$_4$-2-še	Weight of 2 grains
206c	na$_4$-1-še	Weight of 1 grain

(Landsberger and Reiner 1970: 60–61; Robson 2002: 333–334; cf. also in Landsberger and Reiner 1970 *ḫubullu* tablet 16, lines 417–452, pp. 15–16; its Rash Shamra recension, lines 343–374, pp. 49–50; late Old Babylonian forerunner, lines 197–204, p. 53).

Once the scribal student learned some systematic knowledge of measures in subsequences of the thematic noun lists, he moved to study the system as a whole in the standard metrological lists of length, area and volume, weight, and capacity (Robson 335–337). They comprise metrological sections usually in the following ranges:

Capacity:	1/3 sila$_3$ — 1 00 00 gur	c. 0.3 — 65 milion litres
Weight:	1/2 še — 1 00 gun	c. 0.05 g — 1800 kg
Area:	1/3 sar — 2 00 00 bur$_3$	c. 12 m^2 — 47000 ha
Length:	1 šu-si — 1 00 danna	c. 17 mm — 650 km
		(Friberg 1987–90: 543)

In the following example of a standard metrological list the weight notations are disposed in an ascending order from 1/2 še (*uṭṭatum*, "barleycorn") to 2 gú (*biltum*, "talent"); note the consistent repetitive order of the fractions 1/3 to 5/6.

Metrological weight list from 1/2 še to 2 gú (Meer 1935: 32–33, no. 59; Early Dynastic period, cf. Damerow 1981: 83; for similarly ordered fractions in metrological lists, cf. Hilprecht 1906: nos. 29, 37, 38; Neugebauer and Sachs 1984: 249; for lenticular school tablets from the Old Babylonian period with fraction metrological exercises, cf. Al-Fouadi 1979, no. 4, 11, 97, 98, 135, 137, 143).

1/2	še
1	še
1 1/2	še
2	še

2 1/2
3
etc.

28	še	
29	še	
igi 6 gál		(= 30 še)
igi 4 gál		(= 45 še)
1/3	gín	(= 60 še)
1/2	gín	(= 90 še)
2/3	gín	(= 120 še)
5/6	gín	(= 150 še)
1	gín	(= 180 še)
1 igi 6 gál		
1 igi 4 gál		
1 1/3	gín	
1 1/2	gín	
1 2/3	gín	
1 5/6	gín	
etc.		

An Old Babylonian *edubba* text attests that this kind of metrological lists belonged to a standard education of the scribe: "Je veux écrire des tablettes: la tablette (des) mesures d'un gur d'orge jusqu'à six-cents gur, la tablette (des poids) d'un sicle jusqu'à vingt mines d'argent. . . . (lines 40–43; text and transl. Civil 1985: 70, 72).

By listing the numerical values of the weight measures, the student acquired the basic knowledge of arithmetical relations between the measures and of the whole metrological system which constitutes the basis of any more sophisticated mathematical operation. Using the *Document*'s terminology, he studied the established metro-arithmetical "order" (סדר), a necessary basic tool in the administrative and economic functioning of the state and temple.

The "wood calculation" of the *Document*, in which numerical data are tabulated in the descending order of the talent fractions, reflects the elementary level of the scribal education found in the thematic noun lists. The standard metrological lists also contain the numerical sequence of the *Document* but in an ascending order. One should also notice that, except for the last notation (15 minas = 1/4), the fractions 5/6, 2/3, 1/2, 1/3 (Tables 11, 12 and 13) are the ones most frequently used in Babylonian school exercises. The rest of the section in the *Document* (*A.L.D.* 37–46a) is related to the same category of metro-arithmetical school exercises. Note that the same set of fractions in descending order is repeated in *A.L.D.* 37–40a. Thus the whole section *A.L.D.* 32a–46a contain samples of Babylonian type of school exercises on sexagesimal numerical system in connection with weight (*A.L.D.* 32a–36; 45–46a) and capacity (37–44) measures. Similarly to the thematic noun lists, *Document*'s notations do not present an exhaustive list of metrological notations, in contrast to standard metrological lists in Babylonian scribal education. This further suggests that the exercises were intended to give to the students first glimpses of the whole metrological system. Metrological lists of area and length are not reflected in the *Document*.

The number and measure notations of the *Document* do not appear in a column, like the Babylonian exercises, which is due to their incorporation into a literary description of meal sacrifice, a practise not attested in Babylonian literature. Their pedagogical function, however, cannot be overlooked, for they are presented as a wisdom instruction which Levi learns from Isaac (cf. *A.L.D.* 13; 15). One should also note that metrological sections in thematic noun lists were contextualized (boat capacity), certainly for pedagogical reasons. Additionally, contextualisation of metrological units took place in model legal contracts studied by scribal apprentices at Nippur (Robson 2002: 337). Some Sumerian literary compositions studied at scribal schools presented metrological concepts and units as essential part of their narration (Robson 2002: 350–352). Similar pedagogical concerns probably led the author of the Aramaic composition when he incorporated the exercises into the description of the meal sacrifice. This literary move also suggested to priestly apprentices the necessity of studying the metro-arithmetical system for a proper execution of priestly duties.

In *A.L.D.* 32a–36 the *Document* adds a second column of mina multiples parallel to the one with talent fractions, establishing a precise ratio 1:10 between the two, which means that the wood for the fat constitutes 1/10 of the wood assigned to the flesh of the animal. By presenting the exercise as part of Levi's sacrificial activity the author intends to demonstrate how Levitical priestly duties depend on, and are linked to, metro-arithmetical knowledge. Establishing the ratio 1:10 between the two sets of numbers most probably serves the same purpose. The Aramaic term for this numerical relation is מעשר "one tenth," and it may also denote the biblical tithe (cf. *A.L.D.* 3a). In the *Document*, however, Levi's priestly ordination in *A.L.D.* 9 is set in the context of his father's tithing (עשר) of the whole property, and Jacob's assignment of the tithe (מעשר) to Levi is part of the ordination ceremony. The *Document*'s move to establish a מעשר between the two sets of numbers in *A.L.D.* 32a–36 may be seen as a kind of "sacred arithmetics" intended to connect metro-arithmetical calculation with the realm of priestly election and duty.

In the light of this interpretation, the *Document*'s description of the amount of wood assigned for the sacrificed animal and for its fat is a literary device created not only to reflect the sacrificial praxis but also to describe a metro-arithmetical exercise. The biblical tradition, in fact, does not differentiate between wood assigned for the animal and its fat. Fat is offered together with the flesh in the burnt offering, but constitutes the main part of the sacrifice burnt on the altar in the communion offering (שלמים; cf. Lev 3:1–17). The fat of the peace sacrifice is offered together with the burnt offering, cf. Lev 3:5. All fat together with blood belongs to God, and, consequently, it is forbidden to consume them (see Lev 3:16b–17; 7:22–27; cf. *A.L.D.* 56). Similarly, the following amounts of sacrificed material in *A.L.D.* 37–46a constitute a metro-arithmetical exercise on fractions, as the underlying numerical pattern indicates it clearly. The metrological lists of the sacrificed material are transmitted by Isaac to Levi who in this way learns not only how to prepare a sacrifice but also how to count using fractions in the sexagesimal system (cf. *A.L.D.* 31 חושבן "calculation," *A.L.D.* 52 λογισμός "calculation," and *A.L.D.* 88, 90, 98 ספר "scribal craft"). Metrological lists with hieratic fractions and numbers in paleo-Hebrew ostraca from Kadesh Barnea indicate that Egyptian numerical tradition was present in seventh century B.C. Israel (cf. Davies 1991: n° 9.003–9.006; Lemaire 1983: 302–326). The *Document*'s lists, however, unequivocally point to the Babylonian scribal training and Babylonian sexagesimal structure of the metrological and mathematical system.

According to the P classification, the sacrificed animals of the *Document*, bull, calf and bullock, are classified as cattle (בקר; see Lev 1:2, 3–9); ram, he-goat, lamb, and all others, belong to the small cattle category (צאן; see Lev 1:2, 10–13). The *Document* follows this priestly distinction, and the animals listed in *A.L.D.* 32a–36 reappear in the following part of the metro-arithmetical exercise (*A.L.D.* 37–46b). The connection, however, between the animals and computational exercise is completely alien to the P tradition.

3.8.4.2 Salt Quantity—A.L.D. 37–40a

Table 12. Seah Fractions and Salt

Animal	Salt (Seah Fractions)	
full-grown bull	σάτον	a seah
second bull	τὰ πέντε μέρη ἀπὸ τῶν ἓξ μερῶν	the five parts out of the six parts (5/6 of a seah)
bullock	τὸ δίμοιρον	the two parts (2/3 of a seah)
ram or he-goat	τὸ ἥμισυ	the half (1/2 seah)
lamb or kid	τὸ τρίτον	the third (1/3 seah)

Already *A.L.D.* 26 discusses the use of salt with the sacrifice. Note that Ezek 43:24 speaks of sprinkling salt on the burnt offering of ram and bull during the dedication of the altar of burnt offering. The phrase "the covenant of salt" ברית מלח (Num 18:19; 2 Chr 13:5; 11QTᵃ XX 14) may have been coined in connection with the sacrificial use of salt (cf. the expression "salt of the covenant" in Lev 2:13; *Jub.* 21:11). The use of salt with the sacrifices seems to be an ancient custom predating the Priestly source (cf. Zimmerli 1983: 434). No biblical text speaks of salting the skin of the sacrificed animal, a norm introduced in *A.L.D.* 37.

In accordance with the biblical capacity system, the seah measure (סאה, Greek σάτον) corresponds to ca. 12 liters (Powell 1992: 904–905). It is attested in the biblical books (Gen 18:6; 1 Sam 25:18; 1 Kgs

18:32; 2 Kgs 7:1, 16, 18) and at Qumran (2Q24 frg. 4 4; 11Q18 frg. 13 4, 5) on a jar and on many ostraca, but never in connection with salt needed for sacrifice. The analysis of its fractions in the table above suggests that it has a sexagesimal structure (*A.L.D.* 38 "the five parts out of the six parts"). Although *A.L.D.* 44 mentions one eighth of the seah, this fraction does not presuppose a decimal division of the measure but a continuation of the metro-arithmetical exercise on fractions. The seah as the main metric unit is abundantly attested in the *Document*'s metrological exercises for measuring salt (*A.L.D.* 38, 38, 39, 40a), fine flour (*A.L.D.* 41, 42, 42), and oil (*A.L.D.* 43, 44, 44). Applying the seah to measure oil shows that, like the Late Babylonian system, the *Document* does not differentiate between liquid and dry measures (Powell 1992: 905).

Similarly to the talent in *A.L.D.* 32a, the seah constitutes the full unit in the metro-arithmetical exercise, and the following fractions represent again the fraction values frequent in the Babylonian metro-arithmetical exercises and first introduced in *A.L.D.* 32a–36. The fraction terminology here and in *A.L.D.* 40b–47 follows a standard Greek way of expressing fractions (Schwyzer 1953: 599), but is influenced by the Babylonian sexagesimal counting system.

3.8.4.3 *Fine Flour—A.L.D. 40b–42*

A.L.D. 40b–46a describes cereal (40b–44), drink (44b) and frankincense (45–46a) offerings that accompany the burnt offering (cf. *A.L.D.* 30). The following *A.L.D.* 46b–47 establishes relations between different measures. The whole *A.L.D.* 40b–47 stands in close connection with Ezek 45:10–46:15 that, similarly to the *Document*, connects the burnt offerings of different animals with a corresponding amount of cereal offerings (Ezek 45:13, 24; 46:5–7, 11, 14–15) and lays out a particular ratio of different measures (Ezek 45:10–12). Any direct literary dependence is, however, difficult to establish.

Table 13. Seah Fractions and Fine Flour

Animal	Fine Flour (Seah Fractions)	
full-grown bull, second bull, bullock	σάτον	a seah (1)
ram or he-goat	τὰ δύο μέρη	the two parts (2/3 seah)
lamb or kid	τὸ τρίτον	the third (1/3 seah)

After the talent (*A.L.D.* 32a–36) and seah (*A.L.D.* 37–40a) fractions, the exercise continues with resuming the seah unit as the departing point, and continues to note fractions in descending order, similarly to the two preceding sections. It starts with fractional measures of fine flour in *A.L.D.* 40b–42 and continues with seah fractions of oil and wine in *A.L.D.* 43–44. The distinction in the text between its first and second part serves the purpose of discussing two different sacrificial materials used in the exercise. The author of the *Document*, however, treated them as one unit, as the descending order of fraction notation indicates.

The amount of fine flour is close to the data found in the book of Ezekiel (Ezek 45:24; 46:5, 7, 11), where one ephah of fine meal is assigned both to a bull and to a ram. Note, that in *A.L.D.* 46b the *Document* equals the seah with ephah, the Greek text. The amount of one tenth of an ephah of fine flour offered as a daily sacrifice in Exod 29:40 and Lev 6:13; 28:3–8 does not correspond to the *Document*'s description. Similarly, the amount assigned with the burnt offering in Num 15:1–12 differs from the quantities described in the *Document*: one tenth of an ephah for a lamb (v. 4 and Num 28:5); two tenths with a ram (v. 6); three tenths for a bull; for the same corresponding amount offered on different feast days, cf. Num 28:12–13, 20–21, 28–29; 29:3–4, 9–10.

3.8.4.4   *Oil and Wine—A.L.D. 43–44*

Table 14. Seah Fractions and Oil

Animal	Oil mixed with fine flour = Wine (Seah Fractions—Continuation)	
bull	τὸ τέταρτον	the fourth (1/4 seah)
ram	τὸ ἔκτον	the sixth (1/6 seah)
lamb	τὸ ὄγδοον	the eighth (1/8 seah)

That the fine flour should be mixed with oil is a general rule in the biblical sacrificial ritual (Exod 29:40; Lev 2:1; 6:14; 7:12; 23:13; Num 6:15; 7:13, 19, etc.). One part of the cereal offering is set aside for the sacrifice, the other is reserved for the priest (Lev 2:2–3; 9–10; 6:7–11; 7:9–10). This distinction is not made in the *Document*, which does not mention priestly portions at all, cf. *Leviticus* 6–7. The *Document* does not distinguish between raw (Lev 2:1–3) and baked (Lev 2:4–10) cereal offering, although adding frankincense to the fine flour (*A.L.D.* 46a; Lev 2:2) suggests that the raw material is being offered (cf. Lev 2:1–3; Exod 29:40). The oil quantity offered with the burnt offering is listed in Num 15:1–12: a fourth of a hin for a lamb (v. 4); a third of a hin for a ram (v. 6); half a hin for a bull (v. 9). A hin is equal to about 6 liters (cf. Powell 1992: 905).

According to the *Document* the amount of the offered wine (*A.L.D.* 44) should follow the measure of oil. The same ruling may be inferred from Num 15:1–12, where the amount of oil mixed with fine flour corresponds to the wine offered as an accompanying libation offering, cf. also Lev 23:13; Num 28:14. Although the proportion is the same, the quantity is different, see above about the oil. Note that the *Document* uses a technical term for the drink offering σπονδή (*A.L.D.* 44; Hebrew נסך, see Exod 29:40, 41; 30:9; Lev 23:13, 18, 37, etc.; cf. *A.L.D.* 30 l. 13). The particular amount of drink offering accompanying the burnt offering is listed in Num 15:1–12: a fourth of a hin.

3.8.4.5 *Frankincense—A.L.D.* 45–46a

Table 15. Multiples of a Shekel

Animal	Frankincense (Multiples of a Shekel)	
bull	ἕξ	six (shekels)
ram	τὸ ἥμισυ αὐτοῦ	the half of it (3 shekels)
kid	τὸ τρίτον	the third of it (2 shekels)
fine flour	δύο	two shekels (1/3)

This is the last part of the fraction exercises, where six is the basic unit and the rest of the notations constitute its fractions in a descending order. The fine flour amount seems to be unrelated to the first three numerical notations, but the comparison with the frankincense value assigned to the kid (1/3 of 6) allows the conclusion that these two are equal.

Nowhere in the biblical text is frankincense added to the burnt offering. Neither is it added to the cereal offering accompanying the burnt offering in Num 15:1–12. However, the rite of the separate cereal offering reports adding frankincense on top of the sacrifice (see Lev 2:1, 15; 6:8). The author of the *Document* probably builds his argument on this biblical reference, for he assigns two shekels of frankincense to the fine flour offered separately from the fat.

3.8.4.6 *Metrological Table—A.L.D. 46b–47*

Table 16. Metrological Relations

τὸ τρίτον τοῦ σάτου	τὸ τρίτον τοῦ ὑφή
τὰ δύο μέρη τοῦ βάτου	ὁλκῆς τῆς μνᾶς ν΄ σίκλων
τοῦ σικλίου τὸ τέταρτον	ὁλκὴ θερμῶν δ΄
ὁ σίκλος	ις΄ θέρμοι

the third of the seah (1/3 seah)	= the third of the ephah (1/3 ephah)
the two parts of the bath (2/3 bath)	= the weight of the mina = 50 shekels
the fourth of the shekel (1/4 shekel)	= the weight of 4 thermoi
the shekel (1 shekel)	= 16 thermoi

The last part of Isaac's metro-arithmetical instruction in *A.L.D.* 31–47 is given as help in the proper administration of the sacrificial material. It should be noted, however, that this set of metric relations between different units may be used in any other economic and social context. It is evident, that without knowledge of relations between capacity measures Isaac's exhortation to keep Levi's work in order, measure, and weight (*A.L.D.* 30–31) could not take place. Levi's execution of "just/true judgment" (*A.L.D.* 1a v. 18) depends on this knowledge that is part of his judicial authority (דין *A.L.D.* 14) as codified in Isaac's teaching (*A.L.D.* 14–47).

The full importance of this section of the *Document* appears in the context of the Neo-Sumerian tradition which associates the proclamation of the system of weights and measures and their reciprocal relations with the royal legislative activity, the purpose of which was to establish justice and truth in the country. In the laws ascribed by scholars first to Ur-Nammu (2112–2095 b.c.), then to Šulgi (2094–2047 b.c.; cf. Kramer 1983: 453–456), Sumerian kings of Ur III dynasty, one section is dedicated precisely to this topic.

"The seven . . . he fixed. He fashioned a bronze *sila*-measure, standardized the *mina*-weight, (and) standardized the silver and stone shekel *in relation to* the mina." (lines 142–149; text and transl. Finkelstein 1969: 67)

The standardized system of weights and measures became a corner stone of the administrative reforms undertaken by royal authority. Levi is presented in the *Document* as a student of the metrological relations so that he might properly exercise his professional duties. In both cases the knowledge of the metrological system and their reciprocal relations belong to the sphere of exercise of justice (cf. the comment on *A.L.D.* 30 and 31).

V. 46b *one third of the seah is one third of the ephah.* The equal value for the fractions of the seah and ephah means that the ephah most probably corresponds in the *Document* to ca. 12 liters, a seah capacity in the post-exilic period (cf. the comment on *A.L.D.* 37–40a). Since this relation does not correspond to its estimated post-exilic size (ca. 36 liters), and 3:1 ratio with the seah (3 seah = 1 ephah/bath = 36 liters, cf. Powell 1992: 904), one should consider the possibility that the Greek translation is corrupt here. According to Ezek 45:13; 46:14, the ephah has a sexagesimal structure, like the seah in the *Document*. One tenth of the ephah is also attested (Lev 5:11; 6:13; Num 5:15; 28:5) indicating that the decimal division has also been in use.

V. 47 *the two parts of a bath and of the weight of a mina are of fifty shekels.* The bath (βάτος/בת) serves to indicate a volume measure in 1 Kgs 7:26, 38; 2 Chr 4:5 (Powell 1992: 902), while in Ezek 45:10, 11, 14 it may also mean a capacity measure and its size is equal to the ephah, as is the case in the *Document* (see above). As a capacity unit it also serves for liquids (2 Chr 2:9; Isa 5:10) but in the *Document* it is not clear whether it denotes a dry or liquid measure. Since the *Document* refers to the capacity units in *A.L.D.* 37–44, it is reasonable to assume that the bath should also be classified in this category. The "two parts" of the bath denote a fraction unit 2/3 in accordance with the Greek fraction notation system—when the numerator is less by one than the denominator, only the article, the numerator, and μέρη are used (Smyth 1984 § 353; for the same fraction notation see *A.L.D.* 42). Since one bath measure in the post-exilic period holds about 36 liters (Powell 1992: 904), its two parts should, therefore, correspond to about 24 liters.

A mina of fifty shekels is attested at Ugarit (Parise 1981: 155–159) and in 1st millennium Assyria (Powell 1992: 906). The *Document* equals the two parts of a bath with a mina of fifty shekels, a relation that may denote a price for 24 liters of grain. That price, however, would be disproportionately high for any kind of grain for, according to the interpretation of Powell (1992: 904), the biblical data suggest the relation 1 ephah = 1 shekel = 12 liters of barley. The Greek text of the *Document* may be corrupt here. One possible interpretation is to treat the bath – mina – shekel relation as nothing else but a part of a theoretical exercise on fractions without any real metrological value. Note that the numerical values in *A.L.D.* 46b–47 are presented first in ascending order (1/3 – 2/3 – 1 = 50), then the *Document* establishes a ratio between the shekel and its fractions (1:16).

one fourth of a shekel is the weight of four thermoi. The noun in plural θέρμοι denoting a weight fraction of a shekel has not been attested in Greek literature. It is, therefore, probable to assume that the Greek translator borrowed the Aramaic lexeme and remodelled its morphological structure to fit the Greek pattern. The reconstructed Aramaic term in singular would be *תרם* (*tǝram*). The Babylonian or Aramaic literature, however, do not attest any occurrence of this form for a shekel fraction (cf. Powell 1979: 93–103). Neither does there exist any technical term for 1/16 of the shekel, a value unequivocally assigned by the *Document* to one "thermos."

The Hittite metrological terminology seems to be helpful in tracing the linguistic origin of the reconstructed Aramaic word. In the Hittite metric capacity system the name of a unit *tarna-* corresponds to the consonants of the Aramaic term with a minor shift of the labials *n > m* in Aramaic. It becomes plausible, therefore, to claim that the reconstructed Aramaic term in the *Document* is a Hittite loan-word that lost its original reference to the capacity system, for it denotes in the *Document* a shekel fraction. Although the metric value of the Hittite *tarna-* has not been established with precision, the available evidence suggests that the term indicates the smallest unit in the whole Hittite capacity system (see van den Hout 1987–90: 523–524). Note that in the *Document*'s metric table it also indicates the smallest shekel fraction. The presence of the Hittite term in the Jewish *Document* comes as no surprise, for the influence of the Hittite culture on the biblical cult, law, and customs has long been recognized and discussed (cf. Weinfeld 1993: 455–472 and the bibliography there). The Hittite loan words are also attested in Hellenistic Greek and Latin (cf. Neumann 1961).

The subdivision of shekel into 16 *thermoi* should not be treated as an actual metrological division, but, in light of the whole section of exercises on fractions (*A.L.D.* 32a–46a), it is only part of the calculation process. The "thermos," therefore, is rather a calculation unit, and not an actual metrological shekel subdivision. In fact, in the Babylonian weight terminology there exist shekel fractions of 3/4 and 5/6 that do not reflect any metrological reality but serve as units of calculation only (Powell 1979: 100–101).

3.8.5 *Final Exhortation—A.L.D. 48–50*

De Jonge's opinion (1953b:39) that *A.L.D.* 48–61 is one literary unit is debatable, because, from the literary point of view, *A.L.D.* 48–50 end Isaac's instruction which began in *A.L.D.* 14. Becker (1970: 89) affirms that *A.L.D.* 40–50 are parallel to *A.L.D.* 57–60. The structure and vocabulary analysis does not confirm his assertion. *A.L.D.* 57 repeats much of *A.L.D.* 50 and adds an observation concerning blood, a dominant topic of the whole section, vv. 51–57. *A.L.D.*

58–61 are not exhortatory in nature and lack the key term of *A.L.D.* 48–50 that is ἐντέλλομαι.

V. 48 *And now.* The expression forms an *inclusio* (*A.L.D.* 49; 51) that marks off the section. *A.L.D.* 48–50 constitute the closing part of the Isaac's speech (*A.L.D.* 14–50) and its vocabulary is linked to the beginning of the instructions (cf. "my son" [*A.L.D.* 14, 15, 16 and 48], "holy priest" [*A.L.D.* 17 and 48], "law" [*A.L.D.* 13, 15, 49; cf. 15], "to instruct, command" [*A.L.D.* 13 פקד and 49, 50, 50 ἐντέλλομαι]).

listen to my words and hearken to my commandments. The Greek verbs ἀκούω and ἐνωτίζομαι most probably translate the Aramaic שמע and הצית, cf. *A.L.D.* 83b. The clause belongs to a common stock of biblical language (see especially Exod 15:26 [LXX]; Num 23:18 [LXX] Bar 3:9; cf. also Judg 5:3; Ps 49:2; Job 33:1, 31; 34:2; Hos 5:1; Joel 1:2, etc.). Here it is part of a sapiential literary pattern that may be dubbed "teacher's closing formula," (*A.L.D.* 48–50; cf. the comment on *A.L.D.* 15 and 83b). Isaac finishes his wisdom instruction with an exhortation to observe his teaching (*A.L.D.* 48) and to transmit it to the future priestly generations (*A.L.D.* 49) in the same way as he received it from Abraham (*A.L.D.* 50). Note that the Enochic *Astronomical Book* (*1 En.* 72–82) containing astronomical calculation ends with the same sapiential pattern (cf. the comment on *A.L.D.* 15).

let these my words not leave your heart. Levi's "heart," a Semitic metaphor for "mind," is a privileged storeroom of both his visionary experience (7:13) and Isaac's priestly instruction. In his prayer (1a v. 14) he requests that God purify his heart from every impurity as a necessary condition of staying close to the Lord of heaven who knows every human heart (1a v. 5). When instructing his children in the wisdom poem, he teaches them everything that was in his heart (82:6–7). This introduction to the poem makes clear that Levi intends to teach his sons/disciples priestly wisdom transmitted to him by Isaac (cf. *A.L.D.* 82 and 83b).

you are a holy priest of the Lord. For Levi's holiness, cf. the exposition of *A.L.D.* 17. Note that Isaac connects Levi's holiness with his whole wisdom instruction: that is, with the due order (סרך *A.L.D.* 30–31) of priestly activity and the rules concerning priestly endogamy (*A.L.D.* 17) and purity in general (*A.L.D.* 14; 16; 18).

V. 49 *and all your seed will be priests.* This statement assumes that the whole Levitical tribe (Gershon, Qahat and Merari) inherits the priestly vocation, in contrast to *A.L.D.* 64 where Gershon is excluded from the priesthood.

and command your sons. The dominant concept in *A.L.D.* 49–50 is ἐντέλλομαι "to command" (49, 49, 50) that most probably translates the Aramaic פקד (13 l. 7; 82 l. 6; 84 l. 9). The Greek term also appears in the following redactional addition (*A.L.D.* 51–57) with Isaac (*A.L.D.* 52) and Abraham (*A.L.D.* 57) as subjects. The transmission of priestly teaching becomes a condition of priestly service and is rooted in Abraham's authority, cf. *A.L.D.* 22 ll. 11–12; 57.

The Greek term ἐντέλλομαι is an important notion in *T. 12 Patr.*, but its meaning there differs from the use of the *Document*. The Greek term in the *T. 12 Patr.* sometimes summarizes the whole Testament (*T. Reu.* 1:1, 5; 7:1; *T. Sim.* 8:1; *T. Levi* 19:4; *T. Naph.* 9:1), or introduces the last wish of the dying patriarch (*T. Ash.* 8:1; *T. Benj.* 12:1; *T. Jud.* 26:4; *T. Iss.* 7:8; *T. Ash.* 8:2; cf. *T. Naph.* 9:3). The third application of the term in the *Testaments* refers to the patriarch's moral teaching and underlines the necessity of passing it down to next generations to assure a future for them (*T. Reu.* 4:5; 6:8; *T. Sim.* 7:3; *T. Levi* 10:1; 13:1; *T. Jud.* 13:1; 17:1; cf. *T. Reu.* 6:2). None of the *Testaments'* uses of the term apply to the context of the *Document*. Although the biblical references suggest the testamentary setting for Isaac's speech, the *Document* does not mention it at all (cf. *A.L.D.* 13). His instructions, therefore, are not his last will but constitute a teaching necessary to perform priestly and administrative functions. Levi is to command his sons not to assure a future for them but because they too are to be priests (*A.L.D.* 49); additionally, Levitical priesthood is eternal, without limits in time (see *A.L.D.* 3b; 6; 58–60; *A.L.D.* 100). Furthermore, when Levi transmits the commandments to his sons (*A.L.D.* 82–98), he does not do it on his deathbed, a detail characteristic to testamentary literature, but in the year 118 of his life on the occasion of Joseph's death (cf. *A.L.D.* 82). The redactor(s) of the *Testament of Levi* greatly reduced Isaac's speech to a few verses (9:6–14) simply because its content and purpose did not correspond to the characteristics of the *Testaments* and their concentration on exclusively moral or ethical issues (cf. Hollander and de Jonge 1985: 31–32). Similarly, Isaac's order to commend the priestly precepts to Levi's children (*A.L.D.* 49–50) became Levi's general exhortation set in the context of future apostasy (*T. Levi* 10:1–5).

according to this law. For the term κρίσις "law," see the comment on *A.L.D.* 13 and 15.

as I have shown you. The verb ὑποδείκνυμι "to show, indicate" underlines the sapiential character of Isaac's instructions (cf. *A.L.D.* 15). Note that the Greek ὁ πατήρ stands without any pronominal suffix, and thus it supposes Aramaic אבא (see *A.L.D.* 10 l. 23).

V. 50 *For thus father Abraham commanded me to do.* Cf. *A.L.D.* 22–23.

3.8.6 *Sacrifice, Ablution, Blood, and Blessing—A.L.D. 51–61*

Form and Structure

Stylistically, *A.L.D.* 51–61 is divided into two parts (*A.L.D.* 51–57 and 58–61) by an *inclusio* "and now, (my son; child Levi)" in *A.L.D.* 51, 58 and 61. The section is a redactional addition to the main speech of Isaac (*A.L.D.* 14–50) stemming from a reflection on the *Document*'s teaching. *A.L.D.* 51–57 were composed to expressly root

Levi's authority in the teaching of Noah concerning blood. This teaching is not the only connection of the *Document* with the Noahic literature (see the comment on *A.L.D.* 1c, 7 and 73). *A.L.D.* 51–57 can be thematically divided into two parts. The first one (*A.L.D.* 51–53a, 54) has many vocabulary contacts with the preceding Isaac's speech and serves as a connection with the Noahic teaching presented in the second one (*A.L.D.* 53b, 55–57). This teaching has its counterpart in *Jub.* 7:30–32 which belongs to the Noahic section in the book of *Jubilees*. The following verses (*A.L.D.* 58–61) discuss the eternal election of Levi and his sons to the priesthood. The frequent occurrence of the lexeme πᾶς "all, every" in *A.L.D.* 51–59 (52; 52; 53; 53; 54; 54; 55; 55; 56) marks a generalizing tendency of the section different from the particular prescriptions in *A.L.D.* 14–47.

De Jonge (1953b: 39) considers *A.L.D.* 48–61 to be a repetition of what has been said before. Becker (1970: 89–91) criticizes de Jonge's opinion and affirms that *A.L.D.* 51–60 forms a separate speech (A II) that is close to *Jub.* 21. His analysis concentrates on the similarity of the discussed topic (blood) and similarity of the consecutive order of the discussed themes: wood (*Jub.* 21:11–15 and *A.L.D.* 52), ablutions (*Jub.* 21:16f. and *A.L.D.* 53f.), and blood (*Jub.* 21:6, 17–20 and *A.L.D.* 55–57). This is a reversed order of *A.L.D.* 14–50, 61 (A I) which discusses the ablutions first, and then gives the list of trees for the sacrifice. Becker is right in indicating *A.L.D.* 51–60 as a separate unit, but his attempt to present it as a separate speech parallel to *Jub.* 21 cannot stand a critical scrutiny. The vocabulary of *A.L.D.* 51–54 has many contacts with *A.L.D.* 14–50 and some items cannot be understood without reference to the preceding part of the speech. Additionally, *A.L.D.* 51–57 does not run parallel to *Jub.* 21 as many exceptions in Becker's list indicate (1970: 90). He also does not explain the presence of *A.L.D.* 58–60 in the complex section of *A.L.D.* 51–61. These three verses do not correspond to any part of *Jub.* 21.

According to Becker (1970: 89), *A.L.D.* 61 is the closing sentence of Isaac's first speech, *A.L.D.* 14–50, 61. However, the vocabulary analysis indicates that *A.L.D.* 61 is linked to *A.L.D.* 59 (eternal blessing on earth for Levi's descendants); there is, therefore, no reason to dislocate it from its present position in the *Document*. The *inclusio* "and now . . . son" (*A.L.D.* 58 and 61) marks off the section. There is no corresponding material for *A.L.D.* 58–61 either in the book of *Jubilees* or in the *Testament of Levi*.

V. 51 *I rejoice that you have been chosen for the holy priesthood.* In *A.L.D.* 12 Isaac rejoices when he meets the whole family arriving at his place. Here his joy stems from Levi's election to the priesthood (cf. *A.L.D.* 12; and also *Jub.* 31:21; *T. Levi* 18:5, 14). The lexeme ἐκλέγω in the LXX often translates the Hebrew בחר (see, e.g., Gen 6:2; 13:11, etc). Levi's election to priesthood is sanctioned in the *Document* by the visionary revelation and earthly ordination. The verse echoes *A.L.D.* 9–10 where Levi is chosen by his father and ordained a priest of God the most high to whom he offers sacrifice. The reason for the election is made clear in *A.L.D.* 58–61. He enjoys his father's preferential love, he is God's holy one, and his name is brought into the book of remembrance of life forever. *T. Levi* 4:2 suggests that the election took place as an answer to Levi's prayer. Although Levi's prayer in *A.L.D.* 1a is in fact a plea for priesthood, the *Document* is not as explicit as the *Testament*, which may be due to the fragmentary state of the visionary material. Neither does his zeal in executing righteousness and judgment appear as the motif of divine election to the priesthood (see *Jub.* 30:18).

and to offer sacrifice. The term θυσία (*A.L.D.* 51, 52) translates in the LXX an array of sacrificial concepts (cf. Behm 1965: 181; Daniel 1966: 203–246); it is best understood here as referring in a general sense to any offered sacrifice. In *T. Reu.* 6:8 Levi disposes of judgment and sacrifices (κρίσιν καὶ θυσίας) for all Israel (cf. also *T. Levi.* 9:7, 11, 13, 14). Note, however, that the *Document* discusses only the burnt offering of a bull (*A.L.D.* 25a l. 21). The nominalized passive perfect participle of προστάσσω suggests that Isaac mainly refers to the already expounded instructions. The next v. 52 further clarifies that instructions laid down in *A.L.D.* 31–47 are meant here.

In Deut 21:5 the election of Levitical priests is connected with their judicial authority. Their additional functions consist in serving God and blessing his people. For the use of בחר in relation to Levitical priesthood and to liturgical functions, see Deut 18:5; Num 16:5, 7; 17:20; 1 Chr 15:2; 2 Chr 29:11 (cf. Preuß 1992: 56). 4Q545 4 19 speaks of Aaron (?) who "will be chosen as eternal priest" יתבחר לכהי עלמין. In the *Document*, however, Levi is chosen to priesthood as "God's servant," παῖς (*A.L.D.* 1a v. 17). This fact makes his election similar to Jacob's choice as God's servant in Isa 41:8–9; 42:1 (LXX); 44:1–2.

V. 52 *to make before the Lord from every flesh.* The verb ποιεῖν has a cultic connotation here as in *A.L.D.* 31, 49, 50, 51. The expression ἀπὸ πάσης σαρκός may denote either human beings (*A.L.D.* 14) or the sacrificed flesh (*A.L.D.* 54; cf. *A.L.D.* 55). Here it undoubtedly points to *A.L.D.* 31–47 with their enumeration of sacrificed animals.

accept thus as I order you. Levi is instructed to proceed according to Isaac's commands concerning reckoning of wood and receive from the offerers salt, fine meal, wine, and frankincense. This verse refers to the instructions given in the preceding section *A.L.D.* 31–47. Reckoning of wood is discussed in *A.L.D.* 31–36, salt in *A.L.D.* 37–40a, fine meal in *A.L.D.* 40b–42 and 45–46a, oil and wine in *A.L.D.* 43–44, and frankincense in *A.L.D.* 45. The expression "from their hands" most probably refers to lay offerers who bring their gifts to the altar. In contrast to Lev 1–5, their participation in the sacrificial ritual is reduced to a minimum in the *Document*.

V. 53 *wash the hands and the feet*. Ritual ablutions mentioned here and at *A.L.D.* 54 refer to ablutions discussed earlier in the composition. *A.L.D.* 53a has its counterpart in Levi's second ablution (*A.L.D.* 21), while *A.L.D.* 54, set in the context of blood contamination, is closely related to *A.L.D.* 26.

let no blood adhere to your garment. The instructions concerning blood (*A.L.D.* 53b, 55–56) discuss only two topics: prohibition to have priestly garments stained with blood (*A.L.D.* 53b and 55a) and prohibition to eat meat with blood (*A.L.D.* 56). The first one recalls Lev 6:20 which rules that if the blood of the sin offering touches the garment, the priest has to wash it in the temple court.

V. 55 *the blood is the soul in the flesh*. The rule that regards blood as a life's principle (*A.L.D.* 55b) is also a common biblical *topos* (see Gen 9:4; Lev 17:11, 14; Deut 12:23). Differently from the *Document*, however, it justifies there the prohibition to eat blood (cf. Schwartz 1991: 43–45, 48–50). The *Document* uses the rule to explain why any contact with blood is to be avoided.

V. 56 *hide its blood in the earth first*. The order not to eat blood and to cover it with earth is found in Lev 17:13 (cf. Ezek 24:7–8; 11QTᵃ LIII 5–6). This rule stems most probably from the conviction that what offends God should be hidden from his sight (cf. Gen 37:26; Deut 23:14; 1 Sam 26:20; Isa 26:21; Job 16:18). The general prohibition of eating with blood is found in the historical books (1 Sam 14:32–34), in the Pentateuch (Gen 9:4; Lev 3:17; 7:26–27; 17:10, 12; 19:26; Deut 12:16, 23; 15:23), and in the prophetic writings (Ezek 33:25).

V. 57 *my father Abraham ordered me*. Abraham's authority for the legal pre-scriptions is also recalled in *A.L.D.* 22 and 50. The first part of the verse copies *A.L.D.* 50a, the second part points to the book of Noah as the source of Abraham's knowledge.

the writing of the Book of Noah. The Greek expression ἐν τῇ γραφῇ τῆς βίβλου τοῦ Νῶε is easily retroverted into Aramaic: בכתבא די ספר נוח (cf. 1QapGen V 29 פרשגן כתב מלי נוח[ן] "Copy of the writing of the words of Noah["). Ezra 6:18 preserves the *Document*'s expression with a reference to Moses. On the day of the dedication of the temple, the priests and Levites are set for the service of God at Jerusalem "according to the writing of the book of Moses" κατὰ τὴν γραφὴν βιβλίου Μωυσῆ (LXX), ככתב ספר משה (MT). In the light of this comparison, it is certain that the *Document* considers the *Book of Noah* as an authoritative text. Note that, according to *Jub.* 6:11, Noah's covenant is stipulated in the third month, in which the Sinaitic covenant also took place (see Exod 19:1). In the NT the lexeme γραφή in singular denotes an OT passage (e.g. Mark 12:10; Luke 4:21; John 7:38, 42) or Scripture as a whole (e.g. John 2:22; 17:2; 20:9).

For other titles of Aramaic books, cf. 4Q534 1 i 5 "three books" תלתת ספריא (cf. Puech 2001: 137–138); 4Q204 frg. 1 vi 9 "book of the words of truth," ספר מלי קושט]א; 4Q541 frg. 7 4 "books of wisdom," ספרי חכמ]תא, cf. *Jub.* 12:27; 4Q542 1 ii 12 (Qahat's books); 4Q543 1a, b, c, 1 "Copy of the writing of the words of the vision of Amram" כתב מלי חזות עמרם פרשגן; 4Q529 1 1 "Words of the writing that Michael said to the angels" מלי כתבא די אמר מיכאל למלאכיא (cf. Puech 2001: 4).

According to *Jub.* 7:38, Noah is the repository of the Enochic wisdom passed down to him in the books given to him by his father, Lamech. In *Jub.* 10:14 Noah passes his books to his son, Shem; in *Jub.* 21:10 Abraham states that he found the instructions concerning sacrifices and eating meat in the words of Enoch and Noah. In *Jub.* 45:16 Jacob passes all his books and the books of his fathers to Levi that he might preserve them and renew them for his children. Mentioning of the book of Noah in the *Document* serves to connect the priestly wisdom Isaac passes to Levi with the prediluvian patriarch. On the other hand, it makes clear that Levi is the only depository of this wisdom.

concerning the blood. Although prescriptions concerning blood in *A.L.D.* 53b, 55–56 are close to Lev 6:20 and 17:13, the *Document* ascribes them to the *Book of Noah.* In *Jub.* 7:30–32 they belong to the Noahic section of the book, and the supposition that they were part of a separate Noahic book cannot be excluded altogether. Large portions of *1 Enoch, Jubilees,* and 1QapGen extensively discuss and exegetically develop the Genesis account concerning Noah and the flood story (see García Martínez 1992: 24–44). *A.L.D.* 7 and 73 indicate some parallelism with the Noahic section of 1QapGen.

Similarly to the *Document,* the *Apocalypse of Weeks* traces the origins of the dietary rules back to Noah. The first week of world history in which Enoch is born is still characterized by righteousness (4Q212 iii 23–24 = *1 En.* 93:3). In the second week, however, deceit and violence (שקרא וחמסא) spring up (4Q212 iii 25 = *1 En.* 93:4). Then will come the first end and one man (Noah) shall be saved (*1 En.* 93:4). Then in the same second week unrighteousness grows and Noah makes a law (*śərat*) for the sinners (*1 En.* 93:4; for the text-critical problems, cf. Black 1985: 289; Dexinger 1977: 111–112). This law may be considered as a reference to the dietary rules in Gen 9:1–6 in the context of the Noahic covenant (Gen 8:20–9:17), or it may refer to *Jub.* 7:20–39 where Noah's teaching is separate from the covenantal context. Since Isaac's speech in *A.L.D.* 51–61 is influenced by *Jub.* 7:20–39 from the ideological and literary points of view, the reference to the Noahic law in the *Apocalypse of Weeks* may only refer to Noah's teaching in the book of *Jubilees* (cf. Dexinger 1977: 124).

V. 58 *beloved son.* This verse justifies Levi's election to the holy priesthood, cf. *A.L.D.* 51. He is proclaimed a beloved son, a holy one of the Lord most high, and beloved more than all his brothers. Levi's appellative τέκνον ἀγαπητόν most probably translates the Aramaic בר חביב, cf. *A.L.D.* 14 and

84 l. 10 (חביבי "my beloved"; see 4Q539 2 2; 4Q204 1 vi 16 [*1 En.* 14:6 G]; *T. Sim.* 4:7). It is used in the Pauline letters to express not physical but faith relationship (1 Cor 4:14, 17; Eph 5:1; 2 Tim 1:2). Only here, however, it is used in the context of election to the eternal priesthood and underlines Levi's status—he is beloved by his father and beloved by God (see *A.L.D.* 83b l. 9). The affirmation that Levi is chosen to be God's son in *T. Levi* 4:2 most probably stems from the reflection on these two titles of Levi in the *Document* and not from a scribal error (Greenfield and Stone 1990: 157). Given the fragmentary state of the *Document*'s visions, it cannot be excluded *a priori* that Levi has actually been called God's son in his visions.

Levi is proclaimed beloved by his father more than the rest of his brothers. Gen 37:3–4 affirms that Joseph enjoys Jacob's preferential love and the *Testaments* faithfully follow this tradition (see especially *T. Dan* 1:5 and also *T. Sim.* 2:6; *T. Gad* 1:5; *T. Jos.* 1:2; 10:5). The *Document* changes this option in line with Jacob's election of Levi from among his brothers (see *A.L.D.* 9 l. 18). Note that the LXX uses the nominalized pass. participle ὁ ἠγαπημένος for Jacob (Deut 32:15; 33:5, 36; Isa 44:2), Abraham (2 Chr 20:7); without the article: Benjamin (Deut 33:12), Moses (Sir 45:1); Samuel (Sir 46:13). The expression ἄγιος κυρίου ὑψίστου (קדיש לאל עליון?) not only underlines Levi's holiness (see *A.L.D.* 17), but suggests his closeness to angels defined in *A.L.D.* 18 l. 22 as "His holy ones" קדישוהי. For the word-pair ἠγαπημένος and ἄγιος in the context of divine election, see Col 3:12.

Levi's designation as God's beloved ידיד אל in *A.L.D.* 83 l. 9 should be interpreted in the context of *A.L.D.* 58. It makes clear that Levi's election to the priesthood is rooted not only in Jacob's preferential love for him, but in God's love as well. The expression is taken from Deut 33:12 (ידיד יהוה) where it refers to Benjamin and is translated by the LXX with ἠγαπημένος ὑπὸ κυρίου (see also Isa 5:1, 1; cf. Jer 11:5). Also Solomon bears a similar title ידידיה in 2 Sam 12:25 and 4Q522 9 ii 8. The adjective ידיד is also rendered by ἀγαπητός in Ps 59:7; 107:7; 126:2. In the *Document*'s expression, the nominalized adjective ידיד stands in a construct chain פקודי ידיד אל with the following relation [N₁ + [N₂ + N₃]]. In the syntagm ידיד אל, the adjective is nominalized and serves as *nomen regens* for אל. It could be rendered in Greek with the article ὁ ἠγαπημένος/ἀγαπητὸς (τοῦ) κυρίου, cf. *T. Benj.* 11:2. In 4Q379 1 2, Levi is placed in the list of the twelve tribes before the firstborn Reuben, and is called "Levi, the beloved" לוי ידיד. The context, however, is broken and does not allow a closer examination. Note that when the *Testament of Amram* describes the future ideal priest, most probably Aaron (cf. 5Q545 frg. 4 15), it describes him as the "seventh among the men of [his] pleasure" שביעי באנוש רעות]ה (4Q545 4 18).

V. 59 *There will be blessing by your seed on the earth.* This clause constitutes an implicit reference to the blessing promised to Abraham by God in Gen 12:3: "and by you all the families of the earth will bless themselves." Levi's children become the source of blessing for the earth.

the book of the memorial of life. The priestly election is further confirmed by the affirmation that Levi's descendants will be recorded forever in the book of the memorial of life. This is motivated by Levi's holiness (*A.L.D.* 17; 58) and his election to the holy priesthood (*A.L.D.* 51, cf. *A.L.D.* 3b; 9; 13). Sinners do not find place in the book written by God, but will be blotted out from it (see Exod 32:32–33). In Mal 3:16 a book of remembrance is written before God about those who fear the Lord and think of his name; they, therefore, belong to God and constitute his special property (סגלה), God will spare them as a man who spares his son (Mal 3:17). The *Document's* expression βιβλίον μνημοσύνου ζωῆς is related to Mal 3:16 ספר זכרון (LXX βιβλίον μνημοσύνου), and to the expression found in Ps 69:29 ספר חיים (LXX βίβλος ζώντων). The Psalmist makes a case against his oppressors and asks God to blot them out from the book of the living, so that they may not be enrolled with the righteous. Note that the Hebrew חיים in Ps 69:29 may also be rendered in Greek by ζωή as is most probably the case in the *Document.* Both Exod 32:32 and Ps 69:29 use the verb מחה/ἐξαλείφω that strengthens the connection with the *Document's* passage. *A.L.D.* 60 states that Levi's name and that of his descendants will not be blotted out (ἐξαλειφθήσεται) forever (contrast *A.L.D.* 3a l. 6). There is no reason to suspect that the concept of life here refers to eternal life. The formula, however, appears to bridge the exegetical gap between the biblical texts referred to above, and later apocalyptic literature in which the term "book of life" is widely used (cf. *1 En.* 108:3; *Jub.* 30:22; 36:10; Rev 13:8; 17:8; 20:12; 21:27; for the Hebrew ספר החיים, see 4Q381 frg. 31 8; 4Q504 frgs. 1–2 vi [Puech col. XVII] 14). Although Levi is instructed to keep the commandments (*A.L.D.* 48) and to teach them to his descendants (*A.L.D.* 49; cf. *A.L.D.* 83b l. 8), recording of Levi's offspring in the book of the remembrance of life does not explicitly depend on keeping the commandments. Consequently, the principle of keeping the commandments in order to have life established by Lev 18:5 seems not to apply here. Levi's recording in the book of the remembrance of life is God's pure gift, based on Jacob's predilection and God's love for Levi (cf. *A.L.D.* 58).

The origins of the metaphor of the heavenly book of life are most probably connected to the presentation of God as judge of humanity (cf. Ps 149:9; Dan 7:10; Rev 20:12; Koep 1952: 28–30). Mentioning of the book of remembrance of life in the *Document* serves another purpose, however. It expresses the belief that Levi's election to the priesthood will last forever. Even the sinful future described in *A.L.D.* 101–104 cannot cancel God's election of the holy and beloved one (*A.L.D.* 58) to the holy priesthood (*A.L.D.* 51). His name and the name of his descendants will never be blotted out from the book. It is the reason why, after the period of sinfulness, a future restoration is assured (*A.L.D.* 102 ll. 8–9).

V. 61 *your seed will be blessed on the earth for all the generations of the ages.* Blessing bestowed on Levi's descendants is another sign of divine election to an eternal priesthood (see *A.L.D.* 1a v. 16 and 3b l. 3; 8; cf. *Jub.* 30:18; 31:13–17). In the *Testament of Qahat* (4Q542 1 ii 2–3) the patriarch promises his sons that all the words of truth shall come upon them and "the eternal blessings shall dwell on you" ברכת עלמא ישכונן עליכון. This particular blessing stands in the context of Qahat's teaching, and most probably its fulfillment depends on whether his sons follow the truth transmitted to them (cf. 4Q542 1 i 4, 8; 1 ii 1–2).

3.9   *Genealogy and Autobiography—A.L.D. 62–81*

Form and Structure

Table 17. Literary Structure of the Birth Account—*A.L.D.* 63–72

	Gershon	Qahat	Merari	Yochebed
1. Conception	63	66	69a	71 l. 18
2. Birth	63	66	69a	71 l. 19
3. Naming	63	66	69a	71 ll. 19–20
4. Midrash on the name	63–64	67	69a; 69b	71 ll. 20–21
5. Year of Levi's life	65	68	70 ll. 16–17	72 l. 22
6. Birth month	65	68	70 l. 17	72 l. 23
7. Hour of the day	65	68	omitted	omitted

The narrative section interrupted by Isaac's speech (*A.L.D.* 14–50) and redactional additions (*A.L.D.* 51–61) continues with the description of Levi's marriage and birth of his children (*A.L.D.* 62–73 l. 2); then another section is dedicated to the marriage of his sons and the birth of the grandsons (*A.L.D.* 73 l. 2–77) with special attention given to Amram (*A.L.D.* 75–77). The third part (*A.L.D.* 78–81) reviews more important events of Levi's life and ends with a statement concerning the total number of years of his life span. Redactional activity is also detectable in *A.L.D.* 69a, 69b and 75. The genealogical interest of the *Document* corresponds to the preoccupations of the post-exilic community to trace its roots to the forefathers. The genealogies of 1 *Chronicles* may serve here as an example. In Neh 7:63–65 a group of priests is excluded from the priesthood as unclean (נאל) because their names have not been found written in their family records. *A.L.D.* 62–81 constitutes such a record for Levi and his descendants to justify the priestly origin for the future priestly generations. It also reinterprets biblical data to justify the *Document*'s claim to scribal hierocracy in the post-exilic Judean community (for the ideological motivations in the genealogical compositions in the ancient Near East and in the Old Testament, cf. Wilson 1977; for the role of Levitical genealogies in the formation of the post-exilic Judean community, cf. Laato 1994).

The autobiography section concentrates on Levi's person, but it assigns to Qahat and Amram leading positions in the future continuation of the Levitical priestly line. Levi in his prophetic visionary experience foresees their future (64, 67, 76) and the future of his priestly descendants in *A.L.D.* 99–104. The chronological details deal mostly with Levi's life and its main events, agreeing in most cases with the priestly chronology preserved in the *Testaments of the Twelve Patriarchs*, the *Testament of Amram*, and, it seems, 4Q559 as well (for a detailed study of the testamental chronology and its relation to the biblical text, cf. Grelot 1971: 383–394; Grelot 1975: 559–570; for 4Q559, cf. Wise 1997: 3–51). In the following commentary the third century B.C. Demetrius' chronology has been compared with the *Document* only to find an essential difference in chronological approach over against the *Document*. The *Jubilees* chronology is mostly flawed in the text translation and transmission (cf. the note to *Jub.* 28:11–24 in Charles 1902: 170–172).

Testament of Levi 11–12 presents a shorter form of the *Document*'s section. *T. Levi* 11 reflects *A.L.D.* 62–73 l. 2, that is, Levi's marriage and the birth of his children; *T. Levi* 12:1–4 corresponds to *A.L.D.* 73 l. 2–75 that deals with the marriage of Levi's sons and Amram, Qahat's son; *T. Levi* 12:5–6 is close to *A.L.D.* 78–81 that reports important facts in Levi's life. From the literary point of view, the *Testament* is far less elaborate than the *Document*. The regular literary structure of the birth account in *A.L.D.* 62–73 l. 2 is lost in the *Testament*, which concentrates on the midrashic explanations of the names. There also occur some chronological differences between the *Levi Document* and the *Testament* (see *A.L.D.* 78–81). *Jub.* 30–32 omits the section altogether.

Table 18. The Chronology of Levi's Life

Event	Day	Month	Year	A.L.D. Reference
Entry into Canaan			18th	78
Killing of the Shechemites			18th	78
Priesthood			19th	79
Marriage			28th	62; 79
Gershon's birth	at sunset	10th	30th	65
Qahat's birth	at sunrise, 1st	1st	34th	68
Merari's birth		3rd	40th	70
Entry into Egypt			48th	80
Yochebed's birth	1st	7th	64th	72
Amram's birth	on the same day as Yochebed			77
Marriage of Amram and Yochebed			94th	75
Living in Egypt			89	80
Joseph's death			118th	82
Death			137th	81

3.9.1 Marriage and Children—A.L.D. 62–73

V. 62 *And when four weeks were fulfilled*. Mentioning of four weeks of years indicates that the *Document* utilizes the time division into weeks of years attested in *Daniel* 9, *Ethiopic Enoch*, *Jubilees*, and some Qumran writings (cf. VanderKam 1998). This suggests that the *Document* follows the solar calendar used by the authors of these books. According to Greenfield and Stone (1979: 224), another indication for that calendar option is that the months are numbered, not named (*A.L.D.* 65; 68 l. 9; 70 l. 17; 72 l. 23).

I took a wife for myself from the family of Abraham my father. Levi appears to obey the command of his grandfather to marry a woman from Abraham's family. The principle of endogamy is thus confirmed in his life and set as an example for future priestly generations (cf. the comment on *A.L.D.* 17). Levi also takes care that his sons intermarry within the family (*A.L.D.* 73 ll. 2–4), and his daughter Yochebed marries her nephew, Amram (*A.L.D.* 75).

Melcha, a daughter of Bathuel, son of Laban, brother of my mother. The purpose of Melcha's genealogy is clear, but the comparison with biblical data creates some problems. By introducing Melcha's genealogy the author of the *Document* intended to show that Levi continues the example of his grandfather and father, whose wives, Rebecca, Lea, and Rachel, came from the same branch of Abraham's family. In the *Document*, however, Laban is Bathuel's father and Melcha's grandfather, hence the genealogy does not follow the biblical data. In Gen 11:29; 22:23; 24:15, 24, 47, Melcha is a daughter of Haran and wife of Nahor, Abraham's brother. She is also mother of Bathuel, Rebecca's father. Consequently, Laban, Rebecca's brother, is also Bathuel's son (see Gen 28:5), while Laban is the father, not the brother, of Lea, Levi's mother (see Gen 29:16).

In order to solve these incongruencies one may recur to the well attested Semitic custom of papponymy (naming a son after his grandfather). In that case, the clause in the *Document* "brother of my mother" would refer to Bathuel, son of Laban, and grandson of Bathuel, son of Nahor. The author thus expands Laban's biblical genealogy which does not mention any of Laban's sons by name (cf. Gen 31:1). He also introduces another, non-biblical Melcha, a daughter of Laban's son. This exegetical move was necessary to create for Levi a wife whose age would approximate that of Levi and who would come from the family of his mother. The name of Levi's wife is also cited by *Jub.* 34:20, but not by biblical sources. Note that the Greek βαθουήλ and Μελχά follow the LXX vocalization and not the one of the MT בְּתוּאֵל and מִלְכָּה.

Table 19. Melcha and Levi's Genealogy

```
                            Terah
        ┌───────────────────────┴───────────────────┐
      Haran                                   Abraham = Sarah
   ┌────┼──────────────────┐                         │
 Iscah  Lot        Melcha = Nahor                     │
                          │                           │
                       Bathuel                        │
   ┌──────────────────────┴───────┐        ┌──────────┴──────────┐
 Laban                        Rebecca = Isaac                 Ishmael
   ┌──────┬──────────────┐         ┌────────┴──────────┐
 Bathuel  Rachel    =    Lea = Jacob                 Esau
   │              ┌──────┴──────┐        ┌──────────┴──────┐
 Melcha = Levi  Reuben      Simeon    Judah, etc.
```

V. 63 *And she conceived by me, bore the first son, and I called his name Gershom.* The set of expressions ἐν γαστρὶ(συλ)λαμβάνω/הרה, τίκτω/ילד, and κάλεω τὸ ὄνομα/שם קרי (*A.L.D.* 66; 69a; 71) is frequent in the biblical birth narratives and often it occurs with an onomastic midrash (see Gen 16:11; Isa 7:14; 8:3; Gen 29:32, 33, 34, 35; 1 Sam 1:20; Isa 8:3; Hos 1:6; 11 Chr 7:23; Luke 1:31). The elaborate birth accounts in *A.L.D.* 63–73 l. 2 are related to this biblical midrashic tradition but develop it into a regular literary pattern.

The verse is an adaptation of Exod 2:22, which recounts the birth of Gershom, son of Zippora and Moses, ויקרא את שמו גרשם כי אמר בן ותלד‎ גר הייתי בארץ נכרי‎ "She bore a son, and he called his name Gershom; for he said, 'I have been a sojourner in a foreign land.'"; cf. Exod 18:3. The play on words in a popular etymology is evident ("stranger, sojourner" גֵר‎ and "there" שָׁם‎, LXX Γηρσάμ). The name of Levi's son is always spelled in the Pentateuch with the final *nûn*, גרשון‎ (see, e.g., Exod 6:16, 17; Num 3:17, 18, 21; 4:22, etc). Only in the post-exilic book of the Chronicles does the shift to the final *mêm* occur, see גרשום‎ in 1 Chr 6:1, 2, 5, 28, 47, 46; 15:7. The LXX renders the latter in 1 Chr 15:7 with Γηρσάμ, the form with the vocalization that is certainly more ancient than the masoretic tradition (cf. LXX Exod 2:22; 18:3, etc. for the same translation of the name of Moses' son). The Greek translator of the *Document* rendered this proper noun with Γηρσώμ, while A 74 l. 5 reads גרשון‎, thus following the Pentateuchal tradition but making the phonetic play on words impossible.

my seed will be sojourners in the land where I was born. The onomastic midrash on Gershon's name develops the same thought as Exod 2:22; the reference is however, totally different. In the Exodus text, Moses refers to his stay in the land of Midian; the *Document* builds on the parallelism of experience assigned to Levi and his descendants. They will be strangers in the land where he was born; that is, in Mesopotamia where Jacob married Lea and Rachel (see *Genesis* 29) and where Levi was born (Gen 29:34). Levi's prediction about the fate of his sons may only refer to the exile of Israel in Babylon, and not to the stay of Jacob's family in Canaan or Egypt. Gen 15:13 makes a similar prediction about Abraham's offspring: "Know of a surety that your descendants (זרעך‎) will be sojourners (גר‎/πάροικον) in a land that is not theirs, and will be slaves there, and they will be oppressed for four hundred years." The *Document* parallels the experience of being strangers in exile in Mesopotamia with Levi's experience of being stranger in the land of Canaan where he dwells at the time of Gershon's birth.

The Levitical status as a sojourner גר‎ in the land, either in Mesopotamia or in Canaan is rooted in premonarchic tradition which indicates that the Levite was not attached to the land but to a sanctuary (cf. de Vaux 1960: 215; Gunneweg 1965: 14–29). The Levite in Judg 17:7 dwells in Bethlehem of Judah but he has a status of a sojourner there (והוא גר שם‎; cf. Judg 19:1). He is then hired by Micah and installed as priest in the hill country of Ephraim (Judg 17:8–13), but then he follows the Danites when they move further north (Judg 18). Curiously, Judg 18:30 identifies this Levite with Jonathan, son of Gershom, son of Moses (cf. *A.L.D.* 64).

V. 64 *I saw in my vision.* The future destiny of Levi's sons is set in the context of his visionary experience (see *A.L.D.* 67 l. 5). This step is necessary to explain the foreknowledge of his children' destiny and does not necessarily suppose that he had only one vision in the *Document. A.L.D.* 98 l. 9 deals again with the future destiny of his sons revealed to him in a visionary experience (cf. *A.L.D.* 1b ll. 15–16; 7).

he and his seed will be thrown out from the chief priesthood. The Greek ἐκβάλλω in the LXX often translates the Hebrew נרש (see, e.g., Gen 3:25; 4:14; 21:10; Exod 2:17; 6:1, etc.). If it underlies the Greek in the *Document* (Beyer 1984: 203), then prediction of Gershon's future should be qualified as the second onomastic midrash on his name נרוש—נרשם. The *Document* follows a general biblical tradition according to which Gershon's Levitical family does not exercise any priestly functions. His name figures in the Levitical genealogies (Gen 46:11; Exod 6:16–17; Num 3:17, 18, 21; 1 Chr 6:1), and his family serves in the tabernacle in the desert (Num 3:25; 4:41) and as the singers in the temple in the Chronicler's account (1 Chr 23:6). On the other hand, the *Document's* affirmation that Gershon will be expelled (ἐκβάλλω/נרש) from the priestly office assumes that he once exercised it, cf. 1 Kgs 2:27; 2 Chr 11:14. The attempt to dissociate Gershon's name from the priesthood may stem from a conscious doctrinal move to correct the tradition in Judg 18:30, according to which Jonathan, son of Gershom, son of Moses became the priest of the idolatrous worship of the tribe of Dan. The Masoretic textual tradition tried to remedy this problem by insert-ing a *nûn* in Moses' name to read "Manasseh" מנשה, the name of the idol-atrous king of Judah (2 Kgs 21:1–18; cf. 2 Chr 33:1–17). Note that there is a possible word play on Gershom's name when Judg 18:30 נרשם is read in the light of Judg 17:7 שם גר והוא (cf. Gunneweg 1965: 20–21).

V. 65 *at sunse[t]*. Gershon's birth at the sunset of the day has a symboli-cal meaning by setting his fate in contrast with Qahat who is born at sun-rise (*A.L.D.* 68). While Gershon is excluded from the priestly office, Qahat's place in the royal high priesthood is assured (cf. *A.L.D.* 67).

V. 66 [*Qahat*]. The Greek vocalization of Qahat's name follows the LXX pattern against the MT קְהָת, cf. Gen 46:11; Exod 6:16, 18; Num 3:17, etc.

V. 67 *his [would b]e the congregation of all the [people]*. Like the description of Gershon, the onomastic midrash is based on what Levi saw concerning the future fate of his second son. The explanation of his name is based on Jacob's blessing of his fourth son Judah in Gen 49:10 וְלוֹ יְקְהַת עַמִּים = καὶ αὐτὸς προσδοκία ἐθνῶν (LXX). The LXX translates the form יְקְהַת with a noun προσδοκία "expectation" which supposes the Hebrew root קוה "to expect, wait for" (cf. Harl 1992: 186). The author of the *Document* makes a connection between Qahat's name קהת and the form in Gen 49:10 יקהת interpreting it as כנשת "congregation." By choosing this Aramaic noun he clearly refers to the meaning of the Hebrew root קהל "to congregate, assem-ble." Other targumic and midrashic traditions interpret the verbal form יְקְהַת in the same way (cf. Greenfield and Stone 1979: 223). From the stand-point of the ancient exegete Qahat's name is more suitable for an ono-mastic midrash on Gen 49:10 than Judah's. This may be one reason why the Genesis text serves for the author of the *Document* to illumine Qahat's destiny. The other reason is the *Document* exegetical tendency to apply to the Levitical priesthood biblical texts that delineate a future salvific figure coming from the tribe of Judah (cf. the comment on *A.L.D.* 1a v. 8). Here Judah's royal blessing is applied to Qahat and connected with his high priestly vocation, contrast 4Q252 V 1–7 where the whole verse Gen 49:10 receives a messianic and Davidic interpretation. The next line in *A.L.D.* 67, preserved only in Greek (MS E 18,2), makes clear what the verse has already stated implicitly, that the priestly vocation is understood as a royal office. Note that in the Genesis account the idea of a congregation of nations is also connected with Jacob. In Gen 28:3 Isaac invokes God's blessing upon Jacob "so that you may become a congregation of peoples" והיית לקהל עמים. In Gen 48:3 Jacob recalls God's promise in Luz (Bethel) to make him "a congregation of peoples" לקהל עמים.

a supreme kingship, a priesthood [for all Is]rael. The idea that Qahat exercises priestly and royal office is connected with *A.L.D.* 3c l. 2 where Levi's sons receive the promise of a priestly kingdom מלכות כהנותא. In *A.L.D.* 99 l. 15 they are priests and kings כהנין ומלכין, and the next verse speaks of their kingship מלכותכן. One of the reasons why this royal priesthood is assigned to Qahat's line is because he is the father of Amram and grandfather of Aaron and Moses, two important leaders of the nation (cf. the comment on *A.L.D.* 76). Qahat's descendants will play a crucial role in liberating the people from the Egyptian slavery. Another way of exercising their royal office is the judicial authority assigned to them (see *A.L.D.* 1a v. 18; 14 l. 10; 99 ll. 13–14). Note, that the priestly kingdom of eternal peace (*A.L.D.* 3c–4 ll. 2, 6) is opposed to the kingdom of the sword (*A.L.D.* 4 ll. 2–5) that indicates the changing fortune of the sinners. Responsibility to uphold the priestly kingdom of peace free from any impurity lies with Levi and his sons (see *A.L.D.* 102 ll. 3–4). The royal function of the Levitical priesthood consists, therefore, not only in giving the people freedom from the external foes (leaving Egypt under the guidance of Amram—*A.L.D.* 76), but also in keeping themselves free from any impurity and sin by keeping and teaching the sapiential tradition of the forefathers concerning due order of liturgical actions and metro-arithmetical knowledge (*A.L.D.* 14–50; 83b–98). Both topics, keeping the tradition of the fathers and exercising the function of eschatological judges, dominate the Aramaic *Testament of Qahat* 4Q542.

a supreme kingship. In the Aramaic *Vorlage* of the Greek ἀρχὴ βασιλέων lit. "beginning of kings" (*A.L.D.* 67 l. 7), the genitive in plural βασιλέων (*מלכין) is best interpreted here as expressing an abstract concept (cf. Brockelmann 1961: 59–60; מלכותא, cf. *A.L.D.* 3c ll. 2, 2; 4 l. 2; 100 l. 16). Note that the syntagm ἀρχὴ βασιλέων stands in apposition to ἱεράτευμα, a Greek nominal form with the ending -μα which expresses an abstract notion (cf. Smyth 1984: 840a). Semantically, therefore, the Levitical supreme kingship is parallel to the Levitical priestly function. This parallelism corresponds to the *Document*'s presentation according to which Levi and his sons are responsible for both keeping liturgical order (*A.L.D.* 30–31) and eliminating lawlessness from the earth (*A.L.D.* 1a v. 13; 78).

It is very probable that the Greek expression goes back to the Aramaic ראש מלכיא, where ראש "head, beginning" may be interpreted temporarily.

Greenfield and Stone (1985: 466) render the expression with "the beginning of kings." Their translation suggests that Qahat is the first king over Israel, and that can hardly be accepted for obvious historical reasons. Hence it should rather be interpreted together with ראש [כהנו]תה (*A.L.D.* 9 l. 17) and ἀρχῆς ἱερωσύνης (*A.L.D.* 64) where ראש/ἀρχή expresses the "sum" or highest and most perfect expression of the priestly office. In this sense the expression ἀρχὴ βασιλέων is similar to God's title *rəsa mawāʿəl* preserved in Ethiopic (*1 En.* 46:2; 47:3; 48:2; 55:1; 60:2; 71:10, 12, 13, 14) but most probably stemming from the Aramaic original. Charles (1912: 85) translates it as "sum of days," that is "Everlasting," when it occurs as God's attribute in *1 En.* 46:1, but then translates other occurrences literally: "Head of days."

V. 68 *In the fou[r and th]irtieth year of my life he was born.* Levi is thirty-four years old when Qahat is born, a date partially found also in 4Q559 frg. 3 2. In *T. Levi* 11:4 Qahat is born in the 35th year of Levi's life. Becker suggests that differences in dating events of Levi's life go back to the time when the oral tradition which underlies both texts had not been established in detail (1970: 101). However, the dates preserved in the *Document* are coherent, while the possibility of errors in redactional process and transmission of the *Testament* should also be considered as a cause for discrepancies (cf. Comments on *A.L.D.* 78–81 in § 2.1.12). *A.L.D.* 70 l. 17 affirms that Merari is born in the third month, whereas 4Q214a 2 i 3 gives here another month—probably ninth (cf. § 2.2.5). Like other instances of the *Document*'s manuscript transmission, this only proves that the written form of the *Document* underwent several changes, additions, or even errors (see also *A.L.D.* 78 and 80). According to Demetrius' chronological synopsis, Levi was eighty years old when he fathered Qahat, in the year in which Jacob died in Egypt (Eusebius, *Praep. ev.* 9.21.19). Demetrius' counting does not agree at all with the chronology of the *Document*.

in the first month on the [fir]st day of the mon[th]. When describing a chronological order of religious festivals, the *Temple Scroll* assigns to the first day of the first month of the year a particular importance (11QTᵃ XIV 7–9). Then follows the rite of the priestly ordination (XV 3–XVII 4) that lasts seven days (XV 4, 14). Although the beginning of the ordination rite is not specified, from the order of festivals in the text it is evident that it happens within the first fourteen days of the first month of the year, before the Passover celebration begins. Since Qahat's birth falls on the first day of the first month, it would naturally predispose him for priestly consecration. Due to the lack of precise dating of the priestly ordination in the Temple Scroll, much uncertainty about this interpretation remains. However, it is certain, that the first day of the first month has a particular importance in the cultic life in Israel. According to Exod 40:2 the erection of the tent of meeting took place on that day, cf. Exod 40:17. Ezek 45:18 orders the cleansing of the temple to take place on the same day, cf. 2 Chr 29:17.

at sunris[e]. By being born at sunrise Qahat is contrasted with Gershon who is born at sunset (*A.L.D.* 65). This symbolic reference to sunrise recalls the metaphor, which compares Levi with the sun (see *T. Levi* 4:3; 14:3; 18:4; cf. *A.L.D.* 101; 1QSb IV 27). 4Q541 9 3–4 uses the metaphor of sun and fire in relation to someone who probably comes from the tribe of Levi. In 4Q542 1 i 1 Qahat addresses his sons telling them that "He will make his light shine on you" וינהר נהרה עליכון. The subject here is most probably God himself, and the phrase constitutes an allusion to the priestly blessing in Num 6:25, "The Lord will make his face shine upon you" יאר יהוה פניו אליך (cf. Puech 2001: 272).

V. 69a *for I was exceedingly bitter on his account.* The verses 69a and 69b have two very similar explanations of Merari's name. Both express Levi's bitterness and grief on account of his son's struggle with death after his birth. Following Charles (1907: 568–569) and Lévi (1907: 178, n. 1), Grelot claims that the first one is a *hébraïsante* translation of the Hebrew original, whereas the second one renders the text in good Aramaic (1955: 93). He points out that the syntagm מר לי in the expression מר לי עלוהי לחדה in the first section (*A.L.D.* 69a l. 13) is a Hebraism attested in Ruth 1:13 and rendered by the targum with מריר לי. It should be observed, however, that the verb מר exists in Aramaic sources elsewhere (*Ahiqar* 148), and does not necessarily appear to be a Hebraism. Additionally, the *Document*'s expression מר לי עלוהי is much closer to 1 Sam 30:6 and Zech 12:10 where the verb מר is followed by the preposition על as expression of grief on account of the loss of one's children. Close relation to the biblical text proves that the author is versatile in both Hebrew and Aramaic, and that he bases his exposition on the biblical text and language, as it is evident in all four onomastic midrashim in *A.L.D.* 63–73 l. 2. From a literary point of view, the repetition of a similar explanation of Merari's name is best understood as an attempt to fit into a general literary pattern of the section which requires a double exposition on the names of Levi's children.

V. 69b *And I besought and asked for mercy for him.* The explanation of Merari's name is the most personal one. It does not deal with any prediction of Merari's future, but exposes the paternal anxiety of a father who copes with an imminent death of his son (cf. 1 Sam 30:6; Zech 12:10). Facing this kind of bitterness, Levi turns to God asking for mercy for his son. The implicit conclusion is that Merari is not dead, for he marries and begets children (see Exod 6:16; *A.L.D.* 74 l. 7). His prayerful plea for a priestly appointment (*A.L.D.* 1a) was heard by God as well, and thus Levi's piety and prayer are rewarded for the second time.

V. 70 *In the fortieth year of my life.* Note that Levi's three sons are all born in Canaan. Levi is forty-eight years old when he leaves for Egypt (see *A.L.D.* 80). The biblical text does not provide any data concerning Levi's age when his children are born.

V. 71 *and I gave her the name Yochebed.* Levi's daughter Yochebed (יוכבד) is mentioned only twice in the OT, Exod 6:20 and Num 26:59. One learns there that she is a daughter of Levi, that she married Amram and bore to him three children: Aaron, Moses and Mariam; Num 26:59 specifies that she was born in Egypt. The onomastic midrash particularly underlines that Yochebed brings glory to his father, which is an unmistakable reference to her future role as Amram's wife and mother of Moses and Aaron (cf. *A.L.D.* 75–76). Yochebed's name is interpreted with recourse to synonymous Hebrew (כבוד) and Aramaic (יקר) lexemes meaning "glory." This exegetical move is not a fruit of later textual developments but follows the interpretive line of the *Document.* which has recourse to Hebrew when exegeting the names of Levi's children (*A.L.D.* 63–64, 67). When dealing with the date of Yochebed's birth, the *Document* makes an exception in the general literary pattern in *A.L.D.* 63–73 l. 2 which usually provides only one date for the birth of Levi's children. The second dating of Yochebed's birth in *A.L.D.* 73 ll. 1–2 seems to be a later redactional development relating to *A.L.D.* 80 (cf. Haupt 1969: 84).

3.9.2 *Grandchildren—A.L.D. 73–77*

This section is dedicated to the marriage of Levi's children arranged by the father, and to their descendants. Particular attention is given to the marriage of Amram and Yochebed (*A.L.D.* 75–77) and the onomastic midrash on Amram's name (*A.L.D.* 76) explains also the reason for this interest. The literary structure of the section is based on the Levitical genealogy in Exod 6:16–20, where the names of Levi's grandchildren (Exod 6:17–19) are followed by a mention of Amram's marriage with Yochebed (Exod 6:20), cf. Num 26:57–59. Becker (1970: 101) rightly notes that the onomastic midrash in *A.L.D.* 76 is a later intrusion placed between *A.L.D.* 75 and 77 which both deal with chronological remarks concerning Amram and Yochebed. The number of Levi's years standing at the beginning of the biographical remarks in Exod 6:16 is relegated in the *Document* to *A.L.D.* 81 as a closing autobiographical element. The resumé of Levi's life (*A.L.D.* 78–81) has no counterpart in the biblical text.

V. 73 *And for my sons I to[ok wives] from the daughters of my brothers.* The first part of the clause "and for my sons . . . my brothers" stands in close parallelism with 1QapGen VI 8 לבני נשין נסבת מן בנת אחי "for my sons I took wifes from my brothers' daughters." Levi follows the lead of Noah who took the initiative to find wives for his sons and husbands for his daughters. In the *Genesis* patriarchal stories only Abraham takes care to find a wife for Isaac from his kindred by sending one of his servants to Aram-Naharaim (cf. *Genesis* 24). Note that Rebecca is a daughter of Bethuel, son of Nahor, Abraham's brother (Gen 24:15), she is, therefore, Isaac's kinswoman. The *Document* here follows a more restricted tradition, according to which

Levi's sons marry the daughters of their paternal uncles (cf. *A.L.A* 17 and 62).

V. 74 *The name of the sons of Gershon.* For the list of the names of the sons of Gershon, Qahat and Merari, see Exod 6:17–19; Num 3:18–20; 1 Chr 6:2–4; 1 Chr 23:7, 12, 21. The *Document* is evidently not interested in their future liturgical functions assigned to them in the genealogies in 1 Chr 6:1–23 and 1 Chr 23.

V. 75 *And Amram took a wife for himself.* The *Document* obviously follows the biblical text, which speaks of the Amram's marriage with Levi's daughter: "Amram took to wife Yochebed, his father's sister" ויקח עמרם את יוכבד דדתו לו לאשה (Exod 6:20; see Num 26:59). Levi's age at that moment together with the remark that Amram and Yochebed are born on the same day (*A.L.D.* 77) are the *Document*'s chronological additions. The author of the composition seems not to be aware of the conflict with the marital legislation caused by this union. Amram espouses his father's sister, but Lev 18:12 decrees against such a relationship, "You shall not uncover the nakedness of your father's sister; she is your father's near kinswoman" (cf. Lev 20:20). The *Temple Scroll* is even stricter in this regard: "A man should not take the sister of his father or the sister of his mother, for it is an abomination" (11Q19 LXVI 14–15 = 4Q524 frgs. 15–20 3–4).

  Later midrashic tradition solved the problem of Amram's marriage with his aunt by asserting that Levi had two wives, one of which was Yochebed's mother, and the other—Qahat's. The midrash *Leqaḥ Ṭob* (Ben Eliezer 1880: 2:33) correctly states that Amram married the sister of his father, not of his mother. The midrash then asserts that, since before the revelation of the Torah on the mount Sinai only maternal relationships were taken into consideration, the marriage of Amram and Yochebed did not break the law. Note, that the cited ruling of the *Temple Scroll* excludes also this midrashic solution. The same genealogical problem is dealt with and corrected in *Tg. Neof.* Exod 6:20, which affirms that Yochebed was a daughter of Qahat's brother: "the daughter of the brother of his (Amram's) father" ברת אחוי דאבוי (= LXX Exod 6:20; cf. *b. Sanh.* 58b). This reading is an interpretation of Exod 6:20 which states that Amram married his aunt (דדתו), a relation prohibited by Lev 20:20 (cf. Lev 18:12).

V. 76 *This one will {exalt} <lead> the people <out> of the land of Egypt.* Yochebed bore to Amram Moses, Aaron, and Mariam (see Exod 6:20; Num 26:59; 1 Chr 5:29). The onomastic midrash undoubtedly refers to the role of Moses and Aaron in leading the people out of Egypt: "But the Lord spoke to Moses and Aaron, and gave them a charge to the people of Israel and to Pharaoh king of Egypt to bring the people of Israel out (להוציא) of the land of Egypt" (Exod 6:13; cf. Exod 6:26–27).

V. 77 *On the same day the [children] we[re bo]rn, he and Yochebed.* Amram and Yochebed are born on the same day, that is in the sixty-fourth year of

Levi's life (*A.L.D.* 72). They marry in the ninety-fourth year of Levi's life (*A.L.D.* 75), that is when the bride and groom are thirty years old. Since Qahat was born in the thirty-fourth year of Levi's life (*A.L.D.* 68), he must be thirty years old when he fathers Amram, the number corresponding to Levi's age at the birth of his first son Gershon (*A.L.D.* 65). Consequently, he is sixty years old when Amram marries Yochebed. According to Demetrius, Qahat fathered Amram at the age of forty, and Amram is fourteen when Joseph dies (Eusebius, *Praep. ev.* 9.21.19). The *Document*'s chronology points out that Amram must be fifty four at the moment of Joseph's death in the one hundred eighteenth year of Levi's life (cf. *A.L.D.* 82). Demetrius' chronology does not correspond to the *Document*'s computation once again (cf. *A.L.D.* 68, 80 and 82–83a). 4Q543 frg. 1a, b, c 2–4 and 4Q545 1a i 2–3 further specify that Amram died when he was one hundred thirty-seven years old, in the year one hundred fifty-two of the Israel's exile in Egypt. The chronology of the *Visions of Amram* perfectly concords with the *Document*'s data (cf. the comment on *A.L.D.* 80).

3.9.3 *Autobiography—A.L.D. 78–81*

This is the third and final section of the *Document* dedicated to chronological and midrashic interpretation of the events in Levi's autobiography. The expression שנין בר is repeated five times (*A.L.D.* 78 ll. 15, 16; 79 ll. 18, 19; 80 l. 20) and once only שנין (*A.L.D.* 80 l. 22); a final statement concerning the length of Levi's life follows (*A.L.D.* 81). The purpose is mainly chronological; the most important events in his life are concisely recounted. Becker (1970: 94) considers *A.L.D.* 78–81 a final section of the whole *Document* and the Wisdom poem as a later addition. Caution must be exercised, however, for the section is not a final "Überblick über den Inhalt des Werkes," but sets the main events of Levi's life in a chronological order. Chronological details are present in the preceding two sections (*A.L.D.* 62–73 and 73–77) while *A.L.D.* 78–81 briefly summarizes main events in Levi's life that lead to the final statement of Levi's death (*A.L.D.* 81). The latter part, however, does not serve as a *sui generis* "table of contents" for the whole *Document*, but it constitutes the final section of *A.L.D.* 62–81 (for the literary relationship of the Wisdom poem to *A.L.D.* 78–81 and the *Document*, see Form and Structure of *A.L.D.* 82–98 in § 3.10).

Additionally, one can hardly accept Kugler's opinion that *A.L.D.* 78–81 "reminds the reader that Levi's life has been dominated by zealous pursuit of the priestly office, and by the achievement of that aim through his own purity and the recognition of that personal trait by God, by angels, and by his father and grandfather" (1996a:

117). It appears as Becker's interpretation pushed to its extreme, and an *eisegesis* of this short passage.

V. 78 *I was eighteen years old (when) I was brought to the land of Canaan.* Coming back from Paddan-Aram with his family, Jacob builds a house in Sukkot (Gen 33:17) then arrives to Shechem (Gen 33:18–20), an event immediately followed by the account of Dinah's rape and revenge of the sons of Jacob (*Genesis* 34). The *Document* claims that Levi entered Canaan and killed Shechem when he was eighteen years old. That suggests that its priestly author considered Jacob's stay in Sukkot and Shechem as limited in time and certainly not longer than one year. MS B 78 and *T. Levi* 12:5 affirm that Levi was eight years old when Jacob's family reached Canaan and eighteen at the moment of the killing. That assumes ten years' stay either in Sukkot or Shechem before the vengeance on the Shechemites, and is closer to Demetrius' computation than to the *Document*. According to Demetrius, Levi arrives in Canaan when he is ten years and six months old (Eusebius, *Praep. ev.* 9.21.8) and kills Shechem while being twenty years and six months old (9.21.9). From the standpoint of textual criticism it is probable that early in the text transmission of the *Document* the scribes unintentionally omitted the numeral "ten" עשרה, and that change could have entered both B and the *Testament*'s *Vorlage*. Since the *Document*'s chronology is coherent in its computation, it is unlikely that the *Document*'s date is a mistake and the Greek *Testament* preserves a correct reading (Hollander and de Jonge 1985: 164). The opposite is far more probable.

I killed Sheche[m] and destroyed the doers of violence. Levi states that he was eighteen when he killed Shechem. This event, therefore, precedes Levi's priestly ordination, for in the next verse (*A.L.D.* 79) Levi affirms that he was nineteen when he became a priest. Note that the *Document* does not connect the two events, and it is not self-evident that Levi becomes a priest because of the killing.

Gen 34:26 does not specify who killed Hamor nor his son, Shechem. Additionally, the *Document* does not mention Simeon, a fact that is not strange, for the *Document* is wholly concentrated on Levi. Also *T. Levi* 5:3–4 omits Simeon as taking part in the killing. On the other hand, *T. Levi* 6:6 affirms that Levi killed Shechem and Simeon—Hamor. Theodotus (Eusebius, *Praep. ev.* 9.22.11) says the same, but gives prominence to Simeon who is cited first before Levi.

The second clause adds that Levi destroyed the "doers of violence." Theoretically, the latter expression could denote "works of violence." It corresponds, however, to "Shechem" from the preceding parallel sentence and thus denotes all the Shechemites. It would also be difficult to assume that by killing the Shechemites Levi commits an act of "violence." Rather, by doing so, Levi eliminates the "violence" caused by an unlawful sexual assault that leads to the contraction of impurity by Dinah.

The application of the term חמס to the Shechem incident suggests that the interpretation of the killing has dramatically changed in comparison with Gen 49:5. The latter text indicates that Levi and Simeon are respon-

sible of the חמס, for "their swords are instruments of violence" (חמס; cf.
A.L.D. 78). Their killing of the Shechemites is, therefore, interpreted as a
sinful action, which includes deceit (מרמה Gen 34:13; cf. Isa 53:9; Zeph
1:9) and shedding of innocent blood (Gen 34:25–26; cf. Judg 9:24; Ps 72:14;
Jer 51:35; Ezek 7:23; Hab 2:8, 17). Their action is expressly condemned
by their father (Gen 34:30; 49:5–7).

In *A.L.D.* 78, however, the Shechemites are responsible for committing
the חמס in relation to Dinah. This interpretation of the events in *Genesis*
34 is rooted in the biblical text. Gen 34:2 indicates that Shechem, son of
Hamor, took her, lay with her and violated her (ויענה, cf. Deut 22:24, 29).
By doing so, he defiled her (טמא Gen 34:5, 13) and this appears to be the
main cause of the killing of all the male Shechemites (טמאו Gen 34:27).
Additionally, when accused by their father Jacob, the two brothers defend
themselves by saying in the form of a rhetoric question, "Should he treat
our sister as a harlot (כזונה Gen 34:31)?" In the Hebrew Bible the concept
of חמס has a broad range of meaning. It may refer there to a social crime
(Amos 3:10; 6:1–3; Mic 6:12; Isa 53:9, etc.), unjust judgment (Ps 7:17;
25:19; 55:10; 58:3), bloodguilt (Judg 9:24; Ps 72:14; Jer 51:35; Ezek 7:23;
Hab 2:8, 17), or human sin in general (Gen 6:11, 13). It may also denote
an infringement of the marital law (cf. Gen 16:5). The case of Dinah in
Genesis 34 indicates that sexual immorality causes uncleanness of Jacob's
daughter and thus infringement of God's order is being perpetrated. In this
way the Shechemites violated the laws concerning marriage by treating
Dinah like a harlot זנה (Gen 34:31; cf. Tosato 1982: 56–60).

Hence, the presentation of the Shechemites as the doers of violence stems
from the understanding of their treatment of Dinah in *Genesis* 34 qualified
as an act of violence or lawlessness (see *A.L.D.* 1a v. 13). This understanding
of the concept corresponds to the *Document*'s context. Isaac in *A.L.D.*
16 warns Levi to be free of "any fornication, impurity and harlotry" (מן
כל פחז וטמאה ומן כל זנות). It comes as no surprise, therefore, that Levi kills
those who commit these sins with his sister. The killing, therefore, rises to
the status of a "righteous judgment" (cf. *A.L.D.* 1a v. 18; cf. Ps 74:14), for
it eliminates those who perpetrate impurity. Also one part of Levi's second
vision (*A.L.D.* 3c) apparently deals with the case of a woman who defiles
the house of her father. It is not excluded that in the missing text of the
Document before the Shechem incident (*A.L.D.* 1c–2), an angel expressly
orders Levi to execute the vengeance on the Shechemites, similarly to *T.
Levi* 5:3.

4Q175 refers the sentence of Gen 49:5 not to Levi and Simeon but to
two persons who will rebuild the city of Jericho to make it into a fortress
of wickedness. 4Q175 25 (= 4Q379 22 ii 11) states that "the two of them
will be instruments of violence" כלי חמס לה[ן]יות שניהמה. Mentioning of two
persons as the instruments of violence points to Gen 49:5 as the source of
the expression. This Qumran document arranges different biblical texts in
such a way to suggest the coming of three eschatological figures, a prophet
(Deut 5:28–29 and 18:18–19 cited together as in Exod 20:21 in Samaritan
Pentateuch), a Davidic king (Num 24:15–17), and Levi as an ideal priest

(Deut 33:8–11). However, Gen 49:5 is reinterpreted and refers not to the two sons of Jacob but to the two mysterious oppressors of the people.

The reason why the role of the two brothers in the Shechem incident was reinterpreted by *A.L.D.* 78 (cf. LXX Gen 49:5) is probably caused by two factors. The first lies in the fact that the Levitical priesthood has been accused of misdeeds, which eventually led to the exile. Ezek 22 enumerates the sins of Jerusalem and of the nation. The priests have also their responsibility in this sinfulness. Ezek 22:26 states that, "Her priests have done violence to my law (חמסו תורתי) and have profaned my holy things; they have made no distinction between the holy and the common, neither have they taught the difference between the unclean and the clean (בין הטמא לטהור), and they have disregarded my sabbaths, so that I am profaned among them" (see 4Q390 2 i 10 "their priests will commit violence" כוהניהם יחמסו; cf. 4Q541 9 i 7). Zeph 3:4 declares the sins of the Jerusalem prophets and priests, "Her prophets are wanton (פחזים), faithless men; her priests profane what is sacred, they do violence to the law (חמסו תורה)." In the light of these texts it becomes evident that the authority of the Jerusalem priesthood has been damaged. The reinterpretation of the tradition concerning Levi became a way to create a priest who eliminates "violence" and does not perpetrate it, who is ritually clean and cares for the cleanness of the community by eliminating those who cause its uncleanness.

In the context of the *Document* Levi's act of elimination of violence may be seen as expressing his responsibility for the priestly kingdom (*A.L.D.* 3c l. 2). Ezekiel in his vision of the ideal temple and statehood advises the princes of Israel to eliminate violence and act justly: "Put away violence and oppression, and execute justice and righteousness" (Ezek 45:9). The particular responsibility of destroying the villain and evildoer (*ra-ga-am u ṣēnam ana ḫulluqim*) in the country is a duty of the king in ancient Babylonia (cf. the comment on *A.L.D.* 1a v. 18 and Weinfeld 1985: 25–31).

V. 79 *And I was nineteen years old (when) I became a priest.* This verse makes clear that between killing of the Shechemites and Levi's ascension to priesthood there is a one-year difference. This time distance does not favor the opinion that Levi's elevation to priesthood is due to the killing of the Shechemites. The simple succession of events does not necessarily imply their genetic relationship. The separation of the two events makes the theory of two visions in the *Document* even more plausible. The first vision must have dealt with the divine order to execute God's judgment on the Shechemites, the second dealt directly with Levi's heavenly elevation, followed by an earthly investiture. Levi's age at his marriage is also cited in *A.L.D.* 62.

According to the *Document*'s succession of events, Levi was ordained in Bethel and then the whole family arrived at Hebron and met Isaac. Then his priestly apprenticeship begins, in which Isaac is Levi's teacher. Although the text does not indicate how much time passed between the ordination (*A.L.D.* 9–10) and arrival to the fortress of Abraham (*A.L.D.* 11), the immediate succession of the two events suggests that the time gap was not too extended. When Levi begins his study of professional subjects he must have been at least nineteen years old. This chronological detail concords well with the Babylonian data from the Persian and Hellenistic periods, according to which scribal education began when the students were in their late teens and early twenties (Eleanor Robson, letter to author, 5 August 2002).

V. 80 *And I was forty-eight years old.* MS B 80 and *T. Levi* 12:5 agree in claiming that Levi entered Egypt when he was forty years old. This agreement is for Hollander and de Jonge (1985: 164) a reason why they claim the *Document*'s date wrong. The *Document*'s chronology, however, is coherent and should be followed (see Comments on *A.L.D.* 73 ll. 1–2 in § 2.1.12). It is far easier to explain the omission of the number eight in the text transmission, than its addition. Moreover, the *Testament of Amram*, a composition closely related to the *Document*, confirms in an indirect way the *Document*'s date of entry into Egypt. 4Q543 frg. 1a, b, c 2–4 and 4Q545 1a i 3–4 put the number of Amram's years at his deathbed to one hundred thirty seven, in the year one hundred fifty-two of the exile of Israel to Egypt. That means that Amram was born in the sixteenth year after the entry of the Jacob's family into Egypt. This chronological detail concords with the *Document*'s data. *A.L.D.* 77 states that Yochebed and Amram were born on the same day, that is when Levi is sixty four year old (*A.L.D.* 72), in the sixteenth year from the entry into Egypt (*A.L.D.* 73 ll. 1–2). Additionally, B 80 makes another mistake claiming that Levi spent in Egypt ninety years, and that would amount to a total of one hundred and thirty years of the patriarch's life span. In harmony with Exod 6:16, *T. Levi* 19:4, and *A.L.D.* 81, B 81 affirms that Levi was one hundred and thirty-seven years old at his deathbed. There is, therefore, no doubt that the *Document* preserves Levi's correct age at the moment of his entry into Egypt, and that the *Testament of Levi* together with B do not remain faithful to their Aramaic *Vorlage*. Demetrius claims that Levi was forty-three years old when he entered Egypt (Eusebius, *Praep. ev.* 9.21.17). His chronology differs on many points from the *Document* (cf. the comment on *A.L.D.* 68, 77, and 82–83a).

V. 81 *And all the days of my life were one hundred thirty-seven years.* Levi's age in the *Document* is taken from Exod 6:16, but the phraseology of the verse is related to Gen 50:22–23 where the total span of Joseph's life is followed by the mention that he saw Ephraim's children of the third generation (cf. also Exod 34:7; Job 42:16). This literary parallelism cannot be fortuitous for the next verse mentions Joseph's death in the one hundred eighteenth year of Levi's life. If seeing the second generation is a sign of God's blessing (Ps 128:6), seeing the third one is even more so.

I saw sons of the thi[rd generation]. The natural conclusion is that Levi saw his grandchildren, Moses and Aaron (cf. *Tg. Ps.-J.* Exod 6:16), who played the most prominent role in the exodus story and in the Sinaitic revelation. However, according to Grelot's reconstruction of the *Document*'s chronological details compared with Exod 12:40–41 (1971: 389–391), Moses and

Aaron would be born six and three years respectively after Levi's death.
Grelot's chronological speculation is based on the assumption that the four
hundred thirty years of Exod 12:40–41 end not with the exodus from Egypt
but with the entrance to the promised land. Although his well argued
hypothesis lacks a formal proof or confirmation, as he himself confesses
(p. 391), it does not necessarily contradict the *Document*'s statement. The
reference to the third generation is not a chronological detail but suggests
God's particular blessing of longevity bestowed on Levi. Additionally, in
A.L.D. 76 Levi refers to Amram as to the one who will lead the people
out of Egypt. This constitutes a clear reference to Amram's sons, Moses
and Aaron. The promise of future liberation is attached to Amram for,
according to all probability, Levi died before he could pronounce the same
prophecy over Amram's sons.

Mentioning of Levi's death is an important indication for the literary
genre of the whole Levi composition. He does not address his children
lying on his deathbed, a characteristic of the testamentary literary form.
He speaks from another perspective, of one who is already dead. The redactors of the *Testament of Levi* saw the difficulty and moved mentioning of
Levi's death and years of his life to the closing verses of their testamentary composition in *T. Levi* 19:4 and set it in the third person singular narrative. That proves that the literary form of the *Document* did not fit in the
literary pattern they were struggling to build.

Levi's death here does not constitute any formal literary indication that
the *Document* ends here. However, it unambiguously points out that the perspective of the whole *Document* is otherworldly, and adds greatly to the
eschatological character of the work. Since the beginning and the end of
the *Document* are lost, one cannot *a priori* exclude the possibility that it had
a testamentary frame, the conscious redactional work in the *Testament of
Levi* makes this assumption highly unlikely, though. The literary analysis of
separate parts and the whole structure of the *Document* indicate that this
composition can be classified as a pseudepigraphical text written in order
to impart to the priestly students an educational ideal intended to uphold
the scribal hierocracy in Judea (cf. § 1.5.3.3 and § 1.6).

3.10   *Wisdom Poem—A.L.D. 82–98*

Form and Structure

After the autobiographical section (*A.L.D.* 62–81) there comes the
wisdom poem (*A.L.D.* 83b–98) preceded by a short preamble (*A.L.D.*
82–83a) and followed by Levi's speech directed to his children concerning their future (*A.L.D.* 99–104). The poem opens with a sapiential *Lehreröffnung* formula (*A.L.D.* 83b–84) and ends with Levi's
statement about wisdom inherited by his sons (*A.L.D.* 98). Although
the final part of the poem is fragmentary, it is possible to notice that

A.L.D. 98 is the last verse in this poetical composition. First of all, 4Q213 2 8 (*A.L.D.* 98) has a *vacat* suggesting a break in the exposition, while on the margin of 4Q213 1 ii 11 (*A.L.D.* 98 l. 11) a scribal sign indicates the end of a paragraph. Additionally, the beginning of *A.L.D.* 98 forms an *inclusio* with *A.L.D.* 88, a literary feature marking off a literary unit *A.L.D.* 89–98. Finally, the following fragmentary text *A.L.D.* 99–104 discusses the future of the Levitical priesthood and the word "wisdom" חכמה, frequent in *A.L.D.* 83b–98, does not appear there at all.

The poem is an exhortation to do justice (*A.L.D.* 85–87), to teach and study scribal craft and instruction of wisdom (*A.L.D.* 88–89; 98), and praises the man who teaches wisdom (*A.L.D.* 90–93) and seeks it in his life (*A.L.D.* 97). The studying effort is necessary, for wisdom belongs to the hidden type of knowledge and cannot be acquired with other means like a military expedition (*A.L.D.* 94–96). This wisdom theology is not incompatible with the *Document*'s presentation of the Levitical priesthood, but stems from a sapiential understanding of the priestly ideal and education. Levi and his sons have to hand down the priestly tradition received from the patriarchs, and the long ritual and metro-arithmetical instructions in the *Document* (*A.L.D.* 14–61) are rooted in the sapiential understanding of the priestly function according to which a proper order must be observed to make it acceptable to God (*A.L.D.* 30–31). The wisdom poem does not constitute, therefore, an introduction of a wholly new topic and theological perspective, but expresses the instructional aspects of the priestly function in poetical form.

The poem contains some literary forms characteristic of wisdom literature. The opening verses (*A.L.D.* 83b–84) constitute a "teacher's opening formula," with the second verse underscoring Levi's position as a teacher of truth. One also finds an exhortation to follow truth and justice (*A.L.D.* 85) and to teach and study wisdom (*A.L.D.* 88; 90 ll. 2–4; 98). The verse dedicated to Joseph (*A.L.D.* 90) which opens with a verb in the imperative may also be classified as an exhortation to follow the example of the patriarch to attain the same glory and exaltation. Four separate verses (*A.L.D.* 87; 89; 94; 97) express proverbial wisdom stemming from the observation of human behavior and its consequences, and they underscore the hortatory character of the poem. The section dedicated to the praise of the wisdom teacher (*A.L.D.* 91–93) is roughly analogous to the praise of the scribe in Sir 39:1–11 who studies the wisdom of the forefathers,

travels extensively, and is praised and famous for his wisdom (cf.
Skehan and Di Lella 1987: 451–453). The description of an unsuc-
cessful military expedition to conquer wisdom (*A.L.D.* 95–96) serves
as a didactic narrative intended to exemplify the futility of this attempt
contrasted by the intellectual quest for wisdom, the only appropriate way of approach highly praised in the whole poem.

The literary form of this wisdom composition may be defined as
a didactic poem, the purpose of which is to inculcate a priestly ideal
of professional learning. Levi speaks as a teacher who instructs his
pupils to follow his instructions that culminate in the praise of the
wisdom teacher (*A.L.D.* 91–93). His didactic poem is close in its form
to the Psalter's poetic compositions termed as "wisdom psalms" (Pss
1, 32, 34, 37, 49, 112, 128; cf. Murphy 1963: 159–164; Kuntz 1974:
191–215). They share with the *Document* such formal elements as the
admonitory address to "sons" (Ps 34:12; cf. *A.L.D.* 84; 88; 90; 98),
a simile taken from the realm of nature (Ps 1:3–4; 37:2, 20; cf.
A.L.D. 86–87), admonition (Ps 32:9; cf., *A.L.D.* 83b; 90 ll. 2-4; 98),
proverbial saying (Ps 32:10; cf. *A.L.D.* 87; 89). In the *Document*, however, the instructional ideal of a wisdom teacher comes to the fore
in a much more accentuated way, because the praise of the wisdom
teacher constitutes the kernel of the poem (*A.L.D.* 91–93; cf. 90
l. 22 to 90 l. 2). The insistence on teaching of ספר "scribal craft"
that includes calculation skills (*A.L.D.* 88; 90; 98) constitutes a peculiar characteristic of the poem indicating scribal knowledge as an
important component of priestly education. These particular features
relate the poem to the Sumero-Akkadian school (é-dub-ba-a/*bīt tuppi*)
wisdom compositions, which often in poetic form expressed the importance of scribal learning in general and mathematical preparation,
in particular (Van Dijk 1953: 21–27; Gordon 1960: 142–144; Kramer
1963: 229–248). Scribal education together with mathematical skills
of the wise king in the *edubba* are also mentioned in some royal
hymns of the Old Babylonian period (cf. the comment on *A.L.D.*
90). These hymns propagated the ideal of the wise and learned king
and were most probably composed and studied in a school context
(cf. Sjöberg 1975: 160, 172–176). Of particular interest is here the
Akkadian poem "In Praise of the Scribal Art" that extolls scribal
craft (*ṭupšarrūtum*) learned in the *edubba* as a source of glory and prosperity for the scribe (*ṭupšarrum*; Sjöberg 1972).

The Wisdom poem is the best preserved Aramaic poetry text from
the Second Temple period, and, as the literary analysis demonstrates,

it utilizes the common stock of the ancient Semitic poetical devices. The division into stanzas is based on the thematic change with some formal elements helping discern the overall structure (Watson 1984: 163–164). The dominant strophe pattern is a couplet composed of two lines or cola standing in synonymous parallelism. When compared with classical Hebrew poetry, the poem certainly belongs to a later stage of historical development. The single line in the couplet is of uneven length and the trend towards its expansion is noticeable. Greenfield (1979: 51) proposed to divide the poem into three parts (83; 84–87; 88–94) followed by a prose praise of wisdom (95). Since his division came before the publication of the Qumran fragments and was not based on the analysis of the poetical devices, it does not reflect the actual poetic structure of composition. The reconstructed line number refers to the strophic disposition of the poem (see § 2.1.16).

Table 20. Poetical Structure of the Wisdom Poem—*A.L.D.* 83b–98

Stanza	Strophe	Reconstructed line	*A.L.D.*	Content
I	couplet	1	83b	opening formula
	couplet	2	84	
II	couplet	3	85	exhortation to do
	couplet	4	86	justice
	quatrain	5–6	87	
III	couplet	7	88	exhortation to study
	quatrain	8–9	89	and teach scribal
	quatrain	10–11	90	craft, instruction
	couplet	12	90 ll. 2–4	and wisdom
IV	monocolon	13a	91 ll. 4–5a	praise of a wisdom
	couplet	13b–14a	91 ll. 5b–6a	teacher
	hexacolon	14b–17a	91 ll. 6b–11a	
	monocolon	17b	91 ll. 11b–12a	
	couplet	18	92	
	couplet	19	93	
V	couplet	20	94	wisdom hidden
	tricolon	21–22a	95 ll. 17–20a	treasures
	couplet	22b–23a	95 ll. 20b–21	
	heptacolon?	23b–26b	95 ll. 22–96 l. 3a	
	tricolon?	27–28a	96 ll. 3b–4a	
VI	8 cola	28b–32a	97	praise of a wisdom seeker
VII	6 cola	32b–35a	98	inheriting wisdom

The first stanza introduces Levi as the main speaker and his sons as the recipients of the message. Then the second unit discusses the concept of truth and justice using the metaphor of a sower. The third part is an exhortation to teach and study wisdom marked off by the particle "and now" (*A.L.D.* 88). The exhortation ends in *A.L.D.* 90 ll. 2–4, and the topic changes as well. The next stanza praises the one who leads the others in the study of wisdom and depicts his exaltation and acceptance in foreign lands. The fifth section concentrates on the great value of wisdom and its inaccessibility for those who try to conquer it with military means. The penultimate part praises the one who seeks wisdom, while the last section returns to the exhortatory tone of the third stanza with a similar phrase "and now, my sons, scribal craft, and instruction of wisdom that you study/teach." There is no evident chiastic structure in the composition of the poem, but its division into seven stanzas suggests that the stanza IV occupies a pivotal place.

The strophic division indicates a variety of applied patterns. The couplet composed of two cola is a dominant strophe in Semitic poetry (Watson 1984: 174–176) and is most often represented in the poem. The two monocola in the stanza IV have a structural function, marking off the beginning and end of the stanza section. The second monocolon serves also as a climax of the section explaining the reason of the wisdom teacher's exaltation. A variant of this climactic monocolon ends the whole stanza in 93 l. 15. The tricolon in stanza V constitutes a meristic list to express the totality of military forces coming to conquer hidden places of wisdom (for this function of a tricolon, cf. Watson 1984: 184 and 322). The quatrain in stanza II is based on the repetition of the root זרע "to sow" in the first, third and fourth colon. The first couplet of the quatrain (line 5 = 87 ll. 14b–15a) has a partially chiastic structure ab // b'c; the pattern is lost in the second couplet of the strophe. The first quatrain in stanza III is based on the repetition of the same syntactic sequence "the one who teaches wisdom—the one who despises wisdom" at the beginning of the successive couplets. The second quatrain in the stanza III concentrates on Joseph's exaltation, but *A.L.D.* 90 ll. 2–4 is fragmentary and the literary pattern not certain. The hexacolon in the poem in stanza IV is structured by the repetition of the syntagm בה "in it" referring to "land and province" in the first colon of the strophe (line 13b = 91 ll. 6b–7a). Since the text in *A.L.D.* 94–98 is broken and partially restored, its division into stanzas V–VII remains hypothetical.

Synonymous word-pairs constitute another common element in Akkadian, Hebrew, and Ugaritic poetry (Watson 1984: 128–144), and their presence in the poem is another indicator of the poetic nature of the composition. Since Aramaic poetry is scarce, it is impossible to know if these word-pairs are relatively frequent in other compositions. The list of word-pairs in the sayings of Ahiqar drawn up by Watson (1994: 84–85) does not include any example from the *Document*'s list. The word-pairs occurring in parallel lines should be distinguished from the fixed expressions that stand in the same poetic line. To the latter group belong בסרון–שיטו "contempt–despise" (*A.L.D.* 89); מת–מדינה "land–province" (*A.L.D.* 91; 95). The three-word expression "scribal craft–instruction–wisdom" (*A.L.D.* 88; 90; 98) is best taken as a merismus expressing the totality of the transmitted teaching (cf. meristic lists in *A.L.D.* 90; 95).

Table 21. Poetical Word-Pairs in *A.L.D.* 83b–98

שמע // הצית	"to hear // to hearken"	83b
מאמר // פקוד	"word // command"	83b
פקד // החוי	"to command // to reveal"	84
בר // חביב	"son // beloved"	84
קשטא // צדקתא	"truth // justice"	85
מחל // שבק	"to neglect // to abandon"	90
אלף // בעי	"to teach // to seek"	90
נכרי // כילאי	"stranger // half-breed"	91
רחם // שאל שלם	"friend // well-wisher"	92
שניא // רברב	"many // great ones"	92
עותר // שימה	"wealth // treasure"	94
רב // טב	"great // good"	94
ידע // קני	"to know // to acquire"	94

There are also two examples of antonymic word-pairs used in antithetic parallelism. They do not belong, however, to the same poetic verse but are distributed in the first line of the parallel couplets. This is due to the fact that the antithesis occurs between two couplets of the quatrain that has a gnomic or proverbial form.

טב // ביש	"good // evil"	87
אלף // שיט	"to study // to despise"	89

The poem also uses end-rhyme, an important stylistic device achieved by the repetition of the same suffix or word ending.

324CHAPTER THREE

Table 22. End-Rhyme in *A.L.D.* 83b–98

בני // חביבי	-ay	-ay				84
קשטא // צדקתא	-ṭā	-ṭā				85
בה // בה	bah	bah				91
שניאין // רברבין	-în	-în				92
[[ידעיה]] // קניה	-êhā	-êhā				94
מלכין תקיפין – פרשין – רתיכין סניאין	-în	-în	-în	-în	-în	95

Becker (1970: 95) holds the whole Wisdom poem to be a later addition and *A.L.D.* 82 its "redaktionelle Klammer." He also claims that inserting the Wisdom speech after mentioning Levi's death in *A.L.D.* 81 proves that the redactors understood it as testamentary in character but they situated the speech in the year of Joseph's death because Joseph serves as a parenethical example to Levi's sons. Becker's opinion does not stand critical scrutiny. From a literary point of view *A.L.D.* 82 can hardly be considered as a sign of later redactional activity, it is rather an introductory narrative attested elsewhere in the *Document*. At the beginning of the *Document* Levi's prayer is preceded by a report of his liturgical preparation (1a v. 3–4) and by a formula introducing the direct speech, "and I prayed and said" (1a v. 4). Isaac's speech (*A.L.D.* 14–61) is preceded by the report of the arrival of the family to Hebron (*A.L.D.* 11–12). The following verse (*A.L.D.* 13) ends with the expression "And he said to me" introducing the direct speech. Levi's wisdom speech has a similar introductory narrative (*A.L.D.* 82) with the direct speech formula "I answered and said to my sons" (*A.L.D.* 83a). Although the poem with its introduction stands after the statement of Levi's death in *A.L.D.* 81, this cannot constitute a valid literary argument to claim a clumsy activity of a redactor and the testamentary character of the composition. To the contrary, the chronological details in *A.L.D.* 82 witness to the homogeneity of the literary style with the preceding chronological section 62–81, and the vocabulary analysis in *A.L.D.* 82–83b shows many contacts with the *Document*. There is also no literary evidence to claim the testamentary character of the wisdom speech, and its present location after the information of Levi's death in *A.L.D.* 81 strongly advocates against such an interpretation. The literary form of a testament requires a deathbed scenario, which is simply absent in the *Document*. The logic of the narrative in the *Document* necessitates a location of Levi's speech to his children within his life span, but does not preclude the author to have Levi deliver it on the patriarch's deathbed. Since this testamentary scenario does not appear in the *Document*, one has an additional argument for rejection of a testamentary interpretation. The year of Joseph's death is, indeed, not casual for Levi to deliver his speech because Joseph serves in it as an example of a glorified wisdom teacher associated with kings (*A.L.D.* 90), but, again, the deathbed scenario is absent from the account.

3.10.1   *Introductory Narrative—A.L.D. 82–83a*

V. 82 *In the [hundred and eigh]teenth y[ear] of my life.* From the literary point of view the *Document*'s dependence on Gen 49:1 in vv. 82–83a is noticeable but very slim. In the former text Jacob summons his children before his death and his speech is introduced with a similar formula "he said." The *Document*'s passage is a narrative that introduces the wisdom speech and ends with the formula "I spoke and said," ענית ואמרת, cf. *Ahiqar* 14; 45; 110; 118; 121. A similar literary device is also found at the opening of Levi's prayer (*A.L.D.* 1a v. 3–4) and Isaac's speech as well (*A.L.D.* 13). Levi is not on his deathbed but begins to instruct his sons when Joseph dies. The vocabulary shows many contacts with the rest of the *Document*, cf. לחיי . . . [נ]בש[נ]ת: *A.L.D.* 82 l. 3 and 68 l. 8; 70 l. 16; 72 l. 22; 75 l. 9; יוסף אחי: *A.L.D.* 82 l. 5 and 90 l. 22; שרית לפקדה: *A.L.D.* 82 l. 6 and 13 l. 6; לפקדה: *A.L.D.* 82 l. 6 and 13 l. 7; 84 l. 9; cf. also ἐντέλλομαι *A.L.D.* 49; 50; 52; 57. The words "brother" and "son" are common in the *Document* (see, e.g. *A.L.D.* 1c l. 20; 3 l. 15 for אח and 9 l. 18; 14 ll. 9, 9 for בר).

Levi in his teaching function follows Isaac who instructs Levi in the priestly "law" (*A.L.D.* 13 l. 6), commands him to instruct Levi's descendants in the same way (*A.L.D.* 49), and to keep this instruction in his heart (*A.L.D.* 48). The introductory narrative makes it clear that Levi's wisdom poem is an answer of an obedient grandson to his grandfather or rather of a student who becomes a teacher. The content of his instructions is seemingly different from Isaac's exposition of a detailed sacrificial ritual (19–47; 50–57), but compatible with its sapiential purpose to inculcate a proper order of liturgical action (*A.L.D.* 30 and 31) and with their instructional character of a metro-arithmetical exercise.

the y[ear] in which my brother Joseph died. The *Document* relies on Gen 50:22, 25 for the date of Joseph's death and it comments that it happened when Levi was one hundred and eighteen years old, which means that Levi is eight years older than Joseph. Demetrius affirms that when Jacob leaves Laban Levi is ten years and six months old, whereas Joseph six years and four months; that is, Levi is older by four years and two months (Eusebius, *Praep. ev.* 9.21.8). His chronology is again at odds with the *Document*'s count.

In *A.L.D.* 90 Joseph is depicted as a sage who teaches scribal craft (ספר) and is, therefore, associated with kings. Since the sons of Levi are exhorted to study and teach the same type of scribal knowledge (*A.L.D.* 88; 98), placing the wisdom poem in the year of Joseph's death adds greatly to the instructional character of the poem. Joseph becomes an ideal scribe and teacher whose example must be followed to achieve the status of being glorified and associated with kings. The praise of the wisdom teacher in *A.L.D.* 91–93 may in fact be applied to Joseph's life history—especially rising from the status of a stranger to the status of the one who is seated on the throne of glory (*A.L.D.* 93). When Joseph, the teacher of scribal knowledge, dies, the sons of Levi are to take his place on the throne of the royal glory as the wisdom teachers of the same type of scribal knowledge.

everything tha[t] I had intended. Lit. "everything that was with (עם) my heart." Here the term לבב "heart," refers to the activity of conceptual planning before undertaking any action (cf. Fabry 1995: 424; for the whole idiom היה עם לבב with this meaning, cf. 1 Kgs 8:17, 18; 1 Chr 22:7; 2 Chr 6:7, 8; 24:4; cf. 2 Chr 7:11).

3.10.2 *The Poem—A.L.D. 83b–98*

V. 83b *[Hear] the word of Levi, your father, and obey.* The double exhortation to give ear to Levi's teaching ([שמעו] ... והציתו) is a fixed sapiential "Lehreröffnungsformel" (Wolff 1965: 122–123). It is found at the beginning of a wisdom teaching (Deut 32:1; Isa 28:23; Prov 7:24; Ps 49:2), legal instructions (Prov 4:1; Job 13:6; 51:4), prophetic speeches (Hos 5:1; Isa 1:2, 10; 32:9; 49:1; Jer 13:15; Mic 1:2; Joel 1:2), or even at the opening of farewell discourses in the *Testaments* (Nordheim 1980: 93–94). The same construction also underlies the Greek text of Isaac's address to Levi in *A.L.D.* 49: ἄκουσον τοὺς λόγους μου καὶ ἐνωτίσαι τὰς ἐντολάς μου. A line parallel to *A.L.D.* 83b is found in 4QTJoseph ar (4Q539) frgs 2–3 2 (reconstruction of Puech 2001: 207) וכען ש[מעו למאמר יוסף אבוכון ואצי]תו לי חביבי "and now li]sten, my sons,[to the words of Joseph, your father, and hear]ken to me, my loved ones" (cf. *T. Jos.* 1:2).

the commands of God's beloved. Now Levi takes on himself the teaching role that was required from him by Isaac (see *A.L.D.* 49 and 82). In the *Document*'s context his commandments (פקוד) can only refer to the instructions he received from Isaac (see τὰς ἐντολάς μου in *A.L.D.* 48). The authority of his teaching is strengthened by the title ידיד אל "God's beloved," an expression taken from Deut 33:12 ידיד יהוה. Note the change to אל, the *Document* does not use the tetragrammaton, similarly to other Aramaic writings of the period. Being God's beloved is rooted in Levi's election to the priesthood, and constitutes a title ascribed to a highly elevated priest (cf. *A.L.D.* 6 and 58; see also 4Q542 1 i 7b–10 where Levi's son Qahat exhorts his sons to preserve the teaching of Jacob, the judgments of Abraham, and Levi's righteousness).

V. 84 *I myself command you, my sons.* For similar formulas of the sapiential transmission of learning cf. 1QapGen V 9: אנה אמר ברי ולך אנה {א}לכ וכען מחוה "and now I tell you, my son, and I inform you"; 4Q209 frg. 26 6 (*1 En.* 79:1; cf. 76:14): וכען מחוה אנה לך ברי "and now, I show you, my son."

In the first case the expression is used by Enoch who reveals to his son Methuselah that Noah does not come from the illicit union with the Giants (cf. *1 En.* 106:16–19); the second occurrence is found in the Enochic *Astronomical Book* in which most probably Methuselah is instructed about the movement of heavenly luminaries. Qahat, in his testament, instructs his son Amram: "and now to you, my son, I command" וכען לכה עמרם ברי אנא מפקד (4Q542 1 ii 9; cf. 1 i 13; 1 ii 10). The visionary content of the whole *Testament of Amram* is summarized in the opening verses in 4Q543 frg. 1a, b, c, 1–2 (= 4Q545 1a i 1–2): "[all that] he revealed to his sons and what he ordered them on [the day of his death.] [כל דין] אחוי לבנוהי ודי פקד אנון ב[יום מותה] (cf. 4Q545 frg. 4 14, 16; 4Q204 5 ii 26 = *1 En.* 106:19; for the *hapʿel* of חוי in a different context, see *A.L.D.* 3 ll. 17, 19. Here Levi transmits to his sons and grandsons the truth he himself learned in his visionary experiences and through the teaching handed down to him by Isaac in *A.L.D.* 14–61.

I myself show you the truth. The emphatic position of the independent pronoun אנה underlines Levi's role as a teacher of truth. The syntagm לכון, complement object of מפקד, is emphatically placed before the participle it qualifies; the same procedure is repeated in the second part of the bicolon where the participle is preceded by the direct and indirect object, קושטא לכון מהחוי, cf. Dan 2:16, 24, 27; 1QapGen II 19, 21. The mentioning of truth קושטא as object of Levi's instruction recalls *A.L.D.* 15 where Isaac shows Levi the "law of truth."

my beloved. Levi calls his sons "my beloved" in order to underscore their participation in the priestly election (cf. *A.L.D.* 58–59) as recipients of the truth received by Levi in the visionary experience (*A.L.D.* 1b; 3a–6) on the one hand, and learned through the study of priestly duties, ritual (*A.L.D.* 13–30), and metro-arithmetical knowledge (*A.L.D.* 31–47; cf. *A.L.D.* 88), on the other.

V. 85 *Let the principle of all your actions be truth.* The term ראש lit. "head" denotes in *A.L.D.* 9 l. 17 the priestly office, cf. *A.L.D.* 64, and most probably it underlies the Greek ἀρχή in *A.L.D.* 67 referring to Qahat's royal office. It is, therefore, best rendered here with "principle," for Levi now expounds a rule that should underline his sons' actions as officers ראשין in their royal and priestly quality (cf. *A.L.D.* 99). The exhortation here recalls Isaac's teaching to act in order (*A.L.D.* 30, cf. *A.L.D.* 31); Isaac's principle underlies all his teaching in *A.L.D.* 14–47 which is presented as "the law of truth" (*A.L.D.* 15) or "the priestly law" (*A.L.D.* 13; 15). Hence Levi's teaching of the truth should be interpreted in light of Isaac's instructions.

let justice be established with you. The poetic parallelism צדקתא—קושטא suggests that the latter term "truth" denoting a just order upheld by Levi (cf. the comment on *A.L.D.* 1a v. 18; 30; 31) is synonymous with "justice." In 4Q542 frg. 1 i 12 Qahat defines the inheritance (י[רות]הא, cf. *A.L.D.* 98 l. 9) received from the forefathers in a list that includes truth and justice (קושטא וצדקתא) as well. He earlier exhorts his sons to hold fast to "Levi's justice" ובצדקת לוי (4Q542 1 i 8) as well as his own. A similar parallelism

between God's justice and truth exists in Ps 119:142 צדקתך צדק לעולם
ותורתך אמת "Thy righteousness is righteous for ever, and thy law is true."
God's justice endures forever (Isa 51:8; Ps 111:3). The justice of the man
who fears the Lord stands forever (Ps 112:3, 9).

Vv. 86–87 *And [if you s]ow tru[th] . . . his seed returns upon him.* Both verses
use the same metaphor of sowing and they constitute a comment on the
preceding two verses that point to truth as the principle of Levi's teaching
and action (cf. *A.L.D.* 1a v. 18). Levi's exhortation to make truth the principle of his sons' action is further motivated by the prospect of bringing in
a blessed and good harvest. The next verse enlarges the perspective by for-
mulating a general rule of conduct valid for everyone. The continuity
between *A.L.D.* 86 and 87 is assured by the repetition of the verb זרע (86
l. 13 and 87 l. 14, 15) and עלל *hap̄'el* (86 l. 13 and 87 l. 15).

The metaphor of sowing righteousness is found in Hos 10:12 and Prov
11:18. The biblical pages frequently refer to the idea of a harvest corresponding to one's sowing (cf. Ps 37:28; Job 4:8; Sir 6:18–19; 7:3; Gal 6:7).
The *Document*'s clause, "whoever sows evil, his seed returns upon him"
(*A.L.D.* 87 ll. 15–16), is similar to an Aramaic text from Qumran. In a
fragmentary context 4Q550c 1 iii 6 cites a general rule relating to one's
evil conduct and its consequences: בן]אישא באישתה האבה על [ריש]ה "[e]vil,
his evil returns on his [head]" (Milik 1992: 357).

V. 88 *And now, my sons, scribal craft, instruction, wisdom teach your children.* Here
begins a section dedicated to the study and teaching of wisdom with Joseph
as a model of such a teacher (*A.L.D.* 88–90 l. 2). The section belongs to
a larger unit dedicated to wisdom (*A.L.D.* 88–98), where the lexeme חכמה
is dominant (88 ll. 18, 19; 89 ll. 20, 21, 23; 90 l. 2; 91 ll. 5, 12; 93 l. 15;
94 l. 16; 95 l. 22; 97 ll. 5, 5; 98 l. 9). Professional wisdom appears as a
necessary requirement of the Levitical priesthood. Levi asks God for wisdom in *A.L.D.* 1a v. 8 where it is associated with counsel, knowledge, and
might. Here he becomes a teacher of wisdom, which is a necessary means
of elevation and association with kings (*A.L.D.* 90; 93). This royal glory
assured by wisdom will have no end (*A.L.D.* 100). The concept of wisdom
in the *Document* is inseparable from Isaac's priestly instructions in *A.L.D.*
14–61. Although the lexeme חכמה does not appear there, the introduction
(*A.L.D.* 82–83a) and opening verses of the wisdom poem (*A.L.D.* 83b–87)
make this connection clear. The purpose of Isaac's instructions is to pass
on to Levi a set of liturgical and metro-arithmetical laws whose main principle is the sapiential idea of proper order that must be maintained to make
Levi's liturgical actions and life pleasing to God. The wisdom concept in
the poem, therefore, is not a new development unrelated to the *Document*,
but stems from the sapiential understanding of the law and of the priestly
function as well. Note that Levi exhorts his children to teach scribal craft,
instruction, and wisdom to their children. Only the priestly descendants
are, therefore, meant here. Levi's sapiential instructions concern only the
priestly class and not the whole of Israel.

In the subsequent priestly and apocalyptic literature, wisdom becomes a constant element ascribed to the eschatological priests. In a broken context in 4Q543 frg. 2a–b 2, wisdom is given to Amram or his son Aaron. One should also compare 4Q541 frg. 3 4 הכ[מה יאתה לעליכה] "[wis]dom will come upon you. . . ." 4Q541 frg. 9 i 3 speaks of the wisdom of the mysterious priestly figure who will atone for the children of his generation. In 4Q212 iv 13 (*1 En.* 93:10) wisdom is an eschatological gift to the righteous; in 4Q534 1 i 8 Noah's wisdom will reach all the nations.

scribal craft ספר. Greenfield and Stone (1979: 226) translate ספר as "reading and writing," citing as an example Isa 29:11–12. However, the use of the term in the *Document* cannot be restricted to writing skills only, but includes all knowledge transmitted by Isaac to Levi (*A.L.D.* 14–50; 51–61). Thus it is synonymous with the other two terms, מוסר and חכמה, with which it occurs in the poem, and should be rendered with a term that entails all the aspects of Levitical education in the *Document*. In sum, the term in the *Document* encompasses all scribal craft that is linked to, and dependent upon, the knowledge of writing (cf. Dan 1:4 MT ספר = LXX γράμματα "letters"; *T. Levi* 13:2). Note that in Dan 1:17 God gives the Jewish boys at the Babylonian court learning and skills in all ספר and חכמה. The Septuagint translates the former term with γραμματικὴ τέχνη, "scribal craft."

The scribal craft in the *Document* refers to purity rules, liturgical prescripions concerning the holocaust offering (*A.L.D.* 14–31), and to counting or measuring of specific sacrificial material (*A.L.D.* 32a–47). Consequently, it also encompasses knowledge of specific arithmetical concepts and terminology like sexagesimal structure of the metric system (32a–36), fractions of numbers (37–46a), and ratios between metrological units (46b–47), all necessary skills for the proper disposition of the sacrificial material. In this sense it also contains in its semantic range the concept of חשבן "calculation" in *A.L.D.* 31 l. 19 (cf. *A.L.D.* 52 λογισμός).

The knowledge of counting according to a numerical system similar to the way the Babylonians counted is, therefore, an element of Levitical wisdom and instruction. It is, however, not restricted to a mere knowledge of abstract numbers but refers to their practical use in sacrifice administration. The notion of "scribal craft" ספר in the *Document* also entails a simple enumeration of collated items, like the list of trees fit for the sacrifice (*A.L.D.* 24), the order of sacrificed parts of the bull (*A.L.D.* 28), or the numerical sequences of metric units (*A.L.D.* 32a–46a) set in the sacrificial context. This enumeration recalls the *Listenliteratur* of Mesopotamian inspiration that ordered material phenomena in semantic units by simply recording them in a list (cf. the comment on *A.L.D.* 24). The alphabetic texts from Ugarit contain this literary genre as well and in the headings of various lists one often finds *spr*, which serves as their title (see, e.g., *KTU* 4.33:1; 4.322:1; 4.338:1–3; 4.561:1). The term is translated with "register," "record," "inventory" (del Olmo Lete and Sanmartín 2003: 768), "enumeration," "list" (Mettinger 1971: 44), but it unequivocally denotes the action of enumerating single lexical entries, administrative accounts, or ritual instructions.

The understanding of ספר as "scribal craft" that entails calculation skills is also suggested by the reinterpretation of the story of Joseph by the *Document*. In Gen 41:46–49 he is depicted as the one who stores the grain and measures it, while in *A.L.D.* 90 becomes a teacher of ספר which encompasses in the *Document* the knowledge of weights and measures. Also his rise to the position of power and authority is considered as the result of his teaching of scribal skills and instruction of wisdom. This *Document*'s statement fits well with the general OT tendency to link the knowledge of numbers and counting with the exercise of power (cf. Conrad 1999: 309–310).

The sequence "scribal craft and instruction and wisdom" ספר ומוסר וחכמה never appears together in the MT or LXX, but *Jub.* 4:17 has a similar or perhaps identical expression. The *Jubilees* verse states that Enoch was the first "who learned writing and instruction and wisdom" *taməhra maṣḥafa wa-təmhərta wa-təbaba* (transl. VanderKam 1989b: 25; text VanderKam 1989a: 24). The Syriac Chronicle that preserves fragments of the book of *Jubilees* has in *Jub.* 4:17 an expression similar to the one found in the *Document* ʾylp sprʾ wmrdwtʾ wḥkmtʾ (39:1–3 in VanderKam 1989a: 263). The Syriac *mrdwt* is semantically related to the Hebrew מוסר (see Sir 42:8 MS B mg. מרדות for מוסר [MS B]; Sir 33:25 MS E מרדות translated by the LXX with παιδεία; for a detailed discussion see Skehan and Di Lella 1987: 403). Although it is not certain that there existed a full translation of Hebrew *Jubilees* into Syriac, preserved Syriac fragments are closer to the Hebrew text than the Greek excerpts of the book (see VanderKam 1989b: xv–xvi). One may, therefore, legitimately assume that the Syriac expression in *Jub.* 4:17 reflects the original Hebrew *Vorlage*.

In the context of the parallelism with the *Document* one may ask whether the understanding of *sprʾ* in *Jub.* 4:17 should follow the interpretive line of the *Document*. In the *Jubilees*' verse the term stands in the context of Enoch's astronomical knowledge: "He was the first of mankind who were born on the earth who learned (the art) of writing, instruction, and wisdom and who wrote down in a book the signs of the sky in accord with the fixed pattern of their months so that mankind would know the seasons of the years according to the fixed patterns of each of their months" (transl. VanderKam 1989b: 26). If, as in the *Document*, the underlying Hebrew term ספר denotes scribal craft that includes calculation skills, then it would also refer to the metro-arithmetical knowledge Enoch studies in order to be able to do the astronomical calculations. It is well known that Babylonian astronomy depends on mathematical calculations based on the sexagesimal numerical system. *Jub.* 4:17–18, which constitutes a clear reference to the Enochic *Astronomical Book* (*1 En.* 72–82; cf. Milik 1976: 11), confirms this interpretation. It is probable, therefore, that both Enoch and Levi represent the same stream of Levitical priestly tradition influenced by Babylonian arithmetical concepts and scribal education. Note that the *Testament of Levi* 8:17 bestows on the Levites the title of scribes γραμματεῖς, a term often used by the LXX to render ספר (e.g. Ezra 4:8, 9, 17, 23, etc.). Similarly, Enoch is called "the scribe of righteousness/truth" (ὁ γραμματεὺς τῆς δικαιοσύνης *1 En.* 12:4; γραμματεὺς τῆς ἀληθείας *1 En.* 15:1).

VanderKam (1978: 232–233) finds in *Jub.* 4:17–18 an underlying Hebrew poetical structure that makes the connection with the *Document* even more evident. He understands ספר as denoting Enoch's literary activity only, but is unable to find a precise parallel in other contemporary sources for the *Jubilees*' claim that Enoch was the first writer. If one recognizes that the term ספר includes also calcultation skills necessary not only for accounting practises but for astronomical calculations as well, one finds traces of that Enochic tradition in ancient Jewish writers who suggested that Enoch was the first to invent astrology/astronomy. Pseudo-Eupolemus traces the discovery of astrology to Abraham and ultimately to Enoch: "And Abraham lived with the Egyptian priests in Heliopolis, teaching them many things. And he introduced astrology and other sciences to them, saying that the Babylonians and he himself discovered them, but he traced the discovery to Enoch" (transl. Wacholder 1974: 313). Josephus transmits a similar tradition when he says that Abraham taught the Egyptians arithmetics (ἀριθμητικήν) and astronomy (τὰ περὶ ἀστρονομίαν), sciences of "Chaldean" origin (*A.J.* 1.167–168).

A.L.D. 90 l. 23 and 98 have a variant construction of the three terms ספר ומוסר חכמה "scribal craft and instruction of wisdom" (cf. Prov 15:33 מוסר חכמה; in Prov 1:2, 7; 23:23 מוסר is a synonym of חכמה). It is doubtful whether the tradition attributing to Levi and his children the task of teachers of wisdom derives from Deut 33:10; Mal 2:7; Sir 45:17 (Greenfield and Stone 1979: 226). The latter texts insist on Levi's role as the teacher of the whole of Israel, whereas the *Document* insists that the teaching is restricted to the Levitical tribe only as a means of its glorification. The priestly instruction of *A.L.D.* 14–61 is exclusively connected with Levi and his sons (cf. *A.L.D.* 13 and 15). The priestly role as teachers of scribal skills most probably refers to the Levitical family setting where priestly apprentices learn rudiments of calculation associated with liturgical texts.

According to Babylonian mathematical tradition the study of arithmetical and mathematical notions is necessarily connected with the metric sexagesimal system. In the Sumerian and Old Babylonian scribal tradition metrological and mathematical instruction was part of the standard scholarly curriculum (Sjöberg 1975: 167–168). Scribal education and metro-mathematical training of the scribe have often been emphasized in the Sumerian school (é-dub-ba-a/*bīt tuppi*) literature. In a Sumerian text, *Schooldays*, a father praises the teacher of his son and his teaching achievements:

"You 'open the hand' of my young one, you make of him an expert, show him all the fine points of the scribal art. You have shown him all the more obvious details of the tablet-craft, of counting and accounting (šid-níg-šid). . . ." (Kramer 1949: 203, 206, lines 59–62).

The Sumerian logogram ŠID means in Akkadian *manû* "to count, reckon, calculate." It is frequent in the royal Šulgi hymns and in *edubba* literature where it appears in the context of the mathematical preparation of the scribe (cf. Castellino 1972: 88–89; Nemet-Nejat 1993: 5–10). Commenting on the Babylonian scribal terminology, Landsberger (1956: 123) noted that the earliest Sumerian word for scribe is UMBISAG, written logographically

ŠID; calculation, therefore, appears to be semantically and historically the most fundamental function of the scribe.

instruction. Closely associated with scribal craft and wisdom, the noun מוסר refers here to the totality of the sapiential knowledge that the Levitical teachers are supposed to transmit to their pupils or "sons." The close association with חכמה "wisdom" is already attested in the biblical literature (Prov 1:2, 7; 23:23; Sir 6:22 (MS A); Sir 47:14 (MS B), where the term may also denote a body of knowledge to be assimilated by the students (Prov 1:8; 4:1; 13:1; 15:5).

wisdom. Levi instructs his children to teach scribal craft, instruction, *and* חכמה (cf. *A.L.D.* 90 l. 23; 98 l. 8). This curriculum for Levitical priestly class with its metro-arithmetical elements has deep roots in the Babylonian school system where metrological and mathematical studies went hand in hand with the study of wisdom literature, beginning with the most elementary level. Round hand tablets (lentils) from Old Babylonian Ur contain simple metrological and mathematical computations on their reverse side, while on their obverse the student copied Sumerian proverbs (Robson 1999 § A.5). A more advanced curriculum of scribal education at Ur was based on an array of text types that included Wisdom and proverbs, mathematical and metrological texts, hymns and prayers, etc. (cf. Friberg 2000: 176–179). Our knowledge of Babylonian mathematical training in the first millennium B.C. is limited because the available evidence is rather meager. The number of published texts has, however, been growing (cf. Friberg 1999: 139–140), and their study indicates that the mathematical training of the Old Babylonian period has been preserved relatively intact (Friberg 1987-90: 583; Gesche 2001: 136–140). Similarly, most of the literary texts studied in the Old Babylonian *edubba* continued to be used in the scribal education during the New and Late Babylonian period (Gesche 2001: 172–183).

teach. Levi exhorts his sons to be teachers of the professional priestly and scribal wisdom. They thus imitate Isaac, who is Levi's teacher in the *Document* (cf. *A.L.D.* 13 l. 7; 15 l. 13), follow the example of Joseph (*A.L.D.* 90), and become worthy of praise and glory like the wisdom teacher in *A.L.D.* 91. On the other hand, they are obliged to study wisdom and to seek her ways (*A.L.D.* 90 l. 3; cf. 89 l. 20).

eternal glory. In *A.L.D.* 71 Yochebed's name is midrashically explained as the one who is born to bring glory to Levi and to Israel as a future wife of Amram and mother of Aaron and Moses (cf. *A.L.D.* 76). Here the concept of glory for Levi's sons is dependent on the wisdom instruction that is a condition of Levitical royal glorification. Wisdom as a means of attaining glory is stressed throughout the poem. The one who studies it is glorified (89 l. 20; 91 l. 11), his days are long, his fame precedes him, he is welcome everywhere he goes (91 ll. 5–10), and he is seated on the throne of glory (93 l. 14); Joseph as a wisdom teacher is glorified and associated with kings (90 ll. 1–2). Wisdom itself is a glorious and good treasure for those who know and acquire it (94 l. 16). It seems that the word "glory" is the last word in the poem (see *A.L.D.* 98 l. 11). The royal and priestly glory of the Levitical tribe is eternal (88 l. 19) and will have no end at all (100 ll. [17], [18], 19). The concept of glory in *A.L.D.* 104 ll. 2, 4 is found in a broken context.

Eternal glory is also assigned to priestly descendants as a way of sanctification in the eschatological 1QSb III 4: ין[קדש זרעכה בכבוד ע[ו]לם "[and may he] sanctify your seed with eternal glory." Note, that kingship מלכות is mentioned in the next line, though the context is broken. For the same Hebrew expression כבוד עולם, cf. 1QH[a] V 12; XI 4; 4Q418 frg. 126 ii 11. Additionally, in the praise of Aaron, Sir 45:20 affirms that the Lord increased his glory (LXX: δόξα; MS B: כבוד; cf. Sir 50:13) and Sir 45:25 exhorts the high priests to bless the Lord who has crowned them with glory (MS B: המעטר אתכם כבוד). Phinehas is declared to be the third in priestly glory (Sir 45:23).

V. 89 *Whoever studies wisdom will (attain) glory through her.* The verse establishes a general principle of appropriate retribution for teaching or despising wisdom. Its first part generalizes what has already been expressed in the preceding verse (*A.L.D.* 88 l. 19) in regard to Levi's children: the reward for teaching wisdom is glory.

The second part of the verse antithetically states the fate of the one who holds wisdom in contempt. For the motif of despising wisdom, see Prov 1:7; Qoh 9:16. Here the root שוט "to despise, treat with contempt" is a borrowing from the Akkadian *šâṭu* "to hold in low esteem, to disregard" (AHw 1205a; cf. *CAD* Š 2:242b). Note that the same root with the same semantic value is also attested in Ezek 16:57; 25:6, 15; 28:24, 26; 36:5. The synonymous בשרון "disdain, disrespect" has the typically Hebrew morpheme ון-, but it should not be emended with Charles (1908a: 255, n. 2) to בושרן. The morpheme is already attested in Biblical and Qumran Aramaic and may result from the Aramaic phonological development ā > ø (cf. Fassberg 1992: 56–57). 4Q213 1 i 11 reads a *sāmek* instead of MS A *šîn*, לב[סרון, cf. also 4Q542 1 i 6. In the Syriac Ahiqar 28:6, the passive participles of בסר and שוט are attested together (cf. Conybeare 1898: 43). This supports the opinion that the Qumran expression in 4Q213 1 i 11 לב[סרון ולשיטו is a fixed poetic word pair.

The *Testament of Qahat* also attests the verb בסר (4Q542 1 i 6) in Qahat's admonitions of his children; the reason for disdain and contempt is, however, different. He exhorts his sons not to share their heritage with the strangers for, by doing this, they will be humiliated and foolish in the eyes of the foreigners who would despise (יבסרון) them and become rulers over them.

V. 90 *Joseph my brother [who] taught and the instruction of wisdom.* This verse justifies the location of the whole poem in the year in which Joseph died (cf. *A.L.D.* 82). The *Document* depicts Joseph as an example of a wisdom teacher who, on account of his teaching activity, was granted glory and greatness. The biblical Joseph has been reinterpreted and adapted to the needs of the *Document*'s ideals. This reinterpretation follows the tradition attested on the biblical pages. In Gen 41:39, on account of Joseph's dream explanation, the pharaoh emphasizes his wisdom by stating that there is no one so discreet and wise (נבון וחכם) as Joseph. Then, in Ps 105:20–22 the king (מלך) releases Joseph from prison and assigns him a highly elevated status in his house for the purpose of instruction and wisdom: "he made him lord of his house, and ruler of all his possessions, to instruct (MT לְאָסֹר, conj. לְיַסֵּר = LXX τοῦ παιδεῦσαι; cf. יסר and אסר in *HALOT*: *s.v.*) his princes at his pleasure, and to teach (יחכם) his elders wisdom." Although vocabulary contacts with the *Document* are evident (מלכין—מלך, חכמה—יחכם, מוסר (?)—ליסר), there are important differences as well. While in the psalm interpretation Joseph's exaltation precedes his teaching function, the *Document* reverses the order of events and affirms that, because of his profession as a wisdom teacher, he attained glory and greatness and was associated with kings. This *Document's* change explains the author's exhortatory intent to present Joseph's exaltation as a result of his teaching function.

The Aramaic text also adds another component of Joseph's teaching, that is, ספר "scribal craft," the knowledge of calculation included (cf. *A.L.D.* 88). This Joseph's occupation, as the one who teaches ספר, also proceeds from the biblical tradition similarly modified for the *Document's* purpose. As soon as the pharaoh installed Joseph over the whole land of Egypt (Gen 41:37–45), the latter begins to store up grain in preparation for the coming years of famine (Gen 41:46–49). Finally, his activities are summed up, "And Joseph stored up grain in great abundance, like the sand of the sea, until he ceased to measure it (לספר), for it could not be measured (מספר אין)." The *Genesis* statement about Joseph underscores his success in the preparation for the coming period of famine, and his measuring or counting of stored goods is an expression of Joseph's administrative authority by having these goods at his disposal. For the author of the *Document*, however, this biblical text proves that Joseph knows calculation and the writer makes a further step not warranted by the Genesis account—Joseph teaches the Egyptians this kind of metro-arithmetical knowledge and as a result is associated with kings. The tradition about Joseph's metrological skills is attested in Artapanus (Eusebius, *Praep. ev.* 9.23.3) who claims that Joseph discovered measurements (μέτρα) and because of that he was greatly loved by the Egyptians.

The author of the *Document* adapted existing biblical tradition about Joseph to his purpose of exhorting his children to pursue the ideal of wisdom teachers in order to assure their exaltation. The three terms, "glory," "greatness," and "kings" that qualify Joseph's elevation, describe in the *Document* Levitical priestly, sapiential, and royal dignity (cf. *A.L.D.* 6 [רבו "greatness"], 89 [יקר "glory"], and 99 [מלכין "kings"]). Note that when Daniel describes the royal gifts granted to Nebuchadnezzar by God, he mentions the list that resembles the *Document's*: "O king, the Most High God gave Nebuchadnezzar your father kingship and greatness and glory and majesty" מלכותא ורבותא ויקרא והדרה (Dan 5:18; cf. Dan 4:33). *T. Levi* 13:9 also underlines Joseph's royal characteristic as the one enthroned with the kings because of his teaching activities. The connection with wisdom, however, is lost (cf. Hollander 1981: 57–62).

The *Document*'s reinterpretation of the biblical data concerning Joseph was most probably influenced by Gen 45:8 where he is designated as a "father to Pharaoh," אב לפרעה (cf. 2 Kgs 6:21; 13:14). For the author of the *Document*, this expression could only mean that Joseph was the pharaoh's tutor and the pharaoh was his disciple. The formula itself can actually refer to the setting of a scribal school in Egypt. Brunner (1961: 90–100) has shown that the Egyptian counterpart to Joseph's title, which was "father of god," designated in the 18th dynasty a tutor to the crown prince.

The attendance of a scribal school by a king is also attested in the Sumerian texts where scribal skills are transmitted to the ruler. Although the Mesopotamian kings were mostly illiterate, basing their administration on the scribal groups and their skills, some boast, probably without a real basis, of having attended the school and mastered the scribal knowledge. The Sumerian self-laudatory hymns contain several references to the wisdom and mathematical training of Šulgi (2094–2047 B.C.), king and legislator of the Ur III dynasty.

> 35. In the "House of Wisdom" (é-geštú igi-gál) the supervisor of the land,
> 36. I, Šulgi, truly profess wisdom. (. . .)
> 45. To "illuminate" the lapislazuli tablet,
> 46. Counting and calculating (šid-níg-šid) the (administrative) rules of the country,
> 47. As a man of intelligence, I also penetrated their full value.
>   (Hymn C: Castellino 1972: 250–253, the comment pp. 274, 277–278; cf. Hymn B 11–20: Castellino 1972: 31–33, the comment pp. 78–94).

The hymn indicates that the scribal mathematical knowledge necessary for the just administration of the country was associated with royal authority most probably for ideological reasons. Since scribal knowledge was held in high esteem in ancient society, the king who stands at the head of the centralized administration and bureaucracy is depicted as an ideal scribe versed in wisdom, mathematics, and administrative skills. The goal of this idealized picture of the king was to enhance the position of the king as the center of social values and just order (Michalowski 1991: 45–57). Additionally, since these self-laudatory hymns were composed and studied in Old Babylonian schools (cf. Sjöberg 1975: 160, 172–176; Vanstiphout 1979; Tinney 1999: 162–168), they also conveyed a message to the scribal apprentices—the knowledge of scribal craft in general and of numbers in particular is such an important skill that even kings boast about acquiring them.

Another hymn ascribed to Šulgi further illustrates this tendency to combine the scribal ideal with the royal exercise of justice: "I am a wise scribe of Nisaba. Like my heroism, like my strength, my wisdom is perfected, its true words I attain, righteousness I cherish, falsehood I do not tolerate, words of fraud I hate. I, Šulgi, the mighty king, superior to all" (Hymn A 19–26; text and transl. Klein 1981: 189–191).

In one of the royal self-laudatory hymns propagating the image of the just and wise king, another famous king and legislator Lipit-Ištar (1934–1924

B.C.) of the first dynasty of Isin (2017–1794 B.C.) boasts himself about his
mathematical knowledge and scribal competence: "Der Schreiber der Nisaba,
der die Zahlen kennt, der Jüngling nach dem feststehenden Wort Utus bin
ich . . . der Weise voll der unerforschlichen Pläne, der die Zahlen kennt . . .
(text de Genouillac 1930: 2, no. 48; transl. von Soden and Falkenstein
1953: 127, 129; for the royal hymns of the Isin dynasty, cf. Römer 1965).
The third king in Mesopotamian history who claims to possess scribal education and mathematical knowledge is Ashurbanipal (668–627 B.C.; cf. Sweet
1990: 55–56).

Since the scribal knowledge necessary for the just administration of the
country is part of the Near Eastern presentation of a wise ruler, the por-
trayal of Joseph as a teacher of scribal craft elevated to the royal status
follows the same ideological trend but in a reverse direction. While in the
Mesopotamian society the presentation of the king as a wise scribe enhanced
his image as an ideal wisdom ruler, Joseph is the one who from the status of a learned teacher of סֹפֵר becomes a glorified ruler. The presentation of Joseph as a teacher who rises to a highly elevated status becomes
a pedagogical example of extreme importance for Levitical scribal education. First by learning (*A.L.D.* 32a–47) and then by teaching סֹפֵר (*A.L.D.*
88) they learn how to keep the sapiential order סֶרֶךְ (*A.L.D.* 30–31) and
may thus hold all the important administrative offices in the society (*A.L.D.*
99–100). All the references to the Levitical royal dignity in the *Document*
(3c l. 2; 67; 99 l. 15; 100 l. 16) cannot be dissociated from this aspect of
the *Document*'s standpoint.

and to kings [on their thrones he was joined]. The sentence has been restored
in accordance with *T. Levi* 13:9: "If he teaches these things and practices
(them), he will throne with kings, like Joseph our brother" ἐὰν διδάσκῃ ταῦτα
καὶ πράττῃ, σύνθρονος ἔσται Βασιλέων, ὡς καὶ Ἰωσὴφ ὁ ἀδελφὸς ἡμῶν. It seems
that the redactors of the *Testament* preserved the tradition of the *Document*
according to which Joseph was glorified and associated with kings due to
his teaching activity. It is unfortunate that neither the Cairo Geniza nor
the Qumran manuscripts preserve the whole sentence. However, the link
between the teaching and sitting on the throne is well attested in *A.L.D.*
93: "And they seat him on the throne of glory because they want to hear
the words of his wisdom." Joseph's royal elevation because of his work as
a wisdom teacher is presented in the latter verse in general terms in relation to the man who teaches wisdom to the one who studies it (*A.L.D.* 90
l. 4–5). In a Qumran text (4Q525 2–3 9) wisdom rewards the man who
attains her, meditates on her, and is faithful to her ways: "She will place
a crown of pure gol]d [on] his [he]ad and she will se[at him] with kings
וְאֵטֶרֶת פֵּז זָ[הֵב [תָּשִׁית עַל רֹאשׁ]וֹ וְעִם מַלְכִים תּוֹשֵׁ[יבֶנ]וּ/הוּ. Similarly Wis 6:20:
"So the desire for wisdom leads to a kingdom" ἐπιθυμία ἄρα σοφίας ἀνάγει
ἐπὶ βασιλείαν (cf. also Job 36:7).

Do not neglect to study wisdom. A.L.D. 90 l. 2–4 close the exhortatory part
of the poem with a call to study wisdom and continue seeking its way.
This exhortation acquires its full significance in the light of the future apostasy of Levi's sons predicted in *A.L.D.* 102 ll. 5–8. They will abandon (102

l. 5 שבק) the way of truth and neglect (102 l. 6 מחל) the paths of [wis-dom]. The vocabulary contact with *A.L.D.* 90 ll. 2–4 is evident, and Levi's exhortation here acquires a hint of urgency in view of the future infidelity. In the light of *A.L.D.* 102, neglecting the study of wisdom is tantamount to abandoning the ways of truth and walking in the darkness of satan, and constitutes the major sin of Levi's sons. The Sumero-Akkadian bilingual text "In Praise of the Scribal Art" contains a similar exhortation not to neglect the pursuit of scribal education: "Do not be careless concerning the scribal art (*ṭupšarrūtu*), do not neglect it (l. 6) . . . if you neglect it, they will make malicious remarks about you" (l. 9; Sjöberg 1972: 127).

The lexeme מחל "to neglect" is attested in Syriac with the meaning "to be/become weak" (Brockelmann 1928: *s.v.*); in late Aramaic a semantic shift occurred and made the lexeme a synonym of סלח "to forgo, remit a debt," (Sokoloff 1990: *s.v.*). The occurrence here is a transitive form of the jussive followed by the infinitive למאלף, the direct object of the latter being חכמתא. In *A.L.D.* 102 l. 6 the verb is most probably transitive, the context, though, is fragmentary. Since the verb is transitive here, the translation should be "to weaken," hence "to neglect." Note that in 4Q541 frg. 24 4 the verb most probably means "to weaken" (cf. Puech 2001: 254).

V. 91 *[Whoever teaches wisdo]m (to) a man wh[o] studies [wisdom].* The whole section 91–93 is dedicated to the praise of the wisdom teacher. The dom-inant theme is his positive reception in foreign lands caused by the gen-eral desire to learn wisdom. This vision stems in the poem from the preceding exhortation to teach scribal craft, instruction, and wisdom and deals with the exaltation of Levi's sons as wisdom teachers.

It is worth noting that the Qumran reading "whoever guides" (מהילך [די]) seems to be a scribal correction from מאלף "the one who teaches" (cf. the note on this Qumran reading in § 2.2.6). The *hapᶜel* participle מהילך from the root הלך "to go" denotes Levitical teaching function necessary to transmit wisdom to whoever seeks it (cf. *A.L.D.* 91 ll. 11–12), and is thus related in meaning to *paᶜel* אלף (*A.L.D.* 13 l. 7; 15 l. 13; 88 l. 18; 90 l. 23). In 4Q542 1 i 12 Qahat lauds his sons: "you have kept and carried on (והילכתון) the inheritance which your fathers gave you. . . ." The same root הלך in *hapᶜel* expresses there the action of handing down the inheri-tance to future generations. The wisdom teacher in the *Document* is the one who teaches a priestly and sapiential halakah that includes the knowledge of the purity rules concerning marriage and liturgical service (*A.L.D.* 14–18; 19–21); sacrificial order of the burnt offering (22–30); metro-arithmetical calculations of the sacrificed material (31–46a); established ratios between the metrological units (46b–47); prohibition of blood consumption (55–57).

la[nd] or province. The expression is most probably a fixed word-pair denot-ing all the inhabited regions (cf. also *A.L.D.* 95 l. 20).

a brother or companion. Cf. the comment on *A.L.D.* 1c.

[and he is not] considered a stranger in it. Not being treated like a stranger in a foreign country because of the desire to learn wisdom is most proba-bly an allusion to Joseph's story and his acceptance to the royal court (see

above *A.L.D.* 90). When his brothers eventually come down to Egypt, he initially treats them like strangers (אליהם ויתנכר) speaking roughly to them (Gen 42:7).

a stranger [in it] . . . a half-bree[d]. The word pair "stranger" נכרי and "half-breed" כילאי is also attested in the *Testament of Qahat* where the son of Levi warns his sons not to give their inheritance to נכראין and their heritage to כילאין (4Q542 1 i 5–6). Citing Isa 32:5 (כילי) and 7 (כלי), É. Puech (1991: 39; cf. 2001: 273) first suggested translating the gentilic כילאי with *escroc*, that is, "a scoundrel." Caquot (1995: 41), however, links the term with the Hebrew dual form כלאים "two kinds" indicating the types of animals, seed, or textile that cannot be mixed (cf. Lev 19:19; Deut 22:9; 4QMMT B 76–78 = 4Q396 1–2 iv 6–8; 4Q269 9 2). He notices that the term may refer at Qumran and in the Mishnah to the animal offspring resulting from this kind of illicit unions, and he translates the term with "hybrids." He also points out that the term appears in 4QMMT, where the law of Lev 19:19 is recalled to stigmatize the illicit priestly marriages. In fact, in 4QMMT B 79–82 (4Q396 1–2 iv 8–11) the Leviticus law stands in the context of priestly illicit marriages, and Caquot's interpretation fits well with the *Document* since it prohibits exogamous marriages (see *A.L.D.* 16 and 62).

they all give him glory. Dan 2:37; 5:18; 7:14 use the expression "to give glory" יקר יהב, and the royal glory as a gift from God is intended (cf. *A.L.D.* 90 and 93). Here those who learn from the teacher give him glory due to his wisdom.

[be]cause they all desire to learn from his wisdom. This monocolon in the poetic structure of the fourth stanza occupies the climactic position (see literary analysis in Form and Structure above). It explains the reason for the fame and positive acceptance the wisdom teacher enjoys in foreign lands. The general desire to learn makes him welcome everywhere he goes (91 ll. 6–10) and becomes the cause of his glorification (91 l. 11a). *A.L.D.* 93 similarly connects the glorious elevation of the wisdom teacher with the desire of his pupils to learn wisdom from him.

V. 92 *his well-wishers are great ones.* The verse makes one understand that the sapiential teaching activity leads to building up of friendly relations. For the idiom שאל שלם "to greet," see 4Q197 4 iii 3 (Tob 7:1); cf. Hermopolis 1:3; 6:2. It is a customary expression of greeting in the Semitic literature of the ancient Near East.

V. 93 *And they seat him on the throne of glory.* For the parallel Hebrew expression "throne of glory" כסא כבוד, see 1 Sam 2:8; Isa 22:23; Jer 14:21; 17:12; cf. θρόνος δόξης Matt 19:28; 25:31. Note that the teacher in the Greek school sat on a θρόνος while teaching his pupils in a classroom (Marrou 1956: 145). Here the privileged position of the wisdom teacher is the result of his teaching competence. Those who elevate him are his pupils who desire to learn wisdom from him. The verse summarizes the same thought already expressed in *A.L.D.* 91 where the teacher's elevation is the result of his pupils' desire to learn wisdom from him.

A similar description of the teacher's glorification may be found in a Sumerian composition "schooldays" that deals with the education of a scribe in the Sumerian *edubba*. The text describes the schoolboy's vicissitudes at school and his suggestion to his father to invite the teacher home for a visit. The father readily agrees to his son's desire and the story continues: "The teacher was brought from school; having entered the house, he was seated in the seat of honor. The schoolboy took the . . .???, sat down before him; whatever he had learned of the scribal art, he unfolded to his father." (Kramer 1949: 206, lines 52–56)

The father praises the "school-father" of his son and bestows gifts upon him. Then the teacher gives a speech to his pupil thanking him for the gifts and honor received. It is worth noting that both in Levi's poem and in the Sumerian text the teacher is exalted by being seated in a seat of honor, and in both texts the exalted position assigned to him is due to his profession. The ancient Sumerian motif of the teacher's glorification has been incorporated into Levi's poem and presented to the Levitical priestly students as a motivation for pursuing learning and acquiring the status of a teacher.

the words of his wisdom. For the Greek counterpart of the Aramaic מילי חוכמתה see 1 Cor 2:4 ἐν σοφίας λόγοις; cf. 1 Cor 2:13; 12:8 λόγος σοφίας.

V. 94 This verse begins a new section in the wisdom poem (*A.L.D.* 94–97) which presents wisdom as a glorious, hidden, and good treasure that cannot be acquired by military force but by those who seek her in truth. The definition of wisdom and a proper way of acquiring her is expounded in *A.L.D.* 94 and 97; the impropriety of a military expedition is set out in *A.L.D.* 95–96. The repetition of יקר in 93 l. 14 and 94 l. 16 stylistically conjoins the two sections, similarly to חכמתא למאלף (90 ll. 2–3) and אלף חכמה (91 l. 5) that conjoin the first and second part of the poem.

Great wealth of glory is wisdom. In Esth 1:4 a similar Hebrew expression can be found עשר כבוד מלכותו "wealth of his royal glory" (cf. the Greek πλοῦτος δόξης in Rom 9:23; Eph 1:18; 3:16; Col 1:27). The sapiential literature often conjoins wisdom with wealth and riches. In 1 Kgs 10:23 Solomon is said to excel all the kings of the earth in wealth and wisdom (לעשר ולהכמה). In 2 Chr 1:10–12 Solomon asks God for wisdom and knowledge to judge the people and is granted not only these but wealth, possessions, and glory (ועשר ונכסים וכבוד) as well. The underlying idea is that the knowledge of wisdom comes before and surpasses any wealth and possessions. The *Document* does a step further and metaphorically equates the knowledge of wisdom with wealth of glory. The idea is then developed in the following *A.L.D.* 95–96, where hidden wisdom cannot be plundered by the invading armies, whereas all other possessions of the land and province can.

and a good treasure for all who acquire her. The term "treasure" סימא, in a probable reference to wisdom, is also found in *A.L.D.* 96 l. 3 in a fragmentary context. Its meaning is synonymous to אוצר in *A.L.D.* 95 l. 22; cf. Sir 40:18b MS B אוצר, whereas MS B mg. reads סימה, the same exchange

340 CHAPTER THREE

occurring between Sir 41:14a B and Bmg. agreeing with M; cf. also 4Q200
frg. 2 9 (Tob 4:9). The term קני "to acquire, buy" often denotes a com-
mercial activity (Lipiński 1993: 63–65), but in the reconstructed wisdom
poem (cf. § 2.2.6 and § 2.1.16) it stands in poetical parallelism with ידע
"to know." This parallelism indicates that it metaphorically connotes the
process of learning. Acquiring (קנה) wisdom as a metaphor for learning is
a frequent motif in other wisdom texts (see Prov 4:5, 7; 16:16; 17:16; 23:23;
Sir 51:25 MS B). One verse in Sir 51:21 MS B is particularly close to the
Document's image of acquiring wisdom as a good treasure: "therefore I
acquired her as a good possession" בעבור קניתיה קנין טוב. The metaphor
of "acquiring" wisdom most probably reflects the ancient social custom of
paying the tutor for the education received (cf. Lemaire 1981: 56–57). The
Sumero-Akkadian composition "In Praise of the Scribal Art" similarly values scribal education: "Strive to (master) the scribal art (*ṭupšarrūtu*) and it
will enrich you, be industrious in the scribal art and it will provide you
with wealth and abundance (ll. 4–5) . . . The scribal art is a good lot, rich-
ness and abundance" (l. 10; Sjöberg 1972: 127).

Vv. 95–96 *If mighty kings come and a great army*. The imagery of a military
expedition against any land and province serves the purpose of explaining
the futility of any attempt to acquire wisdom treasures and to find its hidden places with violence. In the context of the *Document A.L.D.* 95–96 belies
the opinion that Levi acquired the right to priesthood through his military
exploits at Shechem as indicated in *Jub.* 30:18. The proper way of acquiring wisdom is to seek it through study (cf. *A.L.D.* 97 and 98). Ezra 4:20
reads the *Document*'s phrase "mighty kings" מלכין תקיפין. Ezek 26:7 describes
Nebuchadnezzar's military expedition against Tyre in a way similar to *A.L.D.*
95 ll. 18–19: "king of kings, with horses and chariots, and with horsemen
and a host of many soldiers" מלך מלכים בסוס וברכב ובפרשים וקהל ועם רב
(cf. Deut 20:1; Josh 11:4).
    and they will plunder everything. *A.L.D.* 95 l. 22–96 l. 3 describes what any
royal military expedition cannot achieve against wisdom, which is metaphorically compared to a besieged city with a hidden treasure. Using this imagery,
the author probably alluded to the siege and destruction of Jerusalem, the
city plundered by the Babylonian troops (cf. Jer 20:5). For the verb "to
spoil, to plunder" בזז (*A.L.D.* 95 ll. 21, 22), cf. 1QapGen XXI 28, 33; XXII
4, 11; 4Q318 frg. 2 ii 8.
    the treasuries of wisdom. The principal obstacles for plundering the wisdom
treasuries consist in an impossibility of finding its hidden places and in
entering its gates. The militants will further be unable to conquer its walls
and to see its treasure (*A.L.D.* 96). The section ends with a statement underlying the priceless worth of wisdom, a treasure that cannot be plundered.
The phrase אוצרות חכמה is also found in Sir 41:12 MS B פחד על שם כי
הוא ילוך מאלפי אוצרות חכמה "Have respect for (your) name for it will stand
by you more than thousands of wisdom treasures." The context, however,
is different with the reference to one's good name. Col 2:3 speaks about
wisdom treasures hidden in Christ: "in whom are hid all the treasures of

wisdom and knowledge" ἐν ᾧ εἰσιν πάντες οἱ θησαυροὶ τῆς σοφίας καὶ γνώσεως ἀπόκρυφοι).

V. 96 *her hidden places.* In the immediate context, the term "hidden place" מטמור from the root טמר "to hide, conceal" is semantically related to "wisdom treasures" אוצרי חוכמתא in 95 l. 22 and "treasure" סימא in 94 l. 17 and 96 l. 3. They all indicate the impossibility to conquer wisdom with a military expedition. The connection of the term with the root טמר "to hide, to conceal" and other applications of the same root in the *Document* explain what this term is referring to in the context of the whole *Document*. In *A.L.D.* 7 l. 12 Levi hides (טמר *pe'al*) in his heart his visionary experience, and in *A.L.D.* 15 l. 12, referring to all his instructions in *A.L.D.* 14–61, Isaac assures Levi that he will not hide (טמר *pe'al*) anything from him. Hidden places of wisdom, therefore, refer both to Levi's visionary experience and to the priestly and metro-arithmetical teaching received from Isaac. For the inaccessibility of wisdom, see Job 28, esp. Job 28:12, 20; Qoh 7:23–25; Bar 3:15, 29–31. According to Job 28:23, only "God understands the way to it, and he knows its place" (מקומה), cf. Prov 2:6; Sir 1:1; Col 2:3; Jas 1:5.

V. 97 *[every] ma[n who] looks for wisdom.* This fragmentary verse indicates a proper access to hidden places of wisdom as contrasted with the military exploits described in *A.L.D.* 95–96. The one who looks for wisdom in truth will find its hidden place and will probably not lack anything. In the context of the *Document*, Levi fully realizes this ideal by asking from God for wisdom in truth (see *A.L.D.* 1a vv. 4, 8). The other way suggested to find wisdom is studying and teaching the instruction of wisdom (*A.L.D.* 88–90; 98), in which Levi again excels. He is first taught by Isaac the true or righteous law (*A.L.D.* 13; 15), and then exhorts his sons to keep his words and instruction concerning sapiential truth (*A.L.D.* 83b–84). 4Q525 2 ii proclaims blessed a man who attains wisdom and walks in the law of the Most High.

V. 98 *[I saw in visions that] you will inherit them.* This is the last verse of the poem in which Levi once again reminds his sons to teach and instruction of wisdom (see *A.L.D.* 88 and 90). Levi then refers to his visions to predict that his sons will inherit "them" אנון. The independent pronoun serving as the object of the verb "to inherit" ירת most probably anaphorically refers to the preceding and instruction of wisdom. The line is fragmentary, though. Note that in 4Q542 1 i 4 Qahat commends his sons to be careful with the inheritance (ירותתא) transmitted to them. In the following lines 12–13, he further advises them to carry on this paternal inheritance, that is truth, justice, uprightness, perfection, purity, holiness, and priesthood קושטא וצדקתא וישירותא ותמימותא ודכ[ותא וק]ודשא וכהנ[ו]נתא (cf. also 4Q542 1 ii 9–13). Except for ישירותא and תמימותא, all the terms are reflected in the *Document* and indicate a continuity of the "inheritance" received from Qahat and transmitted to his sons. It additionally proves the same preoccupation of the *Document* to assure the transmission of this tradition that is formulated in the phrase "scribal craft, instruction, wisdom" ספר מוסר חכמה

(*A.L.D.* 88; cf. *A.L.D.* 90). Note that the last word of the poem is "glory" יקר, an important term in the following account of the Levitical glorious future (see below Form and Structure of *A.L.D.* 99–104).

3.11   *Perspectives for the Future—A.L.D. 99–104*

Form and Structure

Although Levi continues to address his children, it is certain that a new section in the *Document* begins here. The end of the wisdom poem is well marked in the Qumran manuscript with a scribal hook on the margin and a *vacat* after the word "glory" in *A.L.D.* 98 l. 11. Additionally, the clause "and instruction of wisdom that you (?) teach/study" in *A.L.D.* 98 makes an *inclusio* with *A.L.D.* 88. The term "wisdom," so frequent in the poem, does not appear anymore in *A.L.D.* 99–104, while the last term in the poem "glory" evokes another important theme discussed in the wisdom poem (cf. *A.L.D.* 88 l. 19; 89 l. 20; 90 l. 1; 91 l. 11; 93 l. 14; 94 l. 16; 98 l. 11) and then reintroduced in Levi's speech to his children (cf. *A.L.D.* 100 ll. 17, 18, 19; 104 l. 2; cf. 104 l. 4).

Levi's prophetic speech concentrates on another topic absent in the wisdom poem, that is, the future fate of Levi's children, their glory, their function as priests, kings and officials, and their sinful apostasy. Thus the thematic subdivision into two parts (*A.L.D.* 99–100 and 101–104) can easily be established. The available Qumran manuscripts on the base of which this section is reconstructed are fragmentary and make any speculation as to the content of the missing part of the *Document* futile. They do permit, however, to conclude that Levi's speech does not end with *A.L.D.* 104.

3.11.1   *Future Glory—A.L.D. 99–100*

V. 99 *also in the books I re[ad.* Levi reads in the books about the future multiple functions of his sons. In the *Testaments of the Twelve Patriarchs*, the writings of Enoch contain the future predicted by Jacob's sons (see *T. Sim.* 5:4–6; *T. Levi* 10:5; 14:1; 16:1; *T. Jud.* 18:1; *T. Dan* 5:6; *T. Benj.* 9:1). This claim is only a literary device, which does not reflect the actual content of the Enochic books, but rather supposes their undisputable apocalyptic authority (see Hollander and de Jonge 1985: 39–40). Although the literary motif of "the books" containing wisdom and apocalyptic knowledge appears in the Enochic tradition, (*1 En.* 68:1; 104:12–13; 105:1–2; *2 En.* 33:5, 8–9; 40:2; 47:2; 48:6–8), the *Document* is influenced by the biblical book of Malachi in the elaboration of the concept of the books that contain the fate of Levitical progeny (cf. *A.L.D.* 59).

In the context of the *Document*, "the books" ספריא most probably contain all the Levitical wisdom summarized in the expression "scribal art, instruction and wisdom" (*A.L.D.* 88; cf. 90; 98), and the destiny of the Levitical tribe which has been written in the book of the memorial of life (*A.L.D.* 59); they should also refer to the instruction contained in the *Book of Noah* (*A.L.D.* 57). According to 4Q542 1 ii 9–13, Levi receives the books from his forefathers (cf. *Jub.* 45:16) and hands them down to Qahat who passes them to Amram and his sons.

4Q541 frg. 7 4 reports a unique expression ספרי חכמ]תא "the books of wisdo[m]." Although the context is broken, it is possible to notice that this expression is somehow related to the words (line 5 מאמרה; cf. frg. 9 i 3) and teaching (line 6 לפו]נה cf. frg. 9 i 3) of a mysterious priestly figure described in the composition (cf. Puech 1992: 466–467 and 492–499; Puech 2001: 239–240). Note that Levi begins his wisdom poem with reference to his words (83b l. 8 מאמר) and his main indication for his children is to teach (*pacel* אלף) scribal craft, instruction, and wisdom.

you will b]e heads, and magistrates, and ju[dges. This line is similar to *Jub.* 31:15 where Levi's sons are declared by Isaac to be "princes and judges, and chiefs (*makʷānənta wa-masāfənta wa-malāʾəkta*) of all the seed of the sons of Jacob." *T. Levi* 8:11 speaks of three offices (ἀρχαί) assigned to Levi's sons and *T. Levi* 8:17 specifically calls them "high priests and judges and scribes" ἀρχιερεῖς καὶ κριταὶ καὶ γραμματεῖς. In the *Document*, however, there are six different titles that describe the Levitical future role, so they cannot be easily reduced to a later tripartite division of the Levitical offices. Since the verse is fragmentary, it is not excluded that the original list with Levitical titles was even longer. Note, however, that *A.L.D.* 3c l. 1 can constitute an allusion to this tripartite division of the *Testament*.

heads. In early biblical texts, the term ראש indicates those who stand at the head of a tribal house or social group exercising military and judicial leadership and this title is also linked to the royal office (cf. Bartlett 1969: 1–10). Here the title seems to imply that Levi's sons are leaders by their judicial, royal, and priestly authority (cf. *A.L.D.* 1a v. 18; 3c l. 2; 14; 78). Their leading position is also due to their quality of educated wisdom teachers. Note that the term in 4Q213 frg. 1 i 14 (*A.L.D.* 91 l. 4) "the one who guides" מהיליך implies a sapiential leader's function of presiding in the study of wisdom. According to the *Testament of Qahat*, his descendants must be cautious to whom they transmit their inheritance in order to maintain their privileged leading position. Qahat warns his sons not to give their inheritance (ירותתא 4Q542 1 i 4, 5, 12) to foreigners or half-breeds for that would make them leaders ראשין over his sons (see 4Q542 1 i 5–7). The Levitical "inheritance" in the *Document* means precisely scribal and priestly wisdom acquired by learning and transmitted by teaching (see *A.L.D.* 88, 90, and 98; cf. also Neh 12:7 [heads of the priests]; 12:23 [heads of fathers' houses and priests]; 12:24 [heads of the Levites . . . to praise and give thanks]; 12:46 [head of the singers]).

A similar motif of elevation to a high social position due to the scribal wisdom acquired at school is also present in the already cited Sumerian *edubba* composition "Schooldays." After having been bestowed with numerous gifts by his pupil's father, the happy teacher praises his student and wishes him a bright future due to his achievements as a master of scribal art.

> Young man, because you did not *neglect* my word, did not forsake it,
> May you reach the pinnacle of the scribal art, achieve it completely.
> (. . .)
> Of your brothers, may you be their leader,
> of your companions, may you be their chief,
> may you rank the highest of (all) the schoolboys . . . (lines 70–71, 77–79; Kramer 1949: 206)

magistrates and ju[dges. The two terms שפטין ודא[נ]ין (*A.L.D.* 99 ll. 13–14) denote the judicial offices that the sons of Levi are supposed to inherit; for Levi's judicial function, see the comment on *A.L.D.* 14. For the term "servants" עבדין (*A.L.D.* 99 l. 14), see the comment on *A.L.D.* 1a vv. 11, 15a and 17. For the function of a שפט in the administration of justice in ancient Israel, cf. Weinfeld 1977.

also priests and kings you will be[come. The two terms "priests and kings" ומלכין כהנין (*A.L.D.* 99 l. 15) assign to Levi's sons the two offices summarized in the phrase "the priestly kingdom" מלכות כהנותא (cf. *A.L.D.* 3c, 67, and 100).

V. 100 *your kingdom will be[. . . glo]ry.* The term מלכותכן denotes the priestly kingdom of Levi's sons (see *A.L.D.* 3c l. 2 and 99 l. 15). It is set here in connection with the concept of "glory" יקר (*A.L.D.* 100 ll. 17, 18, 19) that will have no end (100 l. 17). The latter statement concords with *A.L.D.* 88 l. 19 that uses the expression "eternal glory" עלם יקר in relation to Levitical wisdom. In both cases the eschatological perspective is quite clear. In *A.L.D.* 88 l. 19 eternal glory is associated with wisdom, a result of Levitical teaching activity. Glory without end that will not be taken away from Levi's sons (*A.L.D.* 100 ll. 17–18) sets the same eschatological standard for their kingdom (100 l. 16). The term "end" סוף may have a temporal meaning (Dan 6:27; 7:26). The expression "there is no end" לא איתי סוף is parallel in meaning to the Hebrew אין קץ (see Isa 9:6; Job 22:5; for non-temporal reference, cf. Qoh 4:8, 16; 12:12; also cf. אין קצה Isa 2:7, 7; Nah 2:10; 3:3, 9). This linear eschatology is characteristic to the whole *Document* about the future exalted position of the Levitical tribe (see the comment on *A.L.D.* 3a). Since the line is broken, the precise relationship is impossible to assess. The subject of the verb "to pass away" עבר is most probably either "glory," or "kingdom." For the expression "for all the generations" (*A.L.D.* 100 ll. 18–19), cf. *A.L.D.* 3a l. 7.

3.11.2 *Future Apostasy—A.L.D. 101–104*

V. 101 *for [you] all the nations . . . [sun, m]oon and stars.* The verse is very fragmentary, the preserved vocabulary allows, however, some speculation about its content. Levi still speaks to his sons, but the perspective is universal and cosmic with reference to all the nations, moon, and stars. Milik reconstructs the verse together with *A.L.D.* 102 on the basis of *T. Levi* 14:3, and translates his reconstruction: "[. . . the sun], the moon, and the stars [. . . shine] above [the earth. Do you not shine as the sun and as] the moon?" (1976: 24). Although the reconstruction may be disputable, there is no doubt that the *Testament*'s text agrees in many points with the *Document*, and, consequently, Milik's interpretation seems plausible. Additionally, the description of the Levitical priesthood with cosmic terminology is attested elsewhere. Sir 50:6–7 MS B describes Simon the high priest with a similar cosmic imagery: "Like a star (כוכב) shining among the clouds, like the full moon (וכירח) at the holy-day season; like the sun (וכשמש) shining on the temple of the King, like the rainbow (וכקשת) appearing in the cloudy sky" (Skehan and Di Lella 1987: 547). 4Q541 9 i 3–4 affirms about the mysterious Levitical person that "his everlasting sun will shine and his fire will burn in all the ends of the earth." Note that according to the *Document*, Qahat is born at sunrise, and thus his bright future as the royal high priest over Israel is foreseen (cf. *A.L.D.* 68).

V. 102 *thus you will darken.* Using the metaphor of darkness and the concept of guilt, *A.L.D.* 102 ll. 1–7 describe Levitical apostasy from the way of truth, while the following two lines (*A.L.D.* 102 ll. 8–9) seem to ascribe to Levi's sons intelligence and justification, changing thus the tone to a positive one. The metaphor of darkness is most probably set in contrast with the vocabulary of the preceding verse (*A.L.D.* 101), which speaks of the moon and stars.

T. Levi. 14:4 uses the concept of darkness in connection with Levitical moral transgressions: "What will all the nations do, if you are darkened (σκοτισθῆτε) through impiety. . . ." The same idea of being in the dominion of darkness is expressed in *A.L.D.* 102 l. 7. Levi foretells that darkness will come over his sons. In the *Visions of Amram* 4Q548 frg. 1 the dichotomy between light and darkness in relation to human beings expresses the moral dichotomy between evil and foolishness on the one hand and truth and wisdom on the other; compare especially 4Q548 frg. 1 12: "for all foolish and ev[il are dark,] and all [wi]se and truthful are brilliant" ארו כל סכל ורש[ע השיכין וכל[הכי[ם וקשיט נהיר]ין. The concept of darkness resurfaces in *A.L.D.* 102 ll. 6–7, which deal with Levitical apostasy (see below).

The particle הלא in *A.L.D.* 102 ll. 2 and 4 introduces two rhetorical questions that most probably deal with the legal responsibility of Levi's priestly descendants for the corruption of humankind. Milik (1976: 24) argued that *A.L.D.* 102 l. 2 is an early allusion to the legal complaint of Enoch against the Watchers (*1 En.* 13–16) who are responsible for the moral corruption of humanity (*1 En.* 13:2 and 16:3). He further suggests that both priests

and angels are supposed to be upholders of wisdom and of the true cult
of God and the corruption of humanity is due to the corruption of these
two groups. Although the text is fragmentary and the allusion to Enoch
questionable (cf. § 2.1.17.2), Milik's interpretation corresponds to the *Document's*
viewpoint. It is quite probable, as suggested by Milik, that the allusion to
the *Book of Watchers* is aimed at equaling the Watchers' responsibility for
the corruption of humankind with the Levitical priestly responsibility for
failing to uphold the divine order inscribed in the creation and reflected
in the liturgy. In *A.L.D.* 18 Levi is placed on the same level with the angels
and legal responsibility of the Levitical priesthood is underlined in *A.L.D.*
14 and 99. Levi's liturgical activity is aimed at maintaining a due sapiential order (*A.L.D.* 30–31). If this order were not upheld, a true cult of God
would be certainly compromised.

] did he not accept[to] go to?[. The verb קבל may mean "to lodge a com-
plaint, accuse" (*pe῾al*, e.g. 1QapGen XX 14; 11QtgJob VIII 2 [24:12]; cf.
Fitzmyer 1962: 19), or "to receive, accept" (*pa῾el*, e.g. Dan 2:6; 6:1; 7:18).
Milik (1976: 23) restores here Enoch's name and prefers the former meaning of the verb. However, since the line is damaged, his restoration is not
certain. Additionally, the allusion to the role of Enoch as an accuser of the
Watchers does not have its adequate reflection in the *Book of Watchers* (*1
En.* 1–36). The spirits of the dead lodge a complaint against the Watchers
(see *1 En.* 9:3 [4Q202 iii 1 קבל], 10, 12; *1 En.* 22:5 [4Q206 frg. 2 ii 4, 4
קבל]; cf. 4Q530 frg. 1 i 4; 4Q203 frg. 8 10). Since *T. Levi* 14:2 actually
mentions Enoch's name, the line in the *Document* could refer to Enoch and
his mission to the Watchers.

and on whom will the guilt be. The lexeme חובה "guilt" stands in parallelism
with חטא "sin" in 4Q534 1 ii + 2 16. It resurfaces in the *Testament of Qahat*
4Q542 1 ii 5–6 in the section dedicated to the future of Qahat's sons
(lines 2–8): ". . . and you will rise to pass the sentence o[n . . .] and to see
the sins of all the sinners of the ages ולמחזיא חובת כול חיבי עלמין. Here the
infinitive "to see" למחזיא is probably parallel to "to judge" למדן from the
preceding line and should be rendered with "to consider, to weigh" in a
juridic inquiry. This future role of Qahat's sons confirms the interpretation
of *A.L.D.* 102 ll. 3–4 in relation to the Levitical priestly and judicial responsibilities. Being guilty of their own corruption and that of the nations, they
make their role in the society untenable. In the context of the *Document*,
their guilt may consist in straying from the sapiential instruction of the forefathers (*A.L.D.* 14–61), and thus committing acts of lawlessness (cf. *A.L.D.*
1a vv. 13 and 78). *T. Levi* 15:5–8 and 16:1–3 list priestly sins that are not
specified by the *Document's* fragmentary text.

behold, they will know it. A.L.D. 102 ll. 3–4 suggest that the corruption of
the Levitical priesthood will be known to the nations and Levi's sons will
be held guilty for the ensuing consequences. The pronominal suffix *he*
attached to the imperfect ידעונה "they will know" most probably refers to
the content of the three following verses that describe Levitical apostasy.
The subject of the verb is most probably all the nations mentioned in *A.L.D.*
101 l. 1. Levitical responsibility in relation to the nations stems from the

juridic and priestly responsibility assigned to Levi and his sons in the *Document* (cf. *A.L.D.* 1a v. 18; 14–50; 99).

the p]aths of righteousness you will abandon. This expression in the *Document* relates to Levi and his exemplary way of life as a just priest, king, and educated scribe. He corrects all his ways (1a v. 2), prays to God for the revelation of the true/just paths (1a v. 6) and true judgment (1a v. 18), and exhorts his children to practice truth in their life (85–86). Abandoning the ways of truth means for his sons to neglect the study of instruction, and wisdom (90 ll. 2–4) and the ideal of the just priest who follows the true law/order of priesthood (14–61). The same expression א[רחת קשטא is also found in 4Q212 1 ii 18 (*1 En.* 91:18); 1 v 25 (*1 En.* 94:1) (cf. also "the just eternal path" ארח קשט עלמא 4Q212 1 iv 22 [*1 En.* 91:14]; "and all his ways in truth" וכל ארחתה בקשוט 4Q246 ii 5). As the construct state suggests, the noun "paths, ways" שבילי was followed by another noun, probably צדקתא, a term related in meaning to קשט (cf. *A.L.D.* 85). The lexeme ארח is quite frequent in the Aramaic literature and in the Old Testament as a metaphor for the life conduct (cf. the comment on *A.L.D.* 1a v. 2). The verb pair "to abandon" שבק and "to neglect" חמל also appear in *A.L.D.* 90 ll. 2-4 where Levi exhorts his sons not to abandon the way of wisdom and not to neglect the study of wisdom.

you will walk in the darkness of satan. This unique expression חשוך שטן proves that the *Document*'s eschatology is related to the light-darkness opposition, characteristic of a dualistic view of the spiritual world. In *A.L.D.* 1a v. 10 Levi prays not to be misled by any satan from God's path, and, while his prayer is heard in his life, the contrary is true in the future of his sons. The term שטן denotes a spiritual being hostile to humanity (cf. *A.L.D.* 1a v. 10). His association with darkness in *A.L.D.* 102 l. 6 recalls Melchirešaʿ from the *Testament of Amram*. He is an angelic being whose dominion is darkness and who rules over humankind (see 4Q543 frgs. 5–9 4–5; 4Q544 frg. 1 13; frg 2 12–15). Walking in the darkness of satan refers, therefore, to being under the power and dominion of spiritual beings hostile to light. Note that in the *Testament of Amram*, there appears another angelic being whose dominion is light and whose name is most probably Melchizedek (see 4Q543 frgs. 5–9 6–8; 4Q544 frg. 1 14; frg. 2 16). Levi, who prays not to be under the rule of satan and is evidently heard by God, is indirectly associated with the person of biblical Melchizedek (see the comment on *A.L.D.* 9). Similar phraseology is attested elsewhere: "to walk in darkness" περιπατεῖν ἐν τῇ σκοτίᾳ (see John 8:12; 12:35; 1 John 2:11); "to walk in the ways of darkness" בדרכי חושך יתהלכו (1QS III 21; cf. IV 11); "those who walk in darkness" (1QS XI 10); "to walk in accord with the rules of darkness" (1QM XIII 12).

You will become intelligent[you will be]come a[ll t]ruthfu[l. *A.L.D.* 102 ll. 8–9 change the tone to a positive one. The term שכל "to have insight, to be clever," is related to "insight" שכלתנו found in association with חכמה (Dan 5:11, 14) or "knowledge" מנדע (Dan 5:12). In 4Q542 1 i 10 Qahat exhorts his sons to walk in uprightness "with a truthful and good spirit" ברוח קשיטא וטבה; in the *Visions of Amram* 4Q548 frg. 1 12 "truthful" is

paired with "wise" חכים, the latter word is partly restored: "for all foolish
and ev[il are dar]k, and all [wi]se and truthful are brillian[t]." For the
expression "truthful man" נברא קשיט[א], see 4Q197 frg. 4 iii 9 (Tob 7:7).
The two sapiential terms suggest that the fall and sin will not cause a total
rejection.

V. 103 *]with them/their people (?) by the [e]vil one.* Since the lines in *A.L.D.*
103 are broken, their content is not certain. The fragment most probably
deals with enemies of Levi's sons, while line 2 suggests an individual who
most probably will oppose them. It might be the prince of darkness,
Melkireša', who appears in the *Visions of Amram.* Line 3, however, speaks
about those who hate Levi's sons. Their opponents, therefore, are many.
For the active participle "those who hate" שאנין, cf. Dan 4:16; 1QapGen
XX 17.

V. 104 *more glorious than the women.* The verbal form "you tell me" תמרון in
A.L.D. 104 l. 3 indicates that Levi is talking to his children and the main
topic is their glory (lines 2 and 4; cf. *A.L.D.* 88). Any further comment
could only be based on sheer speculation. The hypothetical reference to
Dinah (line 3—or judgment, cf. § 2.1.17.4) and women (line 4) could suggest the context of the Shechem killing.

CONCLUSION

The commentary on the text stops where the text itself ends. The present work has presented all the manuscript evidence of the *Document*, reconstructed its fragmentary text, and analyzed its content. The constant preoccupation of the commentary has been to explain the main ideas contained in the *Document* in relation to biblical literature, scribal tradition of the ancient Near East, and post-exilic Jewish history. The interpretive line that has consisted in the literary and historical analysis of the *Document*'s content has opened new perspectives in the understanding of the composition, perspectives that have not hitherto been noticed and explored.

The results of the present research indicate that the constant scholarly comparison of the *Levi Document* with the Greek *Testament of Levi* has not been a proper way to understand and explain the former composition. The comparison between the two is helpful to restore the fragmentary text of the *Document*, but the *Testament* underwent many literary transformations and its literary form and content only partially reflect the literary form and content of the former composition. The literary form and purpose of the *Document* are different from the Greek *Testament* and its literary sources and references point to a different set of ideas that influenced the composers. The *Testament* redactor(s) molded the text of the *Document* into a testamentary form and abbreviated or transformed it heavily, thus eliminating much from its original text and literary form.

The *Document* belongs to the category of wisdom literature, the purpose of which is to present the ideal of a wise priest, ruler, and scribe. The composition is most probably to be situated in a social context of family-based Levitical education from which the composition stems and to which it belongs. Levi is depicted as a student of priestly and metro-arithmetical wisdom his grandfather Isaac transmitted to him. Thus professional knowledge is passed on from one generation to another, and Levi in his wisdom poem appears as a sapiential teacher who exhorts his children/students to hand down the same knowledge to future generations. The pivotal person of Levi's poem is the sapiential teacher whose elevation and international glory stems from his wisdom and his teaching qualities.

Thus, the ideal of a teacher of professional priestly and scribal wisdom stands at the heart of Levi's presentation. The future glory of Levitical priests depends on the acceptance and continual study of this kind of professional knowledge and on the faithfulness to the presented sapiential ideals.

Unfortunately, the text of the *Document* remains incomplete and fragmentary, and the last word concerning its interpretation cannot be formulated. The beginning and the end of the text are lacking, and any attempt to reconstruct them is unavoidably reduced to a mere speculation. If some future discoveries do not bring to light the full text of the *Document*, one will have to be content with the knowledge of what remains from this interesting and difficult composition. The analysis of its literary form indicates that it was carefully composed with literary means that proved the literary skills of its author, his broad learning and education. Although his identity remains hidden to the modern reader, his preoccupation with the education of the priestly class indicates how important this problem was for him. In this respect the *Document* opens a new page in the understanding of the Second Temple priesthood. It reflects actual practices used in the professional preparation of priestly apprentices and ascribes a high social position and fame to the teacher of sapiential matters indicating thus the goals of Levitical education. The priestly class is to occupy the leading role in Israel provided that it keeps the tradition of the forefathers and transmits it to future priestly generations. Neglecting sapiential education leads to abandoning the way of truth and justice, and to the dominion of darkness over the sons of Levi.

The last consideration in this work is dedicated to metro-arithmetical concerns in Levitical education. The study of sexagesimal metrological system by Levi indicates how these introductory elements of mathematical education became a paradigm for Levitical priestly students and part of priestly inheritance and piety. Levi learns how to count so that his liturgical actions may be completed in order, by measure and weight. The priest of God the most high, Lord of heavens, thus expresses his commitment to fulfill his duty of assuring a proper worship of his God. The one who in his prayer asks for wisdom, understanding, and knowledge studies his professional wisdom under Isaac to be close to God and to serve him properly.

St. Augustine, who himself studied mathematics in his childhood and used it later to interpret biblical data, considered knowledge without the knowledge of God as useless and worth nothing. His opinion would certainly have been praised by Levi whose professional studies and skills were meant to serve and worship God in a due manner.

> A man who knows that he owns a tree and gives thanks to you [God] for the use of it, even though he does not know exactly how many cubits high it is or what is the width of its spread, is better than the man who measures it and counts all its branches but does not own it, nor knows and loves his Creator. In an analogous way the believer has the whole world of wealth (Prov 17:6 LXX) and 'possesses all things as if he had nothing' (2 Cor 6:10) by virtue of his attachment to you whom all things serve; yet he may know nothing about the circuits of the Great Bear. It is stupid to doubt that he is better than the person who measures the heaven and counts the stars and weighs the elements, but neglects you who have disposed everything 'by measure and number and weight' (Wis 11:21). (Augustine, *Confessions* 5.4.7 [1991: 75–76])

TEXT AND TRANSLATION

For ease of consultation there follow the translation and reconstructed text of the *Document*. When the translation is based on the Greek version, the text in **bold** indicates the words and phrases preserved in the Aramaic of Qumran or Geniza fragments. The *italics* in the translation indicate the text that has been restored without any manuscript evidence. The order of the fragments and missing texts are discussed in § 1.4.3.

(1a v. 1) τότε ἐγὼ ἔπλυνα τὰ ἱμάτιά μου, καὶ καθαρίσας αὐτὰ ἐν ὕδατι καθαρῷ

(1a v. 2) καὶ ὅλος ἐλουσάμην ἐν ὕδατι ζῶντι· καὶ πάσας τὰς ὁδούς μου ἐποίησα εὐθείας.

(1a v. 3) τότε τοὺς ὀφθαλμούς μου καὶ τὸ πρόσωπόν μου ἦρα πρὸς τὸν οὐρανόν, καὶ τὸ στόμα μου ἤνοιξα καὶ ἐλάλησα,

(1a v. 4) καὶ τοὺς δακτύλους τῶν χειρῶν μου καὶ τὰς χεῖράς μου ἀνεπέτασα εἰς ἀλήθειαν κατέναντι τῶν ἁγίων καὶ ηὐξάμην καὶ εἶπα

(1a v. 5) Κύριε, γινώσκεις πάσας τὰς καρδίας, καὶ πάντας τοὺς διαλογισμοὺς ἐννοιῶν σὺ μόνος ἐπίστασαι.

(1a v. 6) καὶ νῦν τέκνα μου μετ᾽ ἐμοῦ. καὶ δός μοι πάσας ὁδοὺς ἀληθείας·

(1a v. 7) μάκρυνον ἀπ᾽ ἐμοῦ, κύριε, τὸ πνεῦμα τὸ ἄδικον καὶ διαλογισμὸν τὸν πονηρὸν καὶ πορνείαν, καὶ ὕβριν ἀπόστρεψον ἀπ᾽ ἐμοῦ.

(1a v. 8) δειχθήτω μοι, δέσποτα, τὸ πνεῦμα τὸ ἅγιον, καὶ βουλὴν καὶ σοφίαν καὶ γνῶσιν καὶ ἰσχὺν δός μοι

(1a v. 9) ποιῆσαι τὰ ἀρέσκοντά σοι καὶ εὑρεῖν χάριν ἐνώπιόν σου καὶ αἰνεῖν τοὺς λόγους σου μετ᾽ ἐμοῦ, κύριε·

(1a v. 10) καὶ μὴ κατισχυσάτω με πᾶς σατανᾶς πλανῆσαί με ἀπὸ τῆς ὁδοῦ σου.

(1a v. 11) καὶ ἐλέησόν με καὶ προσάγαγέ με εἶναί σου δοῦλος καὶ λατρεῦσαί σοι καλῶς.

(1a v. 12) τεῖχος εἰρήνης σου γενέσθαι κύκλῳ μου, καὶ σκέπη σου τῆς δυναστείας σκεπασάτω με ἀπὸ παντὸς κακοῦ.

(1a v. 13) παράδος διὸ δὴ καὶ τὴν ἀνομίαν ἐξάλειψον ὑποκάτωθεν τοῦ οὐρανοῦ, καὶ συντελέσαι τὴν ἀνομίαν ἀπὸ προσώπου τῆς γῆς.

(1a v. 14) καθάρισον τὴν καρδίαν μου, δέσποτα, ἀπὸ πάσης ἀκαθαρσίας, καὶ προσαροῦμαι πρὸς σε αὐτός·

(1a v. 15a) καὶ μὴ ἀποστρέψῃς τὸ πρόσωπόν σου ἀπὸ τοῦ υἱοῦ παιδός σου Ἰακώβ.

(1a v. 15b) σύ, κύριε, εὐλόγησας τὸν Ἀβραὰμ πατέρα μου καὶ Σάρραν μητέρα μου,

(1a v. 16) καὶ εἶπας δοῦναι αὐτοῖς σπέρμα δίκαιον εὐλογημένον εἰς τοὺς αἰῶνας.

(1a v. 17) εἰσάκουσον δὲ καὶ τῆς φωνῆς τοῦ παιδός σου Λευὶ γενέσθαι σοι ἐγγύς,

(1a v. 18) καὶ μέτοχον ποίησον τοῖς λόγοις σου ποιεῖν κρίσιν ἀληθινὴν εἰς πάντα τὸν αἰῶνα, ἐμὲ καὶ τοὺς υἱούς μου εἰς πάσας τὰς γενεὰς τῶν αἰώνων·

1. *Levi's Prayer*

(1a v. 1) Then **I** washed my garments, and having purified them in pure water,

(1a v. 2) I also ba**thed** myself completely in running water, **and** I made straight **all** my ways.

(1a v. 3) Then **I raised** my eyes and my face **towards heavens** and I opened my mouth and spoke;

(1a v. 4) and I spread out faithfully **the fingers of my hands and my hands** in front of the sanctuary and I prayed and **said**,

(1a v. 5) "**O Lord**, you know all the hearts and all the intentions of the thoughts **you alone know**.

(1a v. 6) And now, my children are with me. And give me all the **ways of truth**;

(1a v. 7) **remove** from me, o Lord, the unrighteous spirit and **evil** intention, **and turn fornication** and pride **away** from me.

(1a v. 8) Let the holy spirit, o Master, be shown to me, and give me counsel and wi**sdom and knowledge and strength**

(1a v. 9) to do what pleases you and fi**nd grace before you** and praise your words with me, o Lord.

(1a v. 10) And **do not allow any satan to rule over me** to lead me astray from your way.

(1a v. 11) And have mercy **on me and draw me near to be your** servant and to serve you properly.

(1a v. 12) Let there be a wall of your peace around me and let your shelter of might protect me from every evil.

(1a v. 13) Therefore, remove and efface lawlessness from under the heavens, and eliminate lawlessness from the face of the earth.

(1a v. 14) Purify my heart, o Master, from every impurity, and I will raise myself **to** you;

(1a v. 15a) and do not turn your face away from the son of your servant Jacob.

(1a v. 15b) You, **o Lord, bl**essed Abraham my father and Sarah my mother,

(1a v. 16) and you said you would give them **a seed of right**eousness, blessed for ever.

(1a v. 17) Listen also to **the voice of your ser**vant Levi to be near to you,

(1a v. 18) and make (him) participate in your words to do **a true judgment for a**ll eternity, (that is) me and my sons for all the generations of the ages.

(1a v. 19) καὶ μὴ ἀποστήσῃς τὸν υἱὸν τοῦ παιδός σου ἀπὸ τοῦ προσώπου
σου πάσας τὰς ἡμέρας τοῦ αἰῶνος. καὶ ἐσιώπησα ἔτι δεόμενος.

(1b)] על אבי יעקוב וכד[י   ] באדין ננדת ב[

] שכבת ויתבת אנה ע[ל   מן אבל מין אדי[ן

] בחזות חזוא וחזית שמ[יא   פתיחין וחזית טור   אדין הזיין אחזית[

תחותי רם עד דבק לשמי[א והוית בה ואתפתחו] לי תרעי שמיא ומלאך

] אמר לי לוי על [חד

(1c) דטמאת לב[נ]י יעקב בזנותה על] דברת די כל א[נש יסב לה לאנתה]

למעבד כדין בכל] ארעא   והתמלכת] יעקב אבי ורא[ובן אחי על דברתא

דא (? [

ואמרנן להון ב[חוכמה ובי]נה די ה[וו] צביין אינון בברתן ונהוי כולן א[חין]

וחברין

(2) נזורו] [עורלת בישרכון והתחמיין כו[אתן] ותהון חתימין כואתן במילת

ק[וש]ט ונהוי לכ[ון]

(3) [וחשיבו למקטל יוס[ף](?) אחי בכל עדן [די השתלח לאה[ן]יא די די הוו

בשכם [למשאל לשלם]אחי ואחוי דן [שמ]ע[י]ן[די אחוהי]בשכם ומה

מ]ית יוס[ף ביד עב]די המסא ואחוי אינון יהודה די אנה ושמעון

אחי אזלנא לה[ן]ה לראובן אחונן די למדנ[ת אש]ר ושור

[י]הודה קדמא [ל]משבק עאנא

(3a) א וכען י[ע]לו מכחשי נבר]יא   ] ° [   ] ° [   ] ° [   ] ° []

]אנתה ותחלל שמה ושם אבוה [ ] ° ח ° עם למש] [כ]ה [ ] °דה

בה]ללה] אבהתא וכל

(1a v. 19) And do not turn aside **the son of your servant from before your count**enance for all the days of eternity." And I became silent, still praying.

2. *First Vision*

(1b) Then I went [   ] Upon my father Jacob and wh[en] From Abel Main, then[   ] I lay down and remained o[n   ] vac Then I was shown a vision [   ] in the vision of visions. And I saw the heav[ens *split open and I saw a moun-tain*] beneath me, high until it reached the heave[ns *and I was on it and opened*] to me the gates of heavens and an angel[*said to me, "Levi, enter"*].

3. *Shechem Incident*

(1c) Since she defiled the so[ns *of Jacob with her harlotry,*] there-fore every m[an *will take a wife for himself*] in order to act according to the law in the whole [*country. I consulted*] Jacob my father and Re[uben *my brother on (this?) matter*] and we said to them with [*wisdom* and under]standing because they desired our daughter, so that we all would become b[rothers] and companions:

(2) "Circumcise the foreskin of your flesh and appear like [us] and you will be sealed like us with the circumcision of tr[u]th. And we will be for y[ou]. . . ."

4. *Selling of Joseph*

(3) [*And they plotted to kill Jose*]ph(?) my brother in every time [*when he was sent to*] the [broth]ers who were in Shechem [*to ask about welfare of (?)*]my brothers. And Dan reported [dis]c[uss]i[*ons of his brothers*] in Shechem and how Jose[ph] died [*by the* do]ers of violence. And Judah reported to them that I and Simeon my brother had gone to j[o]in Reuben our brother who (was) on the east of Asher. And [J]udah jumped forward [to] leave the sheep

5. *Heavenly Elevation*

(3a) [   ]and now the pla[g]ues of men will [befa]ll [   ] a woman and she desecrated her name and the name of her father [ ] with [   ] in de[secrating] the fathers. And

בתו]לה זי חבלת שמה ושׁם אבהתה ואבהתת לכל אחיה ול]אבוה}א{

ולא מתחמא שם חסדה

מן כול עמה}א{ <ה> לעלם [   ]לׁם לכל דרי עלמׁא

ומׁ[   ]חׁ° קדישׁן מן עמאֹ

ל] ואׁ[   ]מׁעשר קודש קרבן לאל מׁן

^(3b) [   ] [ ]°°°[   ] ל[עם]° °[ ] שׁ [ ]כׁהנות עלמׁא

^(3c) מׁן די להׁוין תליתין [   ] לב]נׁיך מלכות כהנותא רבא מן מלכות] חרבא

ל]אׁ]לׁ[עׁ]לׁ[יון

⁽⁴⁾ ו]שלמׁא וכל חמדת בכורי ארעא כולה למאכל ולמלכות חרבא פנשא

וקרבא ונחשירותא ועמלא ונצפתא וקטלא וכפנא

⁽⁵⁾ זמנין תאכול וזמנין תכפן וזמנין תעמול וזמנין תנוח וזמנין תדמוך וזמנין

תנוד שנת עינא

⁽⁶⁾ כען חזי לך הכין רבינך מן כולה והיך יהבנא לך רבות שלם עלמׁא

⁽⁷⁾ וננדו שבעתון מן לותי ואנה אתעירת מן שנתי אדין אמרת חזוא הוא דן

וכדן אנה מתמה די יהוי לה כל חזוה וטמרת אף דן בלבי ולכל אינש לא

גליתה

⁽⁸⁾ וﬠׁלנא על אבי יצחק ואׁף הוא כדן [ברכ]נׁי

⁽⁹⁾ אדין כדי הוה יעקב [אבי]מׁעשר כל מה דיהוה לה כנדרה [ודי כ]ﬠׁן

אנה הוית קדמי בראש

[כהנון]תׁה ולי מכל בנוהי יהב קרבן מׁﬠֹשׁ]ר[לאל ואלבשי לבוש כהנותא

ומלי ידי

והוית כהן לאל לאל על}מין/א { <יון> וקרבית כל קרבנוהי וברכת

לאבי בחזוהי וברכת לאחׁי

every [vir]gin who ruins her name and the name of her fathers, she also brings shame on all her brothers [and on] her father. And the name of her revilement will not be wiped out from all her people for ever. [   ]for all the generations of eternity [   ] the holy ones from the people [   ] and [   ] holy tithe, an offering to God from[

(3b)   [ ] with/people [   ] [   ]an eternal priesthood.

(3c)   ] because they will be three [to] your [s]ons, the kingdom of the priesthood is greater than the kingdom [of the sword for [G]od the [most] h[igh].

(4)   and] peace, and all desirableness of the first-fruits of the earth, all of it to eat. But for the kingdom of the sword (there will be) struggle and battle and slaughter and affliction and hissing and killing and hunger.

(5)   Sometimes it will eat, and sometimes it will hunger; and sometimes it will toil, and sometimes it will rest; and sometimes it will sleep, and sometimes will depart the sleep of the eye.

(6)   Now see how we have made you greater than all, and how we have given you the greatness of eternal peace.

(7)   And those seven departed from me, and I arose from my sleep. Then I said, "This is the vision and I wonder that the whole vision like this one will come true." And I hid also this one in my heart and I did not reveal it to anybody.

6. *First Visit to Isaac*
(8)   And we [we]nt to my father Isaac, and he also thus [blessed] me.

7. *Ordination in Bethel*
(9)   Then, when Jacob [my father] was tithing everything that belonged to him according to his vow, [and because n]ow I was first at the head of the [priesth]ood, then to me from all his sons he gave the offering of tith[e] to God, and he clothed me in the priestly clothing, and he filled my hands. And I became a priest of God the most high, and I offered all his offerings. And I blessed my father in his life, and I blessed my brothers.

(10) אדין כולהון ברכוני ואף אבא ברכני ואשלמית להקרבה קורבנוהי
בבית אל

(11) ואזלנא מבית אל ושרינא בבירת אברהם אבונן לות יצחק אבונה

(12) וחזא יצחק אבונא לכולנא וברכנא וחדי

(13) וכדי ידע די אנה כהן לאל עליון למארי שמיא שארי לפקדה יתי
ולאלפא יתי דין כהנותא ואמר לי

(14) לוי אזדהר לך ברי ברי מן כל טומאה ומן כל חטא דינך רב הוא מן
כל בישרא

(15) וכען ברי דין קושטא אחזינך ולא אטמר מינך כל פתגם לאלפותך דין
כהנותא

(16) לקדמין היזדהר לך ברי מן כל פחז וטמאה ומן כל זנו{ת}

(17) ואנת אנתתא מן משפחתי סב לך ולא תחל זרעך עם זניאן ארי זרע
קדיש אנת וקדיש זרעך היך קודשא ארו כהן קדיש אנת מתקרי
לכל זרע אברהם

(18) קריב אנת לאל וקריב לכל קדישוהי כען {הווֹ} <אֹהר> דכי בבשרך
מן כל טומאת כל נבר

(19) וכדי תהוי קאים למיעל לבית אל הוי סחי במיא ובאדין תהוי לביש
לבוש כהנותא

(20) וכדי תהוי לביש הוי תאיב תוב ורחיע ידיך ורנליך עד דלא תקרב
למדבחא כל דנה

(21) וכדי תהוי נסב להקרבה כל די חזה להנסקה למדבחה הוי עוד תאב
ורחע ידיך ורנליך

(22) ומהקריב אעין מהצלחין ובקר איגון לקודמין מן תולעא ובאדין הסק
איגון ארי כדנה חזיתי לאברהם אבי מיזדהר

(23) מן כל תריעשר מיני אעין אמר לי די חזין להסקה מינהון למדבחה
די ריח תננהון בשים סליק

(24) ואלין איגון שמהתהון ארזא ודפרנא וסנדא ואטולא ושוחא ואורנא ברותא
ותאנתא ואע משחא ערא והדסה ואעי דקתא

(10) Then they all blessed me, and also the father blessed me. And I completed to offer his offerings in Bethel.

8. *Wisdom Instruction*

(11) And we went from Bethel and we settled in the fortress of Abraham, our father, alongside Isaac our father.

(12) And Isaac our father saw all of us and blessed us and rejoiced.

(13) And when he learned that I was a priest of God the most high, the Lord of heavens, he began to instruct me and to teach me the law of the priesthood. And he said to me,

(14) "Levi, beware, my son, of every impurity and of every sin; your judgment is greater than all flesh.

(15) And now, my son, the law of truth I will show you, and I will not conceal from you anything to teach you the law of the priesthood.

(16) First of all, beware, my son, of every fornication and impurity and of every harlotry.

(17) And you, take for yourself a wife from my family so that you may not defile your seed with harlots, because you are a holy seed. And holy is your seed like the Holy One, for a holy priest you are called for all the seed of Abraham.

(18) You are close to God and close to all his holy ones, now be pure in your flesh from every impurity of any man.

(19) And whenever you arise to enter the temple of God bathe in water, and then put on the priestly clothing.

(20) And when you are clothed, repeat (it) again and wash your hands and your feet before you sacrifice on the altar all this.

(21) And whenever you take to sacrifice everything that is fitting to offer on the altar, repeat (it) again and wash your hands and feet.

(22) And sacrifice split wood and examine it beforehand for worms and then offer it up, for thus I saw Abraham my father taking precautions.

(23) From all twelve types of wood that are fitting he told me to offer on the altar, these whose smell of their smoke goes up pleasantly.

(24) And these are their names: cedar and juniper and almond and silver fir and fir and ash, cypress and fig and oleaster, laurel and myrtle and asphaltos.

(25a) אלין אינון די אמר לי די די חזין להסקה מנהון ל[תח]ות עלחא על מדבחה

(25b) וכדי תֻנֻסֻקֻת מן אעי)א(אלין על מדבחא ונורא ישרא להדלקא בהון
והא באדין תשרא למזרק דמא על כותלי מדבחה

(26) ועוד רחע ידיך ורגליך מן דמא ושרי להנסקה אבריה מליחין

(27) ראשא הוי מהנסק לקדמין ועלוהי חפי תרבא ולא יתחזה לה דם נכסת
תורא

(28) ובתרוהי צוארה ובתר צוארה ידוהי ובתר ידוהי ניעא עם בן דפנא
בתר ידיא ירכאתא עם שדרת חרצא ובתר ירכאתא רגלין רחיען עם קרביא

(29) וכולהון מליחין במלח כדי חזה להון כמסתהון

(30) ובתר דנה נישפֻא בליל במשחא ובתר כולא חמר נסך והקטיר עליהון
לבונה ויהוון כן עובדיך בסרך וכל קורבניך [לדען]א לריח ניחח
קודם אל עליון

(31) [וכל די] תהוה עביד בסרך הוי עב]יד במשחה] ובמתקל לא תותר צבו
די לא [חזה] ולא תחסר מן הושבן חזת ד]י[ן[א]ע[י]א חזין להקרבה לכל די
סליק למדב[חא]

(32a) לתורא רבא ככר אעין ליה במתקל ואם תרבא בלחודוהי סליק שיתה
מנין ואם פר תורין הוא די סליק

(32b) πεντήκοντα μνᾶς, καὶ εἰς τὸ στέαρ αὐτοῦ μόνον πέντε μνᾶς·

(33) καὶ εἰς μόσχον τέλειον μ΄ μναῖ·

(34) καὶ εἰ κριὸς ἐκ προβάτων ἢ τράγος ἐχ αἰγῶν τὸ προσφερόμενον ᾖ, καὶ
τούτῳ λ΄ μναῖ, καὶ τῷ στέατι τρεῖς μναῖ·

(35) καὶ εἰ ἄρνα ἐκ προβάτων ἢ ἔριφον ἐξ αἰγῶν κ΄ μναῖ, καὶ τῷ στέατι β΄
μναῖ·

(36) καὶ εἰ ἀμνὸς τέλειος ἐνιαύσιος ἢ ἔριφος ἐξ αἰγῶν ιε΄ μναῖ, καὶ τῷ
στέατι μίαν ἥμισυ μνᾶν.

(37) καὶ ἅλας ἀποδέδεικται τῷ ταύρῳ τῷ μεγάλῳ, ἅλισε τὸ κρέας αὐτοῦ,
καὶ ἀνένεγκε ἐπὶ τὸν βωμόν. σάτον καθήκει τῷ ταύρῳ· καὶ ᾧ ἂν
περισσεύσῃ τοῦ ἁλός, ἅλισον ἐν αὐτῷ τὸ δέρμα·

(38) καὶ τῷ ταύρῳ τῷ δευτέρῳ τὰ πέντε μέρη ἀπὸ τῶν ἓξ μερῶν τοῦ σάτου·
καὶ τοῦ μόσχου τὸ δίμοιρον τοῦ σάτου·

(39) καὶ τῷ κριῷ τὸ ἥμισυ τοῦ σάτου καὶ τῷ τράγῳ τὸ ἴσον·

(40a) καὶ τὸ ἀρνίῳ καὶ τῷ ἐρίφῳ τὸ τρίτον τοῦ σάτου.

(25a) These are the ones that he told me that are fitting to offer from them un[der] the burnt offering on the altar.

(25b) And when you have offered of these trees on the altar and the fire begins to burn them, and then you shall begin to sprinkle blood on the walls of the altar.

(26) And again wash your hands and your feet from the blood and start offering the portions (that have been) salted.

(27) First offer up the head and cover it with fat so that the blood of the sacrifice of the bull may not be seen.

(28) And after this the neck and after the neck its two forelegs and after its two forelegs the breast with the flanks and after the two forelegs the thigh with the spine of the loin and after the thigh the two hind legs washed with the entrails.

(29) And all of them are salted with salt as it is fitting for them, according to what they require.

(30) And after this the fine flour mixed with oil; and after everything pour wine and burn upon them frankincense. And thus your deeds will be in order and all your sacrifices [for deligh]t, for a pleasing smell before God the most high.

(31) [And whatever] you do, do it in order, [by measure] and by weight. Do not add anything that is not [fitting] and do not fall short of the adequate calculation of the wo[o]d (that is) required to sacrifice everything that is offered on the alt[ar].

(32a) For the full-grown bull, a talent of wood by weight. And if its fat alone is offered, six minas; and if a calf of bulls is offered,

(32b) fifty minas, and for its fat alone, five minas;

(33) and for the bullock without blemish, 40 minas.

(34) And if a ram of the sheep or a he-goat of the goats is offered, and for it 30 minas and for the fat three minas;

(35) and if it is a lamb of the sheep or a kid of the goats, 20 minas and for the fat 2 minas;

(36) and if it is a one-year-old lamb without blemish or a kid of the goats, 15 minas and for the fat one mina and a half.

(37) When salt has been brought forward for the full-grown bull, salt its flesh and offer it on the altar; a seah is fitting for the bull; and if some salt is left over, salt with it the skin.

(38) And for the second bull, five out of six parts of a seah; and for the bullock, two thirds of a seah.

(39) And for the ram, a half of a seah, and the same for the he-goat;

(40a) and for the little lamb and the kid, a third of a seah.

(40b) καὶ σεμίδαλις καθήκουσα αὐτοῖς·

(41) τῷ ταύρῳ τῷ μεγάλῳ καὶ τῷ ταύρῳ τῷ β΄ καὶ τῷ μοσχαρίῳ, σάτον σεμίδαλιν·

(42) καὶ τῷ κριῷ καὶ τῷ τράγῳ τὰ δύο μέρη τοῦ σάτου καὶ τῷ ἀρνίῳ καὶ τῷ ἐρίφῳ ἐξ αἰγῶν τὸ τρίτον τοῦ σάτου. καὶ τὸ ἔλαιον·

(43) καὶ τὸ τέταρτον τοῦ σάτου τῷ ταύρῳ ἀναπεποιημένον ἐν τῇ σεμιδάλει ταύτῃ·

(44) καὶ τῷ κριῷ τὸ ἕκτον τοῦ σάτου καὶ τῷ ἀρνίῳ τὸ ὄγδοον τοῦ σάτου καὶ ἀμνοῦ καὶ οἶνον κατὰ τὸ μέτρον τοῦ ἐλαίου τῷ ταύρῳ καὶ τῷ κριῷ καὶ τῷ ἐρίφῳ κατασπεῖσαι σπονδήν.

(45) λιβανωτοῦ σίκλοι ἓξ τῷ ταύρῳ καὶ τὸ ἥμισυ αὐτοῦ τῷ κριῷ καὶ τὸ τρίτον αὐτοῦ τῷ ἐρίφῳ. καὶ πᾶσα ἡ σεμίδαλις ἀναπεποιημένη,

(46a) ἢ<ν> ἄν προσαγάγῃς μόνον, οὐκ ἐπὶ στέατος, προσαχθήσεται ἐπ᾽ αὐτὴν λιβάνου ὁλκὴ σίκλων δύο.

(46b) καὶ τὸ τρίτον τοῦ σάτου τὸ τρίτον τοῦ ὑφή ἐστιν·

(47) καὶ τὰ δύο μέρη τοῦ βάτου καὶ ὁλκῆς τῆς μνᾶς ν΄ σίκλων ἐστίν· καὶ τοῦ σικλίου τὸ τέταρτον ὁλκὴ θερμῶν δ΄ ἐστίν· γίνεται ὁ σίκλος ὡσεὶ ις΄ θέρμοι καὶ ὁλκῆς μιᾶς.

(48) καὶ νῦν, τέκνον μου, ἄκουσον τοὺς λόγους μου καὶ ἐνωτίσαι τὰς ἐντολάς μου, καὶ μὴ ἀποστήτωσαν οἱ λόγοι μου οὗτοι ἀπὸ τῆς καρδίας σου ἐν πάσαις ταῖς ἡμέραις σου, ὅτι ἱερεὺς σὺ ἅγιος κυρίου,

(49) καὶ ἱερεῖς ἔσονται πᾶν τὸ σπέρμα σου· καὶ τοῖς υἱοῖς σου οὕτως ἔντειλον ἵνα ποιήσουσιν κατὰ τὴν κρίσιν ταύτην ὡς σοὶ ὑπέδειξα.

(50) οὕτως γάρ μοι ἐνετείλατο ὁ πατὴρ Ἀβραὰμ ποιεῖν καὶ ἐντέλλεσθαι τοῖς υἱοῖς μου.

(51) καὶ νῦν, τέκνον, χαίρω ὅτι ἐξελέχθης εἰς ἱερωσύνην ἁγίαν καὶ προσ-ενεγκεῖν θυσίαν κυρίῳ ὑψίστῳ, ὡς καθήκει κατὰ τὸ προστεταγμένον τοῦτο ποιεῖν.

(52) ὅταν παραλαμβάνῃς θυσίαν ποιεῖν ἔναντι κυρίου ἀπὸ πάσης σαρκός, κατὰ τὸν λογισμὸν τῶν ξυλῶν ἐπιδέχου οὕτως, ὡς σοὶ ἐντέλλομαι, καὶ τὸ ἅλας καὶ τὴν σεμίδαλιν καὶ τὸν οἶνον καὶ τὸν λίβανον ἐπιδέχου ἐκ τῶν χειρῶν αὐτῶν ἐπὶ πάντα κτήνη.

(53) καὶ ἐπὶ πᾶσαν ὥραν νίπτου τὰς χεῖρας καὶ τοὺς πόδας, ὅταν πορεύῃ πρὸς τὸ θυσιαστήριον· καὶ ὅταν ἐκπορεύῃς ἐκ τῶν ἁγίων, πᾶν αἷμα μὴ ἁπτέσθω τῆς στολῆς σου· οὐκ ἀνήψῃς αὐτῷ αὐθήμερον·

(40b) And the fine flour fitting for them:

(41) for the full-grown bull and for the second bull and for the bullock, a seah of fine flour;

(42) and for the ram and the he-goat, two parts of a seah and for the little lamb and the kid of the goats, a third of the seah; and the oil:

(43) and one fourth of the seah for the bull, mixed with this fine flour;

(44) and for the ram, one sixth of the seah, and for the little lamb the eighth of the seah, and of the lamb, and pour out wine as a drink offering according to the measure of the oil for the bull and ram and kid.

(45) Six shekels of frankincense for the bull and half of it for the ram and one third of it for the kid. And all the mixed up fine flour,

(46a) whenever you offer it up alone (and) not on the fat, the weight of two shekels of incense will be brought on it.

(46b) And one third of the seah is one third of the ephah;

(47) and the two parts of the bath and of the weight of a mina are of fifty shekels; and one fourth of the shekel is the weight of four thermoi; the shekel is of one weight with about sixteen thermoi.

(48) And now, my child, listen to my words and hearken to my commandments, and let these my words not leave your heart all your days, because you are a holy priest of the Lord,

(49) and all your seed will be priests; and command your sons in such a way that they do according to this law as I have shown you.

(50) For thus father Abraham commanded me to do and to command my sons.

(51) And now, my son, I rejoice that you have been chosen for the holy priesthood and to offer sacrifice to the Lord most high, as it is fitting to do, according to what has been commanded.

(52) When you receive the sacrifice to make before the Lord from every flesh, according to the calculation of the wood accept thus as I order you, and the salt and fine flour and wine and incense accept from their hands for the whole cattle.

(53) And each time wash the hands and the feet, when you approach the altar; and when you exit from the sanctuary, let no blood adhere to your garment; do not cling to it on the same day,

(54) καὶ τὰς χεῖρας καὶ τοὺς πόδας νίπτου διὰ παντὸς ἀπὸ πάσης σαρκός.

(55) καὶ μὴ ὀφθήτω ἐπὶ σοι πᾶν αἷμα καὶ πᾶσα ψυχή· τὸ γὰρ αἷμα ψυχή ἐστιν ἐν τῇ σαρκί.

(56) καὶ ὃ ἐάν ἐν οἴκω †ουσης† σεαυτὸν πᾶν κρέας φαγεῖν, κάλυπτε τὸ αἷμα αὐτοῦ τῇ γῇ πρῶτον πρὶν ἢ φαγεῖν σε ἀπὸ τῶν κρέων καὶ οὐκέτι ἔσῃ ἐσθίων ἐπὶ τοῦ αἵματος.

(57) οὕτως γάρ μοι ἐνετείλατο ὁ πατήρ μου Ἀβραάμ, ὅτι οὕτως εὗρεν ἐν τῇ γραφῇ τῆς βίβλου τοῦ Νῶε περὶ τοῦ αἵματος.

(58) καὶ νῦν ὡς σοί, τέκνον ἀγαπητόν, ἐγὼ λέγω, ἠγαπημένος σὺ τῷ πατρί σου καὶ ἅγιος κυρίου ὑψίστου· καὶ ἠγαπημένος ἔσῃ ὑπὲρ πάντας τοὺς ἀδελφούς σου.

(59) τῷ σπέρματί σου εὐλογηθήσεται ἐν τῇ γῇ καὶ τὸ σπέρμα σου ἕως πάντων τῶν αἰώνων ἐνεχθήσεται ἐν βιβλίῳ μνημοσύνου ζωῆς·

(60) καὶ οὐκ ἐξαλειφθήσεται τὸ ὄνομά σου καὶ τὸ ὄνομα τοῦ σπέρματός σου ἕως τῶν αἰώνων.

(61) καὶ νῦν, τέκνον Λευί, εὐλογημένον ἔσται τὸ σπέρμα σου ἐπὶ τῆς γῆς εἰς πάσας τὰς γενεὰς τῶν αἰώνων.

(62) καὶ ὅτε ἀνεπληρώθησάν μοι ἑβδομάδες τέσσαρες ἐν τοῖς ἔτεσιν τῆς ζωῆς μου, ἐν ἔτει ὀγδόῳ καὶ εἰκοστῷ ἔλαβον γυναῖκα ἐμαυτῷ ἐκ τῆς συγγενείας Ἀβραάμ τοῦ πατρός μου, Μελχάν, θυγατέρα Βαθουήλ, υἱοῦ Λάβαν, ἀδελφοῦ μητρός μου.

(63) καὶ ἐν γαστρὶ λαβοῦσα ἐξ ἐμοῦ ἔτεκεν υἱὸν πρῶτον, καὶ ἐκάλεσα τὸ ὄνομα αὐτοῦ Γηρσώμ· εἶπα γὰρ ὅτι πάροικον ἔσται τὸ σπέρμα μου ἐν γῇ, ᾗ ἐγεννήθην· πάροικοί ἐσμεν ὡς τοῦτο ἐν τῇ γῇ ἡμετέρᾳ νομιζομένῃ.

(64) καὶ ἐπὶ τοῦ παιδαρίου εἶδον ἐγὼ ἐν τῷ ὁράματί μου ὅτι ἐκβεβλημένος ἔσται αὐτὸς καὶ τὸ σπέρμα αὐτοῦ ἀπὸ τῆς ἀρχῆς ἱερωσύνης ἔσται τὸ σπέρμα αὐτοῦ.

(65) λ΄ ἐτῶν ἤμην ὅτε ἐγεννήθη ἐν τῇ ζωῇ μου, καὶ ἐν τῷ ι΄ μηνὶ ἐγεννήθη ἐπὶ δυσμὰς ἡλίου.

(66) [ ] והו[ה] כומ[נא הזה לנשין והוית] ע[מ]ה [וה]רת עוד [מני וילידת לי בר] אהרן [וקרא]תי שמה ק[הת]

(67) [והזי]ת די לה [התה]ה כנשת כל [עמא וד]י לה תהוה כהנותא רבתא ל[כל יש[ר]אל

(αὐτὸς καὶ τὸ σπέρμα αὐτοῦ ἔσονται ἀρχὴ βασιλέων, ἱεράτευμα τῷ Ἰσραήλ)

(54) but the hands and feet wash continually from all flesh.

(55) And let not any blood and any soul appear on you, since the blood is the soul in the flesh.

(56) And when you are at home yourself to eat any flesh, hide its blood in the earth first before you eat from the flesh and you will not eat of the blood any longer.

(57) For thus my father Abraham ordered me, because thus he found in the writing of the Book of Noah concerning the blood.

(58) And now, as I tell you, beloved son, you are beloved to your father and a holy one of the Lord Most High and you will be beloved more than all your brothers.

(59) There will be blessing by your seed on the earth and your seed will be brought for all the ages into the book of the memorial of life.

(60) and your name and the name of your seed will not be blotted out for ages.

(61) And now, child Levi, your seed will be blessed on the earth for all the generations of the ages."

9. *Genealogy and Autobiography*

(62) And when four weeks were fulfilled for me in the years of my life, in the twenty eighth year, I took a wife for myself from the family of Abraham my father, Melcha, a daughter of Bathuel, son of Laban, brother of my mother.

(63) And she conceived by me, bore the first son, and I called his name Gershom since I said: "my seed will be sojourners in the land where I was born. We are sojourners as it (will be) in the land which is considered ours."

(64) And concerning the child I saw in my vision that he and his seed will be thrown out from the chief priesthood, his seed will be.

(65) I was thirty years old when he was born in my life, and he was born in the tenth month at sunset.

(66) [And it happen]ed **about the ti**[me appropriate for women, and I was] wi[th h]er], [and she concei]**ved again** [by me and bore me] **another** [son], and I call**ed his name Q**[ahat].

(67) [And I sa]**w that to him** [would belo]**ng** the congregation of all the [people and th]at to him would belong the high priesthood (He and his seed will be a supreme kingship, a priesthood) for [all Is]**rael**.

(68) בשנת ארב[ע ות]לתין לחיי יליד בירדא קמ'א [בח]'ד לירד[א] עם
מדנח שמש[א]

(69a) ועוד אוספת והוית ע[מ]ה וילידת לי בר תליתי' וקראתי שמה מרדי
ארי מר לי עלוהי

(69b) לחדה ארי כדי יליד הוא מית והווה מריר לי עלוהי סגיא מן די ימות
ובעית והתחננת עלוהי והוה בכל מרר

(70) בשנת ארבעין לחיי ילידת ביירדחה תליתי'א

(71) ועוד אוספת והוית עמהא והרת וילידת לי ברתא ושויתי שמהא יוכבד
אמר'ת כדי ילידת לי ליקר ילידת לי לכבוד לישראל

(72) בשנת שתין וארבע לי לחיי וילידת בחד בחודשא שביעיא מן בתר די
הע[לנ[א] למצרים

(73) בשנת שת עש[רה למ]עלינה לארע מצרים ולבני נ[ס[בת נשין] מ[ן בנת
אחי לעדן אשויות זמניהון ו['יל]'דו להון בנין

(74) שם בני גרשון ל'בנ['י ו]'שמעי ושם בני קْהْת עْמْרم ויצהר וחברון ועוזיאל
[ו]'שْם בני מררי מחלי ומושי

(75) ו'ס'ב' לה עמרם אנתא ליוכבד ברתי עד די אנה חי בשנת תשעין
ואר['בע] לחיי

(76) וקריתי שמה די עמרם כדי יליד עמרם ארי אמרת כדי יליד דנה
י'[רים[<פק> עמא מן אר'ע מצרים [כ]דן יתקר'א [שמה <עמ]'א< ראמא

(77) ביום חד יליד['ו בנ]י'א הוא ויוכבד ברתי

(78) בר שנין תמנה עשרה העלת ל'א'רע כנע['ן ובר שנין תّמ'נה עשרה כדי
קטלית אנה לשכ'ם ונמרת לעבדי חמסא

(79) ובר שנין תשע עשרה כהנית ובר שנין תמנה ועסרין נסבת לי אנ'ת'ה

(80) ובר שנין תמנה וארבעין הוית כדי העלנא לארע מצרים ושנין תמנין
ותשע הוית חי במצרי'ם

(81) והוו כל יומי חיי שבע ותלתّין ומّאה שנין וחזיתי לי בנין תל['יתיין] עד
די לא מיתת

(68) In the fou[r and th]irtieth year of my life he was born, in the first month on the [fir]st day of the mon[th] at sunris[e].

(69a) And once again I was wi[th] her and she bore me a third son, and I called his name Merari, for I was exceedingly bitter on his account,

(69b) for when he was born he was dying, and I was very bitter on his account because he was about to die. And I besought and asked for mercy for him and it was in all bitterness.

(70) In the fortieth year of my life she gave birth in the third month.

(71) And again I was with her, and she conceived and bore me a daughter and I gave her the name Yochebed, (for) I sai[d]: "When she was born to me, for the glory she was born to me, for the glory of Israel."

(72) In the sixty-fourth year of my life she was born to me on the first day of the seventh month after that we were brou[ght] to Egypt,

(73) in the sixteen[th] year of our entry into the land of Egypt. And for my sons I to[ok wives] from the daughters of my brothers at the moment corresponding to their ages, and sons w[ere b]orn to them.

(74) The name of the sons of Gershon, Libn[i and] Shimei; and the name of the sons of Qahat, Amram and Yizhar and Hebron and Uzziel; [and] the name of the sons of Merari, Mahli and Mushi.

(75) And Amram took a wife for himself, Yochebed, my daughter, while I was still living, in the ninety-fou[rth] year of my life.

(76) And I called the name of Amram, when Amram was born, for when he was born I said: "This one will {exalt} <lead> the people <out> of the land of Egypt." [Th]us [his name] will be called: "<the> exalted [<peopl]e>."

(77) On the same day the [children] we[re bo]rn, he and Yochebed, my daughter.

(78) I was ei[g]hteen years old (when) I was brought to the land of Canaan and I was eighteen years old when I killed Scheche[m] and destroyed the doers of violence.

(79) And I was nineteen years old (when) I became a priest and I was twenty-eight years old (when) I took a wife for myself.

(80) And I was forty-eight years old when we were brought to the land of Egypt, and eighty-nine years I lived in Egy[pt].

(81) And all the days of my life were one hundred thirty-seven years, and I saw sons of the thi[rd generation] before I died.

(82) ובש[נת מאה] ו[ת]מֹני עשרה לחיי היא שנ[תא]די מית בה יוסף אחי
קריתי לבנ[י ו]לבניהון ושריתי לפקדה הנון כל די הווה עם לבבי

(83a) עניתֹ ואמרתֹ לבנֹי

(83b) [שמ]עֹ[וֹ] למאמר לוי אבוכון והציתו לפקודי ידיד אל

(84) אנה לכון מפקד בני ואנה קושטאֹ לכון מהחוי חביבי

(85) ראש עובדיכון יהוי קושטא ועד עלמאֹ יהֹוֹי קאים עמכון צדקה

(86) וקושטֹ[א הן] תזֹ[ר]עֹוֹן תנחֹעֹלון עללה בריכה ו[טא]בֹא

(87) די זרע טאב מֹהֹנעל ודי זרע ביש עלוהי תאיב זֹרֹעה

(88) וֹכֹען בני ספֹר מוסר חוכמה אליפו לבניכון ותהוי חוכמתא עמכון ליקר
עלם

(89) די אליף חוכמתא ויקר היא בה ודי שאֹיט חוכמתא לבשרון מתיהב

(90) חזו בני ליוסף אחי [ד]מֹאלפאֹ ספֹר ומוסר חכמה [ליקר ולרבו ולמלכין
על כורסיהון מתחד הוא] אל תמחלו חכמתא למֹאֹלף ולארחתה ל[אֹ
[תשב]קֹן] לב[עא]

(91) [די מאלף חוכמ]הֹ נבר דֹ[י] אלֹף [חכמה כל י]ומוהי אֹ[ריכין]
וסנה לֹ[ה שמ]עֹה לכל מאֹ[ת] ומדינה] דין] עֹלֹל לה אֹח אֹו חֹבֹר
הוי בה [ולא מ]תנכר הוא בה ולֹא דמ[ה בה]לֹנכרי ולא דמה בה
לכילאֹ[י]מֹן די כולהון יהבֹי[ן לה בה יקר [ב]די כולה צבין למאלף מן
חוכמתה

(92) רחמוה[י]ן סניאין ושאלי שלמיה רברבין
(93) ועל כורסי ייקר מהותבין לה בדיל למשמע מילי חוכמתה

(94) עותר רב די יקר היא חוכמתה וסימא טאבא לכל קניהא

(95) הן יאתון מלכין תקיפין ועם רב וחיל ופרשין ורתיכין סניאין עמהון
וינסבון נכסֹי מאֹת ומדינה ויבוזון כל די בהון אוצרי חוכמתא לא יבוזון
ולא ישכחון

10. *Wisdom Poem*

(82)   In the [hundred and eigh]teenth y[ear] of my life, this is the y[ear] in which my brother Joseph died, I called [my] so[ns and] their sons and I began to command them everything tha[t] I had intended.

(83a)   I spoke and said to my sons:

(83b)   [Hear] the word of Levi, your father, and obey the commands of God's beloved.

(84)   I myself command you, my sons, and I myself show you the truth, my beloved.

(85)   Let the principle of all your actions be truth and for ever let justice be established with you.

(86)   And [if you s]ow tru[th], you will reap a blessed and [go]od harvest.

(87)   Whoever sows good, reaps good, and whoever sows evil, his seed returns upon him.

(88)   And now, my sons, teach your children scribal craft, instruction, wisdom, and let wisdom be with you for eternal glory.

(89)   Whoever studies wisdom will (attain) glory through her, but the one who despises wisdom, becomes an object of disdain.

(90)   Consider, my sons, Joseph my brother [who] taught scribal craft and the instruction of wisdom, [to glory, and to greatness, and to kings *on their thrones he was joined*. Do not neglect to study wisdom *and* do not] aban[don] a se[arch *for her ways.*]

(91)   [Whoever teaches wisdo]m (to) a man wh[o] studies [wisdom, all] his days are l[ong] and hi[s fa]me spreads. Whichever la[nd] or province he enters, he is a brother or companion in it, [and he is not] considered a stranger in it, and he is not simil[ar to] a stranger [in it], and he is not similar in it to a half-bree[d], for they all give him glory in it; (this is) [be]cause they all desire to learn from his wisdom.

(92)   Hi[s] friends are many, and his well-wishers are great ones.

(93)   And they seat him on the throne of glory in order to hear the words of his wisdom.

(94)   Great wealth of glory is wisdom, and a good treasure for all who acquire her.

(95)   If mighty kings come and a great army, and soldiers and horsemen and numerous chariots with them, then they will carry away the possessions of the land and province, and they will plunder everything that is in them, the treasuries of wisdom they will not plunder and they will not find.

(96) מטמוריה ולֹא יעלון תרעיה ולֹא[ולֹא]
ישכחון למכבש שוריה [ ] ולֹא [ ] ולֹא[
יהזון שימֹחֹה שימחה נֹ[נֹ]דֹהֹ [
ולֹא איתי כֹל מחיר נגדה וֹ[לֹא

(97) כֹל [אנֹ]שׁ דין[בעא הכמֹהֹ] הכ[מתֹא יֹ]שכה [תֹה] [
מטמרה מנֹהֹ[ן פֹל [אֹ לֹ°] [
ולֹא הסֹ[יֹ]רֹ [ ]ן כֹל בעֹיֹ]ן [
בֹקֹשׁט [

(98) וכעֹן בני]ספֹר ומוסר חֹכֹמֹהֹ דֹ אלפֹ[ו [ ] הזית בהזוין די]תֹרֹתון אנון
וֹתֹ] [רבה הֹתֹנון
וֹיֹ]קֹר [

(99) אֹנֹ[[אֹפֹ בסֹפֹרֹיֹא
קֹרֹ[יֹת תֹה]וֹן ראשׁין ושׁפֹטֹין
וֹדֹאֹ[נֹין וֹבֹ]ועבדין
] [אֹפֹ כהנין ומלכין תֹהֹ]וון
(100) [שֹׁ] [ ]ן מלכותכן תֹהוֹאֹ[יֹקֹ]רֹ ולֹא איתי סוף
לֹיֹקֹ]רֹכן ולֹא]תֹעבר מנכן עד כֹל
דֹ[רֹיֹא [ ]ן בֹיקֹר רב
(101) [ ] לֹ[כֹ]ן כֹל עממֹיֹא [ ] שׁמשֹׁא שֹׁ]הֹרֹא וֹכֹוכֹביֹא
] [ ] מן[לֹשֹׁהֹרֹה
(102) [כֹן תהשֹׁכֹוֹן[ ] [אֹ הלֹא קבל [לֹ]מֹהֹךֹ לֹ[ ]נֹא ועל מן תהוא הֹובֹתֹא
] [הֹלֹא עֹלי ועֹליכן בנֹי ארו ידעֹונֹה [ ] אֹ]רֹהֹת קשֹׁ°א תשׁבֹקֹוֹן וֹכֹל שׁבֹילֹי
] [תֹמֹחֹלֹון ותֹהֹכֹון בהשׁוֹךֹ שׁטֹן [וֹ]מֹן הֹ[שֹׁ]וֹכֹה תֹהֹא עֹלֹיכֹוֹן [וֹתֹהֹכֹון
] [שֹׁנֹיֹא]טֹעֹן וֹמֹ[לֹ]לֹ [וֹ]תֹהֹווֹין לֹשֹׁכֹליֹן [תֹהוֹ]וֹן כֹֹל קֹ]שׁיטֹ]יֹן וֹ]תֹכֹהֹלֹ[וֹן

(103) [עֹמֹהֹון בֹ[רֹ]שֹׁעֹא [ ] שֹׁ]נֹאֹיכֹן אֹדֹין יֹדֹי[ֹם]בֹכֹן [
] [לֹשׁנֹין בֹכֹן מן כֹל מֹ[ ] °°

(104) [ ] [°] [°] [ ] ארו מן יקר באֹרֹ[עֹא [ ]אֹנֹה [
די תֹמֹרון לֹי דֹ דֹ[נֹ]ה
יקֹירין מן נֹשֹׁיֹא[ ]הֹלֹ[א [ ]לֹ[

(96) her hidden places, and they will not enter her gates, and [they will] not[and] they will [not] be able to conquer her walls, [ ]and not[and] they will [not] see her treasure. Her treasure c[orresp]onding to it (?)[   ] and [n]o price is adequate for it and [not   ].

(97) [every] ma[n who] looks for wisdom, [wis]dom he will [find] [   ] her hidden place from it/him [   ] [   ] and not la[c]k[   ] all who see[k] truly [   ].

(98) [And now, my sons,] scribal craft and instruction of wi[s]dom that you (?) tea[ch/learn   I saw in visions that   ] you will inherit them and [   ]great you will give [and g]lory.

11. *Perspectives for the Future*

(99) [   ]also in the books I re[ad   you will b]e heads and magistrates and ju[dges   ] and servants/doing [   ]also priests and kings you will be[come].

(100) [   ] your kingdom will be [glo]ry and there will be no end to [your] gl[ory] and it will [not] pass from you until all ge[nerations   ] with great glory.

(101) [   ] for [you] all the nations [sun, m]oon and stars [   ]from (?)[   ]for its moon[   ].

(102) [   ]thus you will darken[   ] did not he accept[to] go to [   ] and on whom will the guilt be   [   ] is that not on me and on you my sons, behold they will know it [the p]aths of righteousness you will abandon, and all the ways of [   ] you will neglect and you will walk in the darkness of satan[ ] da[r]kness will come upon you [   ] and you will walk great[ly] he pleaded and he s[ai]d: "You will become intelligent [you will be]come a[ll t]ruthfu[l and]you will be ab[le   ].

(103) [ ]with them/their people (?) by the [e]vil one [those who h]ate you. Then he will aris[e] against you [   ]languages against you from every [   ].

(104) Behold, more than glory in [the] coun[try   ] I, when you tell me that D[inah/judgment (?)   ]   more glorious than the women [   ].

ARAMAIC CONCORDANCE

The Aramaic concordance also includes the Aramaic lexemes from the non-classified Qumran fragments (cf. § 2.3). The forms that were reconstructed without any material basis in the manuscripts are not included. When an Aramaic lexeme appears both in the Cairo Geniza manuscripts and Qumran fragments, only the Geniza text is cited.

1b l. 12	213a 2 12	אב	על אבי יעקוב וכד[י /
1c l. 18		אב	יעקב אבי ורא[ו]בן אחי /
3a l. 3	213a 3–4 3	אב	ותהלל שמה ושם אבוה /
3a l. 4	213a 3–4 4	אב	בה[ללה] אבהתא
3a l. 5	213a 3–4 5	אב	בתו]לה זי הבלת שמה ושם אבהתה
3a l. 6	213a 3–4 6	אב	ואבהתה לכל אחיה / [ול]אבוה{א}
8 l. 14		אב	ועלנא על אבי יצחק /
9 l. 16	213b 4	אב	יעקב / [אבי]מ̇עשר
9 l. 21		אב	וברכת לאבי / בחיוהי
10 l. 23		אב	ואף אבא ברכני
11 l. 3		אב	ושרינא בבירת אברהם / אבונן
11 l. 3		אב	לות יצחק אבונה
12 l. 4		אב	וחזא / יצחק אבונא לכולנא
22 l. 12		אב	כדנה / חזיתי לאברהם אבי מזדהר
83b l. 8		אב	[שמ]ע̇[ו] / למאמר לוי אבוכון
213 6 1		אב	כאב רם אל[ן
26 l. 3		אבר	ושרי להנסקה אבריה / מליחין
24 l. 17		†אדונא†	ואודנא / ברותא ותאנתא
1b l. 11	213a 2 11	אדין	באדין נגדת ב]
1b l. 13	213a 2 13	אדין	מן אבל מין אדין[/
1b l. 15	213a 2 15	אדין	אדין חזיון אחזית] /
7 l. 10		אדין	אדין / אמרת חזוא הוא דן
9 l. 15		אדין	אדין כדי הוה יעקב / [אבי]מ̇עשר
10 l. 22		אדין	אדין כולהון / ברכוני
19 l. 2		אדין	ובאדין תהוי לביש / לבוש כהנותא
22 l. 11		אדין	ובאדין הסק אינון /
25b l. 1		אדין	והא באדין תשרא למזרק דמא /
103 l. 2	213 5 2	אדין	אדין ידי[ם]בכן /
91 l. 7		או	אה או ח̇בר / הוי בה
95 l. 22		אוצר	/ אוצרי חוכמתא לא יבוזון
214 4 4		אוצר	או]צ̇ריה כ°[
3 l. 21		אזל	אזלנא לה[ה]ד̇ה לראובן / אחונן

Ref 1	Ref 2	Root	Text
11 l. 1		אזל	ואזלנא / מבית אל
24 l. 17		‡אטולא‡	ואטולא ושוחא ואודנא /
1c l. 20		אח	ונהוי כולן א[חין] / וחברין
3 l. 15		אח	יוס[ף](?) אחי בכל עדן [/
3 l. 16		אח	לאח]יא די די הוו בשכם
3 l. 17		אח	אחי ואחוי דן /
3 l. 21		אח	אנה ושמעון / אחי אזלנא
3a l. 5	213a 3–4 5	אח	ואבהתהת לכל אחיה /
9 l. 22		אח	וברכת לאחי
73 l. 3		אח	/ נס[בת נשין] מ[ן בנת אחי
82 l. 5		אח	היא שנ[תא]די מית בה / יוסף אחי
90 l. 22		אח	חזו בני ליוסף אחי /
66 l. 4		אהרן	ויל[ידת לי בר] אהרן/
3 l. 21		אחד	אזלנא לה[ן]ה[]דה לראובן / אחונן
96 l. 4	213 1 ii 4	איתי	/ ולא איתי כל מחיר נגדה
100 l. 17	213 2 14	איתי	ולא איתי סוף /
4 l. 2		אכל	וכל חמדת בכורי ארעא / כולה למאכל
5 l. 4		אכל	זמנין תאכול / וזמנין תכפן
1a v. 10	213a 1 17	אל	ו]אל תשלט בי כל שטן /
214 2 4	27 l. 5	אל	ואל יתחזי ל[ה /
90 l. 2	213 1 i 13	אל	א]ל תמחלו חכמתא למאלף /
213 6 1		אל (?)	/ כאב רם אל[ן
24 l. 15		אלן	ואלין / אינון שמחתהון
25a l. 19		אלן	אלין / אינון די אמר לי
25b l. 22		אלן	/ וכדי הנסקת מן אע(י)א) אלין
13 l. 7		אלף	ולאלפא יתי דין / כהנותא
15 l. 13		אלף	לפותך דין / כהנותא
88 l. 18		אלף (emend.)	ספר מוסר / חוכמה אליפו לבניכון
89 l. 20		אלף	/ די אלף חוכמתא ויקר היא / בה
90 l. 23		אלף	/[ה]מאלפא ספר ומוסר חכמה /
90 l. 3	213 1 i 13	אלף	א]ל תמחלו חכמתא למאלף /
91 l. 4	213 1 i 14	אלף	[די מאלף חוכמ]ה
91 l. 5		אלף	גבר דנ[י] / אלף [חכמה
91 l. 12		אלף	כולה צבין / למאלף מן חוכמתה
98 l. 9	213 1 ii 9	אלף	ס]פר ומוסר / חכמה ד אלפ[ו
32a l. 22		אם	/ ואם תרבא בלהודוהי
32a l. 23		אם	ואם פר תורין הוא די סליק /
1a v. 4	213a 1 10	אמר	ו]אמרת מרי אנתה /
1c l. 19		אמר	/ ואמרן להון בן]חוכמה
7 l. 11		אמר	אדין / אמרת הזוא הוא דן
13 l. 8		אמר	ואמר לי לוי אזדהר / לך
23 l. 13		אמר	אמר / לי די חוין להסקה מינהון

Ref	Ref2	Root	Text
25a l. 20		אמר	אמר לי די חזין להסקה / מנהון
71 l. 20		אמר	אמרת כדי ילידת לי
76 l. 11		אמר	ארי אמרת כדי יליד/
83a l. 7		אמר	ענית ואמרת לבני
104 l. 3	214 3 3	אמר	/ אנה די תמרון לי ד̇ ד[י]נה
213a 6 1		אמר	אמרת מא[/
1a v. 1	213a 1 6	אנה	באדין[אנה /] רחעת לבושי
1b l. 14	213a 2 14	אנה	/ שכבת ויתבת אנה ע[ל
3 l. 20		אנה	אנה ושמעון / אחי אזלנא לה[ח]דה לראובן
7 l. 10		אנה	/ ואנה אתעירת מן שנתי
7 l. 11		אנה	אנה / מתמה די יהוי לה כל חזוה
9 l. 17		אנה	כ]ע̇ן אנה הוית קדמי
13 l. 5		אנה	אנה כהין לאל / עליון
75 l. 9		אנה	/ עד די אנה חי
78 l. 17		אנה	/ כדי קטלית אנה לשכם
84 l. 9		אנה	אנה לכון מפקד בני
84 l. 9		אנה	ואנה / קושטא לכון מהחוי
104 l. 3	214 3 3	אנה	/ אנה די תמרון לי
1c l. 20		אנון	די ה̇[וו] / צביין אינון בברתן
3 l. 20		אנון	ואחוי / אינון יהודה
22 l. 10		אנון	ובקר / אינון לקודמין מן תולעא
22 l. 11		אנון	/ ובאדין הסק אינון
24 l. 16		אנון	ואלין / אינון שמהתהון
25a l. 20		אנון	אלין / אינון די אמר לי
82 l. 6		אנון	/ ושריתי לפקדה הנון
1c l. 16		אנש	על[ן] דברת די כל א[נ]ש
7 l. 13		אנש	ולכל איניש לא נליתה
97 l. 4	213 2 1	אנש	כל [א]נ̇ש די[ן] / בעא חכמה̇]
3a l. 3	213a 3–4 3	אנתה	אנתה ותחלל שמה
17 l. 16		אנתה	ואנת אנתתא מן משפחתי סב לך
75 l. 8		אנתה	ונסב לה עמרם אנתא ליוכבד
79 l. 20		אנתה	נסבת לי אנתה̇
104 l. 4	214 3 4	אנתה	/ יקירין מן נשיא[
1a v. 5	213a 1 10	אנתה	ו]אמרת מרי אנתה /
1a v. 5	213a 1 11	אנתה	א]נתה בלחודיך ידע /
17 l. 16		אנתה	ואנת אנתתא מן משפחתי / סב לך
17 l. 18		אנתה	/ ארי זרע קדיש אנת
17 l. 20		אנתה	ארו כהין / קדיש אנת
18 l. 21		אנתה	קריב אנת לאל̇
22 l. 9		אע	/ ומהקריב אעין מהצלחין
23 l. 13		אע	/ מן כל תריעשר מיני אעין
24 l. 18		אע	/ ברותא ותאנתא ואע משחא /
24 l. 19		אע	/ ערא והדסה ואעי דקתא

25b l. 22		אע	/ וכדי הנסקת מן אע)א(אלין
31 l. 19		אע	/ ולא תחסר מן הושבן חזת ד]י[ן אע]י[א /
32a l. 21		אע	/ לתורא רבא ככר אעין ליה
7 l. 13		אף	וטמרת / אף דן בלבי
8 l. 14		אף	ואף הוא כדן /]ברכ[ני
10 l. 23		אף	ואף אבא ברכני
1a v. 4	213a 1 9	אצבע	]ואצבעת כפי וידי /
68 l. 8		ארבע	בשנת ארב]ע ות[ן]לתין לחיי /
72 l. 22		ארבע	/ בשנת שתין וארבע לי לחיי
75 l. 9		ארבע	בשנת תשעין ואר]בע[/ לחיי
70 l. 17		ארבעין	בשנת / ארבעין לחיי
80 l. 21		ארבעין	ובר / שנין תמנה וארבעין הויתי
17 l. 18		ארי	/ ארי זרע קדיש אנת
17 l. 19		ארי	ארו כהן / קדיש אנת
22 l. 11		ארי	ארי כדנה / חזיתי לאברהם אבי
69a l. 12		ארי	ארי / מר לי עלוהי
69b l. 13		ארי	ארי כדי יליד / הוא
76 l. 11		ארי	ארי אמרת כדי יליד /
102 l. 4	213 4 4	ארי	ועליכן בנ' ארו ידעונה /
104 l. 2	214 3 2	ארי	/ ארו מן יקר בא]ר[עא
24 l. 16		ארז	ואלין / אינון שמהתהון ארזא
1a v. 6	213a 1 12	ארה	]ארחת קשט ארחק /
102 l. 5	213 4 5	ארה	א]רחת קש°א תשבקן[
4 l. 1		ארע	וכל חמדת בכורי ארעא /
73 l. 2		ארע	למ]עלינה לארע מצרים
76 l. 12		ארע	י}רים{ <פק> עמא מן ארע מצרים /
78 l. 16		ארע	העלת / לארע כנען
80 l. 22		ארע	כדי / העלנא לארע מצרים
104 l. 2	214 3 2	ארע	ארו מן יקר בא]ר[עא
73 l. 3		אשויות	לעדן אשויות / זמניהון
95 l. 18		אתי	הן / יאתון מלכין תקיפין
102 l. 7	213 4 7	אתי	ח]ש[וכה תתא עליכן[
7 l. 13; 9 ll. 17, 22; 10 l. 1; 11 l. 2; 19 ll. 2, 2; 22 l. 11; 25b ll. 1, 1; 29 l. 11; 30 ll. 13, 15; 31 ll. 17, 18; 32a ll. 21, 22; 68 ll. 8, 9, 9; 69b l. 16; 70 ll. 16, 17; 72 ll. 22, 23, 23; 73 l. 1; 75 l. 9; 77 l. 14; 80 l. 23; 82 l. 4; 89 l. 21; 91 ll. 8, 8, 10, 11; 95 l. 21; 103 ll. 1 (?), 2, 3		ב	
1a v. 7	213a 1 13	באיש	]בֿאיש° וזנותא דחא /

Ref 1	Ref 2	Lemma	Text
87 l. 16		באיש	ודי זרע / ביש
91 l. 11		בדי	[ב]די כולה צבין /
93 l. 15		בדיל	/ בדיל למשמע מילי חוכמתה
3a l. 5	213a 3–4 5	בהת	ואבהתת לכל אחיה
95 l. 21		בזז	/ ומדינה ויבוזון כל די בהון
95 l. 22		בזז	אוצרי חוכמתא לא יבוזון /
1c l. 19		בינה	ואמרן להון ב[חוכמה ובי]נה
11 l. 2		בירה	ושרינא בבירת אברהם / אבונן
4 l. 1		בכור	ו]שלמא וכל חמדת בכורי ארעא /
1a v. 5	213a 1 11	בלחוד	א]נתה בלחודיך ידע /
32a l. 22		בלחוד	/ ואם תרבא בלחודוהי סליק
30 l. 13		בלל	ובתר דנה נישפא / בליל במשחא
69b l. 15		בעי	ובעית והתחננת / עלוהי
90 l. 4		בעי	ולארהחתה ל[א תשבן]קן / לב[עא]
97 l. 5	213 1 ii 5	בעי	כל]אנ[ש דין / בעא חכמה]
97 l. 7	213 2 4	בעי	[ן כל בעי]ן / [
	214b 1 3	בעי	]בעו מצלין]
22 l. 9		בקר	ובקר / אינון לקודמין מן תולעא
1a v. 19	213a 2 10	בר	/ לבר עבדך מן ק]דמיך
1c l. 15		בר	/ דטמאת ל]ב[ני יעקב
3c l. 2	1Q21 1 2	בר	לב]ניך מלכות כהנותא
9 l. 18		בר	ולי מכל בנוהי יהב קרבן /
14 l. 9		בר	אזדהר / לך ברי מן כל טומאה
14 l. 9		בר	אזדהר / לך ברי מן כל טומאה
15 l. 11		בר	וכען ברי דין / קושטא אחזינך
16 l. 15		בר	היזדהר לך / ברי מן כל פחז
69a l. 11		בר	וילידת לי בר / תליתי
73 l. 2		בר	ולבני / נס[בת נשין] מן בנת אחי
73 l. 4		בר	ו]ילי[ד]ו להון בנין
74 l. 4		בר	שם בני / נרשון ל]ב[ני ו]שמעי
74 l. 5		בר	ושם בני / קהת ע]מרם ויצהר
74 l. 7		בר	ו]ש[ם בני מררי מחלי ומושי /
77 l. 14		בר	/ ביום חד יליד]ו בנ]יא
78 l. 15		בר	בר שנין תמ]נה עשרה העלת /
78 l. 16		בר	ובר שנין תמ]נה עשרה / כדי קטלית
79 l. 18		בר	ובר שנין תשע / עשרה כהנית
79 l. 19		בר	ובר שנין תמנה / ועסרין נסבת
80 l. 20		בר	ובר / שנין תמנה וארבעין הוית
81 l. 2		בר	וחזיתי לי בנין תל]י[תיין]
82 l. 5		בר	קריתי לבנ]י ו]לבניהון /
82 l. 5		בר	קריתי לבנ]י ו]לבניהון /
83a l. 7		בר	ענית ואמרת לבנ'
84 l. 9		בר	אנה לכון מפקד בני

88 l. 17		בר	וכען בני ספר מוסר / חוכמה אליפו
88 l. 18		בר	ספר מוסר / חוכמה אליפו לבניכון
90 l. 22		בר	חזו בני ליוסף אחי /
98 l. 8	214a 2 ii 5	בר	/ וכען בני [ספר ומוסר חֻכמה
102 l. 4	213 4 4	בר	הֹלא עלי ועליכן בנֹ[י
1c l. 20		ברה	די הֹ[וון] / צביין אינון בברהתן
71 l. 19		ברה	והויתי עמהא והרת / ויֹלֹדת לי ברתא
73 l. 3		ברה	ולבני / נֹסֹ[בת נשין] מֹן בנת אחי
75 l. 8		ברה	/ ונֹסֹב לה עמרם אנתא ליוכבד ברתי /
77 l. 15		ברה	בנֹ[יא הֹוא ויוכבד / ברתי
1a v. 15b	213a 2 6	ברך	/ מרי בֹ[רכת
8 l. 15		ברך	ואף הוא כדן / [ברכ]ני
9 l. 21		ברך	וברכת לאבי / בחיוהי
9 l. 22		ברך	וברכת לאחי
10 l. 23		ברך	אדין כולהון / ברכוני
10 l. 23		ברך	ואף אבא ברכני
12 l. 4		ברך	וחזא / יצחק אבונא לכולנא וברכנא
86 l. 14		ברך	תֹנֹהֹעלון / עללה בריכה
24 l. 18		ברת	/ ברותא ותאנתא ואע משחא /
23 l. 15		בשים	ריח תננהון בשים סליק
2 l. 21		בשר	נזורן]]עורלה בישרכון /
213b 1	6 l. 8	בשר	הן]כֹה רֹביתֹך מן כל בשרֹ[ן]
14 l. 11		בשר	דינך רב הוא מן כל / בישרא
18 l. 23		בשר	כען {הֹוֹי}<אׁהֹר> דכי / בבשרך מן כל טומאת
214b 7 1		בשר	[מן כול בשרֹ[א
89 l. 21		בשרון	ודי שאיט חוכמתא לבשרון / מתיהב
3a l. 5	213a 3–4 5	בתולה	בתו]לה זי חבלת שמה
28 l. 6		בתר	ובתרוהי צוארה /
28 l. 7		בתר	/ ובתר צוארה ידוהי
28 l. 7		בתר	ובתר ידוהי / ניעא
28 l. 8		בתר	בתר ידיא / ירכאהא
28 l. 10		בתר	/ ובתר ירכאהא רגלין
30 l. 12		בתר	ובתר דנה נישפא / בליל במשחא
30 l. 13		בתר	ובתר כולא חמר נסך /
72 l. 23		בתר	מן בתר די הֹעֹלֹנֹ[א] למצרים
1a v. 8	213a 1 14	נבורה	ח]כמה ומנדע ונבורה /
3a l. 2	213a 3–4 2	נבר	וכען יֹ[ע]לֹו מכחשי גבריא
18 l. 23		נבר	מן כל טומאת כל נבר /
91 l. 4		נבר	נבר דֹ[י] / אלֹף [חכמה

214 4 2		נבר	[°ונברי]ה/א
2 l. 21		נזר	נזורון]עורלת בישרכון /
7 l. 13		נלי	ולכל אינש לא נליתה /
78 l. 17		נמר	ונמרת / לעבדי חמסא
1a v. 9	213a 1 16	ד	[דשפיר ודטב קדמיך /
1a v. 9	213a 1 16	ד	[דשפיר ודטב קדמיך /
1a v. 16	213a 2 7	ד	זרע דק[שט /
1c l. 15		ד	/ דטמאת ל[ב]ני יעקב
20 l. 5		ד	עד דלא תקרב למדבחא /
213 1 i 8	87 l. 14	ד	דזרע טב טב מעל /
1b l. 17	213a 2 17	דבק	רם עד דבק לשמי[א
1c l. 16		דברה	על] / דברת די כל א[נש
1a v. 7	213a 1 13	דחי	[באיש* וזנותא דחא /
3 l. 16		די	לאה]י*א די די הוו בשכם /
3 l. 20		די	ואחוי / אינון יהודה די אנה ושמעון /
3 l. 22		די	לראובן / אחונן די למדנח אשר
3c l. 1	1Q21 1 1	די	[מן די להוין תליתין]
7 l. 12		די	אנה / מתמה די יהוי לה כל חזוה
9 l. 16		די	כל מה דיהוה לה כנדרה /
13 l. 5		די	וכדי ידע די אנה כהן לאל / עליון
21 l. 7		די	להקרבה / כל די חזה להנסקה
23 l. 14		די	אמר / לי די חזין להסקה מינהון
23 l. 15		די	/ די ריח תנונהון בשים סליק
25a l. 20		די	אלין / אינון די אמר לי
25a l. 20		די	אמר לי די חזין להסקה / מנהון
31 l. 18		די	לא תותר צבו די לא [חזה] /
31 l. 19		די	חושבן חזת ד[י]ן אל*[י]א /
31 l. 20		די	לכל די סליק למדב[חא] /
32a l. 23		די	ואם פר תורין הוא די סליק /
67 l. 5		די	[וחזי]תי די לה / [תהו]ה כנשת
69b l. 15		די	מן די ימות
72 l. 23		די	מן בתר די / העלנ[א] למצרים
75 l. 9		די	ליוכבד ברתי / עד די אנה חי
76 l. 10		די	וקריתי שמה די עמרם כדי / יליד
81 l. 3		די	בנין תל[י]תין] עד / די לא מיתת
82 l. 4		די	היא שנ[תא]די מית בה / יוסף
87 l. 14		די	די זרע / מאב מאב מ*נעל
87 l. 15		די	ודי זרע / ביש עלוהי תאיב ז*רעה /
89 l. 20		די	/ די אליף חוכמתא ויקר היא / בה
89 l. 21		די	ודי שאיט חוכמתא לבשרון / מתיהב
91 l. 10		די	[מ]ן די כולהון יהבי[ן / לה בה יקר
94 l. 16		די	/ עותר רב די יקר היא חוכמתה /
95 l. 21		די	ויבוזון כל די בהון /

98 l. 9	213 1 ii 9	די	סֹפר ומוסר / חֹכמֹה ד̇ אלפֹ]ו[
104 l. 3	214 3 3	די	אנה די תמרון לי ד̇ ד[י]נה /
104 l. 3	214 3 3	די	אנה די תמרון לי ד̇ ד[י]נה /
99 l. 14	213 1 ii 14	דין	תה]ו̇ן ראשין ושפטין / ודא[נין
1a v. 18	213a 2 9	דין	דין קשט לכֹל /
1c l. 17		דין	למעבד כדין בכל] /
13 l. 7		דין	ולאלפא יתי דין / כהנותא
14 l. 10		דין	דינך רב הוא מן כל / בישרא
15 l. 11		דין	וכען ברי דין / קושטא אחזינך
15 l. 13		דין	לאלפותך דין / כהנותא
104 l. 3	214 3 3	דין (?)	אנה די תמרון לי ד̇ ד[י]נה]
18 l. 22		דכי	כען {הו̇ו}<א̇הר> דכי / בבשרך
25b l. 23		דלק	ונורא ישרא להדלקא / בהון
25b l. 1		דם	תשרא למזרק דמא / על כותלי מדבחה
26 l. 3		דם	ועוד רהע ידיך / ורגליך מן דמא
27 l. 6		דם	ולא יתחזה לה / דם נכסת תורא
91 l. 9		דמי	/ ולא דמ[ה בה]לנכרי
91 l. 9		דמי	ולא דמה / בה לכילא̇[ני]
5 l. 6		דמך	וזמנין / תנוח וזמנין תדמוך
7 l. 11		דן	חזוא הוא דן
7 l. 11		דן	חזוא הוא דן וכדן אנה / מתמה
7 l. 13		דן	וטמרת / אף דן בלבי
213a 1 5		דן (?)	ד]ן /
20 l. 6		דנה	עד דלא תקרב למדבחא / כל דנה
22 l. 11		דנה	ארי כדנה / חזיתי לאברהם אבי מיזדהר
30 l. 12		דנה	ובתר דנה נישפא / בליל במשחא
76 l. 12		דנה	/ דנה י̇{ר}ים} <פק> עמא מן אר̇ע / מצרים /
214 4 1		דנה	ד]נֹה[
28 l. 8		דפן	ובתר ידוהי / ניעא עם בן דפנא
24 l. 16		דפרן	ואלין / אינון שמהתהון ארוא ודפרנא /
3a l. 7	213a 3-4 7	דר	לֹ]ם לכל דרי עלמא[
100 l. 19	213 1 ii 19	דר	ולא ת̇עבד]מנכן עד כל / ד[ר]יא
24 l. 19		דקתא	ערא והדסה ואעי דקתא /
102 l. 2	213 4 2	ה	א הלא קב̇ל[ל]מֹה̇ך לן]
102 l. 4	213 4 4	ה	הֹלא עלי ועליכן בנ̇י]
104 l. 5	214 3 5	ה	הֹל]א̇ [לֹ]
25b l. 1		הא	והא באדין תשרא למזרק דמא /
24 l. 19		הדס	/ערא והדסה ואעי דקתא
7 l. 11		הוא	אדין / אמרת חזוא הוא דן
8 l. 14		הוא	ואף הוא כדן / [ברכ]ני
14 l. 10		הוא	דינך רב הוא מן כל / בישרא
32a l. 23		הוא	ואם פר תורין הוא די סליק /

77 l. 14		הוא	בנ[י]א הוא ויוכבד / ברתי
1a v. 11	213a 1 18	הוי	וקרבני למהוא לכה /
1c l. 19		הוי	די ה[וון] / צביין אינון בברתן
1c l. 20		הוי	ונהוי כולן א[חין] / וחברין
1c l. 22		הוי	ותהון חתימין / כואתן במילת ק[וש]ט
1c l. 23		הוי	ונהוי לכ[ון] /
3 l. 16		הוי	לאה[ן]יא די די הוו בשכם /
3c l. 1	1Q21 1 1	הוי	[מ]ן די להוין תליתין]
7 l. 12		הוי	אנה / מתמה די יהוי לה כל חזוה
9 l. 15		הוי	כדי הוה יעקב / [אבי]מ[עשר
9 l. 16		הוי	כל מה דיהוה לה כנדרה /
9 l. 17		הוי	[אף כ]ע[ן] אנה הוית קדמי
9 l. 20		הוי	והוית כהן לאל על[מין/א } <יון> /
18 l. 22		הוי	{הווי} <א"הר> דכי / בבשרך
19 l. 1		הוי	/ וכדי תהוי קאים למיעל לבית אל /
19 l. 2		הוי	/ הוי סחי במיא
19 l. 2		הוי	ובאדין תהוי לביש / לבוש כהנותא
20 l. 3		הוי	וכדי תהוי לביש /
20 l. 4		הוי	/ הוי תאיב תוב ורחיע ידיך / ורגליך
21 l. 6		הוי	וכדי תהוי נסב להקרבה /
21 l. 8		הוי	/ הוי עוד תאב ורחע ידיך ורגליך /
27 l. 4		הוי	ראשא הוי מהנסק לקדמין /
30 l. 14		הוי	ויהוון כ[ן] / עובדיך בסרך
31 l. 17		הוי	[וכל די] / תהוה עביד
31 l. 17		הוי	בסרך הוי עב[י]ד
66 l. 3		הוי	/ [והו]ה כזמ[נ]א חזה לנשין
67 l. 6		הוי	לה / [תהו]ה כנשת כל [עמא
67 l. 6		הוי	וד[י]י לה תהוה / כהנותא רבתא
69a l. 11		הוי	ועוד / אוספת והוית ע[מ]ה
69b l. 14		הוי	והוה מריר לי עלוהי /
69b l. 16		הוי	והוה בכל מרר
71 l. 18		הוי	/ ועוד אוספת והויתי עמהא
80 l. 21		הוי	ובר / שנין תמנה וארבעין הוית
80 l. 23		הוי	ושנין / תמנין ותשע הויתי חי במצרי[ם /
81 l. 1		הוי	/ והוו כל יומי חיי
82 l. 6 l.		הוי	כל די' הווה / עם לבבי
85 l. 11		הוי	ראש / עובדיכון יהוי קושטא
85 l. 12		הוי	ועד / עלמא יה[ו]י קאים עמכון צדקה /
88 l. 18		הוי	ותהוי / חוכמתא עמכון ליקר עלם /
91 l. 8		הוי	אח או ח[ב]ר / הוי בה
91 l. 8		הוי	[ולא מן]תנכר הוא בה /
99 l. 16	213 1 ii 16	הוי	[א]ף כהנין ומלכין / תה[וון]
102 l. 3	213 4 3	הוי	ועל מן תהוא חובתא /

102 l. 8	213 4 8	הוי	[ו]תהוון לשכלין /
102 l. 9	213 4 9	הוי	תהו]ון כ]ל ק]שיט]ין
213 1 i 15	91 l. 7	הוך	לכל מת ומדינה די יהך לה /
102 l. 6	213 4 6	הוך	ותהכון בחשוך שׁטן /
102 l. 7	213 4 7	הוך	ה]ש]וכה תתא עליכ]ן [ו]תהכון /
82 l. 4		היא	היא שנ]תא]די מית בה / יוסף אחי
89 l. 20		היא	/ די אליף חוכמתא ויקר היא / בה
94 l. 16		היא	/ עותר רב די יקר היא חוכמתה /
6 l. 8		היך	והיך יהבנא לך רבות שלם / עלמא
17 l. 19		היך	וקדיש / זרעך היך קודשא
213b 1	6 l. 7	היכה	הי]כה רביתך מן כל בשר]ן
6 l. 7		הכין	כען חזי לך הכין רבינך / מן כולה
91 l. 4	213 1 i 14	הלך	מ]אלף <מהלך> נבר די אלף חכמה
66 l. 4		הרי	/ [וה]רת עוד [מני
71 l. 18		הרי	והוויתי עמהא והרת / וילידת לי ברתא
		ו	

1a v. 2 (213a l 7); 1a vv.
4, 4 (213a l 9, 9); 1a v. 7
(213a l 13); 1a vv. 8, 8
(213a l 14, 14); 1a v. 9
(213a l 16); 1a v. 11 (213a
l 18); 1b ll. 12, 14, 16, 18;
1c ll. 18, 19, 20, 21; 2
ll. 22, 22, 23; 3 ll. 15, 17,
18, 19, 20, 22; 3a ll. 2, 3,
3, 4, 5, 5, 6; 4 ll. 1, 2, 3,
3, 3, 4, 4, 4; 5 ll. 5, 5, 5,
6, 6; 6 l. 8; 7 ll. 9, 10,
11, 12, 13; 8 ll. 14, 14; 9
ll. 18, 19, 20, 20, 21, 21,
22; 10 ll. 23, 23; 11 ll. 1,
2; 12 ll. 3, 4, 5; 13 ll. 5,
7, 8, 9; 15 ll. 11, 12; 16
ll. 15, 15; 17 l. 16, 17, 18;
18 l. 21; 19 ll. 1, 2; 20
ll. 3, 4, 5; 21 ll. 6, 8, 8;
22 ll. 9, 9, 11; 24 ll. 15,
16, 17, 17, 17, 17, 18, 18,
19, 19; 25b ll. 22, 23, 1; 26
ll. 2, 3, 3; 27 ll. 5, 5; 28
ll. 11, 7, 7, 10; 29 l. 11; 30
ll. 12, 13, 14, 14, 15; 31
ll. [16], 18, 19; 32a ll. 22,
23; 65 l. [2]; 66 ll. [3, 4,

4, 5]; 67 l. [5, 6]; 68 l. [8];
69a ll. 10, 11, 11, 12; 69b
ll. 14, 15, 15, 16; 71 l. 18,
18, 18, 19, 19; 72 ll. 22,
22; 73 ll. 2, 4; 74 ll. 5, [5],
5, 6, 6, 6, [7], 7; 75 ll. 8,
9; 76 l. 10; 77 l. 14; 78
ll. 16, 17; 79 ll. 18, 19, 20;
80 ll. 20, 21, 22, 23; 81
ll. 1, 1, [1], 2; 82 ll. 3, [3],
[5], 6; 83a ll. 7; 83b l. 8;
84 l. 9; 85 l. 11; 86 ll. 13,
14; 87 l. 15; 88 ll. 17, 18;
89 l. 20; 90 ll. 23, 1, 1; 91
ll. 6, [8], 9, 9; 92 l. 13; 93
l. 14; 94 l. 17; 95 ll. 18,
19, 19, 19, 20, 21, 21, 23;
96 ll. 23, 1, 2, 4, 4; 97
l. 7; 98 ll. 8, 8; 99 ll. 13,
14, 14, 15; 100 l. 17; 101
l. 2; 102 ll. 3, 4, 5, 6, 7,
8; 214 4 2.

14 l. 8		זהר	אזדהר / לך ברי ברי מן כל טומאה
16 l. 14		זהר	היזדהר לך / ברי מן כל פחז
22 l. 12		זהר	/ חזיתי לאברהם אבי מיזדהר /
3a l. 5	213a 3–4 5	זי	בתו]לה זי חבלת שמה
5 l. 4		זמן	זמנין האכול /
5 l. 5		זמן	/ וזמנין תכפן
5 l. 5		זמן	וזמנין תעמול
5 l. 5		זמן	וזמנין / תנוח
5 l. 6		זמן	וזמנין תדמוך
5 l. 6		זמן	וזמנין תנוד / שנת עינא
66 l. 3		זמן	[והו]ה כזמ[נ]א חזה לנשין
73 l. 4		זמן	לעדן אשׁיות / זמניהון
17 l. 17		זניה	ולא תחל זרעך עם זניאן /
1a v. 7	213a 1 13	זנו	[בּאישׁ וזנותא דחא /
16 l. 16		זנו	מן כל פחז וטמאה ומן כל / זנו{ת}
86 l. 13		זרע	/ וקושטׄ[א הן] תזֹ[ן]עֹׄוֹן
87 l. 14		זרע	די זרע / טאב טאב מֹהֹנעל
87 l. 15		זרע	ודי זרע / ביש
1a v. 16	213a 2 7	זרע	/ זרע דק[שט
17 l. 17		זרע	ולא תחל זרעך עם זניאן /

17 l. 18		זרע	/ ארי זרע קדיש אנת
17 l. 19		זרע	וקדיש / זרעך היך קודשא
17 l. 20		זרע	קדיש אנת מתקרי לכל זרע / אברהם
87 l. 16		זרע	עלוהי תאיב זרעה /
25b l. 1		זרק	באדין חשרא למזרק דמא /
84 l. 10		חביב	ואנה / קושטא לכון מההוי חביבי
3a l. 5	213a 3–4 5	חבל	בהחן‍לה זי חבלת שמה
1c l. 21		חבר	ונהוי כולן א[חין] / וחברין
91 l. 7		חבר	אח או חֹבר / הוי בה
1b l. 18	213a 2 18	חד	תרעי שמיא ומלאך חדן
68 l. 9		חד	יליד בירהא קמיא [בח]ד לירה[א] /
72 l. 23		חד	וילידת / בחד בחודשא שביעיא
77 l. 14		חד	ביום חד יליד[ו בנ]יא
12 l. 5		חדי	וברכנא / וחדי
72 l. 23		חודש	וילידת / בחד בחודשא שביעיא
102 l. 3	213 4 4	חובה	ועל מן תהוא חובתא
3 l. 17		חוי	[אחי ואחוי דן /
3 l. 19		חוי	ואחוי / אינון יהודה
84 l. 10		חוי	ואנה / קושטא לכון מההוי חביבי
21 l. 7		חזה	/ כל די חזה להנסקה למדבחה /
23 l. 14		חזה	חזין להסקה מינהון למדבחה /
25a l. 20		חזה	אמר לי די חזין להסקה / מנהון
29 l. 12		חזה	כדי / חזה להון כמסתהון
31 l. 19		חזה	מן הושבן חזת ד[ן] אע[ן]א /
31 l. 20	(emend.)	חזה	/ חזין להקרבה לכל די סליק
1b l. 16	213a 2 16	חזו	בהזות חזיוא וחזית שמ[י]א
1b l. 16	213a 2 16	חזו	/ בהזות חזיוא
7 l. 11		חזו	אדין / אמרת חזוא הוא דן
7 l. 12		חזו	אנה / מתמה די יהוי לה כל חזוה
98 l. 9	214a 2 ii 6	חזו	חזית בחזוין
1b l. 15	213a 2 15	חזי	אדין הזיון אחזית]
1a v. 16	213a 2 16	חזי	/ בהזות חזיוא וחזית שמ[י]א
6 l. 7		חזי	כען הזי לך הכין רבינך / מן כולה
12 l. 3	(emend.)	חזי	והזא / יצחק אבונא לכולנא
15 l. 12		חזי	וכען ברי דין / קושטא אהזינך
22 l. 12		חזי	דנה / הזיתי לאברהם אבי מזדהר /
27 l. 5		חזי	ולא יתחזה לה / דם נכסת תורא
67 l. 5		חזי	[והזין]תי די לה / [תהון]ה כנשת
81 l. 2		חזי	והזיתי לי בנין תל[ן]יתיין]
90 l. 22		חזי	הוו בני ליוסף אחי /
96 l. 3	213 1 ii 3	חזי	/ יהזון שימ[ח]ה שימתה נ[נ]דה]

98 l. 9	214a 2 ii 6	חזי	/ חזית בחזוין דן[י
1b l. 15	213a 2 15	חזיון	אדין חזיון אחזית[ן
14 l. 10		חטא	ומן / כל חטא דינך רב הוא
75 l. 9		חי	/ עד די אנה חי בשנת
80 l. 23		חי	ושנין / תמנין ותשע הוית חי במצרים /
9 l. 22		חיין	וברכת לאבי / בחיוהי
68 l. 8		חיין	בשנת ארב[ע ות]לתין לחיי /
70 l. 17		חיין	בשנת / ארבעין לחיי ילידת
72 l. 22		חיין	/ בשנת שתין וארבע לי לחיי
75 l. 10		חיין	בשנת תשעין ואר[בע] / לחיי
81 l. 1		חיין	/ והוו כל יומי חיי שבע ותלתין
82 l. 4		חיין	ובש[נת מאה] ו[ת]מני / עשרה לחיי
95 l. 19		חיל	/ וחיל ופרשין ורתיכין סניאין /
1a v. 8	213a 1 14	חכמה	ח]כמה ומנדע ונבורה
88 l. 18		חכמה	ספר מוסר / חוכמה אליפו
88 l. 19		חכמה	ותהוי / חוכמתא עמכון ליקר עלם /
89 l. 20		חכמה	/ די אליף חוכמתא ויקר היא / בה
89 l. 21		חכמה	ודי שאיט חוכמתא לבשרון / מתיהב
90 l. 23		חכמה	[ד]מאלפא ספר ומוסר חכמה /
90 l. 2	213 1 i 13	חכמה	אל] תמהלו חכמתא למאלף /
91 l. 4		חכמה	די מאלף חוכמ[ה]ה נבר
91 l. 5	213 1 i 14	חכמה	נבר די אלף חכמה
91 l. 12		חכמה	כולה צבין / למאלף מן חוכמתה
93 l. 15		חכמה	/ בדיל למשמע מילי חוכמתה /
94 l. 16		חכמה	/ עותר רב די יקר היא חוכמתה /
95 l. 22		חכמה	/ אוצרי חוכמתא לא יבוזון /
97 l. 5	213 1 ii 5	חכמה	כל]אנ[ש די]ן / בעא חכמה[ן
97 l. 5	213 1 ii 5	חכמה	חכ]מתא י[שכח
98 l. 9	213 1 ii 9	חכמה	]ספר ומוסר / חכמה ד אלפו[
3a l. 3	213a 3–4 3	הלל	]אנתה ותהלל שמה
3a l. 4	213a 3–4 3	הלל	בח]ללה[ן אבהתא
17 l. 17		הלל	ולא תחל זרעך עם זניאן /
4 l. 1		חמדה	וכל חמדת בכורי ארעא /
2 l. 22		חמי	/ והתחמיון כו[ן]את[ן
3 l. 19		חמס	ביד עב]די חמסא
78 l. 18		חמס	ונמרת / לעבדי חמסא
30 l. 13		חמר	ובתר כולא חמר נסך /
69b l. 15		חנן	ובעית והתחננת / עלוהי
3a l. 6	213a 3–4 6	חסד	ולא מתחמא שם חסדה
97 l. 7	213 1ii 7	חסיר	/ ולא חסן[י]ל[
31 l. 19		חסר	/ ולא תחסר מן חושבן הזהא אע[י]ן[/
27 l. 5		חפי	/ ועלוהי חפי תרבא
4 l. 2		חרב	ולמלכות חרבא פנשא / וקרבא

Ref 1	Ref 2	Root	Text
28 l. 9		חרץ	/ ירכאהא עם שדרת חרצא /
31 l. 19		חושבן	/ ולא תחסר מן חושבן חזתא אׄעׄׄיׄ]ׄן[/
102 l. 1	213 4 1	חשך	]כן תחשכׄוׄן[
102 l. 6	213 4 6	חשוך	ותהכון בחשוך שׁׂטׁׂן
102 l. 7	213 4 7	חשוך	]מן חׄ]שׄ[וכה תתא עליכׄן[
2 l. 22		חתם	ותהון חתימין / כואתן
1a v. 9	213a 1 16	טב	]דׁׂשפיר ודטב קדמיך /
86 l. 14		טב	/ עללה בריכה וׁׂ]טׁׂא[בא
87 l. 15		טב	די זרע טאב טאב מׁׂהׁׂנעל
87 l. 15		טב	די זרע / טאב טאב מׁׂהׁׂנעל
94 l. 17		טב	/ וסימא טאבא לכל קניהא
214 5 4		טב (?)	א]טׄׄׄבׄהׄ[
214a 2 ii 3		טב	טבה וׁׂ]לׁׂ[א
1c l. 15		טמא	/ דׁׂטׁׂמאת לׁׂבׁׂ]נׁׂ[י יעקב
14 l. 9		טמאה	ברי ברי מן כל טומאה
16 l. 15		טמאה	/ ברי מן כל פחז וטמאה
18 l. 23		טמאה	מן כל טומאת כל נבר /
7 l. 12		טמר	וטמרת / אף דן בלבי
15 l. 12		טמר	ולא אטמר / מינך כל פתנם
102 l. 8	213 4 8	טען	]שׁׂנׁׂ[יׄׄ]א טׁׂעׁׂן[
1a v. 4	213a 1 9	יד	]ואצבעת כפי וידי /
9 l. 20		יד	/ ומלי ידי והוית כהן
20 l. 4		יד	ורחיע ידיך / ורגליך
21 l. 8		יד	ורחע ידיך ורגליך /
26 l. 2		יד	/ ועוד רחע ידיך / ורגליך
28 l. 7		יד	/ ובתר צוארה ידוהי
28 l. 7		יד	ובתר ידוהי / ניעא
28 l. 8		יד	בתר ידיא / ירכאהא
83b l. 9		ידיד	והציתו לפקודי / ידיד אל
1a v. 5	213a 1 11	ידע	א]נׄחה בלהודיך ידע /
13 l. 5		ידע	וכדי ידע די אנה כהן
213 1 i	20 94 l. 17	ידע	לכל] ידעיה ושׁׂימׁׂה טׁׂבה /
102 l. 4	213 4 4	ידע	ועליכן בנׁׂי ארו ידעונה /
6 l. 8		יהב	יהבנא לך רבות שלם / עלמא
9 l. 18		יהב	ולי מכל בנוהי יהב קרבן / מׁׂעׁׂשׁׂ]ר[
89 l. 22		יהב	ודי שאיט הוכמתא לבשרון / מתיהב
91 l. 10		יהב	כולהון יהבׁׂן / לה בה יקר
77 l. 14		יום	/ ביום חד ילׁׂידׁׂ]ו בנׁׂ[יׄׄא
81 l. 1		יום	/ והוו כל יומי חיי שבע ותלׁׂתׁׂין
68 l. 9		ילד	בשנת ארבׁׂ]עׁׂ ותׁׂ]לׁׂתׁׂין לחיי / יליד
69a l. 11		ילד	ויׄלידת לי בר / תליתׄיׄ
69b l. 13		ילד	לחדה ארי כדי יליד / הוא מית
70 l. 17		ילד	בשנת / ארבעין לחיי ילידת

71 l. 19		ילד	והרת / וילידת לי ברתא
71 l. 20		ילד	אמרת כדי ילידת לי
71 l. 21		ילד	ליקר / ילידת לי לכבוד
72 l. 22		ילד	וילידת / בחד בחודשא שביעיא
73 l. 4		ילד	זמניהון ו[יליןדׄו להון בנין /
76 l. 11		ילד	וקרית שמה די עמרם / כדי יליד
76 l. 11		ילד	עמרם ארי אמרת כדי יליד /
77 l. 14		ילד	ביום חד ילידׄ[ו בנׄ]יא /
69a l. 11		יסף	ועוד / אוספת והוית עׄ[מׄ]ׄה
71 l. 18		יסף	ועוד אוספת והוית עמהא והרת
104 l. 4	214 3 4	יקיר	יקרין מן נׄשיא[
71 l. 20		יקר	ליקר / ילידת לי לכבוד
88 l. 19		יקר	ותהוי / חוכמתא עמכון ליקר עלם
89 l. 20		יקר	די אליף חוכמתא ויקר היא / בה
90 l. 1	213 1 i 12	יקר	ליקר ולרבו ולמלכין
91 l. 11		יקר	כולהון יהבׄיׄן לה בה יקר
93 l. 14		יקר	ועל כורסי ייקר מהוחבין לה /
94 l. 16		יקר	עותר רב די יקר היא חוכמתה /
98 l. 11	213 2 8	יקר	וׄיׄ[קׄר vacat
100 l. 17	213 2 14	יקר	יקׄ[רׄ ולא איתי סוף
100 l. 18	213 1 ii 17	יקר	ליקׄ[רׄ]רׄכן
100 l. 19	213 2 16	יקר	]ן בׄיקר רב
104 l. 2	214 3 2	יקר	ארו מן יקר באׄרׄ[עׄא
68 l. 9		ירח	לחיי / יליד בירחא קמׄיׄא
68 l. 9		ירח	קמׄיׄא [בחׄ]דׄ לירחׄ[א] /
70 l. 17		ירח	ילידת בייˊˊˊ חה תליתיˊˊˊ /
28 l. 9		ירך	בתר ידׄיˊˊˊ / ירכאתא
28 l. 10		ירך	/ ובתר ירכאתא רגלין רחיען
98 l. 9	213 2 6	ירת	]תׄרתׄון אנון /
13 l. 7		ית	שׄארי / לפקדה יתי
13 l. 7		ית	ולאלפא יתי דין / כהנותא
1b l. 14	213a 2 14	יתב	/ שכבת ויתבת אנה עׄ[ל
93 l. 14		יתב	/ ועל כורסי ייקר מהוחבין לה /
31 l. 18		יתר	לא תותר צבו די לא [חזה] /
1c l. 17		כ	/ למעבד כדין בכלׄ[ן
2 l. 22		כ	/ והתחמיון כו[אתן] ותהון התימין /
2 l. 23		כ	ותהון התימין / כואתן במילת קׄ[וׄשׄ]ט
7 l. 11		כ	וכדן אנה / מתמה די יהוי לה כל חזוה
8 l. 14		כ	ואׄף הוא כדן / [ברכׄ]נׄי
9 l. 16		כ	כל מה דיהוה לה כנדרה /
22 l. 11		כ	ארי כדנה / חזית לאברהם אבי מיזדהר / כ
71 l. 21		כבוד	ליקר / ילידת לי לכבוד לישראל
96 l. 2	213 1 ii 2	כבש	/ ישכחון למכבש שוריה [ ] ולא [

Ref 1	Ref 2	Lemma	Text
1b l. 12		כדי	/ על אבי יעקוב וכד֗ן֗י
9 l. 15		כדי	אדין כדי הוה יעקב / [אבי]מ֗עשר
13 l. 5		כדי	וכדי ידע די אנה כהן
19 l. 1		כדי	/ וכדי תהוי קאים למיעל לבית אל /
20 l. 3		כדי	וכדי תהוי לביש / הוי תאיב תוב
21 l. 6		כדי	וכדי תהוי נסב להקרבה /
25b l. 22		כדי	/ וכדי הנסקת מן אע֗י(א) אלין
29 l. 11		כדי	כדי / הזה להון כמסתהון
69b l. 13		כדי	ארי כדי יליד / הוא מית
71 l. 20		כדי	אמרת כדי ילידת לי
76 l. 10		כדי	שמה די עמרם כדי / יליד עמרם ארי
76 l. 11		כדי	ארי אמרת כדי יליד /
78 l. 17		כדי	/ כדי קטלית אנה לשכם
80 l. 21		כדי	כדי / העלנא לארע מצרים
8 l. 14		כדן	ואף הוא כדן / [ברכ]ני
214b 5–6 i 2	22 l. 11	כדן	[כדן הוית לאברהם
76 l. 13		כדן	[כ]דן יתקר֗א [שמה <עמ]א̇> ראמא /
102 l. 9	213 4 9	כהל	ק]שיט̇י[ן ו]תכה֗ל֗ן ון
79 l. 19		כהן	ובר שנין תשע עשרה כהנית
9 l. 20		כהן	והוית כהן לאל על{מין/א } <יון> /
13 l. 5		כהן	אנה כהן לאל / עליון
17 l. 19		כהן	ארו כהן / קדיש אנת
99 l. 15	213 2 12	כהן	א]ף כהנין ומלכין
3b l. 3	213a 5 3	כהנו	[כהנות עלמא
3c l. 2	1Q21 1 2	כהנו	לב]נ֗י֗ך מלכות כהנותא רבא
9 l. 18		כהנו	אנה הוית קדמי בראש / [כהנו]ת֗ה
9 l. 19		כהנו	ואלבשי לבוש כהונתא /
13 l. 8		כהנו	ולאלפא יתי דין / כהנותא
15 l. 14		כהנו	כל פתגם לאלפותך דין / כהנותא
19 l. 3		כהנו	ובאדני תהוי לביש / לבוש כהנותא
67 l. 7		כהנו	לה תהוה / כ̇הנותא רבתא ל[כל יש]ראל / כהנו
101 l. 2	213 3 2	כוכב	שמשא ש]הרא ו̇כ̇וכביא /
93 l. 14		כורסה	/ ועל כורסי יקר מהותבין לה /
25b l. 2		כותל	למזרק דמא / על כותלי מדבחה
32a l. 21	(emend.)		לתורא רבא ככר אעין ליה ככר
1a v. 2	213a 1 7	כל	אתרחע[נ]ת֗ וכל /
1a v. 10	213a 1 17	כל	ו]א֗ל תשלט בי כל שטן /
1a v. 18	213a 2 9	כל	/ דין קשט ל֗ב֗נ֗ל
1c l. 16		כל	על] / דברת די כל א[נש
1c l. 17		כל	/ למעבד כדין בכל֗[ן אנשי שכם
1c l. 20		כל	ונהוי כולן א[הין] / וחברין
3 l. 15		כל	יוס[ף֗](?) אחי בכל עדן /
3a l. 4	213a 3–4 4	כל	בח[ללה] אבהתא וכל /

3a l. 5	213a 3-4 5	כל	אבהתה ואבהתהת לכל אחיה
3a l. 6	213a 3-4 6	כל	שם חסדה מן כול עמה{א} ‹ה›
3a l. 7	213a 3-4 7	כל	]לﬨ לכל דרי עלמא וﬦ[
4 l. 1		כל	וכל חמדת בכורי ארעא /
4 l. 2		כל	בכורי ארעא / כולה למאכל
6 l. 8		כל	הכין רבינך / מן כולה
7 l. 12		כל	אנה / מתחמה די יהוי לה כל חזוה
7 l. 13		כל	ולכל אינש לא נליחה /
9 l. 16		כל	/ [אבי]מ̇עשר כל מה דיהוה לה
9 l. 18		כל	ולי מכל בנוהי יהב קרבן /
9 l. 21		כל	/ וקרבית כל קרבנוהי וברכת
10 l. 22		כל	אדין כולהון / ברכוני
12 l. 4		כל	וחזא / יצחק אבונא לכולנא
14 l. 9		כל	מן כל טומאה ומן / כל חטא
14 l. 10		כל	מן כל טומאה ומן / כל חטא
14 l. 10		כל	דינך רב הוא מן כל / בישרא
15 l. 13		כל	ולא אטמר / מינך כל פתגם
16 l. 15		כל	היזדהר לך / ברי מן כל פחז
16 l. 15		כל	מן כל פחז וטמאה ומן כל / זנו{ת}
17 l. 20		כל	אנת מתקרי לכל זרע / אברהם
18 l. 22		כל	לאﬥ וקריב / לכל קדישוהי
18 l. 23		כל	כען {הוׄוׄיׄ} ‹אׄהר› דכי / בבשרך מן כל טומאת
18 l. 23		כל	/ בבשרך מן כל טומאת כל נבר /
20 l. 6		כל	עד דלא תקרב למדבחא / כל דנה
21 l. 7		כל	להקרבה / כל די חזה להנסקה
23 l. 13		כל	/ מן כל תריעשר מיני אעין
29 l. 11		כל	וכולהון מליחין במלח
30 l. 13		כל	ובתר כולא חמר נסך /
30 l. 15		כל	וכל קורבניך [לרעו]א̇ / לריח ניחח
31 l. 20		כל	/ חזין להקרבה לכל די סליק למדב[חא] /
67 l. 6		כל	לה / [תהו]ה כנשת כל [עמא
69b l. 16		כל	והוה בכל מרר
81 l. 1		כל	כל יומי חיי שבע ותלתין ומ̇אה /
82 l. 6		כל	הנון כל די̇ הווה / עם לבבי
91 l. 6		כל	לכל מא[ת] [/ ומדינה] די[ן] ﬠﬥﬥ
91 l. 10		כל	כולהון יהבי̇ן / לה בה יקר
91 l. 11		כל	כולה צבין / למאלף מן חוכמתה
94 l. 17		כל	/ וסימא מאבא לכל קניהא
95 l. 21		כל	/ ומדינה ויבוזון כל די בהון /
96 l. 4	213 1 ii 4	כל	/ ולא איתי כֹל מחיר ננדה
97 l. 7	213 2 4	כל	[ן כל בעי]ן
100 l. 18	213 2 15	כל	ולא]ת̇עבר מנכן עד כל

101 l. 1	213 3 1	כל	[לֹ[כן] כל עממיא /
102 l. 5	213 4 5	כל	א]רלחת קשׂ*א תשבקון וֹכל שֹׁבֹילי
102 l. 9	213 4 9	כל	תהו[ן] כֹ[ל ק]ן[שֹׁיטֹ]ין
103 l. 3	213 5 3	כל	[לשֹׁנין בכן מן כל מֹן]
214b 1 1		כל	[מֹין מן כוֹ]ל
214b 1 2		כל	מן]כֹוֹל לבֹיך [
214b 7 1		כל	[מֹן כוֹל בשֹׁר]א
91 l. 10		כֹילֹי	ולא דמה / בה לכֹילֹאֹי
30 l. 14		כן	ויהוון כן / עובדֹיך בסֹרֹך
67 l. 6		כנשה	די לה / [תהֹו]ה כֹנשֹׁת כל [עמֹא
6 l. 7		כען	כען חֹוֹי לך הכֹין רבֹינֹיך /
9 l. 17		כען	/ [וֹדֹי כֹ]עֹן אנה הֹוֹית קֹדֹמֹי
15 l. 11		כען	וכען ברֹי דֹין / קֹוֹשֹׁטֹא אחֹוֹינֹך
18 l. 22		כען	כען {הֹוֹוֹי}<אֹ'הֹר> / בבשֹׁרֹך
88 l. 17		כען	וכען בנֹי סֹפֹר מֹוֹסֹר / חֹוֹכֹמֹה
98 l. 8	214a 2 ii 5	כען	וכען בנֹי]סֹפֹר ומֹוֹסֹר חֹכֹמֹה
1a v. 4	213a 1 9	כף	[ואצבעֹת כפֹי וֹידֹי /
5 l. 5		כפן	/ וֹמֹנֹין תכפֹן וֹמֹנֹין תעמֹוֹל
4 l. 4		כפן	/ ונצפֹתֹא וֹקֹטֹלֹא וכֹפֹנֹא
		ל	

1a v. 3 (213a 1 8); 1a vv. 11, 11 (213a 1 18); 1a v. 14 (213a 2 5); 1a v. 18 (213a 2 9); 1a v. 19 (213a 2 10); 1b ll. 17, 18; 2 l. 23; 3a l. 8; 6 ll. 7, 8; 7 ll. 12, 13; 9 ll. 16, 18, 19, 20, 21, 22; 10 ll. 1, 1; 12 l. 4; 13 ll. 5, 6, 7, 7; 14 ll. 8, 9; 15 l. 13; 16 l. 14, 14; 17 ll. 17, 20; 18 ll. 21, 22; 19 l. 1, 1; 20 l. 5; 21 ll. 6, 7; 22 ll. 10, 12; 23 l. 14, 14; 25a ll. 20, 20, 21; 25b l. 1; 26 l. 3; 27 ll. 4, 5; 29 l. 12; 30 l. 16; 31 l. 21; 32a l. 21; 67 ll. 5, 6, 7; 68 ll. 8, 9; 69a ll. 11, 13, 13; 69b l. 14; 70 l. 17; 71 ll. 19, 20, 21; 72 l. 22; 72 l. 1; 73 ll. 2, 3, 4; 74 l. 5; 75 ll. 8, 8, 10; 78 ll. 16, 17, 18; 79 l. 20; 80 l. 22; 81 l. 2; 82 ll. 4, 5, 5, 6; 83 ll. 7, 8; 84 ll. 9, 10; 88 ll.

18, 19, 21; 90 ll. 22, 1, 1,
1; 90 l. 3; 91 ll. 6, 6, 7, 9,
10, 11, 12; 93 l. 14; 94
l. 17; 96 l. 2; 100 l. 18; 101
ll. 1, 4; 102 l. 8; 104 l. 3;
214 5.

3a l. 6	213a 3–4 6	לא	ולא מהמחא שׄםׄ חסדה
7 l. 13		לא	ולכל אינש לא נליחה /
15 l. 12		לא	ולא אטמר / מינך כל פתנם
17 l. 17		לא	ולא תחל זרעך עם זניאן /
20 l. 5		לא	עד דלא תקרב למדבחא /
27 l. 5		לא	ולא יתחזה לה / דם נכסת תורא
31 l. 18		לא / לא	ובמתקל לא תותר צבו די לא [חזה] /
31 l. 18		לא	לא תותר צבו די לא [חזה] /
31 l. 19		לא	ולא תחסר מן חושבן חזתא אע̇י[ן] /
81 l. 3		לא	בנין תל[יתין] עד / די לא מיתת
90 l. 3		לא	ולארחתה ל[ו]א̇ תשב[קן] / לב[עא]
91 l. 9		לא	ולא דמ[ה בה]לׄנכרי
91 l. 9		לא	ולא דמה / בה לכיל[א]י
95 l. 22		לא	אוצרי חוכמתא לא יבוזון /
95 l. 23		לא	ולא ישכחון מטמוריה
96 l. 23	213 1 ii 1	לא	מטמוריה ולא / יעלון תרעיה̇
96 l. 1	213 1 ii 1	לא	יעלון תרעיה̇ ולא]
96 l. 2	213 1 ii 2	לא	] ישכחון למכבש שוריה [ ] ולא [
96 l. 4	213 1 ii 4	לא	ולא איתי כׄל מחיר נזדה
97 l. 7	213 1 ii 7	לא	ולא הסן[י]רׄ]
100 l. 17	213 2 14	לא	יק]רׄ ולא איתי סוף /
102 l. 2	213 4 2	לא	הלא קבל [ל]מ̇הׄך לׄ[
102 l. 4	213 4 4	לא	]הׄלא עלי ועליכן בנׄי̇
104 l. 5	214 3 5	לא	]הׄל[א לׄ]ן[
214b 1 2		לב	מן]כׄל לביך]
7 l. 13		לב	וטמרת / אף דן בלבי
82 l. 7		לבב	כל די הווה / עם לבבי
30 l. 14		לבונה	והקטיר עליהון לבונה /
9 l. 19		לבוש	ואלבשי לבוש כהונתא /
19 l. 3		לבוש	ובאדין תהוי לביש / לבוש כהונתא
9 l. 19		לבש	ואלבשי לבוש כהונתא /
19 l. 2		לבש	ובאדין תהוי לביש / לבוש כהונתא
20 l. 3		לבש	וכדי תהוי לביש / הוי תאיב חוב
7 l. 9		לות	וננדו שבעתון מן לותי /
11 l. 3		לות	/ אבונן לות יצחק אבונה
69b l. 13		להדה	ארי / מר לי עלוהי
1a v. 5	213a 1 11	להוד	א]נתה בלהודיך ידע /

Ref 1	Ref 2	Lemma	Text
32a l. 22		להוד	ואם תרבא בלחודוהי סליק /
213a 6 1		מא	[אמרת מא /
81 l. 1		מאה	יומי חי שבע ותלתין ומאה / שנין
83b l. 8		מאמר	[שמ]ע[ו] / למאמר לוי אבוכון
20 l. 5		מדבח	עד דלא תקרב למדבחא / כל דנה
21 l. 7		מדבח	כל די חזה להנסקה למדבחה /
23 l. 14		מדבח	די הזין להסקה מינהון למדבחה /
25a l. 21		מדבח	להסקה / מנהון ל[תח]ות עלתא על מדבחה /
25b l. 23		מדבח	וכדי הנסקת מן אע(י)א אלין על / מדבחא
25b l. 2		מדבח	למזרק דמא / על כותלי מדבחה
31 l. 20		מדבח	הזין להקרבה לכל די סליק למדב[חהא] /
91 l. 7		מדינה	לכל מא[ת] / ומדינהן דין עלל לה
95 l. 21		מדינה	וינסבון נכסי מאת / ומדינה
3 l. 22		מדנה	לה[ה]ה לראובן / אהונן די למדנה אשר
68 l. 10		מדנה	[בח]ד לירה[א] / עם מדנה שמש]א [
3 l. 18		מה	[בשכם ומה / ימות יוס]ף
9 l. 16		מה	כל מה דיהוה לה
88 l. 17		מוסר	ולען בני ספר מוסר חוכמה
90 l. 23		מוסר	[ד]מאלפא ספר ומוסר חכמה /
98 l. 8	214a 2 ii 5	מוסר	ולען בני ספר ו[מוסר
3 l. 19		מות	[בשכם ומה / מ]ת יוס[ף
69b l. 14		מות	כדי יליד / הוא מית
69b l. 15		מות	מריר לי עלוהי / סניא מן די ימות
81 l. 3		מות	בנין תל[יתן] עד / די לא מיתת
82 l. 4		מות	שנ[תא]די מית בה / יוסף אחי
3a l. 6	213a 3–4 6	מחי	ולא מחמחא שם ח]סדה מן כול עמה{א} <ה>
96 l. 4	213 1 ii 4	מחיר	ולא איתי כל מחיר נגדה ו[לא
90 l. 2	213 1 i 13	מחל	[א]ל תמחלו חכמתא למאלף /
102 l. 6	213 4 6	מחל	[ת]מחלון ותהכון בחשוך שטן /
96 l. 23		מטמור	ולא ישכחון מטמורייה ולא / יעלון תרעיה
97 l. 6	213 1 ii 6	מטמור	מטמרה מנה[ן
19 l. 2		מי	למיעל לבית אל / הוי סחי במיא
2 l. 23		מילה	ותהון חתימין / כואתן במילת ק[וש]ט
93 l. 15		מילה	בדיל למשמע מילי חוכמתה /
23 l. 13		מן	מן כל תריעשר מיני אעין אמר / לי
1b l. 18	213a 2 18	מלאך	לי תרעי שמיא ומלאך חד[ן
26 l. 4		מלח	ושרי להנסקה אבריה / מליחין
29 l. 11		מלח	וכולהון מליחין במלח
29 l. 11		מלח	וכולהון מליחין במלח
9 l. 20		מלי	ומלי ידי והוית כהן לאל על{מין}א } <יון> / מלי
90 l. 1	213 1 i 12	מלך	ומו[ס]ר חכמה ליקר ולרבו ולמלכין /
95 l. 18		מלך	הן / יאתון מלכין תקיפין ועם רב /
99 l. 15	213 2 12	מלך	[א]ף כהנין ומלכין /

3c l. 2	1Q21 1 2	מלכו	לב]נ̇ך מלכות כהנותא רבא מן מלכות[
3c l. 2	1Q21 1 2	מלכו	לב]נ̇ך מלכות כהנותא רבא מן מלכות[
4 l. 2		מלכו	ולמלכות הרבא פנשא / וקרבא
100 l. 16	213 2 13	מלכו	[ש̇] [ ]ן̇ מלכותכן /
102 l. 8	213 4 8	מלל	ומ̇[ל]ל [ו]תהוון לשכלין /
1a v. 19 (213 a 2 10); 1b l. 13; 3a ll. 6, 7; 3c ll. 1, 2; 6 l. 8; 7 ll. 9, 10; 9 l. 18; 11 l. 2; 14 ll. 9, 9, 10; 15 l. 13; 16 ll. 15, 15; 17 l. 16; 18 l. 23; 22 l. 10; 23 l. 13; 25a l. 21; 25b l. 22; 26 l. 3; 31 l. 19; 65 l. 15; 72 l. 23; 76 l. 12; 91 l. 12; 97 l. 6; 101 l. 3; 102 ll. 3, 5; 103 l. 3; 104 ll. 2, 4; 214b 1 1; 214b 7 l.		מן	
1a v. 8	213a 1 14	מנדע	ח]כמה ומנדע ונבורה /
32a l. 23		מנה	/ ואם הרבא בלהודוהי סליק שיתה / מנין
29 l. 12		מסת	כדי / הזה להון כמסתהון /
3a l. 8	213a 3–4 8	מעשר	[מ̇עשר קודש קרבן לאל מ̇ן /
9 l. 19		מעשר	ולי מכל בנוהי יהב קרבן / מ̇ע̇ש̇[ר] לאל
69b l. 14		מריר	והוה מריר לי / עלוהי סניא
69a l. 13		מרד	וקראתי שמה מרדי ארי / מר לי עלוהי
69b l. 16		מרד	ובעית והתחננת / עלוהי והוה בכל מרד
24 l. 18		משח	/ ברותא ותאנבתא ואע משחא /
30 l. 13		משח	ובתר דנה נישפא / בליל במשחא
214b 7 2		משח	[מ̇שחא ו̊]°
17 l. 16		משפחה	ואנת אנתתא מן משפחתי / סב לך
91 l. 6		מת	לכל מא̇[ת] / ומדינה[ן] דין̇ ע̊לל לה
95 l. 20		מת	וינסבון נכ̇ס̇י מא̇ת / ומדינה
31 l. 18		מתקל	בסרך הוי עב̇[יד במשחה] / ובמתקל
32a l. 21		מתקל	/ לתורא רבא ככר אעין ליה במתקל /
96 l. 3	213 1 ii 3	ננד	/ יהזון שי̇מחה שימחה נ̇[נ]ד̇ה̊ [
96 l. 4	213 1 ii 4	ננד	/ ולא איתי כ̇ל̊ מחיר ננדה ו̇[לא
1b l. 11	213a 2 11	ננד	/ באדין ננדת ב̇[
7 l. 9		ננד	וננדו שבעתון מן לותי /
9 l. 16		נדר	כל מה דיהוה לה כנדרה /
5 l. 6		נוד	וזמנין תדמוך וזמנין / תנוד שנת עינא
5 l. 6		נוח	וזמנין תעמול וזמנין / תנוח
25b l. 23		נור	ונורא ישרא להדלקא / בהון
4 l. 3		נחשירו	הרבא פנשא / וקרבא ונחשירותא

214 5 6		נטי (?)	[אטיון
1a v. 3	213a 1 8	נטל	]נטלת לשמיא
30 l. 16		ניחח	/ לריח ניחח קודם אל עליון
27 l. 6		נכסה (emend.)	ולא יתחזה לה / דם נכסת תורא
95 l. 20		נכסין	וינסבון נכסֹי מאֹת / ומדינה
91 l. 8		נכר	[ולא מן]תנכר הוא בה /
91 l. 9		נכרי	ולא דמנ]ה בה]לנכרי
17 l. 17		נסב	ואנת אנתתא מן משפחתי / סב לך
21 l. 6		נסב	וכדי תהוי נסב להקרבה /
73 l. 3		נסב	ולבני / נס]בת נשין] מֹן בנת אחי
75 l. 8		נסב	/ ונֹסֹב לה עמרם אנתא
79 l. 20		נסב	ובר שנין תמנה / ועסרין נסבת לי אֹנתֹה
95 l. 20		נסב	וינסבון נכסֹי מאֹת / ומדינה
30 l. 13		נסך	ובתר כולא חמר נסך /
28 l. 8		נע	ובתר ידוהי / ניעא עם בן דפנא
4 l. 4		נצפה	/ ונצפחא וקטלא וכפנא
30 l. 12		נשיף	ובתר דנה נישפא / בליל במשחא
98 l. 10	213 2 7	נתן	]רבה תתנון /
91 l. 6		סני	/ וסנה לֹ]ה שמ]עֹה
69b l. 15		סניא	והוה מריר לי עלוהי / סניא
92 l. 13		סניא	רחמוהֹ]י[/ סניאין
95 l. 19		סניא	ורתיכין סניאין / עמהון
24 l. 17		סנד	/ וסנדא ואטולא ושוחא
100 l. 17	213 2 14	סוף	יק]רֹ ולא איתי סוף /
19 l. 2		סחי	למיעל לבית אל / הוי סחי במיא
94 l. 17		סימה	/ וסימא טאבא לכל קניהא
21 l. 7		סלק	כל די הזה להנסקה למדבחה /
22 l. 11		סלק	/ ובאדין הסק אינון
23 l. 14		סלק	די חזין להסקה מינהון למדבחה /
23 l. 15		סלק	/ די ריח תנדהון בשם סליק
25a l. 20		סלק	אמר לי די חזין להסקה / מנהון
26 l. 3		סלק	ושרי להנסקה אבריה / מליחֹין
27 l. 4		סלק	ראשא הוי מהנסק לקדמין /
31 l. 20		סלק	להקרבה לכל די סליק למדב]חא[/
32a l. 22		סלק	/ ואם תרבא בלחודוהי סליק
32a l. 23		סלק	ואם פר תורין הוא די סליק /
88 l. 17		ספר	ולכען בני ספר מוסר / חוכמה אליפו
90 l. 23		ספר	]ד[מאלפֹא ספר ומוסר חכמה /
98 l. 8	214a 2 ii 5	ספר	ולכען בנֹי ספֹר ו]מוסר
99 l. 12	213 2 9	ספר	אֹף בספריֹא /
30 l. 15		סרך	ויהוון כֹן / עובדיך בסרך
31 l. 17		סרך	בסרך הוי עב]יד במשחה] /

3 l. 23		עאן	ושור / [י]הודה קדמא [ל]משבק עאנא /
1c l. 17		עבד	/ למעבד כדין בכל[ן
31 l. 17		עבד	[וכל דין] / תהוה עביד
31 l. 17		עבד	בסרך הוי עב[ן]יד
1a v. 17	213a 2 8	עבד	צלות עב[ן]דך /
1a v. 19	213a 2 10	עב	/ לבר עבדך מן ק[ן]דמיך
3 l. 19		עבד	ומה / מית יוס[ן]ף ביד עב[ן]די חמסא
78 l. 18		עבד	ונמרת / לעבדי חמסא
30 l. 15		עבד	ויהוון כ[ן / עובדיך בסרך
85 l. 11		עבד	ראש / עובדיכון יהוי קושטא
100 l. 18	213 2 15	עבר	ולא]ת̇עבר מנכן עד כל
1b l. 17	213a 2 17	עד	/ תחותי רם עד דבק לשמי[א
20 l. 5		עד	עד דלא תקרב למדבחא /
75 l. 9		עד	/ עד די אנה חי
81 l. 2		עד	בנין תל[ן]יתין[ן] עד / די לא מיתת
85 l. 11		עד	ועד / עלמא יהו̇י קא̇ים עמכון צדקה /
100 l. 18	213 2 15	עד	ולא]ת̇עבר מנכן עד כל /
3 l. 15		עדן	יוס[ן]ף̇(?) אחי בכל עדן /
73 l. 3		עדן	מ̇ן בנת אחי לעדן אשיוות / זמניהון
21 l. 8		עוד	/ הוי עוד האב ורחע ידיך ורגליך /
26 l. 2		עוד	ועוד רחע ידיך / ורגליך /
66 l. 4		עוד	וה]ל̇ת עוד [מני
69a l. 10		עוד	ועוד אוספת והוית ע[מ]ה̇
71 l. 18		עוד	ועוד / אוספת והויתי עמהא
2 l. 21		עורלה	נזורו̇ן]עורלת בישרכון /
94 l. 16		עותר	/ עותר רב די יקר היא חוכמתה /
5 l. 7		עין	וזמנין תנוד / שנת עינא
7 l. 10		עיר	/ ואנה אתעירת מן שנתי
1a v. 11	213a 1 18	על	ע]לי מז̇רי וקרבני /
1b l. 12	213a 2 12	ע	/ על אבי יעקוב וכד[ן]י
8 l. 14		על	/ וע̇לנא על אבי יצחק
25a l. 21		על	ל[ה]ת̇ח̇ן̇ו̇ת עלהא על מדבחה /
25b l. 22		על	ה̇נ̇ס̇ק̇ת̇ מן אני(א) אלין על / מדבחא
25b l. 2		על	למזרק דמא / על כותלי מדבחה
27 l. 5		על	/ ועלוהי חפי תרבא
30 l. 14		על	/ והקטיר עליהון לבונה
69a l. 13		על	ארי / מר לי עלוהי
69b l. 14		על	והוה מריר לי עלוהי / סניא
69b l. 16		על	ובעית והתחננת /עלוהי
87 l. 16		על	עלוהי האיב ז̇רעה /
93 l. 14		על	/ ועל כורסי ייקר מהותבין לה /
102 l. 3	213 4 3	על	ועל מן תהוא ח̇ובתא /
102 l. 4	213 4 4	על	ה̇לא עלי ועליכן בנ̇י̇[

102 l. 4	213 4 4	על	]הלא עלי ועליכן בני
102 l. 7	213 4 7	על	ה]ש[וכה תתא עליכן[
25a l. 21		עלה	להסקה / מנהון ל]תחן[ות עלתא על מדבחה /
3a l. 2	213a 3-4 2	עלל	וכען י]ע[ל]ו מכחשי נבריא
8 l. 14		עלל	/ ועלנא על אבי יצחק
19 l. 1		עלל	/ וכדי תהוי קאים למיעל לבית אל /
72 l. 1		עלל	מן בתר די / העّלנ]א[למצרים
73 l. 2		עלל	בשנת שת / עש]רה למ]ן[עלינה לארע מצרים
78 l. 15		עלל	בר שנין תמ]נה עשרה העלת / לّארע כנעןٔ
80 l. 22		עלל	הויתי כדי / העלנא לארע מצרים
86 l. 13		עלל	תנהّעלון / עללה בריכה ו]טא[בא
87 l. 15		עלל	די זרע / מאב מאב מّהّنעל
91 l. 7		עלל	לכל מא]ת[/ ומדינה]ן[דין עّלל לה
86 l. 14		עללה	תנהّעלון / עללה בריכה ו]טא[בא
3a l. 6	213a 3-4 6	עלם	שّ חסדה מן כול עמה]א{ <ה> לעלם /
3a l. 7	213a 3-4 7	עלם	]לّם לכל דרי עלמא
3b l. 3	213a 5 3	עלם	]כהנות עלמא /
9 l. 20		עלם	והוית כהן לאל על{מין/א } <יון> /
85 l. 12		עלם	ועד /עלמא יّהّוّי קאים עמכון צדקה /
88 l. 19		עלם	ותהוי / הוכמתא עמכון ליקר עלם /
3b l. 2	213a 5 2	עם (?)	]ל עם °]° °[ ]
17 l. 17		עם	ולא תחל זרעך עם זניאן /
28 l. 8		עם	ובתר ידוהי / ניעא עם בן דפנא
28 l. 9		עם	/ ירכאתא עם שדרת הרצא /
28 l. 10		עם	רנלין רחיען עם / קרביא
66 l. 3		עם	והוית ע]מ[הֹ /]וה[רת עוד
68 l. 10		עם	]בה[ד לירה]א[/ עם מדנה שמש]א [
71 l. 18		עם	/ ועוד אוספת והויתי עמהא
82 l. 7		עם	כל די הוזה / עם לבבי
85 l. 12		עם	ועד עלמא / יّהّוّי קאים עמכון צדקה /
88 l. 19		עם	ותהוי / הוכמתא עמכון ליקר עלם /
95 l. 20		עם	ורתיכין סניאין /עמהון
103 l. 1	213 5 1	עם (?)	]עّمהון ב]ר[ّש]עא /
3a l. 4	213a 3-4 4	עם (?)	] אֹ °ٔ ה עם למّש]ן [ ]כה [
3a l. 6	213a 3-4 6	עם	שّ חסדה מן כול עמה]א{ <ה> לעלם
3a l. 7	213a 3-4 7	עם	]לّם לכל דרי עלמّا ומ]ן
76 l. 12		עם	/ דנה י]ّרים{ <פק> עמא מן ארّע מّצרים / עם
95 l. 18		עם	ועם רב / והיל ופרשין ורתיכין סניאין /
101 l. 1	213 3 1	עם	ל]כ[ן כל עממיא [
5 l. 5		עמל	וזמנין תעמול וזמנין / הנוה
4 l. 3		עמל	ועמלא / ונצפהא וקטלא וכפנא
83a l. 7		עני	ענית ואמרת לבני
79 l. 20		עסרין	ובר שנין תמנה / ועסרין נסבת

214b 2–3 2	23 l. 13	עע	תרי ע[שר עעין א]
214b 5–6 i 5	24 l. 19	עע	ע]רא אדסא ועעי
24 l. 19		ער	/ ערא והדסה ואעי דקתא
2 l. 21		עורלה	נזורון [עורלת בישרכון /
9 l. 16		עשר	כדי הוה יעקב / [אבי]מעשר
73 l. 2		עשר	בשנת שת / עש[רה למ]עלינה לארע מצרים
78 l. 15		עשר	בר שנין תמנה עשרה העלת /
78 l. 16		עשר	ובר שנין תמנה עשרה / כדי קטלית
79 l. 19		עשר	ובר שנין תשע / עשרה כהנית
82 l. 4		עשר	ובש[נת מאה] ו[ת]מני / עשרה לחיי
4 l. 2		פנש	ולמלכות חרבא פנשא / וקרבא
16 l. 15		פחז	היזדהר לך / ברי מן כל פחז
13 l. 7		פקד	שארי / לפקדה יתי
82 l. 6		פקד	/ ושריתי לפקדה הנון
84 l. 9		פקד	אנה לכון מפקד בני
83b l. 8		פקוד	והציתו לפקודי / ידיד אל
32a l. 23		פר	ואם פר תורין הוא די סליק /
95 l. 19		פרש	ופרשין ורתיכין סניאין / עמהון
15 l. 13		פתנם	ולא אטמר / מינך כל פתנם
1c l. 20		צבי	די ה[וו] / צבין אינון בברתן
91 l. 11		צבי	כולה צבין / למאלף מן חוכמתה
31 l. 18		צבו	לא תותר צבו די לא [הזה] /
85 l. 12		צדקה	יהוי קאים עמכון צדקה /
28 l. 6		צואר	ובתרוהי צוארה / ובתר צוארה ידוהי
28 l. 7		צואר	/ ובתר צוארה ידוהי ובתר ידוהי
83b l. 8		צות	והציתו לפקודי / ידיד אל
1a v. 17	213a 2 8	צלו	/ צלות עב[דך
214b 1 3		צלי	[בעו מ]צלין]
22 l. 9		צלח	/ ומהקריב אעין מהצלחין
102 l. 2	213 4 2	קבל	א[הלא קבל [ל]מ[הך ל]
1a v. 9	213a 1 15	קדם	לא]שכחה רחמיך קדמיך /
1a v. 16	213a 1 16	קדם	]דשפיר ודטב קדמיך /
1a v. 19	213a 2 10	קדם	/ לבר עבדך מן ק[דמיך
16 l. 14		קדם	לקדמין היזדהר לך / ברי
22 l. 10		קדם	ובקר / אינון לקודמין מן תולעא /
27 l. 4		קדם	ראשא הוי מזהנסק לקדמין /
30 l. 16		קדם	/ לריח ניחה קודם אל עליון
3 l. 23		קדם	ושור / [י]הודה קדמא
9 l. 17		קדמי	הוית קדמי בראש / [כהנן]תה
68 l. 9		קדמי	בירחא קמיא [בח]ד לירח[א] /
3a l. 7	213a 3–4 7	קדיש	ומ[ ]ת[י קדישין מן עמא°
17 l. 18		קדיש	ארי זרע קדיש אנת
17 l. 18		קדיש	וקדיש / זרעך היך קודשא

17 l. 20		קדיש	ארו כהן / קדיש אנת מתקרי
18 l. 22		קדיש	וקריב / לכל קדישוהי
3a l. 8	213a 3–4 8	קודש	[מ‍עשר קודש קרבן לאל מֹן /
17 l. 19		קודש	וקדיש / זרעך היך קודשא
19 l. 1		קום	/ וכדי תהוי קאֹים למיעל לבית אל /
85 l. 12		קום	יהֹוי קאֹים עמכון צדקה /
78 l. 17		קטל	/ כדי קטלית אנה לשכם
4 l. 4		קטל	/ ונצפתא וקטלא וכפנא
30 l. 14		קטר	/ והקטיר עליהון לבונה
94 l. 17		קני	/וסימא טאבא לכל קניֹהא /
17 l. 20		קרי	אנת מתקרי לכל זרע / אברֹהם
66 l. 5		קרי	[וקרא]תי שמֹה קֹ[הת]
69a l. 12		קרי	וקראתי שמה מררי
76 l. 10		קרי	וקריתי שמה די עמרם כדי / יליד
76 l. 13		קרי	ית‍קרֹא [שמה עמֹ]א ראמא /
82 l. 5		קרי	קריתי לבנֹ[י ו]לבניהון /
99 l. 13	213 1 ii 13	קרי	[אֹף בספריא / קֹרֹ]ית
1a v. 11	213a 1 18	קרב	/ וקרבני למהוא לכה /
9 l. 21		קרב	/ וקרבית כל קרבנוהי
10 l. 1		קרב	ואשלמית / להקרבה קורבנוהי
20 l. 5		קרב	דלא תקרב למדבחא / כל דנה
21 l. 6		קרב	להקרבה / כל די חזה להנסקה
22 l. 9		קרב	/ ומהקריב אֹעין מהצלחין
31 l. 20		קרב	להקרבה לכל די סליק למדב[הא] /
4 l. 3		קרב	/ וקרבא ונחשירותא ועמלא
28 l. 11		קרבן	רנלֹן רחׅ‍יֹען עם / קרבׅיא
3a l. 8	213a 3–4 8	קרבן	[מ‍עשר קודש קרבן לאל מֹן /
9 l. 18		קרבן	יהב קרבן / מֹעש[ר] לאל
9 l. 21		קרבן	/ וקרבית כל קרבנוהי
10 l. 1		קרבן	ואשלמית / להקרבה קורבנוהי
30 l. 15		קרבן	וכל קורבניך [לרעֹ]ﬡ / לריח ניחה
18 l. 21		קריב	קריב אנת לאﬥ
18 l. 21		קריב	וקריב / לכל קדישוהי
1a v. 6	213a 1 12	קשט	[א‍רחת קשט ארדק /
1a v. 16	213a 2 7	קשט	/ זרע דקֹ[ש]ט
1a v. 18	213a 2 9	קשט	/ דין קשט לֹכ‍ֹﬥ
2 l. 23		קשט	ותהון התימין / כואתן במילת קֹ[וש]ט
15 l. 12		קשט	וכען ברי דין / קושטא אהזוינך
84 l. 10		קשט	ואנֹה / קושטא לכון מההוי חביבי
85 l. 11		קשט	ראש / עובדיכון יהוי קושטא
86 l. 13		קשט	/ וקושטֹ[א הן] תֹ‍הֹ[ר]‍ﬡֹ‍נֹ
97 l. 8	213 1 ii 8	קשט	ﬢ[ן כל בעﬞ]ן [ ] / בקשט]
102 l. 5	213 4 5	קשט	א]‍ﬡֹדת קשﬡ‍ﬡ תשבקֹוﬥ

102 l. 9	213 4 9	קשט	תהו]ן כ]ל ק]שיט]ין
9 l. 17		ראש	אנה הוית קדמי בראש / [כהנ]תה
27 l. 4	(emend.)	ראש	ראשא הוי מהנסק לקדמין /
85 l. 10		ראש	ראש / עובדיכון יהוי קושטא
99 l. 13	213 2 10	ראש	תהו]ון ראשין ושפטין /
3c l. 2	1Q21 1 2	רב	מלכות כהנותא רבא מן מלכות]
14 l. 10		רב	דינך רב הוא מן כל / בישרא
32a l. 21		רב	לתורא רבא ככר אעין ליה
67 l. 7		רב	/ כהנותא רבהא ל]כל יש]ראל /
94 l. 16		רב	/ עותר רב די יקר
95 l. 18		רב	ועם רב / וחיל ופרשין ורתיכין
98 l. 10	213 2 7	רב	רבה תתנון /
100 l. 19	213 2 16	רב	ן ביקר רב /
214 4 3		רב	כהנ]ה רבה ו]
6 l. 8		רבו	יהבנא לך רבות שלם /עלמא
90 l. 1	213 1 i 12	רבו	ומוס]ר חכמה ליקר ולרבו ולמלכין /
6 l. 7		רבי	חזי לך הכין רבינך / מן כולה
92 l. 13		רברב	ושאלי שלמיה רברבין /
20 l. 5		רגל	ורחיע ידיך / ורגליך /
21 l. 8		רגל	ורחע ידיך ורגליך /
26 l. 3		רגל	ועוד רחע ידיך / ורגליך
28 l. 10		רגל	רגלין רחיען עם / קרביא
103 l. 2	213 5 2	רום	ש]נאיכן אדין ידו]ם]בכן /
1a v. 9	213a 1 15	רחמן	לא]שכחה רחמיך קדמיך /
20 l. 4		רחע	ורחיע ידיך / ורגליך
21 l. 8		רחע	ורחע ידיך ורגליך /
26 l. 2		רחע	ועוד רחע ידיך / ורגליך
28 l. 10		רחע	רגלין רחיען עם / קרביא
1a v. 7	213a 1 12	רחק	א]רחת קשט ארחק /
23 l. 15		ריח	ריח תננהון בשם סליק
30 l. 16		ריח	/ לריח ניחח קודם אל עליון
1b l. 17	213a 2 17	רם	רם עד דבק לשמי]א
76 l. 13		רם	יתקרא [שמה <עמ]א> ראשא
213 6 1		רם	כאב רם אל]
214 5 5	(?)	רם	רם ליש]ראל
30 l. 15		רעו	[לרעו]א / לריח ניחח
103 l. 1	213 5 1	רשע	עמהו]ן ב]ר]שעא
95 l. 19		רתך	ורתיכין סניאין / עמהון
92 l. 13		שאל	ושאלי שלמיה רברבין /
102 l. 5	213 4 5	שביל	א]רחת קש]א תשבקון ו]כל שבילי /
72 l. 23		שביעי	בחודשא שביעיא מן בתר די / העל]ינ]א
7 l. 9		שבע	וננדו שבעתון מן לותי /

81 l. 1		שבע	כל יומי הוי שבע ותלתין ומאה / שנין
3 l. 23		שבק	ושור / [י]הודה קדמא [ל]משבק עאנא /
90 l. 3		שבק	ולארהתה ל[א תשב[ן]קן] / לב[עא]
102 l. 5	213 4 5	שבק	א]רחת קש"א תשבקון
102 l. 8	213 4 8	שניא	[שנ]יא [ ]ט[ע]ן ומ[ן]ל[ל
28 l. 9		שדרה	/ ירכאתא עם שדרת הרצא /
101 l. 2	213 3 2	שהר	שמשא ש[ה]רא וכוכביא /
101 l. 4	213 3 4	שהר	[לשהרה] /
24 l. 17		שוח	ושוחא ואודנא / ברותא
89 l. 21		שיט	ודי שאיט הוכמתא לבשרון / מתיהב
213 1 i 11	89 l. 21	שיטו	לב[ס]רון ולשיטו מתיהב
71 l. 19		שוי	ושויתי שמהא / יוכבד
3 l. 22		שור	ושור / [י]הודה קדמא
96 l. 2	213 1 ii 2	שור	/ ישכחון למכבש שוריה [ ] ולא [
1a v. 10	213a 1 17	שטן	ו]אל תשלט בי כל שטן /
102 l. 6	213 4 6	שטן	[תמחלון ותהכון בחשוך שטן]
96 l. 3	213 1 ii 3	שימה	יהוון שימתה שימחה נ[נ]דה [ ]
96 l. 3	213 1 ii 3	שימה	יהוון שימחה שימחה נ[נ]דה [ ]
1b l. 14	213a 2 14	שכב	/ שכבת ויהבת אנה ע[ל
1a v. 9	213a 1 15	שכח	לא]שכחה רחמיך קדמיך /
95 l. 23		שכח	ולא ישכחון מטמוריה /
96 l. 2	213 1 ii 2	שכח	/ ישכחון למכבש שוריה [ ] ולא [
97 l. 5	213 1 ii 5	שכח	/ בעא חכמה[] הכ[]מתא י]שכה
102 l. 8	213 4 8	שכל	ומ[ן]ל[ל [ו]תהוון לשכלין
1a v. 10	213a 1 17	שלט	ו]אל תשלט בי כל שטן
10 l. 23		שלם	ואשלמית / להקרבה קורבנוהי
4 l. 1		שלם	/ ו]שלמא וכל חמדת בכורי ארעא /
6 l. 8		שלם	יהבנא לך רבות שלם / עלמא
92 l. 13		שלם	ושאלי שלמיה רברבין /
3a l. 3	213a 3–4 3	שם	ותהלל שמה ושם אבוה /
3a l. 3	213a 3–4 3	שם	ותהלל שמה ושם אבוה /
3a l. 5	213a 3–4 5	שם	הבלח שמה ושם אבהתה
3a l. 5	213a 3–4 5	שם	הבלח שמה ושם אבהתה
3a l. 6	213a 3–4 6	שם	ולא מתמחא שם חסדה
24 l. 16		שם	ואלין / אינון שמהתהון
66 l. 5		שם	/ [וקרא]תי שמה ק[והת]
69a l. 12		שם	וקראתי שמה מרדי
71 l. 19		שם	ושויתי שמהא / יוכבד
74 l. 4		שם	שם בני / נרשון ל[בנ]י ו[ן]שמעי
74 l. 5		שם	ושם בני / קהת עמרם
74 l. 7		שם	ו]שם בני מררי מחלי ומושי /
76 l. 10		שם	וקריתי שמה די עמרם
214 5 7		שם (?)	[שם]°

1a v. 3	213a 1 8	שמין	נטלת לשמיא /]
1b l. 16	213a 2 16	שמין	וחזית שמ]יא
1b l. 17	213a 2 17	שמין	רם עד דבק לשמ]יא
1b l. 18	213a 2 18	שמין	תרעי שמיא ומלאך חד]
13 l. 6		שמין	לאל / עליון למארי שמיא
3 l. 18		שמע	ואחוי דן / [שמ]ע[י]ן[
83b l. 7		שמע	[שמ]ע[ן] / למאמר לוי
93 l. 15		שמע	למשמע מילי חוכמתה /
68 l. 10		שמש	עם מדנח שמש[א] /
68 l. 8		שנה	/ בשנת ארב[ע ות]ל[תין לחיי /
70 l. 16		שנה	בשנת / ארבעין לחיי ילידת
72 l. 22		שנה	/ בשנת שתין וארבע לי לחיי
73 l. 1		שנה	בשנת שת / עש]רה למ]עלינה לארע מצרים
75 l. 9		שנה	בשנת תשעין ואר]בע[ן] / לחיי
78 l. 15		שנה	בר שנין תמ]נה עשרה העלת /
78 l. 16		שנה	ובר שנין תמ]נה עשרה /
79 l. 18		שנה	ובר שנין תשע / עשרה כהנית
79 l. 19		שנה	ובר שנין תמנה / ועסרין נסבת
80 l. 21		שנה	ובר / שנין תמנה וארבעין הויתי
80 l. 22		שנה	ושנין / תמנין ותשע הויתי חי
81 l. 2		שנה	כל יומי חיי שבע ותלתין ומאה / שנין
82 l. 3		שנה	ובש]נת מאה] ו[ת]מני / עשרה לחיי
82 l. 4		שנה	היא שנ[תא]די מית בה / יוסף
5 l. 7		שנה	ומנין תנוד / שנת עינא
7 l. 10		שנה	/ ואנה אתעירת מן שנתי
103 l. 2		שני	ש]נ[איכן אדין ירי[ם]בכן /
99 l. 13	213 2 10	שפט	תה]ו[ן ראשין ושפטין /
1a v. 9	213a 1 16	שפיר	ד]שפיר ודטב קדמיך /
11 l. 2		שרי	ושרינא בבירת אברהם / אבונן
13 l. 6		שרי	שארי / לפקדה יתי
25b l. 23		שרי	ונורא ישרא להדלקא / בהון
25b l. 1		שרי	באדין תשרא למזרק דמא /
26 l. 3		שרי	ושרי להנסקה אבריה /
82 l. 6		שרי	/ ושריתי לפקדה הנון
32a l. 22		שת	בלחודוהי סליק שיחה / מין
73 l. 1		שת	בשנת שת / עש]רה למ]עלינה לארע מצרים
72 l. 22		שתין	/ בשנת שתין וארבע לי לחיי
24 l. 18		תאנה	/ ברותא ותאנהא ואע משחא /
20 l. 4		תוב	תאיב תוב ורחיע ידיך /
21 l. 8		תוב	עוד תאב ורחע ידיך ורגליך /
87 l. 16		תוב	ודי זרע / ביש עלוהי תאיב ז[ר]עה /
20 l. 4		תובא	תאיב תוב ורחיע ידיך /
22 l. 10		תולעה	ובקר / אינון לקודמין מן תולעא /

27 l. 6		תור	ולא יתחזה לה / דם נכסת תורא
32a l. 21		תור	/ לתורא רבא ככר אעין ליה
32a l. 23		תור	ואם פר תורין הוא די סליק /
1b l. 17	213a 2 17	תחות	/ תחותי רם עד דבק לשמי[א
25a l. 21		תחות	ל[תח]ות עלתא על מדבחה /
214b 2–3 4	24 l. 18	תככה	בל]ותא ותככה[ ]
3c l. 1	1Q21 1 1	תלתי	מ]ן די להוין תליתין [
69a l. 12		תלתי	וילידת לי בר / תליתי
70 l. 17		תלתי	ילידת ביירהה תליתיא /
81 l. 2		תלתי	והזיתי לי בנין תל[ת]יתין]
68 l. 8		תלתין	/ בשנת ארב[ע ות]לתין לחיי / יליד
81 l. 1		תלתין	כל יומי חיי שבע ותלתין ומ[אה / שנין
7 l. 12		תמה	וכדן אנה / מתמה די יהוי לה כל חזוה
78 l. 15		תמנה	בר שנין תמנה עשרה העלת / ל[א]רע כנען
78 l. 16		תמנה	ובר שנין תמנה עשרה / כדי קטלית
79 l. 19		תמנה	ובר שנין תמנה / ועסרין נסבת לי אנתה
80 l. 21		תמנה	ובר / שנין תמנה וארבעין הויתי
82 l. 3		תמנה	ובש[נת מאה] ו[ת]מני / עשרה לחיי
80 l. 23		תמנין	ושנין / תמנין ותשע הויתי חי במצרי[ם /
23 l. 15		תנן	ריח תננהון בשם סליק
95 l. 18		תקף	הן / יאתון מלכין תקיפין ועם רב /
27 l. 5		תרב	/ ועלוהי חפי תרבא
32a l. 22		תרב	/ ואם תרבא בלחודוהי סליק שיתה / מנין
23 l. 13		תריעשר	/ מן כל תריעשר מיני אעין אמר / לי
1b l. 18	213a 2 18	תרע	/ לי תרעי שמיא ומלאך חד]
96 l. 1	213 1 ii 1	תרע	/ מטמוריה ולא יעלון תרעיה ולא]
79 l. 18		תשע	ובר שנין תשע / עשרה כהנית
80 l. 23		תשע	ושנין / תמנין ותשע הויתי חי במצרי[ם /
75 l. 9		תשעין	בשנת תשעין וא[ר]בע[/ לחיי

Proper Names

1b l. 13	213a 2 13	אבל מין	/ מן אבל מן אדין]
11 l. 2		אברהם	ושרינא בבירת אברהם / אבונן
17 l. 21		אברהם	אנת מתקרי לכל זרע / אברהם
22 l. 12		אברהם	כדנה / חזיתי לאברהם אבי מיזדהר /
10 l. 1		בית אל	ואשלמית / להקרבה קורבנוהי בבית אל
11 l. 2		בית אל	ואזלנא / מבית אל ושרינא
74 l. 5		גרשון	שם בני / גרשון לב[נ]י ו]שמעי
3 l. 17		דן	אחי ואחוי דן /
74 l. 6		חברון	עמ[רם ויצהר וחברון ועוזיאל /

3 l. 20	יהודה	ואחוי / אינון יהודה די אנה
3 l. 23	יהודה	ושור / [י]הודה קדמא
71 l. 20	יוכבד	שמחא / יוכבד אמרת כדי ילידת
75 l. 8	יוכבד	/ ונסב לה עמרם אנתא ליוכבד ברתי /
77 l. 14	יוכבד	ילידן בנ]יא הוא ויוכבד / ברתי
3 l. 15	יוסף	יוס[ף](?) אחי בכל עדן /
3 l. 19	יוסף	ומה / מית יוס[ף ביד עב]די
82 l. 5	יוסף	היא שנ[תא]די מית בה / יוסף אחי
90 l. 22	יוסף	חזו בני ליוסף אחי / [ד]מאלפא
1c l. 18	יעקב	/ יעקב אבי ורא[ו]בן אחי
9 l. 15	יעקב	כדי הוה יעקב / [אבי]מ[עשר
74 l. 6	יצהר	עמרם ויצהר וחברון ועוזיאל /
8 l. 14	יצחק	/ ועלנא על אבי יצחק
11 l. 3	יצחק	/ אבונן לות יצחק אבונה
12 l. 4	יצחק	וחוא / יצחק אבונא לכולנא
67 l. 7	ישראל	/ כהנותא רבתא ל[כל יש]ראל /
71 l. 21	ישראל	/ ילידת לי לכבוד לישראל /
214 5	ישראל	]רם ליש[ראל
78 l. 16	כנען	בר שנין תמנה עשרה העלת / ל[ארע כנע]ן
74 l. 5	לבני	שם בני / גרשון ל[בנ]י ו]שמעי
14 l. 8	לוי	לוי אזדהר / לך ברי
83b l. 8	לוי	[שמ]ע[ו]ן / למאמר לוי אבוכון
74 l. 7	מושי	ו]שם בני מררי מחלי ומושי /
74 l. 7	מחלי	ו]שם בני מררי מחלי ומושי /
72 l. 1	מצרים	מן בתר די / העלנ[א] למצרים
73 l. 2	מצרים	למ]עלינה לארע מצרים
76 l. 12	מצרים	עמא מן אר[ע מ]צרים /
80 l. 22	מצרים	כדי / העלנא לארע מצרים
80 l. 23	מצרים	ושנין / תמנין ותשע הוית חי במצרי[ם /
69a l. 12	מררי	וקראתי שמה מררי
74 l. 7	מררי	ו]שם בני מררי מחלי ומושי /
74 l. 6	עוזיאל	עמרם ויצהר וחברון ועוזיאל /
74 l. 6	עמרם	עמרם ויצהר וחברון ועוזיאל /
75 l. 8	עמרם	/ ונסב לה עמרם אנתא
76 l. 10	עמרם	וקריתי שמה די עמרם כדי / יליד
76 l. 11	עמרם	כדי / יליד עמרם ארי אמרת
66 l. 5	קהת	/ [וקרא]תי שמה ק[הת
74 l. 6	קהת	ושם בני / קהת עמרם ויצהר
1c l. 18	ראובן	/ יעקב אבי ורא[ו]בן אחי
3 l. 21	ראובן	אזלנא לה[ן ח]ד[ה לה לראובן / אחונן
3 l. 16	שכם	לאה[ן]יא די די הוו בשכם /
3 l. 18	שכם	[בשכם ומה / ימות יוס[ף
78 l. 17	שכם	/ כדי קטלית אנה לשכם

3 l. 20		שמעון	די אנה ושמעון / אחי אזלנא
74 l. 5		שמעי	שם בני / נרשון לבנ[י ו]שמעי

Divine Names

3a l. 8	213a 3–4 8	אל	[מ]עשר קודש קרבן לאל מן /
9 l. 19		אל	יהב קרבן / מ[עש]ר[ן] לאל
83b l. 9		אל	והציתו לפקודי / ידיד אל
213 6		אל (?)	כאב רם אל[ן /
1a v. 5	213a 1 10	מרה	ו]אמרת מרי אנתה /
1a v. 11	213a 1 18	מרה	ע]לי מ[רי וקרבני למהוא
1a v. 15	213a 2 6	מרה	מרי ב[ר]כת /
13 l. 6		מרי שמיא	אנה כהן לאל / עליון למארי שמיא
3c l. 3	1Q21 1 3	אל עליון	[ל[א]ל[ן ע]ל[י]ון
9 l. 20		אל עליון	והוית כהן לאל על{מין/א} <יון>
13 l. 6		אל עליון	אנה כהן לאל / עליון למארי שמיא
30 l. 16		אל עליון	לריח ניחח קודם אל עליון /
17 l. 19		קודש	וקדיש / זרעך היך קודשא

GREEK CONCORDANCE

ἀγαπάω

58   τέκνον ἀγαπητόν, ἐγὼ λέγω, **ἠγαπημένος** σὺ τῷ πατρί σου καὶ ἅγιος

58   καὶ **ἠγαπημένος** ἔσῃ ὑπὲρ πάντας τοὺς ἀδελφούς σου

ἀγαπητός, ή, όν

58   νῦν ὡς σοί, τέκνον **ἀγαπητόν**, ἐγὼ λέγω, ἠγαπημένος σὺ τῷ πατρί σου

ἀγιάζω

17   τὸ σπέρμα σου **ἁγίασον** (קדיש?) καὶ τὸ σπέρμα τοῦ ἁγιασμοῦ σου ἐστίν

ἁγιασμός, ὁ

17   καὶ τὸ σπέρμα τοῦ **ἁγιασμοῦ** (קדישא) σου ἐστίν· ἱερεὺς ἅγιος κληθήσεται

ἅγιος, α, ον

1a v. 4   μου ἀνεπέτασα εἰς ἀλήθειαν κατέναντι τῶν **ἁγίων** καὶ ηὐξάμην καὶ εἶπα

1a v. 8   δειχθήτω μοι, δέσποτα, τὸ πνεῦμα τὸ **ἅγιον**, καὶ βουλὴν καὶ σοφίαν

17   ἐκ σπέρματος γὰρ **ἁγίου** (קדיש) εἶ, καὶ τὸ σπέρμα σου ἁγίασον

17   ἱερεὺς **ἅγιος** (קדיש) κληθήσεται τῷ σπέρματι Ἀβραάμ

18   ἐγγὺς εἶ κυρίου καὶ σὺ ἐγγὺς τῶν **ἁγίων** (קדיש) αὐτοῦ. γίνου καθαρὸς

19   καὶ ὅταν εἰσπορεύῃ ἐν τοῖς **ἁγίοις** (בית אל?), λούου ὕδατι πρῶτον

48   ὅτι ἱερεὺς σὺ **ἅγιος** κυρίου, καὶ ἱερεῖς ἔσονται πᾶν τὸ σπέρμα σου

51   χαίρω ὅτι ἐξελέχθης εἰς ἱερωσύνην **ἁγίαν** καὶ προσενεγκεῖν θυσίαν

53   καὶ ὅταν ἐκπορεύῃς ἐκ τῶν **ἁγίων**, πᾶν αἷμα μὴ ἁπτέσθω τῆς στολῆς σου

58   ἐγὼ λέγω, ἠγαπημένος σὺ τῷ πατρί σου καὶ **ἅγιος** κυρίου ὑψίστου

ἀδελφός, ὁ

58   καὶ ἠγαπημένος ἔσῃ ὑπὲρ πάντας τοὺς **ἀδελφούς** σου

62   Μελχάν, θυγατέρα Βαθουήλ, υἱοῦ Λάβαν, **ἀδελφοῦ** μητρός μου

†αδια†

21   καὶ ὅταν μέλλῃς προσφέρειν ὡς **ἀδίαν** (חטה?) ἐνέγκε ἐπὶ τὸν βωμόν

ἄδικος, ον

1a v. 7   μάκρυνον ἀπ᾽ ἐμοῦ, κύριε, τὸ πνεῦμα τὸ **ἄδικον** καὶ διαλογισμὸν

αἴξ, ὁ, ἡ

34   καὶ εἰ κριὸς ἐκ προβάτων ἢ τράγος ἐξ **αἰγῶν** τὸ προσφερόμενον ᾖ

35   καὶ εἰ ἄρνα ἐκ προβάτων ἢ ἔριφον ἐξ **αἰγῶν** κʹ μναῖ

36   καὶ εἰ ἀμνὸς τέλειος ἐνιαύσιος ἢ ἔριφος ἐξ **αἰγῶν** ιεʹ μναῖ

42   καὶ τῷ ἀρνίῳ καὶ τῷ ἐρίφῳ ἐχ **αἰγῶν** τὸ τρίτον τοῦ σάτου

αἷμα, τό

25b   τότε ἄρξῃ κατασπένδειν τὸ **αἷμα** (דמא) ἐπὶ τὸν τεῖχον τοῦ θυσιαστηρίου

26   καὶ πάλιν νίψαι σου τὰς χεῖρας καὶ τοὺς πόδας ἀπὸ τοῦ **αἵματος** (דמא)

27   καὶ μὴ ὀπτανέσθω τὸ **αἷμα** (דם) ἐπὶ τῆς κεφαλῆς αὐτῆς

53   καὶ ὅταν ἐκπορεύῃς ἐκ τῶν ἁγίων, πᾶν **αἷμα** μὴ ἁπτέσθω τῆς στολῆς σου

55   καὶ μὴ ὀφθήτω ἐπὶ σοι πᾶν **αἷμα** καὶ πᾶσα ψυψή

55   τὸ γὰρ **αἷμα** ψυψή ἐστιν ἐν τῇ σαρκί

56   κάλυπτε τὸ **αἷμα** αὐτοῦ τῇ γῇ πρῶτον πρὶν ἢ φαγεῖν σε ἀπὸ τῶν κρεῶν

56   πρὶν ἢ φαγεῖν σε ἀπὸ τῶν κρεῶν καὶ οὐκέτι ἔσῃ ἐσθίων ἐπὶ τοῦ **αἵματος**

57   ὅτι οὕτως εὗρεν ἐν τῇ γραφῇ τῆς βίβλου τοῦ Νῶε περὶ τοῦ **αἵματος**

αἰνέω

1a v. 9   καὶ εὑρεῖν χάριν ἐνώπιόν σου καὶ **αἰνεῖν** τοὺς λόγους σου

αἴρω

1a v. 3   τοὺς ὀφθαλμούς μου καὶ τὸ πρόσωπόν μου **ἦρα** (נטל) πρὸς τὸν οὐρανόν

αἰών, ὁ

1a v. 16   δοῦναι αὐτοῖς σπέρμα δίκαιον εὐλογημένον εἰς τοὺς **αἰῶνας**

1a v. 18   τοῖς λόγοις σου ποιεῖν κρίσιν ἀληθινὴν εἰς πάντα τὸν **αἰῶνα**

1a v. 18   ἐμὲ καὶ τοὺς υἱούς μου εἰς πάσας τὰς γενεὰς τῶν **αἰώνων**

1a v. 19   ἀπὸ τοῦ προσώπου σου πάσας τὰς ἡμέρας τοῦ **αἰῶνος**

59   ‵τὸ σπέρμα σου ἕως πάντων τῶν **αἰώνων** ἐνεχθήσεται ἐν Βιβλίῳ

60   τὸ ὄνομά σου καὶ τὸ ὄνομα τοῦ σπέρματός σου ἕως τῶν **αἰώνων**

61   τὸ σπέρμα σου ἐπὶ τῆς γῆς εἰς πάσας τὰς γενεὰς τῶν **αἰώνων**

ἀκαθαρσία, ἡ

1a v. 14   καθάρισον τὴν καρδίαν μου, δέσποτα, ἀπὸ πάσης **ἀκαθαρσίας**

14   Τέκνον Λευί, πρόσεχε σεαυτῷ ἀπὸ πάσης **ἀκαθαρσίας** (טומאה)

16   ἀπὸ παντὸς συνουσιασμοῦ καὶ ἀπὸ πάσης **ἀκαθαρσίας** (טומאה)

18   ἐν τῷ σώματί σου ἀπὸ πάσης **ἀκαθαρσίας** (טומאה) παντὸς ἀνθρώπου

ἀκούω

48   τέκνον μου, **ἄκουσον** τοὺς λόγους μου καὶ ἐνωτίσαι τὰς ἐντολάς μου

ἅλας, τό

29   καὶ πάντα ἡλισμένα ἐν **ἅλατι** (מלח) ὡς καθήκει αὐτοῖς αὐτάρκως

37   καὶ **ἅλας** ἀποδέδεικται τῷ ταύρῳ τῷ μεγάλῳ, ἅλισε τὸ κρέας αὐτοῦ

52   καὶ τὸ **ἅλας** καὶ τὴν σεμίδαλιν καὶ τὸν οἶνον καὶ τὸν λίβανον ἐπιδέχου

ἀλήθεια, ἡ

1a v. 4   καὶ τὰς χεῖράς μου ἀνεπέτασα εἰς **ἀλήθειαν** κατέναντι τῶν ἁγίων

1a v. 6   καὶ νῦν τέκνα μου μετ᾽ ἐμοῦ. καὶ δός μοι πάσας ὁδοὺς **ἀληθείας**
        (קשׁט)

15   καὶ νῦν τὴν κρίσιν τῆς **ἀληθείας** (קושׁטא) ἀναγγελῶ σοι

ἁλίζω

26   ἀπὸ τοῦ αἵματος, καὶ ἄρξῃ τὰ μέλη ἀναφέρειν **ἡλισμένα** (מלח)

29   καὶ πάντα **ἡλισμένα** (מלח) ἐν ἅλατι ὡς καθήκει αὐτοῖς αὐτάρκως

37   **ἅλισε** τὸ κρέας αὐτοῦ, καὶ ἀνένεγκε ἐπὶ τὸν βωμόν.

37   καὶ ᾧ ἂν περισσεύσῃ τοῦ ἁλός, **ἅλισον** ἐν αὐτῷ τὸ δέρμα

ἅλς, ὁ

37   καὶ ᾧ ἂν περισσεύσῃ τοῦ **ἁλός**, ἅλισον ἐν αὐτῷ τὸ δέρμα

ἀμνός, ὁ

36   καὶ εἰ **ἀμνὸς** τέλειος ἐνιαύσιος ἢ ἔριφος ἐξ αἰγῶν ιεˊ μναῖ

44   καὶ τῷ ἀρνίῳ τὸ ὄγδοον τοῦ σάτου καὶ **ἀμνοῦ** καὶ οἶνον

ἄν

37			καὶ ᾧ **ἄν** περισσεύσῃ τοῦ ἁλός, ἅλισον ἐν αὐτῷ τὸ δέρμα

46a			ἢ<ν> **ἄν** προσαγάγῃς μόνον, οὐκ ἐπὶ στέατος, προσαχθήσεται ἐπ᾽ αὐτὴν

ἀναβαίνω

23			προσφέρε<ιν>, ὧν ἐστιν ὁ καπνὸς αὐτῶν ἡδὺς **ἀναβαίνων** (סלק)

ἀναγγέλλω

15			καὶ νῦν τὴν κρίσιν τῆς ἀληθείας **ἀναγγελῶ** (יחן?) σοι

ἀναπετάννυμι

1a v. 4		καὶ τοὺς δακτύλους τῶν χειρῶν μου καὶ τὰς χεῖράς μου **ἀνεπέτασα**

ἀναπληρόω

62			**ἀνεπληρώθησάν** μοι ἑβδομάδες τέσσαρες ἐν τοῖς ἔτεσιν τῆς ζωῆς μου

ἀναποιέω

30			καὶ μετὰ ταῦτα σεμίδαλιν **ἀναπεποιημένον** (בלל) ἐν ἐλαίῳ

43			τὸ τέταρτον τοῦ σάτου τῷ ταύρῳ **ἀναπεποιημένον** ἐν τῇ σεμιδάλει

45			καὶ πᾶσα ἡ σεμίδαλις **ἀναπεποιημένη**, ἢ<ν> ἄν προσαγάγῃς μόνον

ἀνάπτω

53			πᾶν αἷμα μὴ ἁπτέσθω τῆς στολῆς σου· οὐκ **ἀνήψῃς** αὐτῷ αὐθήμερον

ἀναφέρω

21			καὶ ὅταν μέλλῃς προσφέρειν ὅσα δεῖ **ἀνενέγκαι** (סלק) ἐπὶ τὸν βωμόν

22			καὶ **ἀνάφερε** (קרב) τὰ ξύλα πρῶτον <ἐ>σχισμένα, ἐπισκοπῶν αὐτὰ

25a			ὅτι ταῦτά ἐστιν ἅ σε **ἀναφέρειν** (סלק) ὑποκάτω τῆς ὁλοκαυτώσεως

26			ἀπὸ τοῦ αἵματος, καὶ ἄρξῃ τὰ μέλη **ἀναφέρειν** (סלק) ἡλισμένα

27			τὴν κεφαλὴν **ἀνάφερε** (סלק) πρῶτον καὶ κάλυπτε αὐτὴν τῷ στέατι

31			οὕτως ξύλα καθήκει **ἀναφέρεσθαι** (סלק) ἐπὶ τὸν βωμόν

32			καὶ εἰς τὸ στέαρ μόνον **ἀναφέρεσθαι** (סלק) ἐξ μνᾶς

37			ἅλισε τὸ κρέας αὐτοῦ, καὶ **ἀνένεγκε** ἐπὶ τὸν βωμόν

ἀνατολή, ἡ

68			ἐγεννήθη ἐν τῷ πρώτῳ μηνὶ μιᾷ τοῦ μηνὸς ἐπ᾽ **ἀνατολῆς** (מדנח) ἡλίου

ἀνέρχομαι

11			καὶ **ἀνήλθομεν** (אזל) ἀπὸ Βηθὴλ καὶ κατελύσαμεν ἐν τῇ αὐλῇ Ἀβραὰμ

ἄνθρωπος, ὁ

18			ἐν τῷ σώματί σου ἀπὸ πάσης ἀκαθαρσίας παντὸς **ἀνθρώπου** (נבר)

ἀνοίγω

1a v. 3		τὸ πρόσωπόν μου ἦρα πρὸς τὸν οὐρανόν, καὶ τὸ στόμα μου **ἤνοιξα**

ἀνομία, ἡ

1a v. 13		παράδος διὸ δὴ καὶ τὴν **ἀνομίαν** ἐξάλειψον ὑποκάτωθεν τοῦ οὐρανοῦ

1a v. 13		καὶ συντελέσαι τὴν **ἀνομίαν** ἀπὸ προσώπου τῆς γῆς

ἀπό

1a v. 7		μάκρυνον **ἀπ᾽** ἐμοῦ, κύριε, τὸ πνεῦμα τὸ ἄδικον καὶ διαλογισμὸν

1a v. 7		διαλογισμὸν τὸν πονηρὸν καὶ πορνείαν, καὶ ὕβριν ἀπόστρεψον **ἀπ᾽** ἐμοῦ

1a v. 10		μὴ κατισχυσάτω με πᾶς σατανᾶς πλανῆσαί με **ἀπὸ** τῆς ὁδοῦ σου

1a v. 12		καὶ σκέπη σου τῆς δυναστείας σκεπασάτω με **ἀπὸ** παντὸς κακοῦ

1a v. 13   καὶ συντελέσαι τὴν ἀνομίαν **ἀπὸ** προσώπου τῆς γῆς
1a v. 14   καθάρισον τὴν καρδίαν μου, δέσποτα, **ἀπὸ** πάσης ἀκαθαρσίας
1a v. 15a   καὶ μὴ ἀποστρέψῃς τὸ πρόσωπόν σου **ἀπὸ** τοῦ υἱοῦ παιδός σου Ἰακώβ
1a v. 19   καὶ μὴ ἀποστήσῃς τὸν υἱὸν τοῦ παιδός σου **ἀπὸ** (מִן) τοῦ προσώπου σου
11   καὶ ἀνήλθομεν **ἀπὸ** (מִן) Βηθὴλ καὶ κατελύσαμεν ἐν τῇ αὐλῇ Ἀβραὰμ
14   Τέκνον Λευί, πρόσεχε σεαυτῷ **ἀπὸ** (מִן) πάσης ἀκαθαρσίας
14   ἡ κρίσις σου μεγάλη **ἀπὸ** (מִן) πάσης σαρκός.
15   ἀναγγελῶ σοι, καὶ οὐ μὴ κρύψω **ἀπό** (מִמְּ) σου πᾶν ῥῆμα
16   πρόσεχε σεαυτῷ **ἀπὸ** (מִן) παντὸς συνουσιασμοῦ
16   πρόσεχε σεαυτῷ ἀπὸ παντὸς συνουσιασμοῦ καὶ **ἀπὸ** πάσης ἀκαθαρσίας
16   καὶ ἀπὸ πάσης ἀκαθαρσίας καὶ **ἀπὸ** (מִן) πάσης πορνείας.
17   σὺ †πρῶτος† **ἀπὸ** (מִן) τοῦ σπέρματος λάβε σεαυτῷ
18   ἐν τῷ σώματί σου **ἀπὸ** (מִן) πάσης ἀκαθαρσίας παντὸς ἀνθρώπου
22   ἐπισκοπῶν αὐτὰ πρῶτον **ἀπὸ** (מִן) παντὸς μολυσμοῦ
26   καὶ πάλιν νίψαι σου τὰς χεῖρας καὶ τοὺς πόδας **ἀπὸ** (מִן) τοῦ αἵματος
38   καὶ τῷ ταύρῳ τῷ δευτέρῳ τὰ πέντε μέρη **ἀπὸ** τῶν ἓξ μερῶν τοῦ σάτου
48   καὶ μὴ ἀποστήτωσαν οἱ λόγοι μου οὗτοι **ἀπὸ** τῆς καρδίας σου
52   ὅταν παραλαμβάνῃς θυσίαν ποιεῖν ἔναντι κυρίου **ἀπὸ** πάσης σαρκός
54   καὶ τὰς χεῖρας καὶ τοὺς πόδας νίπτου διὰ παντὸς **ἀπὸ** πάσης σαρκός
56   κάλυπτε τὸ αἷμα αὐτοῦ τῇ γῇ πρῶτον πρὶν ἢ φαγεῖν σε **ἀπὸ** τῶν κρεῶν
64   ἐκβεβλημένος ἔσται αὐτὸς καὶ τὸ σπέρμα αὐτοῦ **ἀπὸ** τῆς ἀρχῆς

ἀποδείκνυμι
37   καὶ ἅλας **ἀποδέδεικται** τῷ ταύρῳ τῷ μεγάλῳ, ἅλισε τὸ κρέας αὐτοῦ

ἀποστρέφω
1a v. 7   καὶ πορνείαν, καὶ ὕβριν **ἀπόστρεψον** ἀπ᾽ ἐμοῦ
1a v. 15a   καὶ μὴ **ἀποστρέψῃς** τὸ πρόσωπόν σου ἀπὸ τοῦ υἱοῦ παιδός σου Ἰακώβ

ἅπτομαι
53   πᾶν αἷμα μὴ ἁπτέσθω τῆς στολῆς σου· οὐκ **ἀνήψῃς** αὐτῷ αὐθήμερον

ἀρέσκω
1a v. 9   ποιῆσαι τὰ **ἀρέσκοντά** σοι καὶ εὑρεῖν χάριν ἐνώπιόν σου

ἀρήν, ὁ
35   καὶ εἰ **ἄρνα** ἐκ προβάτων ἢ ἔριφον ἐξ αἰγῶν κ΄ μναῖ

ἀρνίον, τό
40a   καὶ τὸ **ἀρνίῳ** καὶ τῷ ἐρίφῳ τὸ τρίτον τοῦ σάτου
42   καὶ τῷ **ἀρνίῳ** καὶ τῷ ἐρίφῳ ἐξ αἰγῶν τὸ τρίτον τοῦ σάτου
44   καὶ τῷ κριῷ τὸ ἕκτον τοῦ σάτου καὶ τῷ **ἀρνίῳ** τὸ ὄγδοον τοῦ σάτου

ἀρχή, ἡ
64   αὐτὸς καὶ τὸ σπέρμα αὐτοῦ ἀπὸ τῆς **ἀρχῆς** ἱερωσύνης ἔσται
67   αὐτὸς καὶ τὸ σπέρμα αὐτοῦ ἔσονται **ἀρχὴ** βασιλέων

ἀρχιερωσύνη, ἡ
67   καὶ ὅτι αὐτῷ ἔσται ἡ **ἀρξιερωσύνη** ἡ μεγάλη (כְּהֻנָּה רַבָּה אֹ)

ἄρψομαι
13   δεσπότῃ τοῦ οὐρανοῦ, **ἤρξατο** (שׁרי) διδάσκειν με τὴν κρίσιν ἱερωσύνης

25b   καὶ τὸ πῦρ τότε **ἄρξῃ** (שׂרי) ἐκκαίειν ἐν αὐτοῖς

25b   τότε **ἄρξῃ** (שׂרי) κατασπένδειν τὸ αἷμα ἐπὶ τὸν τεῖχον τοῦ θυσιαστηρίου

26   καὶ **ἄρξῃ** (שׂרי) τὰ μέλη ἀναφέρειν ἡλισμένα

ἀσφάλαθος, ὁ

24   καὶ κυπάρισσον καὶ δάφνην καὶ μυρσίνην καὶ **ἀσφάλαθον** (אשׂי דקהא?)

αὐθημερόν

53   πᾶν αἷμα μὴ ἁπτέσθω τῆς στολῆς σου· οὐκ ἀνήψῃς αὐτῷ **αὐθήμερον**

αὐλή, ἡ

11   καὶ ἀνήλθομεν ἀπὸ Βηθὴλ καὶ κατελύσαμεν ἐν τῇ **αὐλῇ** (בירה) Ἀβραὰμ

αὐτάρκης, ες

29   καὶ πάντα ἡλισμένα ἐν ἅλατι ὡς καθήκει αὐτοῖς **αὐτάρκως** (מסה)

αὐτός, ή, όν

1a v. 1   τότε ἐγὼ ἔπλυνα τὰ ἱμάτιά μου, καὶ καθαρίσας **αὐτὰ** ἐν ὕδατι καθαρῷ

1a v. 14   ἀπὸ πάσης ἀκαθαρσίας, καὶ προσαροῦμαι πρὸς σε **αὐτὸς**

1a v. 16   καὶ εἶπας δοῦναι **αὐτοῖς** σπέρμα δίκαιον εὐλογημένον

18   ἐγγὺς εἶ κυρίου καὶ σὺ ἐγγὺς τῶν ἁγίων **αὐτοῦ**

22   ἐπισκοπῶν **αὐτὰ** πρῶτον ἀπὸ παντὸς μολυσμοῦ

23   ὧν ἐστιν ὁ καπνὸς **αὐτῶν** ἡδὺς ἀναβαίνων

24   καὶ ταῦτα τὰ ὀνόματα **αὐτῶν**· κέδρον καὶ ουεδεφωνα

25b   καὶ τὸ πῦρ τότε ἄρξῃ ἐκκαίειν ἐν **αὐτοῖς**

27   τὴν κεφαλὴν ἀνάφερε πρῶτον καὶ κάλυπτε **αυτὴν** τῷ στέατι

27   καὶ μὴ ὀπτανέσθω τὸ αἷμα ἐπὶ τῆς κεφαλῆς **αὐτῆς**

29   καὶ πάντα ἡλισμένα ἐν ἅλατι ὡς καθήκει **αὐτοῖς** αὐτάρκως

32a   τῷ ταύρῳ τῷ τελείῳ τάλαντον ξύλων καθήκει **αὐτῷ** ἐν σταθμῷ

32b   πεντήκοντα μνᾶς, καὶ εἰς τὸ στέαρ **αὐτοῦ** μόνον πέντε μνᾶς

37   ἄλισε τὸ κρέας **αὐτοῦ**, καὶ ἀνένεγκε ἐπὶ τὸν βωμόν

37   καὶ ᾧ ἄν περισσεύσῃ τοῦ ἁλός, ἅλισον ἐν **αὐτῷ** τὸ δέρμα

40b   καὶ σεμίδαλις καθήκουσα **αὐτοῖς**· τῷ ταύρῳ τῷ μεγάλῳ

45   λιβανωτοῦ σίκλοι ἓξ τῷ ταύρῳ καὶ τὸ ἥμισυ **αὐτοῦ** τῷ κριῷ

45   καὶ τὸ τρίτον **αὐτοῦ** τῷ ἐρίφῳ. καὶ πᾶσα ἡ σεμίδαλις ἀναπεποιημένη

46a   προσαχθήσεται ἐπ᾽ **αὐτὴν** λιβάνου ὁλκὴ σίκλων δύο

52   καὶ τὸν λίβανον ἐπιδέχου ἐκ τῶν χειρῶν **αὐτῶν** ἐπὶ πάντα κτήνη

53   πᾶν αἷμα μὴ ἁπτέσθω τῆς στολῆς σου· οὐκ ἀνήψῃς **αὐτῷ** αὐθήμερον

56   κάλυπτε τὸ αἷμα **αὐτοῦ** τῇ γῇ πρῶτον πρὶν ἢ φαγεῖν σε ἀπὸ τῶν κρεῶν

63   ἔτεκεν υἱὸν πρῶτον, καὶ ἐκάλεσα τὸ ὄνομα **αὐτοῦ** Γηρσώμ

64   ἐκβεβλημένος ἔσται **αὐτὸς** καὶ τὸ σπέρμα αὐτοῦ ἀπὸ τῆς ἀρχῆς

64   ἐκβεβλημένος ἔσται αὐτὸς καὶ τὸ σπέρμα **αὐτοῦ** ἀπὸ τῆς ἀρχῆς

64   ἀπὸ τῆς ἀρχῆς ἱερωσύνης ἔσται τὸ σπέρμα **αὐτοῦ**

67   καὶ ὅτε ἐγεννήθη, ἑώρακα ὅτι ἐπ᾽ **αὐτῷ** ἔσται ἡ συναγωγὴ

67   παντὸς τοῦ λαοῦ καὶ ὅτι **αὐτῷ** ἔσται ἡ ἀρχιερωσύνη ἡ μεγάλη

67   **αὐτὸς** καὶ τὸ σπέρμα αὐτοῦ ἔσονται ἀρχὴ βασιλέων, ἱεράτευμα

67   αὐτὸς καὶ τὸ σπέρμα **αὐτοῦ** ἔσονται ἀρχὴ βασιλέων, ἱεράτευμα

69a   καὶ πάλιν συνεγενόμην **αὐτῇ** καὶ ἐν γαστρὶ ἔλαβεν

69a   καὶ ἔτεκέν μοι υἱὸν τρίτον, καὶ ἐκάλεσα τὸ ὄνομα **αὐτοῦ** Μεραρί

69a   καὶ ἐκάλεσα τὸ ὄνομα αὐτοῦ Μεραρί· ἐλυπήθην γὰρ περὶ **αὐτοῦ**

ἀφίστημι

48   καὶ μὴ **ἀποστήτωσαν** οἱ λόγοι μου οὗτοι ἀπὸ τῆς καρδίας σου

β΄

23   ιβ΄ ξύλα εἴρηκέν μοι ἐπὶ τὸν βωμὸν προσφέρε<ιν>

35   ἔριφον ἐξ αἰγῶν κ΄ μναῖ, καὶ τῷ στέατι **β΄** μναι

41   καὶ τῷ ταύρῳ τῷ **β΄** καὶ τῷ μοσχαρίῳ, σάτον σεμίδαλιν

βασιλεύς, ὁ

67   αὐτὸς καὶ τὸ σπέρμα αὐτοῦ ἔσονται ἀρχὴ **βασιλέων**, ἱεράτευμα

βάτος, ὁ

47   καὶ τὰ δύο μέρη τοῦ **βάτου** καὶ ὁλκῆς τῆς μνᾶς ν΄ σίκλων ἐστίν

βεβηλόω

17   καὶ μὴ **βεβηλώσῃς** (הלל) τὸ σπέρμα σου μετὰ †πολλῶν†

βερωθα

24   καὶ ολδινα καὶ **βερωθα** (ברותא) †καν† θεχακ καὶ κυπάρισσον

βιβλίον, τό

59   ἕως πάντων τῶν αἰώνων ἐνεχθήσεται ἐν **Βιβλίῳ** μνημοσύνου ζωῆς

βίβλος, ἡ

57   ὅτι οὕτως εὗρεν ἐν τῇ γραφῇ τῆς **βίβλου** τοῦ Νῶε περὶ τοῦ αἵματος

βουλή, ἡ

1a v. 8   καὶ **βουλὴν** καὶ σοφίαν καὶ γνῶσιν καὶ ἰσχὺν δός μοι

βωμός, ὁ

20   πρὸ τοῦ ἐγγίσαι τρὸς τὸν **βωμὸν** (מדבחה) προσενέγκαι ὁλοκάρπωσιν

21   καὶ ὅταν μέλλῃς προσφέρειν ὅσα δεῖ ἀνενέγκαι ἐπὶ τὸν **βωμὸν** (מדבחה)

23   ιβ΄ ξύλα εἴρηκέν μοι ἐπὶ τὸν **βωμὸν** (מדבחה) προσφέρε<ιν>

31   οὕτως ξύλακαθήκει ἀναφέρεσθαι ἐπὶ τὸν **βωμὸν** (מדבחא)

37   ἄλισε τὸ κρέας αὐτοῦ, καὶ ἀνένεγκε ἐπὶ τὸν **βωμόν**

γάρ

17   ἐκ σπέρματος **γὰρ** (אר) ἁγίου εἶ, καὶ τὸ σπέρμα σου ἁγίασον

50   οὕτως **γάρ** μοι ἐνετείλατο ὁ πατὴρ Ἀβραὰμ ποιεῖν

55   καὶ πᾶσα ψυχή· τὸ **γὰρ** αἷμα ψυχή ἐστιν ἐν τῇ σαρκί

57   οὕτως **γάρ** μοι ἐνετείλατο ὁ πατήρ μου Ἀβραάμ, ὅτι οὕτως εὗρεν

63   Γηρσώμ· εἶπα **γὰρ** ὅτι πάροικον ἔσται τὸ σπέρμα μου ἐν γῇ

69a   καὶ ἐκάλεσα τὸ ὄνομα αὐτοῦ Μεραρί· ἐλυπήθην **γὰρ** (אר) περὶ αὐτοῦ

γαστήρ, ἡ

63   καὶ ἐν **γαστρὶ** λαβοῦσα ἐξ ἐμοῦ ἔτεκεν υἱὸν πρῶτον

69a   καὶ πάλιν συνεγενόμην αὐτῇ καὶ ἐν **γαστρὶ** ἔλαβεν

γενεά, ἡ

1a v. 18   ἐμὲ καὶ τοὺς υἱούς μου εἰς πάσας τὰς **γενεὰς** τῶν αἰώνων

61   τὸ σπέρμα σου ἐπὶ τῆς γῆς εἰς πάσας τὰς **γενεὰς** τῶν αἰώνων

γεννάω

63   εἶπα γὰρ ὅτι πάροικον ἔσται τὸ σπέρμα μου ἐν γῇ, ᾗ **ἐγεννήθην**

65 λ' ἐτῶν ἤμην ὅτε **ἐγεννήθη** ἐν τῇ ζωῇ μου

65 καὶ ἐν τῷ ι' μηνὶ **ἐγεννήθη** ἐπὶ δυσμὰς ἡλίου

67 καὶ ὅτε **ἐγεννήθη**, ἑώρακα ὅτι ἐπ' αὐτῷ ἔσται ἡ συναγωγὴ

68 ἐν τῷ τετάρτῳ καὶ λ' ἔτει **ἐγεννήθη** (ילד') ἐν τῷ πρώτῳ μηνὶ

γῆ, ἡ

1a v. 13 καὶ συντελέσαι τὴν ἀνομίαν ἀπὸ προσώπου τῆς **γῆς**

56 κάλυπτε τὸ αἷμα αὐτοῦ τῇ **γῇ** πρῶτον πρὶν ἢ φαγεῖν σε ἀπὸ τῶν κρεῶν

59 τῷ σπέρματί σου εὐλογηθήσεται ἐν τῇ **γῇ**

61 εὐλογημένον ἔσται τὸ σπέρμα σου ἐπὶ τῆς **γῆς** εἰς πάσας τὰς γενεὰς

63 εἶπα γὰρ ὅτι πάροικον ἔσται τὸ σπέρμα μου ἐν **γῇ**, ἧ ἐγεννήθην

63 πάροικοί ἐσμεν ὡς τοῦτο ἐν τῇ **γῇ** ἡμετέρα νομιζομένη

γίνομαι

1a v. 12 τεῖχος εἰρήνης σου **γενέσθαι** κύκλῳ μου, καὶ σκέπη σου τῆς δυναστείας

1a v. 17 εἰσάκουσον δὲ καὶ τῆς φωνῆς τοῦ παιδός σου Λευὶ **γενέσθαι** σοι ἐγγύς

18 **γίνου** (היה) καθαρὸς ἐν τῷ σώματί σου ἀπὸ πάσης ἀκαθαρσίας

47 ὁλκὴ θερμῶν δ' ἐστίν· **γίνεται** ὁ σίκλος ὡσεὶ ις' θέρμοι καὶ ὁλκῆς μιᾶς

γινώσκω

1a v. 5 Κύριε, **γινώσκεις** πάσας τὰς καρδίας, καὶ πάντας τοὺς διαλογισμοὺς

13 καὶ ὅτε **ἔγνω** (ידע) ὅτι ἐγὼ ἱεράτευσα τῷ κυρίῳ δεσπότῃ τοῦ οὐρανοῦ

γνῶσις, ἡ

1a v. 8 καὶ βουλὴν καὶ σοφίαν καὶ **γνῶσιν** (מדע) καὶ ἰσχὺν δός μοι

γραφή, ἡ

57 ὅτι οὕτως εὗρεν ἐν τῇ **γραφῇ** τῆς βίβλου τοῦ Νῶε περὶ τοῦ αἵματος

γυνή, ἡ

62 ἔλαβον **γυναῖκα** ἐμαυτῷ ἐκ τῆς συγγενείας Ἀβραὰμ τοῦ πατρός μου

66 ἔτεκεν ἐχ ἐμοῦ κατὰ τὸν καιρὸν τὸν καθήκοντα τῶν **γυναικῶν**

δ'

47 ν' σίκλων ἐστίν· καὶ τοῦ σικλίου τὸ τέταρτον ὁλκὴ θερμῶν δ' ἐστίν

δάκτυλος, ὁ

1a v. 4 τοὺς **δακτύλους** (אצבע) τῶν χειρῶν μου καὶ τὰς χεῖράς μου ἀνεπέτασα

δάφνη, ἡ

24 θεχακ καὶ κυπάρισσον καὶ **δάφνην** (ערא) καὶ μυρσίνην καὶ ἀσφάλαθον

δεῖ

21 καὶ ὅταν μέλλῃς προσφέρειν ὅσα **δεῖ** ἀνενέγκαι ἐπὶ τὸν βωμόν

δείκνυμι

1a v. 8 **δειχθήτω** μοι, δέσποτα, τὸ πνεῦμα τὸ ἅγιον, καὶ βουλὴν καὶ σοφίαν

δέομαι

1a v. 19 πάσας τὰς ἡμέρας τοῦ αἰῶνος. καὶ ἐσιώπησα ἔτι **δεόμενος**

δέρμα, τό

37 καὶ ᾧ ἄν περισσεύσῃ τοῦ ἁλός, ἅλισον ἐν αὐτῷ τὸ **δέρμα**

δεύτερος, α, ον

32a ἀναφέρεσθαι ἒξ μνᾶς· καὶ τῷ ταύρῳ τῷ **δευτέρῳ** πεντήκοντα μνᾶς

38   καὶ τῷ ταύρῳ τῷ **δευτέρῳ** τὰ πέντε μέρη ἀπὸ τῶν ἓξ μερῶν τοῦ σάτου

δή

1a v. 13   παράδος διὸ **δὴ** καὶ τὴν ἀνομίαν ἐξάλειψον ὑποκάτωθεν τοῦ οὐρανοῦ

διά

54   καὶ τὰς χεῖρας καὶ τοὺς πόδας νίπτου **διὰ** παντὸς ἀπὸ πάσης σαρκός

διαλογισμός, ὁ

1a v. 5   καὶ πάντας τοὺς **διαλογισμοὺς** ἐννοιῶν σὺ μόνος ἐπίστασαι

1a v. 7   κύριε, τὸ πνεῦμα τὸ ἄδικον καὶ **διαλογισμὸν** τὸν πονηρὸν

διδάσκω

13   ἤρχατο **διδάσκειν** (אלף) με τὴν κρίσιν ἱερωσύνης καὶ εἶπεν

15   ἀναγγελῶ σοι, καὶ οὐ μὴ κρύψω ἀπό σου πᾶν ῥῆμα. **διδάξω** (אלף) σε

δίδωμι

1a v. 6   καὶ νῦν τέκνα μου μετ᾽ ἐμοῦ. καὶ **δός** μοι πάσας ὁδοὺς ἀληθείας

1a v. 8   καὶ βουλὴν καὶ σοφίαν καὶ γνῶσιν καὶ ἰσχὺν **δός** μοι

1a v. 16   καὶ εἶπας **δοῦναι** αὐτοῖς σπέρμα δίκαιον εὐλογημένον εἰς τοὺς αἰῶνας

δίκαιος, α, ον

1a v. 16   καὶ εἶπας δοῦναι αὐτοῖς σπέρμα **δίκαιον** (קשׁט) εὐλογημένον

δίμοιρος, ον

38   ἀπὸ τῶν ἓξ μερῶν τοῦ σάτου· καὶ τοῦ μόσχου τὸ **δίμοιρον** τοῦ σάτου

διό

1a v. 13   παράδος **διὸ** δὴ καὶ τὴν ἀνομίαν ἐξάλειψον ὑποκάτωθεν τοῦ οὐρανοῦ

δοῦλος, ὁ

1a v. 11   καὶ προσάγαγέ με εἶναί σου **δοῦλος** καὶ λατρεῦσαί σοι καλῶς

δυναστεία, ἡ

1a v. 12   καὶ σκέπη σου τῆς **δυναστείας** σκεπασάτω με ἀπὸ παντὸς κακοῦ

δύο

42   καὶ τῷ κριῷ καὶ τῷ τράγῳ τὰ **δύο** μέρη τοῦ σάτου

46a   προσαχθήσεται ἐπ᾽ αὐτὴν λιβάνου ὁλκὴ σίκλων **δύο**

47   καὶ τὰ **δύο** μέρη τοῦ βάτου καὶ ὁλκῆς τῆς μνᾶς ν΄ σίκλων ἐστίν

δυσμή, ἡ

65   ἐν τῇ ζωῇ μου, καὶ ἐν τῷ ι΄ μηνὶ ἐγεννήθη ἐπὶ **δυσμὰς** ἡλίου

ε΄

36   ἢ ἔριφος ἐξ αἰγῶν ιε΄ μναῖ, καὶ τῷ στέατι μίαν ἥμισυ μνᾶν

ἐάν

56   καὶ ὃ **ἐὰν** ἐν οἴκῳ †ουσης† σεαυτὸν πᾶν κρέας φαγεῖν

ἑβδομάς, ἡ

62   ἀνεπληρώθησάν μοι **ἑβδομάδες** τέσσαρες ἐν τοῖς ἔτεσιν τῆς ζωῆς μου

ἐγγίζω

20   πρὸ τοῦ **ἐγγίσαι** (קרב) τρὸς τὸν βωμὸν προσενέγκαι ὁλοκάρπωσιν

ἐγγύς

1a v. 17   εἰσάκουσον δὲ καὶ τῆς φωνῆς τοῦ παιδός σου Λευὶ γενέσθαι σοι
          ἐγγύς

18   **ἐγγὺς** (קריב) εἶ κυρίου καὶ σὺ ἐγγὺς τῶν ἁγίων αὐτοῦ. γίνου καθαρὸς

18   ἐγγὺς εἶ κυρίου καὶ σὺ **ἐγγὺς** (ק֖רו֖ב) τῶν ἁγίων αὐτοῦ. γίνου καθαρὸς

ἐγώ

1a v. 1   τότε **ἐγὼ** (אֲנִי) ἔπλυνα τὰ ἱμάτιά μου, καὶ καθαρίσας αὐτὰ
13   καὶ ὅτε ἔγνω ὅτι **ἐγὼ** (אֲנִי) ἱεράτευσα τῷ κυρίῳ δεσπότῃ τοῦ οὐρανοῦ
64   ἐπὶ τοῦ παιδαρίου εἶδον **ἐγὼ** ἐν τῷ ὁράματί μου ὅτι ἐκβεβλημένος
            ἔσται

ἐμοῦ

1a v. 6   καὶ νῦν τέκνα μου μετ᾽ **ἐμοῦ**. καὶ δός μοι πάσας ὁδοὺς ἀληθείας·
1a v. 7   μάκρυνον ἀπ᾽ **ἐμοῦ**, κύριε, τὸ πνεῦμα τὸ ἄδικον
1a v. 7   καὶ πορνείαν, καὶ ὕβριν ἀπόστρεψον ἀπ᾽ **ἐμοῦ**.
1a v. 9   ἐνώπιόν σου καὶ αἰνεῖν τοὺς λόγους σου μετ᾽ **ἐμοῦ**, κύριε
63   καὶ ἐν γαστρὶ λαβοῦσα ἐξ **ἐμοῦ** ἔτεκεν υἱὸν πρῶτον
66   καὶ πάλιν συλλαβοῦσα ἔτεκεν ἐξ **ἐμοῦ** κατὰ τὸν καιρὸν τὸν καθήκοντα

μου

1a v. 1   τότε **ἐγὼ** (אֲנִי) ἔπλυνα τὰ ἱμάτιά **μου**, καὶ καθαρίσας αὐτὰ
1a v. 2   ἐν ὕδατι ζῶντι· καὶ πάσας τὰς ὁδούς **μου** ἐποίησα εὐθείας
1a v. 3   τότε τοὺς ὀφθαλμούς **μου** καὶ τὸ πρόσωπόν μου ἦρα πρὸς τὸν οὐρανόν
1a v. 3   τότε τοὺς ὀφθαλμούς μου καὶ τὸ πρόσωπόν **μου** ἦρα πρὸς τὸν οὐρανόν
1a v. 3   ἦρα πρὸς τὸν οὐρανόν, καὶ τὸ στόμα **μου** ἤνοιξα καὶ ἐλάλησα
1a v. 4   καὶ τοὺς δακτύλους τῶν χειρῶν **μου** καὶ τὰς χεῖράς μου ἀνεπέτασα
1a v. 4   καὶ τοὺς δακτύλους τῶν χειρῶν μου καὶ τὰς χεῖράς **μου** ἀνεπέτασα
1a v. 12   τεῖχος εἰρήνης σου γενέσθαι κύκλῳ **μου**, καὶ σκέπη σου τῆς δυναστείας
1a v. 14   καθάρισον τὴν καρδίαν **μου**, δέσποτα, ἀπὸ πάσης ἀκαθαρσίας
1a v. 15b   σύ, κύριε, εὐλόγησας τὸν Ἀβραὰμ πατέρα **μου** καὶ Σάρραν μητέρα
            μου
1a v. 18   σύ, κύριε, εὐλόγησας τὸν Ἀβραὰμ πατέρα μου καὶ Σάρραν μητέρα
            μου
1a v. 18   εἰς πάντα τὸν αἰῶνα, ἐμὲ καὶ τοὺς υἱούς **μου** εἰς πάσας τὰς γενεὰς
48   τέκνον **μου**, ἄκουσον τοὺς λόγους μου καὶ ἐνωτίσαι τὰς ἐντολάς μου
48   τέκνον μου, ἄκουσον τοὺς λόγους **μου** καὶ ἐνωτίσαι τὰς ἐντολάς μου
48   τέκνον μου, ἄκουσον τοὺς λόγους μου καὶ ἐνωτίσαι τὰς ἐντολάς **μου**
48   καὶ μὴ ἀποστήτωσαν οἱ λόγοι **μου** οὗτοι ἀπὸ τῆς καρδίας σου
50   ἐνετείλατο ὁ πατὴρ Ἀβραὰμ ποιεῖν καὶ ἐντέλλεσθαι τοῖς υἱοῖς **μου**
57   οὕτως γάρ μοι ἐνετείλατο ὁ πατὴρ **μου** Ἀβραάμ, ὅτι οὕτως εὗρεν
62   ἀνεπληρώθησάν μοι ἑβδομάδες τέσσαρες ἐν τοῖς ἔτεσιν τῆς ζωῆς **μου**
62   ἔλαβον γυναῖκα ἐμαυτῷ ἐκ τῆς συγγενείας Ἀβραὰμ τοῦ πατρός **μου**
63   εἶπα γὰρ ὅτι πάροικον ἔσται τὸ σπέρμα **μου** ἐν γῇ, ᾗ ἐγεννήθην
64   ἐπὶ τοῦ παιδαρίου εἶδον ἐγὼ ἐν τῷ ὁράματί **μου** ὅτι ἐκβεβλημένος
            ἔσται

ἐγώ / μοι

1a v. 8   δειχθήτω **μοι**, δέσποτα, τὸ πνεῦμα τὸ ἅγιον, καὶ βουλὴν καὶ σοφίαν
1a v. 8   καὶ βουλὴν καὶ σοφίαν καὶ γνῶσιν καὶ ἰσχὺν δός **μοι**
23   ιβ΄ ξύλα εἴρηκεν **μοι** ἐπὶ τὸν βωμὸν προσφέρε<ιν>

50 οὕτως γάρ **μοι** ἐνετείλατο ὁ πατὴρ Ἀβραὰμ ποιεῖν
57 οὕτως γάρ **μοι** ἐνετείλατο ὁ πατήρ μου Ἀβραάμ, ὅτι οὕτως εὗρεν
62 ἀνεπληρώθησάν **μοι** ἑβδομάδες τέσσαρες ἐν τοῖς ἔτεσιν τῆς ζωῆς μου
69a καὶ ἔτεκέν **μοι** υἱὸν τρίτον, καὶ ἐκάλεσα τὸ ὄνομα αὐτοῦ Μεραρί

ἐμέ

1a v. 18 **ἐμὲ** καὶ τοὺς υἱούς μου εἰς πάσας τὰς γενεὰς τῶν αἰώνων

με

1a v. 10 καὶ μὴ κατισχυσάτω **με** πᾶς σατανᾶς πλανῆσαί με ἀπὸ τῆς ὁδοῦ σου
1a v. 10 καὶ μὴ κατισχυσάτω με πᾶς σατανᾶς πλανῆσαί **με** ἀπὸ τῆς ὁδοῦ σου
1a v. 11 καὶ ἐλέησόν **με** καὶ προσάγαγέ με εἶναί σου δοῦλος καὶ λατρεῦσαί
1a v. 11 καὶ ἐλέησόν με καὶ προσάγαγέ **με** εἶναί σου δοῦλος καὶ λατρεῦσαί
1a v. 12 καὶ σκέπη σου τῆς δυναστείας σκεπασάτω **με** ἀπὸ παντὸς κακοῦ
13 ἤρξατο διδάσκειν **με** (רֹז) τὴν κρίσιν ἱερωσύνης καὶ εἶπεν

εἰκοστός, ή, όν

62 ἐν ἔτει ὀγδόῳ καὶ **εἰκοστῷ** ἔλαβον γυναῖκα ἐμαυτῷ

εἰ

34 καὶ **εἰ** κριὸς ἐκ προβάτων ἢ τράγος ἐξ αἰγῶν τὸ προσφερόμενον ἦ
35 καὶ **εἰ** ἄρνα ἐκ προβάτων ἢ ἔριφον ἐξ αἰγῶν κ΄ μναῖ
36 καὶ **εἰ** ἀμνὸς τέλειος ἐνιαύσιος ἢ ἔριφος ἐξ αἰγῶν ιε΄ μναῖ

εἰμί

1a v. 11 καὶ προσάγαγέ με **εἶναί** (היה) σου δοῦλος καὶ λατρεῦσαί σοι καλῶς.
17 ἐκ σπέρματος γὰρ ἁγίου **εἶ**, καὶ τὸ σπέρμα σου ἁγίασον
17 καὶ τὸ σπέρμα σου ἁγίασον καὶ τὸ σπέρμα τοῦ ἁγιασμοῦ σου **ἐστίν**
23 ἐπὶ τὸν βωμὸν προσφέρε<ιν>, ὧν **ἐστιν** ὁ καπνὸς αὐτῶν ἡδὺς ἀναβαίνων>
25a ταῦτα εἴρηκεν ὅτι ταῦτά **ἐστιν** ἅ σε ἀναφέρειν
30 καὶ **ᾖ** τὸ ἔργον σου ἐν τάξει καὶ πᾶσα προσφορά σου εἰς εὐδόκησιν
34 καὶ εἰ κριὸς ἐκ προβάτων ἢ τράγος ἐξ αἰγῶν τὸ προσφερόμενον **ᾖ**
46b καὶ τὸ τρίτον τοῦ σάτου τὸ τρίτον τοῦ ὑφῆ **ἐστιν**
47 καὶ τὰ δύο μέρη τοῦ βάτου καὶ ὁλκῆς τῆς μνᾶς ν΄ σίκλων **ἐστίν**
47 καὶ τοῦ σικλίου τὸ τέταρτον ὁλκὴ θερμῶν δ΄ **ἐστίν**
49 ἱερεῖς **ἔσονται** πᾶν τὸ σπέρμα σου· καὶ τοῖς υἱοῖς σου οὕτως ἔντειλον
55 καὶ πᾶσα ψυχή· τὸ γὰρ αἷμα ψυχή **ἐστιν** ἐν τῇ σαρκί
56 ἀπὸ τῶν κρεῶν καὶ οὐκέτι **ἔσῃ** ἐσθίων ἐπὶ τοῦ αἵματος
58 καὶ ἠγαπημένος **ἔσῃ** ὑπὲρ πάντας τοὺς ἀδελφούς σου
63 εἶπα γὰρ ὅτι πάροικον **ἔσται** τὸ σπέρμα μου ἐν γῇ, ᾗ ἐγεννήθην
63 πάροικοί **ἐσμεν** ὡς τοῦτο ἐν τῇ γῇ ἡμετέρᾳ νομιζομένη
64 εἶδον ἐγὼ ἐν τῷ ὁράματί μου ὅτι ἐκβεβλημένος **ἔσται** αὐτός
64 καὶ τὸ σπέρμα αὐτοῦ ἀπὸ τῆς ἀρχῆς ἱερωσύνης **ἔσται** τὸ σπέρμα αὐτοῦ
67 ἑώρακα ὅτι ἐπ᾽ αὐτῷ **ἔσται** ἡ συναγωγὴ παντὸς τοῦ λαοῦ
67 καὶ ὅτι αὐτῷ **ἔσται** ἡ ἀρχιερωσύνη ἡ μεγάλη
67 αὐτὸς καὶ τὸ σπέρμα αὐτοῦ **ἔσονται** ἀρχὴ βασιλέων

εἰρήνη, ἡ

1a v. 12 τεῖχος **εἰρήνης** σου γενέσθαι κύκλῳ μου, καὶ σκέπη σου τῆς δυναστείας εἰς

1a v. 4	καὶ τὰς χεῖράς μου ἀνεπέτασα **εἰς** ἀλήθειαν κατέναντι τῶν ἁγίων
1a v. 16	καὶ εἶπας δοῦναι αὐτοῖς σπέρμα δίκαιον εὐλογημένον **εἰς** τοὺς αἰῶνας
1a v. 18	τοῖς λόγοις σου ποιεῖν κρίσιν ἀληθινὴν **εἰς** πάντα τὸν αἰῶνα
1a v. 18	ἐμὲ καὶ τοὺς υἱούς μου **εἰς** πάσας τὰς γενεὰς τῶν αἰώνων
30	καὶ ᾖ τὸ ἔργον σου ἐν τάξει καὶ πᾶσα προσφορά σου **εἰς** εὐδόκησιν
32a	καθήκει αὐτῷ ἐν σταθμῷ, καὶ **εἰς** τὸ στέαρ μόνον ἀναφέρεσθαι ἒξ μνᾶς
32b	πεντήκοντα μνᾶς, καὶ **εἰς** τὸ στέαρ αὐτοῦ μόνον πέντε μνᾶς
33	καὶ **εἰς** μόσχον τέλειον μ΄ μναῖ
51	καὶ νῦν, τέκνον, χαίρω ὅτι ἐχελέχθης **εἰς** ἱερωσύνην ἁγίαν
61	εὐλογημένον ἔσται τὸ σπέρμα σου ἐπὶ τῆς γῆς **εἰς** πάσας τὰς γενεὰς

εἷς, μία, ἕν

36	ἢ ἔριφος ἐξ αἰγῶν ιε΄ μναῖ, καὶ τῷ στέατι **μίαν** ἥμισυ μνᾶν
47	γίνεται ὁ σίκλος ὡσεὶ ις΄ θέρμοι καὶ ὀλκῆς **μιᾶς**
68	ἐγεννήθη ἐν τῷ πρώτῳ μηνὶ **μιᾷ** (חה) τοῦ μηνὸς ἐπὼ ἀνατολῆς ἡλίου

εἰσακούω

1a v. 17	**εἰσάκουσον** δὲ καὶ τῆς φωνῆς τοῦ παιδός σου Λευὶ γενέσθαι σοι ἐγγύς

εἰσπορεύομαι

19	καὶ ὅταν **εἰσπορεύῃ** (עלל) ἐν τοῖς ἁγίοις, λούου ὕδατι πρῶτον

ἐκ

17	**ἐκ** σπέρματος γὰρ ἁγίου εἶ, καὶ τὸ σπέρμα σου ἁγίασον
34	καὶ εἰ κριὸς **ἐκ** προβάτων ἢ τράγος ἐξ αἰγῶν τὸ προσφερόμενον ᾖ
34	καὶ εἰ κριὸς ἐκ προβάτων ἢ τράγος **ἐξ** αἰγῶν τὸ προσφερόμενον ᾖ,
35	καὶ εἰ ἄρνα **ἐκ** προβάτων ἢ ἔριφον ἐξ αἰγῶν κ΄ μναῖ
35	καὶ εἰ ἄρνα ἐκ προβάτων ἢ ἔριφον **ἐξ** αἰγῶν κ΄ μναῖ
36	καὶ εἰ ἀμνὸς τέλειος ἐνιαύσιος ἢ ἔριφος **ἐξ** αἰγῶν ιε΄ μναῖ
42	καὶ τῷ ἀρνίῳ καὶ τῷ ἐρίφῳ **ἐξ** αἰγῶν τὸ τρίτον τοῦ σάτου
52	καὶ τὸν λίβανον ἐπιδέχου **ἐκ** τῶν χειρῶν αὐτῶν ἐπὶ πάντα κτήνη
53	καὶ ὅταν ἐκπορεύῃς **ἐκ** τῶν ἁγίων, πᾶν αἷμα μὴ ἁπτέσθω τῆς στολῆς σου
62	ἔλαβον γυναῖκα ἐμαυτῷ **ἐκ** τῆς συγγενείας Ἀβραὰμ τοῦ πατρός μου
63	καὶ ἐν γαστρὶ λαβοῦσα **ἐξ** ἐμοῦ ἔτεκεν υἱὸν πρῶτον
66	καὶ πάλιν συλλαβοῦσα ἔτεκεν **ἐξ** ἐμοῦ κατὰ τὸν καιρὸν τὸν καθήκοντα

ἐκβάλλω

64	**ἐκβεβλημένος** ἔσται αὐτὸς καὶ τὸ σπέρμα αὐτοῦ ἀπὸ τῆς ἀρχῆς

ἐκκαίω

25b	καὶ τὸ πῦρ τότε ἄρξῃ **ἐκκαίειν** (דלק) ἐν αὐτοῖς, τότε ἄρξῃ κατασπένδειν

ἐκλέγω

51	καὶ νῦν, τέκνον, χαίρω ὅτι **ἐξελέχθης** εἰς ἱερωσύνην ἁγίαν

ἐκπορεύω

53	καὶ ὅταν **ἐκπορεύῃς** ἐκ τῶν ἁγίων, πᾶν αἷμα μὴ ἁπτέσθω τῆς στολῆς σου

ἕκτος, η, ον

44   καὶ τῷ κριῷ τὸ **ἕκτον** τοῦ σάτου καὶ τῷ ἀρνίῳ τὸ ὄγδοον τοῦ σάτου

ἔλαιον, τό

30   καὶ μετὰ ταῦτα σεμίδαλιν ἀναπεποιημένον ἐν **ἐλαίῳ** (משׁא)

42   καὶ τῷ ἐρίφῳ ἐξ αἰγῶν τὸ τρίτον τοῦ σάτου. καὶ τὸ **ἔλαιον·**

44   καὶ ἀμνοῦ καὶ **οἶνον** κατὰ τὸ μέτρον τοῦ ἐλαίου τῷ ταύρῳ

ἐλεέω

1a v. 11   καὶ **ἐλέησόν** με καὶ προσάγαγέ με εἶναί σου δοῦλος

ἐμαυτοῦ, ῆς

62   ἔλαβον γυναῖκα **ἐμαυτῷ** ἐκ τῆς συγγενείας Ἀβραὰμ τοῦ πατρός μου

ἐν

1a v. 1   τὰ ἱμάτιά μου, καὶ καθαρίσας αὐτὰ **ἐν** ὕδατι καθαρῷ

1a v. 2   καὶ ὅλος ἐλουσάμην **ἐν** ὕδατι ζῶντι

11   καὶ ἀνήλθομεν ἀπὸ Βηθὴλ καὶ κατελύσαμεν **ἐν** (ב) τῇ αὐλῇ Ἀβραὰμ

18   γίνου καθαρὸς **ἐν** (ב) τῷ σώματί σου ἀπὸ πάσης ἀκαθαρσίας

19   καὶ ὅταν εἰσπορεύῃ **ἐν** (ל) τοῖς ἁγίοις, λούου ὕδατι πρῶτον

25b   καὶ τὸ πῦρ τότε ἄρξῃ ἐκκαίειν **ἐν** (ב) αὐτοῖς, τότε ἄρξῃ κατασπένδειν

29   καὶ πάντα ἡλισμένα **ἐν** (ב) ἅλατι ὡς καθήκει αὐτοῖς αὐτάρκως

30   καὶ μετὰ ταῦτα σεμίδαλιν ἀναπεποιημένον **ἐν** (ב) ἐλαίῳ

30   καὶ ᾗ τὸ ἔργον σου **ἐν** (ב) τάξει καὶ πᾶσα προσφορά σου εἰς εὐδόκησιν

31   καὶ ὅσα ἂν ποιῇς, **ἐν** (ב) τάξει ποίει ἃ ποιῇς ἐν μέτρῳ καὶ σταθμῷ

31   καὶ ὅσα ἂν ποιῇς, ἐν τάξει ποίει ἃ ποιῇς **ἐν** μέτρῳ καὶ σταθμῷ

32a   τῷ ταύρῳ τῷ τελείῳ τάλαντον ξύλων καθήκει αὐτῷ **ἐν** σταθμῷ

37   καὶ ᾧ ἂν περισσεύσῃ τοῦ ἁλός, ἅλισον **ἐν** αὐτῷ τὸ δέρμα

43   τῷ ταύρῳ ἀναπεποιημένον **ἐν** τῇ σεμιδάλει ταύτῃ

48   οἱ λόγοι μου οὗτοι ἀπὸ τῆς καρδίας σου **ἐν** πάσαις ταῖς ἡμέραις

55   καὶ πᾶσα ψυχή· τὸ γὰρ αἷμα ψυχή ἐστιν **ἐν** τῇ σαρκί

56   καὶ ὃ ἐάν **ἐν** οἴκῳ †ουσης† σεαυτὸν πᾶν κρέας φαγεῖν

57   ὅτι οὕτως εὗρεν **ἐν** τῇ γραφῇ τῆς βίβλου τοῦ Νῶε περὶ τοῦ αἵματος

59   τῷ σπέρματί σου εὐλογηθήσεται **ἐν** τῇ γῇ

59   ἕως πάντων τῶν αἰώνων ἐνεχθήσεται **ἐν** Βιβλίῳ μνημοσύνου ζωῆς

62   ἀνεπληρώθησάν μοι ἑβδομάδες τέσσαρες **ἐν** τοῖς ἔτεσιν τῆς ζωῆς μου

62   **ἐν** ἔτει ὀγδόῳ καὶ εἰκοστῷ ἔλαβον γυναῖκα ἐμαυτῷ

63   καὶ **ἐν** γαστρὶ λαβοῦσα ἐξ ἐμοῦ ἔτεκεν υἱὸν πρῶτον

63   εἶπα γὰρ ὅτι πάροικον ἔσται τὸ σπέρμα μου **ἐν** γῇ, ᾗ ἐγεννήθην

63   πάροικοί ἐσμεν ὡς τοῦτο **ἐν** τῇ γῇ ἡμετέρα νομιζομένη

64   καὶ ἐπὶ τοῦ παιδαρίου εἶδον ἐγὼ **ἐν** τῷ ὁράματί μου

65   λ΄ ἐτῶν ἤμην ὅτε ἐγεννήθη **ἐν** τῇ ζωῇ μου

65   καὶ **ἐν** τῷ ι΄ μηνὶ ἐγεννήθη ἐπὶ δυσμὰς ἡλίου

68   **ἐν** (ב) τῷ τετάρτῳ καὶ λ΄ ἔτει ἐγεννήθη ἐν τῷ πρώτῳ μηνὶ μιᾷ τοῦ μηνὸς

68   ἐν τῷ τετάρτῳ καὶ λ΄ ἔτει ἐγεννήθη **ἐν** (ב) τῷ πρώτῳ μηνὶ μιᾷ τοῦ μηνὸς

69a   καὶ πάλιν συνεγενόμην αὐτῇ καὶ **ἐν** γαστρὶ ἔλαβεν

ἔναντι

30 εἰς εὐδόκησιν καὶ ὀσμὴν εὐωδίας **ἔναντι** (קדם) κυρίου ὑψίστου

52 ὅταν παραλαμβάνῃς θυσίαν ποιεῖν **ἔναντι** κυρίου ἀπὸ πάσης σαρκός

ἐνδιδύσκομαι

19 καὶ τότε **ἐνδιδύσκου** (לבש) τὴν στολὴν τῆς ἱερωσύνης

20 ὅταν **ἐνδιδύσκῃ** (לבש), νίπτου πάλιν τὰς χεῖράς σου καὶ τοὺς πόδας σου

ἐνδόσθια, τά

28 καὶ μετὰ ταῦτα τοὺς πόδας πεπλυμένους σὺν τοῖς **ἐνδοσθίοις** (קרבא)

ἐνιαύσιος, α, ον

36 καὶ εἰ ἀμνὸς τέλειος **ἐνιαύσιος** ἢ ἔριφος ἐξ αἰγῶν ιε′ μναῖ

ἔννοια, ἡ

1a v. 5 καὶ πάντας τοὺς διαλογισμοὺς **ἐννοιῶν** σὺ μόνος ἐπίστασαι

ἐντέλλομαι

49 τοῖς υἱοῖς σου οὕτως **ἔντειλον** ἵνα ποιήσουσιν κατὰ τὴν κρίσιν ταύτην

50 οὕτως γάρ μοι **ἐνετείλατο** ὁ πατὴρ Ἀβραὰμ ποιεῖν

50 **ἐνετείλατο** ὁ πατὴρ Ἀβραὰμ ποιεῖν καὶ **ἐντέλλεσθαι** τοῖς υἱοῖς μου

52 ἐπιδέχου οὕτως, ὡς σοὶ **ἐντέλλομαι**, καὶ τὸ ἅλας καὶ τὴν σεμίδαλιν

57 οὕτως γάρ μοι **ἐνετείλατο** ὁ πατήρ μου Ἀβραάμ

ἐντολή, ἡ

48 ἄκουσον τοὺς λόγους μου καὶ ἐνωτίσαι τὰς **ἐντολάς** μου

ἐνώπιον

1a v. 9 ποιῆσαι τὰ ἀρέσκοντά σοι καὶ εὑρεῖν χάριν **ἐνώπιόν** (קדם) σου

ἐνωτίζομαι

48 ἄκουσον τοὺς λόγους μου καὶ **ἐνωτίσαι** τὰς ἐντολάς μου

ἕξ, οἱ, αἱ, τά

32 καὶ εἰς τὸ στέαρ μόνον ἀναφέρεσθαι **ἕξ** (שיחה) μνᾶς

45 λιβανωτοῦ σίκλοι **ἕξ** τῷ ταύρῳ καὶ τὸ ἥμισυ αὐτοῦ τῷ κριῷ

ἐξαλείφω

1a v. 13 ς διὸ δὴ καὶ τὴν ἀνομίαν **ἐξάλειψον** ὑποκάτωθεν τοῦ οὐρανοῦ

60 καὶ οὐκ **ἐξαλειφθήσεται** τὸ ὄνομά σου καὶ τὸ ὄνομα τοῦ σπέρματός σου

ἐπάνω

30 καὶ μετὰ ταῦτα οἶνον σπεῖσον καὶ θυμίασον **ἐπάνω** (על) λίβανον

ἐπί

with gen.:

25a ἅ σε ἀναφέρειν ὑποκάτω τῆς ὁλοκαυτώσεως **ἐπὶ** (על) τοῦ θυσιαστηρίου

27 καὶ μὴ ὀπτανέσθω τὸ αἷμα **ἐπὶ** τῆς κεφαλῆς αὐτῆς

46a ἢ<ν> ἂν προσαγάγῃς μόνον, οὐκ **ἐπὶ** στέατος

56 πρὶν ἢ φαγεῖν σε ἀπὸ τῶν κρεῶν καὶ οὐκέτι ἔσῃ ἐσθίων **ἐπὶ** τοῦ αἵματος

61 τέκνον Λευί, εὐλογημένον ἔσται τὸ σπέρμα σου **ἐπὶ** τῆς γῆς

64 καὶ **ἐπὶ** τοῦ παιδαρίου εἶδον ἐγὼ ἐν τῷ ὁράματί μου

68 ἐγεννήθη ἐν τῷ πρώτῳ μηνὶ μιᾷ τοῦ μηνὸς **ἐπ᾽** ἀνατολῆς (עם?) ἡλίου

with dat.:

55   καὶ μὴ ὀφθήτω **ἐπὶ** σοι πᾶν αἷμα καὶ πᾶσα ψυχή

67   καὶ ὅτε ἐγεννήθη, ἑώρακα ὅτι **ἐπ'** αὐτῷ (ל) ἔσται ἡ συναγωγὴ

with acc.:

21   ὅταν μέλλῃς προσφέρειν ὅσα δεῖ ἀνενέγκαι **ἐπὶ** (ל) τὸν βωμόν

23   ιβ΄ ξύλα εἴρηκεν μοι **ἐπὶ** (ל) τὸν βωμὸν προσφέρε<ιν>

25b   τότε ἄρξῃ κατασπένδειν τὸ αἷμα ἐπὶ (על) τὸν τεῖχον τοῦ θυσιαστηρίου

31   οὕτως ξύλα καθήκει ἀναφέρεσθαι **ἐπὶ** (ל) τὸν βωμόν

37   ἄλισε τὸ κρέας αὐτοῦ, καὶ ἀνένεγκε **ἐπὶ** τὸν βωμόν

46a   οὐκ ἐπὶ στέατος, προσαχθήσεται **ἐπ'** αὐτὴν λιβάνου ὁλκὴ σίκλων δύο

52   καὶ τὸν λίβανον ἐπιδέχου ἐκ τῶν χειρῶν αὐτῶν **ἐπὶ** πάντα κτήνη

53   καὶ **ἐπὶ** πᾶσαν ὥραν νίπτου τὰς χεῖρας καὶ τοὺς πόδας

65   ἐγεννήθη ἐν τῇ ζωῇ μου, καὶ ἐν τῷ ι΄ μηνὶ ἐγεννήθη **ἐπὶ** δυσμὰς ἡλίου

ἐπιδέχομαι

52   κατὰ τὸν λογισμὸν τῶν ξυλῶν **ἐπιδέχου** οὕτως, ὡς σοὶ ἐντέλλομαι

52   καὶ τὸν οἶνον καὶ τὸν λίβανον **ἐπιδέχου** ἐκ τῶν χειρῶν αὐτῶν

ἐπισκοπέω

22   **ἐπισκοπῶν** (בקר) αὐτὰ πρῶτον ἀπὸ παντὸς μολυσμοῦ

ἐπίσταμαι

1a v. 5   καὶ πάντας τοὺς διαλογισμοὺς ἐννοιῶν σὺ μόνος **ἐπίστασαι** (ידע)

ἔργον, τό

30   καὶ ᾖ τὸ **ἔργον** (עובד) σου ἐν τάξει καὶ πᾶσα προσφορά σου εἰς εὐδόκησιν

ἔριφος, ὁ

35   καὶ εἰ ἄρνα ἐκ προβάτων ἢ **ἔριφον** ἐξ αἰγῶν κ΄ μναῖ

36   καὶ εἰ ἀμνὸς τέλειος ἐνιαύσιος ἢ **ἔριφος** ἐξ αἰγῶν ιε΄ μναῖ

40a   καὶ τὸ ἀρνίῳ καὶ τῷ **ἐρίφῳ** τὸ τρίτον τοῦ σάτου

42   καὶ τῷ ἀρνίῳ καὶ τῷ **ἐρίφῳ** ἐξ αἰγῶν τὸ τρίτον τοῦ σάτου

44   καὶ τῷ κριῷ καὶ τῷ **ἐρίφῳ** κατασπεῖσαι σπονδήν

45   τῷ ταύρῳ καὶ τὸ ἥμισυ αὐτοῦ τῷ κριῷ καὶ τὸ τρίτον αὐτοῦ τῷ **ἐρίφῳ**

ἐσθίω

56   καὶ ὃ ἐάν ἐν οἴκῳ †ουσης† σεαυτὸν πᾶν κρέας **φαγεῖν**

56   κάλυπτε τὸ αἷμα αὐτοῦ τῇ γῇ πρῶτον πρὶν ἢ **φαγεῖν** σε ἀπὸ τῶν κρεῶν

56   ἀπὸ τῶν κρεῶν καὶ οὐκέτι ἔσῃ **ἐσθίων** ἐπὶ τοῦ αἵματος.

ἔτι

1a v. 19   πάσας τὰς ἡμέρας τοῦ αἰῶνος. καὶ ἐσιώπησα **ἔτι** δεόμενος

ἔτος, τό

62   ἀνεπληρώθησάν μοι ἑβδομάδες τέσσαρες ἐν τοῖς **ἔτεσιν** τῆς ζωῆς μου

62   ἐν **ἔτει** ὀγδόῳ καὶ εἰκοστῷ ἔλαβον γυναῖκα ἐμαυτῷ

65   λ΄ **ἐτῶν** ἤμην ὅτε ἐγεννήθη ἐν τῇ ζωῇ μου, καὶ ἐν τῷ ι΄ μηνὶ ἐγεννήθη

εὐδόκησις, ἡ

30   ᾖ τὸ ἔργον σου ἐν τάξει καὶ πᾶσα προσφορά σου εἰς **εὐδόκησιν** (רעוא)

εὐθύς, εῖα, ὑ

1a v. 2   καὶ πάσας τὰς ὁδούς μου ἐποίησα **εὐθείας**

εὐλογέω

1a v. 15b   εὐλόγησας (ברך) τὸν Ἀβραὰμ πατέρα μου καὶ Σάρραν μητέρα μου

1a v. 16   εἶπας δοῦναι αὐτοῖς σπέρμα δίκαιον εὐλογημένον εἰς τοὺς αἰῶνας

12   εἶδεν Ἰσαὰκ ὁ πατὴρ ἡμῶν πάντας ἡμᾶς καὶ ηὐλόγησεν (ברך) ἡμᾶς

59   τῷ σπέρματί σου εὐλογηθήσεται ἐν τῇ γῇ

61   καὶ νῦν, τέκνον Λευί, εὐλογημένον ἔσται τὸ σπέρμα σου ἐπὶ τῆς γῆς

εὑρίσκω

1a v. 9   ποιῆσαι τὰ ἀρέσκοντά σοι καὶ εὑρεῖν (אמצא) χάριν ἐνώπιόν σου

57   ὅτι οὕτως εὗρεν ἐν τῇ γραφῇ τῆς βίβλου τοῦ Νῶε περὶ τοῦ αἵματος.

εὐφραίνω

12   καὶ ηὐλόγησεν ἡμᾶς, καὶ ηὐφράνθη (חדי)

εὔχομαι

1a v. 4   εἰς ἀλήθειαν κατέναντι τῶν ἁγίων καὶ ηὐξάμην καὶ εἶπα

εὐωδία, ἡ

30   εἰς εὐδόκησιν καὶ ὀσμὴν εὐωδίας (ניחח) ἔναντι κυρίου ὑψίστου

ἕως

59   καὶ τὸ σπέρμα σου ἕως πάντων τῶν αἰώνων ἐνεχθήσεται ἐν Βιβλίῳ

60   τὸ ὄνομά σου καὶ τὸ ὄνομα τοῦ σπέρματός σου ἕως τῶν αἰώνων

ς′

47   γίνεται ὁ σίκλος ὡσεὶ ις′ θέρμοι καὶ ὁλκῆς μιᾶς

ζάω

1a v. 2   καὶ ὅλος ἐλουσάμην ἐν ὕδατι ζῶντι· καὶ πάσας τὰς ὁδούς μου

ζωή, ἡ

59   ἕως πάντων τῶν αἰώνων ἐνεχθήσεται ἐν Βιβλίῳ μνημοσύνου ζωῆς

62   ἀνεπληρώθησάν μοι ἑβδομάδες τέσσαρες ἐν τοῖς ἔτεσιν τῆς ζωῆς μου

65   λ′ ἐτῶν ἤμην ὅτε ἐγεννήθη ἐν τῇ ζωῇ μου, καὶ ἐν τῷ ι′ μηνὶ

ἤ

34   καὶ εἰ κριὸς ἐκ προβάτων ἢ τράγος ἐξ αἰγῶν τὸ προσφερόμενον ἢ

35   καὶ εἰ ἄρνα ἐκ προβάτων ἢ ἔριφον ἐξ αἰγῶν κ′ μναῖ

36   καὶ εἰ ἀμνὸς τέλειος ἐνιαύσιος ἢ ἔριφος ἐξ αἰγῶν ιε′ μναῖ

ἡδύς, ἡδεῖα, ἡδύ

23   προσφέρε<ιν>, ὧν ἐστιν ὁ καπνὸς αὐτῶν ἡδὺς (בשׂם) ἀναβαίνων

ἥλιος, ὁ

65   καὶ ἐν τῷ ι′ μηνὶ ἐγεννήθη ἐπὶ δυσμὰς ἡλίου

68   ἐγεννήθη ἐν τῷ πρώτῳ μηνὶ μιᾷ τοῦ μηνὸς ἐπ᾽ ἀνατολῆς ἡλίου (שׁמשׁ)

ἡμεῖς / ἡμῶν

11   κατελύσαμεν ἐν τῇ αὐλῇ Ἀβραὰμ τοῦ πατρὸς ἡμῶν

11   ἐν τῇ αὐλῇ Ἀβραὰμ τοῦ πατρὸς ἡμῶν παρὰ Ἰσαὰκ τὸν πατέρα ἡμῶν

12   καὶ εἶδεν Ἰσαὰκ ὁ πατὴρ ἡμῶν πάντας ἡμᾶς καὶ ηὐλόγησεν ἡμᾶς

ἡμεῖς / ἡμᾶς

12   καὶ εἶδεν Ἰσαὰκ ὁ πατὴρ ἡμῶν πάντας ἡμᾶς

12   καὶ εἶδεν Ἰσαὰκ ὁ πατὴρ ἡμῶν πάντας ἡμᾶς καὶ ηὐλόγησεν ἡμᾶς

ἡμέρα, ἡ

48 οἱ λόγοι μου οὗτοι ἀπὸ τῆς καρδίας σου ἐν πάσαις ταῖς **ἡμέραις** σου,

ἡμέτερος, α, ον

63 πάροικοί ἐσμεν ὡς τοῦτο ἐν τῇ γῇ **ἡμετέρᾳ** νομιζομένη

ἥμισυς, εια, υ

36 ἢ ἔριφος ἐξ αἰγῶν ιε' μναῖ, καὶ τῷ στέατι μίαν **ἥμισυ** μνᾶν

39 καὶ τῷ κριῷ τὸ **ἥμισυ** τοῦ σάτου καὶ τῷ τράγῳ τὸ ἴσον

45 καὶ τὸ **ἥμισυ** αὐτοῦ τῷ κριῷ καὶ τὸ τρίτον αὐτοῦ τῷ ἐρίφῳ

θέρμος, ὁ

47 καὶ τοῦ σικλίου τὸ τέταρτον ὁλκὴ **θερμῶν** δ' ἐστίν

47 γίνεται ὁ σίκλος ὡσεὶ ις' **θέρμοι** καὶ ὁλκῆς μιᾶς

θεχακ

24 καὶ βερωθα †καν† **θεχακ** (הכבה) καὶ κυπάρισσον καὶ δάφνην καὶ μυρσίνην

θυγάτερ, ἡ

62 Μελχάν, **θυγατέρα** Βαθουήλ, υἱοῦ Λάβαν, ἀδελφοῦ μητρός μου

θυμιάζω

30 καὶ μετὰ ταῦτα οἶνον σπεῖσον καὶ **θυμίασον** (הקטיר) ἐπάνω λίβανον

θυσία, ἡ

51 προσενεγκεῖν **θυσίαν** κυρίῳ ὑψίστῳ, ὡς καθήκει κατὰ τὸ προστεταγμένον

52 ὅταν παραλαμβάνῃς **θυσίαν** ποιεῖν ἔναντι κυρίου ἀπὸ πάσης σαρκός

θυσιαστήριον, τό

25a ἅ σε ἀναφέρειν ὑποκάτω τῆς ὁλοκαυτώσεως ἐπὶ τοῦ **θυσιαστηρίου** (מדבח)

25b ἄρξῃ κατασπένδειν τὸ αἷμα ἐπὶ τὸν τεῖχον τοῦ **θυσιαστηρίου** (מדבח)

53 ὅταν πορεύῃ πρὸς τὸ **θυσιαστήριον**· καὶ ὅταν ἐκπορεύῃς ἐκ τῶν ἁγίων

ι'

23 ιβ' ξύλα εἴρηκεν μοι ἐπὶ τὸν βωμὸν προσφέρε<ιν>

36 εἰ ἀμνὸς τέλειος ἐνιαύσιος ἢ ἔριφος ἐξ αἰγῶν ιε' μναῖ

47 γίνεται ὁ σίκλος ὡσεὶ ις' **θέρμοι** καὶ ὁλκῆς μιᾶς

65 ἐν τῇ ζωῇ μου, καὶ ἐν τῷ **ι'** μηνὶ ἐγεννήθη ἐπὶ δυσμὰς ἡλίου

ἱεράτευμα, τό

67 αὐτὸς καὶ τὸ σπέρμα αὐτοῦ ἔσονται ἀρχὴ βασιλέων, **ἱεράτευμα**

ἱερατεύω

13 καὶ ὅτε ἔγνω ὅτι ἐγὼ **ἱεράτευσα** τῷ κυρίῳ δεσπότῃ τοῦ οὐρανοῦ

ἱερεύς, ὁ

17 **ἱερεὺς** (כהן) ἅγιος κληθήσεται τῷ σπέρματι Ἀβραάμ

48 ἐν πάσαις ταῖς ἡμέραις σου, ὅτι **ἱερεὺς** συ ἅγιος κυρίου

49 **ἱερεῖς** ἔσονται πᾶν τὸ σπέρμα σου· καὶ τοῖς υἱοῖς σου οὕτως ἔντειλον

ἱερωσύνη, ἡ

13 ἤρξατο διδάσκειν με τὴν κρίσιν **ἱερωσύνης** (כהונא) καὶ εἶπεν

19 καὶ τότε ἐνδιδύσκου τὴν στολὴν τῆς **ἱερωσύνης** (כהונא)

51 καὶ νῦν, τέκνον, χαίρω ὅτι ἐξελέχθης εἰς **ἱερωσύνην** ἁγίαν

64 τὸ σπέρμα αὐτοῦ ἀπὸ τῆς ἀρχῆς **ἱερωσύνης** ἔσται τὸ σπέρμα αὐτοῦ

ἱμάτιον, τό

1a v. 1   τότε ἐγὼ ἔπλυνα τὰ **ἱμάτιά** μου, καὶ καθαρίσας αὐτὰ ἐν ὕδατι καθαρῷ

ἵνα

49   τοῖς υἱοῖς σου οὕτως ἔντειλον **ἵνα** ποιήσουσιν κατὰ τὴν κρίσιν ταύτην

ἴσος, η, ον

39   καὶ τῷ κριῷ τὸ ἥμισυ τοῦ σάτου καὶ τῷ τράγῳ τὸ **ἴσον**

ἰσχύς, ἡ

1a v. 8   καὶ βουλὴν καὶ σοφίαν καὶ γνῶσιν καὶ **ἰσχὺν** (נבורה) δός μοι

κ'

35   καὶ εἰ ἄρνα ἐκ προβάτων ἢ ἔριφον ἐξ αἰγῶν **κ'** μναῖ

καθαρίζω

1a v. 1   ἔπλυνα τὰ ἱμάτιά μου, καὶ **καθαρίσας** αὐτὰ ἐν ὕδατι καθαρῷ

1a v. 14   **καθάρισον** τὴν καρδίαν μου, δέσποτα, ἀπὸ πάσης ἀκαθαρσίας

καθαρός, ά, όν

1a v. 1   ἔπλυνα τὰ ἱμάτιά μου, καὶ καθαρίσας αὐτὰ ἐν ὕδατι **καθαρῷ**

18   γίνου **καθαρὸς** (דכי) ἐν τῷ σώματί σου ἀπὸ πάσης ἀκαθαρσίας

καθήκω

29   καὶ πάντα ἡλισμένα ἐν ἅλατι ὡς **καθήκει** (חוה) αὐτοῖς αὐτάρκως

31   ἐν μέτρῳ καὶ σταθμῷ, καὶ μὴ περισσεύσῃς μηθὲν ὅσα οὐ **καθήκει**

31   οὕτως ξύλα **καθήκει** ἀναφέρεσθαι ἐπὶ τὸν βωμόν·

32a   τῷ ταύρῳ τῷ τελείῳ τάλαντον ξύλων **καθήκει** αὐτῷ ἐν σταθμῷ

40b   καὶ σεμίδαλις **καθήκουσα** αὐτοῖς

51   προσενεγκεῖν θυσίαν κυρίῳ ὑψίστῳ, ὡς **καθήκει** κατὰ τὸ προστεταγμένον

καί

1a v. 1, 2, 2, 3, 3, 3, 4, 4, 4, 4, 5, 6, 6, 7, 7, 7, 8, 8, 8, 8, 9, 9, 10, 11, 11, 11, 12, 13, 13, 14, 15a, 15b, 16, 17, 18, 18, 19, 19; 11; 11; 12; 12; 12; 13; 13; 15; 15; 16; 16; 17; 17; 17; 18; 19; 19; 20; 20; 21; 21; 22; 24; 24; 24; 24; 24; 24; 24 (corrupt), 24; 24; 24; 24; 25b; 26; 26; 26; 27; 27; 28; 28; 28; 28; 28; 29; 30; 30; 30; 30; 30; 30; 31; 31; 31; 31; 32a; 32a; 32b; 33; 34; 34; 34; 35; 35; 36; 36; 37; 37; 37; 38; 38; 39; 39; 40a; 40a; 40b; 41; 41; 42; 42; 42; 42; 42; 43; 44; 44; 44; 44; 44; 44; 45; 45; 45; 46b; 47; 47; 47; 47; 48; 48; 48; 49; 49; 50; 51; 51; 52; 52; 52; 52; 53; 53; 53; 54; 54; 55; 55; 56; 56; 58; 58; 58; 59; 60; 60; 61; 62; 62; 63; 63; 64; 64; 65; 66; 66; 67; 67; 67; 68; 69a; 69a; 69a; 69a.

καιρός, ὁ

66   ἔτεκεν ἐξ ἐμοῦ κατὰ τὸν **καιρὸν** τὸν καθήκοντα τῶν γυναικῶν

κακός, ή, όν

1a v. 12   καὶ σκέπη σου τῆς δυναστείας σκεπασάτω με ἀπὸ παντὸς **κακοῦ**

καλέω

17   ἱερεὺς ἅγιος **κληθήσεται** (מקרה) τῷ σπέρματι Ἀβραάμ

63   ἔτεκεν υἱὸν πρῶτον, καὶ **ἐκάλεσα** τὸ ὄνομα αὐτοῦ Γηρσώμ

66   καὶ **ἐκάλεσα** τὸ ὄνομα αὐτοῦ Καάθ

καλός, ή, όν

1a v. 11 καὶ προσάγαγέ με εἶναί σου δοῦλος καὶ λατρεῦσαί σοι **καλῶς**

καλύπτω

27 τὴν κεφαλὴν ἀνάφερε πρῶτον καὶ **κάλυπτε** (יַפֶה) αὐτὴν τῷ στέατι

56 **κάλυπτε** τὸ αἷμα αὐτοῦ τῇ γῇ πρῶτον πρὶν ἢ φαγεῖν σε ἀπὸ τῶν κρεῶν

καπνός, ὁ

23 ὧν ἐστιν ὁ **καπνὸς** (יַחַן) αὐτῶν ἡδὺς ἀναβαίνων

καρδία, ἡ

1a v. 5 Κύριε, γινώσκεις πάσας τὰς **καρδίας**

1a v. 14 καθάρισον τὴν **καρδίαν** μου, δέσποτα, ἀπὸ πάσης ἀκαθαρσίας

48 καὶ μὴ ἀποστήτωσαν οἱ λόγοι μου οὗτοι ἀπὸ τῆς **καρδίας** σου

κατά

acc:

44 καὶ οἶνον **κατὰ** τὸ μέτρον τοῦ ἐλαίου τῷ ταύρῳ καὶ τῷ κριῷ καὶ τῷ
ἐρίφῳ

49 ἵνα ποιήσουσιν **κατὰ** τὴν κρίσιν ταύτην ὡς σοὶ ὑπέδειξα

51 ὡς καθήκει **κατὰ** τὸ προστεταγμένον τοῦτο ποιεῖν

52 **κατὰ** τὸν λογισμὸν τῶν ξύλων ἐπιδέχου οὕτως, ὡς σοὶ ἐντέλλομαι

66 ἔτεκεν ἐξ ἐμοῦ **κατὰ** (כְּ) τὸν καιρὸν τὸν καθήκοντα τῶν γυναικῶν

καταλύω

11 καὶ ἀνήλθομεν ἀπὸ Βηθὴλ καὶ **κατελύσαμεν** (יָשַׁר) ἐν τῇ αὐλῇ Ἀβραὰμ

κατασπένδω

25b τότε ἄρξῃ **κατασπένδειν** (זָרַק) τὸ αἷμα ἐπὶ τὸν τεῖχον τοῦ θυσιαστηρίου

44 τῷ ταύρῳ καὶ τῷ κριῷ καὶ τῷ ἐρίφῳ **κατασπεῖσαι** σπονδήν

κατέναντι

1a v. 4 καὶ τὰς χεῖράς μου ἀνεπέτασα εἰς ἀλήθειαν **κατέναντι** τῶν ἁγίων

κατισχύω

1a v. 10 μὴ **κατισχυσάτω** (שָׁלַם) με πᾶς σατανᾶς πλανῆσαί με ἀπὸ τῆς ὁδοῦ
σου

κέδρος, ἡ

24 καὶ ταῦτα τὰ ὀνόματα αὐτῶν· **κέδρον** (אֶרֶז) καὶ ουεδεφωνα καὶ σχῖνον

κεφαλή, ἡ

27 τὴν **κεφαλὴν** (רֹאשׁ) ἀνάφερε πρῶτον καὶ κάλυπτε αὐτὴν τῷ στέατι

27 καὶ μὴ ὀπτανέσθω τὸ αἷμα ἐπὶ τῆς **κεφαλῆς** αὐτῆς

κρέας, τό

37 ἅλισε τὸ **κρέας** αὐτοῦ, καὶ ἀνένεγκε ἐπὶ τὸν βωμόν

56 καὶ ὃ ἐάν ἐν οἴκῳ †ουσης† σεαυτόν πᾶν **κρέας** φαγεῖν

56 κάλυπτε τὸ αἷμα αὐτοῦ τῇ γῇ πρῶτον πρὶν ἢ φαγεῖν σε ἀπὸ τῶν **κρεῶν**

κριός, ὁ

34 καὶ εἰ **κριὸς** ἐκ προβάτων ἢ τράγος ἐξ αἰγῶν τὸ προσφερόμενον ᾖ

39 καὶ τῷ **κριῷ** τὸ ἥμισυ τοῦ σάτου καὶ τῷ τράγῳ τὸ ἴσον

42 καὶ τῷ **κριῷ** καὶ τῷ τράγῳ τὰ δύο μέρη τοῦ σάτου

44 καὶ τῷ **κριῷ** τὸ ἕκτον τοῦ σάτου καὶ τῷ ἀρνίῳ τὸ ὄγδοον τοῦ σάτου

44   τῷ ταύρῳ καὶ τῷ **κριῷ** καὶ τῷ ἐρίφῳ κατασπεῖσαι σπονδήν

45   λιβανωτοῦ σίκλοι ἓξ τῷ ταύρῳ καὶ τὸ ἥμισυ αὐτοῦ τῷ **κριῷ**

κρίσις, ἡ

1a v. 18   μέτοχον ποίησον τοῖς λόγοις σου ποιεῖν **κρίσιν** (דִּין) ἀληθινὴν

13   ἤρξατο διδάσκειν με τὴν **κρίσιν** (דִּין) ἱερωσύνης καὶ εἶπεν

14   ἀπὸ πάσης ἀκαθαρσίας· ἡ **κρίσις** (דִּין) σου μεγάλη ἀπὸ πάσης σαρκός

15   καὶ νῦν τὴν **κρίσιν** (דִּין) τῆς ἀληθείας ἀναγγελῶ σοι

49   τοῖς υἱοῖς σου οὕτως ἔντειλον ἵνα ποιήσουσιν κατὰ τὴν **κρίσιν** ταύτην

κρύπτω

15   καὶ οὐ μὴ **κρύψω** (מסר) ἀπό σου πᾶν ῥῆμα. διδάξω σε

κτῆνος,τό

52   καὶ τὸν λίβανον ἐπιδέχου ἐκ τῶν χειρῶν αὐτῶν ἐπὶ πάντα **κτήνη**

κύκλῳ

1a v. 12   τεῖχος εἰρήνης σου γενέσθαι **κύκλῳ** μου

κυπάρισσος, ἡ

24   †καν† θεχακ καὶ **κυπάρισσον** (אַף משה נשא) καὶ δάφνην καὶ μυρσίνην

λ′

34   καὶ τούτῳ **λ′** μναῖ, καὶ τῷ στέατι τρεῖς μναῖ

65   **λ′** ἐτῶν ἤμην ὅτε ἐγεννήθη ἐν τῇ ζωῇ μου, καὶ ἐν τῷ ι′ μηνὶ ἐγεννήθη

68   ἐν τῷ τετάρτῳ καὶ **λ′** (תלתין) ἔτει ἐγεννήθη ἐν τῷ πρώτῳ μηνὶ

λαλέω

1a v. 3   ἦρα πρὸς τὸν οὐρανόν, καὶ τὸ στόμα μου ἤνοιξα καὶ **ἐλάλησα**

λαμβάνω

17   σὺ †πρῶτος† ἀπὸ τοῦ σπέρματος **λάβε** (נסב) σεαυτῷ

62   **ἔλαβον** γυναῖκα ἐμαυτῷ ἐκ τῆς συγγενείας Ἀβραὰμ τοῦ πατρός μου

63   καὶ ἐν γαστρὶ **λαβοῦσα** ἐξ ἐμοῦ ἔτεκεν υἱὸν πρῶτον

69a   καὶ πάλιν συνεγενόμην αὐτῇ καὶ ἐν γαστρὶ **ἔλαβεν**

λάος, ὁ

67   ἑώρακα ὅτι ἐπ᾽ αὐτῷ ἔσται ἡ συναγωγὴ παντὸς τοῦ **λαοῦ**

λατρεύω

1a v. 11   καὶ προσάγαγέ με εἶναί σου δοῦλος καὶ **λατρεῦσαί** σοι καλῶς

λέγω

1a v. 4   ἀνεπέτασα εἰς ἀλήθειαν κατέναντι τῶν ἁγίων καὶ ηὐξάμην καὶ **εἶπα**

1a v. 16   καὶ **εἶπας** δοῦναι αὐτοῖς σπέρμα δίκαιον εὐλογημένον εἰς τοὺς αἰῶνας

13   ἤρξατο διδάσκειν με τὴν κρίσιν ἱερωσύνης καὶ **εἶπεν** (אמר)

23   ιβ′ ξύλα **εἴρηκεν** (אמר) μοι ἐπὶ τὸν βωμὸν προσφέρε<ιν>

25a   ταῦτα **εἴρηκεν** (אמר) ὅτι ταῦτά ἐστιν ἅ σε ἀναφέρειν

58   ὡς σοί, τέκνον ἀγαπητόν, ἐγὼ **λέγω**, ἠγαπημένος σὺ τῷ πατρί σου

63   **εἶπα** γὰρ ὅτι πάροικον ἔσται τὸ σπέρμα μου ἐν γῇ, ᾗ ἐγεννήθην

λίβανος, ὁ

30   καὶ μετὰ ταῦτα οἶνον σπεῖσον καὶ θυμίασον ἐπάνω **λίβανον** (לבונה)

46a   προσαχθήσεται ἐπ᾽ αὐτὴν **λιβάνου** ὁλκὴ σίκλων δύο

52   καὶ τὸν οἶνον καὶ τὸν **λίβανον** ἐπιδέχου ἐκ τῶν χειρῶν αὐτῶν

λιβανωτός, ὁ
45   **λιβανωτοῦ** σίκλοι ἓξ τῷ ταύρῳ καὶ τὸ ἥμισυ αὐτοῦ τῷ κριῷ
λογισμός, ὁ
52   κατὰ τὸν **λογισμὸν** τῶν ξυλῶν ἐπιδέχου οὕτως, ὡς σοὶ ἐντέλλομαι
λόγος, ὁ
1a v. 9   καὶ αἰνεῖν τοὺς **λόγους** σου μετ᾽ ἐμοῦ, κύριε
1a v. 18   καὶ μέτοχον ποίησον τοῖς **λόγοις** σου ποιεῖν κρίσιν ἀληθινὴν
48   τέκνον μου, ἄκουσον τοὺς **λόγους** μου καὶ ἐνωτίσαι τὰς ἐντολάς μου
48   καὶ μὴ ἀποστήτωσαν οἱ **λόγοι** μου οὗτοι ἀπὸ τῆς καρδίας σου
λούομαι
1a v. 2   καὶ ὅλος **ἐλουσάμην** ἐν ὕδατι ζῶντι
19   **λούου** (רחץ) ὕδατι πρῶτον καὶ τότε ἐνδιδύσκου τὴν στολὴν τῆς ἱερωσύνης
λυπέω
69a   καὶ ἐκάλεσα τὸ ὄνομα αὐτοῦ Μεραρί· **ἐλυπήθην** (מר לי) γὰρ περὶ
         αὐτοῦ
μ′
33   καὶ εἰς μόσχον τέλειον **μ′** μναῖ
μακρύνω
1a v. 7   **μάκρυνον** (ארחק) ἀπ᾽ ἐμοῦ, κύριε, τὸ πνεῦμα τὸ ἄδικον
μέγας, μεγάλη, μέγα
14   ἡ κρίσις σου **μεγάλη** (רב) ἀπὸ πάσης σαρκός
37   καὶ ἅλας ἀποδέδεικται τῷ ταύρῳ τῷ **μεγάλῳ**
41   τῷ ταύρῳ τῷ **μεγάλῳ** καὶ τῷ ταύρῳ τῷ β′ καὶ τῷ μοσχαρίῳ
67   αὐτῷ ἔσται ἡ ἀρχιερωσύνη ἡ **μεγάλη** (רב)· αὐτὸς καὶ τὸ σπέρμα αὐτοῦ
μέλλω
21   καὶ ὅταν **μέλλῃς** προσφέρειν ὅσα δεῖ ἀνενέγκαι ἐπὶ τὸν βωμόν (נסב)
μέλος, τό
26   καὶ τοὺς πόδας ἀπὸ τοῦ αἵματος, καὶ ἄρξῃ τὰ **μέλη** (אבר) ἀναφέρειν
μέρος, τό
38   καὶ τῷ ταύρῳ τῷ δευτέρῳ τὰ πέντε **μέρη** ἀπὸ τῶν ἓξ μερῶν τοῦ σάτου
38   καὶ τῷ ταύρῳ τῷ δευτέρῳ τὰ πέντε μέρη ἀπὸ τῶν ἓξ **μερῶν** τοῦ σάτου
42   καὶ τῷ κριῷ καὶ τῷ τράγῳ τὰ δύο **μέρη** τοῦ σάτου καὶ τῷ ἀρνίῳ
47   καὶ τὰ δύο **μέρη** τοῦ βάτου καὶ ὁλκῆς τῆς μνᾶς ν′ σίκλων ἐστίν
μετά
gen:
17   καὶ μὴ βεβηλώσῃς τὸ σπέρμα σου **μετὰ** (עם) †πολλῶν†·
28   καὶ μετὰ ταῦτα τὸ στῆθος **μετὰ** (עם) τῶν πλευρῶν
acc:
28   καὶ **μετὰ** (בתר) τοῦτο τὸν τράχηλον, καὶ μετὰ τοῦτο τοὺς μους
28   καὶ μετὰ τοῦτο τὸν τράχηλον, καὶ **μετὰ** (בתר) τοῦτο τοὺς μους
28   καὶ **μετὰ** (בתר) ταῦτα τὸ στῆθος μετὰ τῶν πλευρῶν
28   καὶ **μετὰ** (בתר) ταῦτα τὴν ὀσφὺν σὺν τῷ νώτῳ
28   καὶ **μετὰ** (בתר) ταῦτα τοὺς πόδας πεπλυμένους σὺν τοῖς ἐνδοσθίοις

30   καὶ **μετὰ** (בתר) ταῦτα σεμίδαλιν ἀναπεποιημένον ἐν ἐλαίῳ

30   καὶ **μετὰ** (בתר) ταῦτα οἶνον σπεῖσον καὶ θυμίασον ἐπάνω λίβανον

μέτοχος, ον

1a v. 18   καὶ **μέτοχον** ποίησον τοῖς λόγοις σου ποιεῖν κρίσιν ἀληθινὴν

μέτρον, τό

31   καὶ ὅσα ἂν ποιῇς, ἐν τάξει ποίει ἃ ποιῇς ἐν **μέτρῳ** καὶ στάθμῳ

44   καὶ οἶνον κατὰ τὸ **μέτρον** τοῦ ἐλαίου

μή

1a v. 10   **μὴ** (אל) κατισχυσάτω με πᾶς σατανᾶς πλανῆσαί με ἀπὸ τῆς ὁδοῦ σου

1a v. 15a   καὶ **μὴ** ἀποστρέψῃς τὸ πρόσωπόν σου ἀπὸ τοῦ υἱοῦ παιδός σου Ἰακώβ

1a v. 19   καὶ **μὴ** ἀποστήσῃς τὸν υἱὸν τοῦ παιδός σου ἀπὸ τοῦ προσώπου σου

15   καὶ οὐ **μὴ** (לא) κρύψω ἀπό σου πᾶν ῥῆμα. διδάξω σε·

17   καὶ **μὴ** (לא) βεβηλώσῃς τὸ σπέρμα σου μετὰ †πολλῶν†

27   καὶ **μὴ** (אל/לא) ὀπτανέσθω τὸ αἷμα ἐπὶ τῆς κεφαλῆς αὐτῆς

31   καὶ **μὴ** (לא) περισσεύσῃς μηθὲν ὅσα οὐ καθήκει

48   καὶ **μὴ** ἀποστήτωσαν οἱ λόγοι μου οὗτοι ἀπὸ τῆς καρδίας σου

53   καὶ ὅταν ἐκπορεύῃς ἐκ τῶν ἁγίων, πᾶν αἷμα **μὴ** ἁπτέσθω τῆς στολῆς σου

55   καὶ **μὴ** ὀφθήτω ἐπὶ σοι πᾶν αἷμα καὶ πᾶσα ψυχή

μηθείς, μηθεμία, μηθέν

31   ἐν μέτρῳ καὶ στάθμῳ, καὶ μὴ περισσεύσῃς **μηθὲν** (צבו) ὅσα οὐ καθήκει

μήν, ὁ

65   καὶ ἐν τῷ ι΄ **μηνὶ** ἐγεννήθη ἐπὶ δυσμὰς ἡλίου

68   ἐν τῷ τετάρτῳ καὶ λ΄ ἔτει ἐγεννήθη ἐν τῷ πρώτῳ **μηνὶ** (ירחא)

68   ἐν τῷ πρώτῳ **μηνὶ** μιᾷ τοῦ **μηνὸς** ἐπ᾽ ἀνατολῆς ἡλίου

μήτηρ, ἡ

1a v. 15b   σύ, κύριε, εὐλόγησας τὸν Ἀβραὰμ πατέρα μου καὶ Σάρραν **μητέρα** μου

62   Μελχάν, θυγατέρα Βαθουήλ, υἱοῦ Λάβαν, ἀδελφοῦ **μητρός** μου

μνᾶ, ἡ

32a   καὶ εἰς τὸ στέαρ μόνον ἀναφέρεσθαι ἓξ **μνᾶς** (מנה)

32b   καὶ τῷ ταύρῳ τῷ δευτέρῳ πεντήκοντα **μνᾶς**

32b   καὶ εἰς τὸ στέαρ αὐτοῦ μόνον πέντε **μνᾶς**

33   καὶ εἰς μόσχον τέλειον μ΄ **μναῖ**

34   καὶ τούτῳ λ΄ **μναῖ**, καὶ τῷ στέατι τρεῖς μναῖ

34   καὶ τούτῳ λ΄ μναῖ, καὶ τῷ στέατι τρεῖς **μναῖ**

35   καὶ εἰ ἄρνα ἐκ προβάτων ἢ ἔριφον ἐξ αἰγῶν κ΄ **μναῖ**

35   καὶ τῷ στέατι β΄ **μναῖ**

36   καὶ εἰ ἀμνὸς τέλειος ἐνιαύσιος ἢ ἔριφος ἐξ αἰγῶν ιε΄ **μναῖ**

36   καὶ τῷ στέατι μίαν ἥμισυ **μνᾶν**

47   καὶ τὰ δύο μέρη τοῦ βάτου καὶ ὁλκῆς τῆς **μνᾶς** ν΄ σίκλων ἐστίν

μνημόσυνον, τό

59   ἕως πάντων τῶν αἰώνων ἐνεχθήσεται ἐν Βιβλίῳ **μνημοσύνου** ζωῆς

μολυσμός, ὁ

22 ἐπισκοπῶν αὐτὰ πρῶτον ἀπὸ παντὸς **μολυσμοῦ**

μόνος, η, ον

1a v. 5 καὶ πάντας τοὺς διαλογισμοὺς ἐννοιῶν σὺ **μόνος** (בלחוד) ἐπίστασαι

32a καὶ εἰς τὸ στέαρ **μόνον** (בלחוד) ἀναφέρεσθαι ἓξ μνᾶς

32b καὶ εἰς τὸ στέαρ αὐτοῦ **μόνον** πέντε μνᾶς

46a ἢ <ν> ἂν προσαγάγῃς **μόνον**, οὐκ ἐπὶ στέατος

μοσχάριον, τό

41 καὶ τῷ ταύρῳ τῷ β′ καὶ τῷ **μοσχαρίῳ**, σάτον σεμίδαλιν

μόσχος, ὁ

33 καὶ εἰς **μόσχον** τέλειον μ′ μναῖ

38 καὶ τοῦ **μόσχου** τὸ δίμοιρον τοῦ σάτου

ν′

47 καὶ τὰ δύο μέρη τοῦ βάτου καὶ ὁλκῆς τῆς μνᾶς **ν′** σίκλων ἐστίν

νίπτομαι

20 καὶ ὅταν ἐνδιδύσκῃ, **νίπτου** (רחץ) πάλιν τὰς χεῖράς σου

21 πάλιν **νίπτου** (רחץ) τὰς χεῖράς σου καὶ τοὺς πόδας σου

26 καὶ πάλιν **νίψαι** (רחץ) σου τὰς χεῖρας καὶ τοὺς πόδας ἀπὸ τοῦ αἵματος

53 καὶ ἐπὶ πᾶσαν ὥραν **νίπτου** τὰς χεῖρας καὶ τοὺς πόδας

54 καὶ τὰς χεῖρας καὶ τοὺς πόδας **νίπτου** διὰ παντὸς ἀπὸ πάσης σαρκός

νομίζομαι

63 πάροικοί ἐσμεν ὡς τοῦτο ἐν τῇ γῇ ἡμετέρᾳ **νομιζομένῃ**

νῦν

1a v. 6 καὶ **νῦν** τέκνα μου μετ᾽ ἐμοῦ

15 καὶ **νῦν** (כעב) τὴν κρίσιν τῆς ἀληθείας ἀναγγελῶ σοι

48 καὶ **νῦν**, τέκνον μου, ἄκουσον τοὺς λόγους μου

51 καὶ **νῦν**, τέκνον, χαίρω ὅτι ἐξελέχθης εἰς ἱερωσύνην ἁγίαν

58 καὶ **νῦν** ὡς σοί, τέκνον ἀγαπητόν, ἐγὼ λέγω

61 καὶ **νῦν**, τέκνον Λευί, εὐλογημένον ἔσται τὸ σπέρμα σου ἐπὶ τῆς γῆς

νωτίζω

48 ἄκουσον τοὺς λόγους μου καὶ **ἐνωτίσαι** τὰς ἐντολάς μου

νῶτος, ὁ

28 καὶ μετὰ ταῦτα τὴν ὀσφὺν σὺν τῷ **νώτῳ** (שדרה?)

ξύλον, τό

22 καὶ ἀνάφερε τὰ **ξύλα** (אע) πρῶτον <ἐ>σχισμένα

23 ιβ′ **ξύλα** (אע) εἴρηκεν μοι ἐπὶ τὸν βωμὸν προσφέρε<ιν>

31 οὕτως **ξύλα** (אע) καθήκει ἀναφέρεσθαι ἐπὶ τὸν βωμόν

32a τῷ ταύρῳ τῷ τελείῳ τάλαντον **ξύλων** (אע) καθήκει αὐτῷ ἐν σταθμῷ

52 κατὰ τὸν λογισμὸν τῶν **ξύλων** ἐπιδέχου οὕτως

ὄγδοος, η, ον

44 καὶ τῷ ἀρνίῳ τὸ **ὄγδοον** τοῦ σάτου καὶ ἀμνοῦ

62 ἐν ἔτει **ὀγδόῳ** καὶ εἰκοστῷ ἔλαβον γυναῖκα ἐμαυτῷ

ὁδός, ἡ

1a v. 2   καὶ πάσας τὰς **ὁδούς** μου ἐποίησα εὐθείας

1a v. 6   καὶ δός μοι πάσας **ὁδοὺς** (אֹרַח) ἀληθείας

1a v. 10   μὴ κατισχυσάτω με πᾶς σατανᾶς πλανῆσαί με ἀπὸ τῆς **ὁδοῦ** σου

οἶκος, ὁ

56   καὶ ὃ ἐάν ἐν **οἴκῳ** †ουσης† σεαυτὸν πᾶν κρέας φαγεῖν

οἶνος, ὁ

30   καὶ μετὰ ταῦτα **οἶνον** σπεῖσον καὶ θυμίασον ἐπάνω λίβανον

44   καὶ **οἶνον** κατὰ τὸ μέτρον τοῦ ἐλαίου

52   καὶ τὸν **οἶνον** καὶ τὸν λίβανον ἐπιδέχου ἐκ τῶν χειρῶν αὐτῶν

†ολδινα†

24   καὶ πίτυν καὶ **ολδινα** (†אַרְזָּן†) καὶ βερωθα †καν† θεχακ

ὁλκή, ἡ

46a   προσαχθήσεται ἐπ᾽ αὐτὴν λιβάνου **ὁλκὴ** σίκλων δύο

47   καὶ τὰ δύο μέρη τοῦ βάτου καὶ **ὁλκῆς** τῆς μνᾶς ν΄ σίκλων ἐστίν

47   καὶ τοῦ σικλίου τὸ τέταρτον **ὁλκὴ** θερμῶν δ΄ ἐστίν

47   γίνεται ὁ σίκλος ὡσεὶ ις΄ θέρμοι καὶ **ὁλκῆς** μιᾶς

ὁλοκάρπωσις, ἡ

20   πρὸ τοῦ ἐγγίσαι τρὸς τὸν βωμὸν προσενέγκαι **ὁλοκάρπωσιν**

ὁλοκαύτωσις, ἡ

25a   ἅ σε ἀναφέρειν ὑποκάτω τῆς **ὁλοκαυτώσεως** (עֹלָה) ἐπὶ τοῦ θυσι-
           αστηρίου

ὅλος, η, ον

1a v. 2   καὶ **ὅλος** ἐλουσάμην ἐν ὕδατι ζῶντι

ὄνομα, τό

24   καὶ ταῦτα τὰ **ὀνόματα** (שֵׁם) αὐτῶν· κέδρον καὶ ουεδεφωνα καὶ σχίνον

60   οὐκ ἐξαλειφθήσεται τὸ **ὄνομά** σου καὶ τὸ ὄνομα τοῦ σπέρματός σου

60   οὐκ ἐξαλειφθήσεται τὸ ὄνομά σου καὶ τὸ **ὄνομα** τοῦ σπέρματός σου

63   ἔτεκεν υἱὸν πρῶτον, καὶ ἐκάλεσα τὸ **ὄνομα** αὐτοῦ Γηρσώμ

66   καὶ ἐκάλεσα τὸ **ὄνομα** (שֵׁם) αὐτοῦ Καάθ

69a   καὶ ἔτεκέν μοι υἱὸν τρίτον, καὶ ἐκάλεσα τὸ **ὄνομα** (שֵׁם) αὐτοῦ Μεραρί

ὀπτάνομαι

27   καὶ μὴ **ὀπτανέσθω** (יְהִיֶה) τὸ αἷμα ἐπὶ τῆς κεφαλῆς αὐτῆς

ὅραμα, τό

64   εἶδον ἐγὼ ἐν τῷ **ὁράματί** μου ὅτι ἐκβεβλημένος ἔσται αὐτὸς

ὁράω

12   καὶ **εἶδεν** (יִרְא) Ἰσαὰκ ὁ πατὴρ ἡμῶν πάντας ἡμᾶς καὶ ηὐλόγησεν ἡμᾶς

55   καὶ μὴ **ὀφθήτω** ἐπὶ σοι πᾶν αἷμα καὶ πᾶσα ψυχή

64   ἐπὶ τοῦ παιδαρίου **εἶδον** ἐγὼ ἐν τῷ ὁράματί μου ὅτι ἐκβεβλημένος ἔσται

67   **ἑώρακα** ὅτι ἐπ᾽ αὐτῷ ἔσται ἡ συναγωγὴ παντὸς τοῦ λαοῦ

ὅς, ἥ, ὅ

23   **ὧν** (אֲשֶׁר) ἐστιν ὁ καπνὸς αὐτῶν ἡδὺς ἀναβαίνων

25a ταῦτά ἐστιν ἃ (רֹ) σε ἀναφέρειν ὑποκάτω τῆς ὁλοκαυτώσεως
31 ἐν τάξει ποίει ἃ ποιῇς ἐν μέτρῳ καὶ σταθμῷ
37 καὶ ᾧ ἂν περισσεύσῃ τοῦ ἁλός, ἄλισον ἐν αὐτῷ τὸ δέρμα
56 καὶ ὃ ἐάν ἐν οἴκῳ †ουσης† σεαυτὸν πᾶν κρέας φαγεῖν
63 πάροικον ἔσται τὸ σπέρμα μου ἐν γῇ, ἧ ἐγεννήθην

ὀσμή, ἡ
30 καὶ πᾶσα προσφορά σου εἰς εὐδόκησιν καὶ ὀσμὴν (רֵיחַ) εὐωδίας

ὅσος, η, ον
31 καὶ ὅσα ἃ ποιῇς, ἐν τάξει ποίει ἃ ποιῇς
31 ἐν μέτρῳ καὶ σταθμῷ, καὶ μὴ περισσεύσῃς μηθὲν ὅσα (צְבֵי) οὐ καθήκει

ὀσφῦς, ἡ
28 καὶ μετὰ ταῦτα τὴν ὀσφὺν (יַרְכָאַ) σὺν τῷ νώτῳ

ὅταν
19 καὶ ὅταν (כַּד) εἰσπορεύῃ ἐν τοῖς ἁγίοις, λούου ὕδατι πρῶτον
20 καὶ ὅταν (כַּד) ἐνδιδύσκῃ, νίπτου πάλιν τὰς χεῖράς σου
21 καὶ ὅταν (כַּד) μέλλῃς προσφέρειν ὅσα δεῖ ἀνενέγκαι ἐπὶ τὸν βωμόν
52 ὅταν παραλαμβάνῃς θυσίαν ποιεῖν ἔναντι κυρίου
53 νίπτου τὰς χεῖρας καὶ τοὺς πόδας, ὅταν πορεύῃ πρὸς τὸ θυσιαστήριον
53 καὶ ὅταν ἐκπορεύῃς ἐκ τῶν ἁγίων, πᾶν αἷμα μὴ ἁπτέσθω τῆς στολῆς σου

ὅτε
13 καὶ ὅτε (כַּד) ἔγνω ὅτι ἐγὼ ἱεράτευσα τῷ κυρίῳ δεσπότῃ τοῦ οὐρανοῦ
65 λ΄ ἐτῶν ἤμην ὅτε ἐγεννήθη ἐν τῇ ζωῇ μου
67 καὶ ὅτε ἐγεννήθη, ἑώρακα ὅτι ἐπ᾽ αὐτῷ ἔσται ἡ συναγωγὴ

ὅτι
13 καὶ ὅτε ἔγνω ὅτι (רֹ) ἐγὼ ἱεράτευσα τῷ κυρίῳ δεσπότῃ τοῦ οὐρανοῦ
25a ταῦτα εἴρηκεν ὅτι (רֹ) ταῦτά ἐστιν ἅ σε ἀναφέρειν
48 ἐν πάσαις ταῖς ἡμέραις σου, ὅτι ἱερεὺς σὺ ἅγιος κυρίου
51 τέκνον, χαίρω ὅτι ἐξελέχθης εἰς ἱερωσύνην ἁγίαν
57 ὅτι οὕτως εὗρεν ἐν τῇ γραφῇ τῆς βίβλου τοῦ Νῶε περὶ τοῦ αἵματος
63 εἶπα γὰρ ὅτι πάροικον ἔσται τὸ σπέρμα μου ἐν γῇ, ἧ ἐγεννήθην
64 ὅτι ἐκβεβλημένος ἔσται αὐτὸς καὶ τὸ σπέρμα αὐτοῦ ἀπὸ τῆς ἀρχῆς
67 ἑώρακα ὅτι (רֹ) ἐπ᾽ αὐτῷ ἔσται ἡ συναγωγὴ παντὸς τοῦ λαοῦ
67 καὶ ὅτι αὐτῷ ἔσται ἡ ἀρχιερωσύνη ἡ μεγάλη

†ουεδεφωνα†
24 κέδρον καὶ ουεδεφωνα (וְדַפְנָא) καὶ σχῖνον καὶ στρόβιλον καὶ πίτυν

οὐ
15 καὶ οὐ μὴ κρύψω ἀπό σου πᾶν ῥῆμα. διδάξω σε
31 καὶ μὴ περισσεύσῃς μηθὲν ὅσα οὐ (לֹא) καθήκει
46a ἢ<ν> ἂν προσαγάγῃς μόνον, οὐκ ἐπὶ στέατος
53 πᾶν αἷμα μὴ ἁπτέσθω τῆς στολῆς σου· οὐκ ἀνήψῃς αὐτῷ αὐθήμερον
60 καὶ οὐκ ἐξαλειφθήσεται τὸ ὄνομά σου καὶ τὸ ὄνομα τοῦ σπέρματός σου

οὐκέτι
56 καὶ οὐκέτι ἔσῃ ἐσθίων ἐπὶ τοῦ αἵματος

οὐρανός, ὁ

1a v. 3   τοὺς ὀφθαλμούς μου καὶ τὸ πρόσωπόν μου ἦρα πρὸς τὸν **οὐρανόν** (שמין)

1a v. 13   παράδος διὸ δὴ καὶ τὴν ἀνομίαν ἐξάλειψον ὑποκάτωθεν τοῦ **οὐρανοῦ**

13   ὅτε ἔγνω ὅτι ἐγὼ ἱεράτευσα τῷ κυρίῳ δεσπότῃ τοῦ **οὐρανοῦ** (שמין)

οὗτος, αὕτη, τοῦτο

24   καὶ **ταῦτα** (אל) τὰ ὀνόματα αὐτῶν· κέδρον καὶ ουεδεφωνα

25a   **ταῦτα** (אל) εἴρηκεν ὅτι ταῦτά ἐστιν ἅ σε ἀναφέρειν

25a   ταῦτα εἴρηκεν ὅτι **ταῦτά** ἐστιν ἅ σε ἀναφέρειν

28   καὶ **μετὰ** τοῦτο τὸν τράχηλον

28   καὶ μετὰ **τοῦτο** τοὺς μους

28   καὶ μετὰ **ταῦτα** τὸ στῆθος μετὰ τῶν πλευρῶν

28   καὶ μετὰ **ταῦτα** τὴν ὀσφὺν σὺν τῷ νώτῳ

28   καὶ μετὰ **ταῦτα** τοὺς πόδας πεπλυμένους σὺν τοῖς ἐνδοσθίοις

30   καὶ μετὰ **ταῦτα** (דנה) σεμίδαλιν ἀναπεποιημένον ἐν ἐλαίῳ

30   καὶ μετὰ **ταῦτα** οἶνον σπεῖσον καὶ θυμίασον ἐπάνω λίβανον

34   καὶ **τούτῳ** λ´ μναῖ, καὶ τῷ στέατι τρεῖς μναῖ

48   καὶ μὴ ἀποστήτωσαν οἱ λόγοι μου **οὗτοι** ἀπὸ τῆς καρδίας σου

49   τοῖς υἱοῖς σου οὕτως ἔντειλον ἵνα ποιήσουσιν κατὰ τὴν κρίσιν **ταύτην**

51   ὡς καθήκει κατὰ τὸ προστεταγμένον **τοῦτο** ποιεῖν

63   πάροικοί ἐσμεν ὡς **τοῦτο** ἐν τῇ γῇ ἡμετέρᾳ νομιζομένῃ

οὕτως

49   τοῖς υἱοῖς σου **οὕτως** ἔντειλον ἵνα ποιήσουσιν κατὰ τὴν κρίσιν ταύτην

50   **οὕτως** γάρ μοι ἐνετείλατο ὁ πατὴρ Ἀβραὰμ ποιεῖν

52   κατὰ τὸν λογισμὸν τῶν ξυλῶν ἐπιδέχου **οὕτως**, ὡς σοὶ ἐντέλλομαι

57   **οὕτως** γάρ μοι ἐνετείλατο ὁ πατήρ μου Ἀβραάμ

57   ὅτι **οὕτως** εὗρεν ἐν τῇ γραφῇ τῆς βίβλου τοῦ Νῶε περὶ τοῦ αἵματος

ὀφθαλμός, ὁ

1a v. 3   τότε τοὺς **ὀφθαλμούς** μου καὶ τὸ πρόσωπόν μου ἦρα πρὸς τὸν οὐρανόν

παιδάριον, τό

64   ἐπὶ τοῦ **παιδαρίου** εἶδον ἐγὼ ἐν τῷ ὁράματί μου ὅτι ἐκβεβλημένος ἔσται

παῖς, ὁ

1a v. 15a   καὶ μὴ ἀποστρέψῃς τὸ πρόσωπόν σου ἀπὸ τοῦ υἱοῦ **παιδός** σου Ἰακώβ

1a v. 17   εἰσάκουσον δὲ καὶ τῆς φωνῆς τοῦ **παιδός** (עבד) σου Λευὶ

1a v. 19   καὶ μὴ ἀποστήσῃς τὸν υἱὸν τοῦ **παιδός** (עבד) σου ἀπὸ τοῦ προσώπου
          σου

πάλιν

20   καὶ ὅταν ἐνδιδύσκῃ, νίπτου **πάλιν** (חוב) τὰς χεῖράς σου

21   **πάλιν** (עוד) νίπτου τὰς χεῖράς σου καὶ τοὺς πόδας σου

26   καὶ **πάλιν** (עוד) νίψαι σου τὰς χεῖρας καὶ τοὺς πόδας ἀπὸ τοῦ αἵματος

66   καὶ **πάλιν** συλλαβοῦσα ἔτεκεν ἐξ ἐμοῦ

69a   καὶ **πάλιν** (עוד) συνεγενόμην αὐτῇ καὶ ἐν γαστρὶ ἔλαβεν

παραδίδωμι

1a v. 13   **παράδος** διὸ δὴ καὶ τὴν ἀνομίαν ἐξάλειψον ὑποκάτωθεν τοῦ οὐρανοῦ

παραλαμβάνω

52   ὅταν **παραλαμβάνῃς** θυσίαν ποιεῖν ἔναντι κυρίου

πάροικος, ον

63   εἶπα γὰρ ὅτι **πάροικον** ἔσται τὸ σπέρμα μου ἐν γῇ, ᾗ ἐγεννήθην

63   **πάροικοί** ἐσμεν ὡς τοῦτο ἐν τῇ γῇ ἡμετέρᾳ νομιζομένῃ

πᾶς, πᾶσα, πᾶν

1a v. 2   καὶ **πάσας** (לכ) τὰς ὁδούς μου ἐποίησα εὐθείας

1a v. 5   Κύριε, γινώσκεις **πάσας** τὰς καρδίας

1a v. 5   καὶ **πάντας** τοὺς διαλογισμοὺς ἐννοιῶν σὺ μόνος ἐπίστασαι

1a v. 6   καὶ δός μοι **πάσας** ὁδοὺς ἀληθείας

1a v. 10   καὶ μὴ κατισχυσάτω με πᾶς **σου** (לכ) σατανᾶς πλανῆσαί με ἀπὸ τῆς ὁδοῦ

1a v. 12   καὶ σκέπη σου τῆς δυναστείας σκεπασάτω με ἀπὸ **παντὸς** κακοῦ

1a v. 18   ποιεῖν κρίσιν ἀληθινὴν εἰς **πάντα** (לכ) τὸν αἰῶνα

1a v. 18   ἐμὲ καὶ τοὺς υἱούς μου εἰς **πάσας** τὰς γενεὰς τῶν αἰώνων

1a v. 19   ἀπὸ τοῦ προσώπου σου **πάσας** τὰς ἡμέρας τοῦ αἰῶνος

12   καὶ εἶδεν Ἰσαὰκ ὁ πατὴρ ἡμῶν **πάντας** (לכ) ἡμᾶς

14   Τέκνον Λευί, πρόσεχε σεαυτῷ ἀπὸ **πάσης** (לכ) ἀκαθαρσίας

14   ἡ κρίσις σου μεγάλη ἀπὸ **πάσης** (לכ) σαρκός

15   καὶ οὐ μὴ κρύψω ἀπὸ σου **πᾶν** (לכ) ῥῆμα

16   πρόσεχε σεαυτῷ ἀπὸ **παντὸς** (לכ) συνουσιασμοῦ

16   καὶ ἀπὸ **πάσης** ἀκαθαρσίας

16   καὶ ἀπὸ **πάσης** (לכ) πορνείας

18   γίνου καθαρὸς ἐν τῷ σώματί σου ἀπὸ **πάσης** (לכ) ἀκαθαρσίας

18   ἀπὸ πάσης ἀκαθαρσίας **παντὸς** (לכ) ἀνθρώπου

22   ἐπισκοπῶν αὐτὰ πρῶτον ἀπὸ **παντὸς** μολυσμοῦ

29   καὶ **πάντα** (לכ) ἡλισμένα ἐν ἅλατι ὡς καθήκει αὐτοῖς αὐτάρκως

30   καὶ **πᾶσα** (לכ) προσφορά σου εἰς εὐδόκησιν καὶ ὀσμὴν εὐωδίας

45   καὶ **πᾶσα** ἡ σεμίδαλις ἀναπεποιημένη

48   οἱ λόγοι μου οὗτοι ἀπὸ τῆς καρδίας σου ἐν **πάσαις** ταῖς ἡμέραις σου

49   καὶ ἱερεῖς ἔσονται **πᾶν** τὸ σπέρμα σου

52   παραλαμβάνῃς θυσίαν ποιεῖν ἔναντι κυρίου ἀπὸ **πάσης** σαρκός

52   καὶ τὸν λίβανον ἐπιδέχου ἐκ τῶν χειρῶν αὐτῶν ἐπὶ **πάντα** κτήνη

53   καὶ ἐπὶ **πᾶσαν** ὥραν νίπτου τὰς χεῖρας καὶ τοὺς πόδας

53   καὶ ὅταν ἐκπορεύῃς ἐκ τῶν ἁγίων, **πᾶν** αἷμα μὴ ἁπτέσθω τῆς στολῆς σου

54   καὶ τοὺς πόδας νίπτου διὰ **παντὸς** ἀπὸ πάσης σαρκός

54   καὶ τοὺς πόδας νίπτου διὰ παντὸς ἀπὸ **πάσης** σαρκός

55   καὶ μὴ ὀφθήτω ἐπὶ σοι **πᾶν** αἷμα καὶ πᾶσα ψυχή

55   καὶ μὴ ὀφθήτω ἐπὶ σοι πᾶν αἷμα καὶ **πᾶσα** ψυχή

56   καὶ ὃ ἐὰν ἐν οἴκῳ †ουσης† σεαυτὸν **πᾶν** κρέας φαγεῖν

58   καὶ ἠγαπημένος ἔσῃ ὑπὲρ **πάντας** τοὺς ἀδελφούς σου

59   καὶ τὸ σπέρμα σου ἕως **πάντων** τῶν αἰώνων ἐνεχθήσεται ἐν Βιβλίῳ

61   εὐλογημένον ἔσται τὸ σπέρμα σου ἐπὶ τῆς γῆς εἰς **πάσας** τὰς γενεὰς
67   ὅτι ἐπ᾽ αὐτῷ ἔσται ἡ συναγωγὴ **παντὸς** (כל) τοῦ λαοῦ
πατήρ, ὁ
1a v. 15b   σύ, κύριε, εὐλόγησας τὸν Ἀβραὰμ **πατέρα** μου
11   καὶ κατελύσαμεν ἐν τῇ αὐλῇ Ἀβραὰμ τοῦ **πατρὸς** (אב) ἡμῶν
11   παρὰ Ἰσαὰκ τὸν **πατέρα** (אב) ἡμῶν
12   καὶ εἶδεν Ἰσαὰκ ὁ πατὴρ (אב) ἡμῶν πάντας ἡμᾶς
50   οὕτως γάρ μοι ἐνετείλατο ὁ **πατὴρ** Ἀβραὰμ ποιεῖν
57   οὕτως γάρ μοι ἐνετείλατο ὁ **πατήρ** μου Ἀβραάμ
58   ἠγαπημένος σὺ τῷ **πατρί** σου καὶ ἅγιος κυρίου ὑψίστου
62   ἐκ τῆς συγγενείας Ἀβραὰμ τοῦ **πατρός** μου, Μελχάν, θυγατέρα
πέντε, οἱ, αἱ, τά
32   πεντήκοντα μνᾶς, καὶ εἰς τὸ στέαρ αὐτοῦ μόνον **πέντε** μνᾶς
38   καὶ τῷ ταύρῳ τῷ δευτέρῳ τὰ **πέντε** μέρη
πεντήκοντα, οἱ, αἱ, τά
32   **πεντήκοντα** μνᾶς, καὶ εἰς τὸ στέαρ αὐτοῦ μόνον πέντε μνᾶς
περί
57   ὅτι οὕτως εὗρεν ἐν τῇ γραφῇ τῆς βίβλου τοῦ Νῶε **περὶ** τοῦ αἵματος
περισσεύω
31   καὶ μὴ **περισσεύσῃς** (אותר) μηθὲν ὅσα οὐ καθήκει
37   καὶ ᾧ ἂν **περισσεύσῃ** τοῦ ἁλός, ἅλισον ἐν αὐτῷ τὸ δέρμα
πίτυς, ἡ
24   καὶ σχῖνον καὶ στρόβιλον καὶ **πίτυν** (שוחא) καὶ ολδινα καὶ βερωθα
πλανάω
1a v. 10   μὴ κατισχυσάτω με πᾶς σατανᾶς **πλανῆσαί** με ἀπὸ τῆς ὁδοῦ σου
πλευρά, ἡ
28   μετὰ ταῦτα τὸ στῆθος μετὰ τῶν **πλευρῶν** (בן דפנה)
πλύνω
1a v. 1   τότε ἐγὼ **ἔπλυνα** τὰ ἱμάτιά μου, καὶ καθαρίσας αὐτα
28   τοὺς πόδας **πεπλυμένους** (רחץ) σὺν τοῖς ἐνδοσθίοις
πνεῦμα, τό
1a v. 7   μάκρυνον ἀπ᾽ ἐμοῦ, κύριε, τὸ **πνεῦμα** τὸ ἄδικον
1a v. 8   δειχθήτω μοι, δέσποτα, τὸ **πνεῦμα** τὸ ἅγιον
ποιέω
1a v. 2   καὶ πάσας τὰς ὁδούς μου **ἐποίησα** εὐθείας
1a v. 9   **ποιῆσαι** τὰ ἀρέσκοντά σοι καὶ εὑρεῖν χάριν ἐνώπιόν σου
1a v. 18   καὶ μέτοχον **ποίησον** τοῖς λόγοις σου
1a v. 18   **ποιεῖν** κρίσιν ἀληθινὴν εἰς πάντα τὸν αἰῶνα
31   καὶ ὅσα ἂν **ποιῇς** (עבד), ἐν τάξει ποίει ἃ ποιῇς ἐν μέτρῳ καὶ στάθμῳ
31   καὶ ὅσα ἂν ποιῇς, ἐν τάξει **ποίει** (עבד) ἃ ποιῇς ἐν μέτρῳ καὶ στάθμῳ
31   καὶ ὅσα ἂν ποιῇς, ἐν τάξει ποίει ἃ **ποιῇς** ἐν μέτρῳ καὶ στάθμῳ
49   ἔντειλον ἵνα **ποιήσουσιν** κατὰ τὴν κρίσιν ταύτην ὡς σοὶ ὑπέδειξα
50   οὕτως γάρ μοι ἐνετείλατο ὁ πατὴρ Ἀβραὰμ **ποιεῖν**

51   ὡς καθήκει κατὰ τὸ προστεταγμένον τοῦτο **ποιεῖν**
52   ὅταν παραλαμβάνῃς θυσίαν **ποιεῖν** ἔναντι κυρίου ἀπὸ πάσης σαρκός
πολύς, πολλή, πολύ
17   καὶ μὴ βεβηλώσῃς τὸ σπέρμα σου μετὰ †**πολλῶν**†
πονηρός, ά, όν
1a v. 7   καὶ διαλογισμὸν τὸν **πονηρὸν** (באיש) καὶ πορνείαν, καὶ ὕβριν ἀπόσ-
          τρεψον
πορεύομαι
53   νίπτου τὰς χεῖρας καὶ τοὺς πόδας, ὅταν **πορεύῃ** πρὸς τὸ θυσιαστήριον
πορνεία, ἡ
1a v. 7   καὶ **πορνείαν** (וזנוא), καὶ ὕβριν ἀπόστρεψον ἀπ᾽ ἐμοῦ
16   ἀπὸ πάσης ἀκαθαρσίας καὶ ἀπὸ πάσης **πορνείας** (זנות)
πούς, ὁ
20   νίπτου πάλιν τὰς χεῖράς σου καὶ τοὺς **πόδας** (רגל) σου
21   πάλιν νίπτου τὰς χεῖράς σου καὶ τοὺς **πόδας** (רגל) σου
26   καὶ πάλιν νίψαι σου τὰς χεῖρας καὶ τοὺς **πόδας** (רגל)
28   καὶ μετὰ ταῦτα τοὺς **πόδας** (רגל) πεπλυμένους σὺν τοῖς ἐνδοσθίοις
53   νίπτου τὰς χεῖρας καὶ τοὺς **πόδας**, ὅταν πορεύῃ πρὸς τὸ θυσιαστήριον
54   καὶ τὰς χεῖρας καὶ τοὺς **πόδας** νίπτου διὰ παντὸς
πρὶν ἤ
56   κάλυπτε τὸ αἷμα αὐτοῦ τῇ γῇ πρῶτον **πρὶν ἤ** φαγεῖν σε ἀπὸ τῶν κρεῶν
πρό
20   **πρὸ** (עד) τοῦ ἐγγίσαι τρὸς τὸν βωμὸν προσενέγκαι ὁλοκάρπωσιν
πρόβατον, τό
34   καὶ εἰ κριὸς ἐκ **προβάτων** ἢ τράγος ἐξ αἰγῶν τὸ προσφερόμενον ᾖ
35   καὶ εἰ ἄρνα ἐκ **προβάτων** ἢ ἔριφον ἐξ αἰγῶν κ΄ μναῖ
πρός
1a v. 3   καὶ τὸ πρόσωπόν μου ᾖρα **πρὸς** (ל) τὸν οὐρανόν
1a v. 14 ἀπὸ πάσης ἀκαθαρσίας, καὶ προσαροῦμαι **πρὸς** (ל?) σε αὐτὸς
20   πρὸ τοῦ ἐγγίσαι **τρὸς** (ל) τὸν βωμὸν προσενέγκαι ὁλοκάρπωσιν
53   νίπτου τὰς χεῖρας καὶ τοὺς πόδας, ὅταν πορεύῃ **πρὸς** τὸ θυσιασ-
          τήριον
προσάγω
1a v. 11 καὶ ἐλέησόν με καὶ **προσάγαγέ** (קרב) με εἶναί σου δοῦλος
46a   ἢ<ν> ἂν **προσαγάγῃς** μόνον, οὐκ ἐπὶ στέατος
46a   **προσαχθήσεται** ἐπ᾽ αὐτὴν λιβάνου ὁλκὴ σίκλων δύο
προσαίρω
1a v. 14 ἀπὸ πάσης ἀκαθαρσίας, καὶ **προσαροῦμαι** πρὸς σε αὐτὸς
προσέχω
14   Τέκνον Λευί, **πρόσεχε** (האזר) σεαυτῷ ἀπὸ πάσης ἀκαθαρσίας
16   **πρόσεχε** (הזהר) σεαυτῷ ἀπὸ παντὸς συνουσιασμοῦ
προστάσσω
51   ὡς καθήκει κατὰ τὸ **προστεταγμένον** τοῦτο ποιεῖν

προσφέρω

20	πρὸ τοῦ ἐγγίσαι τρὸς τὸν βωμὸν **προσενέγκαι** ὁλοκάρπωσιν
21	καὶ ὅταν μέλλῃς **προσφέρειν** (הקרב) ὅσα δεῖ ἀνενέγκαι ἐπὶ τὸν βωμόν
23	ιβʹ ξύλα εἴρηκεν μοι ἐπὶ τὸν βωμὸν **προσφέρε<ιν>**
34	εἰ κριὸς ἐκ προβάτων ἢ τράγος ἐξ αἰγῶν τὸ **προσφερόμενον** ἢ
51	ἐξελέχθης εἰς ἱερωσύνην ἁγίαν καὶ **προσενεγκεῖν** θυσίαν κυρίῳ ὑψίστῳ

προσφορά, ἡ

30	ἢ τὸ ἔργον σου ἐν τάξει καὶ πᾶσα **προσφορά** (קורבן) σου εἰς εὐδόκησιν

πρόσωπον, τό

1a v. 3	καὶ τὸ **πρόσωπόν** μου ἦρα πρὸς τὸν οὐρανόν
1a v. 13	καὶ συντελέσαι τὴν ἀνομίαν ἀπὸ **προσώπου** τῆς γῆς
1a v. 15a	καὶ μὴ ἀποστρέψῃς τὸ **πρόσωπόν** σου ἀπὸ τοῦ υἱοῦ παιδός σου Ἰακώβ
1a v. 19	μὴ ἀποστήσῃς τὸν υἱὸν τοῦ παιδός σου ἀπὸ τοῦ **προσώπου** σου (קדמיך)

πρῶτον

19	λούου ὕδατι **πρῶτον** καὶ τότε ἐνδιδύσκου τὴν στολὴν τῆς ἱερωσύνης·
22	καὶ ἀνάφερε τὰ ξύλα **πρῶτον** <ἐ>σχισμένα
22	ἐπισκοπῶν αὐτὰ **πρῶτον** (לקדמין) ἀπὸ παντὸς μολυσμοῦ
27	τὴν κεφαλὴν ἀνάφερε **πρῶτον** (לקדמין) καὶ κάλυπτε αὐτὴν τῷ στέατι
56	κάλυπτε τὸ αἷμα αὐτοῦ τῇ γῇ **πρῶτον** πρὶν ἢ φαγεῖν σε ἀπὸ τῶν κρεῶν

πρῶτος, η, ον

17	σὺ †**πρῶτος**† ἀπὸ τοῦ σπέρματος λάβε σεαυτῷ
63	καὶ ἐν γαστρὶ λαβοῦσα ἐξ ἐμοῦ ἔτεκεν υἱὸν **πρῶτον**
68	ἐν τῷ τετάρτῳ καὶ λʹ ἔτει ἐγεννήθη ἐν τῷ **πρώτῳ** (קמאה) μηνὶ

πῦρ, τό

25b	καὶ τὸ **πῦρ** (נורא) τότε ἄρξῃ ἐκκαίειν ἐν αὐτοῖς

ῥῆμα, τό

15	καὶ οὐ μὴ κρύψω ἀπό σου πᾶν **ῥῆμα** (פתגם)

σάρξ, ἡ

14	ἡ κρίσις σου μεγάλη ἀπὸ πάσης **σαρκός** (בישרא)
52	παραλαμβάνῃς θυσίαν ποιεῖν ἔναντι κυρίου ἀπὸ πάσης **σαρκός**
54	καὶ τοὺς πόδας νίπτου διὰ παντὸς ἀπὸ πάσης **σαρκός**
55	τὸ γὰρ αἷμα ψυχή ἐστιν ἐν τῇ **σαρκί**

σατανᾶς, ὁ

1a v. 10	μὴ κατισχυσάτω με πᾶς **σατανᾶς** πλανῆσαί με ἀπὸ τῆς ὁδοῦ σου

σάτον, τό

37	καὶ ἀνένεγκε ἐπὶ τὸν βωμόν. **σάτον** καθήκει τῷ ταύρῳ
38	τὰ πέντε μέρη ἀπὸ τῶν ἓξ μερῶν τοῦ **σάτου**
38	καὶ τοῦ μόσχου τὸ δίμοιρον τοῦ **σάτου**
39	καὶ τῷ κριῷ τὸ ἥμισυ τοῦ **σάτου** καὶ τῷ τράγῳ τὸ ἴσον
40a	καὶ τῷ ἀρνίῳ καὶ τῷ ἐρίφῳ τὸ τρίτον τοῦ **σάτου**
41	τῷ ταύρῳ τῷ βʹ καὶ τῷ μοσχαρίῳ, **σάτον** σεμίδαλιν
42	καὶ τῷ κριῷ καὶ τῷ τράγῳ τὰ δύο μέρη τοῦ **σάτου**
42	καὶ τῷ ἀρνίῳ καὶ τῷ ἐρίφῳ ἐξ αἰγῶν τὸ τρίτον τοῦ **σάτου**

43 καὶ τὸ τέταρτον τοῦ **σάτου** τῷ ταύρῳ ἀναπεποιημένον ἐν τῇ σεμιδάλει
44 καὶ τῷ κριῷ τὸ ἕκτον τοῦ **σάτου**
44 καὶ τῷ ἀρνίῳ τὸ ὄγδοον τοῦ **σάτου** καὶ ἀμνοῦ
46b καὶ τὸ τρίτον τοῦ **σάτου** τὸ τρίτον τοῦ ὑφή ἐστιν

σεαυτοῦ, -ῆς
14 Τέκνον Λευί, πρόσεχε **σεαυτῷ** (לך) ἀπὸ πάσης ἀκαθαρσίας
16 πρόσεχε **σεαυτῷ** (לך) ἀπὸ παντὸς συνουσιασμοῦ
17 σὺ †πρῶτος† ἀπὸ τοῦ σπέρματος λάβε **σεαυτῷ** (לך)
56 καὶ ὃ ἐάν ἐν οἴκῳ †ουσης† **σεαυτὸν** πᾶν κρέας φαγεῖν

σεμίδαλις, ἡ
30 καὶ μετὰ ταῦτα **σεμίδαλιν** (ונשיא) ἀναπεποιημένον ἐν ἐλαίῳ
40b καὶ **σεμίδαλις** καθήκουσα αὐτοῖς
41 καὶ τῷ ταύρῳ τῷ βʹ καὶ τῷ μοσχαρίῳ, σάτον **σεμίδαλιν**
43 τῷ ταύρῳ ἀναπεποιημένον ἐν τῇ **σεμιδάλει** ταύτῃ
45 καὶ πᾶσα ἡ **σεμίδαλις** ἀναπεποιημένη
52 καὶ τὸ ἅλας καὶ τὴν **σεμίδαλιν** καὶ τὸν οἶνον

σίκλος, ὁ
45 λιβανωτοῦ **σίκλοι** ἓξ τῷ ταύρῳ καὶ τὸ ἥμισυ αὐτοῦ τῷ κριῷ
46a προσαχθήσεται ἐπʼ αὐτὴν λιβάνου ὁλκὴ **σίκλων** δύο
47 τὰ δύο μέρη τοῦ βάτου καὶ ὁλκῆς τῆς μνᾶς νʹ **σίκλων** ἐστίν
47 γίνεται ὁ **σίκλος** ὡσεὶ ιϛʹ θέρμοι καὶ ὁλκῆς μιᾶς

σικλίον, τό
47 καὶ τοῦ **σικλίου** τὸ τέταρτον ὁλκὴ θερμῶν δʹ ἐστίν

σιωπάω
1a v. 19 πάσας τὰς ἡμέρας τοῦ αἰῶνος. καὶ **ἐσιώπησα** ἔτι δεόμενος

σκεπάζω
1a v. 12 καὶ σκέπη σου τῆς δυναστείας **σκεπασάτω** με ἀπὸ παντὸς κακοῦ.

σκέπη, ἡ
1a v. 12 καὶ **σκέπη** σου τῆς δυναστείας σκεπασάτω με ἀπὸ παντὸς κακοῦ

σοφία, ἡ
1a v. 8 καὶ βουλὴν καὶ **σοφίαν** (חכמה) καὶ γνῶσιν καὶ ἰσχὺν δός μοι

σπένδω
30 καὶ μετὰ ταῦτα οἶνον **σπεῖσον** (נסך) καὶ θυμίασον ἐπάνω λίβανον

σπέρμα, τό
1a v. 16 εἶπας δοῦναι αὐτοῖς **σπέρμα** (זרע) δίκαιον εὐλογημένον εἰς τοὺς αἰῶνας
17 σὺ †πρῶτος† ἀπὸ τοῦ **σπέρματος** (זרע) λάβε σεαυτω
17 καὶ μὴ βεβηλώσῃς τὸ **σπέρμα** (זרע) σου μετὰ †πολλῶν†
17 ἐκ **σπέρματος** (זרע) γὰρ ἁγίου εἶ
17 καὶ τὸ **σπέρμα** (זרע) σου ἁγίασον
17 καὶ τὸ **σπέρμα** τοῦ ἁγιασμοῦ σου ἐστίν
17 ἱερεὺς ἅγιος κληθήσεται τῷ **σπέρματι** Ἀβραάμ
49 καὶ ἱερεῖς ἔσονται πᾶν τὸ **σπέρμα** σου
59 τῷ **σπέρματί** σου εὐλογηθήσεται ἐν τῇ γῇ

59   καὶ τὸ **σπέρμα** σου ἕως πάντων τῶν αἰώνων ἐνεχθήσεται ἐν Βιβλίῳ
60   οὐκ ἐξαλειφθήσεται τὸ ὄνομά σου καὶ τὸ ὄνομα τοῦ **σπέρματός** σου
61   εὐλογημένον ἔσται τὸ **σπέρμα** σου ἐπὶ τῆς γῆς
63   εἶπα γὰρ ὅτι πάροικον ἔσται τὸ **σπέρμα** μου ἐν γῇ, ᾗ ἐγεννήθην
64   ἐκβεβλημένος ἔσται αὐτὸς καὶ τὸ **σπέρμα** αὐτοῦ ἀπὸ τῆς ἀρχῆς
64   ἔσται τὸ **σπέρμα** αὐτοῦ
67   αὐτὸς καὶ τὸ **σπέρμα** αὐτοῦ ἔσονται ἀρχὴ βασιλέων, ἱεράτευμα

σπονδή, ἡ
44   τῷ ταύρῳ καὶ τῷ κριῷ καὶ τῷ ἐρίφῳ κατασπεῖσαι **σπονδήν**

σταθμόν, τό
31   ἐν τάξει ποίει ἃ ποιῇς ἐν μέτρῳ καὶ **σταθμῷ** (מתקל)
32a   τῷ ταύρῳ τῷ τελείῳ τάλαντον ξύλων καθήκει αὐτῷ ἐν **σταθμῷ** (מתקל)

στέαρ, τό
27   τὴν κεφαλὴν ἀνάφερε πρῶτον καὶ κάλυπτε αὐτὴν τῷ **στέατι** (תרב)
32a   καὶ εἰς τὸ στέαρ (תרב) μόνον ἀναφέρεσθαι ἓξ μνᾶς
32b   πεντήκοντα μνᾶς, καὶ εἰς τὸ **στέαρ** αὐτοῦ μόνον πέντε μνᾶς
34   καὶ τούτῳ λ΄ μναῖ, καὶ τῷ **στέατι** τρεῖς μναῖ
35   ἢ ἔριφον ἐξ αἰγῶν κ΄ μναῖ, καὶ τῷ **στέατι** β΄ μναῖ
36   ἢ ἔριφος ἐξ αἰγῶν ιε΄ μναῖ, καὶ τῷ **στέατι** μίαν ἥμισυ μνᾶν
46a   ἢ<ν> ἂν προσαγάγῃς μόνον, οὐκ ἐπὶ **στέατος**

στῆθος, τό
28   καὶ μετὰ ταῦτα τὸ **στῆθος** (נויא) μετὰ τῶν πλευρῶν

στολή, ἡ
19   καὶ τότε ἐνδιδύσκου τὴν **στολὴν** (לבוש) τῆς ἱερωσύνης
53   καὶ ὅταν ἐκπορεύῃς ἐκ τῶν ἁγίων, πᾶν αἷμα μὴ ἁπτέσθω τῆς **στολῆς**
          σου

στόμα, τό
1a v. 3   καὶ τὸ **στόμα** μου ἤνοιξα καὶ ἐλάλησα

στρόβιλος, ὁ
24   καὶ ουεδεφωνα καὶ σχῖνον καὶ **στρόβιλον** (†אשׁולא†) καὶ πίτυν

σύ
1a v. 5   καὶ πάντας τοὺς διαλογισμοὺς ἐννοιῶν **σὺ** μόνος ἐπίστασαι
1a v. 15b **σύ**, κύριε, εὐλογήσας τὸν Ἀβραὰμ πατέρα μου
17   **σὺ** †πρῶτος† ἀπὸ τοῦ σπέρματος λάβε σεαυτῷ
18   ἐγγὺς εἶ κυρίου καὶ **σὺ** ἐγγὺς τῶν ἁγίων αὐτοῦ
48   ὅτι ἱερεὺς συ ἅγιος κυρίου
58   ἠγαπημένος **σὺ** τῷ πατρί σου καὶ ἅγιος κυρίου ὑψίστου
58   ἠγαπημένος σὺ τῷ πατρί **σου** καὶ ἅγιος κυρίου ὑψίστου

σου
1a v. 9   ποιῆσαι τὰ ἀρέσκοντά σοι καὶ εὑρεῖν χάριν ἐνώπιόν **σου**
1a v. 9   καὶ αἰνεῖν τοὺς λόγους **σου** μετ᾿ ἐμοῦ, κύριε
1a v. 10 μὴ κατισχυσάτω με πᾶς σατανᾶς πλανῆσαί με ἀπὸ τῆς ὁδοῦ **σου**
1a v. 11 καὶ ἐλέησόν με καὶ προσάγαγέ με εἶναί **σου** δοῦλος

1a v. 12	τεῖχος εἰρήνης **σου** γενέσθαι κύκλῳ μου	
1a v. 12	καὶ σκέπη **σου** τῆς δυναστείας σκεπασάτω με ἀπὸ παντὸς κακοῦ	
1a v. 15a	μὴ ἀποστρέψῃς τὸ πρόσωπόν **σου** ἀπὸ τοῦ υἱοῦ παιδός σου Ἰακώβ	
1a v. 15a	μὴ ἀποστρέψῃς τὸ πρόσωπόν σου ἀπὸ τοῦ υἱοῦ παιδός **σου** Ἰακώβ	
1a v. 17	εἰσάκουσον δὲ καὶ τῆς φωνῆς τοῦ παιδός **σου** Λευὶ	
1a v. 18	καὶ μέτοχον ποίησον τοῖς λόγοις **σου** ποιεῖν κρίσιν ἀληθινὴν	
1a v. 19	καὶ μὴ ἀποστήσῃς τὸν υἱὸν τοῦ παιδός **σου** ἀπὸ τοῦ προσώπου σου	
1a v. 19	καὶ μὴ ἀποστήσῃς τὸν υἱὸν τοῦ παιδός σου ἀπὸ τοῦ προσώπου **σου**	
14	ἡ κρίσις **σου** μεγάλη ἀπὸ πάσης σαρκός	
15	καὶ οὐ μὴ κρύψω ἀπό **σου** πᾶν ῥῆμα. διδάξω σε	
17	καὶ μὴ βεβηλώσῃς τὸ σπέρμα **σου** μετὰ †πολλῶν†	
17	ἐκ σπέρματος γὰρ ἁγίου εἶ, καὶ τὸ σπέρμα **σου** ἁγίασον	
17	καὶ τὸ σπέρμα τοῦ ἁγιασμοῦ **σου** ἐστίν	
18	γίνου καθαρὸς ἐν τῷ σώματί **σου** ἀπὸ πάσης ἀκαθαρσίας	
20	νίπτου πάλιν τὰς χεῖράς **σου** καὶ τοὺς πόδας σου	
20	νίπτου πάλιν τὰς χεῖράς σου καὶ τοὺς πόδας **σου**	
21	πάλιν νίπτου τὰς χεῖράς **σου** καὶ τοὺς πόδας σου	
21	πάλιν νίπτου τὰς χεῖράς σου καὶ τοὺς πόδας **σου**	
26	καὶ πάλιν νίψαι **σου** τὰς χεῖρας καὶ τοὺς πόδας ἀπὸ τοῦ αἵματος	
30	καὶ ᾖ τὸ ἔργον **σου** ἐν τάξει καὶ πᾶσα προσφορά σου εἰς εὐδόκησιν	
30	καὶ ᾖ τὸ ἔργον σου ἐν τάξει καὶ πᾶσα προσφορά **σου** εἰς εὐδόκησιν	
48	καὶ μὴ ἀποστήτωσαν οἱ λόγοι μου οὗτοι ἀπὸ τῆς καρδίας **σου**	
48	ἀπὸ τῆς καρδίας σου ἐν πάσαις ταῖς ἡμέραις **σου**	
49	καὶ ἱερεῖς ἔσονται πᾶν τὸ σπέρμα **σου**	
49	τοῖς υἱοῖς **σου** οὕτως ἔντειλον ἵνα ποιήσουσιν κατὰ τὴν κρίσιν ταύτην	
53	καὶ ὅταν ἐκπορεύῃς ἐκ τῶν ἁγίων, πᾶν αἷμα μὴ ἁπτέσθω τῆς στολῆς **σου**	
58	καὶ ἠγαπημένος ἔσῃ ὑπὲρ πάντας τοὺς ἀδελφούς **σου**	
59	τῷ σπέρματί **σου** εὐλογηθήσεται ἐν τῇ γῇ	
59	τὸ σπέρμα **σου** ἕως πάντων τῶν αἰώνων ἐνεχθήσεται ἐν Βιβλίῳ	
60	καὶ οὐκ ἐξαλειφθήσεται τὸ ὄνομά **σου** καὶ τὸ ὄνομα τοῦ σπέρματός σου	
60	καὶ οὐκ ἐξαλειφθήσεται τὸ ὄνομά σου καὶ τὸ ὄνομα τοῦ σπέρματός **σου**	
61	τέκνον Λευί, εὐλογημένον ἔσται τὸ σπέρμα **σου** ἐπὶ τῆς γῆς	

σοι

1a v. 9	ποιῆσαι τὰ ἀρέσκοντά **σοι** καὶ εὑρεῖν χάριν ἐνώπιόν σου	
1a v. 11	καὶ λατρεῦσαί **σοι** καλῶς	
1a v. 17	εἰσάκουσον δὲ καὶ τῆς φωνῆς τοῦ παιδός σου Λευὶ γενέσθαι **σοι** ἐγγύς	
15	καὶ νῦν τὴν κρίσιν τῆς ἀληθείας ἀναγγελῶ **σοι**	
49	ἵνα ποιήσουσιν κατὰ τὴν κρίσιν ταύτην ὡς **σοὶ** ὑπέδειξα	
55	καὶ μὴ ὀφθήτω ἐπὶ **σοὶ** πᾶν αἷμα καὶ πᾶσα ψυχή	
58	καὶ νῦν ὡς **σοί**, τέκνον ἀγαπητόν, ἐγὼ λέγω	

σε

1a v. 14 ἀπὸ πάσης ἀκαθαρσίας, καὶ προσαροῦμαι πρὸς **σε** αὐτὸς

15 καὶ οὐ μὴ κρύψω ἀπό σου πᾶν ῥῆμα. διδάξω **σε**

25a εἴρηκεν ὅτι ταῦτά ἐστιν ἅ **σε** ἀναφέρειν ὑποκάτω τῆς ὁλοκαυτώσεως

56 κάλυπτε τὸ αἷμα αὐτοῦ τῇ γῇ πρῶτον πρὶν ἢ φαγεῖν **σε** ἀπὸ τῶν κρεῶν

συγγένεια, ἡ

62 ἔλαβον γυναῖκα ἐμαυτῷ ἐκ τῆς **συγγενείας** Ἀβραὰμ

συγγίνομαι

69a καὶ πάλιν **συνεγενόμην** αὐτῇ καὶ ἐν γαστρὶ ἔλαβεν

συλλαμβάνω

66 καὶ πάλιν **συλλαβοῦσα** ἔτεκεν ἐξ ἐμοῦ κατὰ τὸν καιρὸν τὸν καθήκοντα

σύν

28 καὶ μετὰ ταῦτα τὴν ὀσφὺν **σὺν** (עם) τῷ νώτω

28 καὶ μετὰ ταῦτα τοὺς πόδας πεπλυμένους **σὺν** (עם) τοῖς ἐνδοσθίοις

συναγωγή, ἡ

67 ἑώρακα ὅτι ἐπ᾽ αὐτῷ ἔσται ἡ **συναγωγὴ** (כנשת) παντὸς τοῦ λαου~

συνουσιασμός, ὁ

16 πρόσεχε σεαυτῷ ἀπὸ παντὸς **συνουσιασμοῦ** (פחז)

συντελέω

1a v. 13 καὶ **συντελέσαι** τὴν ἀνομίαν ἀπὸ προσώπου τῆς γῆς

σχίζω

22 καὶ ἀνάφερε τὰ ξύλα πρῶτον <ἐ>**σχισμένα** (הצלה)

σχῖνος, ἡ

24 καὶ ταῦτα τὰ ὀνόματα αὐτῶν· κέδρον καὶ ουεδεφωνα καὶ **σχῖνον**
(סנדא)

σῶμα, τό

18 γίνου καθαρὸς ἐν τῷ **σώματί** (בשר) σου ἀπὸ πάσης ἀκαθαρσίας

τάλαντον, τό

32a τῷ ταύρῳ τῷ τελείῳ **τάλαντον** (ככר) ξύλων καθήκει αὐτῷ

τάξις, ἡ

30 καὶ ᾗ ᾖ τὸ ἔργον σου ἐν **τάξει** (סדר) καὶ πᾶσα προσφορά σου εἰς εὐδόκησιν

31 καὶ ὅσα ἂν ποιῇς, ἐν **τάξει** (סדר) ποίει ἃ ποιῇς ἐν μέτρῳ καὶ στάθμῳ

ταῦρος, ὁ

32a τῷ **ταύρῳ** (הוֹר) τῷ τελείῳ τάλαντον ξύλων καθήκει αὐτῷ

32a ἀναφέρεσθαι ἐξ μνᾶς· καὶ τῷ **ταύρῳ** (פר?) τῷ δευτέρῳ

37 καὶ ἅλας ἀποδέδεικται τῷ **ταύρῳ** τῷ μεγάλῳ, ἅλισε τὸ κρέας αὐτοῦ

37 σάτον καθήκει τῷ **ταύρῳ**· καὶ ᾧ ἂν περισσεύσῃ τοῦ ἁλός, ἅλισον

38 καὶ τῷ **ταύρῳ** τῷ δευτέρῳ τὰ πέντε μέρη ἀπὸ τῶν ἓξ μερῶν τοῦ σάτου

41 τῷ **ταύρῳ** τῷ μεγάλῳ καὶ τῷ ταύρῳ τῷ β΄ καὶ τῷ μοσχαρίῳ

41 τῷ ταύρῳ τῷ μεγάλῳ καὶ τῷ **ταύρῳ** τῷ β΄ καὶ τῷ μοσχαρίῳ

43 τὸ τέταρτον τοῦ σάτου τῷ **ταύρῳ** ἀναπεποιημένον ἐν τῇ σεμιδάλει

44 τῷ **ταύρῳ** καὶ τῷ κριῷ καὶ τῷ ἐρίφῳ κατασπεῖσαι σπονδὴν

45 λιβανωτοῦ σίκλοι ἐξ τῷ **ταύρῳ** καὶ τὸ ἥμισυ αὐτοῦ τῷ κριῷ

τεῖχος, τό

1a v. 12	**τεῖχος** εἰρήνης σου γενέσθαι κύκλῳ μου, καὶ σκέπη σου τῆς δυναστείας
25b	τότε ἄρξῃ κατασπένδειν τὸ αἷμα ἐπὶ τὸν **τεῖχον** (כותל) τοῦ θυσιαστηρίου

τέκνον, τό

1a v. 6	καὶ νῦν **τέκνα** μου μετ᾽ ἐμοῦ. καὶ δός μοι πάσας ὁδοὺς ἀληθείας
14	**Τέκνον** (בר) Λευί, πρόσεχε σεαυτῷ ἀπὸ πάσης ἀκαθαρσίας
48	**τέκνον** μου, ἄκουσον τοὺς λόγους μου καὶ ἐνωτίσαι τὰς ἐντολάς μου
51	καὶ νῦν, **τέκνον**, χαίρω ὅτι ἐξελέχθης εἰς ἱερωσύνην ἁγίαν
58	σοί, **τέκνον** ἀγαπητόν, ἐγὼ λέγω, ἠγαπημένος σὺ τῷ πατρί σου
61	

τέλειος, α, ον

32a	τῷ ταύρῳ τῷ **τελείῳ** τάλαντον ξύλων καθήκει αὐτῷ ἐν σταθμῷ
33	καὶ εἰς μόσχον **τέλειον** μ΄ μναῖ· καὶ εἰ κριὸς ἐκ προβάτων
36	καὶ εἰ ἀμνὸς **τέλειος** ἐνιαύσιος ἢ ἔριφος ἐξ αἰγῶν

τέσσαρες, αἱ

62	ἀνεπληρώθησάν μοι ἑβδομάδες **τέσσαρες** ἐν τοῖς ἔτεσιν τῆς ζωῆς μου

τέταρτος, η, ον

43	καὶ τὸ **τέταρτον** τοῦ σάτου τῷ ταύρῳ ἀναπεποιημένον ἐν τῇ σεμιδάλει
47	καὶ τοῦ σικλίου τὸ **τέταρτον** ὁλκὴ θερμῶν δ΄ ἐστίν

τίκτω

63	καὶ ἐν γαστρὶ λαβοῦσα ἐξ ἐμοῦ **ἔτεκεν** υἱὸν πρῶτον
66	καὶ πάλιν συλλαβοῦσα **ἔτεκεν** ἐξ ἐμοῦ κατὰ τὸν καιρὸν τὸν καθήκοντα
69a	καὶ ἐν γαστρὶ ἔλαβεν, καὶ **ἔτεκέν** (יליד) μοι υἱὸν τρίτον

τότε

1a v. 1	**τότε** ἐγὼ ἔπλυνα τὰ ἱμάτιά μου, καὶ καθαρίσας αὐτὰ ἐν ὕδατι καθαρῷ
1a v. 3	**τότε** τοὺς ὀφθαλμούς μου καὶ τὸ πρόσωπόν μου ἦρα πρὸς τὸν οὐρανόν
19	λούου ὕδατι πρῶτον καὶ **τότε** (באדין) ἐνδιδύσκου τὴν στολὴν
25b	καὶ τὸ πῦρ **τότε** ἄρξῃ ἐκκαίειν ἐν αὐτοῖς
25b	**τότε** (באדין) ἄρξῃ κατασπένδειν τὸ αἷμα ἐπὶ τὸν τεῖχον τοῦ θυσιαστηρίου

τράγος, ὁ

34	καὶ εἰ κριὸς ἐκ προβάτων ἢ **τράγος** ἐξ αἰγῶν τὸ προσφερόμενον ἦ
39	καὶ τῷ κριῷ τὸ ἥμισυ τοῦ σάτου καὶ τῷ **τράγῳ** τὸ ἴσον
42	καὶ τῷ κριῷ καὶ τῷ **τράγῳ** τὰ δύο μέρη τοῦ σάτου καὶ τῷ ἀρνίῳ

τράχηλος, ὁ

28	καὶ μετὰ τοῦτο τὸν **τράχηλον** (צואדה), καὶ μετὰ τοῦτο τοὺς ὤμους

τρίτος, η, ον

40a	καὶ τὸ ἀρνίῳ καὶ τῷ ἐρίφῳ τὸ **τρίτον** τοῦ σάτου
42	καὶ τῷ ἀρνίῳ καὶ τῷ ἐρίφῳ ἐξ αἰγῶν τὸ **τρίτον** τοῦ σάτου. καὶ τὸ ἔλαιον
45	καὶ τὸ ἥμισυ αὐτοῦ τῷ κριῷ καὶ τὸ **τρίτον** αὐτοῦ τῷ ἐρίφῳ
69a	καὶ ἐν γαστρὶ ἔλαβεν, καὶ ἔτεκέν μοι υἱὸν

τρίτον (תליתי)

ὕβρις, ἡ

1a v. 7   καὶ διαλογισμὸν τὸν πονηρὸν καὶ πορνείαν, καὶ **ὕβριν** ἀπόστρεψον

ὕδωρ, τό

1a v. 1   ἔπλυνα τὰ ἱμάτιά μου, καὶ καθαρίσας αὐτὰ ἐν **ὕδατι** καθαρῷ

1a v. 2   καὶ ὅλος ἐλουσάμην ἐν **ὕδατι** ζῶντι· καὶ πάσας τὰς ὁδούς μου

19   καὶ ὅταν εἰσπορεύῃ ἐν τοῖς ἁγίοις, λούου **ὕδατι** (מֵים) πρῶτον

υἱός, ὁ

1a v. 15a   καὶ μὴ ἀποστρέψῃς τὸ πρόσωπόν σου ἀπὸ τοῦ **υἱοῦ** παιδός σου

1a v. 18   ἐμὲ καὶ τοὺς **υἱούς** μου εἰς πάσας τὰς γενεὰς τῶν αἰώνων

1a v. 19   καὶ μὴ ἀποστήσῃς τὸν **υἱὸν** (בר) τοῦ παιδός σου ἀπὸ τοῦ προσώπου σου

49   τοῖς **υἱοῖς** σου οὕτως ἔντειλον ἵνα ποιήσουσιν κατὰ τὴν κρίσιν ταύτην

50   ἐνετείλατο ὁ πατὴρ Ἀβραὰμ ποιεῖν καὶ ἐντέλλεσθαι τοῖς **υἱοῖς** μου

62   Μελχάν, θυγατέρα Βαθουήλ, **υἱοῦ** Λάβαν, ἀδελφοῦ μητρός μου

63   καὶ ἐν γαστρὶ λαβοῦσα ἐξ ἐμοῦ ἔτεκεν **υἱὸν** πρῶτον

69a   καὶ ἔτεκέν μοι **υἱὸν** (בר) τρίτον, καὶ ἐκάλεσα τὸ ὄνομα αὐτοῦ Μεραρί

ὑπέρ

58   καὶ ἠγαπημένος ἔσῃ **ὑπὲρ** πάντας τοὺς ἀδελφούς σου

ὑποδείκνυμι

49   ἔντειλον ἵνα ποιήσουσιν κατὰ τὴν κρίσιν ταύτην ὡς σοὶ **ὑπέδειξα**

ὑποκάτω

25a   ταῦτά ἐστιν ἅ σε ἀναφέρειν **ὑποκάτω** (לתחת) τῆς ὁλοκαυτώσεως

ὑποκάτωθεν

1a v. 13   παράδος διὸ δὴ καὶ τὴν ἀνομίαν ἐξάλειψον **ὑποκάτωθεν** τοῦ οὐρανοῦ

ὑφή, ἡ

46b   καὶ τὸ τρίτον τοῦ σάτου τὸ τρίτον τοῦ **ὑφή** ἐστιν

φέρω

59   καὶ τὸ σπέρμα σου ἕως πάντων τῶν αἰώνων **ἐνεχθήσεται** ἐν Βιβλίῳ

φωνή, ἡ

1a v. 17   εἰσάκουσον δὲ καὶ τῆς **φωνῆς** τοῦ παιδός σου Λευὶ γενέσθαι σοι ἐγγύς

χαίρω

51   καὶ νῦν, τέκνον, **χαίρω** ὅτι ἐξελέχθης εἰς ἱερωσύνην ἁγίαν

χάρις, ἡ

1a v. 9   ποιῆσαι τὰ ἀρέσκοντά σοι καὶ εὑρεῖν **χάριν** (רחמין?) ἐνώπιόν σου

χείρ, ἡ

1a v. 4   καὶ τοὺς δακτύλους τῶν **χειρῶν** μου καὶ τὰς χεῖράς μου ἀνεπέτασα

1a v. 4   καὶ τοὺς δακτύλους τῶν χειρῶν μου καὶ τὰς **χεῖράς** (יד) μου ἀνεπέτασα

20   καὶ ὅταν ἐνδιδύσκῃ, νίπτου πάλιν τὰς **χεῖράς** (יד) σου

21   πάλιν νίπτου τὰς **χεῖράς** (יד) σου καὶ τοὺς πόδας σου

26   καὶ πάλιν νίψαι σου τὰς **χεῖρας** (יד) καὶ τοὺς πόδας ἀπὸ τοῦ αἵματος

52   καὶ τὸν λίβανον ἐπιδέχου ἐκ τῶν **χειρῶν** αὐτῶν ἐπὶ πάντα κτήνη

53   καὶ ἐπὶ πᾶσαν ὥραν νίπτου τὰς **χεῖρας** καὶ τοὺς πόδας

54   καὶ τὰς **χεῖρας** καὶ τοὺς πόδας νίπτου διὰ παντὸς ἀπὸ πάσης σαρκός

ψυχή, ἡ

55   καὶ μὴ ὀφθήτω ἐπὶ σοι πᾶν αἶμα καὶ πᾶσα **ψυχή**

55   τὸ γὰρ αἶμα **ψυχή** ἐστιν ἐν τῇ σαρκί

ὥρα, ἡ

53   καὶ ἐπὶ πᾶσαν **ὥραν** νίπτου τὰς χεῖρας καὶ τοὺς πόδας

ὦμος, ὁ

28   καὶ μετὰ τοῦτο τοὺς **ὤμους** (ד'), καὶ μετὰ ταῦτα τὸ στῆθος

ὡς

29   καὶ πάντα ἡλισμένα ἐν ἅλατι **ὡς** (כדי) καθήκει αὐτοῖς αὐτάρκως

49   οὕτως ἔντειλον ἵνα ποιήσουσιν κατὰ τὴν κρίσιν ταύτην **ὡς** σοὶ ὑπέδειξα

51   προσενεγκεῖν θυσίαν κυρίῳ ὑψίστῳ, **ὡς** καθήκει κατὰ τὸ προστε-
        ταγμένον

52   κατὰ τὸν λογισμὸν τῶν ξυλῶν ἐπιδέχου οὕτως, **ὡς** σοὶ ἐντέλλομαι

58   καὶ νῦν **ὡς** σοί, τέκνον ἀγαπητόν, ἐγὼ λέγω, ἠγαπημένος σὺ τῷ πατρί

63   ἐν γῇ, ᾗ ἐγεννήθην· πάροικοί ἐσμεν **ὡς** τοῦτο ἐν τῇ γῇ

ὡσεί

47   γίνεται ὁ σίκλος **ὡσεὶ** ις΄ θέρμοι καὶ ὁλκῆς μιᾶς

Proper Names

Ἀβραάμ

1a v. 15b   κύριε, εὐλόγησας τὸν **Ἀβραὰμ** πατέρα μου καὶ Σάρραν μητέρα μου

11   καὶ κατελύσαμεν ἐν τῇ αὐλῇ **Ἀβραὰμ** τοῦ πατρὸς ἡμῶν παρὰ Ἰσαὰκ

17   ἱερεὺς ἅγιος κληθήσεται τῷ σπέρματι **Ἀβραάμ**

50   οὕτως γάρ μοι ἐνετείλατο ὁ πατὴρ **Ἀβραὰμ** ποιεῖν καὶ ἐντέλλεσθαι

57   οὕτως γάρ μοι ἐνετείλατο ὁ πατήρ μου **Ἀβραάμ**, ὅτι οὕτως εὗρεν

62   ἔλαβον γυναῖκα ἐμαυτῷ ἐκ τῆς συγγενείας **Ἀβραὰμ** τοῦ πατρός μου

Βαθουήλ

62   Μελχάν, θυγατέρα **Βαθουήλ**, υἱοῦ Λάβαν, ἀδελφοῦ μητρός μου

Βηθήλ

11   καὶ ἀνήλθομεν ἀπὸ **Βηθὴλ** καὶ κατελύσαμεν ἐν τῇ αὐλῇ Ἀβραάμ

Γηρσώμ

63   ἔτεκεν υἱὸν πρῶτον, καὶ ἐκάλεσα τὸ ὄνομα αὐτοῦ **Γηρσώμ**

Ἰακώβ

1a v. 15a   μὴ ἀποστρέψῃς τὸ πρόσωπόν σου ἀπὸ τοῦ υἱοῦ παιδός σου **Ἰακώβ**

Ἰσαάκ

11   ἐν τῇ αὐλῇ Ἀβραὰμ τοῦ πατρὸς ἡμῶν παρὰ **Ἰσαὰκ** τὸν πατέρα ἡμῶν

12   καὶ εἶδεν **Ἰσαὰκ** ὁ πατὴρ ἡμῶν πάντας ἡμᾶς καὶ ηὐλόγησεν ἡμᾶς

Ἰσραήλ

67   καὶ τὸ σπέρμα αὐτοῦ ἔσονται ἀρχὴ βασιλέων, ἱεράτευμα τῷ **Ἰσραήλ**

Καάθ

66   τὸν καθήκοντα τῶν γυναικῶν, καὶ ἐκάλεσα τὸ ὄνομα αὐτοῦ **Καάθ**

Λαβάν

62   Μελχάν, θυγατέρα Βαθουήλ, υἱοῦ **Λάβαν**, ἀδελφοῦ μητρός μου

Λευί

1a v. 17   εἰσάκουσον δὲ καὶ τῆς φωνῆς τοῦ παιδός σου **Λευὶ** γενέσθαι σοι ἐγγύς

14   Τέκνον **Λευί**, πρόσεχε σεαυτῷ ἀπὸ πάσης ἀκαθαρσίας

61   καὶ νῦν, τέκνον **Λευί**, εὐλογημένον ἔσται τὸ σπέρμα σου ἐπὶ τῆς γῆς

Μελχά

62   **Μελχάν**, θυγατέρα Βαθουήλ, υἱοῦ Λάβαν, ἀδελφοῦ μητρός μου

Μεραρί

69a   καὶ ἐκάλεσα τὸ ὄνομα αὐτοῦ **Μεραρί**· ἐλυπήθην γὰρ περὶ αὐτοῦ

Νῶε

57   ὅτι οὕτως εὗρεν ἐν τῇ γραφῇ τῆς βίβλου τοῦ **Νῶε** περὶ τοῦ αἵματος

Σαρρά

1a v. 15b   σύ, κύριε, εὐλόγησας τὸν Ἀβραὰμ πατέρα μου καὶ **Σάρραν** μητέρα
μου

Divine Names

δεσπότης

1a v. 8   δειχθήτω μοι, **δέσποτα**, τὸ πνεῦμα τὸ ἅγιον, καὶ βουλὴν καὶ σοφίαν

1a v. 14   καθάρισον τὴν καρδίαν μου, **δέσποτα**, ἀπὸ πάσης ἀκαθαρσίας

δεσπότης τοῦ οὐρανοῦ

13   καὶ ὅτε ἔγνω ὅτι ἐγὼ ἱεράτευσα τῷ κυρίῳ **δεσπότῃ τοῦ οὐρανοῦ** (שׁמיא
מארי)

κύριος

1a v. 5   **Κύριε** (מרי), γινώσκεις πάσας τὰς καρδίας καὶ πάντας τοὺς διαλογισμοὺς

1a v. 7   μάκρυνον ἀπ᾽ ἐμοῦ, **κύριε**, τὸ πνεῦμα τὸ ἄδικον καὶ διαλογισμὸν

1a v. 9   καὶ εὑρεῖν χάριν ἐνώπιόν σου καὶ αἰνεῖν τοὺς λόγους σου μετ᾽ ἐμοῦ,
κύριε

1a v. 15b   σύ, **κύριε** (מרי), εὐλόγησας τὸν Ἀβραὰμ πατέρα μου καὶ Σάρραν

13   καὶ ὅτε ἔγνω ὅτι ἐγὼ ἱεράτευσα τῷ **κυρίῳ** (אל) δεσπότη τοῦ οὐρανοῦ

18   ἐγγὺς εἶ **κυρίου** (אל) καὶ σὺ ἐγγὺς τῶν ἁγίων αὐτοῦ. γίνου καθαρὸς

48   ἐν πάσαις ταῖς ἡμέραις σου, ὅτι ἱερεὺς συ ἅγιος **κυρίου**

52   ὅταν παραλαμβάνῃς θυσίαν ποιεῖν ἔναντι **κυρίου** ἀπὸ πάσης σαρκός,

κύριος ὕψιστος

30   εἰς εὐδόκησιν καὶ ὀσμὴν εὐωδίας ἔναντι **κυρίου ὑψίστου** (אל עליון)

51   προσενεγκεῖν θυσίαν **κυρίῳ ὑψίστῳ,** ὡς καθήκει κατὰ τὸ προστεταγμένον

58   ἐγὼ λέγω, ἠγαπημένος σὺ τῷ πατρί σου καὶ ἅγιος **κυρίου ὑψίστου**

Reference	Keyword	Context
78:17		
79:20		
78:16		
80:23		
78:15		
78:16		
79:18		
79:19		
80:20		
78:16		
78:15		
78:17		
80:21		
78:16		
78:17		
79:18		
79:19		
80:20		
80:23		
78:15		
78:16		
79:18		
78:15		
78:17		
80:21		
79:19		
79:19		
78:18		
81:1		
78:16		
78:17		
78:18		

Reference	Word	Context
79:20		
80:22		
80:20		
79:20		
78:18		
78:18		
78:15		
80:22		
80:23		
78:17		
81:1		
80:23		
78:15		
78:16		
79:18		
79:19		
80:21		
80:23		
81:1		
81:1		

Proper names

Reference	Word	Context
78:16		
80:22		
80:23		
78:17		

BIBLIOGRAPHY

Aland, Kurt. 1975–1983b. *Vollständige Konkordanz zum griechischen Neuen Testament: Unter Zugrundelegung aller modernen kritischen Textausgaben und des Textus Receptus.* 2 vols. Berlin/New York: Walter de Gruyter.

Al-Fouadi, Abdul Hadi. 1979. *Lenticular Exercise School Texts, Part 1.* Texts in the Iraq Museum 10. Baghdad: Ministry of Culture and Arts.

Albani, Matthias. 1994. *Astronomie und Schöpfungsglaube: Untersuchungen zum Astronomischen Henochbuch.* Wissenschaftliche Monographien zum Alten und Neuen Testament 68. Neukirchen-Vluyn: Neukirchener Verlag.

Albertz, Rainer. 1994. *A History of Israelite Religion in the Old Testament Period.* Translated by John Bowden. 2 vols. London: SCM Press.

Alexander, Patrick. H. *et al.*, eds. 1999. *The SBL Handbook of Style: For Ancient Near Eastern, Biblical, and Early Christian Studies.* Peabody, Mass.: Hendrickson.

Augustine, Saint. 1991. *Confessions.* Translated with Introduction and Notes by Henry Chadwick. Oxford: Oxford University Press.

Avigad, Nahman and Yigael Yadin. 1956. *A Genesis Apocryphon: A Scroll from the Wilderness of Judaea: Description and Contents of the Scroll, Facsimiles, Transcription and Translation of Columns II, XIX–XXII.* Jerusalem: Magnes Press.

Baarda, Tjitze. 1988. "Qehath—'What's in a name?'" *Journal for the Study of Judaism* 19: 220–221.

Bartlett, John R. 1969. "The Use of the Word שאר as a Title in the Old Testament." *Vetus Testamentum* 19: 1–10.

Bauer, Hans and Pontus Leander. 1962. *Grammatik des Biblisch-Aramäischen.* Halle: M. Niemeyer, 1927. Repr. Hildesheim: Georg Olms.

Baumgartner, Walter, ed. 1967–1995. *Hebräisches und aramaisches Lexikon zum Alten Testament.* 5 vols. Leiden: E. J. Brill.

Becker, Jürgen. 1970. *Untersuchungen zur Entstehungsgeschichte der Testamente der zwölf Patriarchen.* Arbeiten zur Geschichte des antiken Judentums und des Urchristentums 8. Leiden: E. J. Brill.

Begrich, Joachim. 1936. "Die priesterliche Tora." Pages 63–88 in *Werden und Wesen des Alten Testaments.* Edited by Paul Volz *et al.* Beihefte zur Zeitschrift für die alttestamentliche Wissenschaft 66.

Behm, Johannes. 1965. "θύω, θυσία, θυσιαστήριον." Pages 180–190 in vol. 3 of *Theological Dictionary of the New Testament.* Edited by Gerhard Kittel and Gerhard Friedrich. Translated by Geoffrey W. Bromiley. 10 vols. Grand Rapids, Mich., 1964–1976.

Beit-Arié, Malachi. 1981. *Hebrew Codicology: Tentative Typology of Technical Practices Employed in Hebrew Dated Medieval Manuscripts.* Paris: Centre National de la Recherche Scientifique, 1976. Repr. Jerusalem: The Israel Academy of Sciences and Humanities.

———. 1993. *The Makings of the Medieval Hebrew Book: Studies in Palaeography and Codicology.* Jerusalem: Magnes Press.

Ben Eliezer, Tobiah. 1880. *Lekach-Tob (Pesikta Sutarta): Ein agadisher Commentar zum ersten und zweiten Buche Mosis.* Edited by Salomon Buber. 2 vols. Wilna: W. & G. Romm.

Bentzen, Aage. 1930/31. "Priesterschaft und Laien in der jüdischen Gemeinde des fünften Jahrhunderts." *Archiv für Orientforschung* 6: 280–286.

Bernstein, Moshe J. 1999. "Pseudepigraphy in the Qumran Scrolls: Categories and Functions." Pages 1–26 in *Pseudepigraphic Perspectives: The Apocrypha and Pseudepigrapha in Light of the Dead Sea Scrolls*. Edited by Esther G. Chazon and Michael Stone. Studies on the Texts of the Desert of Judah 31. Leiden: E. J. Brill.

Bertram, Georg. 1972. "ὕθος, κτλ." Pages 602–620 in vol. 8 of *Theological Dictionary of the New Testament*. Edited by Gerhard Kittel and Gerhard Friedrich. Translated by Geoffrey W. Bromiley. 10 vols. Grand Rapids, Mich., 1964–1976.

Beyer, K. 1984. *Die aramäischen Texte vom Toten Meer samt den Inschriften aus Palästina, dem Testament Levis aus der Kairoer Genisa, der Fastenrolle und den alten talmudischen Zitaten*. Göttingen: Vandenhoeck & Ruprecht.

———. 1994. *Die aramäischen Texte vom Toten Meer samt den Inschriften aus Palästina, dem Testament Levis aus der Kairoer Genisa, der Fastenrolle und den alten talmudischen Zitaten: Ergänzungsband*. Göttingen: Vandenhoeck & Ruprecht.

Black, Matthew. 1985. *The Book of Enoch or I Enoch: A New English Edition with Commentary and Textual Notes*. Studia in Veteris Testamenti Pseudoepigrapha 7. Leiden: E. J. Brill.

Boccaccini, Gabriele. 1998. *Beyond the Essene Hypothesis: The Parting of the Ways between Qumran and Enochic Judaism*. Grand Rapids, Mich.: Eerdmans.

Boecker, Hans Jochen. 1964. *Redeformen des Rechtslebens im Alten Testament*. Wissenschaftliche Monographien zum Alten und Neuen Testament 14. Neukirchen-Vluyn: Neukirchener Verlag.

Bonani, G. *et al.* 1991. "Radiocarbon Dating of the Dead Sea Scrolls." *Atiqot* 20: 27–32.

Bousset, Wilhelm. 1900. "Ein aramäisches Fragment des Testamentum Levi." *Zeitschrift für die neutestamentliche Wissenschaft und die Kunde der älteren Kirche* 1: 344–346.

Brandt, Wilhelm. 1910. *Die jüdischen Baptismen oder das religiöse Waschen und Baden im Judentum mit Einschluß des Judenchristentums*. Beihefte zur Zeitschrift für die alttestamentliche Wissenschaft 18. Gießen: Alfred Töpelmann.

Brinkman, John A. 1977. "Mesopotamian Chronology of the Historical Period." Pages 335–348 in *Ancient Mesopotamia: Portrait of a Dead Civilisation*. A. L. Oppenheim. 2nd ed. Revised by E. Reiner. Chicago: University of Chicago Press.

Brockelmann, Carl. 1928. *Lexicon syriacum*. 2nd ed. Halle: M. Niemeyer.

———. 1961. *Grundriss der vergleichenden Grammatik der semitischen Sprachen: II. Band: Syntax*. Berlin: Reuther & Reichard, 1913. Repr. Hildesheim: Georg Olms.

Brown, Francis *et al.* 1996. *A Hebrew and English Lexicon of the Old Testament*. Peabody, Mass.: Hendrickson.

Brown, Raymond E. *et al.* 1988. *A Preliminary Concordance to the Hebrew and Aramaic Fragments from Qumrân Caves II–X: Vol. 5: Aramaic Part א - ת*. Göttingen: Privately Printed.

Brunner, Hellmut. 1961. "Der 'Gottesvater' als Erzieher des Kronprinzen." *Zeitschrift für ägyptische Sprache und Altertumskunde* 86: 90–100.

———. 1988. *Altägyptische Weisheit: Lehren für das Leben*. Die Bibliothek der Alten Welt, Reihe der Alte Orient. Zürich und München: Artemis.

Buber, Salomon. 1893. *Midrash Mischlé*. Wilna: W. & G. Romm.

Burchard, Christoph. 1965. Review of Marinus de Jonge, *Testamenta XII Patriarcharum: Edited according to Cambridge University Library MS Ff. 1.24 fol. 1.24 203a–262b*. *Revue de Qumran* 5: 281–284.

Buth, Randall. 1990. "'EDAYIN/TOTE—Anatomy of a Semitism in Jewish Greek." Pages 33–48 in *Sopher Mahir: Northwest Semitic Studies Presented to Stanislav Segert*. Edited by Edward M. Cook. Winona Lake, Ind.: Eisenbrauns.

Camponovo, Odo. 1984. *Königtum, Königsherrschaft und Reich Gottes in den frühjüdischen Schriften*. Orbis Biblicus et orientalis 58. Freiburg Schweiz/Göttingen: Univesitätsverlag/Vandenhoeck & Ruprecht.

Caquot, André. 1995. "Grandeur et pureté du sacerdoce: Remarques sur le *Testament de Qahat (4Q542)*." Pages 39–44 in *Solving Riddles and Untying Knots: Biblical,*

Epigraphic, and Semitic Studies in Honor of Jonas C. Greenfield. Edited by Ziony Zevit *et al.* Winona Lake, Ind.: Eisenbrauns.

Castellino, G. R. 1972. *Two Šulgi Hymns (BC).* Studi semitici 42. Roma: Istituto di Studi del Vicino Oriente.

Charles, Robert Henry. 1902. *The Book of Jubilees or the Little Genesis.* London: A. & C. Black.

—————. 1906. *The Ethiopic Version of the Book of Enoch.* Anecdota oxoniensia, Semitic Series. Oxford: Clarendon Press.

—————. 1908a. *The Greek Versions of the Testaments of the Twelve Patriarchs.* Oxford: Clarendon.

—————. 1908b. *The Testaments of the Twelve Patriarchs: Translated from the Editor's Greek Text and Edited, with Introduction, Notes, and Indices.* London: Clarendon.

—————. 1912. *The Book of Enoch or 1 Enoch.* Oxford: Clarendon Press.

Charles, Robert Henry and Arthur Cowley. 1907. "An Early Source of the Testaments of the Patriarchs." *Jewish Qarterly Review* 19: 566–583.

Charpin, Dominique. 1986. *Le clergé d'Ur au siècle d'Hammurabi: (XIXᵉ–XVIII siècles av. J.-C.).* Genève: Libraire Droz.

Chevalier, Marc-Alain. 1958. *L'esprit et le messie dans le Bas-Judaïsme et le Nouveau Testament.* Études d'histoire et de philosophie religieuses 49. Paris: Presses Universitaires de France.

Chyutin, Michael. 1997. *The New Jerusalem Scroll from Qumran: A Comprehensive Reconstruction.* Journal for the Study of the Pseudepigrapha Supplement Series 25. Sheffield: Sheffield Academic Press.

Civil, Miguel. 1985. "Sur les 'livres d'écolier' à l'époque paléo-babylonienne." Pages 67–78 in *Miscellanea babylonica: Mélanges offerts à Maurice Birot.* Edited by Jean-Marie Durand and Jean-Robert Kupper. Paris: Éditions Recherche sur les Civilisations.

Clarke, Ernest G. 1984. *Targum Pseudo-Jonathan of the Pentateuch: Text and Concordance.* Hoboken, N.J.: Ktav Publishing House.

Collins, J. J. 1983. "Sybilline Oracles (Second Century B.C.–Seventh Century A.D.)." Pages 317–472 in *The Old Testament Pseudepigrapha: vol. 1. Apocalyptic Literature and Testaments.* Edited by J. H. Charlesworth. New York: Doubleday.

—————. 1995. *The Scepter and the Star: The Messiahs of the Dead Sea Scrolls and Other Ancient Literature.* The Anchor Bible Reference Library 11. New York: Doubleday.

—————. 1997. *Jewish Wisdom in the Hellenistic Age.* The Old Testament Library. Louisville, Ken.: Westminster John Knox Press.

Conrad, J. 1999. "סָפַר sāpar; מִסְפָּר mispār." Pages 308–318 in vol. 10 of *Theological Dictionary of the Old Testament.* Edited by G. Johannes Botterweck *et al.* Translated by John T. Willis *et al.* 12– vols. Grand Rapids, Mich.: Eerdmans, 1977–.

Conybeare, F. *et al.* 1898. *The Story of Aḥikar from the Syriac, Arabic, Armenian, Ethiopic, Greek and Slavonic Versions.* London: C. J. Clay and Sons.

Cowley, Arthur. 1967. *Aramaic Papyri of the Fifth Century B.C.* Oxford: Clarendon, 1923. Repr. Osnabrück: Otto Zeller.

Crenshaw, James L. 1998. *Education in Ancient Israel: Across the Deadening Silence.* Anchor Bible Reference Library. New York: Doubleday.

Cross, Frank M. Jr. 1963. "The Discovery of the Samaria Papyri." *Biblical Archaeologist* 26: 110–121.

—————. 1966. "Aspects of Samaritan and Jewish History in Late Persian and Hellenistic Times." *Harvard Theological Review* 59: 201–211.

—————. 1974. "The Papyri and Their Historical Implications." Pages 17–29 in *Discoveries in the Wādī Ed-Dâliyeh.* Edited by Paul W. Lapp and Nancy L. Lapp. Annual of the American Schools of Oriental Research 41. Cambridge, Mass.: American Schools of Oriental Research.

Dalman, Gustaf. 1905. *Grammatik des jüdisch-palästinischen Aramäisch.* 2nd ed. Leipzig: J. C. Hinrichs.

Damerow, Peter. 1981. "Die Entstehung der arithmetischen Denkens: Zur Rolle der Rechenmittel in der altägyptischen und der altbabylonischen Arithmetik." Pages 11–113 in *Rechenstein, Experiment, Sprache: Historische Fallstudien zur Entstehung der exakten Wissenschaften.* Edited by Peter Damerow and Wolfgang Lefèvre. Stuttgart: Klett-Cotta.

Daniel, Suzanne. 1966. *Recherches sur le vocabulaire du culte dans la Septante.* Études et commentaires 61. Paris: C. Klincksieck.

Davies, Graham I. 1991. *Ancient Hebrew Inscriptions: Corpus and Concordance.* Cambridge: Cambridge University Press.

Day, Peggy L. 1988. *An Adversary in Heaven: ṣāṭān in the Hebrew Bible.* Harvard Semitic Monographs 43. Atlanta, Ga.: Scholars Press.

de Genouillac, Henri. 1930. *Textes religieux Sumériens.* 2 vols. Musée du Louvre. Département des Antiquités Orientales. Textes Cunéiformes 15–16. Paris: Paul Geuthner.

de Jonge, Marinus. 1953a. "Appendix: The Fragments of a Jewish Testament of Levi." Pages 129–131 in *The Testaments of the Twelve Patriarchs: A Study of their Text, Composition and Origin.* Marinus de Jonge. Van Gorcum's Theologische Bibliotheek 25. Assen: Van Gorcum.

———. 1953b. *The Testaments of the Twelve Patriarchs: A Study of their Text, Composition and Origin.* Van Gorcum's Theologische Bibliotheek 25. Assen: Van Gorcum.

———. 1964. *Testamenta XII Patriarcharum: Edited according to Cambridge University Library MS Ff I.24 fols. 203a–261b.* Pseudepigrapha Veteris Testamenti Graece 1. Leiden: E. J. Brill.

———. 1975. "Notes on Testament of Levi II–VII." Pages 247–260 in *Studies on the Testaments of the Twelve Patriarchs: Text and Interpretation.* Edited by Marinus de Jonge. Studia in Veteris Testamenti Pseudoepigrapha 3. Leiden: E. J. Brill.

———. 1988. "The Testament of Levi and 'Aramaic Levi'." *Revue de Qumran* 13: 367–385.

———. 1997. Review of Robert A. Kugler, *From Patriarch to Priest: The Levi-Priestly Tradition from Aramaic Levi to Testament of Levi. Journal for the Study of Judaism* 28: 115–117.

———. 1999. "Levi in Aramaic Levi and in the Testament of Levi." Pages 71–89 in *Pseudepigraphic Perspectives: The Apocrypha and Pseudepigrapha in Light of the Dead Sea Scrolls: Proceedings of the International Symposium of the Orion Center for the Study of the Dead Sea Scrolls and Associated Literature, 12–14 January, 1997.* Edited by Esther G. Chazon *et al.* Studies on the Texts of the Desert of Judah 31. Leiden: E. J. Brill.

de Jonge, Marinus *et al.* eds. 1978. *The Testaments of the Twelve Patriarchs: A Critical Edition of the Greek Text.* Pseudepigrapha Veteris Testamenti Graece 1.2. Leiden: E. J. Brill.

de Menasce, J. P. 1956. "Iranien *naxčīr.*" *Vetus Testamentum* 6: 213–214.

de Vaux, Roland. 1960. *Les institutions de l'Ancient Testament: II. Institutions militaires, institutions religieuses.* Paris: Cerf.

———. 1964. *Studies in Old Testament Sacrifice.* Cardiff: University of Wales Press.

del Olmo Lete, Gregorio and Joaquín Sanmartín. 2003. *A Dictionary of the Ugaritic Language in the Alphabetic Tradition.* Translated by Wilfred G. E. Watson. 2 vols. Handbook of Oriental Studies: The Near and Middle East 67. Leiden: Brill.

Demsky, Aaron. 1990. "The Education of Canaanite Scribes in the Mesopotamian Cuneiform Tradition." Pages 157–170 in *Bar-Ilan Studies in Assyriology Dedicated to Pinḥas Artzi.* Edited by Jacob Klein and Aaron Skaist. Bar-Ilan Studies in Eastern Languages and Culture. Ramat Gan: Bar-Ilan University Press.

Dexinger, Ferdinand. 1977. *Henochs Zehnwochenapokalypse und offene Probleme der Apokalyptik-forschung.* Studia post-biblica 29. Leiden: E. J. Brill.

Díez Macho, Alejandro. 1968–79. *Neophyti 1, Targum palestinense, Ms de la Biblioteca Vaticana.* 6 vols. Textos y estudios 7–11, 20. Madrid/Barcelona: Consejo Superior de Investigaciones Científicas.

Dillmann, August. 1955. *Lexicon linguae aethiopicae cum indice latino.* Leipzig: T. O. Weigel, 1865. Repr. New York: Frederick Ungar.

Dossin, Georges. 1955. "L'inscription de fondation de Iaḫdun-Lim, roi de Mari." *Syria* 32: 1–28.

Driver, Godfrey R. 1957. *Aramaic Documents of the Fifth Century B.C.* Abridged and Revised Edition. Oxford: Clarendon.

Driver, Godfrey R., and John C. Miles. 1955. *The Babylonian Laws: Volume II: Transliterated Text, Translation, Philological Notes, Glossary.* Oxford: Clarendon.

Drower, Ethel S., and Rudolf Macuch. 1963. *A Mandaic Dictionary.* Oxford: Clarendon.

Elliger, Karl and Wilhelm Rudolph, eds. 1990. *Biblia Hebraica Stuttgartensia.* 4th emended edition by Hans P. Rüger. Stuttgart: Deutsche Bibelgesellschaft.

Endres, John C. 1987. *Biblical Interpretation in the Book of Jubilees.* Catholic Biblical Quarterly Monograph Series 18. Washington, DC: The Catholic Biblical Association of America.

Engel, Edna 1990. "The Development of the Hebrew Script from the Period of the Bar-Kokhba Revolt to 1000 A.D." Ph.D. diss., Hebrew University. Jerusalem. (Hebrew).

Englund, Robert *et al.* 1993. *Die lexikalischen Listen der archaischen Texte aus Uruk.* Archaische Texte aus Uruk 3. Berlin: Gebr. Mann Verlag.

Eph'al, Israel and Joseph Naveh. 1996. *Aramaic Ostraca of the Fourth Century BC from Idumaea.* Jerusalem: The Magnes Press.

Esh, Shaul. 1957. *(כה) הק "Der Heilige (er sei gepriesen):" Zur Geschichte einer nachbib-lisch-hebräischen Gottesbezeichnun.* Leiden: E. J. Brill.

Fabry, Heinz-Joseph. 1995. "לב lēb; לבב lēbab." Pages 399–437 in vol. 7 of *Theological Dictionary of the Old Testament.* Edited by G. Johannes Botterweck *et al.* Translated by John T. Willis *et al.* 12 vols. Grand Rapids, Mich.: Eerdmans, 1977–.

Fassberg, Steven Ellis. 1992. "Hebraisms in the Aramaic Documents from Qumran." Pages 48–69 in *Studies in Qumran Aramaic.* Edited by Takamitsu Muraoka. Abr-Nahrain Supplement Series 3. Louvain: Peeters.

Finkelstein, Jacob J. 1969. "The Laws of Ur-Nammu." *Journal of Cuneiform Studies* 22: 66–82.

Fishbane, Michael. 1985. *Biblical Interpretation in Ancient Israel.* Oxford: Clarendon Press.

Fitzmyer, Joseph A. 1962. "The Padua Aramaic Papyrus Letters." *Journal of Near Eastern Studies* 21: 15–24.

———. 1967. *The Aramaic Inscriptions of Sefire.* Biblica et orientalia 19. Rome: Pontifical Biblical Institute.

———. 1971. *The Genesis Apocryphon of Qumran Cave I: A Commentary.* 2nd, revised edition. Biblica et orientalia 18a. Rome: Biblical Institute Press.

———. 1979. *A Wandering Aramean: Collected Aramaic Essays.* Society of Biblical Literature Monograph Series 25. Missoula, Mont.: Scholars Press.

———. 1999. "The Aramaic Levi Document." Pages 453–464 in *The Provo International Conference on the Dead Sea Scrolls: Technological Innovations, New Texts, and Reformulated Issues.* Edited by Donald W. Parry and Eugene Ulrich. Studies on the Texts of the Desert of Judah 30. Leiden: E. J. Brill.

Fitzmyer, Joseph A., and Daniel J. Harrington. 1978. *A Manual of Palestinian Aramaic Texts: (Second Century B.C.–Second Century A.D.).* Biblica et orientalia 34. Rome: Biblical Institute Press.

Flusser, David. 1966. "Qumrân and Jewish 'Apotropaic' Prayers." *Israel Exploration Journal* 16: 194–205.

Friberg, Jöran. 1987–90. "Mathematik." Pages 531–585 in vol. 7 of *Reallexikon der Assyriologie*. Edited by Erich Ebeling and Bruno Meissner. 8– vols. Berlin: W. de Gruyter, 1928–.

———. 1999. "A Late Babylonian Factorization Algorithm for the Computation of Reciprocals of Many-Place Regular Sexagesimal Numbers." *Baghdader Mitteilungen* 30: 139–161.

———. 2000. "Mathematics at Ur in the Old Babylonian Period." *Revue d'assyriologie et d'archéologie orientale* 94: 97–188.

Friedlander, Gerald. 1981. *Pirkê de Rabbi Eliezer*. 4th ed. New York: Sepher-Hermon Press.

Funk, Franciscus X. 1905. *Didascalia et Constitutiones Apostolorum*. 2 vols. Paderborn: F. Schoeningh.

García Martínez, Florentino. 1992. *Qumran and Apocalyptic: Studies on the Aramaic Texts from Qumran*. Studies on the Texts of the Desert of Judah 9. Leiden: E. J. Brill.

Geffcken, Johannes. 1902. *Die Oracula Sibyllina*. Die griechischen christlichen Schriftsteller 8. Leipzig: J. C. Hinrichs.

Gesche, Petra D. 2001. *Schulunterricht in Babylonien im ersten Jahrtausend v. Chr*. Alter Orient und Altes Testament 275. Münster: Ugarit-Verlag.

Ginzberg, Louis. 1998. *The Legends of the Jews*. 7 vols. Philadelphia: The Jewish Publication Society of America, 1909–38. Repr. Baltimore: The John Hopkins University Press.

Glassner, Jean-Jacques. 1992. "Du bon usage des fractions." Pages 115–127 in *Histoire de fractions, fractions d'histoire*. Edited by Paul Benoit *et al*. Science Networks Historical Studies 10. Basel: Birkhäuser Verlag.

Goldschmidt, Lazarus. 1897–1935. *Der babylonische Talmud*. 9 vols. Berlin: Calvary.

Goodblatt, David. 1994. *The Monarchic Principle: Studies in Jewish Self-Government in Antiquity*. Texte und Studien zum Antiken Judentum 38. Tübingen: J. C. B. Mohr (Paul Siebeck).

Gordon, Edmund I. 1960. "A New Look at the Wisdom of Sumer and Akkad." *Bibliotheca Orientalis* 17: 122–152.

Greenfield, Jonas C. 1974. "Standard Literary Aramaic." Pages 280–289 in *Actes du premier Congrès International de Linguistique Sémitique et Chamito-Sémitique, Paris 16–19 juillet 1969*. Edited by André Caquot and David Cohen. Janua linguarum 159. The Hague/Paris: Mouton.

———. 1978a. "The Dialects of Early Aramaic." *Journal of Near Eastern Studies* 37: 93–99.

———. 1978b. "The Meaning of פחז." Pages 35–40 in *Studies in Bible and the Ancient Near East Presented to Samuel E. Loewenstamm*. Edited by Yitschak Avishur and Joshua Blau. Jerusalem: E. Rubinstein.

———. 1979. "Early Aramaic Poetry." *Journal of the Ancient Near Eastern Society of Columbia University* 11: 45–51.

———. 1988. "The Words of Levi Son of Jacob in Damascus Document IV, 15–19." *Revue de Qumran* 13: 319–322.

———. 1991. "The Verbs for Washing in Aramaic." Pages 588–594 in volume 1 of *Semitic Studies: In Honor of Wolf Leslau*. Edited by Alan S. Kaye. 2 vols. Wiesbaden: Otto Harrassowitz.

Greenfield, Jonas C., and Michael Sokoloff. 1992. "The Contribution of Qumran Aramaic to the Aramaic Vocabulary." Pages 78–98 in *Studies in Qumran Aramaic*. Edited by T. Muraoka. Abr-Nahrain Supplement Series 3. Louvain: Peeters.

Greenfield, Jonas C., and Michael E. Stone. 1979. "Remarks on the Aramaic Testament of Levi from the Geniza." *Revue Biblique* 86: 216–230.

———. 1985. "The Aramaic and Greek Fragments of a Levi Document: Appendix III." Pages 457–469 in *The Testaments of the Twelve Patriarchs: A Commentary*. Harm W. Hollander and Marinus de Jonge. Studia in Veteris Testamenti Pseudepigrapha 8. Leiden: E. J. Brill.

————. 1990. "Two Notes on the Aramaic Levi Document." Pages 153–161 in *Of Scribes and Scrolls: Studies on the Hebrew Bible, Intertestamental Judaism, and Christian Origins presented to John Strugnell*. Edited by Harold W. Attridge *et al.* College Theology Society Resources in Religion 5. Lanham, Md.: University Press of America.

Grelot, Pierre. 1955. "Le Testament araméen de Lévi est-il traduit de l'hébreu? A propos du fragment de Cambridge, col. c 10 à d 1." *Revue des Études Juives* 14:91–99.

————. 1956. "Notes sur le Testament araméen de Lévi (Fragment de la Bodleian Library, colonne a)." *Revue Biblique* 63: 391–406.

————. 1971. "Quatre cent trente ans (Ex XII, 34)." Pages 383–394 in *Hommages à André Dupont-Sommer*. Edited by André Caquot and Marc Philonenko. Paris: Adrien Maisonneuve.

————. 1975. "Quantre cents trente ans (Ex 12,40)." Pages 559–570 in *Homenaje a Juan Prado: Miscelanea de estudios biblicos y hebraicos*. Edited by Lorenzo Alvarez Verdes and E. Javier Alonso Hernandez. Madrid: Consejo Superior de Investigaciones Cientificas.

————. 1983. "Une mention inaperçue de «Abba» dans le *Testament araméen de Lévi*." *Semitica* 33: 101–108.

————. 1991. "Le coutumier sacerdotal ancien dans le *Testament Araméen de Lévi*." *Revue de Qumran* 15: 253–263.

Gunkel, Hermann and Joachim Begrich. 1998. *Introduction to Psalms: The Genres of the Religious Lyrics of Israel*. Translated by James D. Nogalski. Macon, Ga.: Mercer University Press.

Gunneweg, Antonius H. J. 1965. *Leviten und Priester: Hauptlinien der Traditionsbildung und Geschichte des israelitisch-jüdischen Kultpersonals*. Forschungen zur Religion und Literatur des Alten und Neuen Testaments 89. Göttingen: Vandenhoeck & Ruprecht.

Hamp, Vinzenz and G. Johannes Botterweck. 1997. "דין *dîn*." Pages 187–194 in vol. 3 of *Theological Dictionary of the Old Testament*. Edited by G. Johannes Botterweck *et al.* Translated by John T. Willis *et al.* 12– vols. Grand Rapids, Mich.: Eerdmans, 1977–.

Haran, Menahem. 1988. "On the Diffusion of Literacy and Schools in Ancient Israel." Pages 81–95 in *Congress Volume Jerusalem 1986*. Edited by John A. Emerton. Supplements to Vetus Testamentum 40. Leiden: E. J. Brill.

Harl, Marguerite. 1992. *La langue de Japhet: Quinze études sur la Septante et le grec des chrétiens*. Paris: Cerf.

Hatch, Edwin and Henry A. Redpath. 1991. *A Concordance to the Septuagint and the Other Greek Versions of the Old Testament (Including the Apocryphal Books)*. 3 vols. Oxford: Clarendon, 1897–1906. Repr. in 2 vols., Grand Rapids, Mich.: Baker Book House.

Haupt, Detlev. 1969. "Das Testament des Levi: Untersuchungen zu seiner Entstehung und Überlieferungsgeschichte." Ph.D. diss., Martin Luther Universität. Halle.

Hayes, Christine. 1999. "Intermarriage and Impurity in Ancient Jewish Sources." *Harvard Theological Review* 92: 3–36.

Hengel, Martin. 1989. "The Political and Social History of Palestine from Alexander to Antiochus III (333–187 B.C.E.)." Pages 35–78 in *The Cambridge History of Judaism: II. The Hellenistic Age*. Edited by William D. Davies and Louis Finkelstein. Cambridge: Cambridge University Press.

Hilprecht, Hermann V. 1906. *Mathematical, Metrological and Chronological Tablets from the Temple Library of Nippur*. The Babylonian Expedition of the University of Pennsylvania, Series A: Cuneiform Texts 20/1. Philadelphia: Department of Archaeology, University of Pennsylvania.

Hinz, Walther. 1975. *Altiranisches Sprachgut der Nebenüberlieferungen*. Gottinger Orientforschungen. III. Reihe, Iranica 3. Wiesbaden: Otto Harrassowitz.

Holladay, Carl R. 1989. *Fragments From Hellenistic Jewish Authors: Volume II. Poets: The Epic Poets Theodotus and Philo and Ezekiel the Tragedian.* Society of Biblical Literature Texts and Translations 30. Atlanta, Ga.: Scholars Press.

Hollander, Harm W. 1981. *Joseph as an Ethical Model in the Testaments of the Twelve Patriarchs.* Studia in Veteris Testamenti pseudepigrapha 6. Leiden: E. J. Brill.

Hollander, Harm W., and Marinus de Jonge. 1985. *The Testaments of the Twelve Patriarchs: A Commentary.* Studia in Veteris Testamenti pseudoepigrapha 8. Leiden: E. J. Brill.

Hultgård, Anders. 1977. *L'eschatologie des Testaments des Douze Patriarches: I. Interprétation des textes.* Acta Universitatis Upsaliensis: Historia Religionum 6. Stockholm: Almqvist & Wiksell.

———. 1980. "The Ideal 'Levite', the Davidic Messiah and the Saviour Priest in the Testaments of the Twelve Patriarchs." Pages 93–110 in *Ideal Figures in Ancient Judaism: Profiles and Paradigms.* Edited by John J. Collins and George W. Nickelsburg. Septuagint and Cognate Studies 12. Chico, Calif.: Scholars Press.

———. 1982. *L'eschatologie des Testaments des Douze Patriarches: II. Composition de l'ouvrage, textes et traductions.* Acta Universitatis Upsaliensis: Historia Religionum 7. Stockholm: Almqvist & Wiksell.

Hunger, Hermann. 2001. "Zeitmessung." Pages 311–316 in *Changing Views on Ancient Near Eastern Mathematics.* Edited by Jens Høyrup and Peter Damerow. Berliner Beiträge zum Vorderen Orient 19. Berlin: Dietrich Reimer Verlag.

Jacobson, Howard. 1977. "The Position of the Fingers during the Priestly Blessing." *Revue de Qumran* 9: 259–260.

Jastrow, Marcus. 1950. *A Dictionary of the Targumim, the Talmud Babli and Yerushalmi, and the Midrashic Literature.* 2 vols. New York: Pardes Publishing House.

Kaufman, Stephen A. 1974. *The Akkadian Influences on Aramaic.* Assyriological Studies 19. Chicago: University of Chicago Press.

Klein, Jacob. 1981. *Three Šulgi Hymns: Sumerian Royal Hymns Glorifying King Šulgi of Ur.* Ramat-Gan: Bar-Ilan University Press.

Klein, Michael L. 1980. *The Fragment-Targums of the Pentateuch According to their Extant Sources.* 2 vols. Analecta biblica 76. Rome: Biblical Institute Press.

Klengel, Horst. 1992. *Syria 3000 to 300 B.C.: A Handbook of Political History.* Berlin: Akademie Verlag.

Klostermann, August. 1908. "Schulwesen im alten Israel." Pages 193–232 in *Theologische Studien, Theodor Zahn zum 10. Oktober 1908 dargebracht.* Leipzig: A. Deichert.

Koehler, Ludwig and Baumgartner, Walter. 1994–2000. *The Hebrew and Aramaic Lexicon of the Old Testament.* 5 vols. Translated and Edited under the Supervision of M. E. J. Richardson. Leiden: E. J. Brill.

Koep, Leo. 1952. *Das himmlische Buch in Antike und Christentum: Eine religionsgeschichtliche Untersuchung zur altchristlichen Bildersprache.* Beiträge zur Religions- und Kirchengeschichte des Altertums 8. Bonn: Peter Hanstein Verlag.

Kraeling, Emil G. 1953. *The Brooklyn Museum Aramaic Papyri: New Documents of the Fifth Century B.C. from the Jewish Colony at Elephantine.* New Haven: Yale University Press.

Kramer, Samuel Noah. 1949. "Schooldays: A Sumerian Composition Relating to the Education of a Scribe." *Journal of the American Oriental Society* 69: 199–215.

———. 1956. "Die sumerische Schule." *Wissenschaftliche Zeitschrift der Martin-Luther-Universität Halle-Wittenberg—Gesellschafts- und sprachwissenschaftliche Reihe* 5/4: 695–704.

———. 1963. *The Sumerians: Their History, Culture, and Character.* Chicago: The University of Chicago Press.

———. 1981. *History Begins at Sumer: Thirty-Nine Firsts in Man's Recorded History.* 3rd Revised Edition. Philadelphia: The University of Pennsylvania Press.

———. 1983. "The Ur-Nammu Law Code: Who Was Its Author?" *Orientalia, NS* 52: 453–456.

Kraus, Fritz R. 1973. *Von mesopotamischen Menschen der altbabylonishen Zeit und seiner Welt.* Mededelingen der Koninklijke Nederlandse Akademie van Wetenschappen, Afd. Letterkunde, N.S. 36/6. Amsterdam: North-Holland.

Krecher, Joachim. 1969. "Schreiberschulung in Ugarit: Die Tradition von Listen und sumerischen Texten." *Ugarit-Forschungen* 1: 131–158.

Kugel, James. 1992. "The Story of Dinah in the *Testament of Levi*." *Harvard Theological Review* 85: 1–34.

———. 1993. "Levi's Elevation to the Priesthood in Second Temple Writings." *Harvard Theological Review* 86: 1–64.

Kugler, Robert A. 1996a. *From Patriarch to Priest: The Levi-Priestly Tradition from Aramaic Levi to Testament of Levi.* Society of Biblical Literature Early Judaism and Its Literature 9. Atlanta, Ga.: Scholars Press.

———. 1996b. "Some Further Evidence for the Samaritan Provenance of *Aramaic Levi (1QTestLevi; 4QTestLevi)*." *Revue de Qumran* 17: 351–358.

Kuntz, Kenneth J. 1974. "The Canonical Wisdom Psalms of Ancient Israel: Their Rhetorical, Thematic and Formal Dimensions." Pages 186–222 in *Rhetorical Criticism: Essays in Honor of James Muilenburg.* Edited by Jared J. Jackson and Martin Kessler. Pittsburgh Theological Monograph Series 1. Pittsburgh, Pa.: The Pickwick Press.

Kutscher, Eduard Y. 1958. "The Language of the 'Genesis Apocryphon': A Preliminary Study." *Scripta Hierosolymitana* 4: 1–35.

Kvanvig, Helge S. 1988. *Roots of Apocalyptic: The Mesopotamian Background of the Enoch Figure and of the Son of Man.* Wissenschaftlische Monographien zum Alten und Neuen Testament 61. Neukirchen-Vluyn: Neukirchener Verlag.

Laato, Antti. 1994. "The Levitical Genealogies in 1 Chronicles 5–6 and the Formation of Levitical Ideology in Post-Exilic Judah." *Journal for the Study of the Old Testament* 62: 77–99.

Lambert, Wilfred G. 1965. "Nebuchadnezzar King of Justice." *Iraq* 27: 1–11.

Lambros, Spyridon P. 1966. *Catalogue of the Greek Manuscripts on Mount Athos.* 2 vols. Cambridge: University Press, 1895–1900. Repr. Amsterdam: A. M. Hakkert.

Landsberger, Benno. 1956. "Babylonian Scribal Craft and Its Terminology." Pages 123–126 in *Proceedings of the Twenty-Third International Congress of Orientalists, Cambridge, 21st–28th August, 1954.* Edited by Denis Sinor. London: The Royal Asiatic Society.

Landsberger, Benno and Erica Reiner. 1970. *The Series ḪAR-ra = ḫubullu: Tablets XVI, XVII, XIX and Related Texts.* Materials for the Sumerian Lexicon 10. Roma: Pontificium Institutum Biblicum.

Lemaire, André. 1981. *Les écoles et la formation de la Bible dans l'ancien Israël.* Orbis Biblicus et Orientalis 39. Fribourg/Göttingen: Éditions Universitaires/Vandenhoeck & Ruprecht.

———. 1983. "L'ostracon paléo-hebreu n° 6 de Tell Qudeirat (Qadesh-Barnéa)." Pages 302–326 in *Fontes atque pontes: Eine Festgabe für Hellmut Brunner.* Edited by Manfred Görg. Ägypten und Altes Testament 5. Wiesbaden: Otto Harrassowitz.

Leslau, W. 1991. *Comparative Dictionary of Geʿez (Classical Ethiopic): Geʿez-English/English-Geʿez with an index of the Semitic roots.* Wiesbaden: Otto Harrassowitz.

Lévi, Israel. 1907. "Notes sur le texte araméen du Testament de Lévi récemment découvert." *Revue des Études Juives* 54: 166–180.

———. 1908. "Encore un mot sur le texte araméen du Testament de Lévi." *Revue des Études Juives* 55: 285–287.

Levy, Jacob. 1876–89. *Neuhebräisches und chaldäisches Wörterbuch über die Talmudim und Midraschim.* 4 vols. Leipzig: F. A. Brockhaus.

———. 1881. *Chaldäisches Wörterbuch über die Targumim und einen großen Theil des rabbinischen Schritthums.* 3rd ed. 2 vols. Leipzig.

Licht, Jacob. 1965. *The Rule Scroll: A Scroll from the Wilderness of Judaea 1QS 1QSa 1QSb.* Jerusalem: The Bialik Institute. (Hebrew).

Lichtheim, Miriam. 1976. *Ancient Egyptian Literature: Volume II: The New Kingdom.* Berkeley: University of California Press.

———. 1988. *Ancient Egyptian Autobiographies Chiefly of the Middle Kingdom: A Study and an Anthology.* Orbis Biblicus et Orientalis 84. Freiburg Schweiz/Göttingen: Universitätsverlag/Vandenhoeck & Ruprecht.

———. 1992. *Maat in Egyptian Autobiographies and Related Studies.* Orbis Biblicus et Orientalis 120. Freiburg Schweiz/Göttiningen: Universitätsverlag/Vandenhoeck & Ruprecht.

Liddell, Henry G., and Robert Scott. 1940. *A Greek-English Lexicon: Revised and Augmented throughout by Sir Henry Stuart Jones.* 9th ed., with a Revised Supplement 1996. Oxford: Clarendon.

Lidzbarski, Mark. 1915. *Das Johannesbuch der Mandäer.* Giessen: Alfred Töpelmann.

Lipiński, Edward. 1993. "קנה qānāh." Pages 63–71 in vol. 7 of *Theologisches Wörterbuch zum Alten Testament.* Edited by G. Johannes Botterweck and Helmer Ringgren. 10– vols. Stuttgart: W. Kohlhammer, 1973–.

Livingstone, Alasdair. 1986. *Mystical and Mythological Explanatory Works of Assyrian and Babylonian Scholars.* Oxford: Clarendon.

Longman, Tremper. 1991. *Fictional Akkadian Autobiography: A Generic and Comparative Study.* Winona Lake, Ind.: Eisenbrauns.

Loretz, Oswald. 1993. "Opfer- und Leberschau im Israel. Philologische und historische Aspekte." Pages 509–529 in *Religionsgeschichte Beziehungen zwischen Kleinasien, Nordsyrien und dem Alten Testament.* Edited by Bernd Janowski *et al.* Orbis Biblicus et Orientalis 129. Freiburg/Göttingen: Universitätsverlag Freiburg/Vandenhoeck & Ruprecht.

Löw, Immanuel. 1967. *Die Flora der Juden.* 4 vols. Wien und Leipzig: R. Lowit, 1924–1934. Repr. Hildesheim: Georg Olms.

———. 1973. *Aramäische Pflanzennamen.* Leipzig: Wilhelm Engelmann, 1881. Repr. Hildesheim/New York: Georg Olms.

Lust, J. *et al.* 1992–1996. *A Greek-English Lexicon of the Septuagint.* 2 vols. Stuttgart: Deutsche Bibelgesellschaft.

Maclean, Arthur John. 1901. *A Dictionary of the Dialects of Vernacular Syriac.* Oxford: Clarendon.

Mandelkern, Solomon. 1975. *Veteris Testamenti Concordantiae hebraicae atque chaldaicae.* 2nd ed. 2 vols. Berlin: Margolin, 1925. Repr. Gratz: Akademische Druck- und Verlagsanstalt.

Marrou, Henri I. 1956. *A History of Education in Antiquity.* Translated by George Lamb. New York: Sheed and Ward.

Meer, Petrus Emmanuel van der. 1935. *Textes scolaires de Suse.* Mémoires de la Mission archéologique de Perse 27. Paris: Leroux.

Mettinger, Tryggve N. D. 1971. *Solomonic State Officials: A Study of the Civil Government Officials of the Israelite Monarchy.* Coniectanea Biblica: Old Testament Series 5. Lund: CWK Gleerups Förlag.

Metzger, Bruce M. and Herbert G. May, eds. 1977. *The New Oxford Annotated Bible with the Apocrypha: Revised Standard Version, Containing the Second Edition of the New Testament and an Expanded Edition of the Apocrypha.* New York: Oxford University Press.

Michalowski, Piotr. 1991. "Charisma and Control: On Continuity and Change in Early Mesopotamian Bureaucratic Systems." Pages 45–57 in *The Organization of Power: Aspects of Bureaucracy in the Ancient Near East.* Edited by McGuire Gibson and Robert D. Biggs. Studies in Ancient Oriental Civilization 46. Chicago: The Oriental Institute of the University of Chicago.

Milik, Józef T. 1955a. "1Q21. Testament de Lévi." Pages 87–91, Pl. XVII in *Qumran Cave I.* Edited by Dominique Barthélemy and Józef Tadeusz Milik. Discoveries in the Judaean Desert I. Oxford: Clarendon.

————. 1955b. "Le Testament de Lévi en araméen: Fragment de la Grotte 4 de Qumrân (Pl. IV)." *Revue Biblique* 62: 398–406.

————. 1966. "Fragment d'une source du Psautier (4QPs 89)." *Revue Biblique* 73: 94–106.

————. 1972. "4Q Visions de 'Amram et une citation d'Origène." *Revue Biblique* 79: 77–97.

————. 1976. *The Books of Enoch: The Aramaic Fragments of Qumrân Cave 4*. Oxford: Clarendon.

————. 1978. "Écrits préesséniens de Qumrân: d'Hénoch à Amram." Pages 91–106 in *Qumrân: Sa piété, sa théologie et son milieu*. Edited by Matthias Delcor. Bibliotheca ephemeridum theologicarum lovaniensium 46. Paris/Leuven: Duculot/University Press.

————. 1992. "Les modèles araméens du livre d'Esther dans la Grotte 4 de Qumran." *Revue de Qumran* 15: 321–399 + VII Pl.

Mor, Menachem. 1989. "I. Samaritan History: 1. The Persian, Hellenistic and Hasmonaean Period." Pages 1–18 in *The Samaritans*. Edited by Alan D. Crown. Tübingen: J. C. B. Mohr (Paul Siebeck).

————. 1983–84. "The Tell-Fekherye Bilingual Inscription and Early Aramaic." *Abr-Nahrain* 22: 79–117.

————. 1993. "Further Notes on the Aramaic of the Genesis Apocryphon." *Revue de Qumran* 61: 38–48.

Muraoka, Takamitsu and Bezalel Porten. 1998. *A Grammar of Egyptian Aramaic*. Handbuch der Orientalistik I/32. Leiden: E. J. Brill.

Murphy, Roland E. 1963. "A Consideration of the Classification 'Wisdom Psalms'." Pages 156–167 in *Congress Volume, Bonn 1962*. Vetus Testamentum Supplements 9. Leiden: E. J. Brill.

Müller, H.-P. and M. Krause. 1980. "חֲכַם chākham; חָכָם chākhām." Pages 364–385 in vol. 4 of *Theological Dictionary of the Old Testament*. Edited by G. Johannes Botterweck *et al.* Translated by John T. Willis *et al.* 12– vols. Grand Rapids, Mich.: Eerdmans, 1977–.

Nemet-Nejat, Karen R. 1993. *Cuneiform Mathematical Texts as a Reflection of Everyday Life in Mesopotamia*. American Oriental Series 75. New Haven, Conn.: American Oriental Society.

Nestle, Eberhard and Erwin Nestle. 1993. *Novum Testamentum Graece*. Edited by Kurt Aland *et al.* 27th rev. ed. Stuttgart: Deutsche Bibelgesellschaft.

Neubauer, Adolf and Arthur E. Cowley. 1906. *Catalogue of the Hebrew Manuscripts in the Bodleian Library*. Oxford: Clarendon.

Neugebauer, Otto. 1969. *The Exact Sciences in Antiquity*. 2nd ed. New York: Dover Publications.

————. 1975. *A History of Ancient Mathematical Astronomy*. 3 vols. Berlin: Springer Verlag.

————. 1983. *Astronomical Cuneiform Texts: Babylonian Ephemerides of the Seleucid Period for the Motion of the Sun, The Moon, and the Planets*. 3 vols. Sources in the History of Mathematics and Physical Sciences 5. New York: Springer.

————. 1985. "The 'Astronomical' Chapters of the Ethiopic Book of Enoch (72–82)." Pages 386–419 in *The Book of Enoch or I Enoch: A New English Edition with Commentary and Textual Notes*. Matthew Black. Studia in Veteris Testamenti Pseudoepigrapha 7. Leiden: E. J. Brill.

Neugebauer, Otto and Abraham Sachs. 1984. "Mathematical and Metrological Texts." *Journal of Cuneiform Studies* 36: 243–251.

Neumann, Günter. 1961. *Untersuchungen zum Weiterleben hethitischen und luwischen Sprachgutes in hellenistischer und römischer Zeit*. Wiesbaden: Otto Harrassowitz.

Nickelsburg, George W. E. 1981. "Enoch, Levi, and Peter: Recipients of Revelation in Upper Galilee." *Journal of Biblical Literature* 100: 575–600.

————. 2001. *1 Enoch 1: A Commentary on the Book of 1 Enoch, Chapters 1–36; 81–108*. Hermeneia. Minneapolis, Minn.: Fortress Press.

Nissen, Hans J. 1981. "Bemerkungen zur Listenliteratur Vorderasiens im 3. Jahrtausend (gesehen von den Archaischen Texten von Uruk)." Pages 99–108 in *La lingua di Ebla: Atti del Convegno Internazionale (Napoli, 21–23 aprile 1980)*. Edited by Luigi Cagni. Istituto Universitario Orientale, Seminario di Studi Asiatici 14. Napoli.

Nissen, Hans J. et al. 1993. *Archaic Bookkeeping: Early Writing and Techniques of Economic Administration in the Ancient Near East*. Translated by Paul Larsen. Chicago and London: The University of Chicago Press.

Nordheim, Eckhard, von. 1980. *Die Lehre der Alten: II. Das Testament als Literaturgattung im Judentum der hellenistisch-römischen Zeit*. Arbeiten zur Literatur und Geschichte des hellenistischen Judentums 13. Leiden: E. J. Brill.

Palacios, Ludovicus. 1933. *Grammatica aramaico-biblica*. Roma: Desclée & Editori Pontifici.

Parise, Nicola. 1981. "Mina di Ugarit, mina di Karkemish, mina di Khatti." *Dialoghi di Archeologia, n.s.* 3: 155–160.

Pass, Herman L., and John Arendzen. 1900. "Fragment of an Aramaic Text of the Testament of Levi." *Jewish Qarterly Review* 12: 651–661.

Payne Smith, Robert. 1879. *Thesausus Syriacus: Vol. 1:* ܩ - ܐ. Oxford: Clarendon.

Pfeiffer, Henrik. 1999. *Das Heiligtum von Bethel im Spiegel des Hoseabuches*. Forschungen zur Religion und Literatur des Alten und Neuen Testaments 183. Göttingen: Vandenhoeck & Ruprecht.

Philonenko, Marc. 1960. *Les interpolations chrétiennes des Testaments des Douze Patriarches et les manuscrits de Qoumrân*. Cahiers de la Revue d'histoire et de philosophie religieuses 35. Paris: Presses universitaires de France.

Porten, Bezalel. 1968. *Archives from Elephantine: The Life of an Ancient Jewish Military Colony*. Berkeley: University of California.

Powell, Marvin A. 1979. "Ancient Mesopotamian Weight Metrology: Methods, Problems and Perspectives." Pages 71–109 in *Studies in Honor of Tom B. Jones*. Edited by Marvin A. Powell and Ronald H. Sack. Alter Orient und Altes Testament 203. Neukirchen-Vluyn: Neukirchener Verlag.

————. 1992. "Weights and Measures." Pages 897–908 in vol. 6 of *Anchor Bible Dictionary*. Edited by David Noel Freedman. 6 vols. New York: Doubleday, 1992.

Preuß, Horst D. 1992. *Theologie des Alten Testaments: Band 2: Israels Weg mit JHWH*. Stuttgart: W. Kohlhammer.

Pritchard, James B., ed. 1969. *Ancient Near Eastern Texts Relating to the Old Testament*. 3rd ed. Princetown: Princetown University Press.

Puech, Émile. 1971. "Sur la racine 'ṢLḤ' en hébreu et en araméen." *Semitica* 21: 5–19.

————. 1988. "Les écoles dans l'Israël préexilique: données épigraphiques." Pages 189–203 in *Congress Volume Jerusalem 1986*. Edited by John A. Emerton. Supplements to Vetus Testamentum 40. Leiden: E. J. Brill.

————. 1991. "Le Testament de Qahat en araméen de la grotte 4 *(4QTQah)*." *Revue de Qumran* 15: 23–54.

————. 1992. "Fragments d'un apocryphe de Lévi et le personnage eschatologique. 4QTestLevi^c–d(?) et 4QAJa." Pages 449–501 in *The Madrid Qumran Congress: Proceedings of the International Congress on the Dead Sea Scrolls. Madrid 18–21 March, 1991*. Edited by Julio Trebolle Barrera and Luis Vegas Montaner. 2 vols. Studies on the Texts of the Desert of Judah XI.1–2. Leiden: E. J. Brill.

————. 2000. "Sur la dissimilation de l'interdentale ḏ en araméen qumrânien. À propos d'un chaînon manquant." *Revue de Qumran* 19: 607–616.

————. 2001. *Qumran Grotte 4. XXII. Textes araméens: Première partie 4Q529–549*. Discoveries in the Judaean Desert XXXI. Oxford: Clarendon.

————. 2002. "Le *Testament de Lévi* en araméen de la Geniza du Caire." *Revue de Qumran* 20: 511–556.

————. 2003. "Notes sur le *Testament de Lévi* de la grotte 1 (1Q21)." *Revue de Qumran. Forthcoming.*

Rabinowitz, Jakob J. 1956. *Jewish Law: Its Influence on the Development of Legal Institutions.* New York: Bloch Publishing Company.

Rau, Eckhard 1974. "Kosmologie, Eschatologie und die Lehrautorität Henochs: Traditions- und formgeschichtliche Untersuchungen zum äth. Henochbuch und zu verwandten Schriften." Ph.D. diss., Universität Hamburg. Hamburg.

Rengstorf, Karl H., and Leonhard Rost, eds. 1910–. *Die Mishna: Text, Übersetzung und ausführliche Erklärung.* Berlin: A. Töpelmann.

Robson, Eleanor. 1999. *Mesopotamian Mathematics, 2100–1600 B.C.: Technical Constants in Bureaucracy and Education.* Oxford Editions of Cuneiform Texts 14. Oxford: Clarendon.

————. 2002. "More than Metrology: Mathematics Education in an Old Babylonian Scribal School." Pages 325–365 in *Under One Sky: Astronomy and Mathematics in the Ancient Near East.* Edited by J. M. Steele and A. Imhausen. Alter Orient und Altes Testament 297. Münster: Ugarit-Verlag.

Römer, Willem H. Ph. 1965. *Sumerische 'Königshymnen' der Isin-Zeit.* Leiden: E. J. Brill.

Rönsch, H. 1874. *Das Buch der Jubiläen oder die kleine Genesis unter Beifügung des revidirten Textes der in der Ambrosiana aufgefundenen lateinischen Fragmente.* Leipzig: Fues's Verlag (R. Reisland).

Rooke, Deborah W. 2000. *Zadok's Heirs: The Role and Development of the High Priesthood in Ancient Israel.* Oxford Theological Monographs. Oxford: Oxford University Press.

Rudolph, Kurt. 1965. *Theogonie, Kosmogonie und Anthropogonie in den mandäischen Schriften.* Forschungen zur Religion und Literatur des Alten und Neuen Testamentes 88. Göttingen: Vandenhoeck & Ruprecht.

Schaeder, Hans H. 1930. *Ezra der Schreiber.* Beiträge zur historischen Theologie 5. Tübingen: J. C. B. Mohr (Paul Siebeck).

Schams, Christine. 1998. *Jewish Scribes in the Second-Temple Period.* Journal for the Study of the Old Testament Supplement Series 291. Sheffield: Sheffield Academic Press.

Schiffman, Lawrence H. 1975. *The Halakhah at Qumran.* Studies in Judaism in Late Antiquity 16. Leiden: E. J. Brill.

————. 1984. "Purity and Perfection: Exclusion from the Council of the Community in the *Serekh Ha-'Edah.*" Pages 373–389 in *Biblical Archaeology Today: Proceedings of the International Congress on Biblical Archaeology, Jerusalem, April 1984.* Jerusalem: Israel Exploration Society.

Schmid, Hans H. 1968. *Gerechtigkeit als Weltordnung: Hintergrund und Geschichte des alttestamentlichen Gerechtigkeitsbegriffes.* Beiträge zur Historischen Theologie 40. Tübingen: J. C. B. Mohr (Paul Siebeck).

Schulthess, Friedrich. 1924. *Grammatik des christich-palästinischen Aramäisch.* Edited by Enno Littmann. Tübingen: J. C. B. Mohr (Paul Siebeck).

Schwartz, Baruch J. 1991. "The Prohibitions Concerning the 'Eating' of Blood in Leviticus 17." Pages 34–66 in *Priesthood and Cult in Ancient Israel.* Edited by Gary A. Anderson and Saul M. Olyan. Journal for the Study of the Old Testament Supplement Series 125. Sheffield: Sheffield Academic Press.

Schwyzer, Eduard. 1953. *Griechische Grammatik: Allgemeiner Teil, Lautlehre, Wortbidlung, Flexion.* 2nd ed. Handbuch der Altertumswissenschaft 2/1/1. Munich: C. H. Beck.

Scolnic, Benjamin E. 1995. *Theme and Context in Biblical Lists.* South Florida Studies in the History of Judaism 119. Atlanta, Ga.: Scholars Press.

Segelberg, Eric. 1958. *Maṣbūtā: Studies in the Ritual of the Mandaean Baptism.* Uppsala: Almqvist & Wiksells.

Segert, Stanislav. 1975. *Altaramäische Grammatik.* Leipzig: Veb Verlag Enzyklopädie.

Septuaginta: Vetus Testamentum Graecum Auctoritate Societatis Litterarum Gottingensis editum. 1931–. Göttingen: Vandehoeck & Ruprecht.

Simpson, William K. 1973. *The Literature of Ancient Egypt: An Anthology of Stories, Instructions, and Poetry.* New Haven: Yale University Press.

Sjöberg, Åke W. 1972. "In Praise of the Scribal Art." *Journal of Cuneiform Studies* 24: 126–131.

———. 1975. "The Old Babylonian Eduba." Pages 159–179 in *Sumerological Studies in Honor of Thorkild Jacobsen.* Assyriological Studies 20. Chicago: The University of Chicago Press.

Skehan, Patrick W., and Alexander A. Di Lella. 1987. *The Wisdom of Ben Sira: A New Translation with Notes.* Anchor Bible 39. New York: Doubleday.

Slingerland, H. Dixon. 1977. *The Testaments of the Twelve Patriarchs: A Critical History of Research.* Society of Biblical Literature Monograph Series 21. Missoula, Mont.: Scholars Press.

Smith, Morton. 1987. *Palestinian Parties and Politics that Shaped the Old Testament.* 2nd corr. ed. London: SCM Press.

Smyth, Herber Weir. 1984. *Greek Grammar.* Revised by Gordon M. Messing. Cambridge, Mass.: Harvard University Press.

Sokoloff, Michael. 1990. *A Dictionary of Jewish Palestinian Aramaic of the Byzantine Period.* Dictionaries of Talmud, Midrash, and Targum 2. Ramat-Gan: Bar Ilan University Press.

Sperber, Alexander, ed. 1992. *The Bible in Aramaic Based on Old Manuscripts and Printed Texts.* 2nd impression. 4 vols. Leiden: E. J. Brill.

Steingass, Francis. 1970. A Comprehensive Persian-English Dictionary. Beirut: Librairie du Liban.

Stern, Menahem, ed. 1976. *Greek and Latin Authors on Jews and Judaism: Volume One: From Herodotus to Plutarch.* Jerusalem: The Israel Academy of Sciences and Humanities.

Stone, Elizabeth Caecilia. 1987. *Nippur Neighborhoods.* Studies in Ancient Oriental Civilization 44. Chicago: Oriental Institute, University of Chicago.

Stone, Michael E. 1987. "Ideal Figures and Social Context: Priest and Sage in the Early Second Temple Age." Pages 575–586 in *Ancient Israelite Religion: Essays in Honor of Frank Moore Cross.* Edited by Patrick D. Miller *et al.* Philadelphia: Fortress.

———. 1988. "Enoch, Aramaic Levi and Sectarian origins." *Journal for the Study of Judaism* 19: 159–170.

Stone, Michael E., and Jonas C. Greenfield. 1993. "The Prayer of Levi." *Journal of Biblical Literature* 112: 247–266.

———. 1994. "The First Manuscript of *Aramaic Levi Document* from Qumran (4QLevi*ᵃ* aram)." *Le Muséon* 107: 257–281.

———. 1996a. "Aramaic Levi Document." Pages 1–72, Pls. I–IV in *Qumran Cave 4: XVII. Parabiblical Texts, Part 3.* Edited by George Brooke *et al.* Discoveries in the Judaean Desert XXII. Oxford: Clarendon.

———. 1996b. "The Second Manuscript of *Aramaic Levi Document* from Qumran (4QLeviᵇ aram)." *Le Muséon* 109: 1–15.

———. 1996c. "The Third and Fourth Manuscripts of *Aramaic Levi Document* from Qumran (4QLeviᶜ aram and 4QLeviᵈ aram)." *Le Muséon* 109: 245–259.

———. 1997. "The Fifth and Sixth Manuscripts of *Aramaic Levi Document* from Qumran (4QLeviᵉ aram and 4QLeviᶠ aram)." *Le Muséon* 110: 271–292.

Sundermann, Werner. 1984. "Ein weiteres Fragment aus Manis Gigantenbuch." Pages 491–505 in *Orientalia J. Duchesne-Guillemin emerito oblata.* Acta iranica 23. Leiden: E. J. Brill.

Sweet, Ronald F. G. 1990. "The Sage in the Akkadian Literature: A Philological Study." Pages 45–65 in *The Sage in Israel and the Ancient Near East*. Edited by John G. Gammie and Leo G. Perdue. Winona Lake: Eisenbrauns.

Tcherikover, Victor. 1959. *Hellenistic Civilization and the Jews*. Philadephia/Jerusalem: The Jewish Publication Society of America/The Magnes Press.

The Old Testament in Syriac according to the Peshiṭta Version. 1972–. Leiden: J. E. Brill.

Thomas, Joseph. 1935. *Le mouvement baptiste en Palestine et Syrie (150 av. J.-C.–300 ap. J.C.)*. Diss. theol. Lovaniensis, Series II, tomus 28. Gembloux: J. Duculot.

Thompson, Edward M. 1912. *An Introduction to Greek and Latin Palaeography*. Oxford: Clarendon.

Thureau-Dangin, François. 1921. *Les rituels accadiens*. Paris: Ernest Leroux.

Tinney, Steve J. 1999. "On the Curricular Setting of Sumerian Literature." *Iraq* 59: 159–172.

Tosato, Angelo. 1982. *Il matrimonio israelitico: una teoria generale*. Analecta Biblica 100. Rome: Biblical Institute Press.

Tov, Emanuel. 1996. "Scribal Markings in the Texts from the Judean Desert." Pages 41–77 in *Current Research and Technological Developments on the Dead Sea Scrolls: Conference on the Texts from the Judean Desert, Jerusalem, 30 April 1995*. Edited by Donald W. Parry and Stephen D. Ricks. Studies on the Texts of the Desert of Judah 20. Leiden: E. J. Brill.

Tov, Emanuel *et al.* eds. 2002. *The Texts From the Judaean Desert: Indices and Introduction to the Discoveries in the Judaean Desert Series*. Discoveries in the Judaean Desert 39. Oxford: Clarendon.

Tromp, Johannes. 1997. "Two References to a Levi Document in an Epistle of Ammonas." *Novum Testamentum* 39: 235–247.

Ulrichsen, Jarl H. 1991. *Die Grundschrift der Testamente der zwölf Patriarchen: Eine Untersuchung zu Umfang, Inhalt und Eigenart der ursprünglichen Schrift*. Acta Universitatis Upsaliensis. Historia Religionum 10. Uppsala: Uppsala University.

van den Hout, Theo P. J. 1987–90. "Maße und Gewichte: Bei den Hethitern." Pages 517–527 in vol. 7 of *Reallexikon der Assyriologie*. Edited by Erich Ebeling and Bruno Meissner. 8– vols. Berlin: W. de Gruyter, 1928–.

van der Waerden, Bartel L. 1974. *Science Awakening: II. The Birth of Astronomy*. Leiden/New York: Noordhoff International Publishing/Oxford University Press.

Van Dijk, Johannes J. A. 1953. *La sagesse suméro-accadienne: Recherches sur les genres littéraires des textes sapientiaux*. Leiden: E. J. Brill.

VanderKam, James C. 1978. "Enoch Traditions in Jubilees and Other Second-Century Sources." Pages 229–251 in volume 1 of *Society of Biblical Literature 1978 Seminar Papers*. 2 vols. Society of Biblical Literature Seminar Papers 13. Missoula, Mont.: Scholars Press.

———. 1989a. *The Book of Jubilees: A Critical Text*. Corpus Scriptorum Christianorum Orientalium. Scriptores Aethiopici 87. Louvain: E. Peeters.

———. 1989b. *The Book of Jubilees*. Corpus Scriptorum Christianorum Orientalium. Scriptores Aethiopici 88. Louvain: E. Peeters.

———. 1998. *Calendars in the Dead Sea Scrolls: Measuring Time*. The Literature of the Dead Sea Scrolls. London and New York: Routledge.

Vanstiphout, Herman L. J. 1979. "How Did They Learn Sumerian?" *Journal of Cuneiform Studies* 31: 118–26.

Veldhuis, Niek. 1997. "Elementary Education at Nippur: The Lists of Trees and Wooden Objects." Unpublished Doctoral Dissertation, University of Groningen.

Vogt, Ernest. 1994. *Lexicon linguae aramaicae Veteris Testamenti documentis antiquis illustratum*. 2nd ed. Roma: Editrice Pontificio Istituto Biblico.

von Soden, Wolfram and Adam Falkenstein. 1953. *Sumerische und akkadische Hymnen und Gebete*. Zürich: Artemis-Verlag.

Wacholder, Ben Zion. 1974. *Eupolemus: A Study of Judaeo-Greek Literature*. Monographs of the Hebrew Union College 3. Cincinnati: Hebrew Union College-Jewish Institute of Religion.

Waetzoldt, Harmut. 1988. "Die Entwicklung der Naturwissenschaften und des Naturwissenschaftlichen Unterrichts in Mesopotamien." Pages 31–49 in *Naturwissenschaftlicher Unterricht und Wissenskumulation: Geschichtliche Entwicklung und gesellschaftliche Auswirkungen*. Edited by Johann G. Prinz von Hohenzollern and Max Liedtke. Schriftenreihe zum Bayerischen Schulmuseum Ichenhausen 7. Bad Heilbrunn: Verlag Julius Klinkhardt.

Wagner, Max. 1966. *Die lexikalischen und grammatikalischen Aramaismen im alttestamentlichen Hebräisch*. Beihefte zur Zeitschrift für die alttestamentliche Wissenschaft 96. Berlin: Alfred Töpelmann.

Walters, Peter. 1973. *The Text of the Septuagint, Its Corruptions and Their Emendation*. Cambridge: Cambridge University Press.

Watson, Wilfred G. E. 1984. *Classical Hebrew Poetry: A Guide to its Techniques*. Journal for the Study of the Old Testament Supplement Series 26. Sheffield: JSOT Press.

———. 1994. *Traditional Techniques in Classical Hebrew Verse*. Journal for the Study of the Old Testament Supplement Series 170. Sheffield: Academic Press.

Weinfeld, Moshe. 1963. "The Conception of Law in and outside of Israel." *Beth Mikra* 17: 58–63. (Hebrew).

———. 1964. "Universalism and Particularism in the Period of Exile and Restoration." *Tarbiz* 33: 228–242. (Hebrew).

———. 1977. "Judge and Officer in Ancient Israel and in the Ancient Near East." *Israel Oriental Studies* 7: 65–88.

———. 1985. *Justice and Righteousness in Israel and the Nations: Equality and Freedom in Ancient Israel in Light of Social Justice in the Ancient Near East*. Jerusalem: The Magnes Press. (Hebrew).

———. 1993. "Traces of Hittite Cult in Shiloh, Bethel and in Jerusalem." Pages 455–472 in *Religionsgeschichtliche Beziehungen zwischen Kleinasien, Nordsyrien und dem Alten Testament*. Edited by Bernd Janowski *et al.* Orbis biblicus et orientalis 129. Freiburg/Göttingen: Universitätsverlag Freiburg/Vandenhoeck & Ruprecht.

Westermann, Claus. 1981. *Praise and Lament in the Psalms*. Translated by Keith R. Crim and Richard N. Soulen. Atlanta: John Knox Press.

Williamson, Hugh G. H. 1985. *Ezra, Nehemiah*. Word Biblical Commentary 16. Waco, Tex.: Word Books.

Wilson, Robert R. 1977. *Genealogy and History in the Biblical World*. Yale Near Eastern Researches 7. New Haven: Yale University Press.

Wise, Michael O. 1997. "To Know the Times and the Seasons: A Study of the Aramaic Chronograph 4Q559." *Journal for the Study of the Pseudepigrapha* 15: 3–51.

Wolff, Hans W. 1965. *Dodekapropheton 1 Hosea*. 2nd ed. Biblischer Kommentar, Altes Testament 14/1. Neukirchen-Vluyn: Neukirchener Verlag.

Wright, George E. 1965. *Shechem: The Biography of a Biblical City*. The Norton Lectures of the Southern Baptist Theological Seminary. New York: McGraw-Hill.

Wright, W. 1871. *Catalogue of Syriac Manuscripts in the British Museum Acquired since the Year 1838: Part II*. London: Gilbert and Rivington.

Yadin, Yigael. 1962. *The Scroll of the War of the Sons of Light against the Sons of Darkness*. Translated by B. Rabin and Ch. Rabin. Oxford: Oxford University Press.

Zehnder, Markus Ph. 1999. *Wegmetaphorik im Alten Testament: Eine semantische Untersuchung der alttestamentlichen und altorientalischen Weg-Lexeme mit besonderer Berücksichtigung ihrer metaphorischen Verwendung*. Beihefte zur Zeitschrift für die alttestamentliche Wissenschaft 268. Berlin: Walter de Gruyter.

Zimmerli, Walter. 1983. *Ezekiel 2: A Commentary on the Book of the Prophet Ezekiel. Chapters 25–48*. Translated by James D. Martin. Hermeneia. Philadelphia: Fortress.

Zipor, Moshe. 1987. "Restrictions on Marriage for Priests (Lev 21,7.13–14)." *Biblica* 67: 259–267.

Zohary, Michael. 1966. *Flora Palaestina: Part One—Equisetaceae to Moringaceae.* Jerusalem: The Israel Academy of Sciences and Humanities.

———. 1972. *Flora Palaestina: Part Two—Platanaceae to Umbelliferae.* Jerusalem: The Israel Academy of Sciences and Humanities.

———. 1982. *Plants of the Bible.* Cambridge: Cambridge University Press.

INDEX OF BIBLICAL TEXTS

INDEX OF NON-BIBLICAL LITERATURE

RABBINIC LITERATURE

INDEX OF MODERN AUTHORS

SUPPLEMENTS

TO THE

JOURNAL FOR THE STUDY OF JUDAISM

60. Halpern-Amaru, B. *The Empowerment of Women in the* Book of Jubilees. 1999. ISBN 90 04 11414 9
61. Henze, M. *The Madness of King Nebuchadnezzar.* The Ancient Near Eastern Origins and Early History of Interpretation of Daniel 4. 1999. ISBN 90 04 11421 1
62. VanderKam, J.C. *From Revelation to Canon.* Studies in the Hebrew Bible and Second Tempel Literature. 2000. ISBN 90 04 11557 9
63. Newman, C.C., J.R. Davila & G.S. Lewis (eds.). *The Jewish Roots of Christological Monotheism.* Papers from the St. Andrews Conference on the Historical Origins of the Worship of Jesus. 1999. ISBN 90 04 11361 4
64. Liesen, J.W.M. *Full of Praise.* An Exegetical Study of Sir 39,12–35. 1999. ISBN 90 04 11359 2
65. Bedford, P.R. *Temple Restoration in Early Achaemenid Judah.* 2000. ISBN 90 04 11509 9
66. Ruiten, J.T.A.G.M. van. *Primaeval History Interpreted.* The Rewriting of Genesis 1–11 in the book of Jubilees. 2000. ISBN 90 04 11658 3
67. Hofmann, N.J. *Die Assumptio Mosis.* Studien zur Rezeption massgültiger Überlieferung. 2000. ISBN 90 04 11938 8
68. Hachlili, R. *The Menorah, the Ancient Seven-armed Candelabrum.* Origin, Form and Significance. 2001. ISBN 90 04 12017 3
69. Veltri, G. *Gegenwart der Tradition.* Studien zur jüdischen Literatur und Kulturgeschichte. 2002. ISBN 90 04 11686 9
70. Davila, J.R. *Descenders to the Chariot.* The People behind the Hekhalot Literature. 2001. ISBN 90 04 11541 2
71. Porter, S.E. & J.C.R. de Roo (eds.). *The Concept of the Covenant in the Second Temple Period.* 2003. ISBN 90 04 11609 5
72. Scott, J.M. (ed.). *Restoration.* Old Testament, Jewish, and Christian Perspectives. 2001. ISBN 90 04 11580 3
73. Torijano, P.A. *Solomon the Esoteric King.* From King to Magus, Development of a Tradition. 2002. ISBN 90 04 11941 8
74. Kugel, J.L. *Shem in the Tents of Japhet.* Essays on the Encounter of Judaism and Hellenism. 2002. ISBN 90 04 12514 0
75. Colautti, F.M. *Passover in the Works of Josephus.* 2002. ISBN 90 04 12372 5
76. Berthelot, K. *Philanthrôpia judaica.* Le débat autour de la "misanthropie" des lois juives dans l'Antiquité. 2003. ISBN 90 04 12886 7
77. Najman, H. *Seconding Sinai.* The Development of Mosaic Discourse in Second Temple Judaism. 2003. ISBN 90 04 11542 0
78. Mulder, O. *Simon the High Priest in Sirach 50.* An Exegetical Study of the Significance of Simon the High Priest as Climax to the Praise of the Fathers in Ben Sira's Concept of the History of Israel. 2003. ISBN 90 04 12316 4

79. Burkes, S.L. *God, Self, and Death*. The Shape of Religious Transformation in the Second Temple Period. 2003. ISBN 90 04 12954 5

80. Neusner, J. & A.J. Avery-Peck (eds.). *George W.E. Nickelsburg in Perspective*. An Ongoing Dialogue of Learning (2 vols.). 2003. ISBN 90 04 12987 1 (set)

81. Coblentz Bautch, K. *A Study of the Geography of 1 Enoch 17–19*. "No One Has Seen What I Have Seen". 2003. ISBN 90 04 13103 5

82. García Martínez, F., & G.P. Luttikhuizen. *Jerusalem, Alexandria, Rome*. Studies in Ancient Cultural Interaction in Honour of A. Hilhorst. 2003. ISBN 90 04 13584 7

83. Najman, H. & J.H. Newman (eds.). *The Idea of Biblical Interpretation*. Essays in Honor of James L. Kugel. 2004. ISBN 90 04 13630 4

84. Atkinson, K. *I Cried to the Lord*. A Study of the Psalms of Solomon's Historical Background and Social Setting. 2004. ISBN 90 04 13614 2

85. Avery-Peck, A.J., D. Harrington & J. Neusner. *When Judaism and Christianity Began*. Essays in Memory of Anthony J. Saldarini. 2004. ISBN 90 04 13659 2 (Set), ISBN 90 04 13660 6 (Volume I), ISBN 90 04 13661 4 (Volume II)

86. Drawnel, H. *The Aramaic Levi Document*. Text, Translation, and Commentary. 2004. ISBN 90 04 13753 X.

87. Berthelot, K. *L'«humanité de l'autre homme» dans la pensée juive ancienne*. 2004. ISBN 90 04 13797 1

88. Bons, E. (ed.) « *Car c'est l'amour qui me plaît, non le sacrifice …* ». Recherches sur Osée 6:6 et son interprétation juive et chrétienne. 2004. ISBN 90 04 13677 0

89. Chazon, E.G., D. Satran & R. Clements. (eds.) *Things Revealed*. Studies in Honor of Michael E. Stone. 2004. ISBN 90 04 13885 4.

90. Flannery-Dailey, F. *Dreamers, Scribes, and Priests*. Jewish Dreams in the Hellenistic and Roman Eras. 2004. ISBN 90 04 12367 9.

ISSN 1384-2161

PLATES

4

45
(40.490)

0　1　2　3　4 cm

Plate I. 1Q21 1,3,4 (PAM 40.540; Mus. Inv. 647) and 45 (PAM 40.490; Mus. Inv. 647). Courtesy of Israel Antiquities Authority

Plate II. 4Q213 (PAM 43.241; Mus. Inv. 817). Courtesy of Israel Antiquities Authority

2   1

6
(43.243)

3

4

5

Plate III. 4Q213a (PAM 43.242, 43.243; Mus. Inv. 249). Courtesy of Israel Antiquities
Authority

Plate IVa. 4Q213b (PAM 43.242; Mus. Inv. 816).

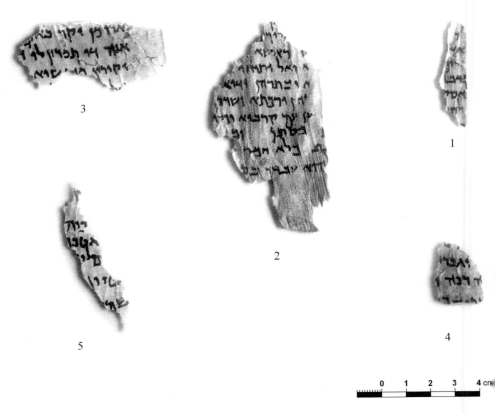

3

1

2

5

4

0 1 2 3 4 cm

Plate IVb. 4Q214 (PAM 43.243; Mus. Inv. 370). Courtesy of Israel Antiquities Authority

214a

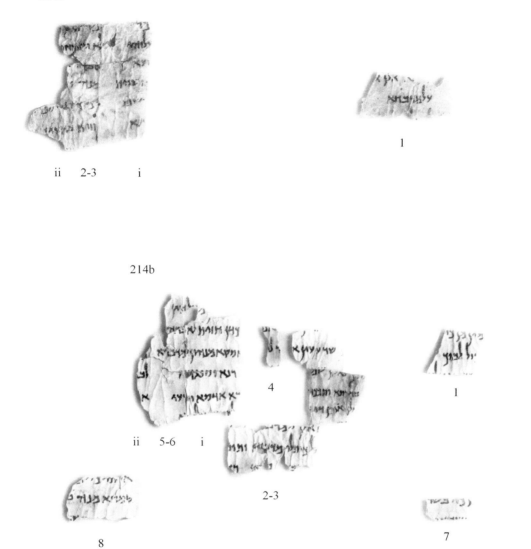

ii   2-3   i

1

214b

ii   5-6   i

4

1

2-3

8

7

0 1 2 3 4 cm

Plate V. 4Q214a and 214b (PAM 43.260; Mus. Inv. 370). Courtesy of Israel Antiquities
Authority

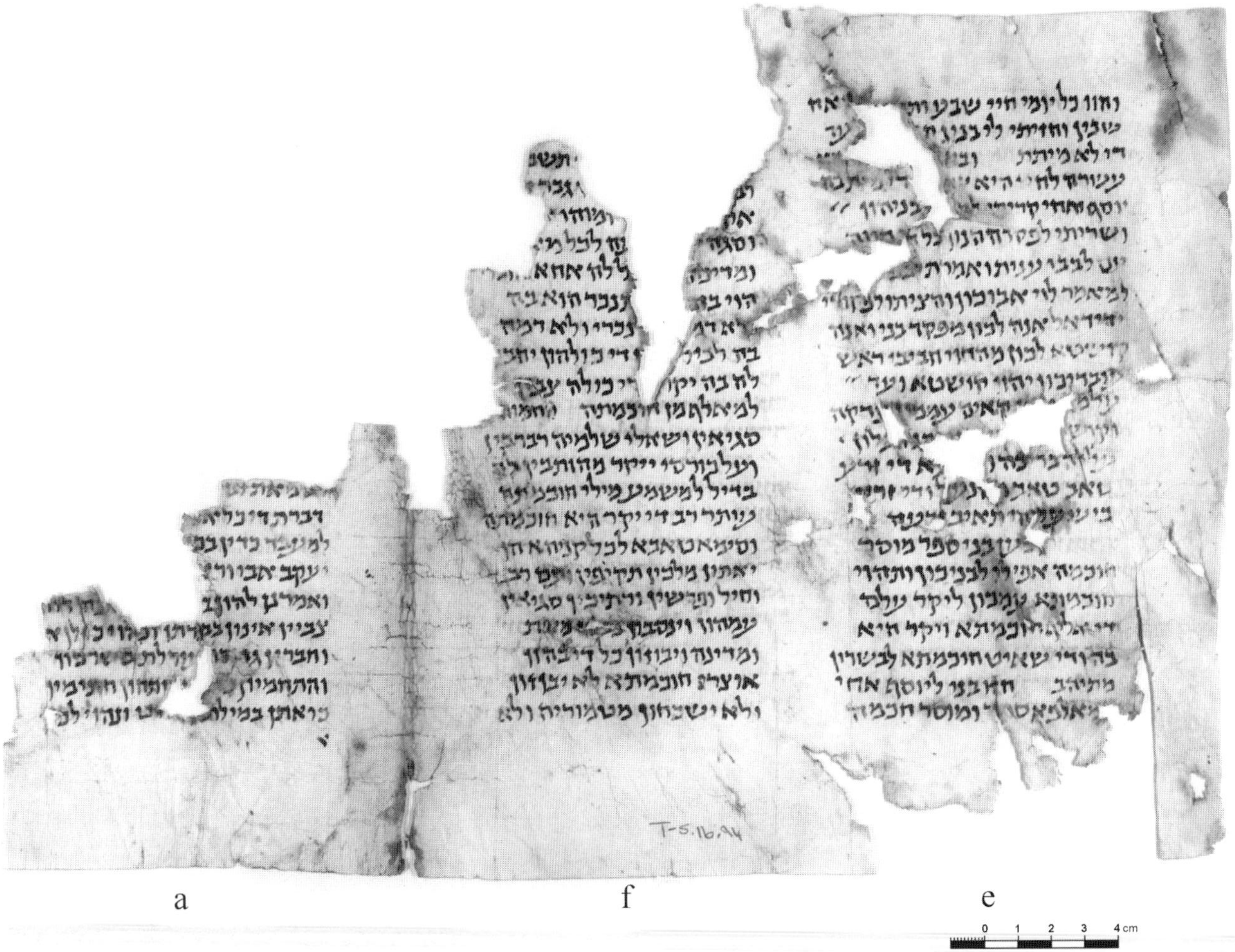

a f e

Plate VI. MS A; *A.L.D.* lc-2; 81-96 (T-S 16.94). Courtesy of Cambridge University Library

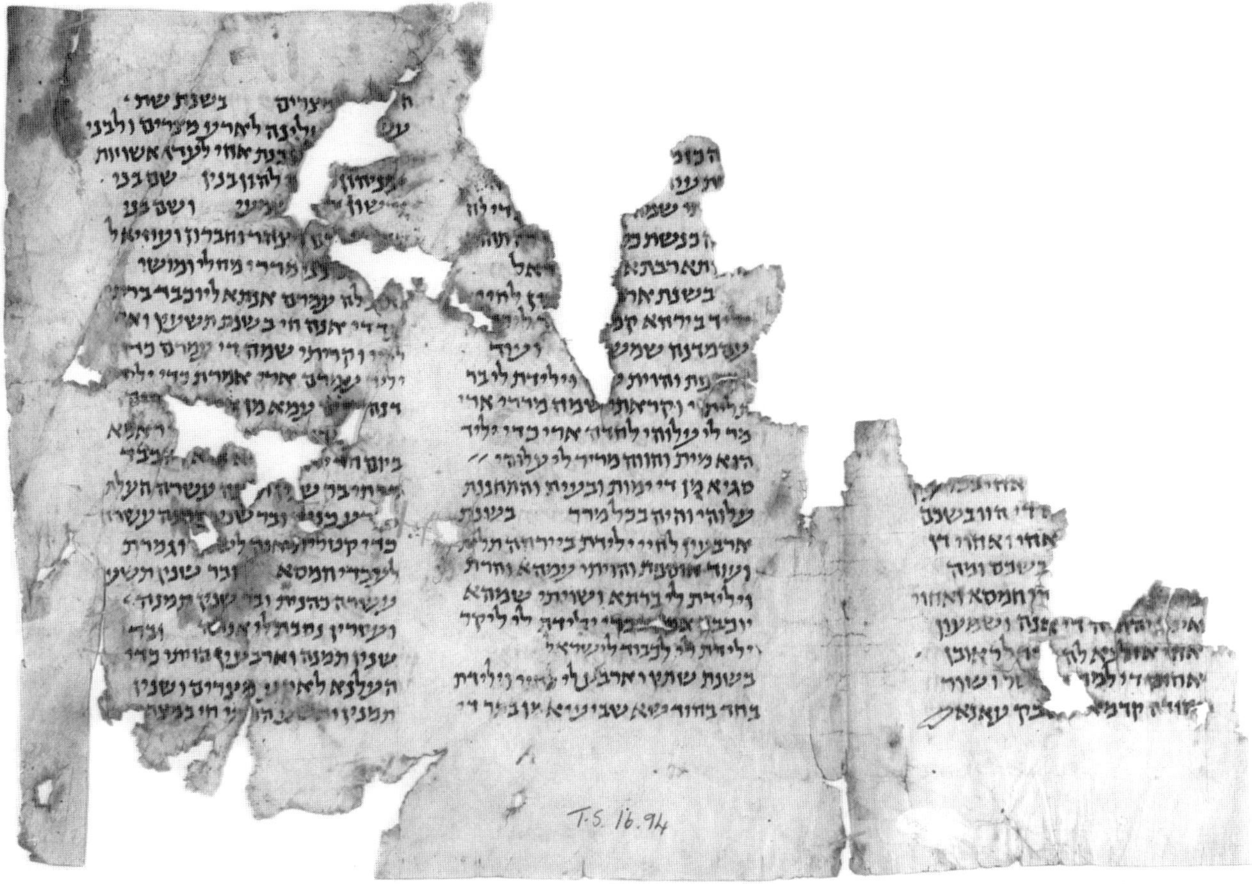

Plate VII. MS A; *A.L.D.* 3; 66-80 (T-S 16.94). Courtesy of Cambridge University Library

b   a

Plate VIII. MS A; *A.L.D.* 4-18 (Ms Heb c 27 f. 56r.). Courtesy of the Bodleian Library, University of Oxford

d   c

Plate IX. MS A; *A.L.D.* 19-32a (Ms Heb c 27 f. 56v.). Courtesy of the Bodleian Library,
University of Oxford

Ἀντίγραφον λόγων Λευὶ ὅσα
διέθετο τοῖς υἱοῖς αὐτοῦ πρὸ
τῆς τελευτῆς αὐτοῦ κατὰ
πάντα ἃ ποιήσουσιν καὶ ὅσα
συναντηθήσεται αὐτοῖς ὅσον λιμβ-
ρας ὁρίσεως· ὑμεῖς μὴ
ὅτε ἐκάλεσεν αὐτοὺς πρὸς
ἑαυτόν· ὡς φθηγαρ αὐτῷ ὅτι
μελλ εἰμὶ ἀποθνήσκειν· καὶ ὅτε
συνήχθησαν, εἶπεν πρὸς
αὐτούς· ἐγὼ Λευὶ ἐν χαρᾷ
συνελήφθην καὶ ὅτε ἐχθην
ἐκᾷ· καὶ μετὰ ταῦτα ὁ λαὸς
σὺν τῷ πρὶ ὁροιλημᾷ λημᾷδ
γερο τεροσυνοτῶν· καὶ ὅτε ἐπὶ
ἡσου μεταϊ συμφῶν τῆϊ ἐκ
δυκλιοιρ τῆς αδελφ θυλιμ-
ληζρας ἀπὸ ὅμμορ· ὡς οδ
ἐποιημένον ὁ νε βθλμα ου λ
πηλου νατε ωκυκιλθεμ ωσ
με καὶ πάντας ὡς ὁρον αιροισ
ἀφ᾽ ἁρμῆ σαμ τας τῆς ὁ δόν αὐτ
καὶ τεϊχ᾽ οἰκοδομῆσαμ ἑαυτὸ
λικακία· το τεϊ ἐγὼ ὁπλυμᾷ
τἀϊρμᾶ πιαμου· καὶ καθαριολο
αὐτὰ ἐν ὕδατι καθαρῷ· καὶ
ὅλος ἐλουσάμην ἐν ὕδατι
ζῶμτι· καὶ πάσας τὰς ὁδοίσ
μου· ὁποίῃσλ ἐν θας· το
τε τους ὁφθαμονσμου καὶ
τὸ πρόσωπον μου ἦρα πρὸς
τὸν οὐνον· καὶ τὸ στομα μου
ἤνοιξλ· καὶ ὁ λαλησλ· καὶ τὴν
δακτύλους τῶν χειρῶν μου·
καὶ τὰς χεῖρας μου ἀνεπέτασα
τὰ εἰσ ἀλήθειαν κατέναντι
τῶν ἁγίων· καὶ ηὐξαμην καὶ
εἶπον

Κε· γηρ οσκας πασας τὰς διᾳ
δίας καὶ πάντας τοὺς οδια
λογισμοὺς ὅμμυ νωμ σὺ μόνος
ὅτι οἶδα σαι· καὶ κρῖμα τε ἐμαρ μου,
μετ᾽ ἐμοῦ· καὶ δὸς μοι πάσας
ὁδοὺς ἀληθίας· μακρυνον
ἀπ᾽ ἐμ κε τὸ πμα τὸ αδικον·
καὶ διαλογισμὸν τὸν πορηρᾷ
καὶ πορνῆας· καὶ ὑψῖν ἀπό
στρεψον ἀπ᾽ ἐμοῦ· δὴ χ μι
το μοι· δᾶτο τᾷ τὸ πμα τὸ αγιον·
καὶ βουλὴν καὶ σοφίαν καὶ
γνῶσιν· καὶ ἰσχυῶ δο ομοι ποι
ῆσαι τὸ ἄρεσκον τα σοι· καὶ
εὑρεῖν χάριν ὁρω πῖο νοσου·
καὶ αἰμῖν τον οσλόγον αυ τον με
τε μου κε· καὶ ἱλικαρτο γυοδ
το με πασ ὁ σατανᾶς· πλαν λὶ
σαιμο ἀπὸ τῆς ὁδοῦ σου· καὶ
ὁλόησον με καὶ προσαγεμρο
εἰ γαισουδ ουλοσ· καὶ λατρ ου
σανσοι καλῶς ο τεϊ χω αρλη λο
σοι ὑρασαι κ υκ λαμου καὶ
ὁκ ωλοου τῆς δυνα ωσφας ο
ὁκ ωλοατο με ἀπὸ παντὸς του
κακου· παρὰ δ ὁσ ο γυ οδλικαι
τῆ ραγομιαν ἐξαλγατον ὑπο
κατω θεν του ουμου· καὶ σω
τελ όσαι τὴν αμγ ομεᾳ ἀπὸ προ
σωπου τῆσ γῆσ· καθαρισον
τὴν καρδίαμ μου δεσπ τᾷ ἀπο
πάσης ακλλθαρσίας· καὶ προσ
αρούμαι προς ε αυτος· καὶ ημι
ἀποστρεψ φᾳσ το πρόσωπον ον μου
ἀπὸ του υιου παιδο σαρ υιᾷ ἀκ ωβ·
συ κε σ ευλογησασ τον αβρααμ
πρα μου· καὶ ὁ σαρραν ιρα μου·
καὶ δ πασ δο υιμαι αὐτοῖσ σπερμα
δίκαιον ευλογημ φον θ οτο υσ
αἰῶρασ· δοακουσον ὁ θ σ· καὶ

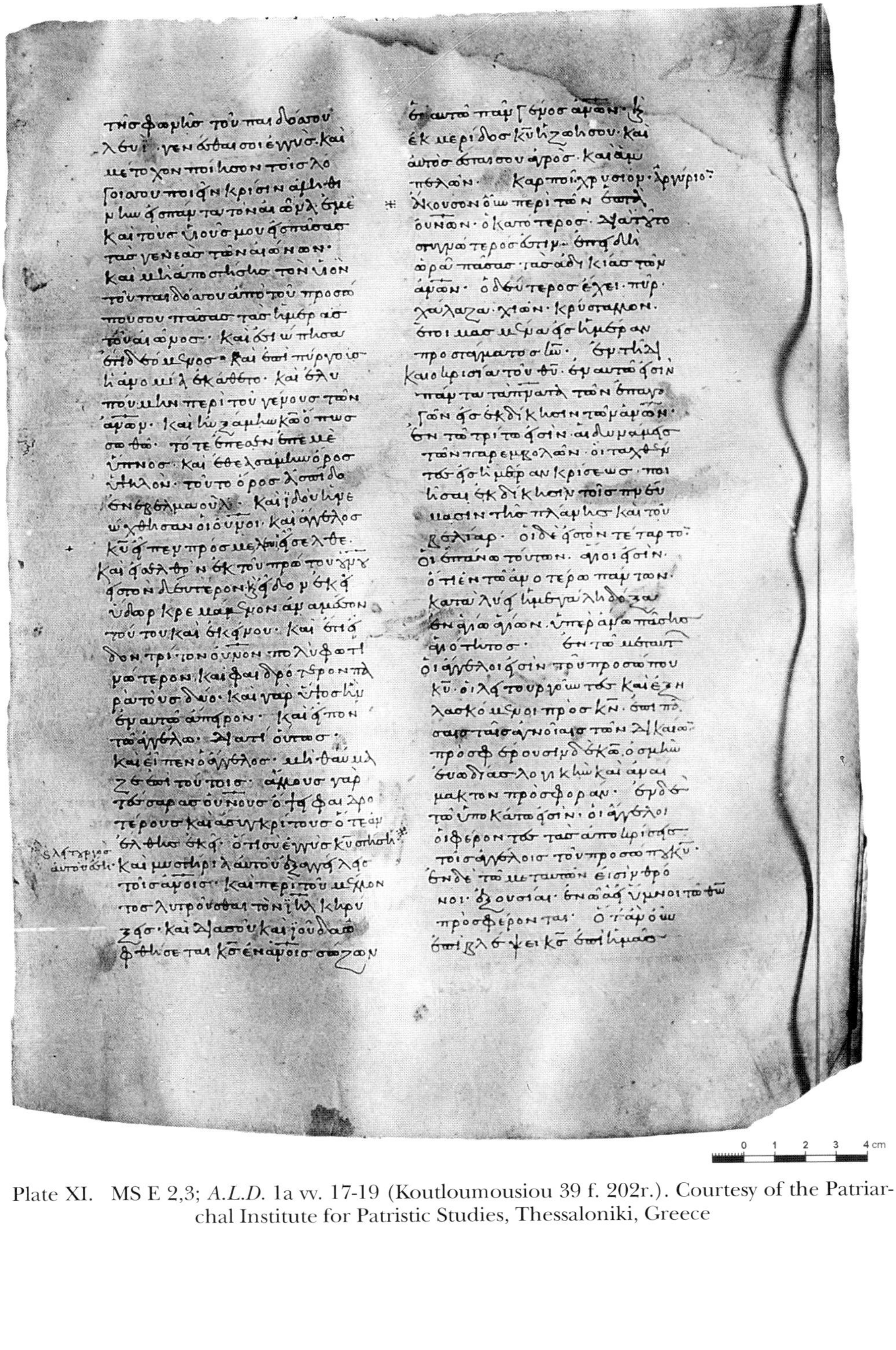

Plate XI. MS E 2,3; *A.L.D.* 1a vv. 17-19 (Koutloumousiou 39 f. 202r.). Courtesy of the Patriarchal Institute for Patristic Studies, Thessaloniki, Greece

Plate XII. MS E 18,2; *A.L.D.* 11-27 (Koutloumousiou 39 f. 205v.). Courtesy of the Patriarchal Institute for Patristic Studies, Thessaloniki, Greece

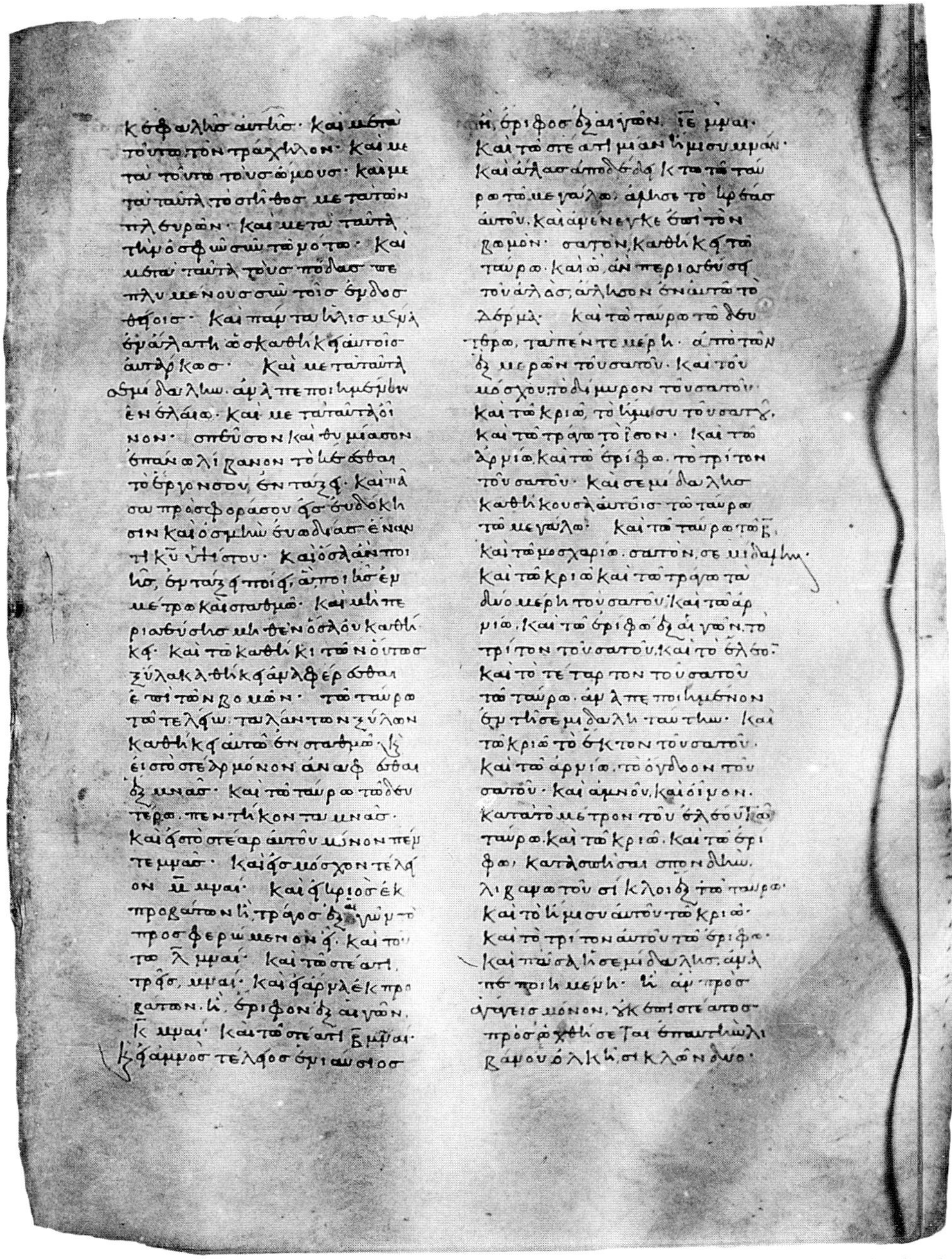

Plate XIII. MS E 18,2; *A.L.D.* 27-46 (Koutloumousiou 39 f. 206r.). Courtesy of the Patriarchal Institute for Patristic Studies, Thessaloniki, Greece

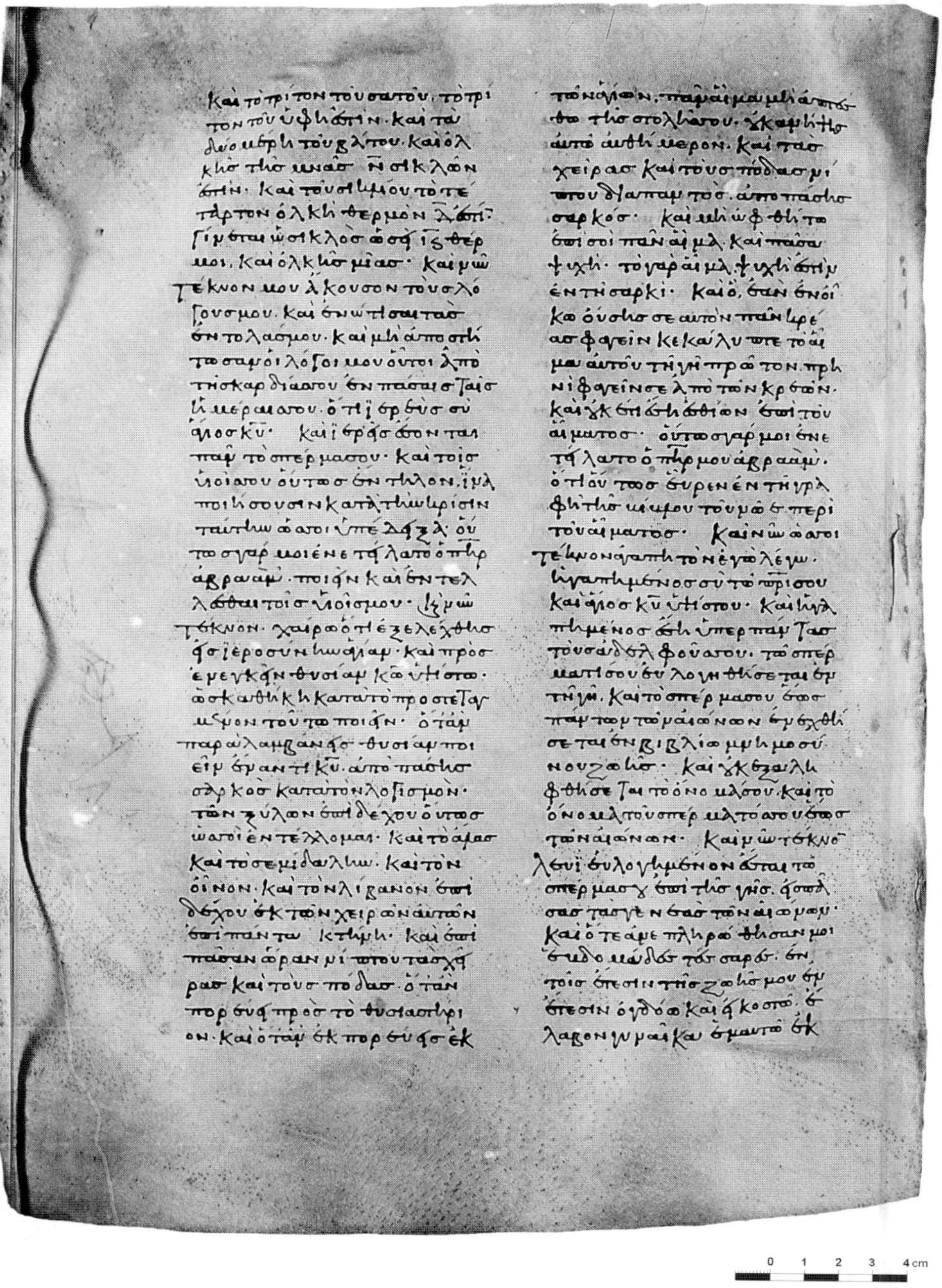

Plate XIV. MS E 18,2; *A.L.D.* 46-62 (Koutloumousiou 39 f. 206v.). Courtesy of the Patriarchal Institute for Patristic Studies, Thessaloniki, Greece

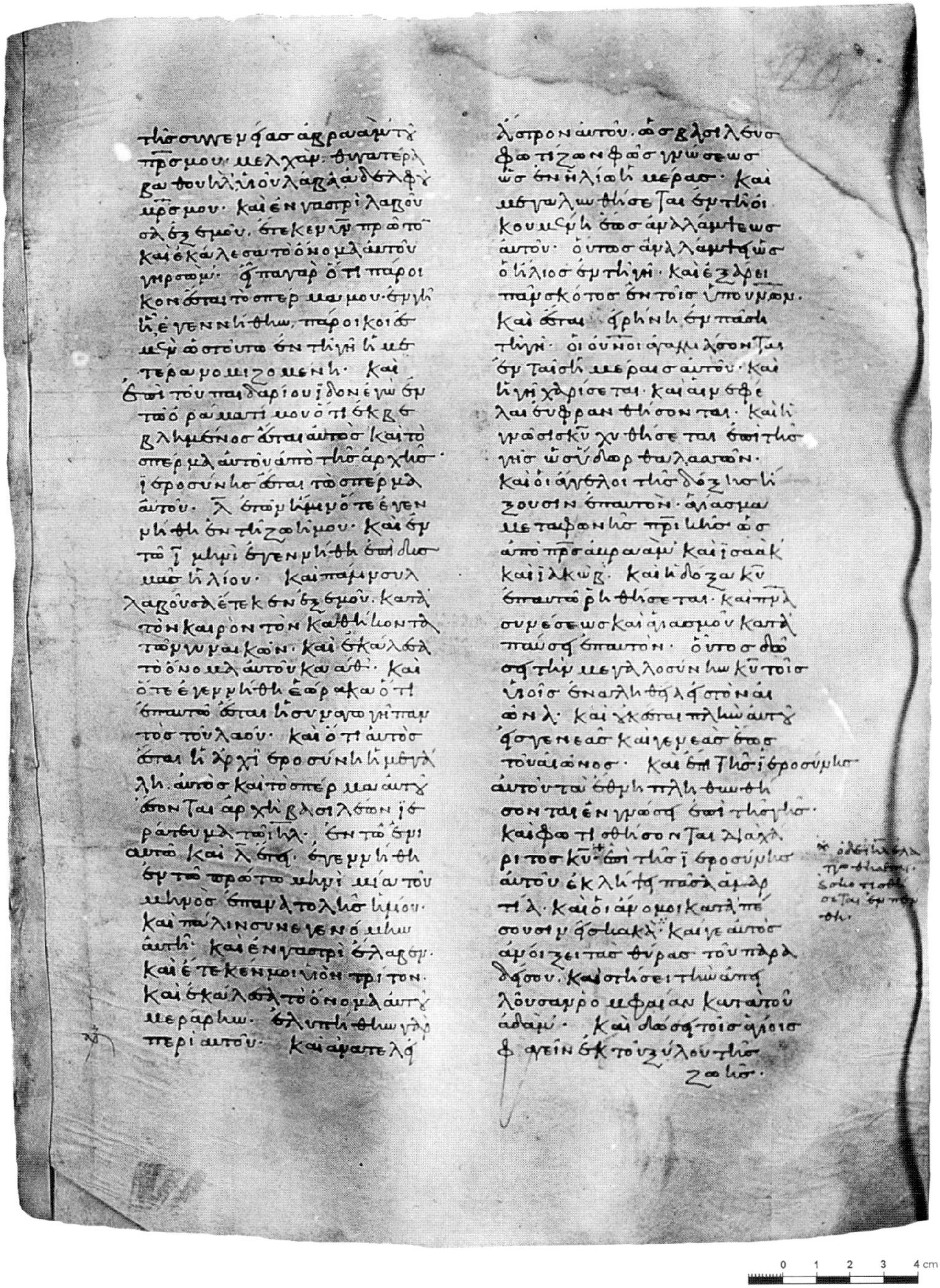

Plate XV. MS E 18,2; *A.L.D.* 62-69 (Koutloumousiou 39 f. 207r.). Courtesy of the Patriarchal Institute for Patristic Studies, Thessaloniki, Greece

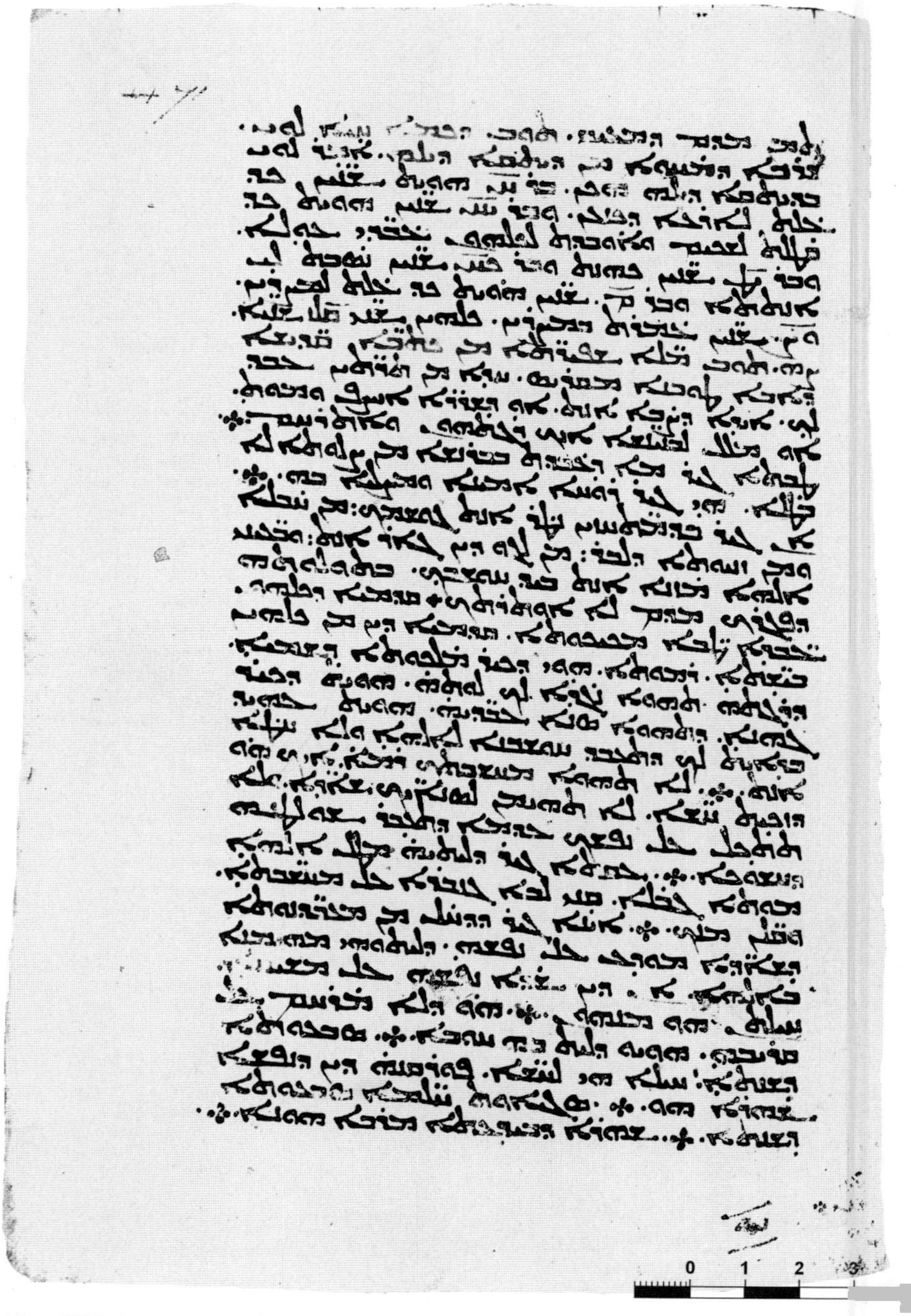

ܠܘܬ ܕܚܕ݂ܪ ܕܡܫܡܠܝ ܘܩܐ ܂ܘܡܫܬܐ ܘܦܫܝܛܐ ܂ ܠܘ ܠܘ

Plate XVI. MS B; *A.L.D.* 78-81 (Add. 17,193 f. 71r.). By permision of the British Library, London